The Double Life of
Bob Dylan

ALSO BY CLINTON HEYLIN

On Bob Dylan:

Bob Dylan Behind The Shades (3 editions)
Dylan Day By Day: A Life In Stolen Moments
Dylan: The Recording Sessions 1960–94
Judas! – From Forest Hills To The Free Trade Hall:
A Historical View Of The Big Boo
No One Else Could Play That Tune:
The Making And Unmaking Of Dylan's 1974 Masterpiece
Revolution In The Air: The Songs Of Bob Dylan 1957–1973
Still On The Road: The Songs Of Bob Dylan 1974–2008
Trouble In Mind: Bob Dylan's Gospel Years

On Popular Music:

All Yesterday's Parties: The Velvet Underground In Print 1966–71 (editor)
The Penguin Book Of Rock & Roll Writing (editor)
The Act You've Known For All These Years: A Year In The Life Of
Sgt Pepper & Friends
All The Madmen: A Journey To The Dark Side Of British Rock
Anarchy In The Year Zero: The Sex Pistols, The Clash And The Class Of '76
Babylon's Burning: From Punk To Grunge
Bootleg! – The Rise & Fall Of The Secret Recording Industry
Can You Feel The Silence? – Van Morrison: A New Biography
Dylan's Daemon Lover: The Tangled Tale Of A 450-Year-Old Pop Ballad
E Street Shuffle: The Glory Days Of Bruce Springsteen & The E Street Band
From The Velvets To The Voidoids: A Pre-Punk History For
A Post-Punk World
It's One For The Money: The Song Snatchers Who Carved Up
A Century Of Pop
Joy Division: Form & Substance (with Craig Wood)
Never Mind The Bollocks, Here's The Sex Pistols (Schirmer Classic Rock
Albums)
No More Sad Refrains: The Life & Times Of Sandy Denny
Rise/Fall: The Story Of Public Image Limited
What We Did Instead Of Holidays: Fairport Convention & Its Extended
Folk-Rock Family

On Pop Culture:

Despite The System: Orson Welles vs. The Hollywood Studios
So Long As Men Can Breathe: The Untold Story Of Shakespeare's Sonnets

The Double Life of Bob Dylan

Volume 1: 1941–66
A Restless, Hungry Feeling

CLINTON HEYLIN

THE BODLEY HEAD
LONDON

13 5 7 9 10 8 6 4 2

The Bodley Head, an imprint of Vintage
One Embassy Gardens
8 Viaduct Gardens
London SW11 7BW

The Bodley Head is part of the Penguin Random House group of companies whose addresses can be found at global.penguinrandomhouse.com.

Copyright © Clinton Heylin 2021

Clinton Heylin has asserted his right to be identified as the author of this Work in accordance with the Copyright, Designs and Patents Act 1988

All unpublished quotes, unless otherwise noted, are reproduced courtesy of the Bob Dylan Archive, Tulsa. Copyright © Bob Dylan
All published quotes are for review, study or critical purposes

Every effort has been made to trace and contact copyright holders. The publishers will be pleased to correct any mistakes or omissions in future editions

First published by The Bodley Head in 2021

www.penguin.co.uk/vintage

A CIP catalogue record for this book is available from the British Library

ISBN 9781847925886

Typeset in 11.5/14 pt Dante MT Std
by Integra Software Services Pvt. Ltd, Pondicherry

Printed and bound in Great Britain by Clays Ltd, Elcograf S.p.A.

The authorised representative in the EEA is Penguin Random House Ireland, Morrison Chambers, 32 Nassau Street, Dublin D02 YH68.

Penguin Random House is committed to a sustainable future for our business, our readers and our planet. This book is made from Forest Stewardship Council® certified paper.

To Beattie Stone (1915–2000) and Maisie Stone (1935–2019),
two remarkable mothers

Contents

That all-important intro ... 2–3–4		1
Prelude – July 29th, 1961: Down By The Riverside		17
Part 1: A Thief Of Thoughts		23
1	January to May 1961: Big City Blues	25
2	Summer 1953 to January 1961: On The Road To Damascus	47
3	May to October 1961: The Kindness Of (Friends & Other) Strangers	75
4	November 1961 to March 1962: The Balladeer Fires Broadsides	99
5	April to October 1962: How Many Roads, So Many Roads	124
6	May 1941 to June 1959: Have You Heard The News?	150
7	October 1962 to April 1963: A New World Singer In Ye Olde Worlde	174
8	April to November 1963: He's Not The Messiah, He's A Very Naughty Boy	202
	Winterlude #1 (November/December 1963): Off The Road	230
Part 2: A Thief Of Fire		239
1	January to June 1964: Becoming Withdrawn	241

2	*June to November 1964: Meet The Beat*	265
3	*November 1964 to April 1965: Walking Down A Crooked Highway*	288
4	*April to June 1965: Call Me Vérité*	312
5	*June to September 1965: The Rites Of Summer*	339
6	*September 1965 to March 1966: Both Kinds Of Music*	366
7	*March to May 1966: I've Been All Around This World*	396
8	*May 1966: Man, I'm Not Even Twenty-Five*	424
	Winterlude #2 (June/July 1966): Off The Road Again	453

Acknowledgements	459
Notes on Sources	462
Index	499

That all-important intro ... 2–3–4

April 26th, 1963. With barely 5,000 album sales to his name, but evidently a prophetic sense of destiny, Dylan is sat with social commentator Studs Terkel in a Chicago radio studio, talking about writing his life story:

Bob Dylan: I'm writing a book now.
Studs Terkel: And what would the book be, an autobiography?
BD: Yeah, it's about my first week in New York.
ST: Oh, that's a very funny song ... a talking song isn't it, 'New York Town'.
BD: It's not that kind of [thing]. It's got more to it than that ... not too much music in it, except maybe a couple of chapters.
ST: This book involves what? Your observations about the Big City?
BD: No, not even about the Big City. The Big City's got nothing to do with it. It's just about somebody who's come to the end of one road, and actually knows it's the end of one road and knows there's another road there, but doesn't exactly know where it is. He knows he can't go back on this one road.
ST: It's [about] a new birth then ...
BD: Yeah, sort of ... it's got all kinds of stuff in it which just doesn't add up ... thoughts in my head all about teachers and school, and all about hitch-hikers around the country, all about these friends of mine too, [and] college kids, and these are all people that I knew. Every one of them [is] sort of a symbol for all kinds of ... people like that. And New York's like a different world. I['d] never been in New York before and I'm still carrying them memories with me, so I decided I oughta write it all down.

★

Thirty-six years later – to the day! – his mind turned again to chronicling his life, as he'd threatened to do in 1963 and 1971. He is in the heartlands of the old Habsburg Empire, between Salzburg and Vienna, on the banks of the Danube 'where the willow hangs down', a place saturated in history, as he knows well.

Linz itself is charming, and the spring tour is going well, opening the curtain on a twelfth year for the subversive construct he had himself christened the Never Ending Tour. It has been eight long (but certainly not wasted) years since the last smartass knowitall tried to tell *his* story. Maybe the time has come for *him* to cover the waterfront. To tell it like it is, as the Neville Brothers once sang.

As is his wont, the man with two names has taken some hotel stationery with him to a smalltown cafe, where he pulls out a pencil and begins to scratch out in that telltale spidery scrawl his world view, his thoughts, his dreams, in that interior voice he alone knows ...

> It used to irritate me when the media portrayed me as a sixties artist. I never wanted for a second to be a sixties artist but an artist for all time. If it's not for all time, it's not worth doing. My mind works in a timeless way, and anyway I'm not good at dates, ages, names and numbers. Everything to me is timeless. 1976 might as well be 2090 – it's all the same to me.

But if the man who is Bob Dylan only when he has to be thinks he is painting over an abiding public image of himself 'as a sixties artist', he is going about it in the most lateral of ways. The following night he will perform an energetic sixteen-song set to the well-fed Austrian burghers, ten of which will be culled from the sixties; all from his pre-accident canon. From the two dozen albums between *Blonde On Blonde* in 1966 and 1997's *Time Out Of Mind*, he will exhume just 'Tangled Up In Blue', and even that song consciously evokes a time when there was 'music in the cafes at night and revolution in the air'. Try as he might, maybe he just can't connect the dots any more ...

*

Both sides of the biographical coin were flipped in 2001, the year of '*Love And Theft*', Dylan's first studio album in four years, and the year he told Mikal Gilmore, 'My story [by] myself would have to be more interesting than [by] anybody else that could look at it from the outside, right?'

Already that year *this* smartass knowitall had dramatically revised the most factually reliable of Dylan biographies – *Behind The Shades* – perhaps just in time. And a former tabloid reporter aka professional dirtdigger, name of Howard Sounes, had decided to out-Scaduto Spitz and go all *National Enquirer* on the man called Alias. The result: a depressingly well-trundled, semi-literate stroll *Down The Highway*.

Dylan, though, was going to take his time. Not until October 5th, 2004 would Simon & Schuster publish *Chronicles Vol. 1*, the sixth Bob Dylan biography, and the least reliable when it came to 'dates, ages, names and numbers'. This bestselling volume – like the sincerer scribblings of Scaduto, Shelton, Spitz and Sounes before – largely concerned itself with events from 1960 to 1969.

Yet the evidence of a mind which 'works in a timeless way' was writ large across the slim volume,* as it jumped backwards and forwards, skipping lightly around the more contentious areas of a life well lived, never once settling down long enough to lay the foundations for a broader narrative or a concerted explication of a body of work that indisputably made its author 'an artist for all time'.

Instead, this endlessly mercurial artist slipped through this invested reader's fingers every time he turned a page. The multitude of personalities Robert Allen Zimmerman first developed as a defence mechanism in his Minnesotan youth remained steadfastly behind closed doors. Even the self-analytical persona dredged up by his psyche down by the Austrian river would be only a fleeting contributor to the final product.

Whether consciously or not, Dylan had elected to emulate the late Graham Chapman, Monty Python's premier pisshead, penning his own *Liar's Autobiography* in the teeth of two biographical portraits foisted on the public in the interregnum between that original righteous thought in Linz and its ultimate expression. Perhaps that was always his plan. As far back as 1971, he'd expressed an intention to play fast and loose with the facts, telling Tony Glover, 'I got a story to tell – but I don't want to tell it the old cornball way. A real writer knows to hold it all up – he can then place his facts wherever he feels like it.'

---

* It could have been slimmer still. The first draft apparently ran to just 40,000 words.

What Dylan made of his most recent chroniclers he wasn't about to say, save by embroidering a couple of the more outlandish stories in Sounes's skim-read till they collapsed 'neath the cumulative weight of his and his biographer's disinformation. But it is possible these other biographies' very existence shaped the tenor and tone of the book he was now (re)writing with renewed urgency, having sealed a seven-figure advance for world rights from the capacious coffers of Simon & Schuster. He implied as much in that detailed 2001 conversation with Mikal Gilmore, 'Because I'm a public figure ... I can mention all kinds of things that have been written about already, but I [can] bring a different resonance to it.'

However, something shifted his autobiographical axis between Linz and Kenosha, the birthplace of Orson Welles, where Dylan came to play in October 2004 just as *Chronicles* was entering the bestseller lists around the world.* Though Dylan had yet to publicly endorse Welles's late period mockumentary, *F For Fake*, on his 2007 radio show, he had chosen to reflect an insight the great composer Bernard Herrmann once offered about Welles as a *raison d'être* for his own memoir, 'Anyone who believes he has caught him in a fantastic lie is apt to find that the fantastic story is the truth. And some unimportant statement, like just having bought an evening paper a half-hour ago, is the lie.'

Examples in *Chronicles* are manifold, but I'll cite just a single instance: the story of how the nineteen-year-old Dylan first came to hear the blues giant, Robert Johnson, and specifically the *King Of The Delta Blues* album. It is a tale worth deconstructing. On page 280 of *Chronicles*, Dylan claims John Hammond Sr gave him 'a thick acetate' of this seminal record – which was 'not yet available to the public' – the day that he was offered a five-year recording contract with Columbia (to which Dylan alleges he took one look and said, 'Where do I sign?').

There are enough documented facts herein which can be checked. And when one does, they don't add up. *King Of The Delta Blues* was released on September 11th, 1961 (forty years to the day before Dylan

---

* The autobiographical writings from the mid-to-late nineties which reside in the official Dylan archive in Tulsa, Oklahoma, have nothing like the same smoke'n'mirrors sheen as the published memoir, but with much of the *Chronicles* material currently embargoed, it is mere guesswork as to when and why this happened.

released 'Love And Theft' and a bunch of jihadists flew into the World Trade Center, killing upward of 3,000 innocent people). Dylan wouldn't sign his Columbia contract until six weeks later, on October 26th, the day after he had been given a first draft, which he asked be amended and extended. Hammond would hardly have given him an acetate at this late date.

Even before I was able to marshal these annoying little facts – which required the resources of Sony Music and Tulsa's Gilcrease Museum – I found it hard to believe Dylan heard Johnson this early, though I accept he was probably the beneficiary of said album courtesy of Hammond. But any such event must have occured in late December 1961 or early January 1962. Why am I so sure? Because there is not a note of influence audible on the twenty-six-song Minneapolis Hotel Tape from December 22nd, but by January 5th he had written his first pastiche of Johnson, 'Standing On The Highway', and four weeks later he was telling Izzy Young he intended to write a song called 'The Death Of Robert Johnson'. The fact that Dylan goes on to describe the impact Johnson had on him in luminescent words, making for one of the best passages in *Chronicles*, in no way abnegates such a wanton disregard for, er, chronology.

Caveat Emptor might have been a better, certainly a more apposite, title for a book in which the song and dance man consciously plays the joker time after time. This alone should have warranted a challenger who respected history a little more, and mythology a little less. But fifteen years on, we're still waiting. Despite bookshelves the world over continuing to groan 'neath a never-ending onslaught of tomes on or about the man and/or his work, Dylan remains an elusive figure in the world of (the rock) biography; even more now that his position in the pantheon is secure and his creative output has slowed to a trickle.

It seems remarkable – to me, anyway – that only five proper (i.e. *researched*) biographies of the man have been published to date, three of which appeared between 1986 and 1991, the absolute commercial nadir of Dylan's six decades of stardom; only one of which was not written in Tabloidese. To put this in context, this is fewer than Janis Joplin, who made just four albums (in four years) and wrote barely a handful of songs before succumbing to one of the manifold ways she found to numb the pain of daily existence. It is as if seventeenth-century controversialist Peter Heylyn were deemed more worthy of biographical study than his near-contemporary, William Shakspeare.*

It seems that the advent of the Internet really has had a deleterious effect on people's intellectual curiosity. It certainly appears as if an avalanche of 'new' information about Dylan (life, the universe and everything) has *dissuaded* people from making sense of this rich pageant, even as the cataloguing of his every endeavour multiplies daily, thanks primarily to the extraordinary resource that is *Expecting Rain*. Meanwhile, misinformation contiguously feeds every other Dylan-related website – from Olof Björner's ostensibly reliable *About Bob Dylan* on down.

This online dystopia, with its search engines and 'egalitarian' dispensation of information *and* misinformation, unfiltered by anything save who pays to advertise, has spawned a new kind of pseudo-historical work: the bedsit biography, of which the most overweening example must be Ian Bell's two-volume account of Dylan's milieu, *Once Upon A Time* (2012) and *Time Out Of Mind* (2014) – though Spencer Leigh's *Outlaw Blues* (2020) runs the late Bell awfully close.

Go to the Amazon website and key in *Once Upon A Time* – as I just did – and one finds vox-pop 'reviews' like this one: 'His level of research and depth of insight is breathtaking.' It certainly takes my breath away. Never in the history of biography has someone done less research for more poundage. Producing nearly 1,500 pages on Dylan without studying more than the five existing biographies and Dylan's own *Chronicles*, and surfing the Web for the odd aside, does not a researcher make, let alone a biographer. It would barely qualify as sufficient for a college freshman's first essay on pop culture.†

This shiny new digital resource – the big bang to Gutenberg's galaxy – surely should be producing something more balanced, more nuanced, more measured by now; as opposed to giving maladroit theories credence while myopically chained to the kind of insidious resource

---

* Despite Heylyn having two faithful biographers writing his life story a good fifty years before Nicholas Rowe, it was Rowe who spawned a mini industry in Shakspere biographies that makes most governments' recycling programmes seem risible by comparison. The next Heylyn biography would not appear until 2007.
† At least Bell almost invariably defers to *Behind The Shades* when it comes to the facts.

Alexander Pope could not have foreseen when he opined, 'A little learning is a dangerous thing; / *Drink deep*, or taste not the Pierian spring.'

On the plus side, at least Bell chose to clash with the dish-the-dirt school of biography, a decade after Howard Sounes produced his protean biographical 'exposé', unlocking even fewer doors of perception than Shelton or Spitz. In that period, the few good books on Dylan came at him from an original angle or focused on one intense period of activity and contextualized it.

Head of the new class was David Hajdu's *Positively 4th Street*, a well-received 'dual biography' of Richard Fariña and Bob Dylan in the lead-up to their 1966 motorcycle accidents – which the latter survived, the former did not. Appearing the same year as *Down The Highway*, it was its very antithesis; well researched, well written and with 'a different point of view' – even if Hajdu distorts the closeness of the connection between Dylan and Fariña, using their joint fascination with both Baez sisters, Joan *and* Mimi, as the hook on which to hang a somewhat tendentious thesis.

Fifteen years later, Barney Hoskyns refracted Dylan through the prism of Woodstock and his ultimately fraught relationship with the Grossmans in *Small Town Talk*. Again, original research vied with head-on myth-demolition as Hoskyns tried to explain why Woodstock became a haven for some, hell for others. In doing so, he tackled a period in Dylan's life others largely skirted over.

Neither Hoskyns nor Hajdu – both accredited biographers before they took on our man – felt like tackling the whole life. Who can blame them? They would have been swimming against a veritable tsunami of first-person rock memoirs, specifically the almost seasonal publication of someone's book-length recollection of time spent with some former rock icon – sometimes penned as the Reaper waved his Scythe – which for a period seemed to swamp publishers' lists.

Despite most publishing houses' penchant for deep discounting and the abandonment of backlists, the modern (auto)biography industry was for a while thriving, in no small measure due to Dylan's own unreliable memoir. As so often, where Dylan trod, legions soon followed. An unholy alliance of commissioning editors, beady agents and rock stars with axes to grind filled the pre-Christmas shelves with ghosted recollections of hapless high jinks on their inexorable way to the remainder bins.

Thus, for a decade after *Chronicles*, the rock memoir flared up like an Independence Day firework display, leaving almost as little to show for it. And while Dylan spent the time fending off enquiries about *Chronicles Vol. 2*, at least three key figures from the pre-accident era *carp*ed the *diem*, scooping up pieces of silver to spill the beans – in the case of Victor Maymudes, Dylan's skirt-chasing bodyguard and occasional drug mule, from beyond the grave and the other side of a lawsuit.

Another Side Of Bob Dylan (2014) was compiled by Victor's son from a sketchy book proposal his father wrote and twenty cassette tapes of his father reminiscing, even though said patriarch had barely known his own flesh and blood. That a mainstream publisher like St Martin's Press would countenance publishing such thin gruel suggested just how fevered this fools' gold rush had become.

If Maymudes' ghost-rider only fitfully recollected a misspent youth convincingly, the memoirs of Dylan's great teen-love, Suze Rotolo (*A Freewheelin' Time*, 2008), and Band leader Robbie Robertson (*Testimony*, 2016), were at least penned by the name on the spine. Each painted a portrait of Dylan which reaffirmed the astuteness of Woodstock cafe owner, Bernard Paturel, who observed of his once-regular customer, 'He's got so many sides, he's round.'

An older, wiser, freer Rotolo – who already knew her days were numbered when the book deal was struck – came across as a modern pushmi-pullyu, caught between an overprotective, uptight mother (the one Dylan famously accused of using 'strings of guilt' to bind her younger daughter) and her spinning dervish of a boyfriend. Throughout it all, her youthful political fervour shines through, suggesting Dylan's determination to detach himself from 'The Cause' by the end of 1963 might have played a role in what tore them apart.

Robertson's memoir is far more of a curate's egg. In his own special way, Robertson chose to be as economical with the truth as the *Chronicle*r, his assumption that the reader would take him as a sympathetic, credible narrator of his own life story only holding true if said reader knows nothing about The Band other than their albums.

Which brings us semi-seamlessly back to Dylan, who in 2004 – before rock-memoir fatigue set in – was relying on reviewers taking his book at face value 'as a sympathetic, credible narrator of his own life story',* even as he littered *Chronicles* with more than enough of what comic genius Peter Cook liked to call 'a thin tissue of lies' to cast doubt on every event described, every feeling recalled.

Witness Dylan's excruciating sign-off to Rotolo at the end of the volume: 'The alliance between Suze and me didn't turn out exactly to be a holiday in the woods. Eventually fate flagged it down and it came to a full stop.' Contrast such overwrought platitudes with Suze's devastating comment at the time, to mutual friend and journalist, Al Aronowitz, 'We keep wearing each other down like pencils', and remind me again which of the two was awarded the Nobel Prize in Literature.

In fairness, Dylan had previously evoked the end of that fateful relationship in words that really did burn like molten coal: 'I still believe she was my twin / But she was born in spring and I was born too late', using a medium he made his own: the song lyric.[†]

He did it again when he penned another of his instantly evocative lines, 'I'm trying to get as far away from myself as I can', within months (or even weeks) of starting to write a memoir of his life, in 1999. This suggests a central paradox at the very heart of the man and his art; one that will serve as a counterpoint to my own narrative, a wholly unauthorised version of the self-same life.[‡]

It is a thread other astute critics of the man have noticed in his more recent work; not just his twenty-first-century music, but in his underappreciated 2003 movie, *Masked and Anonymous* – written at the same time as *Chronicles* – which ex-Poet Laureate Andrew Motion, for one,

---

* Nor would he be disappointed. The reviewers bought into Biographer Bob hook, line and sinkhole: *'It sizzles with biting one-liners and radiates honesty'* – Shusha Guppy, *Daily Mail*; *'The narrator of Chronicles turns out to be a superbly candid and engaging character'* – Ben Thompson, *Independent on Sunday*; *'Peels away some of the enigma that still swirls around Dylan'* – Patrick Humphries, *Sunday Express*; *'Lucid, engaging and incredibly direct. Dylan has taken back his story from his biographers'* – David Sexton, *Evening Standard*. (Methinks not.)
† Dylan actually inverts his and Suze's birth dates. It was he who was born in spring and Suze – like Sara – who was born 'too late', i.e. in November.
‡ This self-referential line, absent from *The Wonder Boys*, would trigger the Oscar-winning song, 'Things Have Changed'.

recognized as 'revelatory, in the paradoxical sense that it allows Dylan to say some important things out loud, and [yet] keep the silences, and retain the elements of mystery, which are essential to his genius'.

Fast-forward sixteen years to the latest celluloid deconstruction of the Dylan myth, *Rolling Thunder Revue* (2019), and we find Dylan continuing to strew enough clues that anything he says in the twenty-first century about what happened in the twentieth should be taken with a truckload of salt. As he revisits the last critical lambasting he received for daring to make a movie about man and myth (1978's *Renaldo & Clara*), he cites the famous Oscar Wilde aphorism 'Man is least himself when he talks in his own person. Give him a mask, and he will tell you the truth.' Could he be trying to tell us to trust the tale, not the artist?

Even Bell grasped the fact that the 2004 memoir, *Chronicles*, 'burns most strongly when he is reaching through the veil of years in the always-doomed effort to touch the lost geography of his childhood and youth'. It just never seems to occur to him that Dylan might be making a conscious choice *not* to tear apart the veil; that maybe that 'effort' is not so much doomed as damned-if-he-will.

On a whole other level, the myth has been enveloping Dylan for so long now that it provides warmth and comfort. Even as he has ventured further and further into his own labyrinthine imagination for emotional succour, so he has left a trail which allows those of us who have followed to reconstruct a way in (and out) of the ongoing odyssey (and I write this as Dylan's 2020 album, *Rough and Rowdy Ways*, just topped charts both sides of the pond, reaffirming his enduring relevance).

He continues to take the savvy view that most folk wish to venture only far enough to say they have been there – not to forge into the unknowable region both he and Rimbaud came to inhabit fleetingly, at a cost to their sanity and their health. Yet there is another contradiction the returning biographer is required to address. Even as Dylan seems determined to blow smoke and hold up cracked mirrors to his own work, past and present, he has allowed his working methods in song and word to be laid bare in a series of approved archival digs.

What no one saw coming two decades ago – least of all yours truly – was Dylan agreeing to release hours and hours of musical discards from a career replete with wrong turns (and yes, I still subscribe to the view some *New York Times* book reviewer castigated me for back in 1991, that I'd have done a better job selecting and sequencing his albums). A brand-new Sony contract in 2012 committed him, and his archivally minded manager Jeff Rosen, to ten annual, *multi-volume* instalments in *The Bootleg Series*, a till-then occasional excavation of largely oft-bootlegged out-takes and near-legendary concert performances.

At the same time, changes in copyright law in Europe forced sixties rock icons to consider issuing limited edition 'copyright collections' of unreleased recordings that would soon be more than fifty years old, and would therefore fall into the public domain unless protected in this way. These copyright collections and *The Bootleg Series* now account for just about every Dylan studio recording of note from 1961 through 1970 – including six CDs' worth of basement tapes – even if historical context is sometimes in short supply.

However, even these expansive collections haven't always included those moments before or after songs – what went on not so much behind the shades as Between the Takes, making it essential that I secured access to the extant session tapes. When I did I uncovered a narrative still being airbrushed by the powers that be; witness the omission of any reference to, or comment by, Dylan's girlfriend and muse Ellen Bernstein during the supposedly complete release of the New York *Blood On The Tracks* sessions, *More Blood, More Tracks* (2018), a rewriting of history which would have made Shakspeare and Holinshed blush.

Instead, the sleeve notes to said Sony set relied primarily on the testimony of an assistant engineer at just two of the four sessions, Glenn Berger, a generous and loquacious man, whose published account of those sessions does not get a *single* material fact right. Whatever his insights – and he has some – they could hardly be a replacement for Ellen's, who not only attended all four sessions *and* the subsequent mixing sessions but was just about the only sounding board to whom Dylan paid any attention at A&R, and whose memory remains fiercely intact.

The main problem for any would-be biographer of a septuagenarian rock star is that memories as good as Ellen's are very much the exception. Not only are Dylan and his contemporaries getting on, their memories are like-as-not shot, whatever their preferred poison back in the day.* Time is not on any true chronicler's side.

This was the fundamental obstacle confronting the likes of Kevin Odegard, Elijah Wald, and Daryl Sanders when they were contracted to tackle, in tome form, those musical landmarks: the *Blood On The Tracks* sessions, the Newport Folk Festival and the *Blonde On Blonde* sessions, from a thirty-, fifty- and fifty-two-year perspective, respectively.[†]

Odegard came closest to enhancing the historical record simply because a) he was actually there himself, at the December 1974 Minneapolis sessions; b) thanks to his many contacts, he managed to interview just about everybody involved musically, including chief engineers Phil Ramone and Paul Martinson, cross-cutting contradictory accounts; and c) there's a quantifiable difference between most folk's memories of past events at fifty and seventy.

Whereas Wald and Sanders set themselves the Sisyphean challenge to slice and dice recollections of historical events which occurred fully half a century earlier, and in Sanders' case from some of Nashville's most notorious bullshitters. (Having read many comments producer Bob Johnston made about working with Dylan, I'm not sure I'd have trusted him to tell the time of day.)

As Dylan himself states at the outset to Martin Scorsese's *Rolling Thunder Revue*, when asked for his memories of that legendary 1975 tour, 'I can't remember a damn thing,' the first and last true statement he offers in that misguided mockumentary.

Tapes, on the other hand, do not lie. And what comes across in those between-take moments at the seminal sessions to *Blonde On Blonde* and *Blood On The Tracks* (both now officially released in their *musical* entirety) is first and foremost the self-assurance of Dylan in the studio. Right from day one – November 20th, 1961, Columbia Studio A – he knew what he wanted and what mattered even as older, stuffier heads remained stuck in their ways and/or congenitally clueless.

If there was an auteur theory which held good for popular music, here would be the smoking gun. It certainly helps explain Dylan's

---

* And yet Richard Alderson, the soundman on the infamous 1966 tour, when I tracked him down in 2016, displayed highly detailed memories of that pill-poppin' time. So, not a hard and fast rule.

[†] The books in question are *Simple Twist of Fate* (2004), *Dylan Goes Electric* (2015) and *That Thin Wild Mercury Sound* (2018), all worthwhile.

choice of producers post-Wilson (i.e. from *Highway 61 Revisited* on). Whereas Dylan instinctively knew what he wanted to bear his name in those 'simple years', producing a body of work that would continue to endure – and sell – in the teeth of incomprehension and condescension in roughly equal measures from the record label, a series of internal Columbia memos from the period – accessed here for the very first time – reveal quite a sting in the tail.

It turns out that certain people at Columbia consistently behaved immorally, and possibly illegally, in their contractual dealings with the once-underage contractee, whereas Albert Grossman did his darnedest to fight Dylan's corner tenaciously, only for his charge to repeatedly sabotage his manager's best efforts and his own self-interest at a cost he would not realize for years.*

So, much has been revealed in the two decades since I last tried to frame Dylan's life and work between hardback covers. However, until March 2nd, 2016, they did not cumulatively demand a volte-face, uber-revisionist take on the Dylan biography I published in 1991 and recast in 2001 (having been gratifyingly informed, in person or print, that it remains the go-to biography for any serious student of the man and his art by writers I rate as highly as James Wolcott, Richard Hell, Jon Pareles, Robert Hilburn, Nick Kent, Francis Wheen, Douglas Brinkley, Sean Wilentz, Jonathan Lethem and Geoff Dyer).

But as a popular poet once said, everything passes, everything changes, and one mad March day in 2016 the world of Dylan studies split open and a great gaping hole at the heart of the master's art was filled if not to the brim, certainly well past the half-full glass of the most optimistic Dylan scholar.†

A story in that day's *New York Times*, called 'Bob Dylan's Secret Archive', was the first breach in a veil of secrecy cast over a clandestine excavation of Dylan's personal archives which had been going on for two or three years, resulting in boxes and boxes of manuscripts dating back as far as his motorcycle accident – housed in any number

---

* If the final section of *Chronicles* is to be believed, Dylan never did fully grasp the consequences of his naiveté.
† Note how Dylan researchers are usually referred to as 'obsessives'; Shakespeare researchers – almost an oxymoron, at this point – as scholars. As both, I baulk at the distinction.

of secure (and not-so-secure) locations from New Jersey to Dylan's Malibu garage – being disinterred.

'Twas the Hitler diaries revisited, with one important difference: this archive was *for real*. The *New York Times* article by Ben Sisario, while hinting of untold riches among the '6,000 pieces', gave us just the tip of a titanic iceberg even as he highlighted a few jewels in this Tulsan crown: two previously unknown *Blood On The Tracks* notebooks; forty pages of draft lyrics to Dylan's discarded late-eighties masterpiece, 'Dignity'; all four filmed performances from New York's Supper Club in November 1993; a typewritten draft to 'Ballad of a Thin Man'.

All the feature could do was whet the appetite of Dylan fans worldwide, prompting them to wonder exactly when the bulk of this material would be on public display, a task the feature effortlessly achieved. Further pieces in *Rolling Stone* and the *Washington Post* filled in further detail, inspiring yet more Pavlovian salivation. Frustratingly, the subtext of all three articles was that general access to the archive was some way off (as indeed it was, and is).

Thankfully, in a welcome break from tradition with the acquisition of such substantive collections, as soon as the Dylan archive found a temporary berth at the Gilcrease Museum – a world-class repository for Americana in all shapes and sizes – it became possible for more, er, accredited Dylan scholars to petition for access. They even let me in. Between October 2017 and September 2019, I was allowed to spend ten weeks, across four distinct trips, working at the archive nine to five each day aided and abetted by librarian/archivist Mark Davidson, helping myself to make sense of this fastidious hoarder I never previously imagine existed.

But contrary to hints in the numerous articles – on- and offline – preceding my visits, it turned out Tulsa had very little manuscript material from the period covered in this volume, the pre-accident years: a fair copy of 'Chimes of Freedom' on Toronto hotel notepaper (already included in *The Bob Dylan Scrapbook*); an early typescript of 'Subterranean Homesick Blues' (reproduced in 1973's *Writings & Drawings*); and a dozen or so hand-corrected typescripts from 1965, most of which had been scheduled to be sold by Christie's in 2011, and were as such reproduced in the auction catalogue. And that was about it.

Where the Tulsa archive did come into its own – and how – in its coverage of the pre-accident years was with the hours and hours of out-take footage it has from the two tour documentaries, *dont look back* and *Eat The Document*, revelatory at every turn; with the uncirculated recordings his Minnesotan friend, Tony Glover, made in August 1962 and July 1963 of a Dylan talking up a storm with his guard down; and a remarkable cache of drafts for his one book-length work of fiction (unless *Chronicles* counts), *Tarantula*. All of these I thoroughly trawled.

How much the portal will open when I, and others, come to the years when there are working lyrics galore, we will have to wait and see. Suffice to say that even though Dylan banked a $22 million cheque, he has retained copyright on all of the written material housed in Tulsa, which means a degree of control in keeping with his character has been retained. The eye-watering sum paid for the archive has not changed *this* leopard's spots.

As it is, the first doorstoppin' result – from my end – is the handsome book you now hold in your hands: volume one of what will be hopefully a 'Double Life' that, taken in tandem, aims to tell the life and times of America's most important twentieth-century popular artist in a way that was unimaginable when I wrote *Behind The Shades*; a new kind of biography written in the same milieu as its subject but with the kind of access to the working processes usually possible only after an artist's death.

I'd like to think my access to the vast archive found behind the Gilcrease's securely locked doors, integrated with my ongoing research across the last decade, notably on auction-house Dylan manuscripts and a slew of Bootleg Series and Sony projects, has produced a cohesive portrait akin to when some Renaissance masterpiece is restored to its truer self – recognizably the same figure but sharper in detail, the colours more illuminated.

As for its author, I hope former readers of *Behind The Shades* will hear the echo of that voice, while at the same time experiencing this 'rockin' reelin' rollin' ride' afresh, as if one had indeed jumped out of a moving vehicle and grabbed a-hold of a subway car, in 'the coldest winter in seventeen' – or is it twenty-eight? – 'years'. Welcome to the Village, in the year of our Lord 1961 . . .

Clinton Heylin, July 2020

Prelude

July 29th, 1961: Down By The Riverside

> Bob Dylan, of Gallup, New Mexico, played the guitar and harmonica simultaneously, and with rural gusto.
>
> Pete Karman, *New York Mirror*, August 6th, 1961

It starts with a lie. The first time Dylan's name is mentioned in print in the context of his music, he is already peddling the legend that he is 'Bob Dylan, of Gallup, New Mexico', which is how the MC introduces him this July afternoon. At least the *Mirror* spells his name right – something that proved beyond the (New Jersey) *Record* when previewing the very concert which would bring the twenty-year-old folk musician mentions in both the *New York Mirror* and the *New York Times*.*

'Bob Dillon' is the name the *Record* gave, a common mistake at the time. Where the *Record*, with remarkable prescience, got it right was in suggesting that the occasion – an eight-hour marathon concert at Harlem's Riverside Church to announce the setting up of a new radio station religiously devoted to folk music – 'should provide a field day for tape recordists'.

For one particular 'tape recordist', amateur folklorist Mell Bailey, the broadcast of the entire concert on WRVR created a serious conflict of interest: whether to attend or stay home and record the event for posterity. In the end, he managed both – we know not how – recording two and a half hours of the ostensible headliners on his Wollensak reel-to-reel while catching his young friend Dylan's performance in person.

---

* The *New York Times*'s Robert Shelton merely describes Dylan as 'a twenty-year-old latter-day Guthrie disciple ... with a curiously arresting mumbling, country-steeped manner'.

Mell and his wife Lillian were already part of a small group of Dylan cheerleaders and they were all there at the Riverside. As attendee Samuel R. Delaney later noted: 'Among the audience of forty-five or fifty people ... there were clearly about ten or twelve who were particularly enthusiastic about him, and had come specifically to hear him – among the dozen [or so] performers that afternoon – and for whom he was clearly playing.'

Mell and Lillian knew what Dylan was capable of, having recorded him a month earlier in their East Village apartment, swapping songs with Ian Tyson (of the folk duo, Ian & Sylvia) and dropping names like billy-o. But what the wider radio audience made of Dylan's five-song performance that afternoon has gone unrecorded.

Thankfully, those mentions in the *Times* and the *Mirror* set the early cabal of Dylan collectors on the trail of a tape, and by 1971 the radio station's own copy had been located and liberated, duly appearing on one of those legendary Trade Mark of Quality bootleg albums cover-artist William Stout emblazoned with his iconic cartoons, *Early 60s Revisited*.

The unknown liberator was evidently interested only in Dylan's performance, so if the full concert was still at WRVR, there it remained. Only with the acquisition of the Baileys' tapes by the Tulsa Dylan archive did their forty-two-song recording of the Riverside broadcast reveal not merely the context, but the entire musicial milieu on which the comet called Dylan had descended six months earlier, when he blew in from Madison, Wisconsin, part of a car-share of folkies bound for glory or bust – his 'mind fixed on hidden interests', as he later put it.

And what a roll call of names the Bailey tapes provide; a veritable who's who of Dylan's peers: Ramblin' Jack Elliott, Bruce Langhorne, Brother John Sellers, Dave Van Ronk, Tom Paxton, the Greenbriar Boys, Annie Bird and Logan English all performed that day alongside stylistic precursors as important to the teenage Dylan as Reverend Gary Davis and Victoria Spivey. Even the son of 'The Father of the Blues' was there to hear Dylan fuse forms, much as his father had half a century earlier, W. C. Handy Jr joining Victoria Spivey on 'St Louis Blues', the very song which gave the big bang to the blues.

Dylan may well have given some thought to the songs he ought to play for his New York radio debut, fully conscious of the fact that so much of his ever-shifting repertoire had been 'acquired' from the very performers with whom he was now sharing this hallowed chancel. Not too much thought, though. He still chose to play 'Po' Lazarus', a song he had learnt from Dave Van Ronk, who'd intended to perform it himself for the radio audience.

Here was perhaps the first indication the young tyke had no intention of respecting the unspoken folkie code of 'dibs on trad arr.' material whenever said arranger was a fellow revivalist. Dylan already knew the song in question was one that showed his belligerent approach to such material in a good light, even compared to Van Ronk's gruff template.

The other two songs with which he verbally assaulted the small audience that afternoon, before turning the microphone over to his Madison friend Danny Kalb, were both ballads familiar to most Village folkies.

'Handsome Molly' was an American derivative of a British broadside ballad ('Courting Is A Pleasure') he was still singing a year later, while 'Omie Wise' (aka 'Deep Water') was a 'judgement' ballad composed shortly after Omie's 1808 murder. An early Dylan tour de force, he would spit out couplets like, 'Go hang him, go hang him, was the brother's command / And throw him in deep water that flows through the land', as eye-for-an-eye justice prevailed in the ballad, which the form demanded – just not in real life, where her killer, John Lewis, escaped scot-free.

Wisely, the one artist on the bill whose repertoire Dylan assiduously avoided was Ramblin' Jack Elliott, even though songs like 'San Francisco Bay Blues', 'Hard Travelin'' and 'Cocaine' – all performed by Elliott at the Riverside – were a key part of this young pretender's daily growin' repertoire. Perhaps he had already heard the echoing Village whispers that likened him to Jack's bastard son, so much had he taken from the Brooklyn cowboy's act.

He also refrained from performing any of his own songs, even 'Song To Woody', perhaps sensing they could not yet stand alongside those his contemporary, Tom Paxton, was already writing and performing; songs like 'The Train For Auschwitz', which Paxton played at Riverside, surely striking a chord with this grandson of East European émigrés.

The twenty-three-year-old Paxton had already set a songwriting bar Dylan would have to clear if he was going to amount to anything. Yet even on this slim evidence – three solo performances, a harmonica accompaniment to one of Kalb's Southern blues and a prom-song pastiche with Elliott – there was something which already set Dylan apart: his delivery. As Village bluegrass aficionados and future Holy Modal Rounder, Pete Stampfel, later noted, 'He was doing all traditional songs, but it was his approach! His singing style and phrasing were stone rhythm & blues.'

All in all, it was a momentous day for the young tyke, topped off when he got talking to the *Mirror*'s Pete Karman and spun a few tall tales angling to secure an introduction to the two sisters who had shared Karman's car on the drive uptown, Carla and Suze Rotolo.

According to the *Chronicler*, he already knew the former slightly because she was fastidious folklorist Alan Lomax's personal assistant. But Dylan wasn't interested in discussing folklore with the elder sister that day. He had eyes only for the golden-haired Suze, and when he was like this, there was no stopping him. It was exactly as an old Minnesotan girlfriend, Ellen Baker, later observed, 'He'd see a girl ... at a party, and it didn't matter ... who he was with – if he was in *that* mood.'

In his memoir, Dylan even admitted that his initial interest was sexual, describing Suze, rather objectifyingly, as 'the most erotic thing I'd ever seen'. Whereas the man-boy Suze described in her own memoir was 'funny, engaging, intense and ... persistent ... He started ... talking backstage ... early in the day and didn't stop until the day was done.' If he was aiming to bowl her over, to make a deep and abiding impression on the seventeen-year-old, he succeeded. He pierced her breast that day.

Barely had the dazed and bemused gal returned home at 4 a.m., after the crowded backstage had relocated downtown to Anne Bird's apartment for an after-hours party, than she wrote to best friend Sue Zuckerman, who had taken a summer job in Connecticut, excitedly telling her all about how 'Dylan gave us a private concert, a repeat of the private one I'd gotten that afternoon in the soundproofed room. He's a good composer, too. He and John [Wynn] sang a song that lasted a half-hour, completely impromptu ... Dylan giggling his adorable giggle all through it.'*

---

* Zuckerman, in her online obituary of her friend, suggests it was John Herald, but in the version she told Scaduto, less than a decade after that party, it was John Wynn, whom I suspect it really was.

The song in question, lost to the evening's alcohol-fuelled air, was called 'The Beautiful People', a satirical send-up of the kind of people the beatniks of Greenwich considered Square. For now, Dylan continued to take the view that 'the only beauty's ugly, man'. His 'alliance' with Suze, which began on this magical night, would change all that. Indeed, many things changed that night.

Here was his first radio show; his first mentions in the press; the first time he had shared a bill with the majority of his peers, enabling him to emerge as someone whose distinctive style set him apart. Just two months later *to the day*, Robert Shelton, folk music critic at the *New York Times*, and one of those who heard someone different from the rest at the Riverside, would let everyone in the Village know he thought this upstart crow could pull the sword from the stone, penning a *Times* review which would trigger a major-label record deal and a great deal of envy and enmity.

For the young Dylan the six months leading up to that Riverside epiphany soon became something of a blur. Yet, as late as 1963, he was still insisting they were so formative that when he did write that memoir, it would be 'about my first week in New York ... I'm still carrying these memories with me.'

When he finally got around to writing these vestigial thoughts down *and* publishing them, a full forty years later, he was still writing about those 'younger days'. But his memory no longer served him well. History would require A. N. Other to gingerly retrace those steps on its behalf, to glean what really happened when it was as yet all up for grabs.

Part 1

A Thief Of Thoughts

Perhaps we are not to look for his Beginnings, like those of other Authors, among their least perfect writings; Art had so little and Nature so large a share in what he did.
 Nicholas Rowe, *Some Account of the Life &c. of Mr William Shakespear*
(1709)

For a Jew, to change your name is to alter your essence.
Elena Poniatowska

Mildred [Peggy Maley]: Hey Johnny, what are you rebelling against?
Johnny Strabler [Marlon Brando]: Whaddaya got?
The Wild One (1953)

To *understand* the *man* you have to *know* what was happening in the world when he was twenty.
Napoleon Bonaparte

1.1

January to May 1961: Big City Blues

You never could pin him down on anything. He had a lot of stories about who he was and where he came from, [but] he never seemed to be able to keep [any of] them straight.

Dave Van Ronk

You could not ask him personal questions. He'd always joke, or he'd tell you something like he used to be a miner – something like that. If you'd ask about his parents, he'd say he had none, or he'd make a joke, or he'd change the subject, or he'd put you on ... [] ... But if you didn't need to get personal with him, you just wanted somebody to hang out with and play music with, he was a ball. He just liked to kid around.

John Herald

One time I asked him about his background. He said he was from New Mexico. I said, 'Do you have parents there?' He said, 'No. I had a lot of foster parents.' I said, 'What was the name of your last foster parents?' He said, 'Aw, there were so many of them, I don't rightly remember.'

Eve McKenzie

I kinda thought he was imitating Woody [Guthrie], but he said that he ... learnt [all] those songs from various hoboes he met on the road. I didn't argue about it.

Ramblin' Jack Elliott

*

Even more momentous than the day Dylan met Suze down at the Riverside was the cold, bright day, half a year beforehand, when he first came to the city that never sleeps. It was the third week in January, and he and his companions of the road had driven 'straight on through' from Madison to Manhattan. The moment he saw its skyline everything changed. As he would write in December 1963, 'I would not be doing what I'm doing today if I hadn't come to New York. I was given my direction from New York ... Jack Elliott ... says he was reborn in Oklahoma, I say I was reborn in New York.'

For the nineteen-year-old Dylan, the past was a foreign country. As he would inform Bill Flanagan in 2009, in a rare moment of twenty-first-century candour, 'I didn't bring the past with me when I came to New York. Nothing back there would play any part in where I was going.' He was a blank slate and he liked it that way; a man without a name, around whom rumours could (and would) freely swirl. A complete unknown.

He had not merely arrived without a past, he had covered his tracks. If any jilted girlfriend or slum landlord had been trying to follow his trail, they'd have given up long ago. In *Chronicles* he would claim he had 'come ... straight out of Chicago'. And he *had* been in Chicago around Christmas looking up a friend he'd met in Denver that summer, Kevin Krown, but he hadn't stayed long, having actually backtracked to Madison, seemingly on his way back to Minneapolis. As he correctly recalled to Randy Anderson in 1978, 'From there I went to New York. That was quite a trip. Another guitar player and myself got a ride with a young couple from the [university] campus, whose parents were from Brooklyn. They were going there and wanted some more drivers.'

What isn't clear is if Krown was the 'other guitar player' in the car. In an earlier account of this cross-country jaunt, to Robert Shelton on a flight to nowhere in March 1966, Dylan spoke of 'a friend ... He's a junkie now. We came to New York together ... I had the guitar,' rather implying that *he* was the itinerant 'guitar player', not his friend.

Krown was certainly more tolerant of Dylan's newly acquired nasal whine than other passengers, one of whom, Dave Berger, was the one whose car it was and was therefore calling the shots. For Berger, the trip would prove memorable but for all the wrong reasons, with

Dylan 'singing all the way ... that weird monotonic kind of style with Woody's twang ... As we got into New Jersey, I finally told him, "Shut the fuck up."'

We know of one other passenger in the car that day: Fred Underhill, a student at the university who shared an apartment with the poet Ann Lauterbach. But Underhill was hardly a close friend of Dylan's (though they stayed in touch till at least 1964); nor did he end up a junkie, moving to England in the mid-sixties with Lauterbach and then staying there.

Assuming Krown *was* indeed that 'friend', as seems likely, the pieces fall into place. He and Dylan *were* friends, and would stay close through 1964 when they began to become estranged, possibly because Krown had indeed taken to hard drugs, as many in that era did. For a short period in 1961, Krown even tried his hand at managing Dylan and seems to have been responsible for convincing Dylan to record himself on the tape recorder of the Gleasons, a family he ended up staying with in East Orange, New Jersey, less than a fortnight after he came to town.

Peter McKenzie, an awestruck kid befriended by the pair, told me that whenever he 'was at the Gleasons' ... Bobby would practise by singing into the tape recorder, learning how to use a microphone. He and Kevin made the tape one day. Kevin sent out several copies.' If so, Krown was responsible for Dylan's first audition tape, the so-called Gleason Tape, an important audio-document featuring three Guthrie tunes, two traditional songs to which Dylan will later put words of his own, 'Gypsy Davey' and 'Trail Of The Buffalo', and Scott Wiseman's 'Remember Me', which he could still remember when song-swapping with Joan Baez at the Savoy hotel in May 1965.

According to a report on the Best American Poetry website, Krown was also one of three people who travelled with Dylan to the Greystone Asylum, near Morristown, New Jersey, on that first weekend in New York, to go see the ailing Woody Guthrie, the ostensible reason why Dylan had just trekked halfway across the country. The significance of this is that Krown, and only Krown, would have known something of Dylan's Minnesotan past, after spending time with him in Denver, Chicago and (presumably) Madison.

Crucially, Krown had known Dylan since before Dylan 'knew' Guthrie, specifically the Guthrie of his own fictional memoir, *Bound For Glory*. He had first met Dylan when he had been playing piano in a strip joint in Central City in the summer of 1960, a long, long way from Folk City USA. He was therefore the one residue of Dylan's past to accompany him to New York.

If they also both made that trip out to Greystone, they shared another common bond, albeit not one that resulted in Krown featuring in Dylan's first-hand account of the historic meeting in the state mental asylum in which Guthrie had been housed ever since a hereditary degenerative disease, Huntington's chorea, had made him need round-the-clock care. Dylan's description of this meeting in *No Direction Home* allows for no third party: 'I took a bus out to Morristown. I think it was an insane asylum ... They put him in a mental home, because he just had the jitters. He asked for certain songs and I'd play them.'

The experience would have been a chastening one for most youths at Dylan's age – barely nineteen – but unbeknownst to anyone outside Minnesota, he had been regularly visiting a crippled friend in hospital back in Minneapolis for the past three years, always playing songs to cheer him up. And as Dylan told a radio audience in 1986, meeting Woody for the first time 'was a thrill. I [had] made a pilgrimage ... and I [had] accomplished what I'd set out to do.'

If Krown was with him on that first occasion – and I suspect he was – they presumably returned to whoever's floor they had found to sleep on in the few days they had spent in Greenwich Village. They were living like beatniks, an idea that appealed to Krown as much as Dylan, with both of them visiting Denver the previous summer for precisely the same literary reason – inspired by the part of Jack Kerouac's *On The Road* set there.

Even in New York Dylan seems to have expected to be taken in by his fellow folkies, later making light of the hardships involved: 'I didn't have any place to stay, but it was easy for me. People took me in.' Having already had a similar experience in Denver, Chicago and Madison, he seems to have assumed the same would apply in New York. So much for 'hard times / living down in New York town'.

He doesn't even seem to have been unduly fazed when, on the day they arrived, he and his travelling companion were offered a place to crash for the night, only to find that their new-found room-mate had a friend who was almost certainly a man, but went by the name of

Dora.* It was a scene straight out of one of Kerouac's road odysseys, and one for the book he planned to write 'about my first week in New York ... [and] somebody who has come to the end of one road, knows there's another road there, but doesn't exactly know where it is'.

These thoughts would stay with him long enough to inspire at least two early talkin' blues, 'Talkin' New York' and 'Talkin' Folklore Center', and three poems for the page: 'My Life In A Stolen Moment' and his sleeve notes for *The New World Singers* LP and Peter Paul & Mary's *In The Wind* – all from 1963 – the same year as the above quote. By then, he was mournfully lamenting 'these times ... for they're gone – an they'll not never come again – it is 'f these times I think about now ... nites when the doors was locked an maybe thirty or forty people sat as close t the stage as they could'.

Initially, he was playing to more like three or four people, and in the earliest draft to 'Talkin' New York', he claimed that when he first 'rolled into this here town, two feet a snow covered the ground / I couldn't find no place to stay, I rode the subway for a couple a days'.

Perhaps this happened after he met Dora, not before. In the version he penned for the following winter's 'Talkin' Folklore Center', he enjoyed yet more adventures on the subway, getting 'out on 42nd Street / I met this fellow named Delores there / He started rubbin' his hands through my hair.' Either his pretty-boy looks were already attracting legions of would-be pederasts or he was reusing his one brush with Dora/Delores at will.†

Either way, he survived unscathed to arrive downtown, where we can be fairly confident that the first Village folk club he performed at

---

* He told the story to Columbia publicist Billy James, that fall: 'I didn't have a place to stay that night. So I asked from the stage and about four hands went up. So my buddy and I, we ... picked out a fellow. He was with a girl. And my buddy says to me, "He looks pretty gay." I didn't really know anything about that kind of stuff. Anyway, he was with a girl. And so we went up with him and the girl got off at 34th Street and we got off at 42nd street [Dylan laughs]. We went in a bar first before we went to [his] place and we met his friend Dora. Dora was his friend who stayed with him. And we all went to a party. That was my first night in New York.'
† He would further embellish the narrative in talking to Shelton in 1966, when he tried to claim he was briefly a rent boy in Times Square when he first came to New York, a Rimbaudian fantasy.

was the Cafe Wha?, for the simple reason that no place else would have let him just turn up and play, save on a hootenanny evening. Having been cold-shouldered by a couple of well-established folk clubs in Denver and Madison, he can't have thought – even in his hyperactive imagination – that the likes of Gerde's Folk City or the Gaslight would open their doors to him readily. But the Wha? was something else:

Bob Dylan: I realized right away that I'd come to the right place, because there were ... places [like this] to play ... Sawdust on the floor, tourist traps [with] a poet, somebody singing a song with a parrot on a shoulder. Tiny Tim-type characters. No one who had any recordings out ever played them. You only played those if you had to. [2000]

I used to play with a guy called Fred Neil ... He would play mostly the types of songs that Josh White might sing. I would play harmonica for him, and then once in a while get to sing a song ... when he was taking a break ... He would be on for about half an hour, then a conga player would get on ... And then this girl ... used to play sweet Southern Mountain Appalachian ballads, with electric guitar and a small amplifier ... Then there'd be a comedian, then an impersonator ... and this whole unit would go around non-stop. [1984]

The girl in question was Karen Dalton, a buxom singer with lung power to spare. Serendipitously, *Village Voice* photographer Fred McDarrah was in the right place at the right time to snap this trio – Neil, Dylan and Dalton – at the Wha? that February. It is Dalton who is centre stage while Dylan plays cupped harmonica, 'blowing his lungs out for a dollar a day', while Neil hollers some harmony and strums a waist-high guitar. Dylan, who had already adopted a cloth, or possibly corduroy, cap and unbuttoned waistcoat as his Village uniform, seems to be having a ball.*

Dylan was not a Wha? regular for long, perhaps less than three weeks. By February 12th, he was telling friends in Minneapolis (by

---

* According to *Chronicles*, Dylan already knew Dalton from 'the previous summer outside of Denver in a mountain-pass town ... folk club'. There is no way of confirming this. Dalton died in 1993, eleven years before his memoir's publication, having wrestled with drug addiction for even longer than her erstwhile nightly accompanist at the Wha? (I mean Neil, a notorious junkie even then).

postcard) that he was visiting Guthrie four times a week – probably an exaggeration – and playing at the Commons, where 'people clap for me'. He was already moving on, literally and metaphorically. In fact, when he pencilled out an outline of possible chapters for *Chronicles* around 2001, he placed his New York experiences as follows:

2. Freddy Neil – Cafe Wha? – Ricky Nelson (flawless intonation)
3. Van Ronk – basket houses – Folklore Center
4. Gaslight

Save for hearing the ghost of his own rock'n'roll past on the radio a whole two months *before* the release of Ricky Nelson's April 1961 45, 'Travelin' Man', this was pretty much how those wintry weeks panned out. He got to meet many of his fellow folkies, most notably Dave Van Ronk, almost the minute he came to town; spent the weekends doing the rounds of the kind of 'basket houses' where the basket was passed more in hope than expectation; and hung out at Izzy Young's Folklore Center and the Gaslight Cafe when he yearned for conversation but couldn't afford a drink – which was most of the time.

However, this is hardly the whole story. He needed to make ends meet, or at least eat, when the basket was empty. And in that 2001 outline, he makes two references to playing for a soul-dance company uptown, suggesting a failed audition of sorts, about which he made no mention at the time. He also kept quiet about another extracurricular activity to his Village friends, though he admitted to Sid (short for Sidsel) and Bob Gleason – the couple whose couch soon provided a home away from home in East Orange – that he took work as a day labourer for the Department of Sanitation, shovelling some of the snow mounting up during that record-breaking winter.

He also described the experience in the first draft of 'Talkin' New York': 'One day I shipped out from 3rd Avenue / Shoveling snow way out there in Rockview / Me and about thirty other men.' If it demonstrated someone who had yet to strip every element of realism from the process of turning life into art, the lines would not survive until the song's appearance on his debut LP, the following March.

For now, talkin' blues was Dylan's preferred medium of expression. A fixed form appropriated by hillbilly singer Chris Bouchillon from blues singers on the ironically named 1926 78, 'Original Talking Blues', its elastic structure enabled verbal asides and elongated verses, improvisation and caustic one-liners to reign.

Dylan's early talkin' blues were the first of his 'originals' to make people sit up and take notice, being perfectly suited to the Village clubs where comedy and folk were frequent bedfellows. However, the idea of using an identical template for multiple lyrics was lost on some, including Dylan's first Columbia producer, John Hammond Sr. When he began recording a talkin' blues about the John Birch Society, at a session shortly after Talkin' New York's release, the experienced producer suggested to Dylan, 'Why not a few different chord changes, 'cause you're using the *exact* same chord changes?' A bemused Dylan replied, 'Yeah, they're the ones I use' – at which point Hammond quietly dropped the subject.*

Originally, 'Talkin' New York' would reference Guthrie twice: once, as the reason Dylan came to the city – 'I rambled to NY one time, came to see a friend of mine' – and then as the 'very great man' who first noted how 'some people rob you with a fountain pen', a line from Guthrie's paean to Pretty Boy Floyd. For now, Guthrie's influence seeped into everything his protégé wrote.

By the time Dylan wrote these lines, he had met the 'great man', and had even apparently attempted to ingratiate himself with the family, turning up at their door in Howard Beach in Queens, perhaps after shovelling snow in Rockview. If he did come to call, it can only have been at Woody's (or Mrs Guthrie's) suggestion, which makes daughter Nora's almost perfect recall of the visit forty years later, to Sounes – describing Dylan as 'a very dusty-looking character' who turned up unexpectedly and 'looked as bad as my dad [did] with Huntington's' – hard to believe.

In 2004, Nora's description seems to have stung the *Chronicler* into telling the kind of story he used to preface his talkin' blues with back in the day. In it, he claimed he needed to cross a swamp to get to the

---

* Dylan had actually been using the form since the fall of 1960, after listening to how Guthrie handled it on records he found at Ellen Baker's parents'. He duly improvised a send-up of his room-mate Hugh Brown, 'the laziest man in town', someone who 'sprained his arm combing his hair', captured on the so-called 1st Minneapolis Tape.

family home, having come to find some manuscripts of lost Guthrie songs their pa had told him about, before gleaning that 'the babysitter was uncomfortable, [so] I stayed just long enough to warm up ... [before] trudg[ing] back across the swamp to the subway platform'.

It's an odd anecdote, made even more peculiar by the fact that Dylan already knew about the weekly Sunday gatherings the Gleasons, old friends of the Guthries, held at their East Orange home; to which Woody would get a day pass from his Greystone 'prison', sitting and listening while various friends sang and shared memories. One must assume Marjorie Guthrie came along on these days.

Dylan certainly met her shortly after he visited Woody, just not in Howard Beach. If it was during his first Sunday at the Gleasons on January 29th – the more likely scenario – it was an auspicious afternoon. Cisco Houston, Woody's sidekick on many a *Bound For Glory* jaunt, was there – as was Ramblin' Jack Elliott, whom Dylan had already met at Greystone's, the second of his early musical idols he could now tell the folks in St Paul he knew.

Elliott, whose Topic albums had been such a lodestar for Dylan back in Minneapolis that he had attempted to take permanent loan of someone else's import copies, had been in England for some time when he came to Greystones to see his old friend and mentor, only to find a 'strange but interesting [young kid with] full, round cheeks and big soulful eyes, sporting a peach-fuzz beard and wearing a funny hat' had got there first.

If it was Elliott who informed Dylan about the Gleasons' weekly gatherings, it was undoubtedly Dylan who 'charmed the heart of the lady' of the house, Sidsel, who would describe the youngster to Scaduto as 'like a choir boy, with that little round face and beautiful eyes'. A real heartbreaker, in other words. Soon he was, in Sid's own words, 'com[ing] out in the middle of the week, when he was really broke, [to] have dinner and stay over sometimes for a day or two'.

Also staying there for days on end was the forty-two-year-old Houston, who had travelled extensively with Guthrie, playing guitar and singing harmony. (They had even joined the merchant marines together during the war.) According to Dylan, talking to some friends in 1963, 'I slept on the couch. He slept on the couch across a room as big as this ... for two weeks out in Jersey. I *knew* Cisco.' It must have been for only a fortnight at the most because – unbeknownst to everyone, including Dylan – Cisco was on his last go round, having been diagnosed with stage-four cancer a few months before.

Houston was due to play his last New York club date at Gerde's Folk City, the Village club run by Mike Porco, on February 16th, a potentially unfortunate choice as it clashed with a 'proper' concert uptown at Carnegie Hall announcing the return of Ramblin' Jack – but a necessary one. Cisco was heading for his sister's home in San Bernardino, California, where he would pass away on April 29th, 1961, eleven months before he was immortalized on vinyl with the line, 'Here's to Cisco and Sonny and Lead Belly, too', from Dylan's first notable original, 'Song To Woody', which according to the untitled fair copy he gave the Gleasons was written 'in Mills Bar on Bleecker St ... on 14th day of February'.

The last line of said song – 'The very last thing that I want to do / Is to say I been hitting some hard travelling, too' – could also be a knowing nod to Houston, who in his last recorded interview, two weeks before his death, spoke about these 'young kids [who] come to me all the time and ask me about my days on the road. It's very romantic to them. I try to dissuade them from just going out like that ... We did that in those days 'cause we *had* to.' He surely had in mind, at least partly, the kid with whom he had just shared a living room in East Orange for a fortnight.

Not that such references would have been understood outside folk circles at the time. This remained a small, insular world; not one in which even an absence of three years in England could stoke enough demand to justify a gig at Carnegie Hall itself. Which is why Jack Elliott had been booked into the smaller Chapter Hall, hidden away up the stairs and seating a couple of hundred at best, as a new venture by the owner of the Folklore Center, Izzy Young, who was still smarting from the fact that Mike Porco had taken the booking of acts at Folk City away from him after he had introduced the club owner to all the upper-echelon folksingers – or so Izzy liked to claim.

Fortunately, uptown concerts generally ended before Greenwich Village clubs had even unfurled their awnings, and Elliott that night went out of his way to tell people to head to Gerde's after the show; as did Marjorie Guthrie, who was there with her thirteen-year-old son, Arlo, and folklorist Alan Lomax, himself recently returned from England.

Marjorie was also doing all she could to fill Gerde's for Cisco's farewell performance, inviting Eve and 'Mac' McKenzie, two stalwarts of the Village scene, to come along.* At the same time, Mrs Guthrie introduced the pair to a young singer who was standing nearby. It was Dylan (thus confirming she knew him by then), whom she introduced as 'a young folksinger from New Mexico', proof that he was already peddling that line.

Eve had already noticed 'this young fellow sitting on a bench to the left of me, wearing this little corduroy hat, very quiet, smoking one cigarette after another, leg jerking up and down'. Her first impression close up was no less striking, 'a character [straight] out of a Charles Dickens novel', a description that was both apposite and intentional.

If Dylan was already soaking up personae like a sponge – from Charlie Chaplin to Bob Cratchit – the chance to see Elliott's act in a concert setting, after listening to his albums till he knew them by heart, was an opportunity too great to pass up. In fact, so profound was its effect that he soon morphed into a person much like the one performing that night at the Chapter Hall. Within days he became Elliott's mirror image, much to the chagrin of the man who had booked the hall that night:

Izzy Young: When he first started singing he stole from Jack Elliott. He imitated him, he looked like [him], he dressed like him ... He's done that with everyone since that time, and not given credit to anyone ... Now people say they knew him when he was a square boy in Minnesota, and he had a regular haircut and business suit ... but he decided to go with that image, the Jack Elliott image. [1965]

---

* According to the *Chronicles*, there was also a farewell party for Cisco, at a woman called Camilla Adams's place, that had the greatest guest list the folk world has ever known. Dylan claims he arrived with his 'part-time girlfriend', the singer Delores Dixon, and in the space of the evening met Pete Seeger, Woody's manager, Harold Leventhal, Moe Asch of Folkways Records, Irwin Silber, Logan English, Harry Belafonte and Mike Seeger. Some eight pages are devoted to this fantastical occasion. Camilla is a fiction, and one suspects it all is. Even Dylan's description of Houston that night, as someone who had 'achieved some great deed, praiseworthy and meritorious', turns out to be lifted verbatim from Jack London's 1906 novel, *White Fang*.

The change also came as something of a shock to Elliott himself, who had heard Dylan sing at the Gleasons', 'The first time Bob got up on the stage and sang, it was such a direct and obvious imitation of my whole style that the people sitting next to me were ... offended *for* me ... I felt like I had to defend him ... because everybody else was so angry about it.'

Elliott never allowed that early affectation to affect their friendship. And nor did another fellow amanuensis of tradition, Dave Van Ronk, just because, as Dylan later put it, 'We sang the same type of songs.' As a matter of fact, not 'the same type', the exact same songs, sometimes the exact same way, thus storing up trouble ahead. Dylan appreciated the way that 'Van Ronk could take the essence of the song and only go after that, not ... the frills'. It was a gift, and Dylan treated it as such. It mattered not for now. They were both scuffling singers scraping a living, who got on like a house on fire. Dylan soon added the Van Ronks to his list of potential crash-pads.

Where and when that first brief encounter happened is not so clear. Van Ronk, in his posthumously published memoir, claimed it was at the Cafe Wha?, Fred Neil was on stage, while 'playing harmonica was the scruffiest-looking fugitive from a cornfield I do believe I have ever seen ... After the set, Fred introduced us. Bob Dylan, spelt D-Y-L-A-N. "As in Dylan Thomas?" I asked, innocently. ... I [also] made my first acquaintance with his famous dead-fish handshake.'

Tom Paxton says otherwise. He insists both Van Ronk and himself first encountered Dylan 'in Gerde's Folk City on a Monday night hootenanny ... the first three songs that he ever sang in New York [*sic*]. They were three Woody Guthrie songs, and he had on a harmonica rack and a black corduroy cap.' Since both singers would have been asked this question a thousand times by the time they put their version down, we should perhaps say simply, the jury is out as to whether it was the Wha? or Gerde's. What is not in doubt is the kinship Van Ronk and Dylan struck up almost immediately, duly noted by the 'Paul' in Peter, Paul and Mary:

Noel Stookey: The intense and insecure Dylan could relax around Van Ronk. Part of the connection with Bobby was that Van Ronk was a historian and Bobby was very well read. Bobby [had] read Balzac, Ginsberg, the poets.

Another key contemporary who became a bosom buddy, with consequences for both further down the line, was the *trad*est of all the trad folksingers. Paul Clayton had been a field-collector and student under the great Virginian folklorist, Arthur Kyle Davis. Just like Elliott, Clayton was someone whose records Dylan had already encountered in Minnesota, recording his 'Gotta Travel On' on the so-called St Paul Tape in May 1960. In a February 1964 interview Dylan gave Clayton the greatest of compliments, crediting Paul with showing him the true meaning of tradition:

> From folk songs I learnt the language, I learnt a lot about people by singing them and knowing them and remembering them ... English ballads, Scottish ballads, I see them in images ... Something like 'Barbara Allen' ... goes deeper than just myself singing it ... [But] the only guy I know that can really do it is Paul Clayton, he's the only guy I've ever heard or seen who can sing songs like this, because he's a medium, he's not trying to personalize it, he's bringing it to you.

Future sidekick Victor Maymudes confirms, 'Clayton [was] definitely one of his teachers', even if the pupil soon surpassed the mentor, who then became more of a conduit to others who, as Dylan put it, were 'authentic nonconformists ... who said ... it was okay to stay at their apartments any time I needed'. At this stage in his peripatetic existence this was the highest praise Dylan could bestow.

But it was not just his contemporaries who frequented the Village in the period when it was the epicentre of the last great US folk revival. As Paul Colby, owner of the Bitter End, recalled in his own memoir, 'The Village [at this time] was where Pete Seeger lived and ... all the men that Dylan adopted as his spiritual fathers. And these people weren't vague, historical figures that lived centuries ago. You could run into most of them right on Bleecker Street.'

Lead Belly might have been long dead, and Cisco and Woody both dying, but great blues artists like Skip James were being (re)discovered daily by the indefatigible Mike Seeger, the younger brother of Pete (and Peggy), and the son of Charles Seeger, who had chanced upon the great folksinger Elizabeth Cotten by the simple expedient of hiring her as a housekeeper.*

If Dylan was always closer to Mike than Pete, and not just in years, the elder brother also took the teen prodigy under his wing once he realized that's what he was. Dylan would proceed to inform Pete he had heard him play at the University of Wisconsin in 1958, when the show was picketed by the right-wing John Birch Society (presumably on the grounds that Seeger was a 'goddamn Commie').† But he certainly was anxious to listen and learn from a man he would laud in print even after he plugged in, breaking Pete's heart (and any hold he still had on the folk revival).

But the piece of advice from Seeger he most took to heart in the year and a half they hung out he got indirectly from a slim book he had spent a few hard-earned dimes on. Called *California to the New York Island*, it was a Woody Guthrie songbook published by Moe Asch's Oak Books. The perfect-bound collection came with an introduction by Seeger, which the impressionable youth pored over repeatedly, highlighting one particular section in his copy, marked in pen, 'property of Bob Dylan'. The ever-didactic Seeger encouraged readers to 'learn from Woody's method of performance ... [a] matter-of-fact, unmelodramatic, understatement throughout ... getting the words out clearly', while admonishing them to 'beware of trying to imitate Woody's singing too closely – it will sound fake and phoney. Don't try and imitate his accent. Don't try and imitate his flat vocal quality. In short, be yourself.'

The first sign that Dylan was slowly learning to be himself came when he wrote that first heartfelt tribute to Guthrie, just a couple of weeks after he met the man. Though he had been adapting and reworking song forms for almost a year, this was the first time he felt like he 'needed to write that [kinda song] and ... to sing it'.

---

* Dylan's pencilled outline of the people and places he planned to write about in the section of *Chronicles* covering his early days in New York includes a reference to 'Lybba Cotton', but she would be absent from the published book. He had already acknowledged her influence, playing 'Shake Sugaree' at shows in 1995.
† This seems unlikely. Perhaps he had heard tell of the historic confrontation when visiting Madison that January and wanted to place himself there.

According to the 'fair copy' of 'Song To Woody' he later gave the Gleasons, he had written the lyric 'in Mills Bar', though he duly contradicted himself by telling *Sing Out!* the following year he wrote it 'in the drugstore on 8th Street ... on one of them freezing days that I came back from Sid and Bob Gleason's in East Orange ... It was a Sunday night.'* If the diction – and the tune, which he self-consciously lifted from Guthrie's own '1913 Massacre', just as Woody had lifted it from Aunt Molly Jackson's 'One Morning In May' – was Woody's, the affected world-weariness was all Dylan's.

At this stage he was delighted to date and sign his own work, even though he would later insist, 'I did not consider myself a songwriter at all.' A lyricist, though, he now was, albeit very much in the Guthrie mould. This is where he would stay for the next six months. In that time he would continue thumbing the pages and memorizing the words of the Oak songbook, perhaps one of only a handful of items he ever purchased at Izzy Young's Folklore Center, a cubbyhole of a shopfront on MacDougal Street, where the proprietor liked to hold court.

Young, a larger-than-life figure, would soon become another mentor for Dylan, who willingly let him vent his many frustrations on this captive audience of one in order to hear suggestions for songs. If *Chronicles* can be believed, the elder statesman of folklore had a plentiful supply, though the examples Dylan quotes – by the Country Gentlemen, Charlie Poole and Big Bill Broonzy – were songs he never did live. In an earlier draft, Young more credibly suggested doing 'Omie Wise', supposedly playing him a version by the Boston bluegrass outfit, the Charley River Valley Boys, who had yet to make a record. That certainly wasn't where this great murder ballad came from.

But Izzy could be real insistent. The way Dylan remembered it, he'd be in his face, saying, 'Ever heard of Charlie Poole?' 'I don't think so.' 'Listen to this.' For now, Dylan was open to all avenues of information, the irascible Izzy included.

By charming Young, he also gained access to the resources of a first-class folk repository that served more as a lending library than the business it purported to be. (As social commentator Oscar Brand

---

* The nearest Sunday would have been the 12th, the third Sunday he had spent at the Gleasons'.

observed, the Folklore Center in those days 'was a social center, like an old Eastern European town square, and just as profitable'.) The perpetually hard-up Dylan certainly wasn't about to make Izzy's store a viable business, prompting the proprietor in later years to cast a rueful backward glance at the boy who became another ingrate as far as he was concerned:

Izzy Young: He used to hang around and be a pain in the ass; he was a hustler, always asking me questions, wanting to meet everybody. I didn't think he was so interesting in those days, but I did know that he was intensive. He ransacked the shelves at the store; read all the magazines; the good, bad, the little tiny things, twelve pages or big things with a hundred pages. He would go through them regularly and consistently; more than anyone I ever met. He absorbed everything, reading non-stop and always [borrowing] records from the store and listening to them. I particularly remember him taking John Jacob Niles records with him. He was always listening to the people in the back room, and ... he would play in the store for anybody who was there, like Dave Van Ronk, Reverend Gary Davis ... [even though] his playing wasn't that hot then!

For someone who spent as much of his time criticizing others as Young would, he wasn't much of a critic. Even at this stage, others felt that Dylan had something which set him apart. The following spring *Village Voice* reporter J. R. Goddard noted his own reaction the first time he heard the young cub at the Folklore Center, just in from out of town, singing 'Muleskinner Blues' à la Jimmie Rodgers: 'He began hopping around a bit. He was funny to watch, [but] anybody with half an ear could tell he [already] had a unique style.'

Barely settled in, Dylan had just made his first media connection, revelling in the Greenwich universe he was determined to bend to his will. For now, as he noted in that 2001 outline, he was 'living the bohemian lifestyle', which meant sleeping on a folding bed; sometimes, a couch. According to a couple of Village habitués, he even resorted to the odd flop house on occasion, hoping some of the *Bound For Glory* spirit might rub off.

Perhaps it did. He wrote another notable original some time in early June, about a tramp lying dead in the street being stepped over by a succession of people in a hurry until a policeman rolled up and informed the body, 'Get up, old man, or I'm a-takin' you down.' The song was called 'Old Man' (later 'Man On The Street'). It was another early indication he was getting a handle on this songwriting lark, even if he'd consciously copped the idea from 'John Doe' by the Almanac Singers, a popular wartime combo Seeger and Guthrie assembled.

But finding subjects about which he could write was not as easy as Dylan had assumed, perhaps because he was stuck in a past of his own making, one full of 'murder ballads & bad men'. Finally, in April, something happened in his neck of the woods about which he – and everyone he knew – was enraged. It was enough to inspire his first topical song. It was called 'Down At Washington Square', and purported to be a piece of first-hand reportage, a modern broadside ballad, detailing the events of Sunday April 9th, 1961.

On this fateful weekend the police – at the behest of some 'pipe-smoking professor types' – tried to shut down the communal singalong gatherings which had been taking place in Washington Square every Sunday afternoon since before the Kingston Trio had made folksong fashionable again. Predictably, at the head of the militant wing of the folksingers' union that day was Izzy Young. On hearing about the planned clampdown, Young set out not to mourn, but to organize a peaceful protest:

> Jerry Silver was there, [as were] Pat Clancy, Cynthia Gooding, Happy and Artie Traum ... And we had [placed] posters in front of my store ... So a group of about 200 people [met up] in front of the store and we marched down MacDougal Street to the park ... The Deputy Police Commissioner came over to me and he said ... 'You know you don't have any right to sing in the square today,' [to which] I said ... 'We've been singing songs since the American Revolution ... We have a perfect right' ... Then I got into the center of the ring and we sang 'The Star Spangled Banner' ... We marched around [some more, but] when we got to the church, I looked back and there was a riot going on ... They arrested about thirteen people ... It was the last gasp of respectable America against folk music. [1965]

Though Dylan's song rather implies he was one of the spartan 200, the 'girl with a banjo' who was trampled to the ground in the lyric was another figment of an already wild imagination. There is no actual evidence he was there. He is certainly nowhere to be seen in the illustrated press reports or the film footage of Washington Square that afternoon, teeming as it was with beards, capos and placards, as well as 'television and newspaper reporters', whom Oscar Brand described as taking 'great delight [when] a melee ensued directly in front of their cameras' – the *Daily News*'s particular delight evident in their headline, 'Park Songfest ... Boils [Over] Into Slugfest'. Dylan preferred to retain an abiding memory of a time when 'people you knew or met congregated every Sunday [in the Park], and it was like a world of music'.

Also absent that day, though she had been driven all the way from Boston by a friend with the express intention of showing solidarity with her guitar-totin' sisters and brothers, was the new darling of the folk revival, Joan Baez, who could pierce the walls of Jericho with her contralto at twenty paces.

Thankfully, she arrived too late to sing her party piece, 'We Shall Overcome'. Instead, she and her younger sister Mimi stayed over at the apartment of civil rights activist Clark Foreman, before heading down to Gerde's to check out the competition at the now-traditional Monday night hootenanny. And much to Baez's amazement, there *was* someone excitingly different. He came in the form of a scruffy young singer in a Huck Finn cap. But if she expected the boy from Minnesota to be in awe of her, she was to be sorely disappointed. In fact, it was with her sister, Mimi, that Dylan was smitten, asking her if she wanted to go to a party with him.

Mimi, who was only about to turn sixteen, was sorely tempted. As she told Howard Sounes, 'I found [Bob] appealing. He was not really the centre of attention that evening, but in fact he was, because even then he was charismatic.' Joan, accustomed to being the centre of attention herself, apparently snapped, 'It is already past your bedtime.'

Six months later, when asked what he thought of Baez's singing, Dylan told Izzy Young, 'Her voice goes through me.' If he still thought 'the only beauty's ugly, man', he was prepared to make an exception when it came to the lovely Mimi, for whom he continued to carry a torch, even though he had a girlfriend, a dancer called Avril (whom he perhaps met at the dance troupe). One imagines she would not have been impressed by the unabashed way Dylan hit on other women.

No matter. By the end of the month his on-off relationship with Avril would be firmly off-piste as the poor unfortunate gal became the first of many to discover that confronting Dylan was not the way to make an honest man of him. Fellow Villager Mark Spoelstra, who knew him from Madison, remembers 'walk[ing] in on them in a restaurant when Avril was breaking up with Bob ... All she wanted was honesty ... The next day he left her a note and simply disappeared ... Avril was really in love with Dylan, but he was intimidated by her honesty and directness.'

What Avril had seemingly not considered was the stiff competition she already faced holding on to her slippery beau. The Village scene was teeming with talented female folksingers, most of whom felt liberated enough to treat men as men had traditionally treated women, and most of the male folksingers were just fine with that.

What singers like Hedy West, Karen Dalton, Jean Redpath, Delores Dixon and Barbara Dane all had in common was a willingness to party, changing partners with aplomb. For the red-blooded Dylan, opportunities to let his libidinous self cut loose were frequent and usually successful. Nor did he ever imagine Avril was 'that special one', just someone with a warm apartment and a body to die for.

And yet, unbeknownst to Dylan, 'that special one' was six feet away at Gerde's on a Monday night in April – possibly on this very night – having been enticed there by her friend Sue Zuckerman, who had already 'witnessed Dylan perform[ing] at an intimate setting of six or seven people in April 1961, not long after he had arrived in New York. I later raved to Suze about this unusual, appealing kid [who invariably] showed up for Monday open-mic nights at Gerde's Folk City.'

When Suze Rotolo did see Dylan play for the first time, what blew her away was not his way with words but 'the way he played the harmonica ... He played with an earthiness that was wonderful.' Still playing harp for others, he'd formed a short-lived duo with Mark Spoelstra which allowed him to blow some harp and 'clown around onstage tuning his guitar'. Meanwhile, Spoelstra got to play twelve-string guitar, singing traditional songs in a voice palatable to the 'folk' tourists who crowded the club for its weekly hoots.

Initially, Suze was more interested in Spoelstra, whom she thought had 'lovely shoulders'. She wasn't that big a fan of Guthrie, preferring traditional ballads and the blues, whereas Dylan's own repertoire was still top-heavy with Woody's words, the very ones he would sing to their author when visiting the ailing folk icon.

And as of April 3rd, he had the chance to see Woody without having to schlep all the way from Port Authority to Morris County by bus, Guthrie having been finally transferred to the Brooklyn State Hospital, close to his wife and family in Howard Beach. Now Dylan just needed to cadge lifts from any Village folkie who could afford, or knew how to borrow, a car:

> **John Hammond Jr**: I had a car and I would drive him to Brooklyn, to the hospital, to see Woody Guthrie. Woody really liked Bob, and Bob really liked Woody. [In fact] he idolized him. Woody was not well at all. He had spasms ... but Bob was really mellow and real calm, and I was very impressed with Bob's ability to handle that whole thing.
>
> **Barry Kornfeld**: He used to go out and see Woody with some regularity at Brooklyn State [Hospital] ... The reason I was there was [because] I had a car ... When we went out there [together, Woody] was pretty far gone. You couldn't understand a word he said. Bobby could but [not me]. He liked having Bobby do [his own] songs, 'cause he couldn't do it. And [when] Bobby brought him a pack of cigarettes, [he'd be] holding onto the wall with both hands, [as] he went around the ward giving out [the] cigarettes. Kept one for himself.

On the downside, the move signalled the end of weekends in East Orange. Fortunately for Dylan, he now had an array of potential girlfriends and mother hens to look after him, all of whom hovered around the Village. As of April 11th, he also had his first paying gig: two weeks supporting the blues legend, John Lee Hooker, at Gerde's. Not that his first week's pay cheque went very far, according to Kornfeld, who like Van Ronk and Paxton caught the pre-Gerde's Dylan shortly after returning from Boston that spring:

> When I got back to New York in 1961, there was [already] a buzz about this guy Dylan. He hadn't started to write yet – he had one song, 'Song To Woody'. There was a coffee house he did sets in, he didn't get paid – Cafe Wha?. He never had any money. Most of us had enough to buy a drink, he didn't have enough to buy a drink. Then he got a gig at Gerde's, [but] he had to spend it all paying back his bar tab.

Although Dylan's parsimony was already the stuff of legends south of Washington, north of Houston, he had acquired another part-time manager, at Kevin Krown's expense. The girlfriend of Van Ronk, Terri Thal towered over Dylan and swore like a sailor, but spoke Clubspeak well enough to convince Mike Porco, the owner of Gerde's, to take a punt on 'the kid', an association he would trade on for as long as he stayed in business.

It wasn't like Porco was taking that big of a risk. It was Hooker who was the draw, not the callow kid propping up the bill. For the first fortnight of Hooker's four-week residency, Dylan just soaked up as much as he could – quite literally – from this older, wiser man who (just like Bobby) had reinvented himself as an acoustic folksinger once playing electric no longer paid the bills:

> I met Bob Dylan in New York at Gerde's Folk City, him and his girlfriend ... He were hangin' round me at the old Broadway Central Hotel. I had this suite there, and he had come to Gerde's to hear me and see me and talk to me ... Every night he'd be right there with me. We'd stay there, we'd party ... drink gin.

Dylan had scrabbled all the way from the Wha? to a billed residency at Gerde's in under three months, an impressively fast trajectory. Which makes his next move a little perplexing: he went home – his real, Midwest home – staying away for most of May, despite previously telling his parents – in a postcard dated April 28th – that he didn't 'know if I can come home then'.* In the version of his adventures he told his mother after he made this unexpected return, he rather implied he had 'made' it against the odds:

> **Beattie Zimmerman**: There were lots of times when he was ready to come back to Minnesota. But he stuck with it. No one helped Bobby – they shut doors in his face, but no one helped him.

---

* In the same postcard he triumphantly informed his parents, 'I've finished my time at Folk City, now I am at the Gaslight ... I am now making $100.00 a week for five nights playing – that's not bad, considering that three months ago I was unknown.'

Precious few in the Village would have recognized this account of her son's first three months in New York. Already the boy wonder was developing his own unique spin on events, casting himself in the role of martyr, put down or put upon. Indeed, if the legend is true, it was when he was on the New Jersey Turnpike, hitch-hiking to Minnesota – possibly via Connecticut – that he sat down to pen 'Talkin' New York', a song from the 'New York is a mean ol' town' school of hard knocks, berating club owners who told him, 'Sorry, we can't use you today, you sound like a hillbilly, we want Folk – with a capital F.'

In truth, he was acting more like the High Plains Drifter who comes into town, paints it red, then disappears into those black hills, dark as night. What no one east knew was that initially he was heading for Minneapolis, the city he had left the previous December to come to see Woody Guthrie.* Oh, how his friends had laughed at the very idea; all except for one, who was stuck in a wheelchair, waiting for word from the friend who had disappeared on a winter's day chasing – or so he thought – the very dream they had once dared to share: becoming a *pop* singer.

---

* Dylan told Henrietta Yurchenco in 1962 that he originally 'planned to return to Wisconsin with his friends ... but [on the] morning Bob watched some children playing in Washington Square Park. "They were so friendly and so warm that I decided New York couldn't be that bad, so I stayed."' Since he also told her the crowd went wild the first time he played a Village club, one should perhaps order some more salt.

I.2

Summer 1953 to January 1961: On The Road To Damascus

When Larry was sixteen, tragedy struck. On a family vacation to Miami Beach, he was with a group of kids diving into the ocean from a high retainer wall. In Minnesota, there are 10,000 lakes but no tides, so Larry was unaccustomed to worrying about variations in the depth of the water. As luck would have it, the tide was out when he took the plunge, diving ten feet into two feet of water: in a mere moment, Larry was paralyzed ... About a week or so after the accident, Bobby and I visited Larry at the University of Minnesota Medical Center in Minneapolis ... As we walked back down the hospital corridors in silence, I saw something I'd never seen before, and would never see again – Bobby with tears in his eyes.

Louie Kemp

Larry: How did I break my neck? Ahh, jumped off a wall into the ocean. And ah, landed on my head in two feet of water. Ah, broke my neck, C-5/6 Lesion. Now I'm laying there, doing a dead man's float, holding my breath. My eyes are open. Seeing the little fish fly by and everything. And I realize that the rest of my life is going to last as long as I can hold my breath. I hear this breathing. But I don't feel anything. I look back and it's this friend that I was diving with, who had swam in and turned me over. He thought I was kidding!

Unproduced screenplay for When Billy Broke His Head

That [accident] must have had something to do with Bobby's career ... That was a real tragedy in Bobby's life.

Beattie Zimmerman, 1968

Writing is nothing; anybody can write really ... if they got dreams at an early age.

Bob Dylan, May 1966

*

When the teenage Dylan started to develop the craft of songwriting seriously in the second half of 1961, two of his best songs – one an 'original' arrangement of a traditional song, 'He Was A Friend of Mine'; the other, his first north country blues, 'Ballad For A Friend' – mourned the loss of friends; one of whom 'died on the road', the other on a railroad track. But he never sang about, or talked about, the 'real tragedy' that ended many of his friend Larry's dreams until one night in November 1980 at San Francisco's Warfield Theater, when he related an incident ostensibly from Carmel, *circa* 1964:

> About fifteen years ago, [Joan Baez] invited me out to her house ... [and] said, 'Let's go out to the beach.' ... The waves were ... crashing up against the rocks ... I started climbing up these rocks, and pretty soon I was in this cave. Things being what they were, I got carried away and sat there for a while. The sun went down and I was still in the cave, and [Joan] was nowhere to be found. And the water started coming in. I looked out of the cave, and all these waves are crashing ... towards the cave, [with] no way to get back to the beach except to jump in the water. And eventually that's what I had to do. I just ... jumped into one of those waves and, sure enough, it just carried me back to the beach. I was lucky, but this friend of mine did the same thing down in Florida, and jumped off a wall ... but he broke himself up pretty bad. He's sitting in a wheelchair now.

Leaving aside whether the above story should be taken at face value, the subtext is undeniable: it could have been *me*. That thought alone made for an unshakeable bond between Bobby and Larry – superglued by five years of teenage friendship – that the passing years and diverging paths would not break.

It all began in the summer of 1953 when a twelve-year-old Robert Allen Zimmerman, plain Bobby to his friends – born May 24th, 1941 in Duluth, Minnesota – was shipped to camp for the summer by his conformist, aspirational parents, Abraham and Beattie. They concurred with a thirty-six-year-old Bob Dylan who told a female reporter that, growing up, 'Other than my family, I didn't have many friends. In a small town, of course everyone is a friend of sorts, but I really only had one close friend all during high school.' The pair hoped he might find some friends among his fellow Jews – who were in short supply in their home town of Hibbing, Minnesota.

What his adult self doesn't say is whether his 'one close friend' attended the same high school, or even lived in the same rinkydink town. Because, by the time he was twelve, there was already a young Bobby who yearned to live in another world. (It is no coincidence that most of his later stories of running away begin when he was twelve.)

The boy who turned up at Camp Herzl in Webster, Wisconsin, that summer was already looking to spread his wings. For the first time, he would be beyond his parents' command and he was determined to make the most of it. Just as with his coming to New York, Beattie had to accept the version of events he gave to her of what went down in Webster. He just needed a couple of co-conspirators for Bobby the Entertainer to blossom. He found them in a boy from Duluth, Louie Kemp, and a kid from Minneapolis, Larry Kegan.

At least one pseudo-biographer has given the impression that Herzl was 'a Jewish Zionist camp' whose 'primary purpose was to endow its youthful participants with a thoroughly Zionist education', campers being enjoined to 'speak Hebrew in the dining hall'. In reality, the only Zionist aspect was the name itself, from a zealot instrumental in the restoration of Israel. One of Dylan's new-found friends, Louie Kemp, has nothing but fond memories of the place and time:

> It was in northern Wisconsin, but it was run by people from Minneapolis; an orthodox rabbi was the director ... who had a good influence on all of us ... We were there for five years. It was a wonderful experience for us [all]. They gave Hebrew names to some of the rooms, but we spoke English. None of us could [even] speak Hebrew. We were in the same cabin the first year, and we stayed together thereafter.

At the tender age of twelve, Bobby had just discovered the recently deceased country singer Hank Williams – his first musical hero – but couldn't as yet emulate him, let alone ask the question, are you sure Hank done it this way? Indeed, some former campers retain a 'vivid memory of Bob ... constantly hugging his guitar' yet never 'actually playing it', perhaps because his mother had just bought him a Silvertone guitar from the Sears catalogue but forgot to buy the requisite amplifier.

But he could still talk about music, notably Hank's, especially to Larry, who shared his passion even at the age of twelve. A scene shot in Kegan's camper van on the Rolling Thunder Revue, used in the 2019 Netflix mockumentary, captures Bobby and Larry duetting on 'Your Cheatin' Heart', probably the first Hank Williams record Dylan ever bought, surely a conscious emulation of what they got up to when the lights went out at Herzl.

If his guitar-picking needed work, it didn't take Bobby long to pick up the basics of another instrument, the piano. When he returned to camp the following summer he was ready for his public debut. By then, he had discovered R&B – as had Larry – the two of them again in sync as to musical taste and an ambition to perform. Kemp sat on the sidelines, proud as punch:

> The 1954 version of the camp's Talent Night ... was ... the first public performance by the prototypical Bob Dylan ... Talent Night was special. It was the night when the entire camp – more than 400 kids, plus rabbis, counselors, and staff – would assemble to witness the best skits, magic acts, and musical numbers we could muster ... Bobby and Larry had decided to perform together, with Bobby on piano ... The tune was called 'Annie Had A Baby', and [it] started out, 'Annie had a baby, can't work no more ...' They went on to list the various things Annie had to do instead of work ... When confronted [by some campers] about his choice of material, Bobby responded tersely ... '[You]'re squares.'

The moment would stay with Dylan, as would the song. When he wrapped up the long, tortuous sessions for his 1981 album, *Shot of Love*, with a jam session of fifties standards, the final song was 'Annie Had A Baby', which he still knew how to vamp on, even if some of these A-list musicians didn't.

From hereon at Herzl, Dylan stuck to the piano even as popular music experienced a series of seismic shifts in sound by those key-poundin' men, Little Richard and Jerry Lee Lewis. By 1956, the young Bobby was telling anyone who would listen that he was going to be a rock'n'roll star, and he wasn't shy of showing 'em just how. As another friend from Herzl, Steve Friedman, recalls: 'He was the star of the camp. He used to sing just like Jerry Lee Lewis ... He'd [even] play piano ... standing up.'

He had finally found an outlet for his prodigious memory – discographical information. Whenever Larry would challenge him about a particular record, he would not only know the singer and/or band, he would know the label and the B-side. It was a party trick of his, with which he didn't really go public until 2006 and the advent of his (and Eddie G's) brainchild, the Theme Hour radio show. Louie was blown away by his friend's facility:

> When we were in the activity room, he would play the piano. The whole company was there, and he'd start playing all these different rock'n'roll songs he knew. He knew many songs, more than any of us. He'd listen to the AM stations coming out of the south at night – Chuck Berry, Little Richard, Jerry Lee Lewis, all these blues people – he knew 'em all.

Bobby also found out real quick that playing and singing was a good way of impressing the girls at camp. He seems to have been particularly smitten by a girl from St Paul, Judy Rubin, for whom he carried a torch right through his college days. Indeed, according to the first reporter to research those Minneapolis days, it was the unnamed Rubin who first 'introduced him into a social whirl of Jewish youth in the Twin Cities'. Not that Judy retained an exclusive on his affections. Even then, he remained open to offers. But at an age when many contemporaries were obsessing about girls, he was obsessing about music, sometimes sharing his rock'n'roll dreams with Louie, more often with Larry.

The trio enjoyed their fair share of adventures and high jinks, and not just at camp. From 1956 on, the twin cities of Minneapolis and St Paul beckoned after Bobby's indulgent parents gave him a motorbike, and with it a first taste of freedom. As Larry told Gene LaFond, a regular travelling companion in later life, 'Bob used to ride his motorcycle down from Hibbing and stay with [me] at [my] parents' home in St Paul. [We] would go to parties, bang on the piano, sing doo-wop songs and get thrown out more times than not.' Most of the time, Louie would tag along; providing excellent cover for the young Bobby, who could tell his parents he was going to visit a friend in Duluth:

> Bob would come to Duluth – he would come down and stay with me. And then sometimes we'd hop the train to Minneapolis and St Paul. You can [do] it in two and a half hours. We'd go down Friday, come back Sunday afternoon/evening. Most of the kids we met at Herzl camp were from Minneapolis and St Paul. So we knew a lot of kids [there]. They'd invite us, we'd go to these open houses. [Judy] lived in Minneapolis.

Bobby would also sometimes stay with cousins in the Highland Park area of St Paul, perhaps to allay his parents' concern that he might be 'up to no good'. But, as Kemp recalls, 'Usually, we would all crash at a friend's house.' There was no shortage of options. Five summers at Herzl exponentially expanded Zimmerman's address book. According to Steve Friedman, the two of them later in Bobby's all-important musical education would sometimes 'hitch-hike down to St Paul, stay in a lousy hotel and look for live music ... [mostly] rhythm & blues – Bob was very into black music'.

But it was usually the terrible trio who ran riot. Not surprisingly, in such austere times, they soon developed something of a 'rep'. As Kemp's 2019 memoir records, 'Eventually, one of our camp friends informed us that we were no longer welcome at his place. "You can't run around with those wild boys anymore," his mother had declared. "Kemp, Kegan, and Zimmerman ... will get you into trouble."' Nor is there any doubt who was the leader of the pack at this time – Kegan.

In fact, the younger Larry could have been Dylan's Neal Cassady to his Jack Kerouac had not fate twisted its blade. The portrait Kemp paints of the pre-accident Kegan instantly conjures up that mythical youth the New York Dylan later transposed to the first person:

> We were all active, but he was *wild* ... By the time he was thirteen, [Larry] was frequently taking off in his parents' car in the middle of the night to go joyriding with friends ... Once Larry even set off for California – [though] he only got as far as Iowa ... [] ... Bobby and I

didn't do things like that. We did things in a more sedate way. Larry just took it [all] a little bit further ... [Then] one of us can't walk anymore – and [it's] the wildest of the three of us – the one who was all over the place.

Without wishing to be reading too much into a single photo, it is all there in a shot of Larry and Bobby in the back seat of a family saloon, from 1957, the year before the accident, used in the *No Direction Home* film. The photo shows two fresh-faced young boys, but it is the younger Larry – with his leather jacket and greaser haircut – who looks like he has seen *The Wild One* more times than he cares to mention, and Bobby who is riding his coat tails all the way to the twin city they named after a Jewish zealot who persecuted Christians before he had a vision on the road.

For Larry, it was not a vision but a lack of vision that changed everything one Floridian day, when he was a little too wild for his own good. Suddenly, for Louie as much as Bobby, those trips to Minneapolis were in the role of ministering angel as they tried keeping their friend's spirits up: 'Larry ... endur[ed] a seemingly endless cycle of surgeries. We worked hard to provide whatever encouragement and comfort we could ... We'd spend most of our time talking about the good old days at Herzl Camp ... Bobby often visited Larry on his own, and would bring along his guitar.'

The experience shook Bobby to the core. According to LaFond, on these Louie-less occasions, 'Bob would come in and wheel Larry into the day room on a gurney where they would sing together', attempting to rekindle the spirit of Herzl, knowing the good times had gone, and with them their dream of forming a band together.

But Dylan remained determined to make it in music, and to make it to Minneapolis, leaving his own private Hicksville behind. And if one close friend and fellow muso from camp couldn't now help make that happen, another maybe could. Fast-forward to the summer of 1959, and an eighteen-year-old Dylan who is now so far beyond his parents' command that he won't even go home.

Larry's tragedy the previous March had temporarily sent him off the rails; his grades at school had plummeted even as he fuelled his rock'n'roll dream with a series of hastily assembled bands of no fixed purpose, at least two of which had Duluth, not Hibbing, as their base: The Satin Tones and Elston Gunn & The Rock Boppers. His parents feared the worst. They may even have sent him to a 'country-club reform school' in Pennsylvania to see if that would straighten him out.*

If they did, it didn't do the trick. Instead, he headed for Fargo, North Dakota the minute that last school bell rang, looking up another ex-camper, Ron Joelson, who one summer at Herzl had become 'friends with Louie Kemp from Duluth, Larry Keegan from St Paul and Bob Zimmerman from Hibbing'. This can only have been pre-accident, i.e. 1957.

Joelson goes on to suggest that the 'following summer [sic] Bob stayed at my house for about three months, during which time I introduced him to local musicians', to whom he now introduced himself as Elston Gunnn, with three n's. We know this was really 1959. Although three months is probably an exaggeration, it does seem as if Bobby was in Fargo for a goodly while, bussing tables and pushing his luck with Mrs Joelson:

> **Ron Joelson**: Zimmerman only played piano at that time and wasn't into writing yet, only performing – mostly Little Richard, Jerry Lee Lewis-type basic early rock'n'roll. My mother couldn't take the way Bob sang or played. ... [She] wanted me to throw him out every time he began warbling!

The final straw, according to Joelson, was when 'Bob, Tom Conoby and Mickey McGuire came over to my house to see if I'd leave Fargo to go to Minneapolis [to make music] with them. I had a big fight with my mother who didn't want me to go with these "no-goods".' Thus was another ex-camper denied the chance to participate in Bobby's rock'n'roll fantasy.

But he was not about to give up on the other part of his plan, making it to Minneapolis and never returning to the dying town he grew up in. By September 1959 he had somehow secured the tacit blessing of his parents, provided that he attend the university; perhaps,

---

* The school was in Deveraux, Pennsylvania, and could be the origin of Dylan's claim to a couple of early confidants that he had spent time in the more notorious Red Wing reform school, which he had not.

as father Abraham hoped, he would study architecture once he got past the usual foundation year. With grades just about good enough to make college, Zimmerman grasped the opportunity with both hands.

The way he tells it in *Chronicles*, he arrived in the Twin Cities feeling 'liberated and gone, never meaning to go back ... I rode in on a Greyhound bus – nobody was there to greet me and nobody knew me and I liked it that way.' Actually, nothing could be further from the truth. He had been escaping to Minneapolis and St Paul on an increasingly regular basis since 1956, and had a veritable frat-house of friends he could call on; as well as assorted cousins, one of whom had been president of one of the two Jewish frat-houses on campus, Sigma Alpha Mu.

Another ex-camper, Dick (or Rich) Cohen kindly put his name forward for the fraternity. According to Kemp, 'The two of them would [often] hang out in Bobby's little room, listening to music.' Cohen was soon co-opted into a collective effort to get Zimmerman 'to shape ... up – [to] make grades, wear the right clothes and fit in'. However, Cohen's camp buddy, truth be told, was no student. Nor was he a joiner, save for when the opportunity arose to poke fun at his fellow SAMmies:

> **Louie Kemp**: When the brothers wanted to put on a skit for their winter party, Bobby – along with two pledges named Bernie and Jerry – volunteered to write the script. The skit was called 'Sammy Claus', and cleverly made fun of the frat brothers ... Bobby played the title role and he was a big hit, playing the piano.

As at camp, Bobby only really seemed to want to participate when he was the centre of attention and could play music, a state of affairs confirmed by a more conformist SAMmy, Jerry Waldman, who described his frat brother as 'quiet ... [except when] he played the piano and everybody would gather around and we'd sing rock'n'roll songs'. Only then did he choose to belong. In fact, he still harboured the same teen dream and was not about to deviate from its course. As Kemp avers, 'Bobby couldn't wait to get out of school so he could put all of his energy into music.'

If anything, being a SAMmy merely focused Bobby's mind on what *not* to be. As he wrote in 1963, part of his first stab at autobiography, 'what I saw connected with the fraternity house summed up the whole established world ... underpants ... cats standin in underpants being inspected by others with serious looks in their eyes'. He even voiced similar thoughts to his father, who told a local reporter that year, 'He had as many friends as he wanted, but he considered most of [his fraternity brothers] phonies – spoiled kids with whom he didn't feel he had much in common.'

According to Abraham, his son quit before he was pledged, but this seems unlikely given that he was still *in situ* well into 1960. The transformation was more gradual, as if he was plotting his escape, but still conflicted as to whether he was going to be a rock'n'roll singer – as he informed a well-known New York folksinger who was passing through that winter (see chapter 1.6) – or a beatnik. Minneapolis girlfriend Ellen Baker suggests, 'Bob was serious about his school work for a while, at the very start ... but it wasn't him. He finally decided he just wanted to play the guitar and party.'

Minneapolis reporter P. M. Cleeper – who set about interviewing folkies and frat brothers in the mid-sixties – described the process thus: 'At first he wore the typical frat uniform, narrow-lapeled suit and a tie. Then he went into a sports coat ... then a sweater ... then a work jacket ... Baggy slacks. Jeans. The white shirt was replaced by a blue workshirt, with the collar turned up.'

Something extracurricular had sent him spinning on a tangential trajectory and this time when he arrived at his destination, Folksong USA, nobody from his past would be there to greet him. As he relates in *No Direction Home*, he was soon 'singing and playing all night. Sleeping most of the morning. I didn't really have any time for studying.'

He was no longer playing piano or looking to join a band. He had become a folksinger, and nobody who saw the transformation firsthand has yet provided a ready explanation, save that one day he wanted to be a cross between Little Richard and Bobby Vee, and the next he wanted to be a cross between Josh White and Lead Belly. Dylan later suggested it wasn't quite that abrupt, 'I'd already discovered Lead Belly and Odetta [before I got to Minneapolis], which was one step beyond Belafonte and the Kingston Trio.' Symptomatic of the switch was a new alias, a new persona to pin a badge on: Bobby Dylan. Among the first to hear of it, back in Hibbing, was an old school friend:

John Bucklen: Bob came back to Hibbing ... just before the Christmas vacation. He had an old acoustic guitar ... and he didn't have any neatness to the way he combed his hair, which was unusual, 'cause he used to be fastidious about that ... He played me this folk song and said, 'Man, this is the thing – folk music!' I think [it] was 'Golden Vanity' ... He said, 'Down there when I play, my name is Dylan ... after Dylan Thomas.'

With that simple gesture, changing his name, Bobby turned his back on the past, this time for good. As he said in 2001, 'I'd forgotten all about the Iron Range [the mining districts around Lake Superior] where I grew up ... It didn't even enter my mind.' But before he could cover his tracks fully, he had admitted to this one former dream-sharer its source: the dead drunk Welsh poet, Dylan Thomas. For Larry Kegan, too, he left a few straggling clues, sometimes turning up at the hospital to talk and play carrying a book of Dylan Thomas poems.

And yet he soon grew to resent the connection, especially after October 1963 when *Newsweek* presented it as fact that 'he picked the name in admiration for Dylan Thomas'; so much so that on the day he first visited the country of Thomas's birth, May 9th, 1966, he told an attendant writer, 'All these people think I got my name from Dylan Thomas, that I got turned on by Dylan Thomas, read his poetry ... and start[ed] writing like Dylan Thomas ... [But] I knew he was a drunkard, so he couldn't be groovy.'

Something about this debt has always rubbed Dylan the wrong way. Even in the twenty-first century, he has continued to deny two plus two equals four, telling his New York manager on camera, 'The name just popped into my head one day. But it didn't really happen any of the ways that I've read about it. I just d[id]n't feel like I had a past.' In an interview promoting *Chronicles*, he ducked the issue completely, merely reiterating that 'some people' are born with 'the wrong names ... I mean, that happens. You call yourself what you want to call yourself.'*

He gave a more credible explanation to Tony Glover in 1971, eleven years after they met in Minneapolis, 'It allowed me to step into the Guthrie [*sic*] role with more character ... It was more or less this idea that ... the character ... had to become [someone] named Dylan ...

---

* Dylan made such a seemingly callous remark only after his mother died.

And [it meant] I wouldn't have to be kept being reminded of things I didn't want to be reminded of, at that time.'

Even in 1960, he delighted in spinning yarns, telling close friend Dave Whitaker that it 'was his mother's name, and that he had taken it because ... he didn't want to be known by his father's name'. The last part of that statement, at least, was true. But since his Jewish mother's family had come from Russia, it must have seemed to the worldly Whitaker rather unlikely that her family name was Welsh for 'son of the sea'.

Already, even among his beatnik friends, Dylan was fast developing a reputation for tall stories. Thankfully, in the circles he was now moving in, it was par for the course. As another St Paul folksinger told Cleeper, putting himself in Dylan's shoes, 'Going to school ... you're [suddenly] responsible for yourself. So you defend yourself with a bottle of wine, or by saying you've just been to Oklahoma gathering folk songs, as Bob did ... You start to miss classes, you have three drinks in the afternoon. You go to a party. And so it goes.'

There is another element to the name change worth mentioning. Fleetingly, Dylan thought he might become a writer like his namesake, not a singer. He was soon immersing himself in extracurricular writers who blew his mind and the minds of an entire generation, his head temporarily turned by the Beats. Dylan Thomas was *not* a beat, but he was a proto-beat of sorts – as was the new Dylan, who in 1966 remembered the moment he saw 'a picture of Allen Ginsberg, Gregory Corso, LeRoi Jones, Kenneth Roxreth and Lawrence Ferlinghetti in *Life* magazine', and wanted to know all about them.

A great deal has been written about Dylan's early musical influences, but little about his literary interests and their formative impact on this troubled troubadour. Yet it was three extracurricular volumes he read in 1959–60, whilst still ostensibly attending college, which would first codify that peripatetic poet/performer persona. Those three books were *Mexico City Blues* and *On The Road* by Jack Kerouac and *Howl & Other Poems* by Allen Ginsberg.

The first of these had just appeared. *Mexico City Blues* – subtitled *242 Choruses* – had been turned down by the publisher of *Howl*, City Light Books, in 1957, finally being published by Grove Press in 1959. And though we would have to wait until 1985 for Dylan to namecheck the book in song ('Something's Burning Baby'), in 1975 he told Ginsberg at Kerouac's Lowell graveside, 'My good friend Dave Whitaker gave me a copy of this book ... in Minneapolis in 1959 ... [and] it blew a hole in my mind.'

To Dylan's impressionable mind, what Kerouac called 'spontaneous composition' 'made perfect sense'. As a result, even as he was developing a folk revivalist repertoire culled from Odetta, Lead Belly &c., he was trying his hand at page-bound poetry. And thanks to the sale at a 2005 Christie's auction in New York of a sixteen-page folio from this time, entitled *Poems Without Titles*, we have a sense of the poet he aspired to be. As the catalogue copy perceptively notes, the young 'Dylan ... [had] created a literary style ... heavily influenced by the beat poets ... [with] a casual humor and a delight in vulgarity that wouldn't be seen again in his work until his so-called basement tapes.'

In one poem, Dylan even mockingly namechecks the curriculum-friendly work of T. S. Eliot, putting the poet's words in the mouth of a pretty coed vainly trying to impress him, unlikely as such a scenario seems:

> I thought she / was hip / When we sat and / Drank / Coffee / And I flipped when / She / Recited / All of *Prufrock* / By Heart / And when she / Clued me in / On all the squares / Down in / Lexington / And when she / Emoted her / feelings / on the / Zen Unities of the Orient / But man, when we / Made it to the door / And she expected me / to / open / The / Damn thing / I puked / Down her sweater / And / Ordered / Some more Coffee.

Conversing with Irish neophyte Bono in 1984, Dylan would cite *Howl*, *On The Road* and *Dharma Bums* – but not *Mexico City Blues* – as books 'that changed me'. Two decades later in *Chronicles*, he would suggest it was a combination of Kerouac, Ginsberg and Gregory Corso, what he called the '*On The Road*, *Howl* and *Gasoline* street ideologies', that to him signalled 'a new type of human existence' not to be found on the radio – or if so, only at night, to the left hand of the dial. For a while, he devoured anything with a City Lights spine but, hardly surprisingly, this college freshman who liked to claim he was expelled from English class for using a four-letter word had yet to find a voice he could call his own.

Though these early poems lack any real literary merit, and have no date, the way that Dylan signs almost every one with his new alias, and even randomly adds the word 'Dylanism', suggests he was still trying the name on for size. For now he would be happy to sign his work.*

Perhaps what Dylan really needed was a muse, preferably not Jewish or Jewish-looking. As he semi-joked to Barbara Kerr in 1978, 'I met a girl [in Minneapolis]; she had long dark hair and leotards. It was the first time I was ever attracted to someone obviously Jewish, but she rejected me, and that probably set my ethnic awareness back for years.'

This wasn't Judy Rubin, who did at least *try* to relate to the new Dylan, gamely going to see him sing at the Ten O'Clock Scholar coffee house, whilst hoping for someone of whom her parents might approve – not a college dropout. Nor was the unnamed girl one of the long litany of names – some real, some fictional – listed in another of the *Poems Without Titles* – beginning with Judy, who 'said / hi to me / when no one else / could take the time ... And I thought I / Loved / Her'. But it could have been Gretel Hoffman, whom he lost to the older, hipper Dave Whitaker; or Lynn Castner's girlfriend, Tova Hammerman, who told Sounes, 'I was too Jewish for him.'

What he really needed was a 'chick' who was equally immersed in the folk universe – because, as he suggests in *Chronicles*, he really 'had no other cares or interests besides folk music'. He met her at the Scholar, the one place in Minneapolis's Dinkytown district where folksong was a constant backdrop and had been ever since Dave Morton had suggested to the owner he might attract a new clientele if he let him sing, early in 1959. Until then, the Scholar had been a place where people sipped coffee and talked, as Dylan and a like-minded friend were doing one afternoon when they were overheard:

> **Bonnie Beecher**: I went into the Ten O'Clock Scholar one day to have my bagel and apple juice, and Dylan and a guy named Harvey Abrams were sitting at the table next to me, talking about music. I recognized some of the names. I didn't know anybody else who knew who Cat Iron was, or Sleepy John Estes, so ... I turned around and I started to join the conversation ... Dylan really perked up, 'Oh yeah? You know

---

* Dave Van Ronk's memoir relates how, during Dylan's days with Suze, the two couples 'used to get stoned out of our minds and do colouring books, and Bob never coloured anything [without] sign[ing] it'. In a 2020 *New York Times* interview, Dylan suggests he never signed his work. Poppycock.

about those people? How do you know?' I said, 'I've got all these records at home.' The next thing I knew, Dylan and I were heading for my house. He finished up borrowing [most of] my record collection – for several years!

Beecher, the 'real' 'girl from the north country', would be a fixture in Dylan's life throughout his time in Minneapolis and for a number of years after – an on-off girlfriend and cheerleader wrapped in one sensual package.

Not that 'his' Bonnie was the only woman who changed his life that fall. He also discovered Odetta, a black folksinger with an operatic range and a voice that could reverberate around canyons; not in person, but on record. As he related in 1978, 'I found th[is] local record store in the heart of Dinkytown. I was looking for ... folk-music records and the first one I saw was Odetta on the Tradition label. I went into the listening booth to hear it ... I learnt almost every song off the record right then and there, even borrowing the hammering-on style.'

From that LP, by his own admission, he 'went to Harry Belafonte, the Kingston Trio, little by little uncovering more as I went along'. If none of these names exactly bespeaks authentic folksinger – and neither did another acknowledgee, John Jacob Niles* – such ersatz folkies really were the singers he initially tried to emulate, their influence being writ large across the two dozen songs on the May 1960 St Paul Tape, almost all of which were 'trad', save for Niles's 'Go 'Way From My Window', Paul Clayton's 'Gotta Travel On', four Woody Guthrie songs and Ewan MacColl's 'Ballad Of Tim Evans'.

Here we hear him trying to sing like the missing quarter of the Kingston Quartet, in a voice his sometime singing partner, Spider John Koerner, described as 'very sweet ... a pretty voice, much different from what it became'. As Koerner has noted, 'He didn't really know what he was trying to do, except be a folksinger.'

Two local scenesters who chafed at any sign of inauthenticity were Paul Nelson and Jon Pankake, hardcore record collectors who were just about to publish their own folkzine as a platform for their 'trad or

---

* Surprisingly, the *Chronicler* owns up to Niles's influence, describing him as 'non-traditional, but he sang traditional songs ... [with a] voice [that] raged with strange incantations'. Not to my ears, it doesn't.

bust' creed when they saw Dylan play in early 1960. As they wrote the year after he reached New York, 'Bob was still a student at the University of Minnesota ... [and] a promising member of a group of singers who performed at ... the Ten O'Clock Scholar. We recall Bob as a soft-spoken, rather unprepossessing youngster ... well groomed and neat in the standard campus costume of slacks, sweater, white Oxford sneakers, poplin raincoat and dark glasses ... Two of his best numbers were Josh White's "Jerry" and Odetta's "Another Man Done Gone".'

Pankake and Nelson gave him the benefit of the doubt – for now. At least neither of these songs were remotely topical, and nor was the rest of his set. Fortunately, Dylan learnt that all-important distinction between folksong and topical song early, and he never forgot it. When – at an April 1966 press conference in Perth – a reporter got the wrong end of the stick, Dylan quickly put him right:

> **Q**: Folk songs are usually written about misery, bombs and racial troubles ...
> **BD**: No. Folk songs are not written about that! Not at all! I'm afraid you don't know much about folk songs. You're speaking of topical songs – 1930 labour movement songs and stuff like that. Those are not folk songs ...
> **Q**: Well, how would you define a folk song then?
> **BD**: Folk songs are traditional songs or ballads. They're not meant to be sung at parties or in crowded rooms where there's noise.

Unfortunately for the young show-off, this was precisely where he was obliged to ply his trade for now – 'at parties' and in coffee houses noisy with the thrum of conversation. When he got up to perform, he was the distraction, not the audience. Indeed, minor writer Stan Gotlieb recollects that, when 'a rather pushy college sophomore named Bobby Zimmerman began dropping in [to the Ten O'Clock Scholar], most of us reacted negatively to him, probably as a balance to his own inflated estimates of his ability as a guitarist and ... poet'.

If Gotlieb's was for now the prevailing view, Dylan was not about to be fazed or forced to shut up. After all, options were few. As Dave Morton told film-maker Marcus Whitman, 'Minneapolis was a small town in those days – [in] Dinkytown, you knew everybody. There was [only] a couple of bars and coffee houses.' Maybe Dylan thought he just needed some help, turning to other musicians to provide it, one of whom he'd played with back in Hibbing:

Jim Propotnick: When I was going to the University of Minnesota, Bob Zimmerman looked me up. He asked me if I wanted to play bass with him down at the Scholar coffee house. I went down to check it out and saw all kinds of beatniks sitting around drinking espresso ... It just wasn't my thing ... His style of music had changed considerably ... I asked Bob what I'd get paid and he replied, '[Well,] you get to eat for free!'

North Dakotan Ron Joelson had also finally made it to Minneapolis, and remembers getting 'together periodically on weekends over at SAMmy's or at the Ten O'Clock Scholar'. But the musician who most regularly provided musical cover in the months before Dylan dared fly solo was local folksinger, Spider John Koerner.

Even the *Chronicle*r acknowledges he learnt a lot from Koerner – and not just specific songs – while Koerner's own abiding memory of the man he fleetingly partnered was someone who 'was not too worried about how he was doing'. The one thing that set Dylan apart, to his mind, was the fact that 'occasionally he'd write a song. I don't remember anything about [the songs] 'cept some of them ... had bite to them. None of ... us were doing that.'

Others, too, later recalled their sense of surprise on discovering Dylan could take a song and make it his own by metempsychosis, even though – to their ears – he could barely play. Harry Weber recalls his version of 'Every Time I Hear The Spirit' being 'like the Negro spiritual he based it on, except it had a rockabilly beat'. And according to Koerner, this was not the only example of Dylan the Jew adapting a gospel song during his time in Minneapolis: 'He was writing some songs ... [that] were like those folksy spirituals that were popular at the time, like "Sinner Man".'

And Gretel Hoffman remembers him writing another song in which 'he was nineteen now and he was not going to live to be twenty-one'. Just such a song can be found on the May St Paul Tape, which he recorded one night that month at the home of the sister of an early fan, Terri Wallace, who loved his (then-)voice and thought 'he just reminded me of a little choir boy, he had such a cute little cherub face'. Sister Karen was not as impressed by his singing but was struck 'with his seriousness, his determination and complete faith that he was going to be somebody'.

He certainly wasn't above simply claiming authorship of a song that was outside the purview of the people he knew. A song he called 'Blackjack Blues', when pressed, he claimed as an original, despite learning it from an early Ray Charles record. Even then, nothing about the boy could be taken at face value, even his seeming lack of musical ability. He stunned one of the better blues guitarists around when he turned up to his house to jam one afternoon and picked up a melodic idea almost instantly:

Dave Ray: I was living in Dinkytown on 4th Street, with my parents, going to high school, college ... I'd been playing the guitar for a couple of years and he came over to my house. [As] we got to know each other a little bit; we got to trade some licks. He was trying to learn how to play the guitar. At that time, even though I was not very good at it, I was light years ahead of him. It was all he could do to clamp on a G chord. So we were fiddling around, showing each other some things ... All of a sudden he just started playing – boom ... His progress on the guitar was [almost] alarming. One minute he couldn't play, the next he was doing *alright*.

If Dylan's guitar playing was still rudimentary, his harmonica playing was positively elementary. And yet, whenever he would invite himself over to Bonnie Beecher's sorority house, after she bought him a mouth organ at Schmidt's, 'he'd play this harmonica, which he didn't know how to play! My friends would come in and they would just go, "Uurgh! Who is this geek?"' while she pleaded for him to play the piano. By now, though, he was going to some lengths to disguise a rock'n'roll past from his folknik friends – unless the college girls giggled. Then the showman would win out; he would lose the twang and rock the joint:

Bob Scroggins: There was an old upright piano at the Purple Onion.*
It was beat-up, but [the owner] Bill [Danielson] had it tuned. Dylan

---

* The Purple Onion was a pizza parlour Dylan began playing in spring 1960 after asking to get paid at the Ten O'Clock Scholar, and being refused.

would sometimes come over in the afternoon, looking for free pizza. He knew ... Bill was a notorious soft touch. Dylan would play that old piano for groups of Hamline coeds, tell[ing] them he played piano for Bobby Vee ... Bill and I were sure he was lying.

The formative Dylan was already going out of his way to ensure no one could see every string to his bow. Nor would he tell even those ostensibly close to him, girlfriends included, where he disappeared to at times. Or if he did, he would like as not tell a bald-faced lie. This was the person another accomplished blues musician – and future long-time musical partner of Dave Ray – met that summer:

> **Tony Glover**: He had short hair, not a crew cut but kinda collegiate. He'd just started to get into Woody Guthrie. He didn't impress me that much musically, but he was real hungry [for] material. He had a bit of a chip on his shoulder, which I later realized was compensating for stuff [that had previously happened]. And there was always stories about going on the road, saying, 'I was down in Oklahoma,' when he was [really] going home to Hibbing. I don't know how seriously people took that stuff, but he would [just] disappear.

Glover was another player from whom Dylan sensed he could learn a great deal. In particular, he could teach him how to play the harp, which was not proving easy to master. It turned out there was a simple explanation – Dylan had the wrong kind of harmonica:

> He was just beginning to play harp with a rack but he had one of those chord harmonicas, where you get an octave [range], two on top of each other, which are good for polkas but not much good for the blues or bend[ing] notes. A lot of the white hillbilly/Guthrie stuff was straight harp. If you're playing a song in C, you use a C harp. [But] with blues you can play a song in C, and use an F harp. We talked about that.

But before they could really develop their friendship, Dylan disappeared again, and this time he really had gone somewhere far away, to locate another self. It seems he had not even told his parents, who came looking for him one day in the room he rented above Gray's

Drug Store in Dinkytown. The property in question was owned by the husband of a friend of Beattie's, Etheldoris Stein. Yet when they came to call, they found the apartment empty. He had upped and split – without telling a soul.

Possessed by a yen to live the life Kerouac depicted in *On The Road*, Dylan had decided to head for Denver. It was no mere whim, being almost exactly 900 miles from the home he sang about in a traditional song he favoured that year. His explanation for this journey seventeen years later, in conversation with Barbara Kerr, was surprisingly free of the usual self-serving mythology:

> I went there because I knew a girl whose floor I could sleep on. That's what I did [back then]: hitch-hike to one place or another, with everything I owned in my guitar case, sleep on someone's floor and play music ... I always tried to keep a couple of dollars in my shoe, but in general money was irrelevant to my life. I stayed around Denver for a while, but there was only one coffee house and they wouldn't give me a job. But then I met a stripper who worked at a bar called the Gilded Garter, and she bought me some clothes and got me a job playing 'Muleskinner Blues' between strip acts.

The Denver 'coffee house' at which he failed to perform was actually a proper folk club, the well-known Exodus, where he first saw Jesse Fuller, though when he 'wrote John Koerner a letter and told him, he thought it was [just] one of my stories.' The venue had just released a showcase album featuring songs by, among others, a young Judy Collins and black folksinger Walt Conley. In keeping with his penchant for put-downs, Dylan later put his feelings of rejection into an early blues, 'East Colorado Blues', describing Denver as 'a mean ol' place to stay'.

Whilst in Denver he befriended another Kerouac acolyte, Kevin Krown, who confirmed (to Scaduto) that Dylan 'was [already] living with this stripper down the road'. He also told said biographer that Dylan came to Denver having already been offered the job at the Gilded Garter. As a result, 'He was the one doing the buying.'*

---

* This certainly sounds more plausible than the story in Sounes, where Gilded Garter owner Sophia St John phones up Walt Conley and says, 'I need a singer up here.' Conley immediately thinks of someone from out of town and not good enough to play the Exodus, somehow knowing Dylan plays the piano. I think not.

The Gilded Garter was hardly across the street, being located in Central City, thirty-eight miles away, a place Kerouac described as 'an old mining town that was once called the Richest Square Mile In The World'. It was no longer that when the writer visited in 1948, but his description of the old prospector town was still enticing enough to draw this folk poet there, knowing that Jack's visit had culminated in his first in-print reference to the term which would define the first noteworthy Cold War literary movement:

> It was a wonderful night. Central City is two miles high; at first you get drunk on the altitude, then you get tired, and there's a fever in your soul. We approached the lights around the opera house ... then we took a sharp right and hit some old saloons with swinging doors ... We started off with a few extra-size beers. There was a player-piano. Beyond the back door was a view of mountainsides in the moonlight. I let out a yahoo ... The night was getting more and more frantic. I wished Dean and Carlo were there – then I realized they'd be out of place and unhappy. They were like the man with the dungeon stone and the gloom, rising from the underground, the sordid hipsters of America, a new beat generation that I was slowly joining.

By the time Dylan got there, Central City was a shell of its former shell. Undeterred, he decided to stick around with this highly accomodating girl, who did not expect him to open even saloon doors for her. But at summer's end, with the next semester approaching, and still undecided about what to do, Dylan returned to St Paul, where he spun stories about his adventures in East Colorado while plotting his next great escape, glad to be 'back in the good ol' USA' ('East Colorado Blues'). Yet something profound had happened, enough to prompt him to return to Central City no fewer than three times in the next six years, without an explanation ever forthcoming.

According to Conley, Dylan took with him back to St Paul a song called 'The Klan', which Conley had foolishly played him the couple of times he needed to memorize it, and a chunk of Conley's record collection. Conley would continue to snipe about Dylan's light fingers to anyone who cared to listen, while back in Dinkytown Dylan just kept shape-shifting and shoplifting. If he had retained any residual goodwill at Sigma Alpha Mu, he was now required to make himself scarce:

Dave Ray: The second or third time I saw him, he came running in and asked if he could go ... down to the basement, where I would [usually] play. And he was kinda nervous. He belonged to the SAMmy fraternity and he was running from 'em. He had taken a load of their steaks from out of their freezer, and sold them to somebody.

The fault lines on the local folk scene were also hardening. Whilst he'd been away, Pankake and Nelson had finally got their folkzine out. Called *Little Sandy Review*, an editorial in their second issue made their stance crystal clear. Their zine would target 'any and all phonies who water, dilute, and pervert American folk music – transforming it into Folkum rather than folksong'. As far as the pair were concerned, 'Folk music should and can only be performed by people in the folk tradition or by people who have taken the trouble to learn it.'

Such an edict placed this particular formative folksinger on the wrong side of their arbitrary divide. And if he was in any doubt he was one of their targets, Pankake apparently told him after seeing the post-Denver Dylan play, 'Maybe you should go back to playing rock'n'roll.' Perhaps it was just such a comment which convinced Dylan the editor should not be allowed to keep some records he felt were gathering dust at Pankake's musical mausoleum. In particular, he had been covetously eyeing up two import albums Ramblin' Jack Elliott had made for England's Topic label.

Unsurprisingly, Dylan's explanation for what happened next (in *No Direction Home*) makes light of his larceny, 'I was listening to [some] records at [Paul Nelson']s house once. I knew they'd be away for the weekend so I went over there and helped myself to a bunch of old records.' In fact, he went into virtual hiding to avoid returning them. As Nelson told me, 'We had like five [addresses], one address would lead to another ... There were a lot of people looking for him, for various reasons.' Dylan surely knew he was never going to get away with it this. Chasteningly, it was his harp teacher who sold him out:

Tony Glover: I was a printer at the time and I was helping these guys put out a fanzine called the *Little Sandy Review*. I [had] met Paul Nelson

[when] he worked at a record shop [that Glover frequented]. Pankake had got a couple of Jack Elliott records from England. It was a big deal. One day those records were missing – and Dylan had [just] stopped by ... Pankake said [straight away], 'You wouldn't have any idea where Dylan might be.' So I made a point of checking out Dylan's record collection next time I was over at his house, [which he shared] with Hugh Brown. Sure enough, there was those two records. Next time I saw Pankake I said, I know where your records are. He decided to go over and get the records and scare Bob a bit. I was [actually] at Bob's place when Pankake showed up with this club about [the length of a baseball bat]. It was getting really heavy. Anyhow, Pankake made a lot of noise, shook Bob up pretty good, grabbed the records, and left ... Bob's position was, 'This guy's a scholar, he's studying these records; I'm a musician, I need them to learn how to play [these songs].'

Dylan may have had a point. As Nelson recalls, 'When we played him the Elliott stuff he came back in a day, or two at the most, and ... from being a crooner, basically ... singing Josh White and Belafonte songs and Odetta songs ... he sounded like he did on the first Columbia record. He had this whole style down that quickly ... He did what it took Elliott ten, fifteen years in two days.' On the other hand, Pankake rightly reckons, 'I felt it expressed a certain amount of contempt for me personally.'

Dylan remained friends with Nelson and Glover – who were both present at the great showdown – but he and Pankake never healed the rift. On the last of the Glover–Dylan home tapes, from July 1963, he insisted, 'Jon Pankake came at me four years ago with a club, for taking some records. Four years ago I was afraid. Now, I couldn't care less.' That final comment was undoubtedly intended to reach Pankake via Nelson, who was again present that night, representing the *Little Sandy Review* in their latest confrontation with the prodigal son for making a record the two editors felt was more Folkum than folksong (*The Freewheelin' Bob Dylan*).

According to Nelson, it wasn't just the Elliott albums to which Dylan helped himself. He told Izzy Young in 1965 he'd actually run 'off with about $400 worth of ... records'. It seems Dylan had now decided to live outside the law, a folknik who took more from Corso than Kerouac. He had also decided that he who was not for him was against him, which came as something of a shock to Glover's playing partner:

Dave Ray: After that, there was an abrupt parting of the ways. He started singularly developing this persona or attitude that he carried on from then on, as far as I could see. This insulated, separatist kinda thing. Almost elitist. It started when he was still in Minneapolis, [and] he was doing a lot of Woody Guthrie stuff, which he mimicked to a T.

Some – Pankake included – actually felt the 'new' Dylan was mimicking Jack Elliott *mimicking Guthrie*. The ten-inch Elliott album he had been particularly keen to relieve Pankake of was called *Talking Woody Guthrie*. It comprised ten Guthrie songs, with a track-listing – 'Talkin' Columbia', 'Pretty Boy Floyd', 'Hard Travelin'', '1913 Massacre' &c. – that could almost be an early Dylan set list.

But the Guthrie Dylan initially locked on to was a writer first, a singer second. As he suggested in 1999, '[Guthrie was] dead serious and I intended to be the same. No fooling around, no fakery.' The 'key work' was Guthrie's own liar's autobiography, *Bound For Glory*, which Whitaker lent him that summer – and never saw again. Dylan later claimed he 'identified with *Bound For Glory* more than I even did with *On the Road*'. After Central City, he perhaps realized he could never be Neal Cassady – he hadn't it in him – but he could see himself as Woody's sidekick real easy. As he states during *No Direction Home*, 'You could listen to his songs, and actually learn how to live.' Woody had written real songs, not 'light fluffy stuff, clever but pointless'.* As he later put it, 'As many of Woody's songs as I could find, I sang.'

The first evidence we have of this Woodyesque wunderkind is a tape Bonnie Beecher made that fall in the near-derelict apartment Dylan shared with Hugh Brown, 'Dirty' Dave Morton and Max Uhler. Morton recalls, 'The apartment next door, there was an R&B band and they would be [constantly] jamming, playing Jimmy Reed riffs, and everybody would say, What's that noise?' Dylan blotted it out, saying goodbye to Jimmy Reed riffs. He had discovered Guthrie's talkin' blues, four of which appear on the so-called 1st Minneapolis Tape, probably all learnt at the home of another girlfriend, Ellen Baker.

---

* The person whose music he is describing in this passage is Cole Porter, someone whose work he would come to appreciate.

Like Bonnie, Ellen was immersed in music. But unlike Bonnie, she had inherited her passion from her father, Mike, who ran the Minneapolis Folklore Society. As Ellen says, 'My father was quite a collector. He had old manuscripts, sheet music and folk magazines ... [Bob and I] would harmonize old tunes from my father's old records ... traditional things, sort of A-minorish folky.'

If Ellen is nowhere to be heard on the 1st Minneapolis Tape, banker's daughter Cynthia Fincher can be heard trying to get Dylan to do some of the songs she likes, to no avail. The scene must have amused Bonnie, who got on with most of Dylan's Twin Cities girl-friends – Ellen, Cynthia, Lorna Sullivan, to name but three – but was under no illusion as to what Bobby's true passion was, or how long he planned to stick around. This was because, as she later confided, they remained 'really close [even] when we were no longer lovers'.

One day that fall he gave (or sent) Bonnie a lyric he had written *for her*. It was his first 'so long, good luck and goodbye' in song, addressed to someone who knows 'what I am doing and where I must go'. He was moving on, not 'know[ing] if I'll see you again'. Nor was it the only song he wrote for her that fall. He had just composed the largely improvised ditty, 'Bonnie, Why'd You Cut My Hair?', after he had to make 'an unexpected trip ... to Hibbing. He wanted me to cut his hair real short, real short so that [his parents] won't know that [he has] long hair. He kept saying, Shorter! Shorter!'

She did what he asked, until it was too short, and too late. For all the humour of the situation, this was a serious matter. Dylan was going home, cap in hand, to tell his parents he was dropping out of school. The way Kemp tells it in his memoir, 'Bobby's parents gave him their blessing to drop out of college and pursue music.' Actually, they *thought* they had gotten their son to agree to a one-year sabbatical before he knuckled down to real life:

Abraham Zimmerman: He wanted to have a free rein. He wanted to be a folksinger, an entertainer. We couldn't see it, but we felt he was entitled to the choice. It's his life, after all, and we didn't want to stand in the way. So we made an agreement that he could have one year to do as he pleased, and if at the end of that year we were not satisfied with his progress, he'd go back to school. [1963]

If any single statement highlights the generational chasm between the son Abraham thought he'd raised and the real Dylan, it is that last sentence. Bobby was telling him what he wanted to hear. He had no intention of going back to school; not now, not ever. But he needed enough funds to head east, bound for Chicago and a potential rendezvous with his friend Krown. Or perhaps not.

According to Ron Joelson, who received a call from Dylan shortly before he split, 'He was leaving for California and wanted me to go with him ... He said he just had to hit the road and play. Quickly. [Then] California turned into New York.' Dylan told Camp Herzl confidant Kemp he headed out on foot to Interstate 35W 'with his guitar over his shoulder, a small suitcase, and five dollars in his sock. As he stuck his thumb out to hitch-hike, the snow was coming down so hard that he had to keep shaking himself off so people would know he was [there].'

It's an evocative picture. But it is probably not what happened. Even to a childhood friend, he was now acting out the movie of his own life. In fact, he had cajoled a girlfriend, Charlotte Jerrusic, into give him a ride to Highway 12, his mind on the future; he felt, as he later said, that he'd learnt as much as he could in Dinkytown 'and used up all my options'. Whilst trying to thumb a ride, he experienced an epiphany of sorts, as he articulated to Tony Glover and friends three years later, when he still felt a kinship he couldn't explain:

> I left this town. I ran away from it. I was on the highway and ... I didn't even think. That was the first of my non-thinking. And I thought, fuck it, and I really meant it. And it didn't matter how cold it got. That was three and a half years ago. I never cared since then about things like talk, rules, words written in a book [or] in a magazine.*

It was a defining moment. Once again, Dylan was travelling to a city several hundred miles away bearing a solitary scrap of paper and a single name, expecting Krown to somehow still be there. Which he was, taking him and his guitar to a party at a girls' dormitory that very first night, at which Krown was shocked to hear the change in his friend, 'Whatever he was before, he wasn't that now.'

---

* Ten years later, he told Glover he felt he'd 'done whatever it was I was supposed to do there.'

This may well be the same party where a guitarist named Mike Michaels introduced himself to 'this guy with a ... funny hat, pudgy face, harmonica in rack, and a guitar ... It turned out that we both loved Woody Guthrie, and we spent a lot of time that weekend playing together in the dorm. Dylan said he was from New Mexico and that his parents were ranchers. I had no reason not to believe him.' Michaels, who had a folk music show on the university radio station, WUCB, later claimed he and Dylan did a show on the radio of 'mostly Guthrie songs'. Sadly, no trace remains.

Within a couple of days – being a fast worker back then – Dylan found an obliging girl who grew pot. According to Krown, he 'moved in with her'. Dylan says not, claiming he 'met [some] woman in [a] bar. She picked me up ... I felt used. I was about nineteen and she was, well, she was old. ... She was wearing a print dress. And a girdle. She made love to me, did it all ... She lived in just one room, with a closet, a sink and ... a dresser with a mirror on top that you can tilt whichever way you want, and a bed with a mattress that sagged clear to the floor in the middle.'

Movie script or real life? Either way, the only person being used was the woman. As in Denver, Dylan seems to have stuck around long enough to find out if there were opportunities for him to make any headway musically, and discovering there were not, headed for another university town, Madison, in the *opposite* direction to New York. Once again, it was a familiar story, reconstructed by Stuart D. Levitan in his 2018 survey of *Madison In The Sixties* (2018):

> Bob Dylan blows into town in early January ... He's got the number for Socialist Club president and banjoist Ron 'Ronny' Radosh, but his apartment ... is too small for Dylan to stay there. So Radosh sends him over to freshman Danny Kalb, a ... folk and blues guitarist, who puts Dylan up in his Huntington Court rooming house for a day or two ... Kalb takes Dylan to a party, where [he meets] Fred Underhill and poet Ann Lauterbach, whose Greenwich Village music teacher had been Pete Seeger ... [They] take him under their collective wing and back to their flat at 430 W. Johnson St, where Dylan crashes for about a week. 'I've been broke and cold,' he writes friends back in Minneapolis ... Kalb takes him to Marshall Brickman and Eric Weissberg's place at 1028 Clymer Street ... For a few nights at the beatnik coffee house the Pad, Dylan

blows harmonica while Kalb sits atop the old upright piano, playing the blues ... After Dylan's been in town about ten days ... Underhill offers him a spot as a relief driver in a car headed for New York.

These were the 'bunch of New York people' – as he described them in a postcard to the Whitakers – who would provide that vital ticket to ride, turning him eastward again. But not before he and Kalb formed a musical bond that would carry over to the Village, where they both were bound, albeit weeks apart. The Dylan Kalb met in Madison was a man in transition, 'a repository of songs, from this sort of generalized left-wing people's songbook ... [But] he was nothing out of the ordinary ... Bob played with me ... on harmonica, at the Pad, a little beatnik coffee house, very small.'

One of the blues Danny boy liked to play was the Bessie Smith standard, 'Backwater Blues' (aka 'It Rained Five Days') about the 1927 Mississippi floods, which eleven months later Dylan would famously feature at his first concert at Carnegie (Chapter) Hall, by which time he had got a handle on the blues.

A tape made by some sage soul 'at a party' that January in Madison contains half a dozen blues by Kalb, as well as more than a dozen songs from Dylan's ever-expanding repertoire. What is remarkable about this tape is Dylan's performance. Kalb may say 'he was nothing out of the ordinary', but this is a fully formed folksinger, playing whooping harmonica and sounding not like a cross between Elliott and Guthrie, but like himself, even on the handful of Guthrie originals, three of them unique in his known canon: 'So Long, It's Been Good To Know You', 'Danville Girl' and 'New York Town'.*

The set list, contrary to legend, is also nicely varied, with traditional material like 'East Virginia Blues', 'Cocaine Blues' and 'Easy Rider', all songs he would continue to play in New York. He even tips his hat to the man who started it all, Hank Williams, singing 'I Heard That Lonesome Whistle', a song which would remain a lodestone for him as late as 1989's *Oh Mercy* sessions.

With hindsight, one choice seems ironic, given its final verse. In 'New York Town', Guthrie insisted, 'Never comin' back to this man's town again'. Just a few days later Dylan took the ride of his life to New York town and, unlike Lot's wife, he didn't look back.

---

* This tape has now been acquired by the Bob Dylan Archive in Tulsa.

1.3

May to October 1961: The Kindness Of (Friends & Other) Strangers

The first thing you noticed about Bobby in those days was that he was full of nervous energy ... [forever] herky-jerky, jiggling, sitting on the edge of his chair.

Dave Van Ronk

Even in those first days he couldn't sit still for more than fifteen minutes. Something was always going on inside him. Outside, too. His leg would shake with nervous energy, almost like a spastic's. He would move in a chair just the way he later moved on stage, a sort of rhythmic bobbing from the waist up. He used to laugh a lot then, and we called him Bobby.

Robert Shelton, July 1965

He ... would give as much as he got, but he was still not easy to get close to. Always there was a feeling of slight detachment, as if he were watching the scene with bemusement.

Robert Shelton, February 1966

When you talked to him, he either told you a story, or he said, 'Yeah? Is that right?', as if what you were telling him was the most amazing thing he'd ever heard.

Jack Nissenson, Village regular and Mountain Four member

*

Having left St Paul 'for good' in December 1960, imagine the ripple of surprise when an unrepentant Dylan turned up in Minneapolis in early to mid-May 1961,* to make 'a brief, but extremely telling, appearance at a university hootenanny', as *Little Sandy Review*'s editors Pankake and Nelson reported:

> The change in Bob was, to say the least, incredible. In a mere half-year, he had learnt to churn up exciting, bluesy, hard-driving harmonica-and-guitar music ... Dylan's performance that spring evening of a selection of Guthrie and Gary Davis songs was hectic and shaky, but it contained all the elements of [a] now perfected performing style.

Pankake later qualified such contemporary ebullience, suggesting, 'Musically, he was just potential [and] his guitar was shockingly out of tune.' The newly confident Dylan cared not. Nor had he returned empty-handed. For Glover, 'he brought back a little flyer from the Gaslight [sic] – John Lee Hooker, special guest: Bob Dylan ... Once I saw that flyer, I knew something was happening.' And so did the rest of Dinkytown.

Bonnie, for one, was anxious to see him and record him again. Having half-jokingly once suggested that a previous recording she had made (and later lost) would be worth $200 to the Library of Congress, he now made the fabled twenty-five-song Party Tape, which over the next half-century would make bootleggers a whole lot more, capturing a large chunk of Dylan's repertoire at a crucial juncture in his development: the exact midpoint between his arrival in New York and making his first LP.

We are fortunate that Beecher made such a tape because blink and this version of Dylan is gone like a turkey through the corn. The only crossover between this and three other known home tapes from the next three months devolves to a single song – 'Young But Daily Growin'', aka 'The Trees Do Grow So High' – which he admitted learning from Liam Clancy, prefacing the song to the Baileys in June.

Though Guthrie is depressingly well represented on Beecher's tape, with ten songs allocated his way (and before 'Pastures Of Plenty' a casually offered remark that Guthrie thinks he does it better than

---

* He played the Indian Neck Folk Festival in Branford, Connecticut on May 6th, so one presumes he arrived in the Twin Cities around the 10th, unless he went home to Hibbing first.

anyone else), the result is certainly more than 'a selection of Guthrie and Gary Davis songs'. Dylan's first serious discographer, Paul Cable, even expressed doubts that the tape dates from this early, citing the plentiful 'vocal idiosyncrasies here that [are now] familiar', evidence that, 'the Dylan we know [is] well on the way to emergence'. May it is, nonetheless.

Predictably, the least interesting inclusions are the Guthrie tunes, all respectfully reproduced but strictly ho-hum. Whereas the three blues tunes are positively gripping, while the seven traditional songs would live with early listeners and Dylan himself the longest. Three of them – 'Wild Mountain Thyme', 'Man Of Constant Sorrow' and 'Young But Daily Growin'' – were being performed and/or rehearsed in the G. E. Smith era (1988–90).

Nor does Dylan forget his audience, setting 'Bonnie, Why'd You Cut My Hair?' down before he forgets it, while providing conclusive evidence, according to Cable, 'that Dylan is a tit man', by the way he sings the salacious 'I Want My Milk'. Yet what he chooses not to perform is almost as telling. Just two of the Guthrie standards tally with the equally fulsome St Paul Tape, the previous May. He also fails to include 'Song To Woody', perhaps because it was the exact same tune and sensibility as the song he had given Bonnie before leaving town, five months earlier.

The Minneapolis Party Tape is certainly a more rounded musical portrait than the one he delivered at a Connecticut folk festival, the week before, when he shared a makeshift stage with the likes of Mark Spoelstra, the Greenbriar Boys, Reverend Gary Davis, Jim Kweskin, Buffy Sainte-Marie, Sandy Bull and Tom Rush. Three Guthrie originals, two of them talkin' blues, was all he felt like offering in his slot at Branford's Montowese Hotel, making no impression on anyone who hadn't seen him before. It was as if his mind was already travellin' on.

At least the all-day festival would prove a useful networking exercise, the interesting stuff all happening away from the microphone. Mid-sixties sidekick Bobby Neuwirth met the other Bobby for the first time while 'standing around the beer barrel ... Kweskin, Robert L. Jones and I were singing some Woody Guthrie songs. Bob came up and he started playing along ... and he had another Woody song, and it went from then until dark – obscure Woody Guthrie and Hank

Williams songs ... I told him ... he should really come up to Cambridge.'

Instead, Dylan set about retracing the path he'd travelled five months earlier – minus the Chicago detour and the red-headed woman. Madison was again used as a stopover (and perhaps more) on the way back from Minneapolis, Dylan once again using the familiar West Johnson Street crash-pad while he reconnected with poetess Lauterbach and others likely to be impressed by his remarkable transformation. According to Stuart D. Levitan, 'By now, Dylan's aura is starting to grow ... Young women are calling and coming on to him when he hangs out behind the Union – he even gets in some time on the piano at Grove's Women's Co-op.'

He lingered in Madison a while; so much so that even after Krown phoned on behalf of Avril, who was wondering where the hell he might be, Dylan made no effort to hurry 'home'. He was enjoying the attention in a city where the competition was less fierce and the women more easily impressed.

But if he was testing his girlfriend's patience, he had overplayed his hand. When he finally returned to the Village at the end of the month, he discovered she had left for San Francisco, and he was obliged to call on the McKenzies' after midnight:

> **Peter McKenzie**: He wasn't sure what to do, 'cause she had closed up the apartment, left town. He was coming to the house to say, Hi, what's happening, and basically found out she wasn't there. There he was with his guitar over his shoulder and his little suitcase, which only had one pair of underwear in it and my mother asked him if he had a place to stay, 'cause it was two in the morning. He said, 'No, I'll find a place.' He never asked to stay ... He just stayed.

By the following morning he was full of remorse and professing to have learnt his lesson, hastily scribbling a lyric to the tune of 'Columbus Stockade', in which he lectured other boys not 'to ramble / ... Get you a gal that really loves you / Stay right there and settle down.' He had no intention of doing anything of the sort himself, but he still called Avril long-distance and played her the song, called 'California Brown Eyed Baby'.

As Eve McKenzie would remark, 'It was the first time we'd heard him sing one of his own songs.' He even started performing this collection of clichés in his live set. No version survives, though, mainly because he fails to respond to a request for it at the Chapter Hall show in November.

In truth, the song added up to one big lie – and he knew it. In fact, most of the songs he was writing after putting his feet under the McKenzies' table that spring – and there were at least twenty-three – fell short of the grade. Almost uniformly derivative, they bear titles like 'Don't Let My Deal Go Down', 'Just As Long As I'm In This World' and 'Mean Ol' Mississippi Blues', the last of which lifted the entire opening verse from Jimmie Rodgers' 'Mississippi River Blues'.

Looking back on this time in February 1964, he admitted, 'What I was writing I was still scared to sing, and there was no one else who was writing ... I wrote a song about Woody Guthrie which ... made a certain amount of sense song-wise, but the rest of the stuff I never did sing.' Even the couple of cast-offs he did slip into a club set, he says he 'didn't think ... were here nor there'. Thankfully, he got into a routine of writing them down. As Eve recalled, 'He would come home ... three or four in the morning ... sit down at the table, close the doors and start writing.'

Quite the worst lyric from the first batch that spring was 'VD Seaman's Last Letter', an attempt to mimic Guthrie's set of VD songs he'd been commissioned to write during the war. Try as Dylan might to muster a tone of regret, a line like 'With siff [i.e. syphilis] as my cargo, I'll dock in your harbor no more' would have had 'em rolling in the aisles for all the wrong reasons. He quietly filed it away.

Wisely, he kept at it. Equally wisely, the McKenzies preserved such juvenilia. But he was still some way off emulating others 'who wrote their own songs', including contemporaries like Tom Paxton and Len Chandler, even if as part of the learning process he did attempt co-authoring a talkin' blues, the idiom he had mastered the most, with Paxton some time that summer: 'Bob and I [were] walk[ing] up 6th Avenue all the way up to the music stores on 48th Street. Bob needed a new harmonica rack, and as we walked we did our one-and-only co-write ... which we didn't even finish. It was ... a riff on "Talking Union" ... Our version was called "Talking Central Park Mugger Blues".'

Dylan also set about penning another of his talkin' blues, his funniest yet, from a story in the June 19th *New York Herald Tribune* regarding an excursion boat to Bear Mountain that was oversold. Meanwhile Paxton continued building a repertoire of mainly orginal songs for his 1962 debut, *I'm The Man That Built The Bridges*, recorded at the Gaslight Cafe.

Dylan was in more of a hurry, though, making his own Gaslight Tape that summer with a purpose all its own. The six-song tape was made at Van Ronk's girlfriend Terri Thal's suggestion, ostensibly to help generate out-of-town gigs. Generally dated to September 6th, the choice of songs suggest an earlier date, perhaps the July residency Shelton says he played there.* The three originals herein – 'Song To Woody', 'Talkin' Bear Mountain Picnic Massacre Blues' and 'Man On The Street' – had certainly all been written by late June, while two of the three covers appear on the May Party Tape.†

The other he had first heard on May 6th, learnt it again in early June, and was now claiming as an original arrangement. The provenance of 'He Was A Friend Of Mine' has always been murky; made murkier still by Dylan's decision to lodge his arrangement with Leeds Music in January 1962, a good nine months after a very similar arrangement had appeared on an album by Eric Von Schmidt and Rolf Cahn.

Though the duo's album had passed Dylan by, Von Schmidt certainly played the song to him in June, when Dylan visited Boston for the first time, though it was not the first time he had heard the song. Jim Kweskin had played it at the Indian Neck festival within earshot of Dylan, after Kweskin credited Von Schmidt as his source in his introduction. 'Twas the circle game, writ large.

This residual memory perhaps prompted Dylan to ask Von Schmidt to teach him the song, from which it was only a short step to recording

---

* David Hajdu also suggests an earlier date, or a different tape, seemingly unaware that Thal recalled the track listing almost perfectly to Spitz. He is trying to force the chronology to fit an apocryphal trip to Boston by Thal. The real issue it raises, if it really is September 6th, is why no 'Sally Gal'?
† 'Pretty Polly' and Guthrie's 'Car Car' (aka 'Car Song'), a duet with Van Ronk.

it for his first album in November, only to 'donate' it to Van Ronk for the Prestige album he would record the following April, perhaps a mea culpa for nicking Van Ronk's arrangement of 'House of The Rising Sun'. Van Ronk later joked he learnt the song from Von Schmidt, who'd learnt it from Dylan, who learnt it from him.*

Sometimes, it seems, Dylan genuinely did not know where a song he was playing had come from. On one occasion, Sylvia Tyson remembers Dylan bursting into the Kettle of Fish and exclaiming, 'Hey, you gotta listen to this song I just wrote ... or at least, I think I wrote it. Maybe I just heard it somewhere.' At this point, it was all grist for the musical mill.

It was clear as soon as he played it that 'He Was A Friend Of Mine' fit perfectly, being another song dealing with death, this one close to home. It quickly became a central ballast in his repertoire. Though it missed out on that debut album, it would be instrumental in him getting a Columbia contract and was one of four traditional arrangements copyrighted for his first songbook, *Bob Dylan Himself*.†

Incredible as this seems, the idea of putting together his own folio of songs actually predates that Columbia contract. Though he rarely played more than a single original at his shows, back at the McKenzies' he had been furiously penning songs all summer. No matter that he duly informed a Columbia publicist, 'I write a lot of songs [but then] I forget them as soon as I write them,' the McKenzies kept his lyrics, and at some point he rifled through them, writing two draft sequences for either an album of wholly original songs – most unlikely – or a songbook. The second sequence runs thus:

1. Dope Fiend Robber 2. Talkin' Bear Mt. 3. Ramblin' Gamblin' Blues 4. Over The Road I'm Bound To Go 5. California Brown Eyed Baby 6. I Hear A Train A-Rolling 7. Rocking Chair 8. Old Man (John Doe) 9. Get Where I'm Going 10. Woody's Song 11. Talkin' New York Town 12. Great Chicagonian.

---

* Just to muddy the waters some more, Dylan told Shelton he had learnt the song from 'a Chicago street singer' when it was still in contention for his vinyl debut.
† The *Bob Dylan* out-take (lodged as a Leeds Music demo) was released in 1991 on *The Bootleg Series Vols. 1–3*.

Having his own folio of songs held an allure for Dylan that may seem mystifying to modern music fans, but he had grown up in an era when such folios – particularly for country artists like Hank Williams, who self-published two such folios before he ever made a record – were commonplace.* The early Guthrie songbook, *California to the New York Island*, further whetted an appetite which would culminate in *Bob Dylan Himself*.†

Such a folio, already on his mind in late August, prompted the above list of a dozen 'largely unknown' Dylan originals. Actually, 'Talkin' Bear Mountain', 'Woody's Song' and 'Talkin' New York' would all make the 1962 songbook, as would 'Old Man', under its new title, 'Man On The Street'; 'Over The Road I'm Bound To Go' was an adaptation of a traditional song he later rewrote and recorded as 'Sally Gal'; while 'California Brown Eyed Baby' was one song anyone who caught him at Gerde's this early might have known.‡

That leaves six songs he does not seem to have performed live, at least two of which were rewrites of songs from that Guthrie songbook. 'I Hear A Train A-Rolling' and 'The Great Chicagonian' – based on 'This Train' and 'Philadelphia Lawyer'. If the latter owes as much to 'The Jealous Lover', the traditional template for Guthrie's song, the former tips its hat to Johnny Cash's 'Folsom Prison Blues' in its opening couplet.

More prescient of the future songwriter, though, is his clever inversion of the traditional 'This Train Is Bound For Glory' so that this train becomes hell-bound; filled to the brim with cheaters, rich men who think they're 'better than you and me', parasites who make their money 'off of all of me and you', and anyone who has 'lied to his fellow man [and] used them for his own needs / To strengthen his own hand', a presentiment of the *John Wesley Harding* Dylan. Already, Dylan was more concerned with the lost than the saved; convinced Satan was alive and well and driving the train.

---

* Grelun Landon, a VP at Hill & Range, Elvis's music publisher, later claimed Dylan visited him that summer, seeking a job as a staff writer at $50 a week, presumably as a day job to fill the downtime from club-hopping.
† See chapter 1.4 for a fuller discussion of the publishing history of *Bob Dylan Himself*.
‡ Mentioned by Izzy Young in *Sing Out!* as a song which was catching on, it was fast dropped by Dylan, lest it did.

'Dope Fiend Robber' also anticipates a later Dylan, one he could perhaps have let be: seeing every criminal as a victim of society. In this case he manages to make the robber a junkie, too. In the final verse, he says to his jailer-cum-doctor, 'Now you fixed my wounds and I am glad / But you didn't fix the habit I had ... I was found guilty at the trial / Judge said I'm condemned to die / Now I'm not asking for sympathy / From anybody in y[o]ur society.'

If this self-pitying Dope Fiend Robber was entirely fictional, it wouldn't take him long to find a historical figure also 'condemned to die'. Donald White would be the subject of his first true topical song, the following February. By then he'd learnt to trim some fat from such songs; the seventeen long, weary verses of 'Dope Fiend Robber' he pruned to ten.

'Ramblin' Gamblin' Blues' also anticipated a song from another folio, six months later. It is the story of a boy 'I once knowed' who was killed on his way back to Utah to see his mother, anticipating both 'Ballad For A Friend' and 'I Was Young When I Left Home'. Whether he subconsciously realized these songs fell short or not, he showed them to few folk, though Young noted, 'One day Dylan walks in [to the Folklore Center] and says he wants me to see some songs he had written. It was still uncommon at that time to do so.'

He would continue to show Izzy some of what he wrote for the next six months, a process documented in Young's diary. Dylan still didn't know what audience he was reaching for. As he said, looking back in 1965, 'I wrote wherever I happened to be. Sometimes I'd spend a whole day sitting at a corner table in a coffee house ... look[ing] at people for hours and I'd make up things about them. Or I'd think, what kind of song would they like to hear, and I'd make one up.'

For now, Dylan decided to focus more on expanding his repertoire till he had the whole folk/blues canon in his hands. Sometimes it did seem like his instinct for which song, what element to purloin was uncanny. As Liam Clancy recently recalled, 'He soaked up everything. He had this immense curiosity, and he was ready to suck up everything that came within his range'; sentiments to which Van Ronk readily concurred, 'His repertoire changed all the time; he'd find something he loved and sing it to death and drop it and go on to something else. Basically, he was in search of his own musical style and it was developing very rapidly.'

Swapping songs with fellow folkies was the very life blood of this insular scene – they even had a name for it: 'the folk process'. But although it has been well documented that Dylan's mind acted like a one-man tape recorder at this time, we only now have hard evidence of what such sessions were like. On June 24th, 1961, Dylan and Ian Tyson, the Canadian folksinger (and, later, a notable songwriter in his own right), convened at Mell and Lillian Bailey's to make a home tape, as others had done because, as Suze recalled, 'Musicians liked making recordings for Mell. Ian and Sylvia, Paul Clayton and others came over to make tapes ... [and] Bob sang many songs into Mell's Wollensak [when] work[ing on] his new material.'

Dylan opens with 'Lang A-Growin', as it is listed, the one song from Bonnie's May Party Tape he does that June evening.* From here, he reels off 'Golden Vanity', Child Ballad 286, the first song he ever played at the Scholar and one he was still singing live in 1992; the traditional 'Jack O'Diamonds', with some bottleneck guitar; and 'Easy Rider', which he teaches to Tyson.† He then pulls out a harmonica and begins to play the freshly minted 'Man On The Street', before Tyson joins him on the *Titanic* broadside ballad, 'The Great Ship' and a couple of improvised party songs.

Apart from its musical significance, such a tape demonstrates that song swapping was a two-way process, in which Dylan gave as much as he took. The Baileys would make two shorter home tapes of him that summer, on which he surprised them by performing his own adaptation of Guthrie's 'This Train', plus obscurer trad songs like 'No Grave Can Hold My Body' and 'Johnny's Gone to High Lea' – a song he had perhaps just learnt from Richard Fariña.‡ He is already starting to develop a fixation with songs about the dead and dying, performing 'See That My Grave Is Kept Clean' for the first time on the same tape. If he had probably taken this from Blind Lemon Jefferson's anthologized 78 – which he doubtless heard at the Van Ronks' – his research into America's folk past was unceasing and indiscriminate.

---

* Other titles include 'Young Craigston', 'Young But Daily Growin'' and 'The Trees Do Grow So High'. But its earliest reference, *circa* 1675, is as 'Long a-growing'.
† Tyson says he learnt this song 'in the course of a long afternoon session with Bob Dylan last summer', in the notes to Ian & Sylvia's eponymous 1962 album.
‡ He references 'High Lea' in the unedited Columbia version of 'Bob Dylan's Blues'.

Among the many folk songbooks he could lay his hands on, he certainly pored over Alan Lomax's 623-page *Folk Songs of North America*, published the previous year, making a numerical list of those songs which interested him. When he found a set of lyrics he liked, he would write them out longhand, and then search for a recording from which he could memorize the tune. Versions of Hank Williams' 'Lost Highway', 'Omie Wise', 'I'm A Rounder Till I Die', and two songs he would not record until 1980 – 'Satisfied Mind' and 'Mary From The Wild Moor' – are extant in Dylan's hand from this summer, proof of catholic tastes even then.

Aware that his new girlfriend had a sister who worked for Alan Lomax, he began to turn up at Carla Rotolo's, 'listening to my records, days and nights. He studied the Folkways *Anthology of American Folk Music*, the singing of Ewan MacColl and A. L. Lloyd, Rabbit Brown's guitar, Guthrie, of course, and blues.' Among the songs he probably found there was an early showstopper called 'Dink's Song', that Alan's father, John, had collected from a woman named Dink on the Brazo River in 1907. If he found the song at Carla's, her sister first heard it by her beau at one of his early out-of-town shows that August – a shared bill with Van Ronk at a Philadelphia coffee house. It gave her chills: 'He stood straight with his head slightly back and his eyes nowhere and began to sing "Dink's Song" ... The audience slowed their chattering; he stilled the room.'

Congenitally perverse, he never got around to recording this paradigm of pure tradition, though it *was* thankfully captured by Cynthia Gooding at Gerde's in October and Tony Glover in Minneapolis in December. (God bless folkies, and their desire to document!) Glover's recording duly appeared on the first ever commercial rock bootleg, *Great White Wonder*, in 1969 from which Jeff Buckley learnt the song, which later became the cornerstone of the Coen Brother's 'Greenwich Village' movie, *Inside Llewyn Davis* (2014); a case of the pop process taking up the slack.

Dylan's constant search for source material also led him to another propitious connection, the *New York Times*'s Robert Shelton, one he assiduously cultivated. Shelton told another early Dylan supporter, *Melody Maker*'s Max Jones, in 1966, when his memory still served him well, that he had first 'met Dylan in [the early] summer of 1961, after he sang in a hootenanny at Folk City in Greenwich Village. I told him whenever he was working somewhere regularly to call me as I'd like to do a feature story on him ... In those days he was doing some traditional songs like "House of the Rising Sun", also a few Woody Guthrie things, [and] was very much under the influence of Jack Elliott and Van Ronk... We used to knock around listening to music together, and that period was interesting because Dylan was listening to every bit of music he could hear. He walked around with his ears hanging out, eager to follow whatever was going on in folk music. He'd come over to my house and play piano and listen to records.'

Shelton even brought Dylan to the odd uptown concert, hoping to further his musical education, taking him to see the Clancy Brothers at the Town Hall shortly after their March 1961 *Ed Sullivan Show* appearance took the country by storm (for which Dylan remained eternally grateful). By the time Shelton finally gave Dylan the big push in late September, he had been watching the boy wonder for some months, till he could cover the full gamut – love lyrics, Anglo-American ballads, Irish drinking songs, gospel and blues.

The scribe wasn't the only one not immediately bowled over by Dylan's early material, yet enjoyed his curioisty and his company:

Maria Muldaur: I remember when he wrote ... 'Talkin' Bear Mountain Picnic Blues' ... Everyone was saying, isn't that clever ... But I was not getting the buzz at all. I'd enjoy sitting and having a glass of wine with him, [but] I was not in awe of him. At the bar near us would be characters like ... Peter LaFarge, Josh Logan; the old-guard leftists.

As with all things new, some Village regulars instantly recognized a true original. Bruce Langhorne, an extraordinary musician who played alongside Dylan at his first ever recording session and would make a telling contribution to both his second and fifth albums, remembered seeing him when 'he had a little hat like a watchcap and was playing Woody Guthrie songs', and what struck him immediately was this 'quality of determination ... that some people have. When they're doing something, they're *really* doing it, and you know you have to pay attention to it.' Pay attention Langhorne did, even if by his own admission they 'never hung out and got drunk or high together'.

There was already a name for what Dylan had: unswerving self-belief. As early as December 1961, he bragged to his Columbia publicist,

Billy James, 'I knew I could sing better than all those people that are singing now. And I knew that I could sing *the same songs* much better.' When he later suggested he simply 'crossed Sonny Terry with the Stanley Brothers with Roscoe Holscomb with Big Bill Broonzy with Woody Guthrie', he was consciously omitting that all-important *ingredient x*.

The latterday *Chronicler* may assert that 'what really set me apart ... was my repertoire ... hardcore folk songs', but it wasn't his *choice* of songs, it was the way he was doing them.* *That* voice, as he gamely admits, tended to 'either drive people away or they'd come in closer to see what it was all about'.

Even back then, it had a rare quality – a precision to its intonation and a preternatural intensity – that prompted one early reviewer to unfavourably compare it to a dog with his leg caught in barbed wire, leaving Dylan to store up an inner resentment till it spumed out at a foolish *Time* reporter in 1965's *dont look back*, who'd suggested Caruso was a better singer: 'I happen to be just as good as [Caruso] ... [You] have to listen closely, but I hit all those notes and I can hold my breath three times as long.'

Which isn't to say that his fast-developing stagecraft didn't soon start to win admirers; it's just that his early performing persona was designed for small clubs and sympathetic audiences. In such a setting, it wasn't just about the songs. One trick he learnt from other folk-singers to win over an audience and break down the barrier between him and them was to borrow a harmonica from someone. It was a trick he was still using when booed at the Newport Festival in July 1965. Even in 1961, it didn't always work. Earl Crabb recently wrote online about a support slot to Reverend Gary Davis Dylan played in early fall 1961 at a college in Bennington, Massachusetts. Crabb had previously caught him at a May folk festival:

> It was clear that the concertgoers were there for Davis, not Dylan. Dylan looked the same as he had ... at Indian Neck, with the hat and harmonica, but actually sounded better ... but the audience was not

---

* In those days, even his guitar-playing was different. He preferred picking or playing slide, especially on the blues.

impressed. They wanted Davis. There were even some boos, which was very unlike Bennington at the time.*

A sympathetic audience invariably got a better show because, as Village regular Jack Nissenson observed, Dylan would 'do these long, long monologues, with no point, and no punchline – except they kept you in hysterics'. He generally had to rely on the sense of humour of those listening. As Shelton revealed to Mr Jones, 'His own stuff then was principally humorous song and commentary, [with] the commentaries being outrageously funny.'

When he was in the right frame of mind, and the setting was right, 'the audience reaction was one of laughing not at but with Dylan' – as club-owner Arthur Kretchmer duly noted. The Dylan Kretchmer briefly knew 'was ... a real country character, and that is what everybody loved about him ... Sometimes he would play piano, or tell a funny story, or just clown around for a few minutes.' Suze concurs, 'All that fumbling around [would be just] the warm-up for a set that was either very down home or hypnotic and distant.'

His early 'clown[ing] around' often resembled a silent-movie comedy routine, reflecting another unexpected influence the later concert performer would have to largely sideline, though he acknowledged it to Billy James back in 1961: 'My biggest idol, goin' through my head all the time, is Charlie Chaplin.' Watching Chaplin shorts – and he would have had plenty of opportunities back home in Hibbing, where his uncle owned four movie houses – he learnt the timing he would use to such galvanizing effect when up against it in 1965–6.

But also, as Nissenson notes, he could be 'distant ... onstage, very into his own thing'. And not just onstage; at parties, at home. It was one of the characteristics his new girlfriend rather admired in him, 'that he could go inside himself so thoroughly and so completely that there was nothing else around but the music he was hearing in his

---

* To slightly belie Dylan's reputation for stinginess – and even Suze says, 'He was not known for his generosity' – Crabb reports, 'Davis was getting $75 and Dylan $50 for that concert. Afterwards, when they were getting paid, Dylan said that Davis should never have to work for less than $100, and gave Davis half of his money.'

head ... He would withdraw anywhere, at any time ... in a noisy room full of people or when it was just the two of us alone together.'

Such empathy was a rare quality, one Dylan couldn't always rely on going forward, even from his nearest and dearest. As he would plaintively enquire on 1977's 'Is Your Love In Vain?': 'When I am in the darkness, why must you intrude?' Suze understood, and it drew them closer. She even liked the fact that in social situations he would stick 'close to me or watch ... me from across a room.' What she found less endearing was that 'he was evasive and secretive with me'. Welcome to the club.

Through that summer and fall, though, it was love, crazy love. Even Dylan was obliged to admit to himself that, for the very first time, 'outside of my music, being with [Suze] seemed to be the main point in life'. What she had not quite realized was the level of ambition which burned within her boyfriend, only later recalling, 'He had ... said he was going to be very big ... but I had no idea what it meant.' Or how determined he was going to have to be to get there.

Even before he and Suze became 'an item', Dylan had been pushing for a record deal from the few specialist folk labels that kept their ears to the downtown ground, doing most of the legwork himself. Only after the fact did self-aggrandizers like Izzy Young and Harold Leventhal endeavour to take credit,* Izzy stating in 1965 that he 'brought [Dylan] up to Jac Holzman [at Elektra Records], and Jac said no ... Then I took him up to Irwin Silber [at Folkways] and ... Moe Asch just kicked him out of the place ... [because of] the way he looked.'

Izzy had already forgotten that in his own October 1961 interview with the man, for the Chapter Hall programme notes, Dylan had told him, 'Someone from Elektra came down [to see me] but nothing happened,' or that he also stated he went up to Folkways of his own accord, and said, 'Howdy, I've written some songs' – suggesting he was hoping they might publish them in the form of a songbook – but 'Irwin Silber didn't even talk to me. Never got to see Moe Asch'.

---

* Shortly before he died, Leventhal offered the following fanciful recollection to John Hammond's biographer, 'I used to invite Dylan up to [Seeger's] recording sessions, and John was always there.'

Dylan's version is supported by Asch, who insisted in 1978, 'He never came to me. I never rejected him.'

In *Chronicles*, Dylan makes yet another unbelievable assertion: that Terri Thal informed him she could get an appointment with Jac Holzman, but he told her he was interested only in Folkways. Actually, Dylan was pushing anyone and everyone he knew to open doors – even Shelton, who later said, 'I ... tried to get several companies to record him, but they were either uninterested or unavailable.'*

Supposedly, two of his more vocal supporters at this juncture – Carla Rotolo, still a fan, and Sybil Weinberger – even tried to get the legendary Columbia producer, John Hammond Sr, to listen to the tape Thal had made at The Gaslight. If this is the case, the audition tape must predate its September 6th attribution. Within a week of that date, Hammond would be working with Dylan, but not because of it.

John Hammond and Bob Dylan were to meet one mid-September afternoon at One Sheridan Square not because of the efforts of Young, Shelton, Terri and Carla but because of Boston connections Dylan had made for himself at the Indian Neck festival in May, cultivated with his first visit to Boston in June, and developed further during an overnight stay in late August.

Never one to knowingly pass up an invite, the Hibbing hustler had taken Bobby Neuwirth and Robert L. Jones at their word, turning up in Boston in early June, fresh from his Midwest travels, hoping to have the same immediate effect on the Boston/Cambridge folk scene he'd had on its less trad cousin, Greenwich Village. The north-east scene, though, was known as a tough nut to crack, especially if one sang like a New Yorker.

Initially, Dylan turned up at Robert L. Jones's apartment, surprising the hell out of him. Jones attempted to fob him off on his brother-in-law, Eric Von Schmidt, which suited Dylan just fine. He'd heard that name before, and when they convened at Von Schmidt's apartment, he got to hear 'He Was A Friend Of Mine' first-hand, as well as versions of 'Wasn't That A Mighty Storm' and 'Baby, Let Me Lay It On You', both songs Von Schmidt had acquired directly from the

---

* In conversation with Izzy, Dylan acknowledged that 'Shelton helped [me] by ... talk[ing] around.'

Library of Congress the previous year, in the era when they would run off an acetate copy of anything you wanted for a small fee.

In those days one only needed to show Dylan a song once. As Von Schmidt wrote in his co-authored 1979 history of the Boston folk scene, *Baby Let Me Follow You Down*, 'It was something, the way he was soaking up material in those days – like a sponge and a half.' Neuwirth proved just as obliging, taking Dylan over to the Club 47, the go-to place for guitar-totin' folkies in the Harvard Square area. Afterwards, he turned to Neuwirth and said, 'I'd like to get a job here.' For now, though, he'd have to bide his time.

Returning for an August visit to the New England capital gave him the opportunity to pump Von Schmidt for more songs. He also finally seized the opportunity to audition live for Club 47 co-owner Paula Kelley, after availing on that night's headliner, Carolyn Hester – whom he had just met on the beach, with her then husband Richard Fariña, in the company of Von Schmidt and his wife, Helen – to let him play a couple of songs between sets. He began with a fail-safe showstopper, 'Talkin' Bear Mountain', but Kelley couldn't hear it – of which she was strangely proud in subsequent years. Dylan didn't feel the need to repeat the gesture, not playing Boston again until April 1963, at which time the hottest property in folkdom would pointedly play two nights at the Cafe Yana.*

The following day, Dylan detached himself from the Von Schmidts and connected with the Fariñas again, bending Carolyn's ear 'about his business situation. He explained that [al]though ... Terri Thal ... [was] trying to help him, he was needing more gigs, and [asking me] did I have any ideas. I told him that right now I wasn't moving around so much, as I was getting ready to make an album over at Columbia.'

One doesn't need to have been there to visualize Dylan's ears perking up at this point, 'An album over at Columbia? Tell me more, tell me more.' Hester proceeded to inform Dylan that earlier that year

---

* Hajdu jumps through historical hoops trying to make Thal's forty-year-old memory of personally trying to get Dylan a booking at Club 47 fit the known chronology and ties it to some equally flawed recollections from Von Schmidt and Hester, determined to reinvent the standard account of Dylan's first meeting with Fariña. Sometimes people just remember things wrong.

she had heard 'her hero', Pete Seeger, had been signed by John Hammond, and that 'there was a rumour [going] around Greenwich Village that John Hammond and Columbia were possibly going to build a stable of folk musicians ... and I was going to get to audition for Mr Hammond, thanks to my young manager, Charlie Rothschild'.

For once, the rumour had some substance. But it was Joan Baez who was preying on Hammond's mind, not Seeger. Yes, he had signed Seeger shortly after returning to Columbia the previous year, even though Seeger was at this time – as Hammond liked to point out – 'still under indictment for contempt of Congress, [and] still being blacklisted by CBS, our parent [TV company]'. He was merely testing the waters, seeing if Columbia had the guts to back him and his judgement, which he could afford to do, having been born a Vanderbilt, and thus by sheer good fortune able to make his passion – jazz and blues – his lifelong vocation.

But if Seeger came relatively cheap, his next attempt at 'build[ing] a stable of folk musicians' hit a brick wall called Baez. By his own admission, he 'passed on Joan Baez ... because she was asking a great deal of money while still a relatively unknown artist'. The 'great deal of money' was in reality just a square deal. As Dylan was about to find out, this was the one thing not on the table as far as Hammond was concerned. Baez, a smart cookie, promptly used the interest of Columbia to get the deal she really wanted at Vanguard Records, one that gave her the kind of control and freedom from interference it would take Dylan fourteen years to emulate.

When her first album remained on the *Billboard* charts all year, peaking at fourteen – astral heights for a folk album – Hammond knew his fabled A&R radar had let him down, and he needed to show the label he had not lost his touch. His solution was to sign Carolyn Hester, someone almost as ravishing as Baez but with a more vanilla appeal, who sang beautifully. She just lacked any *ingredient x*.

Perhaps it was just a case of getting some of Dylan's to rub off on her. Or at least get him on board. By the end of that Boston afternoon, Dylan had scored a far greater coup than playing at Club 47 – he had availed on Hester to let him play on her Columbia debut. It seems husband Fariña had convinced her Dylan had that indefinable something, and 'the fact that Richard was fascinated by Dylan was good enough for me'.

Dylan and Fariña had already enjoyed a little jam session of their own – probably on the beach – with Fariña on the dulcimer, Dylan on guitar and/or harp, improvising riffs and swapping songs. A bond was formed. They agreed to reconvene in New York and begin rehearsals for Hester's debut album, to be produced by the man who discovered Count Basie and Billie Holiday.

At last Dylan would get to meet The Man. Perhaps Hammond already knew his name. After all, there was a family connection. Dylan was friends with John Hammond Jr, a white blues musician who hung around the Village. Not that Junior exactly played up the Senior connection, having never been 'that close with my father' (something of a Vanderbilt tradition). Nonetheless, Hammond Jr would later insist he told his father 'about this guy that was in New York playing at Gerde's, and at other coffee houses, and that this guy was really good'.

If Hammond Sr did indeed check Dylan out, either before their first meeting or before Hester's first Columbia recording session, it changes the narrative. It would even suggest he sometimes did his job. And as Dylan said in 2001, 'There were always talent scouts in the clubs.' Perhaps he *was* lurking in the shadows. Dylan told childhood friend Louie Kemp in 1971 about an early club date where 'there was an older, distinguished-looking guy in the front row who stood out because he was wearing a suit and tie'. Dylan was later informed it was John Hammond.

Certainly, the nonchalant account Hammond gave of their first face-to-face meeting, to *Melody Maker* in January 1965, doesn't quite ring true: 'I heard Bob playing harmonica one day for Carolyn Hester down on West 10th Street I thought he looked like a real character, so I asked him to come up to the studios. He came up and I liked him, so I signed him.' Dylan, in the guise of Liberty Valance, goes along with the legend in *Chronicles*: 'The sessions [sic] went well and as everyone was packing up and leaving, Hammond asked me to come into the control booth and told me that he'd like me to record for Columbia Records.'

There's only one glitch. The two myth-makers are describing two entirely separate sessions: Hammond, a pre-session rehearsal at Ned O'Gorman's apartment on West 10th on September 14th; Dylan, the bona fide Columbia session on the 30th. Hajdu, on the basis of a 1966 recollection by Fariña, posits an earlier rehearsal at Mary Rotolo's where Dylan taught Hester 'Come Back, Baby'.

A recent cataloguing of the 1957–58 John Bucklen tapes has revealed that the young Bob Zimmerman had already learnt the song by 1957, presumably from the Ray Charles album, *Hallelujah I Love Her So*, if not from late-night radio. Unlike Hester, Charles had the wit to credit the traditional song to himself. The material attempted on Bucklen's tapes confirms what Dylan later told Tony Glover, 'I always liked rhythm'n'blues [as much as] country [and] western ... but for r'n'b you just had to listen to radio late at night.'

By September 1961, Dylan had made the song his own, though the idea that Suze's mother would allow Dylan to use her home for this purpose barely six weeks after meeting her younger daughter beggars belief. And Hester herself seems in little doubt that she learnt 'Come Back, Baby' at the rehearsal Hammond attended:

> John Hammond wanted to hear my band: Bruce [Langhorne], Bill [Lee] and Bob, the three Bs. We had a get-together in Greenwich Village. Very informal ... John sat on the same side of the table as Bob. Bill Lee had his big stand-up bass. Bruce and I sat on the other side of the table with our guitars. John liked it ... [but it] felt like I was a song short, so Bob taught me 'Come Back, Baby', a blues John liked a lot. And he liked Bob a lot. He asked him if he wrote songs.

This tallies with Eve McKenzie's generally reliable memory. She specifically recalled Dylan returning from the *practice s*ession and telling her that Hammond had said to him, 'Come and see me. I think you have something.' Surely he would have had to hear Dylan sing more than a single song to express such an interest. Fariña remembered things differently, telling Robert Shelton that he talked to Hammond about Dylan at 'the session', telling him, 'between takes', 'When this is all over you ought to listen to Dylan,' which sounds just like this would-be Homer. Fariña also informed Shelton that his wife had asked Dylan to teach her some blues, 'and he sang around fifteen or twenty at her'. Even allowing for the usual Fariñaesque exaggeration, this suggests more than enough for Hammond to glean the boy had talent, especially at a time when he could whip up a mighty storm on guitar, prompting the producer to suggest he come up to Columbia and see him some time. In *Chronicles*, Dylan confirms that Hammond 'heard me singing a few things in harmony with Carolyn'.

Fast-forward a fortnight, to immediately after the Columbia session. It is early October and two first-hand accounts reveal that Hammond has already offered him a deal. Richard Fariña places himself and Carolyn 'sitting at the Gaslight and Bob said that he had just been offered a Columbia contract, and he came over and hugged me'. The other confidant was Shelton, sat at Gerde's one night when Dylan swore him to secrecy because the deal had yet to be rubber-stamped.

More questions remain. Though in 1965 Hammond made it sound like he heard Dylan play harp at a rehearsal, and on this basis signed him to Columbia – as you do – he was more circumspect to Dylan's first biographer five years later, telling Scaduto that he had asked, 'Can you sing? Do you write? Why don't you come up to the studio? I'd like to do a demo session with you just to see how it is.' Which sounds more like an experienced A&R man.

Unfortunately, no evidence of Dylan doing 'a demo session' in that fortnight resides at Columbia. But what we do have – thanks to one of the Tulsa deposits – is a copy of the *first* draft of Dylan's original recording contract, dated October 25th, 1961. It departs from the final contract, as agreed the following day, in one highly significant way. It describes in surprising detail what the label expected from the (one) album they were contracting Dylan to record at this stage:

> 1. The musical compositions to be recorded are the following:
> SEE THAT MY GRAVE IS KEPT CLEAN, HE WAS A FRIEND OF MINE plus a sufficient number of compositions as designated by us, comprising Woody Guthrie material, Southern mountain and Southwestern songs, to constitute a minimum of 2 long-playing 33⅓ rpm microgroove record sides, or the equivalent thereof.

There it is, in black and white, the names of two songs Dylan played to Hammond which impressed him enough to offer him a deal – a lousy deal, but a deal nonetheless. The specified titles were certainly among his most powerful. How much 'Woody Guthrie material, Southern mountain and Southwestern songs' Hammond also got to hear is now mere conjecture.

Did Hammond actually tape him? Seemingly not. Another Columbia A&R man, George Avakian, has claimed (to Dunstan Prial, Hammond's biographer) Hammond was 'doubtful as to whether to sign him ... [because of] that twangy country singing', which suggests *he* heard *some kind* of audition. But Hammond made sure the label were left with nothing save the word of the man who discovered Billie Holiday to go on. For Columbia's president Mitch Miller that was enough. Avakian could go hang.

Now Hammond just needed to make sure the ragamuffin could perform before an audience. It was an acid test, one he was still applying a decade later, when signing the latest new Dylan, a kid from New Jersey called, er, Springstein. On that occasion, after cutting a full twelve-song audition tape with him, he set up a show at the Gaslight (of all places) the same night to see how he performed in front of people who had never heard him before. The Jersey Devil passed with flying colours.

Fortunately, Hammond didn't need to pull strings to hear Dylan live. He was already booked to play another fortnight's residency at Gerde's, starting September 26th. Who was responsible for getting Dylan this second shot at Folk City is unclear. Both Terri Thal, who was still ostensibly managing Dylan, and Charlie Rothschild, who was managing Hester, have claimed credit. In all likelihood, it was simply time. Dylan was being discussed even by those who could not see what the fuss was about. And this time Shelton was fully prepped to give him the big push – even though Dylan was again not deemed headline material by the ever-pragmatic but tin-eared Porco. The Greenbriar Boys, one of the acts Dylan had blown off the stage at the Riverside, were top of the bill.

Truthfully, it was no contest – as Gooding's October 1st tape of both acts proves. That first night, Shelton saw and heard enough to describe Dylan as someone 'bursting at the seams with talent ... [with] the mark of originality and inspiration, all the more noteworthy for his youth'. But it was the layout editor at the *Times* who did Dylan the bigger favour, coining the headline, 'A Distinctive Folk-Song Stylist', and putting a single-column photo above the copy. The Greenbriar Boys' set that night – and henceforth – became a mere footnote to 'that' review.

Irrespective of whether Shelton asked Izzy to approve his copy – as Young repeatedly claimed – the journalist personally informed Dylan it would run on the 29th. Suze well remembered the two of them staying up late to grab 'the early edition of the paper ... at the newspaper kiosk on Sheridan Square and [going] across the street to an all-night deli to read it. Then we went back and bought more copies.' One of these her incredulous boyfriend sent home to Hibbing. Two years later, his father acknowledged its receipt: '[After] Bobby received a glowing "two column" review in the New York Times ... we figured that anybody who can get his picture and two columns in the New York Times is doing pretty good.'

Abraham's elder son was still high on the moment two nights later, when his old friend, Cynthia Gooding, lugged a reel-to-reel to Gerde's to record Dylan for her popular radio show and caught him still rapping about the review between songs. For anyone wondering, 'Why him?', the first five songs of the set that night were all the evidence required. 'Sally Gal', 'See That My Grave Is Kept Clean', 'The Girl I Left Behind', 'Dink's Song' – introduced as a Brazo River song, confirming that he'd learnt it from John and Alan Lomax's *American Ballads & Folk Songs* (1934) – and 'He Was A Friend Of Mine' were all top-drawer Dylan. A gushing Gooding was over the moon. If Hammond caught this show – and I suspect he caught a set before the Hester session on the 30th – it merely confirmed Shelton's ringing endorsement.

A distinctive stylist, indeed. Now 100% sure, Hammond instructed the label to draw up a standard contract for the boy – and legally, he was just that – to sign. The producer later told Scaduto he promised Dylan, 'I'll get you the best deal possible from the company. We usually start an artist at 2% ... but I'll start you at 4.'

He did nothing of the sort. The contract started at 2%. Only if it was renewed after the first album would it then escalate to 3% and eventually 4%. Crucially, the renewal clause worked only one way – Columbia's. What Dylan signed on October 26th was a contract that gave Columbia five annual options to purchase his 'services at recording sessions at our studios, at mutually agreeable times, for the purpose of making phonograph records', the results of which 'shall be entirely our property, free from any claims whatsoever by' the artist responsible. It was a contract as American as apple pie. The original contract he had been offered on the 25th had been a single-album deal, after which he would have been free to negotiate a better contract with Columbia or its competitors, but Dylan wanted options, even one-way options.

As he writes in *Chronicles* – one of two versions at opposite ends of the book, neither of which shows him to be savvy or streetwise – '[Hammond] put a contract in front of me, the standard one, and I signed it right then and there, didn't get absorbed into details ... I would have gladly signed whatever form he put in front of me.'

If he was relying on Hammond to do right by him, he was dotting the 'i' in naive. Dylan simply asked, 'Where do I sign?' Hammond showed him. 'I trusted him,' he wrote. Having signed Dylan because of his performance of 'He Was A Friend Of Mine', he proved to be no friend of his.

Yet Lady Luck smiled on Dylan, who inadvertently left himself a get-out clause. As he told a French reporter in 1966, 'John Hammond ... wanted my father to sign as well, because at that time I was only twenty. I lied and told him my only relative was an uncle in Nevada, but I didn't know how to contact him. He believed me and I signed a worthless contract.'

This time it was Hammond who proved careless and trusting. More fool him. The experience prompted some lines in a 1966 letter to a Dylan fan complaining about how Dylan 'told me that he had no parents and that for the past [few] years he had been bumming around on the road. The facts, of course, were quite different.' By then, the contract Dylan had signed as a minor in October 1961 was due to expire and an older, wiser Dylan was about to go to war with the label over the terms he had signed when legally a minor, and without the offer of legal representation.

But in October 1961, all the twenty-year-old cared about was making a record. The last thing Hammond said to him that day was, 'Think about what you want to play.' It was all he would think about for the next four weeks as he impatiently counted the days till he returned to Columbia, for what would be something of a rude awakening. Hammond had already demonstrated a blithe disregard for Dylan's inalienable moral rights; he was about to show he was a better talent scout than he was a producer.

I.4

November 1961 to March 1962: The Balladeer Fires Broadsides

He told me so many lies right away, and while my daughters and their friends didn't seem to notice, they were stories that were ... beyond belief to an older woman.

Mary Rotolo, mother of Suze

In Minnesota ... I didn't know him that well, but what little I did know him, he had a strong streak of dishonesty and a strong streak of honesty ... right together, almost inseparable it seemed.

Paul Nelson to Richard Reuss, July 1965

Bob Dylan is a great and original artist, [but] I doubt that he has ever been sincere in his life. Strangely enough, that [does] not take away from his artistry ... I would say that Bob always had fantasies about himself.

John Hammond Sr, 1966

*

As far as Dylan was concerned, he couldn't have timed the record deal more perfectly. Desultory as the advance was, it gave him enough reassurance, personally and financially, to ask Suze to move in with him – just as soon as he had somewhere to move into.

The two contracts Columbia had sent him to sign had been addressed c/o Miki Issacson, another Village mother-hen whose coop was a one-bedroom apartment at One Sheridan Square, but who acted like she had all the room in the world, a world she cordially invited to be her room-mate. As Suze says, 'It didn't bother her that if she had a party the guests never left. There were nights when Peter Yarrow, Jack Elliott, Jean Redpath and Bobby were all camped out on her floor.'

Nor, it seems, did it alarm Suze that Dylan was sharing said tiny apartment with the likes of Redpath, a warm-blooded traditional folksinger who had arrived from a Scottish village that fall to 'sing at Gerde's and give a Fifeshire lesson in tradition'. Suze was presumably unaware that Redpath and Dylan would 'briefly become more than friends', perhaps almost inevitably given Dylan's libertine libido and the cheek-and-jowl existence of all folkies who used Issacson's apartment as a crash-pad. Redpath herself graphically describes the set-up in her own autobiography:

> Don't make the mistake of thinking that Miki's apartment was designed to be a guest house. You came in off the corridor to her studio apartment and on your right was a bathroom, on your left a Pullman kitchen – long and narrow – and then you walked into this 'single end'. There was a double bed and a couch, behind which many bedrolls and sleeping bags were neatly rolled up and tucked out of sight. There were usually eight of us in there – something which I didn't tell too many people back home, because [they'd think I'd] joined a commune. It was anything but. Miki ran her place like an army camp ... Among the other regulars at Miki's [was] Bob Dylan, who hit the big city almost exactly at the same time as I did ... He was just a fresh-faced kid out of the Midwest who was in exactly the same position as I was, which meant mostly raiding, rather than contributing to, the communal fridge.

If Rotolo knew nothing of Dylan's lowland fling, in all likelihood neither did Robert Shelton; who was himself, in Izzy's unvarnished phrase, 'notorious for running after folk-singing women.' Not only did Shelton lack Dylan's personal charm, he was not adverse to using his position of power – the power of the press – in a way that made him as many enemies as friends.

This largely unloved scribe fell for Redpath almost the minute she came to the happening Village, prompting him to write a glowing review of her Gerde's debut in mid-November, proof that reviews like the one he gave Dylan were not restricted to those he thought would shoot lightning through the world of entertainment. He was just as likely to unleash a paragraph or two of hyperbole about 'a big-boned, apple-cheeked radiantly healthy girl' like bonnie Jean, especially if he thought it might charm her into bed.

For as long as Dylan needed Shelton, the only thing that the *Times* man thought 'his' Jean ever gave Bobby was 'a book of Yevtushenko's poems'. Meantime, Redpath cut a swathe through the Village folk scene as rapidly as Dylan. After just two Monday hootenannies at Gerde's, she 'was offered a job by Mike Porco, the owner, for a gig at Gerde's six weeks ahead', the very one at which she sang 'unaccompanied, in long, arcing phrases ... [her] arresting [Scottish] ballads', bowling Bob Shelton over.

Redpath represented an older woman with a store of authentic tradition for Dylan to tap, just Dylan's type – or one of 'em. After all, his success rate with older women was high, whether he was trying to charm a potential landlady or just wanting a bed for the night, whoever occupied it. Even Suze noticed he 'had an impish charm that older women found endearing ... [which] he was aware of ... and used'.

Where he hit a stone wall of open hostility was with Mary Rotolo, mother of Suze and Carla, who from their very first encounter – in Dylan's vivid phrase – 'treated me like I had the clap'. She saw through the layers of charm to someone who was, in her eyes – which burned 'like twin coals' every time he entered the room – not worthy of her daughter. As she informed Suze in no uncertain terms, Mary 'knew right away that his name wasn't really Dylan'.

Suze's mum felt if he was prepared to lie about that, what wouldn't he lie about? Suze, caught in the crossfire, slowly grew to realize that the animosity was mutual: 'He paid her no homage and she paid him none ... They saw through each other in some way that had nothing to do with me.'

Dylan knew he needed to remove his girlfriend from her mother's pernicious influence, and the way to do that was to get an apartment and convince her to come live with him. There was one small impediment – the law. Up until late November, she was still a minor, sweet seventeen; her mother's ward. He would have to bide his time, even as he spent every hour he was not camping at Issacson's, or working on his music, with the new love of his life.

At least it gave him time to break Suze's resistance down and to get her sister on his side. Suze once told Victoria Balfour, 'By the time

I was going out with Dylan, neither [my mother] nor Carla really approved of him at all', but she does her sister's memory a disservice suggesting Carla was hostile to her boyfriend this early. If anything, the elder sister was more impressed with Dylan the performer than the younger sister, going out of her way to help him find the right material for his debut platter.

As Carla later recalled, 'We were all concerned about what songs Dylan was going to do. I clearly remember talking [to him] about it.' She even endeavoured to get him a proper bed for the night, Barry Kornfeld describing how she 'tried to talk to me into taking Bobby on as a room-mate. I hardly knew him at that point.' Barry knew enough to say no, and Dylan was fond enough of him to remain friends.

Carla also brought him to Alan Lomax's place to meet the great man, who, according to Sounes, told the young colt, 'This is what you ought to listen to … if you want to understand American folk music.' It certainly sounds like Lomax, dogmatic and didactic in equal measures.

According to the *Chronicler*, Lomax opened his loft door to more than just young would-be folk scholars. In an early draft of his memoir, Dylan suggests everyone from 'dukes & lords' to 'actors, authors, ca[r] d sharps poets & painters' gathered at Alan's to see and hear the singers Lomax had brought along. Said list of singers supposedly included Mance Lipscomb, John Jacob Niles, Lightnin' Hopkins, Jean Ritchie and Jeannie Robertson.* But although the two Jeannies – the godmothers to a post-war folk revival both sides of the pond – famously met at Lomax's apartment, it was his London apartment, in 1953, while it was Redpath who saw Robertson sing (at the Edinburgh University Folksong Society) and decided to become a folksinger.

Dylan had yet to immerse himself in Robertson's recordings or plunder the great Scottish ballads, though he did attempt two of them at his first album sessions – 'Pretty Peggy-O' and 'The House Carpenter'. If both were heavily Americanized, somebody who knew their Child ballads explained the latter's subtext to him, because his

---

* Dylan spells Robertson correctly in his typed draft but in the published *Chronicles*, it is spelt Robinson. Go figure. Ritchie made no mention of meeting Dylan at Lomax's but got to see him perform, at Izzy Young's instigation, the first week in November.

spoken preface to the studio take – 'This is a story about a ghost come back from outta the sea, come to take his bride away from the house carpenter' – lays it bare. The former, he would tell Hammond at the first session, 'is an American army song ... it might be Irish, though'. It was nothing of the sort, merely a transmuted version of 'The Bonnie Lass Of Fyvie'.

These were just the kind of songs he could come away from Carla's carrying in his head. Yet, for reasons best known to himself, Dylan decided to develop an entirely new repertoire in the lead-up to these make-or-break sessions, something he twice made a joke of, forty years apart; in December 2000 he claimed, 'I just wanted to record stuff that was off the top of my head and see what would happen.' Whereas at the outset to his one billed concert between signing for Columbia and making that first record he informed the small audience, 'Come pretty prepared tonight I got a list on my guitar. This is a new list. I used to have one ... about a month ago, that was no good. Figured I'd get a good list. So I went around ... other guitar players an' I looked at their list, [and] copied down songs on[to] mine. [Pause] Some of these I don't know so good.'

A handwritten provisional list of songs for this album, which at one juncture was going to be called *The Great Divide*, was even more left-field than the one he released. The eleven songs he wrote down – seven on side one, four on side two – included no fewer than three songs betraying Reverend Gary Davis's profound influence – 'Will The Circle Be Unbroken?', 'On My Journey Home' and 'Trying To Get Home' – and two lengthy broadside ballads, 'The Battleship Of Maine' and 'The Lady Of Carlisle' (next performed in 1992), neither aspect featuring on the final artefact.

Indeed, it included just two songs that made the final album, 'Highway 51 Blues' and 'Man Of Constant Sorrow', and three more from his regular club repertoire – 'The Cuckoo Is A Pretty Bird',[*] 'Railroad Boy' and 'Pretty Polly'. But there was space left at the end of side two for a couple of showstoppers. Perhaps this was where 'See That My Grave Is Kept Clean' and 'He Was A Friend Of Mine' were supposed to go.

---

[*] Though this is a song that circulates only from a September 1962 Gaslight recording, Dylan did play it at Carnegie Hall, as a request.

The midtown show he was booked to play on November 4th would hopefully clarify his thinking. And the fact that it included ten of the songs he would record a fortnight later suggests it did. But in a marathon set of twenty-three songs, he also played two originals which were already firm favourites: 'Talkin' Bear Mountain' and 'Sally Gal'; a version of Bessie Smith's 'Backwater Blues' which would make a porcupine sit up straight; and four Guthrie songs he used to do in Minneapolis.

In the half-empty hall on a cold November night, he resolutely refused to drop challenging material like the traditional 'In The Pines' and 'Young But Daily Growin'', or a gripping anti-racist monologue he learnt from a Lord Buckley record, 'Black Cross', even though he discarded all three when the sessions came round. Already his middle name was Perverse. At least he offered an explanation for all the Guthrie songs, prefacing 'This Land Is Your Land' by saying, 'I haven't done too many Woody Guthrie songs since a long time ago, so I'm gonna do a few of 'em tonight.'

It would be fair to say his promoter, Izzy Young, was not greatly amused, calling the concert, in 1965, 'more of a tribute to Jack Elliott and his style', and accusing Dylan of walking on 'so casually that he almost fell off the stage'. Jean Ritchie, in the front row at Young's invitation, remembered Dylan turning up 'forty minutes late', surely an exaggeration, then walking 'up on stage and talk[ing] about ... how he got lost on the subway. Then he started tuning his instruments ... He had a table with about twenty harmonicas on it and he was blowing into each one. After about fifteen minutes [sic] ... he said, "I think I won't sing that song."' Suze also remembered him 'casually wander[ing] around the big stage in the nearly empty hall as if he were in a downtown coffee house'.

Supposedly, there were no more than fifty-three paying customers, though the audience tape that the Baileys made – which includes an 'In My Time Of Dyin'' the board tape omits – suggests it was fuller. There is certainly a sense that those who schlepped uptown were willing him to succeed. All except Izzy himself, it seems, who 'didn't have the nerve to tell him [what he thought] at the concert. [But] the next day he [asked], "What did you think?" ... I said, "Well, you sounded just like Jack Elliott." And his leg stopped. The only time I ever saw it stop.'

If Izzy made a habit of telling people what he thought, the twenty-year-old Dylan could be just as ascerbic. In the two interviews he did with Young a fortnight earlier for the programme notes, he not only dismissed Baez's voice, but took great delight in reporting that 'Woody [also] doesn't like Joan Baez'. Yet he refused 'to criticize big money-makers like [Harry] Belafonte, Kingston Trio', perhaps because both had been entry points for him.

Even in *Chronicles*, he claimed to prefer 'the older women singers – Aunt Molly Jackson and Jeanie Robertson … [who] didn't have the piercing quality … Joan had'. That 'piercing quality' went straight through him, which is presumably why, three and a half years later, at a party at the Savoy, he would raise a glass and challenge Joan to shatter it, and why he was nowhere to be seen when Baez returned to New York a week after Dylan's damp squib of a concert, to play a sold-out show at the 1,700-capacity Town Hall.

But fate kept tracking them down and at the following Monday's Gerde's hootenanny, their paths crossed again, standing in the doorway. Ever the gentleman, Dylan asked where Mimi was. Baez later confessed, 'I was quietly jealous of his interest in her, but managed to laugh and tease him.' Meanwhile, he remained unfazed by all her success, perhaps because he genuinely believed his own breakthrough was just around the corner. After all, in seven days he would be at Columbia's fabled Studio A on 59th Street, recording with the great John Hammond, having already been told that the label expected great things of him.

Even the day Hammond had chosen for work to begin was an auspicious sign – Suze's eighteenth birthday, November 20th, 1961. She happily agreed to come along at Dylan's behest, later writing to her friend, Sue Zuckerman, 'john hammond (the guy who "discovered" the pig and is doing all for him) completely flipped. i swear if dylan vomited into the microphone hammond would have said, great bob, but try it again with harmony.'* Also there to greet Dylan when he stepped inside was John Hammond Jr, whom Columbia staff photographer Don Hunstein caught showing his buddy a few guitar licks.

---

* 'The pig' was Suze's 'endearing' nickname for her beau when in Sue Zuckerman's company. It is unclear whether Suze was there on the first or second day, but it was the same day as John Hammond Jr.

From the very first take, Hammond Sr is all at sea. At the end of a dynamite take of 'You're No Good', he tells a bemused Dylan, 'I wanna make another one right away, 'cause we were fixing the balance as you were going on ... Now we know what's gonna happen, we're all right.' This was Hammondspeak for, We fucked up and you're gonna have to do it again, five times.

If that wasn't bad enough, Dylan then asks to record a spoken intro about a Connecticut Cowboy. First Hammond cuts him short for popping 'the p in planes', and then after the third take, he tells Dylan, 'I hope we can match it [to the song] – I think we can.' There is absolutely no way of editing two such distinct takes together seamlessly. As a result, the spoken intro. is never used.*

And yet it was Hammond who later had the unmitigated gall to say, 'I'd never worked with anyone so undisciplined before.' He also suggested Dylan 'popped every p, hissed every s, and habitually wandered off mike. Even more frustrating, he refused to learn from his mistakes.' In fact, it was Hammond who needed a lesson or two, interrupting Dylan on superb takes for minor technical infractions. He cuts short a moving first take of 'He Was A Friend Of Mine' because Dylan supposedly has 'a couple of frogs' in his throat, then does the same on an exemplary third take of 'Man On The Street' because 'Policeman popped on us.'

Even when Dylan gets on something of a roll at the end of the first session, Hammond curtails a promising first take of 'Song To Woody' to berate him, 'Listen, we got to be careful of all those hard consonants.' Dylan does his best to comply, but it is clear that he is unimpressed by the pernickety producer's concern. For Dylan, it is all about the feel of the performance, and in gauging that, Hammond proves a poor judge. Although Dylan locks into 'Fixin' To Die' immediately, delivering a first take for the ages, Hammond makes him do it again – twice.

By the second session Dylan is getting the hang of things. After Hammond suggests another take of 'See That My Grave Is Kept Clean' – 'We can make it a little better, I think' – Dylan shoots back, 'I think

---

* Michael Krogsgaard's Dylan sessionography, readily available online, starts as it means to go on by listing eight takes of 'You're No Good' when in reality it is five takes of the album opener and three takes of 'Connecticut Cowboy', all three listed as 'complete'.

we can make it a *lot* better.' He now has the measure of his revered producer. He even starts to gently send him up. After a nice first take of 'Man Of Constant Sorrow', he asks Hammond what he thinks. All the producer cares about is clarifying the publishing:

BD: Did you like that one?
JH: Sure … Who wrote that?
BD: I don't know.
JH: Has it been recorded?
BD: Not that way.
JH: How has it been recorded?
BD: A different way, I guess.
JH: Who did it?
BD: Judy Collins did a version. But not like that. On Elektra.
JH: We'll find out from Elektra who wrote the damn thing.

Dylan knows full well that Judy Collins' 'Maid Of Constant Sorrow' is a different song but happily sends Hammond on a wild goose chase, rather than just informing him it's traditional as 'trad arr.' can be.

Although Dylan would tell a reporter the following year 'I just played the guitar and harmonica and sang those songs and that was it', he had put a great deal of thought into the kind of record he wanted to make. The use of spoken intros over guitar was clearly part of his concept. Not only does he use the technique on 'Pretty Peggy-O' and 'Baby Let Me Follow You Down', but also at the start of 'House Carpenter' and as an insert for 'You're No Good' (neither of them ultimately used).

Throughout, his focus is unerring. As Suze later noted, 'Bob was intense, both sure and not sure of what he was doing. Afterward he'd ask: What do you think, what do you think?' He wanted feedback, and he wasn't getting a great deal from Hammond.

Nor was such a lack of input uncharacteristic. John Court, the partner to Dylan's future long-term manager, would attend another Columbia session a year later, almost to the day, reporting back to Albert Grossman, '[Hammond] didn't stop Bob for mistakes, feeling, mood, or anything. He just kept the tape rolling.'

Hammond's attitude seemed to be: if a first take was complete and had no pops, it was usually a keeper. After doing 'In My Time Of

Dyin'' just once, Hammond tells Dylan, 'That's great. That's the master right there.' Dylan isn't sure, querying, 'You want me to do that again?' Hammond can see the clock ticking, 'No, you don't have to. That's it,' making it the last of three single-take performances at the end of the first session. As with 'Baby Let Me Follow You Down' – the first of the three – we have no way of knowing if a better take was just around the corner.

They do return to 'Man Of Constant Sorrow' – also dispatched in a single take on the 20th – with both takes from the 22nd superior. Again, though, Dylan takes a while to get going. The session starts with six takes of 'Man On The Street', after which an unconvinced Dylan pleads, 'You really like the song that much, you think it's worth trying to get it?' Hammond is adamant, 'I do.' Yet there will be no more takes. A complete second take, good enough to be released in 1991, is 'pulled to master', and Dylan gets on with recording the only Guthrie song he does that day, 'Ramblin' Round'.

At the end of this second session, Hammond shows his true colours – and real vocation: accountancy – telling Dylan, 'Gee, I hate to stop recording. It's going too well.' Yet stop he does. Time's up, even though Dylan has just recorded four blazing first takes one after the other – 'Gospel Plow', 'Highway 51', 'Freight Train Blues', culminating in a 'House Carpenter' so hell-bound it could just as easily have been a lost Robert Johnson out-take. So much for evidence of an artist who 'refused to learn from his mistakes'.

They had barely skimmed the surface of the songs Dylan knew, as was demonstrated by the 26-song tape he recorded in Minneapolis a month to the day after that second Columbia session. It would feature just five of the seventeen songs he had recorded in under six hours, with such 'indiscipline'.

Now he and/or Hammond had to decide what songs to include and in what sequence.* Time is on their side. Perhaps the twelve songs given to the art director on acetate at this juncture represented

---

* Such decisions in the sixties were usually left to the producer. Even an album as revered as Van Morrison's *Astral Weeks* was wholly sequenced by its producer, Lewis Merenstein.

the intended artefact; in which case it would have been quite a different album:*

> Talkin' New York. In My Time Of Dyin'. Man Of Constant Sorrow. Fixin' To Die. Highway 51 Blues. Pretty Peggy-O. Baby Let Me Follow You Down. House Of The Rising Sun. Song To Woody. He Was A Friend Of Mine. Ramblin' Blues. House Carpenter.

Intriguingly, the song with which Dylan opened the sessions and the released album, 'You're No Good', isn't here. Neither is album closer, 'See That My Grave Is Kept Clean'. But there were opportunities a-plenty for player and producer to change their minds.

The album could not be released until March 1962, when Dylan's contract was actually activated, Columbia having inserted into the small print a clause that would come back to bite Bob. Though he signed on the dotted line on October 26th, 1961, the first annual term of the contract was scheduled to run from March 1st, 1962 – and then, in a smoke'n'mirrors manoeuvre never challenged in court, March 19th, the release date of his first album.

Dylan was hardly thinking about such things in the immediate aftermath of making his debut statement. Everything was just fine and dandy. In fact, when Suze wrote to Sue Zuckerman in early December, she feared it all might be happening a tad quickly:

> things are going ... unbelievably great for the pig. things are happening to him that only happen in the movies ... EVERYBODY AT COLUMBIA RECORDS (from the PRESIDENT on down) thinks bob dylan is the new GOD. they are dropping everything just to push his record ... they think he's going to be the new idol of the usa. no shit. they are putting his record out in 2 months [sic] ... he'll be on tv, in magazines, etc, etc.

One of these publicity men would feature in Dylan's life for the next five years, Billy James being called into the November sessions

---

* These acetates were recently sold by Sotherby's in New York, having been barely played. Evidently, the art director was not blown away.

to hear Hammond's new protégé. Impressed, he suggested getting an interview for the files, to ensure that the PR department had good copy when the word came down to open the floodgates of hype.

The callow Dylan simply failed to understand the importance of this moment, spinning the same outlandish tapestry of lies, half-truths and youthful braggadocio he did at the Kettle of Fish, as well as to Oscar Brand on his WNYC radio show and Izzy Young for his Carnegie programme notes, the month before. As Ian Bell astutely observes, 'This is no mere showbiz stratagem: he lies outrageously, lies when there is no need, habitually, even compulsively. There is a misaligned facet to this character, an internal contradiction.'

Nor was it a facet he had resolved or discarded forty-three years later, when he gave his own account of that afternoon when tape was rolling and he constructed the first, and most damaging, of his many mythical autobiographies, as – in his own words – James 'tried to get me to cough up some facts, like I was supposed to give them to him straight and square'. No danger of that.

Four years on, James would be sat next to Dylan on a Hollywood rostrum under the TV lights as Dylan was bombarded with questions by the press, and again 'he lies outrageously'. But in December 1965, his defences needed to be up and his answers really were riddles wrapped in an enigma called Dylan. Here, though, he just careens off into a life he never led, gerrymandered from scraps he had read and heard, but never experienced:

> Let me say that I was born in Duluth, Minnesota – give that a little plug. That's where I was born and [I was] out in the Midwest most of my life. Well, about three-quarters of my life around the Midwest and one quarter around the south-west – New Mexico. But then I lived in Kansas – Marysville, Kansas, and Sioux Falls, South Dakota ... I learnt a lot of songs there ... [Actually] I didn't learn songs, I just learnt a way of singing. I learnt the way of singing I do. I didn't really learn so many songs. There was this fella there on a farm right in Sioux Falls, South Dakota – a little bit out – played autoharp. And he was just a farmhand there. He was from Kansas. I learnt just ways of singing from people like that. But I never really heard any other way.

This isn't how he learnt any of his early songs. He acquired them from friends, records and books. But some of those friends had their own records to make and rather wanted to use songs they had made their own – notably Van Ronk, who had jumped labels from Folkways to Prestige. Again, in *Chronicles*, Dylan stretches the truth to breaking point, claiming half of his debut album was 'renditions of songs that Van Ronk did' – as if he was coming clean.

He was doing nothing of the sort. Though it was just 'House Of The Rising Sun' which was unequivocally Van Ronk's arrangement, its inclusion was not, as Dylan suggests, something that 'just happened'. He knew what he was doing when he recorded it that way, having prefaced the song sixteen days earlier with a full and frank disclosure, 'This is a song I knew for many, many years but I never really knew it till I heard a fellow named Dave Van Ronk sing it. He's ... got a moustache hangs right down to his ankles.'

A few weeks later, Van Ronk was at his usual table in the Kettle of Fish when Dylan came in, sat down and asked his friend, 'Hey, would it be okay for me to record your arrangement of "House Of The Rising Sun"?' Van Ronk politely but firmly told him, 'Bobby, I'm going into the studio to do that myself in a few weeks.' 'Uh-oh ... I've already recorded it.' As even Suze observed, it was 'a traitorous thing, breaking the code of honor among thieves ... and Dave was angry for a long time'. As he should have been. Here was another 'misaligned facet to this character, an internal contradiction' others had already experienced and noted, including some he'd left in the dust of Dinkytown:

> **Dave Ray**: I wouldn't say he was a particularly ingratiating person, but he did have a knack for getting himself in the right place to be able to pick things up and he wasn't at all bashful about using whatever came to hand. A lot of people are very timid about [using] something [they learnt], for fear of stepping on somebody else's toes. That's not something that seemed to bother Bob. If you showed him how to do something ... ten minutes later, he was doing it – not necessarily saying it was his own and he just came up with it – [but] there was a suddenness to it which was uncanny. I still don't understand ... that mechanism.

In addressing the cavalier way Dylan treated a close friend, when he still had them, it is important to note, he *could* have pulled the track. As comments during the session suggest, Hammond would have been worried about any copyright claim with so much of the

LP culled from a netherworld of anonymity. Even the original songs had tunes that bore the mark of someone else's copyright *if* it became worth pursuing. (Hence the industry saying, 'if you have a hit, expect a writ'.)*

The album was still months away from release and a couple of the out-takes were as good as anything that made the final cut. Yet Dylan never even considered asking Hammond to pull the track, or convincing Hammond to go back into the studio and cut the other three-quarters of his repertoire, most of which was firmly in the public domain and as yet unrecorded.

He was, however, perfectly happy to unpack a few more gems from that prodigious memory for his friends in Minnesota, a month later. This time the tape not only kept rolling, but proceedings were overseen by someone who knew how to use the right setting (Bonnie's bedroom), the right lubricant (bourbon) and the right mike placement: Tony Glover. Not that Bonnie Beecher was out of the picture – she just needed to be lightly airbrushed for fear of word getting back to the Village, and Dylan's new room-mate:

> **Tony Glover:** By the time he came back [in December], he had really grown. From being this run of the mill player, he turned into this dynamic picker and performer. He was doing bottleneck blues, he could do a harp solo piece. He got Woody Guthrie down to a T when he came back. He had recorded his first album a month before, and he'd come home for Christmas. I got this tape recorder, and said, '[Would] ya like to tape a few things, like a Library of Congress thing?' We bought a pint of Jim Beam. I said into the tape the date, December 22nd, and he [interjected] Beecher's Hotel because he didn't want to say Bonnie's bedroom, 'cause there was certain stuff going on. He was smiling. He mixed a bit of the rock'n'roll drive into the folk-blues stuff. [But] that was done in one night, pretty much straight through.

Glover doesn't make the mistake the McKenzies had made when recording their own home tape the day after the second Columbia

---

* Indeed, Eric Von Schmidt would later claim a share of 'Baby Let Me Follow You Down', after Dylan's injudicious intro gave away the debt he owed, a mistake he would not repeat.

session, when the arrival of Kevin Krown interrupted the flow. As the Sotheby's catalogue copy from when the tape was (unsuccessfully) put up for auction reads, 'Krown requests particular material, and Krown also offers suggestions about Dylan's guitar technique.'

Peter McKenzie, who was there that evening, told me, 'Kevin took over the entire proceedings and you can hear it ... where he basically tells Bob what to sing, [and] how to sing it. Bob had his own agenda and here's Kevin telling him I want you to do this song, I want you to do that song.' Krown will not be the last former confidant to learn the hard way that his friend has not merely moved on, but has entered a dimension he cannot enter.

When Glover sets the tape rolling that December, the pace at which Dylan is moving creatively is frightening. Again, Cable calls it right when suggesting the Hotel Tape contains 'some rather good performances ... a few of [which] would have [been] preferable ... to some of the stuff on the first official album'. The legendary tape is certainly more representative of the fall 1961 Dylan than the imminent official report. 'Dink's Song' and 'Black Cross' are both captured magnetically, as is a 'Baby Please Don't Go' he will never better and an 'Omie Wise' which finds the tragedy in a commonplace melodrama.

And while he does none of the three originals he recorded for *Bob Dylan*, nor a single talkin' blues, let alone his arrangement of 'He Was A Friend Of Mine', Glover does capture 'Sally Gal' when she's still fresh-faced, as well as two new originals that could have brightened the day of the dour John Hammond.

Dylan had mentioned 'Hard Times In New York Town' to Billy James as 'a new song ... I wrote ... last week about New York. I wish I would have recorded it. Some people are singing it now at the Blue Angel.' Based on the traditional 'Down On Penny's Farm', it is a precursor to 'Maggie's Farm', which is perhaps why it opens 1991's *The Bootleg Series Vols. 1–3*.

The other 'original' song he does in Bonnie's boudoir highlights another character flaw, one he admitted to Billy James – forgetfulness: 'I write a lot of songs and I forget them. As soon as ... I write them or sing them out loud to myself ... I forget 'em.' 'I Was Young When I Left Home', not released until 2001, is actually the best thing Dylan had 'written' to date. Although the song is another Depression-era fantasy, with its references to pawning his watch and chain and going home (lifted clean from the trad '900 Miles') and being in debt to the commissary store, one section catches in the throat, suggesting he had a very specific audience in mind, one he had returned to the Midwest to see: 'I used to tell my Ma sometimes, when I see them ridin' blinds / Gonna make me a home out in the wind.' The unique Minneapolis performance is gut-wrenching, Dylan inhabiting the song in a way that at this point he is doing only with other people's songs.

And yet, when he records his first publishing demo-tape exactly two weeks later, he doesn't even consider it for inclusion, preferring pseudo-traditional pastiches like 'Poor Boy Blues' and 'Standing On The Highway'.* Dylan's description of the technique he applied to the songs he would demo for Lou Levy's Leeds Music on January 5th, 1962 – 'rearranging verses to old blues ballads, adding an original line here or there, ... [and] slapping a title on it' – is a pretty accurate description of all three songs, as well as most of 2001's *Love and Theft*.

In fact, the line between the 'original' compositions on said demo tape and the four arrangements also copyrighted with Leeds – 'He Was A Friend Of Mine', 'Gospel Plow', 'Pretty Peggy-O' and 'Man Of Constant Sorrow' – is wafer-thin, as evidenced by the credits in the resultant folio – Dylan's first official songbook, *Bob Dylan Himself* – which varies from 'music and new lyrics' to 'arrangement of music'.

He even adds a composite of commonplace verses to the three album cuts, as if this will somehow reinforce his own copyright, coming up with a final verse to 'Man Of Constant Sorrow' that both references Robert Johnson and introduces a soon-to-be common companion: 'It's a hard, hard road to travel / When you can't be satisfied / I've got a rope that's hanging o'er me / And the Devil's at my side.'

The inclusion of 'Standing On The Highway' offers further proof Dylan has now been introduced to the late, great king of the Delta blues singers, author of 'Crossroad Blues', Mississippi's answer to Faust. Yet it is a debt Dylan will only fully acknowledge with his first

---

* Dylan was presumably perfectly aware that his song had been partly lifted from Hedy West's own adaptation of '900 Miles', '500 Miles', copyrighted that year after being covered by Gerde's favourites, The Journeymen. Even when Dylan copyrighted the song in 2001, he erred on the side of caution, crediting it as a 'Trad arr. Dylan' composition.

proper collection of lyrics, 1973's *Writings & Drawings*, which he dedicates 'To the magnificent Woody Guthrie and Robert Johnson who sparked it off.' It was his way of saying, yes, Guthrie opened the door on my songwriting, but it was Johnson who shoved me through.

Dylan further acknowledges Johnson's importance in a four-page section of *Chronicles* in which he effuses on the man's greatness. But back then, when he played the 'acetate' he'd gotten from Columbia's own commissary store to Dave Van Ronk, the elder statesman of folk-blues proceeded to point 'out that this song comes from another song and that one song was an exact replica of a different song'.

Van Ronk is right as right can be. Johnson was as brazen a song-snatcher as the man he'd invited into his apartment. But, as the *Chronicler* notes, he also 'put his own spin on' the songs he stole. Dylan had long needed someone other than Guthrie to show him how to do just that, prompting him to nail this particular debt to the masthead, 'If I hadn't heard the Robert Johnson record when I did, there probably would have been hundreds of lines of mine that would have been shut down.'

However, none of those lines inhabit 'Standing On The Highway', of which he still seemed worryingly proud a few weeks later on Cynthia Gooding's WBAI radio show, *Folksinger's Choice*. Fortunately, it was not the only blues song he had in his locker when he came to call on Lou Levy that first week in January. To the five Guthriesque songs from the year before, he added three new blues from the fortnight just gone. That Johnson record had hit him hard, enabling him to tap into his own emotional core and 'put his own spin' on a blues that was so fresh off the page it went through three titles in a month: 'Sitting On The Railroad Track', 'Reminiscence Blues' and (the copyrighted) 'Ballad For A Friend'. Once again, he fleetingly references his true roots in a single verse – 'We['d] go up in that North country / Lakes and streams and mines so free / I had no better friend than he' – before wrapping it in a bubblewrap of blues clichés. But even that solitary hint conveys a hurt an order of magnitude removed from a song like 'Poor Boy Blues'.

And yet, it is 'Standing On The Highway' Dylan includes on the Gooding show the following month, having the temerity to slot it alongside Howlin' Wolf's 'Smokestack Lightning' and Big Joe Williams' (wife's) 'Baby Please Don't Go'. One can't help but wonder what the cigar-puffin' Levy thought. He had, after all, just coughed up a $200 advance for a folio of songs from the promising penman, at Hammond's behest.*

Hammond was probably trying to generate a small revenue stream to supplement the penny-pinching contract from Columbia. Hammond also presumably had a hand in Dylan getting his second official session work for the label, a day's work on February 2nd, 1962 with box-office baritone Harry Belafonte; according to Dylan, 'the only ... memorable recording date that would stand out in my mind for years to come'. If so, it was presumably because the session was so interminable.

If Dylan already had a deserved rep. for his harmonica-work, 'Midnight Special' was a song he could play in his sleep, being as traditional as a day at Angola Prison was long – which hadn't stopped John Lomax appropriating it on Lead Belly's behalf. It took Belafonte and his steel-drivin' crew twenty takes, and one recorded rehearsal, to master it as Dylan blew his lungs out all day for a few dollars. After take fifteen, producer Hugo Montenegro – of *The Good, The Bad & The Ugly* fame – asks, 'Hey, Bob, maybe you can start off with one of those boom-chakka-chak things. [You know,] start off with something exciting.' The blast of blues harmonica that follows is as far from 'boom-chakka-chak' as an intro could be.

Dylan had a whole lot more fun four weeks later, recording four songs in a single afternoon with Victoria Spivey, Lonnie Johnson and Big Joe Williams, three legends of the very blues he now had a feeling for. The version of the Mississippi Sheiks' 'Sitting On Top Of The World' – which Big Joe Williams impertinently took the credit for, presumably because his missus was not around† – presents the harpman-for-hire at his wailin' best.

While Dylan was waiting impatiently for his own album to appear, he was working on his own songs, which had now started to flow forth, something he duly acknowledged in *No Direction Home*: 'I wrote a lot of songs in a quick amount of time. I could do that then, because

---

* According to the 2004 Dylan, it was 'Song To Woody' which sold Levy on the project and 'hooked me up with Leeds Music'.
† Williams' most famous song, 'Baby Please Don't Go', was reportedly written by his wife. I refer interested readers to the perfectly splendid *It's One For The Money* (Constable, 2015) for the full story.

the process was new to me. I felt like I'd discovered something no one else had ever discovered.'

Dylan was so bowled over with one song that he went back to Lou Levy and got him to add it to the folio of songs, thirteen days after he cut the original Leeds demos.* It was originally called 'Rambling Willie', before a 'Gamblin'' was added to explicate the subject of the song: a glorified card shark who meets his end when dealt the dead man's hand – 'aces backed with eights'. Its traditional template was an old Irish ballad the Clancys did, 'Brennan On The Moor', about an Irish Dick Turpin who was hanged about the time Omie Wise was breathing her last. Still mired in a mythical past, what Dylan felt he gleaned from the Clancys was the ability to inhabit exactly these kind of 'rousing, rebel songs – Napoleonic in scope'.

Not only did he play this outlaw ballad to Levy before the ink was dry, he also called in at the Folklore Center to play it to Young, who memorialized the moment in his next *Sing Out!* column, describing the song as being 'as good as any badman ballad I can think of', and suggesting the tyke 'has a true poetic touch that smacks of the best folk tradition'. It was a ringing endorsement which prompted the singer to briefly make a habit of previewing new songs to Izzy.

Suze remained his main sounding board, though, now that he and she were living like two proverbial peas in their own pad, a walk-up on West 4th Street. The way her boyfriend put it, it seemed to make sense to pool resources and Suze went along with it. As she told Hajdu, 'I didn't have a place of my own, and he didn't have a place to live. [But] we were both not very verbal.'

Both kept secrets, too. Although Dylan had taken it for granted that she would want to live with him, when Suze wrote to Sue Zuckerman in December, she had already begun voicing inner fears about subsuming her sense of Self to Bobby's career:

> i don't want to get sucked under by bob dylan and his fame. it really changes a person completely when they become well known by all and

---

* Oddly enough, 'Rambling Willie' does not come last on the Leeds Music demo-tape that first circulated in the early 1970s. But its omission from the original bootleg LP, *Early 60s Revisited*, perhaps suggests there was once a version of the tape which omitted it altogether.

sundry. they develop this uncontrollable egomania. I can see it happening to bobby. and I've tried to tell him in so many ways, but it's useless, it really is. he's beginning to love me only in relation to himself ... i am in need of advice, friendship, and all around shit.

Suze proceeds to ask Zuckerman when she arrives in town and whether they could 'share an apt. ... i'm serious.' Needless to say, this never happened. But the fact that Suze suggested sharing an apartment with her best friend just a matter of weeks after moving in with Dylan suggests the bloom was already fading on *la belle romance*. Not that there is the slightest clue in the photos Ted Russell took of the couple in their apartment that December, some of the most intimate Dylan ever allowed to be developed. As Russell writes, 'They must have just moved into the apartment, which was ... largely lacking any furniture. They may, in fact, have still been in the process of moving in.' Through Russell's lens – and indeed, Joe Alper's the following month – his adoration of Suze is there for all to see. It's all rather touching, with both kids looking frighteningly young. Their black and white selves shall not grow old.

Suze was the one person Dylan wanted to impress, and be impressed by. That aspect of the relationship – mutual intellectual interests – would shape and mould the man in the formative years of his own artistry. As Suze put it, 'We went back and forth, feeding each other's curiosity.'

Suze was very well read for someone who was barely eighteen, with the French symbolists particular favourites of hers. So when she started reading Rimbaud, 'it piqued his interest,'* even if Dylan qualified this a few weeks before his 1997 health scare, insisting 'Everybody influenced me', and suggesting it was François Villon who was really his man because he 'didn't hold his opinions back' and 'was prejudicial as hell'.

Three years later he talked about 'stay[ing] at a lot of people's houses wh[o] had poetry books and poetry volumes and I'd read what

---

* I dismiss out of hand the claim by writer Mark Spitzer that he used to withdraw books by Rimbaud from the University of Minneapolis in the early 1960s and 'the mythic name of Zimmerman was always there, scrawled in the same ink in which passages were underlined in French as well as English'.

I found: Verlaine ... or Rimbaud'. This was a time when folkies were the New Left, and nearly every West Village apartment had the latest City Lights or New Directions paperbacks. (Indeed, 1961 saw the latter publish important editions of Rimbaud, Alfred Jarry and Kenneth Roxreth.)

As for the highly opinionated François Villon, he was someone to whom Dylan was introduced by the no less opinionated Van Ronk. John Cohen, who also photographed Dylan at this time, solo, had heard some of his new songs and told him straight out, 'This is no longer like a Woody Guthrie folk song, it's more like ... Rimbaud and Verlaine.' Dylan professed to not 'know who they were, [so] he came over to my loft in New York and I showed him some books.'* Cohen's was one of several private leanding libraries Dylan sourced as the songs poured forth and he passed from poetaster to poet, all the while developing – with a little help from his girlfriend – a social conscience.

The first evidence of a newly politicised poet can be found in a song he wrote at the end of January specifically for a CORE (Campaign of Racial Equality) benefit in three weeks' time. He would tell Tony Glover in 1963, he 'had a dream one night that these people from CORE wanted me to write a song for them'. One suspects the truth was more prosaic.

As Suze duly admitted, 'I was working for CORE and went on youth marches for civil rights.' Inevitably, 'the concerns that were on my mind were inevitably passed to him ... [but] if he were not interested, he wouldn't have been interested.' Methinks she doth protest about protestin' too much. Eve McKenzie had no doubt about Suze's input: '[She] wanted him to go Pete Seeger's way ... to be involved in civil rights ... Suze was very much with the cause ... She influenced Bobby considerably that way.'

What Dylan needed at this juncture, above all else, was *subject matter*. So when Suze told him about the infamous murder of Emmett Till in 1955 by white bigots who took umbrage at the way he talked to a white woman in a Mississippi general store, tortured him and 'threw him in deep water that flows through the land' (a deft touch

---

* Cohen conflates this occasion with when he heard 'A Hard Rain's A-Gonna Fall' for the first time in September 1962.

and a nod to 'Omie Wise'), Dylan saw not a civil rights banner but a modern broadside ballad.

He debuted the song on Cynthia Gooding's *Folksinger's Choice*, in early February.* Gooding's gushing reaction confirmed he was on to something, though the song itself – even with the terrific electric arrangement McGuinness Flint gave it ten years after – is more black and white than the race divide it sought to highlight. Dylan also gets a number of material facts wrong; not because he didn't do enough homework, but because he did none.† A complete disregard for the *facts* was just another 'misaligned facet to this character', tainting every protest song he would set out to write in the next twenty-two years.

Two years later to the day, he would dismiss 'Emmett Till' as 'a bullshit song'. But for now he kept writing ones just like it, right down to its smug moralizing coda. He even turned the talkin' blues into a medium for political satire, penning the barbed 'Talkin' John Birch' the week before he tilled Emmett's soil. As ever, he was most at home using humour as a weapon, and with the far-right John Birch Society it was like shooting whitefish in a barrel. This one he didn't offer to Lou Levy. Indeed, he later told Cynthia Gooding, 'I [simply] didn't think Leeds would publish John Birch.'

By now, Pete Seeger – the Old King Cole of folk, ever convinced songs could change the world – had introduced Dylan to a couple of tame editors who would happily publish it, and indeed emblazon it across a new mimeographed zine for topical songs, *Broadside*, a highly appropriate name given the standard of most contributions, which rarely rose above what rolled off seventeenth-century black-letter presses.

Sis and Gordon Friesen would publish their 'topical' magazine for over a decade but the half-life of its cultural impact was past by 1964, as both Dylan and Phil Ochs moved on to bigger and better gigs,

---

* One continues to see this show dated January 13th, 1962, a patent impossibility. Gooding's own papers give no such date and 'Emmett Till' was not written until late January, let alone Dylan's mention of his album coming out 'next month'. I know not why that date has been given to it. February 13th, possibly.
† Notably, he suggests that the two brothers 'confessed that they had killed poor Emmett Till', something they did not do till *after* they were acquitted and could not be retried.

Dylan telling friends in private, 'I'm sick and tired of writing songs for *everybody*.' By September 1965, Dylan was even placing the blame for his volte-face in subject matter in winter 1962 squarely at the Friesens' door. In conversation with Frances Taylor – an old friend of Seeger's, and as such on the opposite side of the Newport barricade – he asserted, 'In the Village there was a little publication called *Broadside* and with a topical song you could get in there. I wasn't getting far with the things I was doing ... [and] *Broadside* gave me a start.'*

At least Dylan generously repaid the Friesens for their faith and charity by allowing them to use some of his better 'topical' discards on two various-artist albums issued on Folkways – *Broadside Ballads Vol. 1* (1963) and *Broadside Reunion* (1972) – the latter of which featured ballads on both Emmett Till and the next martyr to injustice he chanced upon at home, watching a TV documentary with Suze about a convict called Donald White. White was altogether less deserving than Till, being a convicted murderer who blamed society for his own character deficiencies until society pulled the switch. The song was even less worthy, but still gratefully received by *Broadside*.

Fortunately, his next idea for a song he got not from watching TV documentaries or attending a CORE benefit. Rather, it was a subject he had been carrying around in his head for a while. In fact, he would tell Nat Hentoff that December it came to him when he 'was going through some town ... and they were making this bomb shelter right outside of town ... I was there for about an hour, just looking at them ... I carried it with me for two years ... I finally wrote it down.'

The actual trigger, though, seems to have been another broadside ballad, which he heard for the first time during a December 1961 trip to Toronto in the company of Gil Turner. The song in question ('Strontium 90') was erroneously christened 'Strange Rain' by Izzy Young after Dylan informed Izzy on February 7th, 1962 it had inspired him 'to say something about fallout and bomb-testing, but ... not ... a slogan song. Too many of the protest songs are bad music.'

---

* Dylan's comment to Taylor stung Friesen to remark in 1968, 'There were some people ... who cast doubt on Bob's sincerity ... [which] stemmed mainly from the often quoted interview by Frances Taylor ... [in which he] sounded like he *only* used *Broadside* ... to get him started on the road to fame.'

He had evidently now started to write 'Let Me Die In My Footsteps', but unlike the other songs he wrote that month, it did not come quickly. He would not play Izzy the finished song till March 19th, by which time what he had was a punchy antidote to the satirical song he'd heard with Turner, which dated back to 1959 and two Californian sisters, Ann and Marty Cleary, as he explained to Tony Glover the following August:

Tony Glover: Who'd you write the Shelter Song [i.e. 'Let Me Die In My Footsteps'] for?
Dylan: I wrote that for some people that asked me. You saw it printed wrong.
TG: [It] looked like a song [where] someone said, 'Dylan, why don't you write ...'
BD: [No,] I just thought you'd got all these stupid fallout songs, [like] 'Strontium 90', fallout will get you two heads, six eyes, seven pricks. That's a phoney song ... People were saying how terrible the fallout shelter was. I took a different point of view – how great the land was.

The verse of the Clearys' composition Dylan chooses to ridicule asks, 'What will we get from radiation? ... No necks, two necks or maybe three / Each one will have his own mutation / Nobody else will look like me', making a joke of something Dylan was deadly serious about; hence his opening couplet: 'I will not go down under the ground / 'Cause somebody tells me that death's coming round'.

He had found his inner voice, even if he seems dismissive of the result in *Chronicles*, calling it 'a slightly ironic song ... based on an old Roy Acuff ballad ... [that] was personal and social at the same time, though ... [it] didn't break down any barriers for me or perform any miracle'. This could even be a conscious rebuttal of my own evaluation in *Behind The Shades*, where I suggest the song 'may well be Dylan's first masterpiece'. As far as Dylan was concerned, 'I still hadn't written what I wanted to.'

Even after he wrote his very next song, which would make him a wealthy man, he 'was never satisfied', dismissing it as something he 'wrote in ten minutes'. (Also not true.) His secret goal remained the grandiose one he told Robert Hilburn forty years later: 'Popular culture usually comes to an end very quickly. It gets thrown in the grave. I wanted to do something that stood alongside Rembrandt's paintings.'

Having gone from 'Hard Times In New York Town' to 'Let Me Die In My Footsteps' in less than three months – waiting for Columbia to get his earlier songs into the microgroove – by March 19th, the day he played Izzy the finished song and *Bob Dylan* was released, he knew that the album bearing his name and former image, was not it. As he would say in February 1964, 'I made that [record] two and a half years ago, that's an old, old record. I wasn't even *me*. I was still learning language then.' The question most preying on his mind now was: would he get a second chance?

1.5

April to October 1962: How Many Roads, So Many Roads

He was a sponge, soaking in the information. He was like an electrical condenser, a capacitor filling up with information and ultimately exploding on paper with songs. We could ramble about how barns were built one moment and be talking about Woody Guthrie lyrics the next.

Victor Maymudes

He was very shy. He would ask Suze [to] tell [me he'd] like a cigarette ... Suze was absolute sunshine ... They would [constantly] whisper between themselves. She was his insulation between him and real life ... [But] there was always a guitar. He was not shy about playing that.

Steve Wilson, to author

*

If Dylan had been assiduously cultivating the 'folk press' since coming in from the cold the previous January – and could as such include *Sing Out!*'s Izzy Young, the *New York Times*'s Robert Shelton and the *Village Voice*'s J. R. Goddard among his early proselytizers – with the March 1962 release of *Bob Dylan*, it was time for Columbia to step up to the plate. And they could have started by getting some promo copies out. At the end of the month Cynthia Gooding, who wanted to play some selections on her influential radio show, had to borrow Dylan's own copy of the LP to do so.

Not surprisingly, with such a limited supply of 'promos', reviews were few and far between. Part of the problem was that there was as yet no established music press, save for Music Biz weeklies like *Billboard* and *Cashbox*. Though *Seventeen* and *Hifi Stereo Review* both gave Dylan space, they were poles apart in their demographics and critiques, *Seventeen*'s brief, positive review running under the unlikely headline, '[What] Teens Are Listening To'.

The best of the reviews would come from writers converted by Dylan and/or Hammond, not Columbia's marketing dept. Of these, perhaps the most surprising, and certainly the most glowing, came from the *Little Sandy Review*. Nelson and Pankake let bygones begone. They described the ex-Dinkytown deadbeat as 'probably the most exciting, most potentially great, new city folksinger in recent years', before cautioning him to avoid the topical song trap:

> This LP is a magnificent debut, [but] we sincerely hope that Dylan will steer clear of the Protesty people, continue to write songs near the traditional manner, and continue to develop his mastery of his difficult, delicate, highly personal style.

Also on his side was Nat Hentoff, the *Village Voice*'s jazz critic, who first heard him at Gerde's, remembering in 2004, '[He] wore a leather cap, blue jeans and well-worn desert boots. I was not impressed with his voice, and certainly not with his rather rudimentary guitar playing, but the lyrics to his original songs were intriguing.' He was pushed to play the LP by Hammond himself, admitting, 'It was only after John made me listen to that album that I [really] started paying attention.'

Pay attention Hentoff did, writing the sleeve notes to Dylan's next album and consistently championing him in print till he was free and clear of folk. While Goddard was assigned to review the album in the *Voice*, calling it 'one of the best to come from the boiling folk pot in a long, long time', Hentoff found his own outlet, the *Reporter*, to herald a distinctive, highly personal stylist:

> Accompanying himself on guitar and taking an occasional whooping break on the harmonica, Dylan plunges into Negro blues, plaintive mountain songs, updated Scottish tunes and sardonic folklike pieces of his own composition. He adapts his sound and phrasing to the varying needs of the material, but throughout he is unabashedly himself.

Columbia used Hentoff's quote in a full-page ad they finally ran in the October–November *Sing Out!*, by which time they were already telling its readers to 'Watch For His New Album – To Be Released Soon'. If Columbia's PR was slow out of the blocks, they did manage to score something of a coup by getting Dylan an audition for the *Ed Sullivan Show* – the very show that had made Elvis a national phenomenon. This, though, was as far as it got, as the singer later bemoaned to a friend over a drink or three:*

> Six men sat and listened to Dylan talking the blues, harshly mourning over lost wanderers, and singing mockingly of the seduction of Pretty Peggy-O. They were obviously bewildered by his raw, craggy style ... The agent told Dylan, 'They've never heard anyone like you before. They need time to decide what you are.' ... 'I was right in front of them. They either like me or they don't.' 'It's not that simple,' said the man from MCA. 'They figure you're far out, but they don't know yet whether you're the kind of far out that sells.' ... He proceeded to McGowan's bar in the Village. 'Well,' he told a friend after several drinks ... 'I'm not going up there again.' 'They'll call you,' said the friend ... 'Maybe,' said Dylan, 'but they ain't gonna tell me what to sing.'

Yet despite Columbia's stuttering publicity campaign, the album began to pick up converts by simple word of mouth in the folk underground. Dylan himself was shocked when he began to 'get fan letters from ... little towns in Idaho, or Michigan ... places I hadn't even heard of'. Village folkie Adele Sushi sent a copy to a girlfriend in Montreal, Anna McGarrigle, who immediately realized Dylan 'didn't sound like anybody else'. When Dylan played local folk-spot, the Potpourri, in July, she would stun him by requesting 'Baby Let Me Follow You Down'. It even made it to those London record shops which specialized in imports, where both Rod Stewart and Marc Feld (aka Bolan) succumbed early to its earthy charms, Stewart later suggesting, 'Nothing had altered the air around me like that [first] Dylan album. I would play it over and over on the family radiogram.'†

---

* Almost certainly, the 'friend' was Hentoff, who related the above story just weeks *before* Dylan's infamous second Ed Sullivan audition, the following May.
† Stewart would cover 'Man Of Constant Sorrow' on his own first solo album, the evergreen *An Old Raincoat Won't Ever Let You Down* (1969).

By October 1962, John Hammond Sr was boasting to David Kapralik in a Columbia memo that Dylan's 'first album is over 4,000 and I think it will continue to sell'. He also pushed for a bump in the miserly royalty rate he'd originally offered. This suggests the oft-quoted figure of 5,000 domestic sales in the first year was hardly a source of alarm. Yet Kapralik told Hajdu, 'We almost didn't release [the first album] at all. John fought for it tooth and nail'. Not a shred of evidence supports such a self-aggrandizing assertion. The album was released at the earliest possible date contractually, two months *before* Carolyn Hester's, despite going through various cover slicks, alternate sequences and a change of title (from *Freewheelin'*) – hardly indicative of cold feet on Columbia's part.

Which brings us to the much-propagated myth that Dylan was dubbed 'Hammond's Folly' inside Columbia. There isn't a single contemporary reference to this perjorative nickname, and the whole thing rings wrong. The earliest mention in print I can find comes from Robert Shelton, who told Max Jones in 1966, 'For a while Bob was known as Hammond's Folly', something he can only have heard second-hand, probably from Hammond himself, who told Karl Dallas in 1968, 'Bobby's first album didn't sell at all well and the company were thinking of dropping him. For a while they called him "Hammond's Folly".' By then, it very much suited Hammond to make such a claim.

Actually, Hammond's position at Columbia, as long as Mitch Miller remained in charge, was rock solid, no matter how much others in A&R, Kapralik included, had it in for him. Also, nothing in what Hammond wrote in 1962 internal memos suggests Dylan was in disfavour. The very reverse, in fact. Within just six months of his debut, the label was fighting tooth and nail to hang onto Dylan, aware now that the contract he signed a year earlier was not worth the paper on which it was written.

Do the math. Dylan's first album cost $402 to record. The contract was boilerplate. Where was the risk, let alone the folly? Certainly, when Glover came to town the month after the album's release and Dylan took him up to Columbia, Glover recalled 'these people in suits were real deferential' to their potential new meal ticket.

In fact, Columbia seemed to be expecting another album asap, this being an era when two albums per annum was the norm. As such,

Dylan found himself back at Studio A less than five weeks after his debut, perhaps something he pushed for himself, being 'way past that [previous] record'.

Again, he would end up recording for two afternoons – April 24th and 25th – with Hammond occasionally looking up from his paper to curtail a take. When the producer cuts off a first take of 'Rocks And Gravel', a traditional blues Dylan was looking to claim as his own, the singer knows what's coming and pre-empts Hammond, 'Esses?' Dylan is already starting to resent Hammond's obsession with mike placement. After a fine second take of 'Ramblin' Gamblin' Willie', Hammond says, 'Listen, I want to do it again. It was much better but "the people" just whacked us. You put your head up when you say People; put your head *down* when you say People,' prompting Dylan to shoot back, 'Woody Guthrie told me [to] always pronounce my words clear.'

But the first real sign of growing antipathy with Hammond's recording methods comes after a second take of 'Talkin' Bear Mountain Picnic Massacre Blues' – which Dylan has finally decided to get on tape – breaks down. Hammond suggests, 'Just do that verse. You only get screwed up on that thing.' Displaying the first signs of a lifelong aversion to inserts, Dylan insists, 'No, I wanna do the whole thing'. Finally, somewhat reluctantly, he goes along with Hammond, recording the insert, only to blow the whole song ending.

His annoyance is audible, 'See, I lost a whole verse in there someplace.' Hammond tries to placate him, 'OK, Bob, we'll skip it for now,' at which point the tape stops. One must assume words are exchanged because when the tape starts rolling again, Dylan is laying down a word-perfect take of 'Talkin' Bear Mountain'. Perhaps Dylan is already starting to sense the folly of retaining Hammond as his producer.

Despite the producer's pedantry, the two sessions produced seven songs apiece, including shiny new originals like 'Let Me Die In My Footsteps', 'Talkin' John Birch', 'Death of Emmett Till' and 'Ramblin' Gamblin' Willie', as well as three leftovers from his 1961 club set: 'Sally Gal', 'Talkin' Bear Mountain' and 'Talkin' Hava Nagilah'. Dylan also does a favourite Hank Williams cover, 'I Heard That Lonesome Whistle', while his new-found love of the Delta blues (and its king) finds expression in a version of 'Corrina Corrina' that owes more to Robert Johnson than the tradition they both habitually pillaged, and a 'Milk Cow Blues' that crosses its ostensible author, Kokomo Arnold, with Johnson, Lead Belly and Elvis Presley.

Dylan starts out doing the latter on the piano, à la the Million Dollar Quartet, but soon switches to guitar and by take four even Hammond is moved to observe, 'Oh, that's ever so much [better]', before closing down the day's proceedings. Three of the originals will be earmarked for the second album, while two of the acoustic blues must await revival, rockabilly-style. For now, that all-important second album is put on hold.

Also placed on hold is Dylan's desire to bring in other musicians to accompany him, as Bill Lee had at the first of these April sessions. Lee, whose instrument was stand-up bass, was really a jazz musician who, as Suze observes, 'didn't ... relate to this folk stuff easily ... but Bob [would go] over to talk to him ... bringing him into the scene'. Lee reciprocated, making him hip to some of the jazz scene which shared the same downtown milieu.

Dylan at this point was prepared to listen to anything – from Moondog at the Living Theatre to Coltrane at the Village Gate, to Charlie Mingus at the Five Spot – and would play with anyone. Indeed, after wrapping up proceedings at Columbia on the 25th, he apparently hightailed it over to 52nd and 8th, six blocks away, to perform at 'A Folk & Jazz Concert' in Palm Gardens, scheduled to also feature Archie Shepp and Cecil Taylor who had their own way of connecting musical dots.

It was a night off from another residency at Gerde's that had seen Dylan perform some of those just-recorded songs. One he played most nights, though he refrained from donating it to Columbia, perhaps because he sensed he was not quite done with it. It was called 'Blowin' In The Wind', and as of the week before the Columbia sessions, when it ran to just two verses (the first and the third), he was prefacing it with a disclaimer, 'This here ain't a protest song, or anything like that, 'cause I don't write protest songs.'

He already disliked the association. As he says in *No Direction Home*, 'They were trying to build me up as a topical songwriter. I was *never* a topical songwriter.' Sounds like semantics to me. The idea for the song certainly came from a protest song, the anti-slavery negro hymn, 'Many Thousands Gone' aka 'No More Auction Block', purportedly composed by runaway slaves who escaped to Nova Scotia – a safe British haven – in the early nineteenth century.

According to Shelton, Dylan learnt his arrangement of the traditional song – which that September he performed at the Gaslight, for a show he was recording – from a great-great-granddaughter of African American slaves, Delores Dixon. Dixon sang with the New World Singers and according to *Chronicles*, was his 'part-time girlfriend', suggesting he turned to her sometimes when Suze was outta town – as she was about to be for quite a while.

For now, 'Blowin' In The Wind' remained just another song, nothing special. Dylan even said as much, when Glover later tried to get him to admit that it changed things, 'I was writing songs all the time then. Every day I'd be writing songs – some I'd remember, some I wouldn't ... Blowin' In The Wind just happened to be the lucky one, the one that stuck. But I probably wrote a song the night before that, and I probably wrote one or two the next day ... which were in the same vein.' He must have thought there was something about the song, because untypically he continued tinkering with it.

By the time he played it to the Friesens in May, for inclusion in *Broadside* #6, it had a third verse that vainly reached for the same pantheistic feeling as the final verse of 'Let Me Die In My Footsteps'. If a handwritten manuscript on Taft Hotel stationery, recently sold privately, also dates from this time, Dylan was even toying with a fourth verse that lent heavily on Jack Rhodes's 'Satisfied Mind', the lyric of which exists in Dylan's handwriting from 1961.*

Even though he doesn't appear to have played the song to Tony Glover when he came to town that April, he did play him 'Let Me Die In My Footsteps', perhaps because he was genuinely proud of that one.† Glover recalled, 'He was living in this fifth-floor walk-up. I got in touch with Bob – he showed me around [the Village]. He had me over for dinner one night – we had hot dogs Suze made. We [even]

---

* Though the manuscript is unquestionably in Dylan's handwriting and was authenticated by Jeff Rosen, the use of Taft Hotel stationery raises questions. It was the very hotel where Jimmie Rodgers died, but no irrefutable explanation for why Dylan should be using its paper in April 1962 has yet been provided. As we shall see, it is the first of a series of seemingly authentic drafts of classic Dylan lyrics to emerge in the 21st century, pre-Tulsa.

† Glover dates the visit to May. However, the *Little Sandy Review* of Dylan's LP, published in April, includes Guthrie's own comment to Dylan about the album, 'It's a good 'un, Bobby,' which must have come from Glover.

went to ... some afternoon game show. He said, "You [ever] been to Times Square?" People were handing out tickets. Bob said, "D'ya wanna check this out?"' Dylan was out to impress Glover with the songs he was writing, the bohemian life he was living and the connections he was making. He even took him to meet Woody, an occasion Glover vividly remembered a quarter of a century later:

> [Woody] was in this facility somewhere in Brooklyn, and it was hard to get there on the subway, so he was gonna [ask] his friend with a car, John [Cohen]. [During the drive,] Bob handed me a poem he'd just written about Big Joe Williams [which ended], 'Did he teach me how to respect the blues / No, he taught me how to sleep in my shoes.' This building was [surrounded by] wire mesh. Double-locked door.* John brought along his guitar because Woody liked people to play for him. We were sitting in the day room, and this guy shuffled out ... Bob introduced us. Some guy was muttering something in Russian. We went into Woody's room to get some privacy. Bob said, 'D'ya like the record?' Woody said yeah. Woody could barely talk. He'd get out a few words. Bob did a few songs.

Dylan knew only too well that Glover would report back to the Midwest mafia that he really did know Woody, after they had learnt not to always take the man at his word. When he and Suze went on what was ostensibly a song-collecting trip to Virginia in late May, with Paul Clayton as their guide, Dylan was hoping to meet the legendary blues singer, Etta Baker, famous for her version of 'Railroad Bill'. Though Suze later insisted it never happened, Dylan suggested, 'We should say we met her.'

Sure enough, the next time he was in Minneapolis, he regaled Glover and friends with the story of how he was recently 'visiting Elizabeth

---

* It turns out Glover had the foresight to keep this 'poem', all six lines of it, which was auctioned in November 2020 as 'an unfinished Dylan song'. I think not. Reproduced in the auction catalog in facsimile, it ran thus: 'My eyes are cracked I think I been framed / I can't seem to remember the sound of my name / What did he teach you I heard someone shout / Did he teach you to wheel & wind yourself out / Did he teach you to reveal, respect and repent the blues / No jack, he taught me how to sleep in my shoes.' Line two reappears three months later in 'Tomorrow Is A Long Time'.

Cotton in Washington ... me and Paul Clayton. We all went down to see Mrs Etta Baker after that. She's got a bunch of cousins. I was playing them "Deep Elem Blues". Cora Phillips. Great family. If you're ever down in North Carolina, go see 'em,' confident his becalmed friends in Dinkytown never would.

If Dylan struck out in his attempt to meet these old-time folksingers, Clayton did introduce him to Steve Wilson – Clayton's college friend, who would come to New York later in the year. Wilson's house in Waynesboro, Virginia, was where Dylan would spend his twenty-first birthday. Suze recalled, 'We had a real good time listening to music and making music.' Dylan, though, seemed preoccupied; Wilson knew not why.

Suze knew. She was leaving for a three-month Italian sojourn in a fortnight's time to study, and was already being subjected to severe pressure from her paramour not to go. Yet go she did, cajoled by her Italian mother to *carpe diem*. Only when she arrived in Italy, after a brief stopover in Paris, did she experience 'a sinking sensation that I had fallen for my mother's wicked scheme to get me away from Bob – whom she hated, I now saw clearly'.

Already, a letter was waiting for her from Dylan, describing standing on the dock and watching the ship sail beyond the horizon, an image he would revisit, most notably in a song he wrote seven months later which overtly captured his feelings of despair that June morning, 'Boots Of Spanish Leather'.

Almost immediately, Dylan's support network kicked in. The evening after she sailed, he had dinner at 'the Macs', Eve attempting to reassure him 'that he shouldn't be angry, that he had to understand that [Suze] was only going for a short while and that she'd be back. He was quiet. He didn't answer.' He did not believe her. She was *gone*. Worse still, if he wished to discover her whereabouts, he would have to go see her mother Mary and her 'waspy professor husband', Suze's stepfather; a visit that was filling him with dread.

A letter Bob sent Suze on Independence Day confirms he had swallowed his pride and paid a call. It was swiftly followed by a report from Carla of what transpired, confirming the elder sister's ongoing support of the couple by providing an account of a public dressing-down of Bobby by mother Mary. Not surprisingly, it brought an immediate rebuke from the shores of Italy, Suze asking her mother to consider her feelings, even as she admits to being 'homesick lately' and crying herself to sleep nightly because she misses her boyfriend 'so much'.

Carla's detailed account of the beau's visit was clearly designed to paint their mother as the villain, prompting Suze to note how her mother never gives 'her Bobby' a chance. According to the sibling, their mother had taken umbrage at Dylan calling her Mary, berating him about his manners. How could his parents have not taught him to address his girlfriend's mother as *Mrs Rotolo*? At this point, she apparently turned to her friend, Mrs Evans, and said, 'This is the jerk Bob *Zimmerman* Dylan, the one Suze likes.'

But if Mary thought she had headed Dylan off at the pass by spiriting Suze all the way to Italy, her daughter's July 10th letter contained the worrying news that her boyfriend had again hinted at marriage, a prospect that set Mary off on another anti-Dylan rant to Mrs Evans – this time without the poor boy *in situ*. Carla, still present and correct, continued to report as their mother told the redoubtable lady, 'There are plenty of good Catholic boys. My daughter has no sense.'

Suze's angry response probably reached Mary about the time Dylan sent Suze one of his own, describing his latest Columbia session and the songs he had been writing for it – and *her*: 'I sang six [*sic*] more songs – you're in two of them – Bob Dylan's Blues and Down The Highway … and another one too – I'm In The Mood For You – which is for you, but I don't mention your name. I [also] wrote a song about that statue we saw [together] in Washington of Tom Jefferson.'

The session was on July 9th, a month and a day after Suze sailed, a week after Dylan played five nights in Montreal and the day before his absent girlfriend sent her fiery letter home. It appeared to indicate personal concerns had indeed risen to the fore. Dylan even offered an explanation for this change to Tony Glover, the following month:

> I figured I'd been writing too many songs for other people. I was on a big kick there for about five months where I was writing songs … just to bring out a *point* … I finally said to myself, 'Gee Dylan, you ain't written any songs about *you*.' … So I wrote a bunch of songs about myself … about ten songs in a week. I recorded one of 'em, Bob Dylan's Blues.

He actually recorded five of 'em, as well as all three verses of 'Blowin' In The Wind' and an exquisite cover of Hally Wood's 'Worried Blues' in the three hours Hammond and Columbia allocated.

This time, it is down to business from minute one, with Hammond keeping most of his opinions to himself save for telling Dylan, 'You can do a whole lot better,' after a second take of 'Babe, I'm In The Mood For You' – resulting in two more attempts before admitting defeat – and an exclamation, 'That's the one, Bob!' after take three of 'Blowin' In The Wind', destined to be fixed in perpetuity.

But the most radical surgery was done to 'Bob Dylan's Blues', which lost two verses, the first of which namechecked those trad. landmarks Shenandoah and Lea Highway, the second of which could have easily slotted into 1965's 'On The Road Again': 'I got a clock in my stomach, Lord, and a watch in my head / I'd better watch out or I'll wind up dead.'

For now, such surreal couplets were kept at bay, Dylan preferring to devote himself to the Pentecostal fervour of 'Quit Your Lowdown Ways', a ribald rewrite of Henry Thomas's 'Honey, Just Allow Me One More Chance' and the one original to address acute feelings of loss at this time, 'Down The Highway'; all three dispatched in single takes at the afternoon's meridian. Four of the seven tracks would make it to the second album proper, a productive day's work that mostly hid the hurt he felt inside. Dylan let Hally Wood express how he really felt, 'I got the worried blues / I'm a-going where I never been before.'

There was another cause for concern. He was stockpiling original songs at a rate of knots, and a single Columbia session every three months was never going to keep track of 'em all. The song about Jefferson's statue is now lost, as is one he wrote that summer about John Henry Faulk's lawsuit, brought against AWARE's McCarthyite blacklist, which in late June resulted in a $3.5 million award in Faulk's favour – proof that songs written 'just to bring out a point' had not been entirely forsaken.*

---

* The song was called 'Gates Of Hate'. This being America, the award was appealed until it was reduced to a miserly half a million or, after costs, a pitiful $75,000. Dylan discussed the case with Faulk in person.

When Dylan recorded a second home tape with Tony Glover, five weeks after this July session, he had five brand-new songs he wanted to get down, none of which he would record for his second album. Fortunately, three of them would be scooped up by his new music publisher, Witmark Music, after they signed him that July in one of the shadiest publishing deals this side of the free-for-all days of Ralph Peer.*

How the Witmark deal came about is shrouded in mist'n'mirk, partly because of a long list of claimants who later sought credit, the first of whom was chancer Roy Silver – 'a hustler on the street', in Dylan's choice phrase – who apparently got the foolhardy folksinger to sign a piece of paper saying he was his manager that spring.†

With Thal long out of the picture, Dylan was evidently looking for representation. According to Arline Cunningham – an employee of Guthrie's manager and music publisher, Harold Leventhal – Dylan even 'came in and did a little audition' for Leventhal, though whether he was aiming to be managed or published by the notorious Ludlow Music is unclear. If the fast-talkin' Silver did not last long, it was long enough to bring Dylan to Artie Mogull at Witmark Music and play him what Silver was calling 'the greatest song I've ever heard', or at least the greatest song he'd heard that week:

Artie Mogull: When I heard, 'How many ears must one man have before he can hear people cry?' I flipped. I said, 'Okay, that's it. I want you. I'll give you a thousand-dollar advance. You'll sign a seven-year [sic] writer's contract' ... We got a contract ready and he signed it. The next day, he and Roy [Silver] came back and they said, 'Listen, does it mean anything that we also signed a contract with Leeds Music?' ... So I gave them another thousand dollars and told them to go back and see if they could buy their way out of the old contract.

Already, the fog of faulty memory begins rolling in. Whereas Mogull has Dylan coming in with his guitar and harmonica and playing 'Blowin' In The Wind' in the office, Silver insists he'd already cut the

---

* In 2015, Dylan would describe the A&R pioneer, in a blurb for Barry Mazur's biography, as 'an overwhelming character in the music field, a true visionary who realized the potential power of common music long before anyone else'.
† Jeff Rosen's brief, bullshit-laden interview with Roy Silver for the *No Direction Home* project was included as a 'bonus' DVD to the deluxe edition of 2009's *Together Thru Life*.

song to acetate before he called Mogull. (Indisputably, a stand-alone publishing demo of 'Blowin' In The Wind' was lodged when the song was registered for copyright on July 30th, just eighteen days after Dylan signed what was actually a *three*-year deal with Witmark, for that thousand-dollar advance.)

Dylan would not record any (more) demos for his new publisher until December. As such, the mere existence of a July publishing demo suggests a) it was made for, not by, Witmark, and b) that the deal largely revolved around this one catchy song.

Where fog lights really are required is when the bulky figure of Albert Grossman heaves into view, muscling in on the deal with his usual bull-in-a-china-shop charm. Whatever Mr Silver's arrangement had been with Dylan, formal or informal, he was soon removed from the equation by a pincer movement from Mogull and Grossman. The legendary thousand-dollar pay-off to buy Dylan's already-expired contract with Leeds Music – mentioned in Scaduto's 1971 biography and reiterated, almost verbatim, by Dylan in *Chronicles* – never happened. If any contract needed buying out before Grossman and Mogull could really start cooking the books, it was the one Dylan injudiciously signed with Silver.*

By July 1962, everyone in the folk world knew (of) Albert Grossman, and had an opinion about him. What few knew was that he had graduated from Roosevelt University, Chicago, with a bachelor's degree in commerce, before cutting his teeth running the fabled folk club, the Gate of Horn. As one former colleague described him, '[Grossman] came off at first glance as a sweetheart of a guy, but underneath the charming veneer, he was a killer through and through. If he was on your side ... [all] you saw [was] the jovial, friendly, dope-smoking safe haven.' As far as Van Ronk was concerned, the man's character flaws were obvious: 'He took a sort of perverse pleasure in being utterly unscrupulous.'

If Grossman's own musical taste tended towards the traditional, his degree had already taught him that the real money lay in music publishing. Charlie Rothschild, who was one of those who stood back and let Grossman cherry-pick the scene, knew that 'Albert wanted to get into music publishing ... and he started looking to sign folksingers who could write.'

---

* Shelton later suggested it cost as much as $10,000. I think we can remove a nought.

In the period when Dylan's own songs were starting to create a buzz downtown and Silver was on the prowl, the Chicago businessman was busy cultivating people like Mogull as a way of paving the yellow brick road. In the spring of 1962, Mogull introduced him to Herman Starr, the head of Witmark's parent company, Warners Music, who agreed to a deal by which Grossman 'would receive 50% of the publisher's net profits from the publishing of every performing artist whom he attracted to Witmark'. So if it was Silver who really brought Dylan to Mogull, Grossman's deal with Starr would be null and void – *unless* he and Mogull jointly agreed to paper over the truth.

It wasn't just Starr they kept the facts from. Dylan knew nothing about this arrangement, carefully timelined so that his Witmark signing predated any management contract with Grossman, ensuring no conflict of interest in the legal sense. Morally, what Grossman did was at the very least underhand.

Which is why he went to such lengths to ensure Dylan never found out. Never, however, was a long time; longer, even, than the term Witmark (and therefore Grossman) could now commercially exploit the songs Dylan would write in the next three years, from 'Blowin' In The Wind' to 'Like A Rolling Stone'. Under US copyright law, that term was twenty-eight years, after which it could be renewed, twice.

A stroke of good fortune ensured that said options would reside solely with Dylan, adding millions ultimately to his net worth. Barely months before Paul McCartney and John Lennon signed away large chunks of their future income to music publisher Dick James – which they have yet to get back – Dylan's Witmark contract was drafted by M. William Krasilovsky (who would later write the classic textbook on music and copyright, *This Business of Music*). Krasilovsky attached to it the so-called '1947 Revised Uniform Popular Songwriters Contract', which ensured that 'copyrights [automatically] revert to [the] composer at the end of the original copyright term or twenty-eight years'. It meant that by 1993 Dylan would own – and more importantly, control – all of his publishing, making him the sole passenger on his own gravy train.

However, he would not be so lucky with the management contract he signed with Grossman the following month. Before he was in a position to sign the next seven years away, though, he needed to return home and attend to some business there, no matter how much it hurt his nearest and dearest. Having been advised to change his name legally to Bob Dylan, presumably by Grossman, he returned to Hibbing to do the necessary with a Minnesotan registrar. On August 9th he did the deed at the St Louis County Court in Hibbing.*

Apparently, the person he asked to witness this legal change was his father, Abraham, who was moved to tears at what was for any Jew a moment pregnant with symbolism, his son and heir's renouncement of the family name. Somehow, his father went through with it, but he was now under no illusion: his son was beyond his command. He would never see a poem Bobby wrote at the time which ends with the following telling passage:

> Yes father I understand
> that you dont have time
> You are a very busy man
> an you are runnin many places
> where you have your many interests
> but put the batteries back
> in your flashlight
> an shine it
> in the bushes.

While in Hibbing saying hi to the family, Dylan also decided to reconnect with somebody else from his past life as Bobby Zimmerman: high school sweetheart, Echo Helstrom. In fact, she accompanied him to Minneapolis, where a party was being laid on for her ex's benefit by his friends, the Whitakers, another opportunity for him to remind Dinkytown how far he'd travelled since leaving town twenty months earlier, and for Glover to again delineate that distance on tape and in interview:

He came here again in August ... He stopped a couple of days ... The trip before, it was real quiet, just Whitaker and a few people. This was [more] like, Dylan Returns! The star returning to his home town; there was a bit of that. Whitaker was having this big open-house party. Bob was pretty drunk, [playing this] real shitty guitar. A dizzy blonde [called] Echo showed up ... She was coming on pretty heavy, and he was going,

---

* Whatever source suggests he changed his name legally in a New York court on August 2nd is clearly not reliable.

'Wait a minute, I got a girlfriend back in New York.' Dave [Whitaker] and his wife Gretel were having a fight. At one point, [when] there were only three or four people left, Bob started doing 'Corrina Corrina'; Dave and Gretel were wailing at each other.

Dave Morton – who had already run into Dylan at the Scholar, where he showed Morton a new arrangement of 'House Of The Rising Sun' and they improvised a blues tune trading insults with each other – confirms that Dylan stayed in town for what he called 'a long weekend'. Morton ended up driving Dylan 'and the girl he was with' to the airport after they had crashed at his place. Morton's account suggests that either Dylan's protestations at the party about having 'a girlfriend back in New York' were for others' benefit or that his attack of conscience had not lasted long in the face of Echo's importuning.

Even when back in New York, he was not entirely convincing as the bereft boyfriend waiting chastely for his true love. Indeed, he later affirmed this long-standing moral ambivalence when conversing with Liam Clancy, who at this time had become involved with a girl called Kathy Perry, only to find out that when he went on the road she started seeing Dylan. The Minnesotan's explanation to his old friend was simple: 'She was lonesome for you, man. I just offered her comfort. She missed you, man, and you weren't there. I was.' His later autobiographical song, 'Simple Twist Of Fate', shows a similar lack of moral compass as he looks back at a '4th Street Affair' (its original subtitle) – probably with a prostitute – shortly after Suze sailed away in the morning.

It seems he just couldn't face being alone and returning home merely accentuated the negative. Dave Van Ronk vividly remembered 'a phone call from him at four or five o'clock in the morning ... Bobby said he was standing in a phone booth some place in Minneapolis. It was nineteen degrees below zero and he was crying, "I want Suze."' He also told Glover, with the tape rolling and the Whitakers yelling, 'My girlfriend's in Europe right now. She'll be back September 1st ... Till she's back, I['ll] never go home. Sometimes it gets bad.'

Determined to prove how deep his feelings for Suze went, he offered to play Glover a song he had barely started, one that exemplified him self-consciously 'thinking about' Suze, even if he immediately insists, 'This is way out of my style.' The song was 'Tomorrow Is A Long

Time', and though he only really has the last verse, he announces he's 'gonna make up the first two verses'. He then almost changes his mind, saying, 'I don't know who [you're] gonna play this to. I might incriminate myself.'

In the end, he doesn't just sing it, he improvises a second verse unique to this version, with the feel of a man crying in a phone booth at 4 a.m.: 'Only if the highway stopped its ramblin' / Only if the ocean turned to sand / Only if the blind could see me singing / Then I might fall down on my knees and cry'.

Though this is the one overt mention of Suze that evening, another partly improvised rendition of 'Corrina Corrina' includes the verse, 'I love [my] baby more than I love myself [x2] / You'd break my heart into pieces if you were with anyone else', a standard to which he was disinclined to hold himself. The final song of a long, drunken night – probably called 'Blue Eyed Baby' – also claimed, 'If I don't get my blue-eyed baby, don't want nobody at all.' But he couldn't always help himself. He missed her, and she wasn't there. Sometimes, someone else was.

Glover's own 1971 description of this tape, 'Recorded at party at Whitakers' on a very shitty buzzy guitar ... some drunken rapping', does the twenty-one-year-old Dylan a slight disservice. He is enjoying himself, choosing particular songs because he wants to 'get this on tape to see how it sounds', as he does with 'Tomorrow Is A Long Time' and 'Motherless Children', both as yet unrecorded. Even he admits he doesn't 'know what kinda tape we're gonna make tonight – a pretty drunken tape – [though if] you want me to talk, I can *talk* on key' (a reference to the problems he's having tuning this guitar).

It's all good-humoured, even when someone asks if he knows 'any put-down songs'. He sings one called 'Talkin' Hypocrite', 'for Bill Barth', an otherwise lost song from this prolific period. Fortunately, the slightly juiced versions of 'Long Ago Far Away' – introduced, tongue firmly in cheek, as 'a song about how great we are now 'cause all the bad things that used to happen don't happen no more' – and 'Long Time Gone' are not the only ones we have. In both cases, the later Witmark versions are superior, Dylan admitting after the former, 'I forgot most of the verses.'*

---

* Dylan was still willing to do the latter during an April 1963 home session at the McKenzies'.

The days when Dylan would willingly make such tapes was drawing to a close, and with it the happy-go-lucky guy who could still on occasion steal back to his good ol' used-to-be. Glover would capture the last sighting of that unselfconscious man the following July, but for now it was time to drop Echo off and return to 4th Street, where a letter from Suze was a-waiting, announcing she would not be coming home on September 1st after all.

There had come a point when he had called her and she 'didn't want to go to the phone, 'cause I was enjoying life ... I [had] got over the terrible sadness of leaving my love at home.' Only now did Dylan's thoughts turn bitter; the letter seemingly prompted an immediate riposte, though it was not one Suze would hear for a few months. As the roosters crowed on Thompson Street, not knowing they were slated for somebody's dinner plate, he got flashbacks to a time of togetherness. But this time he picked up his pen and dipped it in bile. This was a new Dylan, one who had discovered how to write 'put-down songs' that cut to the very quick, even as he casually declared, 'Don't think twice, it's all right.'

Perhaps it was the company he was now keeping. A few weeks earlier, he had been introduced to Victor Maymudes, who had helped run the Unicorn in LA with Herb Cohen since 1957. An imposing, often brusque dude, Maymudes claimed in his curtailed memoir that Jack Elliott suggested he was 'the right kind of producer-manager type' for Dylan, which suggests Grossman had yet to sign him up.

Although Maymudes claimed they met in 1961, he remembered Phil Ochs playing at the Gaslight the night they met, and that Dylan 'wasn't performing like everyone else was at this time; he would wait till closing, then ask if he could do a song or two'. So we are clearly talking about the summer of 1962.

By then Gaslight head honcho, Sam Hood, knew he had someone special. Tom Paxton confirms that by that summer, Dylan 'was never actually on the bill at the Gaslight, [but] he was there most nights and usually got up for a set toward the end of the evening. A lot of his [new] songs were heard there first.' Maymudes' only clear memory of Dylan's brief set was 'his own take on "Corrina, Corrina", a bluesy version that ... was closer to what Robert Johnson was doing', which also nails it down, date-wise, to the spring or early summer of '62.

Afterwards, the pair rapped about Woody, Lead Belly and Cisco, and all points between, finding common ground, before they 'walked to Cafe Figaro and played chess till the sun came up'. Dylan was already known around the Village as something of a 'chess hustler', who would loudly exclaim, 'I don't know what I'm doing,' shortly before announcing, 'Er, checkmate.'

Though Maymudes presumably soon realized the job of 'producer-manager' was no longer on offer, he still wanted to know how far Dylan planned to go. Dylan told him, 'I want to go the distance.' The flame of ambition burned brightly enough for Maymudes to stick around and be a thorn in the side of Suze, as and when she returned, and a founding member of the entourage his new friend would soon use as a crutch.

Dylan was having to adjust his lifestyle to take account of a new-found, highly localized 'fame', surrounding himself with tall dudes who could handle confrontation when so required. Maymudes fitted the bill. Thankfully, club owners like Sam Hood at the Gaslight and Paul Colby at the Bitter End respected Dylan's desire not to be hassled when hanging out, Colby's club usually proving to be the 'place to go and listen and to take it all in'. Whenever the Kettle of Fish was overcooked and the Gaslight was on fire, as Colby recalls, the Bitter End 'was where he hung out'.

Despite being heartsick, Dylan was in a good space creatively. If the West Coast cowboy was chilled enough to hang out, smoke and drink with Dylan, he got a free pass to meet and greet the likes of Chip Monck, the man who stagelit every club downtown, Richard Alderson, soundman extraordinaire, and those *bon vivants*, Fred Neil and Hamilton Camp.

All of them would hole up at Monck's basement apartment to blow smoke. Dylan still remembered its location and decor in 1971: 'At the bottom of the Village Gate ... a real cruddy apartment but it had wall-to-wall carpeting and the carpeting even ran up the walls.' If Bitter End boss Paul Colby has the six of them sitting 'around [at Chip's] on weekends, passing guitars and singing and talking', Alderson has a more straightforward explanation for these gatherings: Monck had the best weed in town, and privacy was assured.

Dylan has even suggested he wrote 'A Hard Rain's A-Gonna Fall' there. But he did not. Monck's place was for chilling and chatting.

Upstairs at the Gaslight was where he occasionally hammered out a song or three, when not playing cards or chess. As Paxton recalls, 'There was a little apartment that the Gaslight rented or owned ... [a] kind of a storage room. And we set up a table in there. We had this penny-ante poker game that was continuous.' Kornfeld concurs, 'The Gaslight had four regular acts – and they rotated. There was an annex above the stage – we used to play poker there: John Hammond Jr, Hugh Romney, Tom Paxton, Noel Stookey, Van Ronk, [Dylan and I].'

It was here where Dylan would let the rain wash over him, leaving Kornfeld, for one, agog: 'He wrote wherever. It amazed me to watch him write 'cause he used to just sit at a typewriter.' Hanging out with fellow folkies until lightning struck, when it did he would throw in his hand, get up, move over to where Hugh Romney had left his portable typewriter, and begin tapping away, seemingly oblivious to any hubbub around him. Steve Wilson recalls seeing it happen, and confirms all the material elements in Kornfeld's account:

> There was no doubt that he had unique musical skills ... He was [somehow] able to write his song material at a typewriter without any collaboration from a musical instrument. His ability to both remember complex lyrics of great length, and to scan words so they fit the meter of the line, was highly unusual. He had little need to practice or work up his material, because it arrived in his head largely formed, not requiring further negotiation. Every once in a while he would change a word, or make some trivial adjustment, but his ability to conceptualize and remember very intricate constructions was quite remarkable. Paul [Clayton] thought he had the Devil in him.

Maymudes, who also witnessed the process at work, was equally thunderstruck. He had his own take on the working methodology: 'It's not like he's hammering nails, it's more like he's thinking over coffee, while at his desk with his guitar. Typing and handwriting between smoking cigarettes, and he can do that for longer than anybody.'

But neither Wilson nor Maymudes were there the September night Tom Paxton climbed the stairs from the Gaslight – where he had recently recorded his own debut album – and 'found Bob finishing a four- or five-page poem on Hugh's typewriter. "What's this?" I asked. "Just a poem or something." Bob was a guy who could shrug with his voice. I ... asked him if he was going to put a tune to it ... "Think I should?" "Hell, yes. Then you got a song. This way you just have something ... in some little magazine."' 'A Hard Rain's A-Gonna Fall' – the song in question – was at this stage little more than a series of images. But already it had a hook – the ballad commonplace, 'O whar hae ya been' – on which Dylan hung its irregular verses.

That it was always somewhere between a song and a poem is most forcefully indicated by something Dylan said in 1968 to John Cohen – one of a number of folkies crammed into this 'storage room' that September night: 'The language which [the Beats] were writing you could read off the paper and somehow it would begin some kind of tune in your mind.' The well-read Cohen knew right away 'Hard Rain' was more 'Howl' than 'Lord Randal'.* This time, though, it wasn't just the best minds of a generation facing annihilation. As Dylan told Studs Terkel the following April, 'Every line in that is really another song ... I didn't know how many other songs I could write'.

According to Colby, he initially just recited the song, 'with Hamilton Camp backing him on guitar'. If so, it was a fleeting whim. Paxton was not alone in thinking it should be set to a melody. Cohen was also 'wondering how it fit into music'. Yet, according to Dylan (in July 1963), it was 'Pete Seeger [who] convinced me to sing it. I wrote it as a poem, and Pete told me to sing it. I just talked it, then finally it became a song.'

Colby alone recollects hearing him recite it that first time, something wholly at odds with the first line of the hand-corrected typescript, later retrieved by Hugh Romney and put up for auction in London in 2015, which reads:[†]

---

* As did Ann Charters when she compiled *The Penguin Book of the Beats* in 1993, which included the lyric.

[†] This typescript with manuscript corrections was put up for auction by Sotheby's on September 29th, 2015, with an estimate of £150,000–200,000, but failed to make its reserve. A handwritten manuscript that was clearly a later copy, with nothing like the same provenance – this one coming from Romney's son – had sold in New York fifteen months earlier for $400,000, reaffirming the fetishistic obsession of collectors with manuscripts, whatever their provenance, over an earlier, more historically significant hand-corrected typescript.

IT'S A HARD RAIN'S GONNA FALL – Words-Music B. Dylan '62

Nor does Colby's claim sit easily with the way a three-line refrain is marked out at the end of each verse: 'And it's a hard / It's a hard / It's a hard rain's gonna fall.' Perhaps the twenty-one-year-old Dylan didn't decide which form suited it best till he had finished with it. But when he finished it, it was a song. And thank the Lord, it was. In the July 1963 conversation with Tony Glover, Dylan at one point turned to an attendant Paul Nelson and asked:

Did I sing you a song I wrote for a poet-friend of mine who got killed in Peru, Eddie ... It never did come out as a song, 'cause I never memorized it. I wrote it as a poem ... I wrote a lot of stuff like that. I can't remember it. At one time I remembered it all but then I got hung up writing poems. You don't have to remember them, or do nothing. You write a poem you wanna sing, you gotta memorize it – especially if it's very long. Sometimes I write too fast and I forget what I'm writing. By the time I'm done with it, I don't even know what it was all about.

The above seems almost perfectly to describe the likely writing process for 'A Hard Rain's A-Gonna Fall'. Van Ronk was one of those stunned when he heard Dylan sing it 'during one of the hoot nights at the Gaslight. I could not even talk about it. I just had to leave the club and walk around for a while. It was unlike anything that had come before it.' Thankfully, the poem was soon introduced to the world of song, and at Pete Seeger's insistence a few days later, on September 22nd (still some weeks before the so-called Cuban Missile Crisis) it made its 'official' live debut at a multi-act show Seeger was MC'ing at Carnegie Hall. The show was called 'Travelin' Hootenanny' and it seems Dylan's inclusion had been arranged by Dylan's new manager, Al Grossman, who as of August 20th now claimed a 20% share of his income for the next *seven* years on both 'contracts then in place and those entered into while under Grossman's management'.

Not content with this, and the considerable kickback he was getting from Witmark Music, Grossman also insisted on receiving 25% 'on all incomes received by the Artist from recordings', even though he'd had zero input into the contract Dylan had signed with Columbia, a situation he was determined to change. The first enemy he made on

Dylan's behalf was Izzy Young, whose idea the Travelin' Hootenanny really was:

> That's another time when Albert Grossman never came through. [It was] the Folklore Center presents [Travelin'] Hootenanny, but I never got any money ... Dylan sang at that concert ... and he already sounded then like a character [version] of himself. I even have it written down in my notes [from] that evening. He sounded already like *A Face In The Crowd*.

If Young thought Dylan had already sold out, John Hammond was impressed by Dylan's performance and couldn't wait to get him back in the studio. As he wrote to his bosses a fortnight later, 'I think he will be the most important young folk artist in the business. He got rave notices in the *New York Times* for his concert on September 22, and he literally broke up the show, taking the play away from more established artists on the bill.'

Unbeknownst to Hammond, his great discovery was about to be asked to choose between his new manager and the man who made him sign a slave contract eleven months earlier. Grossman's first gambit in a carefully choreographed game plan was to get his new artist to record the audition tape he never made for Hammond, a showcase for his talents. Rather than booking a studio, Grossman elected to record Dylan live, using the same intimate surroundings which captured Paxton at his best earlier in the year: the Gaslight. He immediately knew who could do the recording, someone Dylan trusted implicitly, Richard Alderson, who seems to think it was the Gaslight's co-owners who approached him to make the famous Second Gaslight Tape (Dylan's second *audition* tape there):

> Sam Hood and his father, Clarence ... said, 'Well, Dylan's written these great new songs and he's going to be performing them for the first time at this private, afterhours gig at the Gaslight. [So] you gotta ... bring your tape machine.' So I did. It was over two nights. It was invitation only, and there were probably [no more than] twenty-five people in the room. It started around midnight, after the Gaslight had closed for business. The first night was all sort of conventional, original Bob Dylan folk-music stuff. The second night was the beginning of the Bob Dylan everybody knows. It was one of the first times he

performed 'A Hard Rain's A-Gonna Fall' … I was sitting right in front of Dylan, stage right … The stage was maybe two feet high … I used a portable Nagra, which was … made for early film work. Which is why [some of] the songs begin and end oddly … It was really an audition kinda thing for him, testing to see how people would react to this stuff … [Afterwards,] Dylan wanted to hear it … I had a little one-room studio at Carnegie Hall with some big speakers that I'd built, and [so] I brought him up [there]. We got stoned together, and we were very relaxed … He wanted Albert Grossman to hear them, and [so] … I gave copies to Grossman.

Alderson's fulsome 2014 description of the circumstances behind this oft-bootlegged (and Starbucked) recording goes some way to explaining the cross-section of material, everything from Robert Johnson to Lord Buckley; the sheer sonic quality of a mere 'club tape'; and the fact that Dylan played no fewer than four originals on which the ink was barely dry: 'John Brown', 'Ballad Of Hollis Brown', 'A Hard Rain's A-Gonna Fall' and 'Don't Think Twice, It's All Right'. It also helps explain why Dylan would be playing the tiny cafe between appearances at midtown's Carnegie and Town Halls. Those fortunate enough to catch one or both Gaslight shows were universally blown away. It certainly made one Village folkie believe in magic:

John Sebastian: I remember … this one cataclysmic moment. Dylan walked into the Gaslight Cafe and played 'Hard Rain' and 'Masters Of War' [sic].* He was trying out this new material … It was still a moment when he could be this endearing, Chaplinesque character, but that was changing. As much as people invested in his songs emotionally, that's how much they seemed to have invested in *him*.

Why, though, would Dylan need an audition tape in late September 1962 – unless Grossman thought he could get him away from Columbia?† Clearly, he thought he could, and this was a way of flexing his management muscles.

---

* The misremembered 'Masters Of War' was probably 'John Brown', another anti-war song with a trad tune.
† A recently attributed date for this tape – October 15th – has no factual basis and can be discounted. No such date features on the master reels.

As Dylan's mid-sixties road manager, Jonathan Taplin, recently noted, 'In those days contracts were essentially indentured servitude for five or seven years with a fixed royalty rate. Albert introduced the idea that you could renegotiate a record deal in the middle of the contract ... Albert would say, "We're gonna go on strike." He threatened that with Dylan at Columbia.'

It had been three months – two of them under Grossman's tutelage – since the last Columbia session, and still no new recording date had been fixed. It was Grossman's way of turning the screw. Dylan had already fulfilled that year's obligations under the contract he signed a year earlier, with twenty-one songs currently in the can. He had all the leverage. At the very least, his manager was determined to get a bump in the royalty rate and for Columbia to start marketing Dylan to a popular, not just a folk, audience. Just like Dylan, 'he wanted to go the distance'.

On one front at least, he and John Hammond saw eye to eye, the producer writing in a memo that month, 'Grossman and I would ... like an immediate single release by Bob Dylan.' Where Hammond and Dylan/Grossman were less in sync. was the kind of 'single release' they had in mind. Hammond felt he already had 'plenty of stuff in the can that would be suitable for a single release,' whereas Dylan wanted to re-record the song that single-handedly invented rock'n'roll, his first love.

'That's All Right Mama' – a song he would revisit at Columbia studios in 1963, 1969 *and* 1975 – had been the A-side of Elvis Presley's first Sun 78; a song Presley had learnt from an Arthur Crudup 45 – unlike Dylan, who would not hear the Crudup original until he visited a certain English record shop.* It would be the second 'Elvis Sun' single Dylan had recorded in the past six months. He was about to come out of the closet.

Not that secret rock'n'rollers were in short supply, hiding in plain sight all over the Greenwich hamlet. When Fred Neil sang, 'I've Got

---

* Dylan told bandleader Spencer Davis backstage in London in 1966, he 'found this Arthur Crudup record over here – all those Elvis Presley songs, about four of 'em, were taken off the Arthur Crudup record. [He does] "That's All Right Mama" in a high tenor voice. "My Baby Left Me" he plays in open-tuning.'

A Secret', he wasn't kidding. In a former life, he'd cut a series of rockabilly singles and wrote songs for Buddy Holly and Roy Orbison:

> **Steve Mandell**: At the time, you would never admit that you liked rock'n'roll. When I first met Dylan at a party, he was secretly introduced to me as 'a really good rock'n'roll piano player'. You had to be a closet rock'n'roller.
>
> **John Sebastian**: [Some of us] knew that [Dylan had] had teenage rock'n'roll bands back in Minnesota; that was an experience common to those of us of a certain age. Some of my earliest memories of Bob involve the two of us sitting in the basement of Gerde's Folk City playing all kinds of non-folk songs – old rock'n'roll, obscure Johnny Cash records on Sun, gospel, surf music! Buddy Holly was a[nother] big favourite.

According to Richard Fariña, Buddy Holly was 'the first person that Dylan and I ever talked about, when we hung out together'. Dylan may even have been clearing the way for his coming out ball when he told Gil Turner, for a *Sing Out!* cover story that fall, that his influences included Hank Williams, Muddy Waters and Jelly Roll Morton, three of rock'n'roll's most vital progenitors. Turner even dared to describe Dylan in the article as the 'Elvis Presley of folk music'.

It had been eight years since Elvis had thrown the whole of traditional song – and Crudup's song is as much a composite of traditional tropes as any Robert Johnson track – into a musical melting pot and stirred it up. For most of that time, Dylan had been valiantly trying to make the whole thing blend. The only question on his – and presumably Grossman's – mind was whether now was the time to unveil his true musical roots, or was the folk world not quite ready to take him at his hip-shakin' word.

1.6

May 1941 to June 1959: Have You Heard The News?

Cynthia Gooding: I first heard [you]... three years ago in Minneapolis, and at that time you were thinking of being a rock'n'roll singer ...
Bob Dylan: I was making pretend I was going to school out there – I'd just come in from South Dakota.

Folksinger's Choice, February 1962

[We] always knew that Bobby had a real streak of talent, but we didn't know what kind. We just could not corral it.

Abraham Zimmerman, October 1963

He never wanted anyone to know *anything* about him.

A Hibbing High School classmate

We were sitting around shooting the bull with Barry Kornfeld ... and somehow it came out that Jack [Elliott] had grown up in Ocean Parkway, [Brooklyn] and was named Elliott Adnopoz. Bobby literally fell off his chair ... A lot of us had suspected that Bobby was Jewish; after that we had no doubts.

Dave Van Ronk

I found out for sure that his name was Robert Allen Zimmerman when I saw his draft card. In spite of myself, I was upset that he hadn't ever said anything about it.

Suze Rotolo*

---

* It may have been the *Little Sandy Review*'s May 1962 article on Dylan which blew his cover among Village contemporaries, referring as it did to 'Bob [being] listed in official university enrollment records as Robert Zimmerman'.

Bob and I were good friends, but I ... must say he was always a little eccentric. He sort of lived with the times, or better yet, made up his own times.

Ron Joelson

I used to listen and play music [all the time in Hibbing]. That really took me to where I thought I wanted to go.

Dylan, to Tony Glover, January 1971

*

1954 had been an important year for popular music – not that one would necessarily glean this from the *Billboard* Hot Hundred, which failed to register either the release in Britain of the Lonnie Donegan-led Chris Barber Jazz Band's loose adaptation of Lead Belly's 'Rock Island Line' or of Elvis Presley's rocked-up reinvention of Arthur Crudup's 'That's All Right Mama' in Memphis, Tennessee, both recorded in July of that year; the twin pivots on which the music of the sixties will hinge.*

It was also an important year for the thirteen-year-old Robert Allen Zimmerman, a Jewish boy living in Hibbing, Minnesota, with his parents, Abe and Beattie, and his six-year-old sibling, David. He became a man in Jehovah's eyes, after a highly traditional bar mitzvah two days before his thirteenth birthday (May 24th), while learning to play rudimentary boogie-woogie piano. The two could conceivably have crossed over. According to Dylan *circa* 1985, he undertook instruction in Hebrew from Rabbi Reuben Maier in his rooms above 'a rock'n'roll cafe where I used to hang out'. Though the L&B Cafe on Howard Street was a good two years away from recognizing rock'n'roll, there was a piano in the back room and a jukebox.

Bobby would soon use both as a way to connect with his (mostly Christian) contemporaries in a world divided in two – Family and 'others' – which his mother tried to bridge on his behalf. According to Beattie, her attempt to assimilate into Hibbing society extended to the guest list for her son's bar mitzvah, in the ballroom of the Andro Hotel, 'The Grand Old Lady of Howard Street', which included not

---

* 'Rock Island Line' did go Top Ten stateside, but in April 1956, much to Alan Lomax's chagrin, after Donegan claimed copyright on a traditional song Alan and his father John had already assigned to themselves.

only Jewish friends and relatives but Christian friends and neighbours, too. Family and friends of both faiths reported how impressively Bobby read from the Torah and chanted the requisite traditional melodies.

It was young Bobby's largest audience to date. Of the 400 folks in attendance, many from his extended Jewish family in nearby Connor's Point and places as far-flung as his birthplace, Duluth, Minnesota, and Superior, Wisconsin, named after the great lake on the edge of which both towns sat, which would provide him with some of his earliest memories.

Bobby's boyhood friend Louie, also from Duluth, remembers 'a thriving Jewish community ... Bobby spent his early years in the heart of it, on 3rd Avenue East ... just blocks away from two synagogues that everybody called the 3rd Street Shul and the 4th Street Synagogue. ... [Even after] he had moved with his family to Hibbing ... Bobby often spent weekends in our home town.'

Even before he met Louie in 1953, Bobby felt himself being repeatedly called 'home', suggesting in *Chronicles*, 'Sometimes on weekends my parents would drive down from the Iron Range to Duluth and drop me off at [my grandmother's] place for a couple of days.' From her window, 'on the top floor of a duplex', he could supposedly see Lake Superior and hear the sound of foghorns in stereo, rolling across the lake.*

Five years later, he remembered 'the way the wind blows around the grain elevators. The train yards go on forever, too. It's old-age industrial ... You'll see it from the top of the hill for miles and miles before you get there.' He was no less impressionistic in 2017: 'I was born in Duluth – industrial town, shipyards, ore docks, grain elevators, mainline train yards, switching yards. It's on the banks of Lake Superior, built on granite rock. Lot of foghorns, sailors, loggers, storms, blizzards.'

In fact, Bobby never really accepted Hibbing as home. Uprooted at the age of six and planted in the midst of a town less than a fifth the size of Duluth,† he withdrew into himself, his behaviour all the more

---

* Presumably, Dylan means his paternal grandmother, Anna Zimmerman, née Greenstein, who was born in Odessa and emigrated to America in 1910. However, any such visits must have ended when Dylan was pretty young. Anna died in St Paul in April 1955, having lived with her son, Maurice, in Hibbing for 'some years'.
† Hibbing had a post-war population of about 18,000, Duluth was close to 105,000 in 1950.

marked because his mother was, in the words of local musician Kevin Odegard – who came to know both mother *and* son – 'everything Bob [i]s not: outgoing, effusive, warm, charming and socially adept'.

Beattie welcomed one and all, even in times of mourning. As she told a journalist in 1990, 'I got on with everyone. When a Christian friend died, [and] they wanted to have the wake in my house, instead of in a funeral home, I said, "Okay, but I don't serve ham."' Later on, she suggested that 'living in a town like Hibbing made me all the more conscious of living in the outside world'. If Christian neighbours were invited to the Zimmermans' for potato pancakes on Hannukah, the Zimmermans in turn attended midnight mass at the Catholic church on Christmas Eve, an experience which may have made a deeper impression on her elder son than Beattie perhaps realized.

But no matter how integrated the Zimmermans tried to be, the Iron Range's unique demographic told against them. In 1910 – when Grandma Zimmerman arrived from Odessa – out of a population of 77,000 on 'The Range', Jews numbered fewer than a thousand, joint sixteenth with Bulgarians. The Finns were the largest group, numbering over 11,000, followed by Slovenians. Both groups had a long-standing tradition of working open-cast mines like the one encircling Hibbing, making it the iron-ore capital of the USA.

The attraction of the place for the Zimmermans was not the mines. Rather, it was the miners and the family Beattie had left behind when she married Abraham on June 10th, 1934, and moved to Duluth. Dave Engel, trying to depict post-war Hibbing through Bobby's eyes in his 1997 study *Dylan in Minnesota*, described how 'everywhere Bobby goes is family. At the clothing store, Grandma and Uncle Lewis Stone ... At this new Chisholm furniture store, Uncle Henry Goldfine; Uncle Henry and Aunt Irene buy a nice two-storey house on the west side of Hibbing. Not far away are Uncle Paul Zimmerman and Grandma Zimmerman. At the theaters, at school and all around town are numerous Edelsteins representing several generations.' When Grandma Zimmerman died in April 1955, she left five sons, one daughter and fourteen grandchildren, including Bobby and David. As Dylan himself would relate, 'My grandmother had about seventeen kids on the one side ... So there was always a lot of family-type people around.'

There were real commercial opportunities in Hibbing, too, thanks to a war boom in iron ore that had – temporarily, it turned out – given the miners disposable income to spend on goods like the ones they sold at the Zimmermans' electrical store in Hibbing. Bobby, though, wasn't the only Zimmerman who didn't want to be there. His father, who had contracted polio in the mid-forties, a decade before the Salk vaccine was developed, had been obliged to give up a good job in the oil industry and take something less physically demanding, joining his two brothers running their Hibbing store. Dylan later suggested, 'My father was a very active man, but ... the illness put an end to all his dreams.' Dylan wasn't going to allow that to happen to *him*.

Kemp told me his friend just 'dealt with [his father's polio] – it didn't affect Bob', but I rather suspect it did. However, the real dark cloud hanging over Bobby, leaving his mind 'black with soot', was the town itself, and the pervasive sense of torpor and irremediable decline seeping into every crevice as the iron reserves ran low and munition industries curtailed their orders in peacetime. It was captured in its most unambiguous form in that otherwise highly ambiguous work, *Tarantula*, particularly in an early draft:

<u>youve never been here</u>. where
i live. <u>theres nothing to do here</u>.
the only thing that keeps the area going is
tradition. <u>there certainly isnt
any work</u> ... everything around
me <u>is rotting</u> ... i refuse to be
a part of it ... i'll do anything to leave here ...*

What he omits on publication only serves to explicate a later passage which represents the thoughts of a fifteen-year-old boy on the Iron Range: 'i dont know how long it has been this way, but if it keeps up, soon i will be an old man – & i am only 15 – the only job around here is mining – but jesus, who wants to be a miner.' Such frank autobiography, hidden within the rap-tap-tapping of a mind going off the rails in this impenetrable impasse of a 'novel', sticks out like Tom Thumb.

It was probably put here because few would realize that the 'real' Bobby Zimmerman had such thoughts, then or now. Only in 2001 did he again attempt to come clean, telling an interviewer, 'I was born

---

* The sections underlined were subsequently deleted or rewritten.

very far from where I [was] supposed to be ... on the way to nowhere. You probably couldn't find it on a map.' As a result, 'Mostly what I did growing up was bide my time.'

Between 1948 and 1953, he did little else but bide his time – and read to escape. If what he wrote in an early draft of *Chronicles* is true, he tore through Grimm's Fairy Tales and the works of Jules Verne, H. G. Wells and Edgar Allan Poe. All of them – even Poe – created worlds wholly alien to the one Bobby daily inhabited. If he would later develop a taste for the gritty realism of John Steinbeck, it was only after he was exposed to the Hollywood version – James Dean in *East of Eden* – by which time his moodiness manifested itself in teenage angst, externalized by the music on the local cafe's jukebox.

For now he kept it all hidden, save for the occasional poem he began to write around the age of eight or ten. According to his parents, interviewed in 1963, 'He was always fond of poetry and started writing verses, which [we] ... saved, when he was only eight.' A year later, Dylan himself spoke of a need 'to get back to writing like I used to when I was ten – having everything come out naturally'.

In fact, between 1964 and 1966 he talked a lot about what he called his 'insanity poetry', the stuff he wrote 'at the age of eight and ten' – the wild mercury years. The most lucid of those comments came on the *Les Crane* TV show in February 1965, where he made a clear distinction between 'these insane things [one writes] down when you really don't know what else to do' and the period 'when I started writing songs', which he dated quite specifically to '*after* I heard Hank Williams', which was probably 1953, when he was eleven or twelve.

Dating that epiphany accurately is no sea breeze. In a 1966 conversation, Dylan insisted, 'I played Hank Williams songs when I was ten years old,' i.e. 1951, while in the unreliable *Chronicles*, he suggests he first 'heard Hank ... singing on the Grand Ole Opry ... [He] sang "Move It On Over", a song about living in the doghouse ... [and] spirituals like "When God Comes And Gathers His Jewels" and "Are You Walking And A-Talking For The Lord?"'* But 'Move It On Over'

---

* He asserted in a 2015 interview that he heard Hank 'way early, when he was still alive'. His brother David has suggested that Bobby's 'preoccupation with death' came 'out of Hank Williams's'. Dylan's comments on *Les Crane* and elsewhere suggest any real interest was posthumous.

was released in 1947, when Bobby was six, and two years before Hank played at the Grand Ole Opry.

He didn't need to hear Hank to know he was different. As he told Victor Maymudes, 'I knew I was on fire when I was eleven.' He just hadn't yet made a song and dance about it. Beattie preferred to paint a picture for the Minnesota Historical Society of 'a quiet and polite boy, sitting on the couch during ... [social] gatherings at her home, writing poems that [she] would later find scattered throughout the house'.

The first family member to really take notice of his early scribblings was not Beattie. Rather, it was her sister, Irene, who told his mother that she believed Bobby would become a writer. High school changed all that, perhaps inspiring a comment Dylan jotted in a notebook the year after his motorcycle accident: 'To kill the creative child who writes creative things ... send him to a creative school.' If he had no intention of doing this with his own, his parents conformed to the norm. For eternal outsiders like them and their forefathers, there was nothing more desirable than belonging.

For the young Bobby, belonging was never an option. As he openly admitted in 1978, 'Other than my family, I didn't have many friends.' A lot of the time he didn't necessarily feel like letting even his family in. According to brother David, 'When he was nine or ten, he put his pajamas on backward, [put on] an old fedora of his father's ... and strapped on a cap-gun holster. "Who are you supposed to be?" [I] asked. "If you don't know," Bob said, "I'm not gonna tell you."'

If Bobby the Elder already had Mystery written across his forehead, he did try to participate in some of the other kids' games. One of the more popular proved a little too rich for his blood, although he remembered it well enough to describe it in the early stages of *Chronicles*. It involved using guns that fired rubber pellets which from ten feet away 'could maim somebody', and from a greater distance could still leave welts that hurt for days. He even alleges that a couple of his contemporaries got blinded in these rubber gun fights, presumably those who failed to protect themselves with garbage can shields, as he did.

This being the summer, and hot as hell, single-layer clothing provided no protection at all, whereas in the winter – *No Direction* Dylan recalls – 'you just wore two or three shirts at a time – slept in your clothes', because the Midwest was a place where the climate was extreme: 'Frostbite in the winter, mosquito-ridden in the summer, no air conditioning when I grew up, steam heat in the winter.' Many years later, when he paid a private visit to John Lennon's Liverpudlian childhood home, and sat in his old friend's cold bedroom, he told the guide his one memory of his own childhood was 'the cold'.

In both *Chronicles* and *No Direction Home*, he cites another big chill which pervaded the fifties – the Cold War. Even in the Midwest, far away from any strategic centre, it was a part of his daily reality: 'Back then people feared the end of time. The big showdown between capitalism and communism was on the horizon.' As a result, teachers 'would show you in school, how to dive for cover under your desk'.

Though the *Chronicler* suggests that growing up under such a cloud of fear 'robs a child of his spirit', that was one thing no one could take away from Bobby. Anyway, 'Rock'n'roll made you oblivious to the fear, busted down the barriers . . . ideologies put up', or so he came to believe.

If he had any ambitions pre-rock'n'roll, it was to be a lawyer or a soldier, or so he informed Jeff Rosen: 'I thought about going to military school . . . I could always envision myself dying in some heroic battle.' He may have begun taking an interest in military school because his own Neal Cassady had been dispatched to just such a school. As Kemp recalls, the father of their mutual friend had 'finally got so fed up with having to pick him up from St Paul Central High School for misbehaving that he enrolled Larry in military school'.

When the realization dawned on Bobby that he did not have what it took to be eligible for West Point – his name didn't have a 'de' or 'Von' before it – he began to conceive of becoming a trial lawyer, modelling himself on Charles Darrow, if not Orson Welles's version of Darrow in 1959's *Compulsion*. As he wrote in that Austrian spring of 1999, realization soon dawned that even this was wholly impractical.

What was left to him, or so he thought, was sport or entertainment, and his build and stature was not condusive to the former. By the age of thirteen, when Bobby and Larry were reunited at camp, the third option – the world of Entertainment – not merely loomed large, but had become all-consuming, for both of them.

In the mythical biographies he would create over the next decade and a half, Dylan would invariably begin running away from Hibbing at the symbolic age of twelve – the age he was when he met Larry and heard his first Hank Williams record. In conversation with a French reporter – the day he turned twenty-five – he colourfully attributed his epiphany to another Williams – someone he would know later on:

> **Q:** At what age did you leave home?
> **BD:** At twelve, when I had had enough of helping my father moving refrigerators. I became the manager of a very famous popular blues singer, Big Joe Williams. It was the first time I ran away.

It was a witty twist on the version of autobiography most often quoted – Dylan's 1963 bio-poem, *A Life In Stolen Moments* – in which he described Hibbing as 'a good ol'' town / I ran away from it when I was 10, 12, 13, 15, 15½, 17 an 18'.*

He never did run away, save in his imagination, the part of him that had opened wide thanks to Hank Williams and now teemed with possibilities. This was, according to the 1997 Dylan, 'The reason I can stay so single-minded about my music ... because it affected me at an early age in a very, very powerful way and it's all that affected me. It's all that ever remained true for me.' He went as far as expressing relief 'that this particular music reached me when it did because frankly, if it hadn't, I don't know what would have become of me'.

The 'particular music' he means was not rock'n'roll, though. His bond with Larry (and Hank) predated rock'n'roll by a good two years. Which is why, when asked, 'Why did you change your style to the big beat?' at one of those conference contretemps from 1966, he was at pains to put the pressman right: 'You don't understand, people in the United States who are my age now have been raised on ... country & western music ... It's something I played when I was twelve years old. I was raised on Hank Williams and Lefty Frizzell. That's all I could hear on the radio.'

The radio was young Bobby's lifeline, a link to this other world. And thanks to a father who worked at an electrical store, he lived in

---

* This poem appeared in a number of press packs and concert programmes from 1963 through 1965.

a household where it was part of the furniture. One day in 1953, he turned it on and heard a voice speaking directly to *him*:

> I heard Hank Williams. I think [it was] 'Kaw Liga', and [the DJ] said he was dead. Hank's voice stopped me in my tracks. It was from the same world as the Stanley [Brothers] but from [a] more focused part of it – it was more explanatory [*sic*] and less mysterious, more jolting and spine-tingling, especially the voice, [which] was coming from one man instead of many – I went to the record store and the store had a few of his records – I asked the man to play them and went into the listening booth to hear them.

In another autobiographical vignette, written in the late nineties, he attempted to describe the first song he learnt to play, suggesting that hearing Hank and picking up a guitar happened almost simultaneously. According to this older Zimmerman, from this day on he listened to Hank Williams on the radio until he had the money to buy one of his records. At the same time, his doting mother ordered a Silvertone guitar for her elder son from the Sears catalogue, not realizing it needed amplification. Undeterred, Bobby would place the top of the guitar-neck against the frosted window to get some kind of sound while he taught himself 'My Son Calls Another Man Daddy'. But when he played it to some school chums, they informed him they didn't 'get' the song. Convinced they were rolling their eyes at him behind his back, this was the last time he sprung a song on a hometown audience without testing their level of musical appreciation first.

The choice of song itself is suggestive. 'My Son Calls Another Man Daddy' was hardly one of Hank's top pop picks, being the B-side to 1950's 'Long Gone Lonesome Blues'. But it was just one of a series of songs 'the sound of [which] made me feel like I was somebody else and that I was maybe not even born to the right parents', a chilling remark he made after his mother passed in 2000. Others which conjured up a similar feeling included a version of a well-known gospel hymn, 'Driftin' Too Far From Shore' – probably Roy Acuff's – and a song called 'The Drunkard's Son' he found on a Hank Snow record, the lyrics of which he transcribed and signed, as if they were his very own.

'The Drunkard's Son', credited to 'Clarence E. Snow' on Snow's 1950 single, was in fact a thinly veiled rewrite of a song by the father of country, Jimmie Rodgers, 'A Drunkard's Child'. Soon the young Bobby became immersed in both country artists, probably after purchasing Snow's 1953 album, *Hank Snow Salutes Jimmie Rodgers*. Describing that album in 1997, he noted, 'The songs were different than the norm. They had more of an individual nature and an elevated conscience.'

Snow was one Hank he really could have heard a number of times on the Grand Ole Opry. If so, he was one of the last. The Opry had become complacent about its position, and proved slow to react when its radio rival, the Louisiana Hayride, out of Shreveport, Louisiana, showed the way ahead. By 1955, the Opry was only for those in need of a nostalgia fix, as the Hayride rode the coat tails of a new country sound. Having taken Hank Williams back in September 1952, just three months before his untimely and unglamorous demise, dead drunk in the back of a limousine on New Year's Day 1953, the Hayride soon began to champion a country blues artist called Elvis Aaron Presley, starting October 16th, 1954. Both sides of Presley's debut Sun single, 'That's All Right Mama' b/w 'Blue Moon of Kentucky', were performed that evening, blowing a hole in teenage listeners' minds.

Whether Bobby was attuned enough to hear that seminal broadcast, we don't know. But Elvis performed the A-side no fewer than five times on the Hayride over the next ten months, including his final appearance in August 1955, by which time he had surely crossed an attuned Bobby's radar. By then, there was not just Elvis. The tsunami of fledgling rockers who emerged in the eighteen months after his Sun debut was something to behold, and hard to grasp, though Dylan came close in an autobiographical note he wrote in the late 1990s:

> In a blinding flash ... in the middle fifties these faces: Elvis, Jerry Lee, Carl Perkins, Little Richard, Fats Domino, Buddy Holly, and ... others, but in a lesser way, sent the most powerful messages; were [in fact] the most powerful people on the planet, even if each of them only made one record. This was the era when the atom bomb was unleashed, and these people reflected it – they came forth with power, truth and beauty ... and all of us who were there can still feel it.

It was not just these artists who were breaking rules. The labels themselves had started developing sounds all their own. As Dylan opined on his *Theme Time Radio Hour* show, in 2007, 'When you dropped the needle on a Speciality Record, you knew it was a Speciality Record. Same with Imperial, Chess, King and a million others. [But] perhaps the most distinctive were those that came out of the Sam Phillips Memphis Recording Studio and were put out on the Sun record label.'

For him, the Sun sound would never be topped. And as of 1956, there was another Sun recording artist who would shape his own cosmology forever and a day: Johnny Cash, whose debut single, 'I Walk The Line', Dylan remembered being 'played all summer on the radio, and it was different from anything else you had ever heard. It was profound, and so was the tone of it, every line: deep and rich, awesome and mysterious all at once.'

After his experience playing a Hank song to his fellow Hibbingites, the more adult concerns of Cash were to remain a private passion, largely confined to bedroom listening sessions, some with John Bucklen, a high school pupil from the year below, whose father was a musician and ex-miner. Later, he would produce the guitar he rarely brought out, and play along.

By 1956, Dylan had switched to piano for public performances, in love with Little Richard's Speciality sound. In a world where he still helped his dad move refrigerators – presumably in return for all the records he put on his father's account at the local music store, Crippa's – he was found by school friends like Pat Mestek in 'his father's store. There was an old piano in the back and ... Bobby was supposed to be stocking shelves, or sweeping or something. But he would be pounding on that piano, making his own melodies [while] his father would say, "Don't make so much noise!"'

By December 1956, his piano-playing was deemed sufficiently competent – at least by his close friend Larry – to make a record. It was Christmas Eve and Bobby was in St Paul, of all places, with Kegan and a cousin named Howard Rutman, when they decided to pay the five dollars necessary to make a double-sided, eight-minute acetate of the three of them singing a medley of their favourite songs.

They called themselves The Jokers, an apposite name considering what they proceeded to do to 'Let The Good Times Roll', 'Boppin' The Blues', 'I Want You To Be My Gal', 'Lawdy Miss Clawdy', 'Ready

Teddy', 'Confidential', 'In The Still Of The Night' and 'Earth Angel'. With Bobby frequently drowned out by the atonal acrobatics of his off-key friends, the record hints at, well, nothing but three friends hopped up on Christmas bonhomie.

Compare it with two similar acetates an undiscovered Elvis made at Sun in 1953–4, and they are an ocean apart. Although the Ten O'Clock Scholar, where *Dylan* would be born in three years' time, was just a few blocks from the Terlinde Music Shop's recording booth, in terms of potential the kid was light years away.

Perhaps the type of material was holding him back. If 'Lawdy Miss Clawdy' was meant to suggest Elvis, and 'Boppin' The Blues' Carl Perkins, it was in name only. Most of the others were doo-wop standards, which required harmony singing – a talent Dylan would never fully master.*

According to Rutman, The Jokers was a real combo, playing high-school dances and dreaming of greater things, 'We were hugely ambitious and we really wanted to do stuff.' Yet Kemp rightly dismisses his account: 'Larry and Bob would sing at camp all the time, and in the city they would jam together. But that record was a one-off. That guy Howard may have sung with them the odd time, [but] he lived in St Paul.'

Bobby was going to have to find a backing band nearer, a lot nearer, to his Hibbing home if he was going to make it. But make it, he insisted he would. As Kemp affirms, 'He was one of the most determined people I'd ever met. He always would tell me – and the other people at the camp – that he was going to be a rock'n'roll star, that was his goal. It never wavered in all the time I knew him.' Even those at his high school soon knew about his dreams. He even passed a note to a friend in English class that read, 'I'm going to make it big. I know it for sure, and when I do, you bring this piece of paper and for two months you can stay with me, no matter where I'm at.'

Also captured on one of John Bucklen's 1957 tapes is an exchange in which Bucklen and the young Zimmerman pretend to be in a recording studio, and the young Bobby is saying, 'I make up a song. I know it's gonna sell a million copies. I start to record it and some

---

* When an optimistic legatee tried to auction said record after Kegan's death in 2001, it failed to reach its six-figure reserve.

bum comes along and says to stop "songing", because it's not gonna sell.' Already, he is imagining obstacles he must overcome even as he has begun writing songs in his head.

Yet he took his own sweet time putting together a home-town band, as if still unsure whether to emerge from his bitterly cold chrysalis. One challenge he was still struggling to resolve six decades later had not arisen during his impromptu sessions at Herzl: finding musicians who'd play *his way*. There was another, more practical concern – where to play if one doesn't want to simply (re)play the hits of the day. As he later said of the 'small dance bands' who did exactly that, 'It always seemed like background music.' As a result, a still-vexed Dylan noted in 2000 that his early combos 'rehearsed and played where we could play, [but] there wasn't much opportunity to really break out of that area'.*

He wanted to make an *impression*. Easier said than done. Jim Dickinson – who was raising hell with The Regents at the exact same time, and would finally record with Dylan in 1997 – quickly found 'other bands ... played ... more acceptable music ... There was nothing acceptable about the music that we played, and there was certainly no way to make it into a career.' And that was when one came from *Memphis*!

In mid-fifties Hibbing, they still played polkas in the taverns on a Saturday night. At least the polka bands were loud, but not as loud – by all accounts – as Bobby's first *serious* Hibbing band, The Golden Chords, formed in the fall of 1957. Even in 1986 Dylan liked to boast that the Chords were 'just the loudest band around ... What we were doing, there wasn't anyone else around doing.' Rock'n'roll was here to stay, and the town elders could go hang.

In forming the Chords, Bobby stuck to a three-piece – piano, guitar and drums – recruiting Monte Edwardson, the hottest guitarist in school, and Leroy Hoikkala, who liked to hit things. They began playing regularly at Van Feldt's snack bar and a small barbecue-joint called Collier's on Sunday afternoons, in preparation for the big day – February 6th, 1958 – when they would play the Jacket Jamboree in

---

* His first band, The Shadow Blasters, lasted just long enough to play a talent show at the high school in April 1957. 'A sensational novelty number', mentioned in the school paper's preview, turned out to be Bobby doing Little Richard's 'Jenny Jenny' till he broke the piano pedal, perhaps his way of saying he wasn't a novelty act.

front of the whole high school. Second on the bill to the coronation of the homecoming queen, it was a scene that wouldn't have been out of place in *National Lampoon's Animal House*. Those who knew the band from Collier's dug it. The rest of the place – and the capacious auditorium could hold 1,800 – looked like they'd just witnessed *Springtime for Hitler*.

Remarkably, photos from this performance survive, preserved by Hoikkala. They capture the moment perfectly. There is Bobby, sporting a Penniman pompadour, while most of the girls crowding the wings either have their mouths agape or are thinking about it. Yet, according to his current girlfriend, Echo Helstrom, 'Bob was sort of oblivious to the whole fact that people were not turned on by his music … There was this cat, playing like they were clapping, when they were really booing.' In this freeze-frame moment, he already knew that this is where he belonged. Notoriety was a whole lot better than being a nonentity.

Three weeks later, the Chords played a headlining gig at the National Guard Armory, which the local newspaper saw fit to advertise as a 'Rock'n'Roll HOP FOR TEEN-AGERS … Intermission Entertainment by Hibbing's Own GOLDEN CHORDS FEATURING: Monte Edwardson Leroy Hoikkala [and] Bobby Zimmerman.' This was as good as it got, for now.

But he had made a tactical mistake getting people to back him who could actually play. Edwardson and Hoikkala were good enough to be lured away by the promise of more regular gigs. And lured away they were, something which still bugged Bob a quarter of a century later: 'Lead singers would always come in and take my bands, because they would have connections, like, maybe their fathers would know somebody.' The hackles stay up unto *Chronicles*: 'I couldn't understand how this was possible … These guys weren't any better at singing or playing than I was.'

It never seems to have occurred to him that Edwardson and Hoikkala might have *wanted* out. They weren't in this for the long haul. They were in it to have fun. To play, not just rehearse. By the end of 1958, the pair had joined the newly formed Rockets, a two-guitar, no piano combo featuring Jim Propotnick and Rod Taddei, that aimed to play what people wanted to hear, not what their singer had discovered at Crippa's or by mail order from Virginia, Minnesota, that week.

By late 1958, Dylan's real passion was R&B, as he expressed on one of the home tapes his friend Bucklen made, 'Rhythm and blues is something that you can't quite explain ... [but] when you hear a good rhythm and blues song, chills go up your spine.' That is the effect he was presumably reaching for when performing his first original song live. 'Big Black Train' ordered a locomotive which has 'got my woman ... [to] bring her back to me'.

The essential problem, one noted by his brother's classmate Bill Berg – who saw Bobby's new combo, The Satin Tones, at the St Louis County Fairgrounds Grandstand in September 1958 (and would play with Dylan in somewhat more auspicious circumstances in December 1974) – was that most folks weren't 'quite into the things Bobby was doing. He was ahead of his time, even then.' It was back to the future with Bobby.

At the show in question, the Tones went head to head with the newly fired up Rockets, whose bass guitarist remembers, 'Zimmerman did a good job on Little Richard songs.' But in the end, Bobby's 'wild Elvis rendition', duly noted by the local newspaper, lost out to The Rockets in any popularity contest, prompting Bobby to ditch the Tones.

When Rod Taddei left for college, Bobby swallowed his pride and auditioned to rejoin his own band – as he saw it – on *guitar*. The audition went surprisingly well, Propotnick recalling, 'We went over our songs and he seemed to fit right in'. But Bobby was never going to be content playing second fiddle – or plain ol' electric rhythm – something he never quite mastered. As Propotnick recalls, 'Bob had eclectic tastes, even back then ... He'd go from one thing to the next, always looking for something different – changing out players, instruments etc.' He was looking to do some of his own stuff. Again, Propotnick recalls he was met with short shrift: 'Occasionally, he'd try to get us to do one or two of his own songs and we always blew him off.'

All too soon, he was deemed surplus to the Rockets' requirements, replaced by Dave Karakash, putting The Rockets into reverse thrust and consigning them to music history's footnotes. If his fellow Rockets had found Bobby hard to handle, by the end of 1958 they were not alone in noticing a new edge to the former goody two-shoes.

Bobby the poet had even penned what he called (semi-seriously) a 'good poem'. Though it was anything but, it did betray a rare gift for self-analysis, describing 'a boy in school / Who don't live by no rule /

He hands everyone lots of sass / Thinking no one will kick his ass ... / Jimmy, he thinks himself like / Just 'cause he owns a motorbike / He's a little, fuzzy kid, not too tall / And boy, is he heading for a fall.'

The acquisition of a motorcyle sometime in 1956 or 1957 had turned Abe and Beattie's blue-eyed son into something of a terror around town as he self-consciously became Hibbing's very own hologram version of the biker Brando played in *The Wild One*, a 1953 movie that gave teen rebellion an image a full year and a half before it had a concomitant soundtrack.

He even had Black Rebels Motorcycle Club – the name of Brando's gang in the movie – stencilled to his leather jacket as he played 'chicken' with his uncomprehending brother, a game he had learnt from another movie he caught at one of his uncle's movie houses, this one released in October 1955, *Rebel Without A Cause*. The 'Jimmy he thinks himself like' was, of course, James Dean, Dylan admitting in 1971 that he didn't ever 'think I wanted to *be* James Dean, but there was a time when he blocked out everybody else.' This was that time. The method-acting rebel in that generation-defining movie learns his lesson only when a game of 'chicken' results in another kid driving off a cliff while a disconsolate Dean looks on. The only one traumatised by Bobby's own variant was brother David:

> **Kevin Odegard**: There's a thin line to being terrorised, and being taunted by an older brother, and that motorcycle was the line. He'd run right up into the driveway and head for David, and veer off at the last minute ... David told that to me ... I'm not the only person you'll hear that from. You'll hear that from childhood friends in Hibbing ... There was sibling rivalry, but David was more plaintive than [amused]. He was telling me, 'It's not easy being this guy's brother. It never has been and it never will be.'

Bobby became particularly difficult after Larry Kegan's tragic accident in March 1958, which seemed to send his buddy temporarily off the rails, as if the mantle of wild child had now passed to him. At the same time, his grades began to dip and for the first time he failed to make his year's honor roll. His parents may even have tried a short, sharp shock, sending him briefly to a kind of 'country club reform school'. Dylan certainly mentioned to Maymudes (and Al Aronowitz) about 'going to juvenile hall'. And in a 1962 poem later auctioned from Suze Rotolo's private collection, he suggested that in such a place one 'quickly realized there was a social structure ... either you're going to get along or you really shouldn't be there'. He even hinted to early confidants that he spent time at Red Wing, the reform school – which he certainly never did.

Abe and Beattie hinted at the difficulties their elder son had presented in his youth in a 1963 interview with a local journalist, portraying their Bobby as someone who 'impressed his peers and adults alike as being intelligent but unsettled, even [if] his parents concede that they found some of his ways distressing'.

If he was really sent somewhere other than Camp Herzl in the summer of 1958 – and it seems he was – it had negligible effect, though his grades in his final high school year did improve as the realization dawned that he would need good grades if he was ever to escape, to college – and freedom.

In preparation for the great breakout, throughout his final two years of school he undertook a series of trial runs for the great escape which centred on the bright lights of Duluth and St Paul, in that order. As Louie Kemp recalls, 'Bobby grew more restless the older he got. When he couldn't take it anymore, he'd bum a ride or hop a Greyhound from Hibbing to Duluth in search of a little action. The minute he arrived, we'd take my dad's car and head out to the East End to grab burgers at the London Inn Drive-in, the primo hangout for the youth of Duluth.'

And when Bobby didn't have the time or the funds to head for St Paul, there was always Superior, 'the notorious red-light, gambling town' of his fertile imagination, just across the suspension bridge from Duluth – but now in Wisconsin, which is where he later claimed to have had his first experience of live R&B, in a bingo parlour, as some unnamed conduit belted out Little Willie John's 1956 classic, 'Fever'.

At both the Duluth–Superior axis and the St Paul pitstop there were also *girls*. Bobby the performer liked to entertain 'em, to make 'the girls wiggle ... making them jump up and down / And mingle in their socks and [in] their britches', as he lasciviously put it in an impromptu 1967 rewrite of Bobby Bare's 'All American Boy', released in 1958.

He soon found he had something of a gift for it – and for infidelity. Through much of 1957 and 1958 he had been 'going steady' with the bashful blonde of Swedish descent, evocatively called Echo. But, as she later ruefully recalled, 'He began taking off every weekend, going down to Minneapolis or St Paul – to listen to music, he said – but I knew he was seeing other girls.'

Hers would become a familiar mantra. Echo was not the first, nor the last. According to Dylan, the former honour was reserved for Gloria Story, a girl from camp, which was where he also became smitten by Judy Rubin, the St Paul girl he mooned over for most of the late fifties. Simply put, in John Bucklen's words, 'He was ... very successful with girls ... this little pudgy-faced kid, you know.' The self-confidence it took to mount a stage determined to do his own thing had found another outlet, one where success was measurable and often immediate. Bucklen was impressed by his peer: 'If he wanted to talk to some [girl], he wouldn't be shy about going up and talking with them ... He had a kind of quiet manner about him like he was shy ... [but] he was *bold*.'

It helped that Bobby grew up surrounded by female cousins – some of whom, real or imagined, would later turn up on tour, much to the amusement of a sceptical road crew. One of these, called Reenie in *Chronicles*, would 'come along ... when I played at different places ... One time she asked me why I was using a different name when I played ... in the neighboring towns ... "Who's Elston Gunn? That's not you, is it?"' It was.

Echo also later described an occasion when her boyfriend ran all the way to her house to announce he had thought of a stage name. Years later, she convinced herself he'd said Dylan, but it was surely Elston Gunn (with just two n's for now). Bobby even fleetingly put together his own, Duluth-based band with assorted cousins in the days of '59, and called it Elston Gunn & The Rock Boppers.

In the rock'n'roll era, aliases were all the rage. All three of the acts Bobby went to see play the Duluth Armory on January 31st, 1959 were hiding behind nom de plumes. Charles Hardin Holley, J. P. Richardson and Richard Valenzuela hardly had the same ring as Buddy Holly, the Big Bopper and Ritchie Valens.* Bobby loved them all, but he had a special place in his heart for Buddy, rock's first great white singer-songwriter.

---

* Valens' valedictory hit, 'La Bamba', would later form the basis for Dylan's own radical reinvention of rock, 'Like A Rolling Stone'.

He would famously claim, during a Grammy acceptance speech in 1998, that on this very night he was standing just 'three feet away from him, and he *looked* at me'. He made no mention of his friend, Louie, who was stood alongside him, noticing how 'Bobby stood there mesmerized, never taking his eyes off of Buddy ... Perhaps time has embellished my memory of that night, but Buddy [really] seemed to be smiling down on Bobby.'

Whether or not Buddy did notice Bobby, the symbolism of the moment – just three days before 'the music died' in a flaming plane festooned across an Iowa farm – was not lost on a soon-distraught Dylan. He had lost Hank Williams and Jimmie Rodgers before he was even aware of them; he had lost James Dean and almost his friend Larry to freak accidents; and now, the Winter Dance Party – as Buddy's tour was billed – had become the last dance.

For Bobby, though, the dream was still alive – with the name of his new band a tacit tip of the hat to the late Big Bopper. But if he was going to become 'the jester' in Don McLean's eight-minute paean to rock'n'roll, something needed to change. Well, according to another autobiographical sketch from the late nineties, it did – almost immediately. The day after the Armory gig, Dylan says he heard a song by the Kingston Trio on the radio.*

'Hang Your Head Tom Dooley' was Bobby's introduction to one of America's finest original art forms: the traditional murder ballad. As he went on to write, 'Not long after that, somebody gave me a Lead Belly record. The stuff was pure rock'n'roll.' Bucklen dates this moment specifically to 'just after he'd left high school, but before he left for Minnesota'.† He also recalls it being 'one of [Bobby's] relatives [who] had given him some rare Lead Belly records, old 78s', and that Bobby was so consumed with this new passion, he called him up. 'He thought it was great. I thought, This isn't great.' It was a poignant parting of the ways for two friends who shared a passion for the same kinda music until one of them didn't.

Dylan has also said, 'Before leaving the Iron Range, I'd heard John Jacob Niles.' His introduction to folk music thus came about thanks to three of the post-war revival's most visible proponents of what

---

* Given that it was released in August 1958, and topped the *Billboard* charts in November, it is unlikely it took Dylan this long to hear the song.
† He probably means Fargo, which is where Bobby went after leaving high school.

Dave Harker labels 'fakelore'. In all three instances, the artists bastardized tradition and copyrighted the results – in Lead Belly's case, brilliantly, and with one foot on a tree with roots; the other two, by ersatzing oral tradition till it bled dollars and wept salt tears.

For now, Bobby just filed the stuff away, even as he packed his bags and headed for the destination Buddy Holly et al. were bound on that fateful night in early February: Fargo, North Dakota. He later wrote, 'Got out of high school and left the very next day ... I was gonna try to join some other band.'

He didn't do anything of the sort, though he did leave soon enough, and when he did, he did not envisage returning, as comments he wrote in two female classmates' 1959 yearbooks suggest. He explicitly wrote to one Judy Jane, 'I doubt if I'll ever see you again after school's let out', before wishing Gail 'a real lot of luck in whatever you are gonna do', rather implying their paths would not cross again.* To Jerry, meanwhile, he fondly recalled 'sessions down at Colliers', and suggested he 'keep practicing the guitar and maybe someday you'll be great!' – advice he should perhaps have heeded himself. Instead, he reverted to piano, still bent on 'join[ing] Little Richard', an ambition emblazoned in perpetuity below a photo of him in that 1959 high school yearbook.

According to Engel, the Zimmermans threw a large graduation party for their son, who had made the senior honour roll. Bobby did not stay long. Nor did he stay long in Hibbing. After a brief trip to St Paul to see his aunt and/or renew Herzl acquaintances, he headed for Fargo, where he had somehow inveigled a camp friend into letting him stay at the family home while he indeed tried 'to join some other band':

Ron Joelson: Zimmerman only played piano at that time and wasn't into writing yet, only performing – mostly Little Richard, Jerry Lee Lewis-type basic early rock'n'roll ... After several months [*sic*], Bob ... got an apartment in town. He also got a job bussing tables at the Red Apple Cafe in Fargo ... I remember vividly when he explicitly told me to stop calling him Zimmerman. He was now Elston Gunnn – with three n's.

---

* His inscription to Judy Jane betrays some of the confusion he was feeling as he admits, 'I'm kinda lost for words ... I can't think strait ... my head's going round n round.'

It was while 'bussing tables' that Bobby got a gig with a local band, The Poor Boys, Fargo's answer to The Rockets, thanks to the ever-vigilant Joelson. Just like The Rockets, The Poor Boys came from nowhere, made one abysmal single for a local label, and went straight back there. Joelson's friend didn't even make it to Gig #2:

Bob Becker: Ron mentioned that Bob played piano and said we should give him a try, so we did, but found Bob only played in the key of C and sometimes in the key of A. We used him at Crystal Ballroom in downtown Fargo one Saturday night. This ballroom was tops in Fargo and if you worked for [the owner] Doc Chinn, you were a top band ... He did *not* like rock'n'roll, but had to book some of us because big bands were slowly fading out and combos were becoming popular ... Anyway, [when] Doc came to pay us [he] heard Bob sing[ing] a song and play[ing] piano ... As I approached ... to get our money, he ... said, 'That guy's gotta go!'

Barely was his piano stool pulled away from under him by The Poor Boys than Bobby was back bussing tables. But not for long. Again, a Tonto-less Joelson rode to the rescue, this time selling Bobby's credentials to another local singer, Bobby Vee (né Velline). Vee had just cut his first single, 'Suzie Baby', on the back of a well-received live debut by him and his pick-up band, The Shadows, on February 3rd at a gig in Moorhead, Minnesota, replacing the original headliner, a certain Buddy Holly, who was unavoidably deceased.

By the time Elston showed his face in Fargo, Vee and The Shadows had been trundling around the Midwest for nigh-on six months, hoping 'Suzie Baby' would break on radio and go national – which it eventually did. The Fargo-born Vee had convinced himself that if they added a piano player, 'we would probably have the ultimate rock'n'roll band. So we asked around the Fargo area and a friend of ours suggested a guy that had been staying at his house and working at a cafe ... He was a kinda scruffy little guy, but he ... loved to rock'n'roll ... He wanted us to use the stage name of Elston Gunnn for him. We went out and played a couple of small jobs in North Fargo, then decided ... not to use a piano ... He was a bit disappointed.'

An earlier account of the fateful meeting with Elston removed Joelson entirely from the equation. Rather, Vee asserted, 'One day my brother Bill came home and said he was talking with a guy at Sam's Recordland who claimed he played the piano and had just come off of a tour with Conway Twitty. So Bill made arrangements to audition him at the KFGO studio. ... [He] played "Whole Lotta Shakin' [Goin' On]" in the key of C. Bill [had] said he was a funny little wiry kind of guy and [that] he rocked pretty good ... His first dance with us was in Gwinner, North Dakota ... [but] we decided we didn't need a piano player.'

The outcome was the same: the man who had formed The Shadow Blasters three years earlier was asked to leave The Shadows. Though he told Billy James he was indeed 'a bit disappointed', folksong's Liberty Valance wasn't quite ready to admit his tenure was over before it really began:

I played piano when I was seventeen ... for this rock'n'roll singer. His name is Bobby Vee and he's a big star now, I guess ... That was in Fargo, North Dakota. Then we went all around the Midwest. Went to Wisconsin, Iowa, toured around there and then I left. I was with him ... just about every night, for about a month or two. And then as soon as I left him he got on another recording label and then I saw his picture in big picture magazines ... not too long after that. So that was sort of a disappointment.

A month earlier, Dylan had already boasted to Izzy Young that he 'played piano with Bobby Vee – would have been a millionaire if he stayed with him. Played piano [from] North West to Montana.' He even put a novel spin on his demotion to his parents, his father telling Bob Shelton, 'Bobby went to Fargo to play with him ... [Vee] had his brother and his relatives in the group and he never had room for Bobby. He wrote him a letter and said if any of the boys ever quit, [he] would like to have [him back].' Running into Bucklen on his return to Hibbing, Bobby seemed unchastened. When his school friend asked him what he'd been doing, he said, 'I've been recording for this record label by the name of Bobby Vee.'

Even in the Village he would drop Vee's name as evidence of a prelapsarian interest in rock'n'roll. But what he didn't tell anyone, not even Vee and his band, was that he later snuck into a gig of theirs in New York. The *Chronicle*r would insist this was in early April 1961, a week before his Gerde's debut, and that Vee was playing his 'current' hit, 'Take Good Care Of My Baby' – which was a good three months away from release – on a bill that included The Shirelles, Danny and the Juniors, Jackie Wilson, Ben E. King and Maxine Brown.

There was indeed an Easter Parade of Stars advertised to run for five nights, starting March 31st, at Brooklyn's Paramount Theater. However, Jackie Wilson – though advertised to appear – never played that show. Dion DiMucci did. It is inconceivable that such a long-standing fan of Dion would not remember him appearing at the same show, especially as the last time he would have seen him would have been at the Duluth Armory, on January 31st, 1959.

Perhaps Dylan was outside, chatting to the other Bobby, who – he now tells us – 'was as down-to-earth as ever, was wearing a shiny silk suit and narrow tie, [and] seemed genuinely glad to see me'. All of which is distinctly at odds with what Vee told a Floridian reporter in 1972. According to this Bobby, it was not in Brooklyn but on Staten Island that Dylan came to see them play, and 'he never did come backstage to see us ... Our main thought was wonder[ing] how he had managed to get so far east.'

The truth is Dylan turned his back on rock'n'roll after Buddy died, Elvis joined the army and Bobby Vee turned his back on him. And he was not alone. As he said in 1966, 'At a certain time the whole field got taken over into some milk ... Frankie Avalon, Fabian and this kind of thing ... So everybody got out of it. And I remember when everybody got out of it.'

What can't be known is whether, as of October 1962, Dylan felt he had just been biding his time – as his alter ego Bobby had been, all those years in Hibbing – waiting for Opportunity to come a-knockin'. Or had he always seen what he did then and what he planned to do now as one and the same, and his preordained role was to tie a lover's knot around the red, red rose of folk and rock'n'roll's thorny briar?

1.7

October 1962 to April 1963: A New World Singer In Ye Olde Worlde

When I was seventeen, I started playing folk music. Because it was easier. And the people in it were all very unknown at the time.

Perth press conference, April 1966

I'm a rock'n'roll singer, man. I started out playing rock'n'roll music when I was ten, and I quit when I was seventeen 'cause it was drag. I came from the Midwest. Folk music, pacifist, I learnt these words when I got to New York.

Bob Dylan, May 1966

When Dylan first came to New York, he was just scuffling to get work. He was into different music then – protesting and all that – but ... I believe that he just wanted to be a rock'n'roll star right from the beginning ... His influences are all media and communication.

Mike Bloomfield, June 1968

Dylan [told me] bluntly [at Newport] that he had used topical songs as a vehicle to get to the top and always considered them as a means to an end.

Paul Nelson, July 1965

*

On October 26th, 1962, Dylan resumed recording for Columbia, his (manager's) contract negotiations not so much resolved as self-sabotaged. At least his manager had extracted one important concession: an agreement to record and release a single. With Hammond on board, and a five-piece backing band which included Bruce Langhorne and jazz pianist Dick Wellstood, Dylan clearly intended a major musical departure.*

Over the next two sessions Dylan and the musicians would work on just four songs, two of which he had tackled back in April acoustically: 'Corrina Corrina' and 'Rocks And Gravel'. Both used bluesified arrangements of traditional standards (and were copyrighted accordingly), an acid test for both Dylan and his backing musicians. After the first, incomplete take of the former, Hammond cuts in to inform Dylan, 'You're not doing the traditional thing here, so there's a clash between you and the bass on occasion.' The matter is quickly resolved. They proceed to cut four complete takes (2–4 and 6), before Hammond presses rewind, 'The other one was good, Bobby.'

The intention seems to have been to get a version suitable for the well-advanced second album, which to Dylan's mind needed a couple of electric tracks to signal a possible future direction. Instead, take four would appear on Dylan's next 45.

Now the fun could really start. After what is really just a rehearsal for 'Mixed Up Confusion' – a song Dylan told Izzy Young he wrote on the way to the session† – it is straight into 'That's All Right Mama', already clearly earmarked for a single – hence Hammond's comment at the end of a rockin', reelin' first take, 'That was 3.20. You wanna have it quite that long?' Dylan's response is to tell Hammond, 'Just fade it out when you think', singles being three minutes, a hard-and-fast rule he would shatter irrevocably with his next but one single.

But if Dylan thought that was that, he was quickly disabused. After a second take breaks down, Hammond admonishes Dylan, 'When you do something like this, start it with some *life*! Sounds like you were thinking [about] what you're gonna do two choruses from now.' It is a most uncharacteristic outburst, as if he is not entirely convinced by the choice of song. The chastened singer protests, 'It's hard to feel

---

* Wellstood had recently done arrangements for another of Grossman's clients, Odetta, on her jazz-folk album, *Odetta And The Blues*, so was perhaps his suggestion.
† In his invaluable study *The Formative Dylan* (Scarecrow Press, 2001), Todd Harvey posits that there was a Witmark demo of the song, now lost, throwing some doubt on Dylan's assertion.

that way ... at the beginning,' and launches into a third (unlogged) take, which breaks down even more precipitously, prompting an exchange which is positively headmasterly in tone from Hammond – not that the musicians take a blind bit of notice, having all worked with him before:

John Hammond: You were certain, but the other guys didn't know *what* the hell you were going to do. So, c'mon, get with 'em.
Unknown musician: I think that little intro's nice.
JH: It's nice, Bobby. But do it like you mean it.
Musician: Let's establish your thing with four bars, then come right in with the vocal.
Dylan: You guys wanna come in with me?
Musician: Nah, we'll sneak in. We're waiting for a definite spot.

The dressing-down over, everyone pulls together for two fully focused takes, the second of which is deemed good enough to be lodged with Dylan's music publisher as a reference demo.*

Only now can work really start on what was intended as the A-side of Dylan's 45 debut, 'Mixed Up Confusion'. It would be the start of a long haul, longer even than his next 'single as a single', in June 1965, even if, initially, things go well. After the very first take, Hammond exclaims, 'We almost got something!' After just one more breakdown, they capture it again, Hammond exclaiming, 'I think we got a good one.' It is the end of a long afternoon, but Hammond seems content. Albert Grossman would not be so convinced. This was probably the session to which he dispatched his partner John Court (see chapter four), whose own report read, Could do better.

Hammond later told Scaduto, 'Albert Grossman and John Court insisted on coming up to all the sessions and Court was trying to tell Bobby what to do ... I ordered them out of the studio ... [But] Albert stayed around and ... had the brilliant idea that Bobby ought to be recorded with a Dixieland band ... It was a disaster.' We now know

---

* In February 1963 Dylan had the chutzpah to copyright his arrangement – which was really Elvis's arrangement – of a song Arthur Crudup copyrighted in 1947, suggesting he intended to either release it or publish it. He did neither. Hence, why the copyright was never challenged.

this is a parcel of lies. There is no Dixieland take, nor can Grossman be heard between takes on any of the three sessions it took to get the single both men had pushed for.* Hammond's later animosity towards Grossman – the result of the manager excommunicating him for steering his client wrong not once, but twice – lies behind his jaundiced account.

Actually, Hammond himself seemed to admit he did not have a handle on what Dylan wanted because after the first take on the next session, six days later, he announces, 'I'm gonna have George Barnes in here this time, so he can hear what you're doing, Bob.' Though Barnes will end up credited with just guitar, he can be heard on talk-back for the five remaining takes of 'Mixed Up Confusion' that day, after which he tells Dylan, the 'other take' (confusingly labelled 'take 10') is the one. With Dylan and Langhorne trading guitar licks, Barnes confines himself to shaping the side sonically. He certainly knew how to make a guitar sound *electric*, having made the first commercial recording of an electric guitar back in March 1938 with Big Bill Broonzy; a connection surely (made) known to Dylan.

If the session seemed to have gone well, what Barnes made of Dylan's November 1st 'That's All Right Mama' – dispatched in a single take – one would love to know. Even 'Rocks And Gravel' came easily, in two takes. But someone felt they still needed to declutter 'Mixed Up Confusion', and a third session was scheduled for the 14th.

Meanwhile, Grossman was starting to wonder whether he and the producer were on the same page, or even if Hammond was acting in good faith. Events of the past month rather suggested not, after Hammond had received a letter in late September, signed by Dylan, drafted by his lawyer David Braun, to the 'effect that since his Columbia contract was signed when Dylan was a minor, it was null and void and he wished the return of all his material'.

Grossman, looking after his client's (and his own) interests had got Dylan to sign this letter, repudiating the contract he signed on October 26th, 1961 – a smart move all round. But Hammond had headed him off at the pass. As he boasted in an internal Columbia memo, dated

---

* Grossman can be heard commenting on sessions in 1963, but by then, Hammond is gone.

October 9th, 'The following day I got Bob Dylan into my office [alone] and had him sign a letter repudiating the previous one and reaffirming his original contract.'

He had gone behind Grossman's back, making a perennial enemy of someone he needed on his side. In acting like a true Vanderbilt, Hammond showed he did not have the measure of the manager. But he did know Dylan who, sure enough, signed his third ill-advised legal document of the year. In *Chronicles*, Dylan rather presents the showdown in terms that suggest personal integrity lay at the heart of his about-turn: 'Hammond had believed in me ... There was no way I'd go against him ... Hammond said that we should straighten this contract situation out right here and now ... A new young counsel for the record company came in and ... an amendment to the old contract was drawn up and I signed it right then and there.'

What he did was sheer lunacy. If, as Dylan later claimed, Grossman 'just about went berserk', who can blame him? Yet most of his (and his lawyer's) righteous anger was not directed at Dylan, but rather at Hammond. As David Braun pointed out in a later deposition, 'I thought it was a violation of the canons of ethics since Mr Dylan was represented by an attorney when the disaffirments were sent in and when the reaffirments were signed they didn't contact us.'

Grossman was never going to let such a stunt go unchallenged. Hammond was soon obliged to inform his boss, Dave Kapralik, 'Subsequent[ly], Al Grossman and Bob Dylan came to my office and Grossman made the following point: there is a statutory limitation of three years' duration for contracts signed by minors in New York State.' It seemed like Columbia would have to negotiate to keep their artist, after all; an artist who, according to Hammond, just six months earlier Kapralik wanted to drop.

Only at this point did Hammond go to bat for Bob, whom he described to his boss as 'a very hot songwriter [whose songs] Tennessee Ernie Ford and The Kingston Trio, among others, are recording'. He began to push for Columbia to raise the publishing on all original songs from 1% in the original contract to 1.5% (less than Grossman wanted). He further requested the royalty on record sales should rise to 5% *retrospectively* on renewal of his contract in March 1963. Finally, he pushed Columbia to agree 'an immediate single release by Bob Dylan'.

These terms, Hammond hoped, would satisfy Grossman and lead to a newly drafted five-year contract with the twenty-one-year-old. Indeed, according to Hammond's recent biographer, Dunstan Prial, 'Columbia signed off on the amended deal.' They did nothing of the sort. Five months later, when Dylan became embroiled in a censorship row with his label, he found he had left himself unable to bargain by reaffirming the rogue contract from a year earlier.

By then, he knew Columbia had failed to really follow through on the single. Yes, they allowed him to complete 'Mixed Up Confusion', only to release it two days after Christmas without telling a soul, letting it die an unnatural death. And a disenchanted Dylan let them, having told Izzy, he 'was disgusted after the third session and left, not know[ing] which of the three versions they'll use'.

They picked one from the 14th, putting an out-take of 'Corrina Corrina' on the B-side, rather than 'That's All Right Mama', as Dylan originally intended. 'Mixed Up Confusion' third time around had again taken up an inordinate amount of time, not helped by Hammond's assurance, after a series of false starts, 'We got all the time in the world. We'll just take it till we got it.' An exasperated Dylan even broke into an impromptu blues after eleven takes, unaware that Hammond had stopped rolling tape. As it came to an end, Hammond sheepishly informed Dylan, 'Well, we got *most* of that.'

Yet there would be no walkout from Dylan. Instead, he discharged the band, kept Langhorne on retainer and used the rest of the afternoon to get the album he was supposedly finishing back on track. No longer hamstrung by band arrangements, he cut four acoustic tracks with consummate ease, including a quasi-traditional original based around the familiar 'who's gonna shoe your pretty little feet?' commonplace, set in Kingsport Town Jail, the same setting as a poem written at around the same time, which began, 'Oh yes I could've gotten the money / I suppose / t pay my fine / out 't the King's port jail.'

Two other songs recorded that afternoon gave Langhorne room to riff: 'Ballad Of Hollis Brown', which featured some terrific guitar interplay but was discarded for now,* and 'Don't Think Twice, It's All

---

* Dylan seems to have always intended some additional accompaniment for the song. When he played it on his first TV appearance, the following March, Barry Kornfeld would provide it. Yet by the time he revisited it for the third LP, it was strictly solo.

Right'. Both had been previously previewed at the Gaslight, solo. Although Langhorne later defended Dylan's guitar-playing – '[he] was actually doing some very interesting things with guitar ... He wasn't a virtuoso guitarist, but he had some very creative ideas' – Dylan struggled with the latter's guitar part in the studio until Langhorne overdubbed the guitar and saved his blushes, and time.*

Dylan could never have played said part with the technical aplomb of Langhorne. Instead, he put his very soul – which the lover in the song prefers to his heart – into the vocal, dispatched in a single take, cursing every moment Suze was away and wanting her to know it. As he wrote to Suze just a few days after composing said song: 'I'm hating time – I'm trying to push it by – I'm trying to stab it – stomp on it – throw it on the ground and kick it – bend it and twist it with gritting teeth and burning eyes – I hate it I love you.' When he wrote to her after the Cuban Missile Crisis, his only thought, or so he claimed, had been, 'If the world [was about to] end ... all I wanted was to be with you.'

Bereft without her, he wrote letters 'with [an] honesty and clarity that [was] unexpected after so much time together ... about his family, his feelings growing up, his name change, and about truth and lies'. He also sent Suze a small volume of Lord Byron poems for her November birthday, knowing that her idols were Edna St Vincent Millay and Lord Byron, not some vacuous film star. But no matter how much of himself he revealed to her, he was none the wiser as to when she'd be coming home again.

Not surprisingly, his alcohol consumption soon began to rise as he spent too many evenings at the Kettle of Fish, and not enough at home. These evenings were usually spent in the company of his musical peers as Dylan rose to every challenge they threw at him – liquid or lyrical. One evening, according to Van Ronk, after a discussion about 'joke song titles' he bet Dylan he couldn't write a song with the recurring punchline, 'If I Had To Do It All Over Again, Babe,

---

* On the four-track session tape, there is no bleed from the vocal on the guitar track, which confirms it was an overdub, presumably over Dylan's original part.

I'd Do It All Over You'. Within a few hours, Dylan had written the song and donated it to Dave, for use on his next album.*

According to biographer Marc Eliot, Phil Ochs – who, although six months older than Dylan, had only recently arrived from Cleveland, hoping to steal the protest crown (the minute his nemesis surrendered it) – spent a similarly memorable evening at the Kettle:

> Shortly after Dylan had signed with Albert Grossman ... Phil [was] telling Dylan he'd really made it. 'Bobby, you really are the biggest thing right now.' 'Nah, nobody knows who I am.' Dylan decided to test his popularity. Blind drunk, he staggered down the stairs to the front door of the Gaslight, leaning against the gigantic coffee urn. Everybody who entered the club was questioned by Dylan. 'Do you know who I am?' He'd mark their answers in his notebook. When someone would say, 'Yeah, you're Bob Dylan,' he would squint his eyes and burn into theirs, sneering, 'You don't know who I am.'

Unlikely as such a contretemps seems, his reported response to anyone who thought they knew him sure sounds like Dylan the mind-game master. But if Ochs thought he could match him in the righteous-lyric department, Dylan was about to give him – and all other contributors to *Broadside* – a crash course in topical songwriting that would set the bar way high.

The song was called 'Oxford Town', Dylan's direct, if slightly belated, response to a constitutional crisis caused by the enrolment of black student James Meredith at the University of Mississippi on October 1st. Meredith's much delayed enrolment – held up by an unashamedly racist governor – had led to rioting and two deaths from gunshots. Dylan personalized the mayhem, painting him, his gal and her son (an odd family unit for 1962) as innocent bystanders 'met with a tear-gas bomb'. He played it for a delighted Sis Cunningham and Gordon Freisen in November, after an informal competition was

---

* Dylan demoed the song for Witmark, and performed it on the so-called Banjo Tape in February 1963 and at Town Hall two months later, but never recorded it officially. It remains one of his best early comic songs. (As an alien put it in Woody Allen's *Stardust Memories*, 'We like your movies – especially the early, funny ones.').

launched in the pages of *Broadside* #14 for 'a good lasting song in [Meredith's] honor'.

The first entrant, by pushy Phil himself, was published in issue #15, Ochs's second contribution to the topical-song zine. Five more ballads that were pure Grub Street followed, before Dylan made his point in just five four-line verses, without mentioning Meredith once. As he said about the song, the following April, 'It deals with the Meredith case, but then it doesn't.' He was applying a broader brush now to his topical songs – as evidenced by another song he demoed for *Broadside* that month, 'Paths of Victory'.

'Oxford Town' was another of the five tracks he cut on December 6th, 1962 at what was supposed to be the final session for his second album, and one of three dispatched in single takes. ('Whatcha Gonna Do?' – already cut at the previous session – and 'A Hard Rain's A-Gonna Fall' were the others.)

Court may have been there again to keep an eye on things. He later described Hammond as a producer who 'every once in a while looked up over the magazine to say, "Okay, are you through, Bob? Is that it?"' – pretty close to Hammond's actual response to 'Oxford Town': 'Don't tell me that's all.' His response to 'Hard Rain' – the last song of the session and a near faultless performance – has gone unrecorded, but it surely rendered him speechless.

The songs were again pouring out of Dylan, so much so that in the three weeks separating the last two Columbia sessions of the year, he recorded no fewer than eight songs for *Broadside* and a daunting thirteen for Witmark Music, without duplication. The *Broadside* songs were almost all tailor-made – save for the whimsical 'I Shall Be Free' – and when not topical, tub-thumping. Most were never in serious contention for Columbia, with three cuts not even demoed for publishing purposes: 'Train A-Travelin'', 'Cuban Missile Crisis' and 'Ye Playboys & Playgirls', suggesting that Dylan wasn't being entirely disingenuous when later claiming he wrote almost to order for 'sis and gordon' to a sceptical Paul Nelson, who recalled him saying, 'The easiest way to get published if you wrote your own songs was to write topical songs, 'cause *Broadside* wouldn't publish [it] if you didn't.'

The best of the bunch – 'Oxford Town' excepted – was a 'come all ye' call to join the march of progress, 'Paths Of Victory' and its flipside, a highly personal plea for independence of thought, 'Walkin'

Down The Line'. As with the earlier 'Ain't Gonna Grieve', 'Paths Of Victory' was a fairly blatant rewrite of a gospel hymn (known as both 'Deliverance Will Come' and 'Palms Of Victory'), delivered like the last of the true believers. It is also the only song done here still on his mind nine months later.

In the case of the Witmark session – and he really does seem to have cut the lot in a single visit – it was essentially a mopping up exercise from the year that'd been. But there was still room for three new songs of real merit. Two of these, 'Tomorrow Is A Long Time' and 'Long Time Gone', had been previewed to Glover back in August; the former, now an exquisite exegesis on love and loss, would become one of his most covered songs, without him cutting a studio version till June 1970.

The cutting of demos seems to have been Dylan's idea, a necessity born of the fact that he could not read or write music (and never would learn). A callow Witmark engineer, Ivan Augenblink, had been asked by Artie Mogull to get Dylan to write out the lyrics, but the young songwriter declined, asking Augenblink to transcribe them instead and he would hand correct them, a practice he would perpetuate into the eighties.

If Dylan never asked for acetates himself, copies were usually forwarded to Grossman, who sometimes would attend in person. Yet these were first and foremost *publishing* demos. Once they outlived their purpose, they were junked. Indeed, Mogull actually directed Augenblink 'to discard demos after they were on album, and to use the LP version'.

According to Augenblink, Dylan would sometimes come in and do half a dozen songs, other times just one.* Again according to

---

* The emergence of paperwork in Tulsa which reveals seventeen songs registered for copyright on December 7th, 1962 throws into disarray a whole number of presumptions about the dating of Witmark demos I made in an article in the *Telegraph* #16 in 1984, which several foolhardy souls – including sleeve-note writer, Colin Escott – seemed to consider *fact* when compiling the official release of the Witmark Demos as *The Bootleg Series Vol. 9*. 'Seven Curses', previously dated to spring 1963, is one of five songs now known to have been misassigned, the others being 'Bound To Lose', 'Bob Dylan's Blues', 'Long Time Gone' and 'Talkin' John Birch'. Two other demos, also cut this day, 'Down The Highway' and 'Honey Just Allow Me One More Chance', were subsequently destroyed as per Mogull's instructions.

Augenblink, when Dylan did come in to record on the fifth floor of 488 Madison, across the street from Columbia, 'arrangers would shut their doors and ask him to shut [the] studio doors'. Dylan returned the favour with a dig at their kind in the spoken intro to 'Bob Dylan's Blues'.

What these arrangers shut out on that November afternoon was a new original unlike anything they referenced, one suggesting Dylan was still soaking up trad. songs like a sponge. 'Seven Curses' was the first of a small but select body of his songs that paint judges in a bad light.* That he had it in for these esteemed dispensers of 'justice' is clear from a contemporary poem in which the narrator, as he is about to be sentenced, insists 'I swear I saw the judge nod / as if he was the hand 'f God / touchin one 'f the children / 'f his favourite religion.'

The judge in 'Seven Curses' is surely his most venal law official, threatening to hang a man for stealing a horse unless his daughter sleeps with him. After she agrees, he hangs her father anyway, at which juncture the daughter lays seven curses on him, the last of which is that 'seven deaths will never kill him'. It is a magnificent reworking of tradition – in this case a Hungarian folk song called 'Anna Fehrer' – that he performed at both Town Hall and Carnegie Hall showcases in 1963, and recorded for his third album, but failed to release, another masterpiece cast aside; by no means, the last.

What is a matter of dispute is where exactly he heard the Hungarian original, or variant thereof. The most likely source would have to be Judy Collins, who recorded her version of the traditional original, as 'Anathea', on her third Elektra album, but had been playing it since 1961. Though a regular at Denver's Exodus in summer 1960, Collins doesn't seem to have met Dylan until 1962, by which time she was desperate, in her own words, 'to meet ... the mind that created all those beautiful words. We set something up ... had coffee ... When it was over, I walked away thinking, "The guy's an idiot, he can't make a coherent sentence."'

Collins was still smart enough to co-opt Dylan's better discards. Even before Baez, she had begun to read the writing on the wall,

---

* In the next year he will write the superlative 'Percy's Song' and 'The Lonesome Death Of Hattie Carroll', both of which take potshots at a judge.

Abraham and Beattie Zimmerman at Niagara Falls, 1939 (The Bill Pagel Archive).

Three babes in the north country: (*from left to right*) unknown girl, Dennis Pryor and Bob Zimmerman. Bettie Zimmerman is directly behind her son, 1944 (The Bill Pagel Archive).

Dale Boutang and Bob Zimmerman plot their next game of chicken, 1957
(The Bill Pagel Archive).

Bob Dylan, Karen Dalton and Fred Neil at the Cafe Wha, February 1961 (Getty Images).

A smokin' Bob Dylan busks along with fellow folkies, Ralph Rinzler (*left*) and John Herald (*right*), 1961 (Getty Images).

John Hammond Junior, Bob Dylan and Suze Rotolo at Columbia Studio A, November 20, 1961 (Sony Archives).

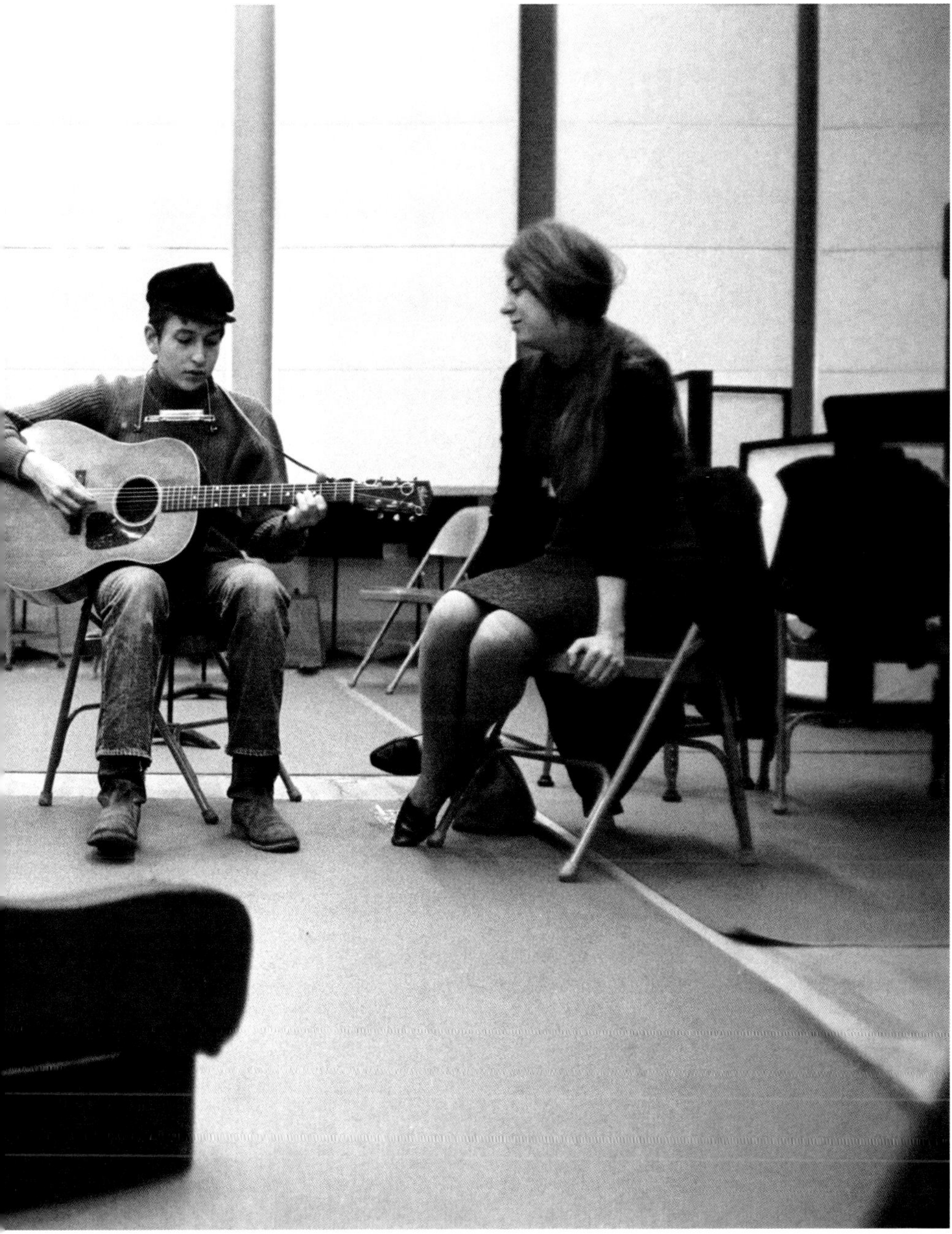

The irascible Izzy talkin' Folklore Center bull, early 1960s (Getty Images).

Suze Rotolo and Dylan enjoying themselves at Mark Spoelstra's wedding reception, 1962.

Suze and Bob, the most photogenic couple in the West Village, 1963 (Getty Images).

Dylan ruffles some southern feathers at the July 1963 Columbia convention in Puerto Rico (Sony Archives).

recording contemporary songs from the likes of Ewan MacColl and Pete Seeger. She now acquired several unreleased Dylan originals, probably from the man himself or Witmark,* her 1963 album featuring not just 'Anathea' but two then-unreleased Dylan songs, 'Farewell' and 'Masters Of War', perhaps some form of *quid pro quo*.

Whatever Dylan's source for 'Seven Curses', he immeasurably improved on tradition, aka 'the only true valid death you can feel today'. He was getting the hang of how to shape and tailor tradition just in time because in mid-December he headed for London, capital of Albion since the Romans and the font of Anglo-American song.

Before that, he started enquiring what had happened to his first songbook, nudging his lawyer to fire off a letter to Lou Levy's lawyer, asking about *Bob Dylan Himself*.† Evidently, he had no inclination to disown such songwriting juvenilia. Levy's lawyer, the well-informed Arnold A. Gurwitch,‡ assured Braun that 'Duchess Music Corp. is fully prepared to comply with its agreement with Mr Dylan to publish a collection of the original compositions and arrangements in question.' Fully prepared or not, the slim volume would still take more than two years to appear.

If Dylan had written up a storm in the days before he cut those Leeds demos back in January 1962, it was as nothing to the songs that poured forth after immersing himself in a three-week crash course in British folksong. One of them, 'Girl From The North Country', based on the veritably ancient 'Scarborough Fair' (aka 'An Acre of Land'), even included a weather report, 'The wind hits heavy on the borderline', as he again arrived in a town in gridlock from an unprecedented cold front that closed London Airport for days and made south-east England a frosty facsimile of the Midwest, the 'real' north country.

---

* In *Baby Let Me Follow You Down*, Baez's manager Manny Greenhill claims he was sent an acetate of 'a dozen or so of Bob's songs and ... gave it to Joan with the suggestion she gave it a listen'. One must assume these were Witmark demos. Ian & Sylvia recorded 'Tomorrow Is A Long Time' in 1963.

† The programme notes for the September 22nd Travelin' Hootenanny at Carnegie Hall reported that Dylan already had 'a folio of his own compositions', presumably because that information was conveyed when it was thought to be imminent.

‡ Gurwitch, in his reply to Braun's latter, dated December 26th, notes that Dylan himself 'left for overseas on December 16th, 1962'. He probably got this information from the December 19th *Variety*.

The trip to London soon turned into an adventure against which even Denver and Madison paled. When next he saw his Minneapolis friends in July, he regaled them with London story after London story, beginning with this Minnesotan, inured to such wintry conditions, checking out of the luxurious and warm Piccadilly hotel the BBC had booked him into, rather than perpetuate the feudal tipping system there:

> On the first day there we checked into this hotel, the Mayfair. [It] has these hooded little guards who take your bags into the hotel, then some guy takes your bag to the stairs then some guy to the elevator. You gotta tip 'em. The elevator guy opens the door, puts your bags in the elevator, you tip him, you get out the elevator, there's a cat waiting to take your bags, you get to the door, some guy takes your bags to the bed. The first day, man. So I split. The second day I check[ed] out.

The director of the play the BBC had commissioned him to appear in was Philip Saville.* In 1989 he would suggest different reasons for Dylan having to leave the Mayfair: '[The] hotel were worried about his appearance ... playing a guitar in the foyer, staying up all night and dragging ... girls off the street.' By 2005, he'd added another, 'The management asked him to refrain from *that* type of smoking.'

By now, Dylan noted, 'It's snowing out, very cold. I [now] know what it feels like to be a negro – I'm over there and I'm segregated.' Saville, trying his best to make this citizen of the world feel at home, suggested introducing him to an American he knew. The scene Dylan described to Glover was almost the rap equivalent of 1965's 'On The Road Again':

> He told me there's an American cat living with an English chick, and they're both living with her mother ... We walk in the door and the American cat is sitting in this big armchair, weighs about 300 pounds, [eating] popcorn. I circle him and the director says, 'This is Bob Dylan.'

---

* According to Saville, he first saw Dylan in New York after NY resident W. H. Auden sent him to a club that summer, where he saw 'an extraordinary spastic poet giving out raw chunks of what was going on in America'.

He ain't listening, he's watching television. Just then the granny comes in at about half a mile an hour. She's got a cane. It takes her almost ten minutes to get from the door to the television set. [As] she walks by the television set for just a second ... he says, Get the fuck out. She's about to sit down on the stool and he yanks it out. She crashes to the floor – the granny ... got up at a hundred miles an hour, shaking her finger at him. I thought, I must be in a movie. He laughs. Just then I hear a noise from the kitchen. Do you want some coffee? Yeah. The girl came in, she was really good-looking, looked about seventeen ... very French ... with this big tray of coffee and tea. He was watching the TV. He went bang. Tray went across the room, every cup and saucer broke. She [just] laughed and went back in the kitchen. By that time I was scared. I didn't know where I was. She came back with more coffee. He punched granny in the stomach ... threw a cup against the wall ... stuffed the turkey down his girlfriend's mouth. Sat in this room like a king. Place was a mess ... I told Phil I couldn't stay there.

Evidently, if Saville had been looking for the real *Madhouse on Castle Street* – the title of the play he was directing – he'd been looking in all the wrong places. Having failed to make Dylan feel at home once, his second suggestion was a house full of English proto-hippies, who provided yet more material for those early comic songs:

Bob Dylan: We go ... into this room and there's a fireplace and about fifteen people in this room. It's very cold, and they're all wearing short-sleeve shirts ... The fireplace is burning up. I learn ... these are the English hippies. They say, Do you wanna dance? I say, Sure. They put on the Everly Brothers and they start to twist ... with one leg ... After about an hour, they ask me to play. I play ... 'Hollis Brown' and ... 'Hard Rain' ... And they froze, they were solid, [said] they never heard anything like that before ... I put down the guitar, I start putting my hands in the fire, and they're twisting again. [1963]

Just as he was making himself comfortable, one of the girls whispered, 'Would you like to see my paintings?' He didn't have to think twice. Suze hit the nail on the proverbial head when she later observed how he skilfully projected an 'image of himself as the abandoned, wounded lover [while] I'm sure he was having a fine time'. At this point, Dylan forgot all his true love ways:

> I think I've scored – in London! I won't have to go back to America thinking I really failed. We walk outta the room, through a bathroom, we climb up a ladder, we go down a balcony, swing down a rope, jump down, we're in a corridor. We get down the hall. We're standing on this balcony as big as this room, and we walk to the end and see her room [through] these huge high windows, two fireplaces. I thought, 'Here is where I [want to] stay the rest of my life. Wait till the cats in New York see what I latched onto.' We walk down[stairs]. It's completely dark. She turns on the light and says, 'These are my paintings.' I look up at the paintings and I know nothing about paintings – good or bad. Nothing. [But] these paintings were *so bad* ... I just looked at her paintings and thought, how can she paint these? She's so beautiful, [I try to convince myself] she must be helping someone out. And all of a sudden she says, 'That's my baby boy.' I expected to see a photo of the kid. It was a painting of the kid. It looked like a piece of lettuce on a tomato with a garbage bag over the top ... everything except a kid. I said, Hey, I'll see you later, waved a fond farewell and I ran down the hall. I had to find a place to stay for myself. Those people are weird.*

What a shame Dylan didn't use such material at his one and only appearance at London's fabled satire club, the Establishment, the result of a chance meeting with theatrical agent Willie Donaldson, who convinced co-owner Peter Cook to let Dylan do a short set in exchange for dinner. According to Donaldson, 'It was a disaster. Nobody wanted to know.' If Dylan performed 'Talkin' John Birch' – a song he was still championing that month at the King & Queen's and the Troubadour – it's no wonder. Its US-centric references would have been lost on many a diner.

At this point Saville surrendered to the inevitable, letting Dylan stay at his house while he canvassed more lugubrious hotels. According to the director, his charge continued 'playing guitar ... [and] staying

---

* In a recent conversation with historian Doug Brinkley, Dylan suggested he would like to write about this trip in *Chronicles Vol. 2*. One can only hope he revisits both madhouses.

up all night', until, 'At about five [in] the morning, the first night he stayed, I could hear this song, "How many roads ... "'

Rather unlikely. If Dylan was working on anything that cold, grey dawn, it would have been 'Masters Of War', a song we can confidently date to Dylan's first week in London, thanks to an impromptu spoken intro he gave before recording it for Alan Lomax that winter: 'I wrote it in London ... I was at this rehearsal place in Putney and I kept seeing the papers every day, putting down Macmillan, [suggesting] Kennedy's gonna screw him on these missiles ... They got headlines in the papers, underneath Macmillan's face, saying, "Don't mistrust me. How can you treat a poor maiden so?"'*

The song itself came easily, as did the tune, a marginal rearrangement of Jean Ritchie's famous rendition of 'Nottamun Town' that would mean trouble ahead. Dylan later insisted, the song was not 'antiwar. It has ... to do with the military industrial complex.' It seems this was indeed his target, and he now had 'em in his sights. As he told Richard Fariña in London, 'Man, there's things going on in this world you got to look at, right? You can't pretend they ain't happening ... You can keep on singing about "Railroad Bill" ... or you can *step out*.' (The message was evidently meant for Fariña's future sister-in-law, Joan Baez.)

If 'Masters Of War' was Dylan stepping out, he added another dimension shortly afterwards. Writing out a fair copy of the finished lyrics, he attached a crude drawing of a man with a guitar standing over a grave 'to make sure that [they]'re dead'. There is something otherworldly about this man, as if he has just returned from the salt, salt sea. A closer look reveals a cloven hoof, proof that Satan was alive and well and already on Dylan's mind.

But for now he had more pressing matters – some rehearsals – to attend (to). The 'place in Putney' was St Mary's Hall, hired by the BBC,†

---

* Dylan is referring to nuclear-missile talks held between Harold Macmillan and President Kennedy in the Bahamas, December 17th–20th. The 'Lomax' version appears, minus Dylan's spoken intro, on the 2016 six-CD set, *Root Hog Or Die*.
† According to BBC files, three weeks of play rehearsals were due to start there on December 11th. I simply don't believe Dylan was in London that early. I think he arrived later in the week, whether because rehearsals were delayed, or because he turned up after they started.

and almost immediately after Dylan's belated arrival, there was a problem. *Madhouse* author Elvin Jones later recalled how, during their first read-through, 'We got to [Dylan's character] Lennie's first speech and Philip nodded to him, and he [just] said, "I don't know what I'm doing here. *These* guys are actors."' Dylan confirmed something similar occurred to his Minnesotan friends:

> I had lines to read and play[ed] guitar and everything. They paid round-trip transportation, [but] I didn't care whether I did the thing or not ... I said, I can't do it. And they said, 'You gotta do it. We wrote this part especially for you.' ... I couldn't do it. I'm sat around this table with all these famous actors from England, reading my part, really shitty, the worst possible actor in the world. And they're saying, 'That's good.' I knew it wasn't good. So I cop out on the second day.

Saville had stuck his neck out, big time, to bring Dylan over to play this key role in the play. The BBC, not known for its fiscal generosity, were paying him 500 guineas plus fifty guineas a week expenses and a return air fare of £173 – a grand total of £856, twice what the playwright was getting, only for Saville to belatedly realize, 'Dylan wasn't able to deal with the dialogue at all.' As an alternative, he began to talk to him 'about various songs that he could add to the production'.

Jones, meanwhile, suggested splitting the Lennie character in two, giving the spoken parts to RSC actor David Warner and creating Bobby the Hobo out of thin air. Dylan convinced them to scrap Jones's own song, 'Cut Me Down, My Love', replacing it with two traditional songs he felt more comfortable doing, 'The Cuckoo' and 'Hang Me Oh Hang Me'. He also proceeded to rewrite Jones's 'Ballad Of A Gliding Swan', oddly uncomfortable with lines like 'The doctor gave Sally a sad surprise, a thalidomide baby with no eyes' and 'My father has cancer, my mother's insane, the girl I'm in love with takes cocaine'. His new role agreed, Dylan opted out of most rehearsals, leaving him with a great deal of time on his hands:

> So I have all these days. I was [now playing] his friend. All I had to do was say the last line of the play and play a few songs. There's a big explosion, I'm sitting on the steps and he comes up to me and says, 'What do you think about it, Bobby?' – they even called me Bobby –

and I said, 'If I was you, I wouldn't think about it.' Every day I got nothing to do. I go to bed at six in the morning, I get up ... say my line, and run out. I walk around all day ... I'd ask the director ... 'You gonna get around to me today?' 'No, no.' And I'd split.

He was a free man. Now he just needed a place to stay where his nocturnal lifestyle did not wreak havoc. Having rapidly outstayed his welcome at the Savilles', and with fifty guineas a week expenses burning a hole in his jeans, Dylan settled on the Cumberland Hotel off Marble Arch, a step down from the Mayfair, but still walking distance from the whole West End. From here, he could start to look up some names he had been given by more well-travelled New Yorkers. Jack Elliott had suggested Max Jones, the folk/jazz critic at *Melody Maker*, but when he called on Jones, he was informed he was out by Bob Dawbarn, who later described the visitor to Jones as 'some bloody folker ... with a cowboy hat ... [who'd] walked up the turnpike'.

He was still at the Cumberland when he became the subject of a two-page picture story in *Scene* magazine, 'perched on his bed ... a pile of rolled up shirts erupt[ing] from an open suitcase and a large sheepskin jacket in dire need of cleaning ... beside the bed, where it had obviously been dropped the night before'. The *Scene* story was the one scoop a man who later claimed 'there's no such thing as bad publicity' managed. Andrew Loog Oldham – not yet The Rolling Stones's manager – had turned up at the Cumberland and convinced Grossman, also *in situ*, to pay him £5 for a week's work as Dylan's publicist.

Other chance meetings on this madcap trip included one with poet-classicist Robert Graves, arranged by the poet Rory McEwen. Dylan was reading Graves's 'historical grammar of poetic myth', *The White Goddess*, having probably been turned onto it by Suze. If, as the *Chronicler* claimed, 'invoking the poetic muse was something I didn't know about yet', he was presumably also unaware that Graves had taught a class in traditional ballads and published a Child Lite collection in the twenties. According to Jack Elliott, Dylan 'wanted to get his approval ... [and] came on a little too strong'. As per.

There was also almost a feature in *Vogue*. Polly Devlin, their young features editor, was an early Dylan fan and 'when a press release came in saying that he was ... to act in a BBC drama, I asked for an interview.

He came to Vogue House ... and I trolled off with him to a basement bar in Maddox Street. We more or less hung out for the day ... talking for a long time.' But in January 1963 Dylan was not *Vogue* material.

It was time he went back to his own kind of people – folk people. He struck lucky right away, thanks to one of Pete Seeger's suggestions, Anthea Joseph, who ran the Troubadour in Earls Court of a Tuesday evening. Dylan might have been able to walk the streets of London unrecognized, but English folkies knew *Sing Out!*, and guess who was on the cover of the latest issue. Anthea called him out, and then asked him to play. He did 'Masters Of War', and rendered the Court's late-night regulars mute. He was up and running.

A couple of days later, as Martin Carthy recalled in 1965, 'He strolled into the King & Queen pub, near Euston, where I was playing with a folk group called The Thameside Four. He sat sipping a beer and listened to the group. He said he liked us – and after that we became good friends.' Dylan asked him, What else is going on? The Home Counties man told him about all the folk clubs that had sprouted wings during the late-fifties folk revival. He was back where he belonged.

Of these clubs, the most prestigious – and potentially prickly – to play was the Singers, run by Ewan MacColl and Peggy Seeger, both insufferable folk-snobs. Lady Seeger later wrote, 'Perhaps we were not welcoming enough,' something of an understatement considering Dylan came with a ringing endorsement from her two brothers. Fortunately, Dylan had the towering Anthea and that doyen of English folksong, A. L. Lloyd, standing him a round before he got up to play. And play. As Anthea patiently explained, 'When you got up off the floor your maximum was five minutes really. [Dylan did] twenty! And he did it on purpose. I'm sure of it ... And brought the house down ... He did "Masters Of War" and [then] "Ballad Of Hollis Brown", which goes on forever.'

He was determined to make his mark, and not just at the Singers. By December 30th, the night he played for the MacColls, three days of studio rehearsals had started for that irksome BBC play, before they recorded the actual broadcast on the fourth, in a session that overran even before Bobby sang 'Blowin' In The Wind' over the end credits.

By January 5th, he was a free man again. This time he decided to follow one of his favourite women to the shores of Italy; not Suze but the lung-bustin' Odetta, also represented by Grossman, who was playing a show in Rome. Suze was already back in New York, their letters to each other detailing travel plans having crossed in the mail, after Dylan's flight to London landed just as Suze was sailing home. He still wanted to see Italy, though, which he described in glowing terms to Glover that July:

> Over there, you can walk down the street [even if] you ain't got nuthin', you don't have to worry about it. Because they don't *sell* you things. They're not hammering at your door. And they serve wine for three cents a glass. Four places on a block. And all the groovy food they serve. You're going over there to live off them. It's a poor country. They [think] all Americans have ... a lot of money.

But his trip 'down to Italy' was not *entirely* carefree. Talking to an Italian translator in 1966, he remembered, 'On street corners, walking up and down behind all these chicks with blonde hair, going up to intersections, were like a hundred very dark gentlemen with their shoes polished and their keys dangling. They would sit there and stick toothpicks in their mouths and they would whistle at all these chicks and ... give me the worst time possible'.

In the land of the alpha male, an alien hound like Dylan needed to watch himself. Where exactly he travelled in the few short days he was there is unclear. In a postcard to Suze, he said he was planning to go to Turin, but he mostly stayed in Rome, where he told her he had a 'meeting with the Pope about all the colored people coming over here'. More plausibly, he said he found time to visit the catacombs, a place where 'the people who don't work live'; as well as the rounds of the one folk club, getting up to play 'three or four songs' at Folkstudio to 'no more than fifteen people' (according to co-owner Giancarlo Cesaroni). He evidently enjoyed himself. The following month he improvised an original song called 'Going Back To Rome'.*

---

* In 2006, Christie's auctioned a postcard Dylan sent to Suze from Rome, mailed from 'Poste Roma Centro' (the main post office). The postmark read February 22nd, 1963, six weeks too late. It is possible Dylan gave the postcard to someone who forgot to mail it. But it has also been suggested he returned to Rome to continue a liaison, unlikely as that seems, for purely financial reasons.

Although Suze was long gone, she remained on his mind as he finally got around to writing a song from an idea which he'd had 'for a long time, but it just wasn't the right time ... When the right time finally did come, the song was in my mind and it was ready.' This was 'Girl From The North Country', which was as much for Bonnie Beecher (and maybe Echo) as it was for Suze, an idea that seems to upset some. As Bonnie has said, 'It seems to be very important to some people who that song is about.' The one time Dylan dedicated a live rendition to a north-country girl in the audience, it was in Oakland in November 1978. That girl was Bonnie.

More overtly 'about' Suze, albeit a mythical Suze, was another song Dylan began around the same time, 'Boots Of Spanish Leather', set to almost the same tune: Martin Carthy's one-off arrangement of 'Scarborough Fair'. Thankfully, Carthy appreciated Dylan's gift for tailoring tunes to lyrics – 'He doesn't learn the tune, he learns the idea of the tune and he can do something like it' – and gave him the benefit of the doubt.

Unlike others from whom Dylan learnt things on this trip through Anglo folk tradition – notably Dominic Behan, whose arrangement of 'The Nightingale' he appropriated for 'With God On Our Side', along with Behan's nebulous notion of 'The Patriot Game' – Carthy was delighted with what Dylan had done. Hilariously, when Dylan attempted to show his friend what that was, he had to abandon it halfway through, too embarrassed to continue. At least he didn't nip down to the local post office and register Carthy's arrangement as his own.

But he would have to learn to be selective as to the people to whom he played some of these new songs. If Jean Ritchie should be MC'ing a songwriters workshop at a folk festival, probably not a good idea to play 'Masters Of War'. If the Clancys are in town, better they don't hear what he's done to 'The Leaving Of Liverpool' (made it into 'Farewell'). And if Suze is at a session or show, best to steer clear of a song about a girl from Liverpool he met one time in London.

That this 'Liverpool Gal' was probably real is strongly suggested by Dylan's long spoken intro to his one documented performance, to Minnesotan friends that July: 'She was one of the most beautiful girls in the world ... like a dream ... beautiful to look at, beautiful to talk to, beautiful ideas', a sentiment which comes across in a song which begins much like 'When First Unto This Country', before the singer starts 'thinking thoughts and dreaming dreams / The kind when you're all alone / But most of all I was thinking about / The land I'd left back home.'

Taken in by the Scouse lassie, they pass the time platonically, 'We talked for hours by the inside fire / 'Bout the outside world so cruel', until the chastened singer concludes, 'One thing I found out / Of walkin' and ramblin', I know too hard / But love I knew nothing about'. Though Dylan never recorded the song officially, Glover captured it in July, and Dylan kept a copy among a set of contemporary lyrics and poems.*

For someone who had been whining for months about how much he missed Suze, he seemed in very little hurry to go back home, continuing to hit the London folk clubs on his return from Rome, either on his own or – according to resident folkie Jim McLean – 'with that lassie with the long blonde hair'.

On the one occasion he turned up mob-handed, though, the blonde lass was nowhere to be seen. Instead, doorkeeper Anthea was confronted by Dylan, Dick Fariña, Eric Von Schmidt and fiddle player Ethan Singer all arriving at the Troubadour one Tuesday night 'about eleven o'clock, absolutely out of their gourds except for Ethan … [who] was straight as a die and very embarrassed by this collection of bozos that he was looking after … The Troubadour has … a platform – less than a foot. [But Bob] was [still] falling off it.'

Four days earlier, on his return from Rome, Dylan had joined Fariña and Von Schmidt, both passing through town, at the Hotel de France, BBC funds having dried up. He found the cognac and brown ale was already a-flowin'. Cue three days of well-oiled mayhem – Fariña describing it to Mimi by letter as a lot of 'grass all over the place, singing, jumping [and] yelling'. Such jollies were suspended just once, at 9 p.m. on Sunday the 13th while *Madhouse On Castle Street* was broadcast (and critically panned).

---

* These were the so-called Margolis & Moss papers. Could 'Liverpool Gal' perhaps be the unknown song Dylan played to Rosemary Gerrette in Perth in April 1966, of which he said, 'I'll never have it published, recorded. I wrote it for this way-out moon chick. We just sat on these mattresses … and for two hours I spoke to her with my guitar'?

Their collective high jinks culminated in two afternoon sessions for a Fariña and Von Schmidt LP downstairs at Dobell's, probably the first UK record shop to stock Dylan's debut LP. 'Blind Boy Grunt' – contracted to Columbia under his legal name – offered his services on harmonica and backing vocals, and a good time was had by all.

When they decided to reconvene at the Troubadour after the second session, for what was their fond farewell to London town, they were already sloppy drunk. Nonetheless, they were determined to perform, whatever the audience or that night's act (the unfortunate Judy Silver) thought. When Scottish folksinger Nigel Denver tried to get Dylan and his friends to relinquish the stage, he found out Dylan could not be moved, or talked down. He also discovered that Dylan had a rare gift for performing under the influence.

Even back in Minneapolis, Dave Whitaker remembered, 'He used to get really fucking drunk, we all did. But he would always play that guitar. When he couldn't even stand up, ... he would stand up and play that guitar.' This preternatural instinct for performing trashed had also been displayed in Montreal the previous June. Anna McGarrigle, future singing sister of Kate, 'asked him to sing "Baby Let Me Follow You Down", and he ... wanted to know where we'd heard the song. [He said] he'd sing [it], but that he was drunk ... He did it – with his guitar in one key and his harmonica in another. He knew he was doing it and even if there had been a hundred people in the audience – [and] there were only four people there that night – he would have done it anyway. [Somehow] he carried it off.'

And he carried it off at the Troubadour. As eyewitness Peter Stanley told Hajdu, 'The others got stoned and played while they were fucked up, and they gave fucked-up performances. Dylan got stoned, and he instinctively *used* it.' Denver never forgave him, later writing an open letter in *Folk Music* – the first of its kind – to the trailing comet, suggesting he 'come back to this country, and ... while you are here, study the writings of Ewan MacColl. You could learn a lot.' The only contribution to Dylan's craft MacColl had to offer after their one stone-faced meeting was the odd traditional tune.

Dylan would return to London sixteen months later, but not to the Troubadour, the Singers or the King & Queen. The days of busking round town were drawing to a close everywhere in the English-speaking world, and especially so in New York, to which he returned to a still-radiant Suze, who was surprised to find 'Whatever it was that held us together hadn't dissipated. He wanted to be part of my world as much as he wanted me in his.'

For the next couple of months he diligently worked at retying the bond, asking Suze to accompany him on a photo-shoot with Columbia house photographer Don Hunstein as he clung to her tightly, walking the slush-filled streets of the Village. Perhaps he was just trying to keep warm having, as Suze noted, put on that dirty suede jacket as 'an "image" choice ... That jacket was not remotely suited for the weather'. He froze right to the bone. Ten months later, Suze was still nagging him to 'get a newer warmer coat / i [just] shake my head'.

The couple also visited old friends Ian and Sylvia in Toronto, where Dylan perhaps played them 'Tomorrow Is A Long Time', impressing old friends and reminding his girlfriend how much he had been a-hurtin'. Back home, they took in movies like *Pull My Daisy*, Kerouac's adaptation of *The Beat Generation*, and Francois Truffaut's *Shoot The Piano Player* – two powerful influences on Dylan the cineaste – the latter featuring Charles Aznavour as the piano-playin' character 'with a heartbreaking acceptance of how things are in the world'. Not surprisingly, Dylan related.

They also visited art shows, including many at MoMA, Suze delighted that 'he was able to look at something for as long as I could'. Suze also encouraged him to make his own drawings (of which 'Masters Of War' seems to be early evidence), Dylan duly acknowledging in *Chronicles* it was a lifelong habit he 'picked up ... from Suze, who drew a lot'.

Fortunately, he had time on his hands – and a lot of relationship repairwork to do – as he waited for the impasse that was his second Columbia album to be resolved. It had all gone quiet at the label, who were perhaps hoping that Grossman had forgotten all about the underhand reaffirmance of his client's original contract. He had not, and on March 13th, a letter landed on Walter Dean's desk from his lawyer David Braun, sparked by a conversation with Grossman 'concerning the Bob Dylan matter':

> Al did point out ... that he permitted Bob Dylan to record for Columbia only after he had received assurances from John Hammond that the existing agreement would be reduced in term, that a 2% license fee would be paid for Dylan's compositions, that a 5% royalty would be

paid, and that the boilerplate language in the agreements would be modified to reflect contract language that would have resulted had Dylan been represented by an attorney when the agreement was signed. The assurances, by the way, given by John Hammond ... were made in the presence of certain witnesses.

Only now did the scales fall from Dylan's eyes, as Columbia informed him that they were pulling 'Talkin' John Birch' from the second album after receiving legal advice that it was potentially libellous to suggest the ultra-right-wing organization 'agreed with Hitler's views'. They did, but only in broad brushstrokes.

When Dylan went to see Columbia attorney Clive Davis to have this decision explained to him, John Hammond was present as a furious artist demanded to know, 'What is this? What do you mean I can't come out with this song?' Astonishingly, Hammond would later claim, 'He has had remarkable freedom to work without censorship here at Columbia', clearly not the case. It was not a decision Dylan was going to take lying down. He threatened to go on strike for the second time in six months:

> **Izzy Young:** He told me the reason for the delay in the [release] of the record was because they refused to put ['Talkin' John Birch'] on, and he refused to let the record come out without the song. He said, 'Over my dead body, Izzy, will that record come [out] without that song on it.' [But] then it came out without the song.

In truth, there wasn't a lot Dylan could do about it. As Suze observed, 'Early in his career, Bob didn't have much control over how his work was presented and marketed.' Who does? But he could sure make the song Columbia wanted to remove a cause célèbre, starting with an April 12th showcase that Columbia were planning to record at the Town Hall. Now called 'Talkin' John Birch Paranoid Blues', it was sandwiched between the jocular 'All Over You' and a heartbreaking 'Boots Of Spanish Leather' (perhaps there at the expense of 'Girl From The North Country').*

---

* 'Girl From The North Country' – or as he calls it 'North Country Girl' – was on Dylan's handwritten provisional set-list, as was 'Fare Thee Well' and 'Playboys & Playgirls'.

Dylan also saw fit to sing 'Tomorrow Is A Long Time' and 'Don't Think Twice', while a teary-eyed Suze gazed on, flanked by Bob's parents, who had come to see their son and have dinner with the pair before the show. Suze had not known quite what to expect, her boyfriend failing to prep her beforehand, but it passed off smoothly enough. As did the show, a tour de force of this new Dylan: twenty-three songs and a seven-minute poem as a second encore (plus another bio-poem in the programme).

Dylan was determined to make his previous Chapter Hall bust a career footnote, playing just two songs – 'Talkin' New York' and 'Pretty Peggy-O' – from that set seventeen months earlier. The other twenty-one songs were fifty shades of Dylan, prompting his ever-faithful *New York Times* cheerleader to call it 'a memorable evening of new songs by an incredibly gifted songwriter'. Meanwhile, Barry Kittleson's *Billboard* review added to the growing typecasting of Dylan as someone whose 'primary purpose is to speak [out], not to entertain', a perception echoed by the *Village Voice*, in its July review of *Freewheelin*': 'What he sings is more important than how he sings.' Any dissenters were a thousand miles away.

Columbia, who set up Don Hunstein to shoot the show and a 4 p.m. soundcheck – which the label recorded and then duly wiped – weren't quite sure what to do, though they quickly rejected half the songs that night from consideration for a live album, including 'Blowin' In The Wind', 'Hard Rain', 'Talkin' John Birch', 'Don't Think Twice' and a riveting 'Seven Curses', still not knowing what they had.

Others there that night came away more impressed and motivated than Dylan's own label. Jackie Deshannon, one of the more original singer-songwriters in US pop, immediately canvassed the ironically named Liberty label – unsuccessfully – to let her do a whole album of Dylan songs,* while Bert Berns, co-author of 'Twist And Shout' and esteemed producer, was inspired to buy Dylan's debut and to add beat musicians to one particular song, 'Baby Let Me Follow You Down', a demo of which he gave to his fellow producer, Mickie Most, for his Geordie band, The Animals. Thus was folk-rock born.

---

* Instead, Deshannon cut an album of folk standards, confusingly called *In The Wind*, opening with three Dylan songs, 'Blowin' In The Wind','Don't Think Twice' and 'Walkin' Down The Line', as well as including songs with a Dylan connection like '500 Miles' and 'Baby Let Me Follow You Down'.

Dylan, meanwhile, just wanted to get his second record – given an advance plug by *Billboard* – into the shops. When his (lawyer's) March shot across the bows yielded no strategic change, Grossman played his ace: if Columbia wanted to cut 'Talkin' John Birch', his client wanted to reconfigure the album completely by recording some new songs. As Dylan told Nat Hentoff, whose sleeve notes had already been delivered, 'There's too many old-fashioned songs in there, stuff I tried to write like Woody. I'm goin' through changes. Need some more finger-pointin' songs in it, 'cause that's where my head's at.'

This time, though, there would be *no* John Hammond. After the meeting with Davis, he was *persona non grata*. As Hammond ruefully recalled two years later, 'I produced most of [the album], but ... then professional management came into the picture and I went out.' What, pray tell, did he expect? The label now had a problem – a lack of other folk producers. So they turned to a six-foot-four, black, Harvard-educated, jazz producer called Tom Wilson, confident he would get a break from Bob if for no other reason than the colour of his skin:

Tom Wilson: I was introduced by David Kapralik at a time when I was not properly working for Columbia ... He said, 'Why don't you guys stick around and do a coupla things?' I said, 'What do you mean? I don't even work for Columbia.' ... I didn't even particularly like folk music. I'd been recording Sun Ra and Coltrane ... I thought folk music was for the dumb guys ... But then these words came out.

Singer and producer struck up an immediate bond that would last through June 1965. As Dylan said in 2017, fifty-two years after their association ended and thirty-nine years after Wilson's premature death, 'When I met [Wilson] he was mostly into offbeat jazz, but he had a sincere enthusiasm for anything I wanted to do.'

What Wilson brought to the process was not technical. As long-time friend Al Kooper said of him, 'Tom was sort of a spectator-sport producer. He didn't do all that much ... [but he] got the job done. He didn't interfere in anything ... He was a very well-educated black man, but he didn't lose his black thing ... He was still a soulful and funny guy.'

First and foremost, Dylan's new producer had a sense of humour and a long fuse. Their first session together was scheduled for April

23rd, eleven days after the Town Hall and two days after *Billboard* announced the album they were calling *The Free Wheeling Bob Dylan* was being 'readied for May release'. In fact, Columbia had already pressed a previous version of the album, sending out promo copies and a few stock copies in a box to Berkeley, California, where a teenage Greil Marcus purchased one, saw the track listing did not tally with the LP itself, and returned it to the store.

Dylan really did want more finger-pointing songs on there, replacing 'Talkin' John Birch' with 'Talkin' World War III', proof that he meant it when he said, 'There's things going on in this world you got to look at.' 'Masters Of War' made it on there, too, though only after Dylan returned to it at session's end, Wilson having stopped take one with the immortal line, 'Hold it, Bob. We didn't know that was coming.'

After this, the session proceeded without any real hiccups until Dylan decided there were too many finger-pointing songs. He abandons 'Walls Of Redwing' without ever completing it, saying, 'Ah, I don't want to sing this,'* and announcing, 'I'd like to do this [one] instead.' He promptly delivers a riveting 'Girl From The North Country', a song that will haunt its subject, whomever she might be, for decades. At the end of the morning session, squeezed into a busy Studio A schedule, Dylan had an album for the ages. As did Columbia, even without the one song they'd made him remove, but he wasn't about to renounce.

---

* The 'Walls Of Redwing' on *The Bootleg Series Vols. 1–3* is not from this session, whatever the notes – and Dr Krogsgaard – may say.

1.8

April to November 1963: He's Not The Messiah, He's A Very Naughty Boy

People make the mistake to think that *he's* the guy that sings 'The Times They Are A-Changin''. [But] the guy that wrote [that song] only existed for that moment, for that righteous thought. It took me a while to realize that. But he actually convinces you that yes, it is me who is talking to you, and I'm being sincere about it ... In reality he's just singing a song and just playing.

Cesar Diaz, Never Ending Tour guitar-tech, to author

[When] me and Koerner got signed to Elektra, they flew us out to New York – my first time on an airplane – and I went to see Bob. He was still living on 4th Street. I remember there was some typed pages, song lyrics ... lying on the table. I picked one up and it said, 'Come senators, congressmen, please heed the call.' And I said, 'What is this shit, man?' And the guy shrugged and said, 'Well, you know, it seems to be what the people like to hear.'

Tony Glover

Joan had no expectations of Bob. Or if she did, she kept them in check.

Barry Kornfeld, to author

*

It didn't take long. Yet, even by Dylan's standards, the affair that started with a trip to Boston the week after Town Hall, was ill-advised. If both guilty parties liked to take the high moral ground in their songs, neither had any qualms inhabiting the dark end of the street. Unable to quit his lowdown ways, Dylan connected with Joan Baez of all people after two shows at the Cafe Yana, and arranged to reconnect in Monterey of all places in four weeks' time. Monogamy, it seems, just wasn't in his DNA, even when it came to 'the fortune-teller of my soul', Suze.

So where was Suze? She was supposed to join her beau in Boston, having written to her displaced friend Sue Zuckerman earlier that month, 'we'll probably be in boston (cafe yana) april 19–20 (definitely, not probably)'. And yet she was nowhere to be seen – unlike everyone who was anyone on the Boston folk scene. Had Dylan dissuaded her from coming along?

By now, Dylan's brief Club 47 cameo, twenty months earlier, had become the stuff of legend. This time when he got up, there was no holding him – or the crowd's appetite for him – back. When Baez heard him sing 'With God On Our Side', she was 'bowled over. I never thought anything so powerful could come out of that little toad. It was devastating.' Mitch Greenhill, who'd witnessed that Boston debut and thought 'he was imitating Ramblin' Jack Elliott imitating Woody Guthrie', now concluded 'he wasn't imitating anyone'.

If the locals were easily impressed by topical songs masquerading as folk songs, so was former Guthrie imitator Ramblin' Jack Elliott, who was among those crowded into Geoff and Maria Muldaur's apartment after the Club 47 closed its doors, as Dylan continued reeling off songs on which the ink was still wet, including – Elliott recalled – 'Who Killed Davey Moore?', an almost tuneless anti-boxing sermon from a man who would later own a boxing gym.* The song, like 'Walls Of Redwing', was one Dylan found hard to get out of his system. Yet he never recorded it in the studio – not even when he finally found a tune for it.

Dylan was fast becoming the darling of the 'Protesty' folk Nelson and Pankake had warned him to steer well clear of, even if they failed to mention any attendant physical threat. So Dylan was taken aback when 'With God On Our Side' sparked a near 'riot' at his next concert, bringing the curtain down prematurely on a promising new venue. Located in Grossman's home town of Chicago, the place was called

---

* Moore had been outboxed and beaten senseless by Sugar Ramos on March 22nd and died three days later, without regaining consciousness.

The Bear. Dylan had been invited by an old friend of Albert's, Howard Alk, an important future collaborator:

Bob Dylan: I opened it, groovy place, ran for about three months ... Howard ... wanted me ... for a week, but I could only play for two nights. It was this old mansion, converted into a hotel upstairs and three nightclubs downstairs ... I played there first night, and ... Howard's got this megaphone, he's going around telling people to sit down. I play '[With] God On Our Side' ... That was the last song. And this guy from the [far] end starts [up], 'Fucking communist, unpatriotic son of a bitch.' Starts yelling these nasty things. I'm just getting off the stage – I'm tired – and this guy in front of me ... gets up and says [to the heckler], 'Shut your fucking mouth,' and takes a salt shaker and crashes it across his mouth. This guy's face is bleeding ... Howard grabs the megaphone. It was a riot! The cops did everything they could to close it – [for] being a beatnik hangout.

A board tape of the show circulates, but cuts before any such imbroglio. It also fails to document a pre-show showdown between Dylan and local blues guitarist Michael Bloomfield, for the simple reason that there wasn't one, despite Bloomfield going down to the Bear intending to give the cub writer a mawling:

I went down there because I had just read the liner notes on one of his albums that described him as a 'hot-shot folk guitar player, bluesy, blah-blah-whee, Merle Travis picking, this and that'. The music on the album was really lame, I thought. He couldn't sing, he couldn't play. I went down to the Bear to cut him with my guitar ... and we just talked. He was the coolest, nicest cat. We talked about Sleepy John Estes and Elvis's first records and rock'n'roll.

Bloomfield became a convert after spending 'the whole day jamming with him and singing old songs. [Then] that night I heard him perform, and I don't know what it was he had ... but it knocked me out, even though it was not especially the kind of music I loved.' The audience, though, lapped it up. As Dylan entered his second Protest Phase, with capital Ps, college-age audiences were lapping it up. In that sense, at least, he was right-on when he told Glover bluntly, 'it seems to be what the people like to hear'. The seven-song Bear tape features just two examples of Dylan *not* steppin' out – 'Honey, Just Allow Me One More Chance' and 'Bob Dylan's Dream', a lovely valedictory to lost youth set to the tune of 'Lady Franklin's Lament'.*

Another seven-song set at the Brandeis University folk festival, a fortnight later, maintained the same quotient of topical versus folk sensibility. Perversely, though, it included three talkin' blues, one of which dated back to June 1961 ('Talkin' Bear Mountain'), another to February 1962 ('Talkin' John Birch'). It was Indian Neck all over again.

He was now quite insistent on performing 'Talkin' John Birch', though he already knew it would not feature on *Freewheelin'*. Perhaps he was warming up for his *Ed Sullivan Show* debut on May 12th, when he planned to slip the song across CBS-TV and into millions of American homes.

TV had recently become the new battleground for any songs-of-freedom quorum, thanks in part to an article by Nat Hentoff in the March 14th *Village Voice* entitled 'That Ole McCarthy Hoot!', exposing the real reason why Pete Seeger would not be appearing on ABC's *Hootenanny*, the TV station's shameless cash-in on the 'folk craze'. An associate producer had let it slip to a college reporter that 'pressure from advertising agencies, sponsors and stations' was behind the ban.

Suddenly, ABC found itself on the receiving end of someone else's blacklist. Jack Elliott led the charge, telling *Variety*, 'If I did the program, I couldn't stand up and sing again, or sit down to dinner again, with Pete Seeger.' In danger of broadcasting a folk-music programme with no folksingers, ABC's executive producer Richard Lewine held a press conference to insist there was no blacklist. He had simply listened to Seeger's records – surely above and beyond the call of duty – and decided, 'Pete Seeger just can't hold an audience.' It fooled no one.

Baez, never shy of mounting a bandwagon, told Hentoff, 'It's disgusting that there are city folksingers – including some who don't need the bread or exposure – who perform on those programs. They should know what it's about.' She had found her cause, announcing the formation of a *Hootenanny* boycott committee, which apparently

---

* Bloomfield specifically remembered him also playing 'Walls Of Redwing', absent from the tape.

already ran to fifty names – including Dylan's. Who exactly was trying to impress whom?

It was in this febrile climate that Dylan arrived at CBS's midtown studio the afternoon of May 12th for the *Sullivan* rehearsals, the high praise from Hentoff in a recent *Playboy* piece ringing in his mind: 'Dylan, the most vital of the younger citybillies ... draws his audiences into his stories as if he were an ancient bard.' Not on his first TV appearance of the year, he hadn't. *Folk Songs and More Folk Songs*, recorded in March and broadcast in May on the Westinghouse syndicate, was MC'd by John Henry Faulk, who knew a blacklist when he saw one. It featured a single song each from Dylan's first three albums (including a symbolic 'Blowin' in the Wind'), though only one of those albums was out.

As with the later *Les Crane Show*, Dylan had the off-the-wall notion of adding accompaniment to a bleak, mid-wintry 'Hollis Brown' and asked Barry Kornfeld to oblige on banjo.* He should perhaps have asked the gifted jazz guitarist Jay Berliner – who was also on the show – rather than making fun of Berliner's versatility, shouting, 'Hey, Jay, can you play that Warsaw Concerto?' When Berliner duly obliged, Dylan cracked up. As Kornfeld notes, 'Bob used to do stuff like that [all the time] – but with a friendlier tone.'†

It was Dylan who failed to see the funny side when the CBS censor told him to drop his John Birch song, telling friends, 'They wouldn't let me do it on the show. But Ed Sullivan dug it. Man, I walked off that show because they passed that song. The producer dug it. Brenda Lee dug it. The cameraman dug it. We rehearsed that program three times. The sponsor dug it. But the censor didn't dig it. One man ... It was all in the papers the next day. But I didn't do anything.'

Not quite true. Dylan had been spoiling for a fight with CBS. He may even have calculated that a non-appearance on *Ed Sullivan* would generate more publicity than an actual appearance. Certainly, he already knew that he had been stopped from releasing the song by

---

* The tune of 'Hollis Brown' was adapted from 'Pretty Polly', the definitive version of which remains B. J. Shelton's 1927 'Bristol Session' Victor recording, accompanied by his plangent banjo.
† It would take until 1969 for Dylan to really appreciate what he'd missed, when Berliner's guitar work shaped Van Morrison's timeless *Astral Weeks*.

another arm of the same organization. Both the *Times* and the *Voice* ran stories, with Dylan obliging the latter with a quote, telling Hentoff, 'I could have sung a substitute song ... but I just couldn't do it after coming so close to doing the "John Birch" thing. Those other John Birch songs, you can listen to the beat ... But mine, you've got to listen to the words. That's what I wanted the people to hear.'

Although Suze recalled him calling her 'from the rehearsal studio in a fit', that famous temper also remained the perfect smokescreen for a man on a mission. Certainly, Billy James – the one person to accompany him that day – recalled 'leaving the studio, with him not too terribly disappointed. Because he was tough – he was used to rejection.' Perhaps because this time he'd instigated it, having reinvented himself as the Prince of Protest in the eyes of his activist girlfriend/s. The feeling didn't last. When Izzy Young – at Grossman's behest – organized a protest outside the CBS building, Dylan cried off. Young 'called Dylan [on the day] and he didn't know if he could come down. He wasn't feeling so good.' He had made his point and moved on. ('Talkin' John Birch', though, would stay in the set for the next eighteen months, just to bang those credentials home.)

Through the summer of 1963, Dylan would milk this protest persona dry, little realizing it would define him well beyond any half-life it provided creatively. Thankfully, for now he kept his fun-loving side and his topical songwriting distinctly separate. As Peter Yarrow (of Peter, Paul & Mary) observes, 'Out of him would spout these extraordinary, earth-shaking songs, but in personal terms he was laughing all the time.'

Knowing he remained good company, Yarrow personally invited Bob and Suze to his Catskills cabin for a spring break in the little upstate hamlet of Woodstock. The cabin even had an old upright piano, which prompted Dylan to start writing on it; so much so that, as Suze saw first-hand, 'He kept a notebook beside him on the piano bench as he worked on songs, which were coming out of him rapid fire.' For her, it was like a revelation: 'I had no idea he could play piano so well.'

The others would sometimes leave him to it, only for them – in Yarrow's words – to 'come back with a picture, and Bobby would have written [something like] "Only a Pawn in Their Game"' – just about the only song we know he *didn't* write here. He also wasn't writing about his love life, perhaps because it might give the game away, but mainly because he suddenly felt exposed. People had started prying into what he perceived – naively – as his private life. That naiveté was on display during one of the more extraordinary exchanges from an evening with Tony Glover and Paul Nelson that July, when Dylan chastised Nelson for mentioning the personal background to 'Girl From The North Country' in his *Little Sandy* review of *Freewheelin'*, which was finally released while Dylan was upstate:

> When you reviewed my record you mentioned Dylan wrote this song when his girlfriend went to Italy. I wish you['d] never have done that, because that's ... *too* personal. It's like me telling [about] something in your life, that means something to you [but] I know nothing about ... It's not right. It's a sickness, and you don't dwell on people's sickness ... That's the only thing in the article I disagree with, [pertaining] to me.

Given that Dylan himself had already explicated the circumstances in another *Freewheelin'* cut, 'Down The Highway', it was a churlish complaint. Perhaps he was still sore that *LSR* had 'outed' him as Robert Zimmerman, the year before. Dylan was certainly taking the whole thing personal, more concerned about a review that would be read by a few hundred folk at most than what *Time* and *Newsweek* had to say. Evidently, comments like 'Dylan bases everything here almost 100% on his own personality' hit their mark.

Nor were Nelson and Pankake the only unregenerate folkies to take potshots at the album. In Blighty, Nigel Denver pointed the finger in a *Folk Music* open letter, suggesting 'a young contemporary writer should give hope in his songs and not accept the system as it is. The writer should be superior to the subject he is writing about; e.g., in ... "Masters Of War" ... you point out ... how they hide in their mansions and run at the first sign of trouble. But you are accepting again the fact that people are going to put up with it.' However much such comments stung, though, the album was turning into a slow-burn commercial smash both sides of the pond, eventually topping the charts in Britain, albeit two years later.

Nor was he turning off the tap, just redirecting the spray to douse the deceivers, those who 'hide in their mansions' while minions carried out their bidding, which was the subject of a song he wrote in mid-June, some days after Peter Yarrow sat with Dylan in Woodstock on June 12th, watching the news that Medgar Evers, a field secretary for the National Association for the Advancement of Colored People, had been gunned down outside his home in Jackson, Mississippi.

Yarrow insists Dylan duly got up and 'wrote a ballad about it', à la 'Donald White'. But whatever Yarrow thought he saw, it wasn't 'Only A Pawn In Their Game', which a few days later Dylan played to Maria Muldaur and Annie Bird in New York, probably on the day he wrote it. Muldaur would remember the occasion in detail in a letter to its author. She and Annie Bird were practising their Carter Family duets at the Third Side when he rushed in, bleeding from a finger cut. After the requisite tea (actually, coffee) and sympathy, Dylan asked his two friends if they wanted to hear a song he just wrote.

For Muldaur, it was an epiphany: 'I distinctly remember my mind busting open and a whole new world of consciousness coming over me.' Yet this 'new world of consciousness' was an increasingly paranoid one, triggered for Dylan and others by the film of Richard Condon's 1959 novel, *The Manchurian Candidate*. Released in October 1962, at the height of the Cuban Missile Crisis, it imagined a president being assassinated by a brainwashed Korean War veteran, played by Laurence Harvey. Dylan – who would later befriend David Amram, whose memorable score fits the film like a glove – portrayed Evers' assassin as a Manchurian candidate of bigotry.

But he still required an editorial in the June 16th *New York Times* to connect the dots. Dylan wrote the song only after reading a report of the speech NAACP executive secretary Roy Wilkins gave at Evers' funeral, undeniably the hairpin trigger for Dylan's song:*

> We are here today in tribute to a martyr in the crusade for human liberty, a man struck down in mean and cowardly fashion by a bullet in the back ... The lurking assassin at midnight June 11th ... pulled the trigger, but in all wars the men who do the shooting are trained and indoctrinated and keyed to action by men and by forces which prod them to act. The Southern political system put him behind that rifle: the lily-white Southern governments, local and state; the senators,

---

* It's possible Dylan heard a first-hand account of Wilkins's speech. Among the mourners was John Hammond.

governors, state legislators, mayors, judges, sherriffs, chiefs of police, commissioners.

The culprit had not even been arrested as yet. When he was, ten days later, Wilkins's thesis, co-opted by Dylan, was shown to be fatally flawed. Byron De La Beckwith, a high-ranking official in the Ku Klux Klan, paid the $10,000 bail the judge set in cash. He was no pawn. Just a bigot, who ran for lieutenant governor of Mississippi four years later, after he was twice acquitted of Evers' murder. It took a deathbed confession to confirm what everyone already knew. It really *was* him who 'fired the trigger'.

Dylan, though, would continue to champion the idea behind the song, telling Max Jones in May 1964, 'He's been taught there's only one way; he's been sheltered. He's gonna get uptight ... when he sees something different. We have to ask why these people have ... taught him this.' And the following year, he all but absolved Beckwith and his ilk: 'Some people have been taught to care what people look like. People who hate [others] have been taught that way. It's not their fault.'

In June 1963, though, Dylan was spoiling for a fight, insisting his response to 'see[ing] friends of mine sitting in Southern jails, getting their heads beat in' was to 'get mad'. He certainly seemed angry when he wrote 'Only A Pawn' and was still as mad as hell a month later, when he told Paul Nelson he wrote it 'for me and people like me. I can't write the kinda song you're thinking of, [something like] "Stand, Fall, Billy Saul". This song ... I saw work. I saw people get moved enough to kill that fuckin' white guy – and that's what I want ... I want them to get off their ass, whether it takes guns to do it, to have a gun in their hand for the betterment of themselves. But hey, I'm young, man. I believe that way right now. That's a fight song and I seen it work ... It's too easy to sit back in a box in the suburbs.'

Here is a uniquely unguarded moment of belligerence. He would never let the mask drop like that again, even if he still informed the left-leaning *National Guardian* in September, 'What comes out in my music is a call to action.' By then, he had experienced the South in the midst of its civil rights struggle, at the sharp end. In fact, it was probably this very song that actor and activist Theodore Bikel heard one night – a fortnight before the flight he described to Sounes – which prompted him to take Dylan aside and say, 'Bobby, you shouldn't just write songs about this stuff. You should experience it first-hand ... Come down south with me.' Supposedly, Dylan cried poverty.

Bikel was not so easily dissuaded and told Grossman he'd pay for the ticket: 'Just don't tell Bobby.' Bikel later convinced himself that when they both boarded an evening flight in early July to Jackson via Atlanta, and saw 'Bob scribbl[ing] ... lyrics on the backs of envelopes', that it was the already-completed 'Only A Pawn In Their Game' he was working on. It was not.

The trip down to Greenwood, Mississippi, where Dylan publicly debuted the song on July 6th to a voter-registration rally and news film crew, has been presented as a case of him stepping up, not just steppin' out. Certainly, Evers' death had heightened tensions exponentially, sparking riots that resulted in twenty-seven arrests – of mostly black 'agitators'. However, when Dylan got up to sing his song, on the back of an NAACP truck, he was in no real danger.

As Pete Seeger – who needed no such persuading to make the trip – wrote in his first-hand account in *Broadside*: 'Because reporters were present from *Life* magazine and the *NY Times* as well as press and television cameramen, the police were on their guard against any rough stuff taking place. They [even] dispersed a crowd of vengeful Dixiecrats who tried to assemble across the highway from the field.'

It was still a real eye-opener for Dylan. In future, he would confine himself to providing rabble-rousing, finger-pointing songs – and not even those for much longer – while privately visiting friends like Len Chandler, a black folksinger savagely beaten in a racist attack, in Bellevue Hospital. Hospital visits, he could handle.

But he still knew which side he was on when making his last trip to Minneapolis as a folksinger, on the back of a death in the family: his beloved maternal grandmother, Florence, who had lived with the Zimmermans ever since her husband, Ben, had died. The trip brought home to Dylan what he had escaped, producing one of his most haunting early ballads, 'North Country Blues', written in the first-person as a Hibbing miner's wife, his worst nightmare.

Meanwhile, he had another Midwest score to settle, summoning Paul Nelson to a soirée at the Whitakers' to answer for his (and Pankake's) *LSR* review of *Freewheelin'*. It was a last gathering of the Scholar clan, with Morton and Koerner in attendance, too.

While Dylan found the time to play (and Glover to record) more than a dozen songs – including eight written in the last half-year – as the taper later noted, 'The talk is almost better than the songs.' When things got too heavy – and they did – dissenting voices, not just Nelson's, were raised, but Dylan would not be moved. As Glover recalled, 'They got into some really interesting shit. Whitaker would be saying, C'mon, let's lighten up. How about a song? [only for] Bob [to] play a song to illustrate a point, like "Who Killed Davey Moore?"'

As Nelson recalled, 'It went on and on. We were sort of the anti-topical-song people ... [But, to me] it [was] like patting yourself on the back music, it just seemed so obvious ... And Dylan was arguing, "No, no, this is really where it's at." ... He was really a brilliant talker then. He'd play "Who Killed Davey Moore?" and he'd say, "Whaddya think about that?" "I don't like it much." Everybody would give me a hard time. And Dylan'd say, "You've almost got it." But it was a very uncomfortable night.' Nelson stood his ground, though, consoling himself with the thought that he was 100% right:

> I kept saying, 'You're way too talented to be in this blind alley. You can only express A thru B by writing [like] this. Why would you want to stay there? ... And you won't.' It didn't take a genius to figure that. We sorta made friends that night, because I showed up and because I did argue and I didn't cave in ... Jon just didn't want to go. He figured it right, 'If you go, you're gonna have twenty of Dylan's friends all aiming their guns at your head, and he's gonna be out to wipe you out.' [But] we did take this stand against topical songs, [so I thought] we oughta go and answer it, and I think he respected me for coming ... He was kinda drunk and ... he was out to impress everybody, and I wasn't a very impressive talker. He wiped the floor with me ... He out argued me a hundred to one.

Nelson does himself a disservice with the above remark, made decades after he last heard Glover's judiciously edited tape.* A sequence sandwiched between Dylan singing the turgid 'With God On Our Side' and the tender 'Girl From The North Country' serves

---

* As Nelson informed me, Glover only 'turned on the tape ... when it got interesting'.

to demonstrate that the singer didn't always get the best of the verbal ding-dong or take the philosophical high ground, resorting to saying things he would renounce before the leaves were even off the trees:

Dylan: It's too easy to sit and write about what's wrong [with songs]. Would you like it if everybody sat around and sang 'East Virginia' all day, the same way? What would you have to criticize? ...
Glover: Why don't you play 'With God On Our Side'?
Dylan: [Okay,] this ain't got nothing to do with folk music, man. I wrote this song because I feel that way. Gonna be no more Woolworth's building. No more *Little Sandy Review*. Hey, where's all that wine? ... I'd like to dedicate this now ...
Nelson: To posterity.
Dylan: Hey, you should dig Joan Baez. If you knew her, you wouldn't put her down ... which is awful easy.
Nelson: That's all I'm trying to do.
Dylan: But you're losing [out]. I'm not criticizing. I'm just talking to you as a friend. There has to be people like you, to ... just criticize from your point of view. But you lose out on so much by just sticking to the rules. I wouldn't want to have your job. I'd split in a week. But it takes a lot of courage to stay and write a magazine.
[Plays 'With God On Our Side']
Nelson: I liked it fine but I wouldn't say it was any better than 'East Virginia', which you were talking about before ...
Dylan: I didn't say it was better. Nothing's better than nothing. These are different times, but you gotta understand it all. You see ... everybody [I know] reads ya.
Nelson: It's hard to do all these things.
Dylan: But it's gotta be done. Here's a writer, Dave Morton. He sang a couple [of songs] to me when he came to New York, [and] they're groovy songs. I got as much respect for him as Bascar Lunsford.
Morton: Thanks a million!
Dylan: It's easy to make rules for folk music. You're giving people advice in your magazine. You gave me some advice. You said, get back to the fifty-fifty [split of traditional and original material]. Well, I'll tell ya right now, I'm never gonna do it. And the next record you can put down more. It'll make no difference.

Nelson: You did it in that song. The melody was pure folk music ...
Dylan: We can be friends but you gotta know when you ask me who I'm writing my songs for ...
Nelson: ... A lot of people write for themselves.
Dylan: Woody didn't. Woody wrote for people like him ... so I write for people *like me*. I write for Tony Glover and Courtney Cox, from Jackson, Mississippi. You're writing for people taking [their] finals on Friday. None of my friends go to college. All my friends are either in New York or bumming across the country. I don't want you to get hung up. You got one step to go. Izzy Young puts you down. Lot of people put you down. That's nothing. But ... as soon as you do something, you got all these people latching on, so they can make their living, too.
Nelson: I'm not making a living. I'm doing what I believe it's right for me to do.
Dylan: All I'm asking you to do is travel around without the sense of rules. You're living by rules. Listen, man, I can't convince you of nothing. I'm trying to come up to your door and bang it and run back to New York. 'Cause you need it banged. I got no doors in front of me. I'm walking naked. There's no doors. You can swipe at me but when I wake up in the morning, there's no doors. You got doors, man ... You put down a lot of people in your magazine – a lot of good people.
Nelson: I'm not putting down these people, I'm putting down what's on the record.
Dylan: ... All I'm saying is, don't take yourself or your magazine too seriously ... Do something with that magazine. Get those rules and them chains and get them outta there. It ain't gonna help a soul putting down Harry Belafonte. He's too far gone – leave him to himself. You got a name – forget putting down Judy Collins. It don't look good [you saying], We think she could be a folksinger in a couple of years if she gets back in line ...
Nelson: It's a critical magazine of record reviews and that's where I want it to be. Though you seem to want to convert me.
Dylan: You run a magazine ... [so] why don't you check all these people's feelings before you write?
Nelson [incredulous]: You want me to check all these feelings before I write?

Dylan: Sure I do. I look around and see how people feel about things. I don't just look at my backyard ... You don't understand what I'm doing.
Nelson: I understand what you're doing.
Dylan: No you don't. Have you seen the people I talk to, I bum around with, [because] I know the people you write for ...
Glover: Sing a song that he didn't like in the review ...
Dylan: You put down 'Bob Dylan's Dream' and 'Girl From The North Country'. I think 'Girl From The North Country' is beautiful. Not because I wrote it. [Girl: Play it.] I'll play it. I feel very close to that. I wrote that song with somebody else who knew what it was all about ...
[Plays 'Girl From The North Country']
'Please see for me if her hair hangs long.' Man, [that]'s a gut-pulling line for me ... and I wouldn't write it, if not. I was thinking about the whole thing. I'm not thinking [of] 'yonder sits little maggie' as a love song. I can't think of a love song as this and that. I'm gonna sing Paul a song. [It's] called 'Boots Of Spanish Leather'. I want you to hear this one. I don't pretend this [is] folk music ... You can call me anything you want, but I got a thing to do and I do it.

If it was an uncomfortable evening for Nelson, the experience also left Dylan ruminating for weeks afterwards. He had already written a long free-verse apologia for the position he took that night, one which elaborated on his claim that he couldn't think of 'Little Maggie' 'as a love song'. It took the form of a letter to Glover. But this time, the private conversation went public, after 'somebody called me up and asked me to write something in the Newport Festival book. He said, You got anything you could submit right away? ... I had this letter I was writing ... and I [just] said, "Well, as a matter of fact I do have something" ... I finish[ed] the letter and I said, "Here, man, print it all." The next thing Glover knows, there is a prose poem addressed to him in the festival programme – 'i can't sing little maggie with a clear head / i gotta sing seven curses instead / i can't sing john henry / i gotta sing hollis brown ...'

'For Dave [sic] Glover' could just as easily have been called Last Thoughts To Tony Glover. As proof that things had changed, Glover even remembers, 'When he was getting ready to leave [town] – he had to be somewhere for a gig – ... I had this feeling, as he got on the plane, [that] this was some kind of turning point.' Reviewing the tape in 1971, at Dylan's request, Glover described the experience as 'very nostalgic for me to hear'. That man without a five-foot-nine psychological fence around him would soon be a half-remembered chimera. It was certainly back in place the next time he played 'Only A Pawn In Their Game', two or three days later, to a more hostile audience:

> **Tom Wilson**: In the first Columbia convention, in '63, I had two acts, Dylan and Terry Thornton. I'd just joined the company ... Dylan had just written that song about Emmett Till [sic] ... He sang it and half the cats in the convention got up and split ... They didn't want to hear this.

Dylan had flown to Puerto Rico at the label's expense, with Suze and Carla along for the ride, their way of showing him some perks they would bestow on him if he was a good boy. But, as Suze stated, 'He didn't schmooze with the suits [or] make small talk with the executives or salesmen.' Instead, he sang songs which made Southern reps. walk out.

But if Columbia had ever thought he might be more trouble than he was worth, it only took one glance at *Billboard*'s Hot Hundred to see 'Blowin' In The Wind' at number two. The following week he was playing to 10,000 earnest young things with spending power and a shared point of view at the third 'annual' Newport Folk Festival.*

Yet even here, Dylan's first real moment of triumph, he could feel himself constricted by an already unrealistic level of expectation. As he told WBAI DJ Bob Fass that festival weekend, 'Suddenly I just can't walk around without a disguise. I used to walk around and go wherever I wanted. But now it's gotten very weird. People follow me into the men's room just so they can say that they saw me pee.' He found himself needing to reiterate that he was just a songwriter, as he did in both his contribution to the festival programme and in conversation with *Boston Broadside*:

---

* There had actually been a two-year hiatus prior to the 1963 festival, which ran from July 26th–28th.

I'm not writing Folk Songs, Protest Songs, Freedom Songs or any other category. I have certain things that just have to be said. People can judge my songs in whatever way they want and get out of them whatever they see in them [but] these are just the thoughts that are honest and real to me.

Already, his relationship to the tradition he was fastidiously mining was being stretched to breaking point. When he was invited to appear at a ballad workshop on the Saturday afternoon, having written in the programme that he 'can't sing john johannah cause it's his story an his people's story / i gotta sing with god on our side', he was obliged to admit he was using the same tune an earlier workshop performer, Jean Redpath, had employed for 'The Patriot Game'. Said workshop was MC'd by Jean Ritchie, which is perhaps why Dylan refrained from performing 'Masters Of War'.*

If lines were being drawn, Dylan was too much in sync. with the times to be left on the wrong side of the fence – unlike the Kingston Trio, whose manager was told by a certain Albert Grossman, 'in the rudest [possible] terms', that they had no right to be there. When 'Blowin' In The Wind' joined hands with 'We Shall Overcome' for the communal encore, everyone on stage knew Dylan had found his fan base.

Yet the next time he played to a similar size crowd, three weeks later on August 17th, at Forest Hills Stadium, the response was altogether more ambivalent. According to an attendant (and wholly unknown) Paul Simon, 'I remember [when] Joan took him on at a concert in Forest Hills, he sang two numbers at the end ... and got booed off stage.'

Just as he had at Newport, Dylan was sharing a stage with Baez, but this time it was her show to her fans, many of whom were audibly appalled at the 'upstart crow' she would gushingly introduce at shows for the next year. Nor would Dylan's growing reputation lessen others' opprobrium when she relinquished stage after stage to the singing hobo. A particularly scathing critic of Dylan's incursion would be thirty-two-year-old John Updike, who called him to account after a show in Massachusetts:

---

* He saved it – more appropriately – for the following day's Topical Songs workshop.

> The unkindest cut of all [was when] Miss Baez yielded the stage, with a delight all too evident, to a young man ... in tattered jeans and a black jacket, three months on the far side of a haircut, whose voice you could scour a skillet with ... [Yet] it must be acknowledged that his plangent strumming and bestial howling gave the Baez concert what vitality it had. Miss Baez, this admirer was pained to observe, visibly lit up with love-light when he came onto the stage, and even tried to force her way, in duet, through some of the impenetrable lyrics ... Dylan composes as abundantly as poison ivy puts forth leaves.

Whether or not Updike was speaking for the many, mattered not. For the next eighteen months, Baez would continue turning on that 'love-light'. Having previously had quite a reputation for, in Eric Von Schmidt's words, 'want[ing] to be on stage all the time, and ... not lik[ing] anybody else being there', she now couldn't wait to introduce her protégé, easing the Queen's audience into Dylan's distinctive style with her own histrionic version of 'Don't Think Twice, It's All Right', a song she introduced at Newport as 'about an affair that has gone on too long'.

Hoping to supersede Suze, she stayed on after Newport, stopping at Grossman's home overnight with Dylan on her way back to New England. But it was their joint impromptu appearance at Gerde's one night early in August, performing the newly mined 'Troubled & I Don't Know Why', that really set tongues a-waggin'. Subsequently, Baez would cling to her memory of this time, 'and it wasn't a long time, when he was on my tour with me and we were getting close, it was very sweet between us ... and he was incredibly vulnerable and endearing'. Or it seemed that way, for a while.

Set to the tune of 'What Did The Deep Sea Say?', 'Troubled & I Don't Know Why' was another 'tell all about my troubled mind' song; strictly frivolous fare. But if Baez wanted something more powerful, a spat with a hotel clerk a week later over Dylan's shabby attire sent him into overdrive. The result was his first apocalyptic masterpiece, 'When The Ship Comes In'.

Again, the idea had been percolating for weeks, if not months; ever since Suze started work at the Sheridan Square Playhouse on Brecht and Weill's *Threepenny Opera*. Suze noticed her boyfriend 'was very affected by the song "Pirate Jenny"', made famous by Lotte Lenya, who played a maid who dreams of a black ship's crew sailing 'into the quay'. When asked, Who has to die?' she responds, 'All of them!' The violence of When The Ship's imagery would again prove unsettling to some, but Dylan clearly felt he needed to write a call to arms – or two. Three months *before* JFK's assassination, he sensed a change had gotta, gotta, gotta come.* The idea of a ship saving only the worthy appealed to Dylan – even then – which he admitted to Nelson in a particularly illuminating part of their July exchange:

Dylan: Do you like the song 'Black Freighter' that Brecht [*sic*] wrote? ... In this country there's a terrible fucking thing going on. There are certain people who are gonna have to throw away everything and join the boat. Otherwise, they're gonna be blown away by the boat. You're close to the boat and that's why I wanna tell you, Hey, get on the boat 'cause I know you can see it. The people that are far away are gonna get killed. The people that just walk along to campus and think about last year's prom, or writing their exam so they can join the law firm in the morning, they're gonna die, man.
Nelson: You think I'm that far off.
Dylan: You gotta be close to the boat, because you write about what you write about.

'When The Ship Comes In' was written almost to order, not for *Broadside* but rather a truly historic performance: the Washington Civil Rights March, scheduled for August 28th, 1963, eleven days after the brief Baez East Coast tour ended and the prodigal boyfriend came home to Suze, only to discover she had flown the coop.

Returning to an empty nest, Dylan found himself having to re-evaluate their relationship afresh. Suze was at her sister's, having come to feel she 'could no longer cope with all the pressure, gossip, truth and lies that living with Bob entailed'. But Dylan was not about to take the hint. He essentially moved in with her sister, too, 'which was rough on Carla'. Really rough. Even turning down his invitation

---

* Sam Cooke's 'A Change Is Gonna Come' was also written after he was refused admission to a hotel in Shreveport that fall, having been so inspired by 'Blowin' In The Wind' that he had incorporated it into his repertoire. Dylan returned the compliment in 2004, performing Cooke's song at a one-off show at the Apollo.

to join him on the Washington March didn't make the penny drop or make him drop Baez.

Instead, he arrived at the Lincoln Memorial with Joan, who sat with him on the dais and even tried to turn 'When The Ship Comes In' into a duet, while Suze looked on from a teeming throng of likeminded believers. She and Zuckerman had travelled there together on an Actors Equity union bus. But the Baez association continued to bother Suze, who told her friend, more in hope than with conviction, 'Bobby could never love anybody more famous than he is,' even someone as keen to change the world.

Baez would later claim, 'I had to use [a] cattle prod to get him up there, practically ... It wasn't really his thing, but he did it.' It never occurred to her that maybe Dylan knew how it would look to a face in the crowd. Whether Dylan bought into the optimism which permeated that day, he has never said, but recently he has implied he related more to Malcolm X than Martin Luther King.

Still the apocalyptic streak of songs continued – for now. Barely had he returned to his 4th Street apartment than he leafed through the Gospel according to Matthew, the most apocalyptic of the synoptic gospels, and found the line, 'The many that are first will be last, and the last first.' The result would be 'The Times They Are A-Changin', a song he would have to qualify more times in the next two years than any other, until he revealed to *Melody Maker*'s Ray Coleman that he had had the idea 'on 42nd Street ... There was a bitterness about at that time. People were getting the wrong idea. It was nothing to do with age ... [but rather] the type of person who sticks his nose down and doesn't take you seriously, but expects *you* to take *him* seriously ... I don't know if the song is true, but the feeling's true.'

It certainly spoke to people the country over. No sooner did he play the song live than the clamouring began. When, in December 1963, he reappeared at Bennington College – where two years earlier he'd been booed – poet Anne Waldman, then a student, asked him to write out the lyrics for the college's own literary magazine, *Silo*.

---

* It bears little resemblance to another so-called working MS offered for auction in March 2020, with its fantastical extra verse, 'Come all you magicians of illusion and deceit / With hundred-pound weights tied to your feet ...'

He duly obliged, signing it, 'Me, Bob Dylan'.* By then, Circumstance and a grassy knoll had already ensured it took on a life of its own.

If something specific prompted Dylan to leaf through his New Testament, perhaps it was an experience he had that month in, of all places, North Platte, Nebraska, in the company of photographer Barry Feinstein, as the two of them were driving Al Grossman's latest purchase, a gleaming Rolls-Royce, across country. Feinstein, who was at the wheel that day, later recalled:

> We doubled back to Denver and then went north to Cheyenne, Wyoming, where we stopped at a western clothing store for some shirts, pants and a vest for me. Then we picked up Route I-80 ... across Wyoming into Nebraska. On the way into North Platte, Nebraska, we saw this big sign for a revival meeting. We parked [up] ... Once inside the first door, we found ourselves in a pressurized chamber in an inflatable tent. We closed the outside door, opened the inside one, and stepped into a gale-force revival meeting: organ, drums, bass and choir, with singing and preaching side by side. We sat down and were revivalized. I was starting to mumble along ... when Bob and I exchanged a look. Then, moving with the music and the words of the Lord, we made for [the] door. I told Bob to stay with me but he was moving with the Lord. I stepped through the first door into the chamber and then opened the next door before Bob had closed the first door [which depressurised the tent] ... We walked fast to the Rolls giggling, trying not to stare at the dented tent behind us, when one of the preachers came out to see who'd let God's wind escape. He followed us to the middle of the parking lot, and watched us ... roll away.

Dylan himself would write about the self-same event thirty-five years later. He also remembered the tent caving in, but what he mainly recalled, with startling clarity, was what the preacher had to offer as his own apocalyptic subtext to the ship coming in:

> War is everywhere, friends. We are born into it. It has a life of its own. Peace is stillness and quiet and meditation. Freedom of the mind. Just because bombs aren't falling in your backyard, don't think that the mind of war is not working ... It's working on your jealousy, envy and fear. It is a demon spirit ... It's working on greed and blasphemy of

the spirit. It's working on your nasty jokes and your barnyard humor. It is waiting to be kindled. You are at war daily. Your inability to control your thoughts and desires is the mind of war at work ... Life is war. We are a lil' nation at war. We live and thrive in it. Jesus is the answer. In Him there is no war. Man himself is sin – sin [is] embedded in the soul of man ... Enmity is in the land, creeping through it.

Quite how much of this preacher's words sank in that day, not even Feinstein could say. But he did recall his friend 'moving with the Lord', perhaps thinking back to times spent in churches in Hibbing.

The stop in Denver also triggered a nostalgic trip to the Exodus, 'where people began noticing Bob. That really amused him.' Last time he couldn't get arrested, even when he stole someone's record collection. On leaving Denver, Dylan turned to Feinstein and said, 'I'd like to see a place I worked at in Central City.' Forty-five minutes later, they pulled up outside the dilapidated saloon: 'I played piano for a stripper in there.' 'You want to go in?' 'Nah, they fired me. I just wanted to see it.'

Whatever had happened in Central City in 1960 continued to bother him. Five months later, he would be back again – as he would in March 1966 – without ever finding what he was looking for. Kerouac's America, perhaps? Certainly, the jaunt with Feinstein was a way of seeing if it was still possible for him to travel around, masked (by perennial dark shades) and anonymous.

One night they raced a freight train across the Nebraska plains, as Bobby used to do on his motorcycle back in Minnesota, and for that brief moment Feinstein felt 'it was as if we had the same ideas about cars and trains, maybe life and death. An hour went by like a minute.' They got to eat dinner at truck stops, where truckers marvelled not at Dylan's appearance but at the car. Because back then, 'People in Iowa never saw a Rolls-Royce.' When 'Masters Of War' and 'Don't Think Twice' came on the radio in Illinois, they pulled over to listen, the experience still quite novel.

When they got to Chicago, the pair 'took a day off', and went their own way, Dylan perhaps going in search of Bloomfield and/or Alk, as well as a telephone box from where he could phone Suze, just to hear her voice. Whenever he was out of town, and whoever he was with, he would always phone: 'It was like an addiction – he needed to know I would be there for him.'

Yet no sooner was he back in New York than he was planning a trip west to play some shows with Suze's nemesis, the caterwauler from Carmel. It still suited Dylan to ride the waves of interest coming from Baez, hoping they would wash away any undertow of doubt about his own personal behaviour, doubts that saturate his one true love song that summer, the heartbreaking 'One Too Many Mornings'.

Carmel, where Baez had made her home, would prove therapeutic enough to inspire his most pantheistic song to date, 'Lay Down Your Weary Tune'. It was written, Richard Fariña recalled, one evening after the two writers had been 'out surfing ... He rode the motorcycle back and wrote the tune ... [Joan] was on her way to do a concert at the Hollywood Bowl, and he was very keen that she should sing it with him.'

Richard and Mimi would join Bob and Joan on the trip down the coast, Mimi recalling, 'He was obviously [still] very interested in me, and [was] being kind of flirtatious in his mumbling Bob way. So it was kind of weird between the three of us.' For Joan, it was bad enough that she had a love rival in Suze; should she have to fend off her sister, too?

In the end, both sisters had to fend off a debauched Henry Miller instead, after the writer ended up backstage at the Bowl playing table tennis with Dylan, trying to figure out which sister he most desired. As Fariña joked, 'He went after them both,' much as Fariña's own literary alter-ego, Gnossos Pappadopoulis, would have. ('Avoid my gaze, ladies, for you read my wish well enough.')

Fortunately, both sisters were still in awe of their own man's literary brilliance, as Fariña worked hard on his first novel and Dylan wrote songs 'like ticker tape' – to use Joan's expression – while she fed him 'salad and red wine'. To her lovesick mind, it was all 'brilliant stuff', especially 'The Lonesome Death of Hattie Carroll'.

Dylan had held off writing about the 'brutal beating by a wealthy socialite' of a black Baltimore barmaid, Hattie Carroll, at the time of the incident, back in February, awaiting the June trial of William Zantzinger and the judge's sentence to be passed. When it *was* delivered, on the day of the March on Washington – a six-month sentence for involuntary manslaughter – Dylan was reminded of an earlier poem of his, where the rich paid a fine and the poor did time:

> high degree family blood carryin charactors
> an the rest just had all the money by themselves
> an all 'f 'm walked out free
> just like that ...
> across the floor
> out the door
> down the steps
> an up the street
> round the bend an back again
> they bought their freedom ...
> [but] the answer dont lie with money
> no
> it lies with the judge.

Only now did he turn that ticker-tape in Zantzinger's direction. So easily did the song flow that the facts of the case were yet again as chaff blowing in the wind. The man who had told Paul Nelson, 'Don't take yourself or your magazine too seriously,' took an article by Roy H. Wood about the 'slaying' (his word) of Carroll at face value, though the whole piece was 'fake news', long before there was such a term.

When Dylan sang the song to his largest audience to date, on Steve Allen's TV show in February 1964, he told Allen, 'I took [it] out of a newspaper. It's a true story. I [just] changed the reporter's view.' He took far more liberties than that, fictionalizing the 'high office relations', Carroll's background and Zantzinger's response to the news of her death. But the most egregious libel was that Zantzinger beat Carroll with 'a cane that he twirled round his diamond ring finger'. The cane he was carrying was a hollow toy cane, and witnesses testified at the trial that even that 'weapon' had been snapped in two by another guest before a worse-for-wear Zantzinger verbally berated the grossly overweight Carroll, who actually died of a chronic heart condition after uttering the immortal words, 'That man has upset me so, I feel deathly ill.'

The judge's conclusion, unlike Dylan's, was measured and judicious: 'Here is an unfortunate set of circumstances. If the deceased had been a well person, we would not have heard anything about it. We don't feel Mr Zantzinger is an animal type.' What he was, to Dylan's closed mind, was guilty. And guilty he would remain, the songwriter insisting to Bob Hilburn forty years later, 'Who wouldn't be offended by some guy beating an old woman to death?' Answer: any halfway decent investigative journalist.

Dylan wrote another song about a judge's sentencing policy that month, but 'Percy's Song' took the opposite tack: deriding a ninety-nine-year sentence for being at the wheel when a car crashes, killing four, as unjust. Sadly, it would fall into the same molten pit as 'Lay Down Your Weary Tune', 'Seven Curses', 'Eternal Circle' and 'Moonshine Blues', four other gems melted down to make way for the likes of 'With God On Our Side', 'Hollis Brown' and 'Only A Pawn In Their Game', songs already past their sell-by date.

Once again, he was not sure what kinda album he intended but after the last LP, where songs came in all shapes and sizes, he generally preferred jabbing listeners in the ribs with a near-lethal dose of moralizing. Yet the *Times* sessions were the smoothest to date, spanning just five afternoons across August and October 1963, while producing enough out-takes for another, possibly better album.*

It did not start auspiciously. On the afternoon of August 6th he cut eight tracks in three hours, but used just one, a raw 'North Country Blues'. The problem may well have been in Dylan's head. He opened proceedings with an exquisite single-take 'Boots Of Spanish Leather', at least the equal of the album take, before he allowed himself to get bogged down by 'Only A Pawn In Their Game', 'North Country Blues' and 'Hollis Brown' as mike placement again became an issue, Wilson telling Dylan after three false starts to 'Pawn', 'Stay lined up, Bob, 'cause if you change around, it's gonna change the sound of your voice.'

After two false starts on 'North Country Blues', Wilson is on his case again: 'Bob, just back up about two inches and I think we can

---

* Aside from the five grade-A songs already mentioned, he recorded usable takes of 'Only A Hobo', 'Paths Of Victory', 'New Orleans Rag', 'Farewell' and 'Walls Of Redwing'.

get the "p" in there.' At the end of a promising third take of 'Hollis Brown' – logged as complete but breaking down on 'shotgun in his hand' – Dylan's frustration apparent in his voice, he offers to 'do it again. I stopped.' Instead, he does 'Seven Curses', and it is magnetic. But then he kills the mood again with 'God On Our Side'.

It requires an attendant Grossman to suggest, 'Hey Bob, what about "Farewell"?' He senses his client needs to lighten up, and after some stumbling, an unlogged fifth take nails it. Thinking he might be back on track, Dylan revisits 'Hollis Brown' and does 'New Orleans Rag', both on guitar, in single takes. But the whole vibe of the session feels wrong, prompting him to revisit five of these songs the next day, convinced he'd wasted almost a whole afternoon at Studio A.

The following afternoon, a change has come. The first five songs are all dispatched in single takes, four of them becoming album cuts. Almost everything works. Dylan even breaks into an enjoyable piano/harmonica instrumental he calls 'Direct To You From Carnegie Hall' after 'Eternal Circle'; one of three instrumentals at these sessions. He even rediscovers his love of the piano, recording versions of 'Keys To The Highway', 'New Orleans Rag', a new, improved 'That's All Right Mama' and 'Hero Blues' at the ol' johanna.*

A third August session on the 12th yields usable takes of 'Hero Blues', 'Moonshiner Blues' and 'Eternal Circle', but Dylan seems unsure whether he should even be doing (six-month-)old songs like 'Hero Blues', 'Paths Of Victory' or 'Only A Hobo', knowing he has plenty in reserve for a commercial successor to the chart-climbing *Freewheelin'*.

By the time two sessions are booked for October 23rd/24th, nothing old or borrowed will be allowed to blur his unerring focus. Aside from a valiant attempt to recapture 'Eternal Circle', work is confined to songs he'd written since August. At least he has now figured out that, if a song ain't workin', move on and return to it later. On day one he does this with three songs destined for the album: 'Hattie Carroll', 'When The Ship Comes In' and 'Times' itself. After the first take of 'Times', which has all the words but breaks off during Dylan's harp

---

* Perhaps surprisingly, he doesn't attempt either 'When The Ship Comes In' or 'The Times They Are A-Changin'' at the piano, as he had for Witmark, an indication that they were probably written at the keys.

outro, he says, 'I ain't in the mood to sing that.' Likewise, after take two of 'When The Ship', he informs Wilson, 'I don't feel like singing that. I'm searchin' and I shouldn't do that.'

In both cases, he returns later in the session and tries again. On the latter, he even does an extended harmonica intro, only to then record it with no intro at all. Feel is everything as he continues insisting on complete takes – no inserts! – even when a second take of 'Percy's Song' on day two breaks down eight minutes in, Dylan exclaiming, 'Shit! Man, I forgot the words. What the fuck am I doing here? We'll start it *all* over.'

He knows such things only happens when his mind is a-wanderin'. And if proof were needed of this rule, either side of 'Percy' Song' he dispatches 'Times' and 'Lay Down Your Weary Tune' in single takes, the latter a performance which could and should have graced the album; the former, one that did.

He has just one more song to get through, 'One Too Many Mornings', the only song directly addressing Suze, who is there that afternoon to hear him pour his heart out. Having done so, Dylan breaks into a Mexican Rag and a 'New Orleans Rag', both on the piano.*

When the second take of the latter breaks down, Wilson informs him, 'We can use it another time. They're kicking us out 'cause they got someone coming in.' Dylan has just recorded an album that will fill Columbia coffers for the next half-century but The Banjo Barons – I kid you not – have been booked for Studio A at 2.30 and Bob and Tom must leave. So much for Columbia respecting the artistic process!

Actually, Columbia could have saved itself the few dollars expended on five three-hour sessions if it had just made Dylan's next album a live LP, like the one they recorded at Carnegie Hall two days after The Banjo Barons twanged away the afternoon. Of the nineteen songs Dylan performed that night, five were from *Freewheelin'*, the rest were all newly framed, save for the now ubiquitous 'Talkin' John Birch'. Dylan even unleashed exemplary versions of the three best songs not to make the cut: 'Seven Curses', 'Lay Down Your Weary Tune' and a positively gripping 'Percy's Song', in a show that was a quantum leap on Town Hall, performance-wise.

---

* The former would be logged, and released in 1991, as 'Suze' but was always bootlegged as 'The Cough Song' because Dylan coughs to signal Wilson to 'fade it out'.

Dylan was becoming a mesmeric performer. As Suze later noted: 'Grossman, Dave Van Ronk, Terri Thal and ... I watched and absorbed what was happening [sidestage]. We all sensed a sea change.' Also there to see their son stun a sell-out crowd were his parents, who had already told a journalist from the *Duluth News Tribune* they were 'particularly proud that Bob will perform in Carnegie Hall ... and ... plan to be there'. As Beattie later said, 'We knew he was gifted when we went to Carnegie ... and that he was really enjoying what he was doing.' Suze again played the official girlfriend as Dylan took the folks out for dinner. This time, Beattie recalled, 'We stayed for a few days.'

However, the interview the couple had given to the local paper the week before had appeared with an unfortunate headline: 'My Son, the Folknik: Youth from Hibbing Becomes Famous as Bob Dylan'. Uh-oh. And they were presumably in New York on the 28th, when the latest issue of *Newsweek* appeared on the stand, turning the *Duluth Tribune*'s scoop into national news.

Newsweek reporter Andrea Svedberg – cut from the same cloth as Roy H. Wood – had been chasing Dylan for weeks. When a scheduled interview on the 23rd or 24th became a slanging match, she slung as much mud as she could, before going back for seconds.

Svedberg took the usual tabloid journalist's delight in juxtaposing Dylan's claim not to 'know my parents ... I've lost contact with them' with the news they had come to see him play at Carnegie. And she used the few quotes she squeezed out of his brother to make them sound estranged: 'We were kind of close ... [But] Bobby is hard to understand.' Maliciously, she repeated an earlier libel 'that Dylan did not write "Blowin' In The Wind" ... it was written by a Millburn High student named Lorre Wyatt', which was not only a lie but legally indefensible on her (and *Newsweek*'s) part. Svedberg didn't care.

Suze remembers Dylan 'felt violated and his parents ... were very upset', though not half as upset as Dylan was at them for talking to the press about him. That was not gonna happen again. Capisce! The publicist who set up the interview, Billy James, was also deemed culpable for just doing his job. As James says, the tenor of the piece was 'snide [and] vengeful ... forever colour[ing] his relationship with reporters and editors'.

But if Dylan was angry, Wyatt was mortified. He had told the *Millburn High School Miller* the previous December – having learnt the song from *Sing Out!* – that 'a well-known folksinger ... bought the song and the rights to it for $1,000', never expecting any more would come of this lil' white lie. But *Newsweek* kept pestering him, hammering on the disquieting questions. Even when he 'denied authorship of the song,' Svedberg still hinted that *he* had written 'Blowin' In The Wind'.

Dylan, who had been guilty of a fair share of appropriation himself, was having his most famous, lucrative composition taken away from him in print. For those like the irascible Izzy, he had it coming: he 'has never given one single person credit for a musical idea or a literary idea. And the reason for that is economic ... The image of a genius is that they don't copy.' It was time Dylan came clean, and in the process write his own restless epitaph. The press wars had begun.

Winterlude #1 (November/December 1963): Off The Road

> I used to get scared that I wouldn't be around much longer, so I'd write my poems down on anything I could find – the backs of my albums, the backs of Joan's albums, anywhere.
>
> Bob Dylan, 1965

> I think [Grossman] was one of the few people that saw Dylan's worth very early on, and played it absolutely without equivocation or any kind of compromise. He refused to let him go on any rinkydink TV shows, refused to let Columbia do bullshit things with him ... And Dylan in his early stages required that kind of handling – 'cause [he] himself would go off at spurious tangents.
>
> D. A. Pennebaker

*

In the months after Svedberg's character assassination, one of those 'spurious tangents' became letter-writing. Far from escaping 'the deadly rhythm of his own private thoughts', though, Dylan now succumbed to them.* As he wrote at the top of the typescript to the solitary song he wrote in those months, 'the time cant be found t fit / all the things i want t do'.

For this 'restless soul', the letters and poems he wrote between December 1963 and the summer of 1964 – usually in free form verse, à la 'For Dave Glover' – would come in all shapes and sizes, before Dylan just as suddenly turned off the tap. So much so that by May

---

* 'All men must escape at times from the deadly rhythm of their private thoughts' – Raymond Chandler, 1944.

1965 he would place top of a personal list of hates, in UK magazine *Jackie*: 'Writing letters. I just never do that.'

Yet the year before, he corresponded with fellow singers Johnny Cash and Joan Baez, fellow poet Lawrence Ferlinghetti, folkzine editors Sis Cummingham and Gordon Friesen at *Broadside* and Irwin Silber at *Sing Out!*, (ex-)girlfriend Suze Rotolo, female fan Tami Dean, Minnesotan friend Tony Glover and the Emergency Civil Liberties Committee, to name just the ones we know about. Some of these came in the form of open letters, meant for publication or circulation; some were so private they remain under wraps to this day.*

If he had spent part of 1963 contributing liner notes to friends' album sleeves, in the next nine months he preferred plastering them across his own; writing eleven poems for *The Times They Are A-Changin'* – obliging Columbia to include a double-sided insert to contain them all – and eleven more for *Another Side*, released a mere seven months later.†

Nor were these the only typewritten torrents pouring off of every page. He had begun work on the autobiography he had talked to Studs Terkel about in April, as well as at least two plays, while contributing a couple of columns to Robert Shelton's short-lived *Hootenanny* magazine.

At the same time he took a break from conventional songwriting, something to which he openly alludes in a free-verse letter he wrote to Tony Glover on December 6th:

> My guitar strings have escaped my eyesight ...
> they remain with me now as a friend who stands in front a me
> makin me look better ...
> an its gettin so now that I'm growin not to need
> it ... an soon I expect I will shout my words
> with out it. for its colors are wearin off on
> me an soon I myself will vanish into the sound
> hole ... an all that will be going down will be
> stark naked undressed obscene flesh colored songs.

---

* Both Cash and Rotolo kept his correspondence, but neither revealed its contents. The Silber letter ended up among the Paturel papers.
† Columbia did their best to oblige again, but cut more than half of what Dylan gave them. The full content did not appear until 1973's *Writings & Drawings*.

Meanwhile, he continued trying to jam into song form the first of a series of 'epitaphs' to a former self. 'Bob Dylan's Restless Epitaph' – as 'Restless Farewell' was called in typescript – really belongs with the Eleven Outlined Epitaphs he would spend November writing. One of these dealt with Newsweek's accusations far more poetically than 'Restless Farewell': the famous 'i am a thief of thoughts'. Another addressed the north-country roots Svedberg had 'exposed', claiming, 'the town i was born in holds no memories ... the town i grew up in is the one / that has left me with my legacy visions' – a half-truth, at best.

Six weeks later, he insisted in an open letter, 'my songs speak for me ... I write them / in the confinement of my own mind an have t cope / with no one except my own self.' If only that were true. With a sizeable, definable audience, he stumbled at the first hurdle – writing a song which made sense to others. 'Restless Farewell' took a traditional template – in this case, celebrated Irish drinking song, 'The Parting Glass'* – and tried to make it strictly personal, jamming the words into the ill-fitting tune. Had traditional templates outlived their usefulness? Or was it that the rhymes were painfully forced, Dylan jamming 'wrongfully' with 'forcefully' and 'harmfully' with 'knowingly', while simultaneously disappearing down his own metaphoric tunnel with clumsy neologisms like 'The time ain't tall / Yet on time you depend'?

Dylan was soon aware that changing the face of song would be a struggle. As he told Nat Hentoff at the first (and last) session for his next album, 'A song has to have some kind of form to fit into the music. You can bend the words and the metre, but it still has to fit somehow.'

Making 'Restless Farewell' the album closer would give him the opportunity to repent at leisure the haste with which he tried to marry a poem more suited to the page with traditional song. And his haste in composing would extend to the studio, too, where a session had been scheduled for All Hallows' Eve – just three days after Svedberg published her poison-pen epistle – solely to record what was little more than a rough draft. Indicative of a new clout at Columbia, the

---

* It's the closing track on the Clancy Brothers' live album, *In Person at Carnegie Hall*, released on September 16th, 1963, Dylan's probable source.

album had been put on hold while Dylan and Wilson cut eight takes, four of them complete, each progressively more mannered, as Dylan accentuated rather than ameliorated the dislocation between tune and words. He was determined to do it his way.[*]

With only a provisional sequence for that difficult third album, he had written his first self-conscious album-closer. He had a plethora of songs from which to choose nine more, but not a panoply of styles. In the quest for a little musical variety, Dylan even considered including a piano 'Hero Blues' – instead of 'One Too Many Mornings', one of his best love songs – long enough for a test-pressing to be sent out. A December 1st sequence also added 'Seven Curses' to side one, making for a fifty-minute album.

In the end, he plumped for relentless finger-pointing, making for a slightly gruelling listen, if hopefully an edifying one – assuming one liked being hectored. Some didn't. When the album was released on January 13th, it sold noticeably less than *Freewheelin'*, in the teeth of a growing public profile.

Through November and December, Dylan would continue to attend to performance duties but there would be no new songs in the live set. Not that audiences knew this. To them, half the set was new, i.e. unreleased, as he continued opening each and every show with his clarion call, 'The Times They Are A-Changin'', even after the times dramatically changed with the assassination of President John F. Kennedy on November 22nd, 1963 by a still-unknown hitman (or two) in Dallas, aka Redneck Central.

The next time Dylan performed the title track to his forthcoming album, the meaning had changed for good: 'I thought, How can I open with that song? I'll get rocks thrown at me ... But I had to sing it, my whole concert takes off from there ... They [started] applauding that song, and I couldn't understand why they were clapping or why I wrote that song, even.'

Having reconfigured his second album to *add* finger-pointing songs, he was already unhappy with how many he'd allowed on his third, telling Barry Kornfeld, 'All people want from me now are finger-pointing

---

[*] The analogy was not lost on Sinatra, who at his eightieth birthday bash in 1995 asked Dylan to perform 'Restless Farewell', and was rewarded with a performance for the ages.

songs and I only have ten fingers.' Too late. Columbia's corporate wheels were in motion.

Still seeing himself as part of the Village demi-monde, Dylan spent a harrowing weekend with Suze at Carla's Avenue B apartment, as people came and went, talking of JFK. Paul Clayton, who was now dating Carla, swung by, as did the Van Ronks and Kornfeld, who remembered 'He spent a lot of time at the typewriter', seemingly sunk in his own thoughts. These thoughts festered for three weeks before they spewed out of a nervous, swaying Dylan at a charity event at the Hotel Americana on December 12th, expressing aloud a thought he had previously tapped out: 'there is no right or left / there is only up an down / an the bullet came from somewhere below level'.

He seems to have quickly rejected the 'lone assassin' theory, even before Jack Ruby gunned down the appointed patsy, typing out the line, 'it had t be done with more guns than one', while also telling Bob Fass that weekend, 'They are trying to tell you, don't even hope to change things. If you try to put yourself up against the forces of death ... you're done for.'* He had learnt the hard way topical songs could be overtaken by events in the blink of a sniper's gunsight.

Kennedy's assassination led to an outpouring of grief, and verse, from a devastated Dylan – just not initially in song. He sympathised with Mrs Kennedy 'crawlin / on all fours ... after you knew your / husband was shot'; felt a sense of futility as he 'recall[ed] the day once more in my mind'. And he remembered, 'the colors of Friday', as he thought of 'cathedral bells ... gently burnin / strikin for the gentle / strikin for the kind / strikin for the crippled ones / an strikin for the blind'. He had found the apposite imagery, but as with 'When The Ship Comes In' he put it on the backburner.

Instead, he continued his sabbatical from song. For a minute or two he thought he could be a playwright, the Shakespeare of the alley cats. Inspired by Brechtian thoughts, he began writing a play,

---

* As early as December 1963 he would write, 'I was not speakin of [Oswald's] deed *if* it was his deed.' In 2020, he would address all the various conspiracy theories head-on in the scattershot, sixteen-minute 'Murder Most Foul', exciting fevered debate on-line and clocking up three million listens on YouTube in the first week, generating his first number one US 'single' ever.

set in a combination barroom/church: 'it is early evenin ... November 21st', i.e. the day before Kennedy paid for the sins of the father. The lead characters include a whore called Annastacia, John B. Pimp and a 'barroom philosopher', Thomas Drum. Though the play was abandoned fifteen pages in, it was not before he told *Broadside*, 'I'm wrapped in playwritin / for the minute my songs tell only about me an how / i feel but in the play all the characters tell how / the[y] feel.'

As Dylan continued inwardly processing this decade-defining event, thoughts tumbled out of him, unedited and unformulated, notably at the Hotel Americana in an ill-advised address to an audience of his elders. The ECLC had decided to give him the Tom Paine Award for his contribution to the civil rights struggle, a rather left-field choice. Dylan was no spokesman, as he discovered looking out at a sea of bald heads. Forgetting his gift for euphony he called a spade a spade, before suggesting they should all be at the beach with a bucket.

In describing the occasion to poet Allen Ginsberg a fortnight later, he said he had 'declared a sort of independence of any specific political allegiance and that upset them a bit'. What really upset them was his suggestion that their day was done, something he tried to qualify in a written apologia: 'when i speak of bald heads, i mean bald minds / when i speak of the seashore, i mean the restin shore / i d[o]nt know why i mentioned either of them.'

Unaware that the dinner was essentially a fund-raising event, he slipped the catch off and let rip, telling a middle-aged liberal elite they should move over and let the young remake the world, prompting a chorus of boos. No matter. He'd been booed before and he'd be booed again. However, when he learnt from his friend Geno Foreman that his speech had hit the ECLC in the pocket, he felt compelled to write 'a message to the ECLC', in the style of the Beats:

> oh God, i'd a given anything not t be there ...
> people were coughin an my head was poundin
> an the sounds of mumble jumble sank deep in
> my skull from all sides of the room
> until i tore everything loose from my mind
> an said just be honest, dylan, just be honest.

In a room full of elders, he had seen no mentors. So when he met the inspirational Ginsberg, the day after Christmas, he was mightily relieved to find someone on the same wavelength. Reading 'Howl' and learning about the ensuing obscenity trial had been defining moments for Dylan and he was anxious to talk poetics. In fact, according to the elder statesman of verse, they covered the waterfront, 'We talked about poetry and politics, how poetry was just a reflection of the mind, independent of politics. We made friends that night.'

Unfortunately for Ginsberg, a notorious homosexual hoping for more, Dylan was (and is) as hetero as could be. It didn't stop Allen. It would take Al Aronowitz, the hip *Post* journalist who had brought the two cultural icons together – something of a hobby of his – to read the elder poet the riot act:

'From the time we left [bookseller] Ted Wilentz's party until we ended up in front of Bob's pad on West 4th Street, Allen wouldn't let up. When Bob got out of the car to go upstairs, Allen got out of the car, too ... I said, 'C'mon Allen, stop coming on [to him].' ... I told him he wasn't acting like a famous poet [while] Allen jumped up and down like a disappointed kid having a tantrum ... 'What's the use of my getting famous if I *can't* come on to him?'

Ginsberg later admitted the validity of Aronowitz's charge: 'He was this nice, beautiful-looking kid. I immediately had a crush on him.' But he also felt kinship with a like-minded thinker: 'I'd [already] heard his music through Charlie Plymell ... I remember I laughed when I heard ["A Hard Rain's A-Gonna Fall"]. It seemed like the torch had been passed on to another generation.' When Dylan invited him to please come to Chicago for a show at the Orchestra Hall the following night, a wary Ginsberg politely declined, 'afraid I might become his slave or ... his mascot'. He saw the danger, and he baulked.

For Dylan, who had continued ruminating about his own love life, a fraught few months wrestling over his relationship with Suze led him to admit in another outlined epitaph, 'i think of Sue most times ... with her long hair spread out', and telling friends at *Broadside*, 'i should love everybody like i love sue / [but] in all honesty i dont', two public statements that must have cut Baez to the quick.

His most touching display of affection, though, came in a private inscription to 'Moohead' on Suze's twentieth birthday, two days before Dallas:

I pictured visions / In the midst of dreams / 'f a little girl chugging an puffin / Her way across the kitchen / With one hand graspin / A colour crayon/ And the other clingin titely / t a penny / Singing t herself / 'I'm twenny I'm twenny' / With the voice sounds 'f a small child / Complete with runny nose an snorts / Wide eyed with a playground grin / Bitin her tongue with concentration / Gettin so sleepy / Finally exhausted she dropped her tools / An stretched / An climbed slowly t her feet / An yawned / With curled mouth an bowed face / An teasingly I heard her say / In a shy whisper / 'OK I'm all done bein twenty I wanna play' / An I went with her because I loved her / An I asked myself when I woke up / Who was this strange sandbox birthday girl? / That has changed thru my dreams? / An it was you Moohead / An it will always be / You.

What went unsaid, even in his art-book inscription, was the shadow cast two months earlier, when Suze had found herself pregnant. Dylan – who was, in Suze's own words, 'confused and very upset at the idea of an illegal – read dangerous – abortion' – reluctantly agreed that now was not a good time to bring a baby into the world.

One imagines the relief in the Rotolo household was palpable. But it probably coloured Dylan's thoughts on the A-word permanently. As guilt mingled with an increasingly combustible mix of emotions, he bought Suze a handmade, embroidered Romanian sheepskin jacket he found in an East Village store for Christmas, hoping they still had a future, even as he typed out a section of his resurrected autobiography that recalled a Christmas in Minneapolis when erstwhile girlfriend Judy Rubin said 'not t call at certain times' because 'her ma hates me'. Even with History repeating itself, Dylan refused to learn from his mistakes.

For him and Suze, the end was nigh, and with it the anchor that tied him to that Village he had known long before his ship came in. With a new year dawning, Dylan toasted 'his' Suze at a party at Robert Shelton's. But he was troubled, and this time he knew why. As he told Sis and Gordon 'an all broads of good sizes': 'i have my fears but mine are fears of / the mind. the fears of the head / a lonely person with money is still a lonely person'.

Just as he set about turning his back on the folk family that had taken him to their bosom, he was telling himself, in the last of those Eleven Outlined Epitaphs, 'mine shall be a strong loneliness / dissolvin' deep / t' the depths of my freedom / an that, then, shall / remain my song'. No longer a mere thief of thoughts, he was about to become a Rimbaudian thief of fire.

Part 2
A Thief Of Fire

There are two classes of poets – the poets by education and practice, these we respect; and poets by nature, these we love.

Ralph Waldo Emerson

The poet makes himself a seer by a long, prodigious, and rational disordering of all the senses. Every form of love, of suffering, of madness; he searches [for inside] himself ... Therefore, the poet is truly the thief of fire.

Arthur Rimbaud to Paul Demeny, May 15th, 1871

If the fate of twentieth-century man is to live with death from adolescence to premature senescence, why then the only life-giving answer is ... to divorce oneself from society, to exist without roots, to set out on that uncharted journey into the rebellious imperatives of the self.

Norman Mailer, 'The White Negro' (1957)

We all got high. But not everybody went home and did something. A lot of people went home and did nothing or did more drugs. Only a few people ... accomplished something.

Victor Maymudes

2.1

January to June 1964: Becoming Withdrawn

One day he was a respected young songwriter, the next he was this *thing*. The Voice Of A Generation. The Man With All The Answers. People were at him all the time ... It was *relentless*. You or I couldn't have stood that kind of pressure. We'd have been crushed by it. Dylan not only stood up to it, he continued to do great work on his own terms in spite of it.

David Blue

For all his bravado, Bobby was a very sensitive and delicate entity and needed to be protected. People wanted to get high with him and get busted with him or get into bed with him. Being the object of that kind of fame and pursuit was not a comfortable thing.

Peter Yarrow

While you were on your own with him, he was an absolute delight to be with, but when his henchmen and his minders and his hangers-on came into view, he turned into 'Bob Dylan'.

Ken Pitt

*

Through the first half of 1964, Dylan would talk about – and talk up – projects galore, none of them his true métier. By the time he was writing to his *Broadside* buddies at the turn of the year, that proto-autobiography had become a novel, one that 'dont even tell a story / it's about a million scenes long / an takes place on a billion scraps / of paper', an almost perfect description of the book it became after everything he'd written before the fall had been consigned to the waste bin, having suggested to Glover back in December that he was 'going up t woodstock t finish my book', as if he was almost there.

By April 1964 he was telling his preferred publisher, Lawrence Ferlinghetti at City Books, 'as of now I am in the midst of destroyin all I've done ... I do got things of songs an stories for you. my hangup is tho that I know there will be more. I want to send the more more than I want t send the got', a frank admission he was already unhappy with the direction of his first book; a dissatisfaction that would never fully abate.

Likewise, his plan to write a play or two was fast heading in diametrically different directions, even as he was telling 'sis and gordon', 'I'm wrapped in playwritin / for the minute.' He simply couldn't keep his mind on track long enough to shape and reshape a narrative for weeks or even months, jumping from idea to idea like a fakir skipping over hot coals.

John B. Pimp and his friends would be left in the limbo of their barroom/church – part of a substantial discarded folder of poems and sketches, the Margolis & Moss mss. – even as he began a more Dylanesque play possibly called *Mother Revisited*, a title namechecked at least twice in 1965–6.* This time the ubiquitous prostitute character is joined by a cowboy and a young couple, Jewel and Pork Meatball, fresh from Highway 61.

If the dialogue suggests someone warming up for next year's surreal travelogues, this is not yet the rightful place or the time. What resides at Tulsa is little more than a fragment but it conveys the gist, each character asking after mother, and then wanting to know how the others know the absent Madonna, before the cowboy – a self-confessed 'freak for tits' – begins relating a story about a girl he met on the street whose tits were 'like mountains'. They escape in a pick-up which she asks him to floor – a premonition of the only song Dylan ever co-wrote with a real playwright – as they head 'for the woods'. Already, the lumberjacks are coming.†

---

* In conversation with *Melody Maker*'s Max Jones in May 1964, Dylan suggests he is still working on 'two plays', but does not provide specifics. Only the fifteen-page John B. Pimp typescript, which would constitute part of the Margolis & Moss papers, can be confidently dated to fall 1963.
† Six non-sequential pages of the *Mother Revisited* play ended up among the Tulsa papers. It is sheer happenstance even these survived.

A number of elements necessary for the alchemical change are there, just not in the right order. Before he could provide an apposite setting – a new kinda oral poetry – he would need to shift and shape Song itself. That process began at the end of January in a Toronto hotel room. Rather than taking 'one of the thousand million little points I can ... pick out – something bad, like segregation ... and explode it' – a description of his former approach he gave within hours of landing – he now tried to write a song for 'every hung-up person in the whole wide universe'.

He got as far as the first four verses, applying a narrative hook to a song about church bells tolling in a storm while ticking off a checklist of like-minded miscreants, the 'countless confused, accused, misused, strung-out ones', as he heard 'the chimes of freedom flashing'. He had not lost a sense of ambition, though he would need time to complete the lyric, adding verses five and six in pen at a later point.*

Nor had he stopped listening to the songs of freedom his friends sang, one of which, Van Ronk recalled, was among 'my grandmother's favourites, "The Chimes of Trinity", a sentimental ballad about Trinity Church, that [included the line] "Tolling for the outcast" ... He made me sing it for him a few times until he had the gist of it.'

Actually, the song – dating from 1882, with music attributed to a Sam Rosenberg – contains no such line, though it does provide the melodic gist for 'Chimes Of Freedom', a song that put a ton of gelignite beneath the protesty platitudes found on Dylan's latest platter, released just a fortnight earlier. Yet these were the songs he was in Toronto to promote, appearing on a half-hour CBC TV special, *Quest*, that filmed a disinterested Dylan to a backwoods backdrop even more stilted than the performance. Already, he was hinting at a dissatisfaction with the treadmill of live performance, telling a Toronto journalist, 'I don't work that much. I don't play concerts that much. I'm in this accidentally ... because [of] the songs I write.'

He still needed to find a way to make touring part of the experience of life, so much so that the minute he returned from Toronto on February 2nd he set off on a twenty-one-day, partial recreation of Kerouac's inspirational 1948 cross-country sortie, during which he

---

* The 'Chimes' manuscript is reproduced in *The Bob Dylan Scrapbook* (2005).

returned to both Denver and Central City, three and a half years on. It was a trip he later depicted to friends thus, 'We hit forty-six halls from Augusta, Ga. to Berkeley, Calif. We talked to people in bars, miners. Talking to people – that's where it's at, man.' Actually, before Berkeley he played just one show in Denver as he travelled to California from the New York island, via New Orleans.

As he travelled across America with hipster friends like the burly Maymudes and the pill-poppin' Paul Clayton, he was slowly turning inward. Realization was fast dawning that the days of travelling anonymously from place to place 'with everything I owned in my guitar case, [to] sleep on someone's floor and play music' were all but gone. His was already a fame ten times that which drove Kerouac to drink himself into an early grave.

He was now public property, something brought into sharp relief by one particular incident at a record store in Charlottesville, when he stopped off to see if they were carrying his new album. Pete Karman, the man who introduced him to Suze and gave him his first press mention, was along for the ride in the unfamiliar role of chronicler. When Dylan was recognized in the store, Karman recorded his reaction, 'Man, there's a lot of *people* in here. Let's split.' Outside the store, he exclaimed, 'They're closin' in on us,' before the quartet jumped in the car and made their getaway, Dylan exhaling 'Man, they almost got me.' So much for 'talking to people'.

If Karman was a strange choice, so was Clayton, who by now was dealing with deep-rooted psychological issues by consuming industrial quantities of speed, a recipe for psychosis. As their mutual friend Steve Wilson notes, 'Paul [had] tried to attach himself through Carla to Bob, by dating her, making him an ersatz brother-in-law, even though he was gay.' In Wilson's view, 'Bob was everything [Paul] wanted to be', save heterosexual.

Clayton kept any pederastic yearning from his travelling companion/s, as well as keeping at bay a burning resentment toward the thief of thoughts, something he would on occasion express to others. 'Don't Think Twice', fast becoming one of Dylan's most covered songs, had clearly been based on Clayton's 1960 recording of the traditional 'Who's Going To Buy You Ribbons' – and everyone who knew them, knew it. Yet Dylan did nothing to acknowledge his debt, either morally or financially – unless inviting him to act as his 'mind-guard' on this cross-country tour, all expenses paid, qualified.

If employing someone whose mind was disintegrating as a 'mind-guard' was not the smartest move, Dylan hoped Clayton might at least introduce him to folk-collecting aristocracy, as he had in May 1962, starting with Pulitzer-winning poet Carl Sandburg, whose 1927 folk collection, *American Songbag*, had blazed a trail for many like him.

Clayton was already 'known to Sandburg'. However, according to Sandburg's housekeeper, when the dusty travellers turned up at her employer's North Carolina home, they appeared unannounced. Dylan, holding a copy of his new album under his arm, asked to speak with the octogenarian, introducing himself as 'a poet' and telling Sandburg how much he admired his folk song collection and poetry. But as with his earlier meeting with Graves, there would be no symbolic passing of the baton. As an attendant Maymudes noted, 'Sandburg ... was in his late eighties and tired easily. Bob was hoping he was going to ... indulge us. [But] after about an hour, Carl said his goodbyes and politely gestured that he planned to retire inside ... Bob [had] wanted to spend some significant time with him.'

Afterwards, Karman and Dylan started to argue about poetry, Karman challenging him, 'How d'ya write the stuff you do when you don't even understand what it means?' This wasn't quite what Dylan had in mind when he originally plotted this beat pilgrim's progress: recognized by gushing fans, unrecognized by precursors and challenged to explain himself by a companion of the road.

Thankfully, the bright lights of N'Orleans beckoned. In Victor's words, 'Mardi Gras loomed like a safe haven and a proper stomping ground for stoned whitenecks on tour', as they arrived at the hotel to find a single room reserved for the four of them in a city booked solid.

They headed for the Seven Seas Bar, aka Los Siete Mares, but even with some margueritas to take the edge off room-sharing, they needed an early night ahead of Fat Tuesday's annual revelries, when Dylan would become just another face in the Cajun crowd, accosting the odd transvestite, chasing girls down the street in semi-serious pursuit and arguing poetics with schoolteacher Joe B. Stuart. As the drink flowed, he returned to a mantra he had already tried out on Karman,

'Rimbaud's where it's at. That's the kind of stuff means something. That's the kind of writing I'm gonna do.'

Sure enough, he rolled into his room in the wee small hours with the germ of an idea for a song about a musical muse, a Pied Piper-figure wielding a tambourine and offering the singer a trip on his 'magic swirlin' ship' (Dylan's version of Rimbaud's *le bateau ivre* – perhaps Arthur's most fabled illumination), a genesis he finally acknowledged in the 1985 *Biograph* notes.

Indeed, if a two-page manuscript that emerged around 2013 on Royal Orleans Hotel notepaper, indubitably in Dylan's hand, can be believed, 'Mr Tambourine Man' came to him whole and entire in the bone-weary aftermath of a night on the French Quarter tiles. 'Cept it didn't.* The manuscript was a later concoction.

Such moments would become rarer and rarer going forward, even as Dylan consciously cultivated the notion that his greatest songs came in a blaze of inspiration,† a mythology he first propagated on the radio as early as June 1962. By now he has learnt to allow ideas underlying important songs to ferment and form. 'When The Ship Comes In' and 'Hattie Carroll' had both taken shape at the back of his mind for weeks before being hammered out in a rush of ribbon. Likewise, 'Chimes Of Freedom' had begun life as a six-line response to Kennedy's assassination but it took two months for the rain to unravel.

Anyway, Dylan was out of Louisiana time. His Mardi Gras pitstop had left the ex-revellers little margin for musal meditation. The singer needed to be in Denver, 1,300 miles away, in seventy-two hours, on February 15th, for another symbolic homecoming. Time to turn the radio on, rev that engine and put the pedal to the floor, even as every station they tuned to was playing this British bubblegum his girlfriend and their hip friend at the *Post* had been trying to foist on him:

Al Aronowitz: Suze Rotolo thought The Beatles were great ... and she and I used to gang up on Bob about them. To him, The Beatles

---

* The Royal Orleans hotel did exist in 1964, just not under that name or with that notepaper.
† As late as February 1990, when Leonard Cohen asked him how long it took him to write 1983's 'I And I', he delightedly replied, 'Fifteen minutes.'

were 'bubblegum'. But then, Bob had a habit of turning up his nose at most everything that everybody else liked.

Dylan and the gang had been in a (TV-less?) motel in Meridian, Mississippi – Jimmie Rodgers' birthplace – on February 9, when an unprecedented 78 million Americans tuned in to see The Beatles' debut on the *Ed Sullivan Show*. As such, his own epiphany had to wait till he was 'driving through Colorado ... and eight of the top ten songs were Beatles songs ... Their chords were outrageous, just outrageous, [but] their harmonies made it all valid ... I knew they were pointing the direction of where music had to go.'

Serendipitously for the sixties, The Beatles themselves had reached much the same conclusion about Dylan's music three weeks earlier, in Paris. All but barricaded in at the George V Hotel by Beatlemania, the Fab Four used this time to assimilate *The Freewheelin' Bob Dylan*, leaving one to wonder, where did they find it? The album had yet to be released in France (or England), and Lennon's April 1965 claim that 'we cadged [it] off a DJ who came to interview us' was almost immediately contradicted by John himself, who told *Melody Maker*, 'Paul got [the Dylan albums] off whoever they belonged to.'

As with most musical trends, McCartney had the jump on Lennon, who gamely admitted, 'Paul had heard of him before, but until we played [*Freewheelin'*] his name did not really mean anything to [the rest of] us.' 'Macca' could well have brought the album with him to Paris, having 'borrowed' it from his brother, Mike McGear, who had borrowed it from a girl he had been (vainly) trying to impress, someone hip enough to own an import copy. McGear's first reaction on hearing *Freewheelin'* at her place – or so he claims – was 'This guy can't sing.' But he was real keen on this Liverpool gal, so he persevered; to the extent that he eventually asked to borrow the album to listen to at home, where he was caught in flagrante by his brother, who opined, 'What is this shit? This guy can't sing.' Mike replied, 'It kinda grows on you.' Fast-forward to January 1964. Mike has come to raise the siege of George Cinque, only to be stunned to hear, upon entering the boys' palatial suite, Dylan's dulcet tones. He challenges Paul, 'Hey, I thought you said he couldn't sing.' The remark engendered a slightly sheepish, 'It kinda grows on you.'

Already looking beyond the he-loves-you-blah-blah-blah platitudes of *Please Please Me*, Paul had the sense to realize the guy with the nasal whine was 'pointing the direction of where music had to go', with a little help from his fab friends, who were just as anxious to meet him as he them.*

Even as The Beatles' presence gridlocked Manhattan through the first half of February, Dylan continued heading west to a rendezvous with Baez and the Berkeley radicals. His February 22nd Community Theater concert would make a lifelong convert of the *Chronicle*'s informed jazz critic, Ralph J. Gleason, and convince Joan's brother-in-law that Dylan was now the real deal, so much so that at a post-gig soirée at the Baez home, Fariña began to talk to the singer about the two of them making a film together.

Fariña's idea, according to his biographer, was 'a western about a peace-loving cowboy who never carried a gun but had to take up arms to save his father', which sounds like a cross between *Shane* and *Saving Private Ryan*. The following February, Dylan informed a national TV audience he was making 'a horror cowboy movie' called 'Mother Revisited' only for the idea to disappear in a puff of aromatic smoke.

Nor was this the first time Dylan prematurely promoted the idea of him becoming a movie actor. As early as August 1963, Albert Grossman had written to Walter Dean at Columbia to inform him he had met with CBS president Goddard Lieberson 'to discuss an exciting motion picture venture, [a] motion picture [called] *Daffy*, the script by Les Pine and starring Bob Dylan ... The script is owned by Pennebaker Inc., Marlon Brando's company ... Bob Dylan will not only star in *Daffy*, but will also write all of the music. The picture will have scope and breadth and it will be shot mainly outdoors in many different locations in the United States, and will have the "feel" of a large budget picture in addition to an excellent story.' It's the last we hear of any such project, but not Dylan's cinematic ambitions.

Evidently, it wasn't just Dylan who was inclined to go off at 'spurious tangents'. Nor was Fariña the only one co-opted into his celluloid pipedream. Writing to Irwin Silber in June 1964, Dylan claimed, 'friends

---

* All parties, though, would have to bide their time. Though Dylan would visit London in May, it coincided with a secret holiday in the Virgin Islands for the Scousers.

of mine an me made or started makin this movie over in paris ... its all about us (for art's sake) ... an we go to blow up the arc of triumph'. Perhaps it was related to a movie idea he discussed with Maymudes that spring, 'based on the sense of alienation that couples with fame'.

While The Beatles were making *Hard Day's Night* with an actual moviemaker, real actors and a snappy script, Dylan was still at the stage where he was impressed to be partying at the former Hollywood house of Bogart and Bacall. The party in question came after another landmark show, at the Santa Monica Civic Auditorium, a week after Berkeley, at which the first shoots of Dylanmania appeared, catching Dylan and a Village friend by surprise:

Maria Muldaur: I was backstage when the concert ended. ... It was a big deal for him. 3,000 people, sold out ... He's glad to see a face from home ... People were saying they were his uncle, cousin, long-lost best friend from high school ... With the help of security we formed a V with Maimudes and [Neuwirth] in front and got through the crowd to our car ... That night I witnessed the beginning of what would become his enormous stardom ... I saw women throwing themselves at him, and he was just this scruffy guy.*

Muldaur had sat next to Clayton at the show that evening when Dylan announced a new song, 'Chimes Of Freedom', that helped her 'see the world in an ever-unfolding new way'. Dylan was fast outstripping his contemporaries, and the pair knew it. Also there that night were a quorum of Minnesotans. Tony Glover and Dave Morton had followed Dylan down from San Francisco, where they had been hanging out with Dylan and Maria's husband, Geoff, who had been playing with Jim Kweskin at a club in Oakland. Already in LA was Bonnie Beecher, with whom Dylan was especially delighted to reconnect. However, as Morton ruefully recalls, 'That was the last time we [all] really hung out.'

Dylan was due to make his prime-time national TV debut, on the *Steve Allen Show*, where he would find yet another reminder of his

---

* Perhaps they took the view expressed by Mati Klarwein to Miles Davis: 'The girls ... know what is good when they hear it and they believe that what is good vertically must be good horizontally, too.'

prediluvian youth. Howard Rutman, a former member of The Jokers, was a production assistant on the show. He quickly discovered the old Bobby and the new Dylan still had something in common: 'He was [always] terrible at small talk.'

Nor had he got any better at explaining his work, being stumped for words when Steve Allen asked him to explain what 'Hattie Carroll' was about. But he certainly got the song itself across, delivering one of his best performances in a medium with which he would never fully get to grips. Unfortunately, if his new-found fame was making it easier to find a warm bed for the night, it was alienating him from the person he cared about the most:

> **Suze Rotolo**: Bob ... was a beacon, a lighthouse. He was also a black hole ... At parties I [now] noticed that people would approach him with reverence and tell him involved stories about their lives ... They wanted him to suggest solutions ... to enlighten them in some way. It made him uneasy ... We both needed protection from the outside world, but in the end I needed it more ... Bob had an aura of darkness and intensity that enveloped me when I was near him.

What drove Suze particularly crazy was the idea of being 'his chick', not a person in her own right. As Dylan himself began to develop a way of twisting words back upon the speaker in a way that belittled them, she realized he was crossing into a dark place, where the people he surrounded himself with already resided:

> Suddenly Bob had advisers and consiglieri in his corner, smiling and shuffling about ... [] ... There were a lot of people around him that I didn't like at all ... bodyguards and managers ... bloodsuckers ... I began to see everyone as wanting my friendship ... just to get close to Bob ... I knew that I [was] losing Bob to his fame ... Then he began snubbing his old friends. But it was all so understandable.

Dylan's two most regular enablers, Bobby Neuwirth and Victor Maymudes, were both at his side on the West Coast; the latter returning with him to New York in early March, much to Suze's chagrin. Here was someone she described perfectly in her memoir as 'Bob's silent and creepy buddy-bodyguard ... so cool, so hip, so cold.' Maymudes' predatory persona always gave *her* – and a fellow Scorpio now about to enter the picture, Sara Lownds – the creeps.

Nor were these sisters under the skin the only girlfriends set on edge by Dylan's enablers. Introduced to Neuwirth for the first time in LA, Beecher came to dread every meeting, 'Because he was always parrying [words at] me and I would go blank. I would ... leave a room ... on the verge of tears.'

In Suze's case, when the post-Dylanmania Dylan turned up at her sister's Avenue A apartment in mid-March to impart some home truths in Carla's direction, she 'had kind of a nervous breakdown'. By the time the cavalry arrived, she had already tuned out:

> **Barry Kornfeld**: [Carla] had been rooming with Suze. Her and Bobby never got along. [By then] they really were at odds ... Clayton was nominally affianced to Carla, which is particularly strange [given] that he was gay. Anyway, he was staying at my apartment and we got a call in the middle of the night. It's Carla, and she's in hysterics. I grabbed Paul's coat, gave it to him, and we jumped in a cab and went over to the Lower East Side, and God, Suze was in shock. Carla and Bobby were standing there, practically frothing at the mouth at each other. I left Paul there to [pour] oil on troubled waters, and I grabbed Carla, brought her back to my apartment, put her on the couch ... It was never clear to me which side of the break-up Suze saw herself on, [even after] I talked to her about it.

So much for Dylan's suggestion, in *Chronicles*, that 'the alliance between Suze and me' came to an end because 'fate flagged it down'. He had burnt his bridges by going away for six weeks, staying with Baez some of the time and flaunting his infidelities by sleeping with a coed at Emory University when Suze's friend, Pete Karman, was around. As Kornfeld smartly concludes, 'I think the real break-up was when she could no longer [deny] the fact that Bobby was not being faithful.'

Add to this Dylan pouring gasoline on the tinderbox that was his relationship with the Rotolos, and it was bound to blow up. The animosity between Carla and Dylan, which had developed over time, turned to verbal glycerine that night in March. While Suze was caught in the blast, Bob and Carla argued semantics like it was life and death, firing words back and forth, her with 'many grievances', him with 'truths to tell'.

For a while, the Jack of Hearts convinced himself he could put all the pieces back together again, but it was no good. Try as he might, from hereon Suze was her own person and Dylan would have to meet up on her terms, not his. The price, for her, was a rift with Carla that never fully healed; for him, a general estrangement from the West Village milieu which had given him much-needed camaraderie and succour.

In a highly symbolic gesture, Dylan would distance himself from all participants that night. For Clayton, this was particularly painful. Kornfeld was just baffled: 'We used to hang out and play chess all the time, and once upon a time he [even] recorded the message on my answering machine, [a version of] Bob Gibson's "Who's That Calling".'* It was like Dylan had become a folk Arkadin, methodically erasing his past,† removing anchors when he needed them most. Dave Van Ronk was next:

> Bobby had always been kind of paranoid, and now he felt he had to surround himself with people he could trust. But ... he never felt he had to be trustworthy himself. He was always testing the loyalty of the people who were near him ... Bobby and I reached our parting of the ways fairly early. Shortly after his ... fourth record ... he was holding court in the Kettle of Fish and he got on my case and started giving me all this advice about how to manage my career, how to go about becoming a star ... I was polite and even asked him a couple of questions, but it became obvious that he was simply prodding and testing me ... Finally ... I walked out ... We were never close again.

At least, Dylan's first abortive attempt at reconciliation with Suze would result in one of his greatest songs. According to Suze, 'Mr Tambourine Man' was 'written about a lonely night Bob ... spent wandering the streets after the two of us had quarreled'. But it was no quarrel. Dylan was actually attempting to patch up their seismic

---

* The correct title of the song in question is 'Well, Well, Well'.
† *Mr Arkadin* is a 1955 Orson Welles film about a man who hires an investigator to track down figures from his past, whom he then has assassinated.

split, having been dropped off by Al Aronowitz, with whom he had been hanging out. And according to the journalist, writing in 1973, Dylan did not so much wander the streets as raid a fridge:

> He had stopped in to see [Suze], briefly, while I waited outside in the car. They had tried hard to stay close. The drive out to Jersey ... was a gloomy ride. At my house, we talked, listened to some records and [he] raided my refrigerator. You've never known a refrigerator raider like Bob. He'd stand there for what seemed like an hour ... and pick a full-course meal off the shelves, running some kind of insane, hilarious, non-stop dinner conversation as he kept chomping away ... He kept coming back to the subject of Suze. I remember him talking about what it had been like having her to turn to ... He said he had to write a song. He already had the music, he just needed the words. The next morning ... he sung me some of the lines and we had talked about the song, 'Who was Mr Tambourine Man?' – my wife asked those kinds of questions ... I found a wastebasket full of crumpled false starts.

The melody, both original and memorable, could well date from the morning after Mardi Gras, evoking the same power of song as 'Lay Down Your Weary Tune'. But this time Dylan tied his pantheistic conceit to the quixotic figure of the Tambourine Man. How ironic that just as he was becoming an occasional presence in the Village, he should recall how another memorable Village character, Bruce Langhorne, was prone to wandering its streets playing – in Langhorne's own words – 'this giant Turkish tambourine. It was about [four inches] deep ... very light and it had a sheepskin head and ... jingle bells around the edge ... I used to carry it around with me and pluck it out and play it anytime.' Nor was this Langhorne's last important contribution to the song, or Dylan's career.

Convinced he had 'consumed all the poisons in [him], and kept only their quintessences' – as Rimbaud had advocated in his famous 'seer manifesto' of 1871 – Dylan knew he'd shattered another glass ceiling and went looking for the benediction of his fellow songsmiths. Jack Elliott would hear the song from the man himself, at an apartment his former wife was sharing with Grossman's feisty new girlfriend, Sally Buehler.

And just like old times, Phil Ochs got a knock at the door one night soon after midnight from Dylan who insisted that the three songwriters already there play what they have been working on before unveiling 'Mr Tambourine Man'. Ochs would subsequently suggest 'it was the first time he had played the song for anyone.' So would Eric Andersen, who in 2005 claimed that what the two of them heard that night was not yet a song:

> I was at Phil Ochs's apartment, sitting around with Phil and David Blue ... and in rushes Bob with Victor Maymudes. They'd literally rolled into town minutes before. Bob sat down on the couch and spread out all the writing he'd done on the road. Pages and pages and pages. Poems, songs, notes, it went on and on. Everything seemed of epic proportions. This was the raw material, and it was amazing to see it all spread out like that. He sang 'Chimes Of Freedom' and stunned everyone. He [also] had bits of 'Mr Tambourine Man'. He knew he'd tapped into something significant, and the work was pouring out of him.

It was 'Hard Rain' all over again. Everyone wanted to lay claim to the moment of creation, while Dylan proudly basked in the afterglow. When he visited Eric Von Schmidt at his second home in Sarasota, Florida for a few days that spring, in need of some r'n'r, he even allowed his old friend to roll tape – the last such home tape we know of – before playing the newly completed 'Tambourine Man' in the middle of a jam session that otherwise recalled the pair's earlier London waltz, both in its choice of covers – a smattering of rock'n'roll and country songs – and un-PC asides (Dylan calls Jackie Deshannon, a notable singer-songwriter in her own right, 'this Hollywood chick').

Still curious about the competition, Dylan cajoled Von Schmidt into playing his most notable song, 'Joshua Gone Barbados', about a 1962 plantation strike, even as he was telling the likes of Ochs, 'Politics is bullshit. It's all unreal. The only thing that's real is inside you. Your feelings. Just look at the world you're writing about and you'll see that you're wasting your time. The world is ... just absurd.' Although Von Schmidt's gripping narrative was almost as much of a fantasy as 'Tambourine Man' – the 'three people lying dead' was a fiction on Von Schmidt's part – it stayed with Dylan, coming out three years later at Big Pink, when he was consciously trying to recreate the vibe of those early home tapes, and the man he used to be.

Fame, aligned closely in his mind with losing Suze, changed all that. As Aronowitz, an important confidant at this time, would write, the break-up signalled 'a long step further into loneliness, a personal loneliness over, above and beyond the loneliness that had to do with his career, with his destiny, with all that abstract crap which makes ... an idol out of a man'.

Perhaps inevitably, this double-edged pain pushed Dylan to experiment with more physiological means of escape. Indeed, many who heard 'Tambourine Man' while it remained under wraps commercially assumed it was inspired by the still-legal LSD. Shortly after writing to Lawrence Ferlinghetti, admitting 'I have nothin to do. an no place t go', Dylan seems to have lysergically indulged himself at the end of an April north-east tour, in the safe house that was Grossman's Woodstock home.

According to Maymudes, 'Sally Grossman was there. Sara Lownds was there ... [But] Albert wasn't around that night. Tom Law had the acid and gave it to me ... We had a four-foot ... roll of paper that we unfurled and filled [with drawings] ... When the sun came up, we all crawled into bed.' Producer Paul Rothchild, also there that night, has suggested the acid was already on hand, in Grossman's fridge, perhaps put there for just such an occasion.

It was one of a number of sleepless nights that spring, usually when 'the forsakeness of high-degree romance overtakes me' (as he put it in a letter to Tami Dean days after the break-up). Such was his new-found vulnerability that he even saw himself on the end of a truth-attack from that most unlikely source, Suze. It happened, 'one night after some party ... when Bob and I were still unable to definitively separate. We ended up back at Albert's place, Bob wanted me to stay. I refused, [but] continued to talk a lot of shit ... I don't know what got into me that night ... [but] I needed to hurt him.'

Dylan took it all on the chin, perhaps processing it the way he always did by writing a song in the first person, pointing a finger at a second person, while a third person listened in. This one was called 'It Ain't Me Babe', one of two classic love songs he began in Woodstock that April. Predictably, he turned a real-life situation around so that it's 'she' who begs *him* to stay and he says, no can do. For now, he had just the barest of outlines:

Please go from my window baby
Without using vulgar words
Please go from my doorway
You'll only be let down
You say that you are looking for someone who stands strong
t protect you and defend you constantly ...

Already, he has the 'go from my window' motif, drawn from a sixteenth-century cuckold folk song of the same name.* Though he has yet to explicate his ongoing infidelity with the withering line, 'An' anyway I'm not alone', the narrator of this wish-fulfilment song has moved on.

Another song-outline in the same slim black notebook confirms the singer himself has not. The nerves remain red raw when he writes, 'I could be with you but not be there writing/ tho you havent been in my breath nor thought / you're in my [mind].' 'Mama You Been On My Mind' – probably the last song he began ahead of his May trip to Europe† – would suffer the same fate as 'Walls of Redwing' and 'Eternal Circle', two other songs he was still playing at shows after rejecting them from the vinyl record.

Yet he worked on this affecting song long and hard, excising lines that insisted he was 'not pleading for lost love I can't get' – which was precisely what he *was* doing when he wrote to Suze within days, telling her he 'rode alone ... thru the hills on backroads,' as he was when he wrote an extra verse in London, protesting, 'I am not putting any pressure on you t come back to me at all,' after she failed to answer his long-distance call.

Ultimately, he decided to put both 'Mr Tambourine Man' and 'Mama You Been On My Mind' aside, even though (for the first time)

---

* This first draft, which resides at Tulsa, proves that Dylan originally referenced 'Go From My Window', not John Jacob Niles's 'Go 'Way From My Window'. He later disguised its true origins by substituting 'Way' for the weak opening word, 'Please'.
† 'Spanish Harlem Incident' and 'My Back Pages' were evidently composed stateside, but it is unclear when.

he lacked a surfeit of worthy alternatives. He would later suggest he left 'Tambourine Man' off his fourth album 'because I felt too close to it'. This allowed a hastily assembled LA folk combo, Jet Set, to use a demo of the song to secure their own Columbia record deal (as The Byrds).*

The other gem he would leave two familiar *chansonniers*, Joan Baez and Judy Collins, to record, all the while retaining enough affection for the song to still be playing it in the 1990s. But he was never going to pass over 'Tambourine Man'. He knew it was a break (on) through song. In fact, he couldn't wait to play it to an awestruck Martin Carthy on landing in London, having turned up at Al Aronowitz's to get a lift to the airport, intending to head 'off to Europe for a week or two, with only an eight-pound zippered bag as his luggage'.

He was finally ready to debut some of his new songs live, arranging for Pye to record the sold-out May 17th Royal Festival Hall show (at his own expense). As a result, even those Brits who had invested in an import copy of the third album were treated to no fewer than seven unreleased songs in the eighteen-song set, five of which came in a mid-set burst: 'It Ain't Me Babe' – which he introduced as 'a moment song. I feel this way at moments' – 'Walls Of Redwing', 'Chimes Of Freedom', 'Eternal Circle' and a heavenly 'Mr Tambourine Man'. And this time, he prefaced 'Talkin' John Birch' with an explanation of what the John Birch Society was – 'an organization for *very* paranoid people' – while 'Who Killed Davey Moore?' was a song about boxers, not boxing, and 'Hattie Carroll', roundly applauded by the hip Londoners, was 'a song about people who cry too soon, too much and about the wrong thing'.

Once again, a post-concert crush to touch the metaphorical hem of this new prophet ensued, for which Dylan seemed entirely unprepared. UK publicist Ken Pitt recalled, 'It was the very first time Bob experienced fan hysteria. We'd ordered a taxi after the show, but when we got there, there was an enormous crowd between us and the cab. Bob was chuckling with delight, going "Wow!" ... [The taxi driver] put his foot down and tried to zoom off, but Bob was having a great

---

* Although Dylan himself demoed both songs, along with 'I'll Keep It With Mine' at his last Witmark session in June, it seems The Byrds were given an acetate of the 'Another Side' out-take, now released on *The Bootleg Series Vol. 7*.

time, thoroughly enjoying his new experience, shaking hands, kissing girls.' Maymudes, another soul caught up in this chaotic situation, had also 'noticed Bob ... was in ... thrall to the moment', as if they both simultaneously knew 'that his life never would be the same ... This really was ... the first time Bob was introduced to the crazed fan, something that would [soon] have a significant impact on his personality.'

At least they didn't lay siege to his hotel. Dylan had returned to the Mayfair, where he left the tipping to others and got on with putting the hotel stationery to good use, finishing the two songs he had begun in Woodstock and starting four more songs – 'Black Crow Blues', 'Denise, Denise', 'Ballad In Plain D' and 'To Ramona' – during the twelve days he spent in England, while recording two TV shows, giving interviews to Max Jones and Maureen Cleave, and generally holding court. Other song ideas remained stillborn, including one with the burden 'Oh babe, I'll let you be you', and another with the potentially promising opening: 'early on one foggy morning / upon the phantom ship I spied'.

He would need more stationery to take to Europe, where he planned to travel for the next fortnight as he shaped material that was still raw, emotionally and literally, for his fourth album, because his label were pressuring him to record after seven months of radio silence.

First stop, Paris, where he had two potential contacts, a French singer called Hugues Aufray, who had translated some of his songs into French, and the German model-actress, Nico.* It was just like old times, save for the presence of a burly handler to now carry his dope. It was Aufray who enabled them to top up supplies, thanks to his pretty cousin who had married an infamous American writer and co-author of *Candy* (1958), a hilariously picaresque, semi-pornographic update of Voltaire's *Candide*, and as such someone Dylan was bound to want to meet. Initially, the feeling wasn't entirely mutual:

Mason Hoffenberg: The first time Dylan did a London concert, he wanted to see Paris and ... naturally, they came over to my house, because I was an American who smoked dope. And I didn't know who

---

* Her contact details appear in the same Tulsa notebook as 'It Ain't Me Babe' and 'Mama You Been On My Mind', suggesting that their meeting was prearranged.

Dylan was. That was about the last point in his life when he could still meet people normally. [But] we had a ball. I liked him a lot. I actually thought he was a hillbilly.

Nico, on the other hand, couldn't wait to meet the songwriter – 'He was like a god to me' – even offering to let him and his shadow stay at her studio flat, where he played her pieces of his new songs, including 'It Ain't Me Babe', which he gave her the impression he had just composed, and engaged her in animated conversation, struck by her Germanic beauty and recognizing a rare kindred spirit:

> He spoke a lot that first time. At first, he [was] very open. Then suddenly he['d] go back into his shell. We all went back to my studio flat ... and I cooked a meal. They decided to stay ... They were staying in a terribly dark, dismal hotel. It was not a good place to work. During the week he stayed, he wrote many songs ... I didn't know what to expect.

As a now familiar act of courtship, Dylan wrote a song 'about me and my little baby' for the lady. Although 'I'll Keep It With Mine' does not appear in any of the *Another Side* papers, nor was it attempted at the June 9th Columbia session, it really does appear that he wrote it and gave it to Nico, and forgot about it – for now. But Dylan still demoed it for Witmark that month along with two other piano-man songs, 'Mr Tambourine Man' and 'Mama You Been On My Mind', his last Witmark demo session.

Ironically, it was just the kind of song his new abum needed – one that wasn't about 'sex and excitement and foolish things, which can only happen in a man's mind'.* Rather, it was, as Paul Cable once wrote, 'the least patronising way ... of saying, I'm older than you, therefore I know better' – even if Nico was actually two and a half years older.

Instead, Dylan was consumed by two songs he saw as bookends to that difficult fourth album: one, the exquisite 'To Ramona', riddled with regret and sorrow on *her* behalf, 'stemmin from forces an friends that define', wishing those 'cracked country lips' were still his; the other, the ill-advised 'Ballad In Plain D', his myopic account of the

---

* Dylan's 1969 description of *Tarantula*, the book he now started to conceive.

break-up with Suze, in which he looked to skewer both sister and mother on the bayonet of 'truth' only to come out as the real villain of the piece.

The 'parasite sister' maintained her dignity even when Dylan phoned her up twenty years later to 'make peace', after admitting to Bill Flanagan, 'I must have been a real schmuck to write that.' As for Suze, she merely noted that her erstwhile beau had found a place for the Chinese cookie philosophy he'd espoused one evening at their favourite pizza parlour, Emilio's, when 'all fired up about the concept of freedom', he asked rhetorically, 'What defines the essence of freedom? Are birds really free? Or are they chained to the sky?'

By the time Dylan had wrestled 'Plain D' into submission, he was in Greece, at the finishing end of a grand tour which had encompassed a trip to Berlin – where, according to Hoffenberg, they 'picked up this German girl . . . Dylan asked her "What's your name?" She said, *"Vas?"* [i.e. "What?"] . . . [After that] Dylan says to her, "You know what time it is, Vas?"' Dylan's own account, the following month, had them 'lookin for . . . vagrants of high caliber. droolin. seekin', as the German girl 'took us around. told us what was happenin.'

He also passed through Rome, where he 'visited some people who lived outside of a wall' and spent a day at the Coliseum, wasting time, before stopping off in Athens, in the company of Nico and Maymudes. The latter suggested they find a local coastal resort, somewhere to chill and compose: 'What Bob wanted was a quiet place where he could write, so I suggested that we just drive out into the country . . . A small village called Vouliagmeni sparked our interest and we decided it was the spot for our vacation. We found a small, comfortable place to stay in a bunker left over from the First World War, situated on a rocky beach at the edge of the Aegean Sea.'

Here, Dylan found the peace he needed to complete the jigsaw, constructing an album reflecting all the inner turmoil the last nine months had brought. He already had a title, *Another Side of Bob Dylan*. But for the first time, he had a bunch of songs he'd barely completed, let alone tried out on a vox pop of like-minded souls. Even Maymudes, who had been on hand most of the time, recalled how the new Dylan 'wrote by himself and never sang them in front of anybody until . . . we got to the studio [and] he just blurted it out'. Which sounds remarkably close to the truth.

Dylan had decided to record his latest contractual high-wire act without a safety net: to make a record like he imagined Robert Johnson used to, in a single night, fuelled solely by adrenalin and red wine. Unfortunately, as Aronowitz noted, 'Back [then] Bob always had trouble holding his liquor. From the time I met him, alcohol was Bob's drug of choice but ... many were the nights Bob'd spend the ride back home from New York barfing out the window ... of my station wagon.'

Barely pausing to unpack his travel bags in Woodstock, Dylan reported to Columbia on June 9th intending to expel all the poisoned-pen letters he'd written himself in the past four months. That was how long he had been working on *Times*'s successor – and it showed. It was not an album he had lived with in its creation, nor shaped in performance. Nothing save 'Chimes' was tried and tested.

As Tom Wilson confided to Nat Hentoff, there to write a profile for the *New Yorker*, 'I'm somewhat concerned about tonight, [as] we're going to do [the] whole album in one session.' He was right to be concerned, just as he was when informing Hentoff – out of Dylan's earshot – that his 'main difficulty has been pounding mike technique into him. He used to get excited and move around a lot and then lean in too far, so that the mike popped.' Actually, Wilson's primary problem going forward would be Dylan beginning to exercise his growing clout, which included ignoring any producer who questioned his mike technique at the expense of feel.

It didn't take long that June night for them to lock horns, with Wilson asking Dylan before the fourth song, 'Spanish Harlem Incident', 'Hey Bob, try to hold the same position.' Two songs later, before 'I Don't Believe You', he is at it again, 'Get Back, Bob, so you won't pop,' which leads to the first showdown of the evening. Having delivered a terrific take three, save for a single line where he blew the words, Dylan starts again rather than singing an insert, only for Wilson to stop the take because of a problem with 'the word wall'. He asks Dylan to 'move a little to your right'. Dylan responds by asking, 'Whatever it was [about the word wall], I want you to *show* it to me.'

Dylan's patience is wearing thin. Wilson perseveres. When a third false start to 'Motorpsycho Nitemare' is curtailed, he pleads, 'Back up, Bob. You popped. I want the words to come out good.' However, Dylan is not in the mood for criticism from anyone – constructive or otherwise. When someone audibly suggests he switches to another song after a third false start on 'Chimes Of Freedom' – the one song he should have known inside out – he snaps, 'No, I got to do it. Play me back the words.'

Likewise, when Mason Hoffenberg – who had returned to the States with or immediately after Dylan, using family funds – tells him he shouldn't use the image of 'flashing diamond teeth' in 'Spanish Harlem Incident', he takes no notice. But he doesn't forget. Meeting again in Paris in 1966, he reminds Mason, 'Remember when you came to my recording session and you said, "That song, man, you shouldn't put those words in that song" ... You're the only cat that [ever] said that.' As a proper writer, he was the only one who would dare.

The fiercest critic of Dylan's work, though, remained the man himself. The fifth song of the evening he was calling simply 'Poem'. After a single false start, he prefaces take two by confessing, 'I don't know if I can make it through this.' And nor can he, not because of ill-fitting rhymes or questionable mike technique, but rather poor crowd control. During the take, a friend's child breaks into the studio, prompting Dylan to warn the naughty Joel, 'I'll rub you out. I'll touch you – you'll turn to dust.' He then tells Wilson he's gonna 'start again – with this *dumb* song'. The song in question? 'Ballad In Plain D'.

If 'Plain D' is plain dumb, he introduces the jocular 'Black Crow Blues' (aka 'Weird Consumption') by claiming, 'This is a serious one,' attempting it twice on guitar, 'to give you an idea', and once on piano, which successfully breaks the downbeat mood of the session.

Throughout the six-hour session Dylan refuses to spend a great deal of time with any single song. If anything, he is rushing. And it shows. When he gets through a song, it is invariably a keeper – the only exception being 'Spanish Harlem Incident'. At one point he makes the seemingly impromptu suggestion to an attendant Jack Elliott, 'Hey Jack, sing on this. [Just] the chorus,' and begins strumming 'Mr Tambourine Man', which Wilson (correctly) cuts short to tell Elliott, 'If you're gonna sing that much, you need to be behind him,' a diplomatic way of saying, You're ruining the song. Second time round, they complete the take but the experiment is a bust.

An unperturbed Dylan just keeps leafing through lyrics and rolling tape. At session's end, he even allows Wilson to convince him to sing an insert, rather than redo the whole of 'I Shall Be Free #10' – a tenth-as-funny remake of 'I Shall Be Free' – after stumbling over the ending to take four. Initially inclined to 'maybe ... do another one', Wilson says it will screw up the running order. So Dylan agrees to sing an insert – the first time he allowed an edit of two takes on record.

These were very different times: an album was usually a series of *recorded* performances. As Dylan himself recalled in 2017, 'Back then I don't think I was ever allowed to talk to an engineer. The board was simple – two, at the most four, tracks. In those early years you went into the studio and recorded live, take after take. If someone made a mistake you had to start over, or you just had to work your way through a song until you got the right version.'

Such a methodology was not ideal for any albums made in a day, though. Recording since seven in the evening, it is nearly 1.30 a.m. before the singer announces the last song, 'Ancient Memories'.* He has just dispatched 'Mama You Been On My Mind' in a single, sensitive take, as he starts strumming the album's restless farewell to protest, only for Wilson to cut him short and the camel to collapse:

Wilson: Let's start again, Bob. You're a little too close to the horn.
Dylan: Hey man, don't stop me!
Wilson: Have to.
Dylan: Well, okay, but don't stop me any more. Because I won't be able to do it. If you stop me once more, I can't do the song. [Pause, more conciliatory] It's a weird song.
Wilson [wearily]: Okay, Bob. Just try to hold your position. Take two ...

Wilson thus receives a stay of execution, but it is only that. Both he and engineer Roy Halee are on notice: this artist won't be retaking songs because of mike placement any more. The next time they share a studio together, Wilson will try another tack, but even with Dylan a whole lot more focused, he knows he is skating on thin ice.

For now, Columbia have their album, albeit one that is treading water musically, and missing the finest two compositions of the past

---

* The song will appear on the album under the title 'My Back Pages'.

few months. Dylan, though, seems disinclined to return to the studio to smooth out any rough edges left dangling from a session where, as Paul Cable notes, 'Dylan had consumed something in the region of two bottles of Beaujolais.' He left it to Wilson to put it together, preferring to spend the two-month period the album is in production filling up another rear sleeve with what he chose to call 'some other kinds of songs'. He still sees himself as a poet, just one who is now using nouns and adjectives interchangeably.

2.2

June to November 1964: Meet The Beat

He was rarely tender, and seldom reached out to anticipate another's needs, though occasionally he would exhibit a sudden concern for another outlaw, hitch-hiker, or bum.

Joan Baez

Acquiring personal possessions doesn't bother him ... but he does live in a big house at Bearsville, just outside New York ... on the edge of a forest ... He likes the secluded life. For this reason, he moved out of Greenwich Village. Phoney artists bug him. He was glad to get away from them.

Martin Carthy, 'The Dylan I Know', *Disc*, April 10th, 1965

As soon as he began to get famous in late '63, there were a lot of obsessive fans who would come up to him on the street in an almost aggressive way. Whereas he could hang out at the [Cafe] Espresso and not be bothered.

Jonathan Taplin

Before he met Albert, Bob was really accessible. Then Grossman began creating a mystique of exclusiveness. He secluded him away up in Woodstock and that changed Bob.

John Hammond Jr

In Woodstock, Albert partially created this division between the people that were in and the people that were out.

Peter Yarrow

*

Through the summer of 1964 that restless, hungry feeling continued eating away at Dylan, manifesting itself – as it had nine months earlier – in a flurry of poems he wanted his label to attach to the album he'd just delivered. Meanwhile, all new lyrics – save for a single song of innocence *and* experience – remained on hold.*

Nor was his growing dissatisfaction with the limitations of song lost on those who on occasion felt the same. Friendly rival Phil Ochs gave an interested observer's thoughts in notes he contributed to that year's Newport Festival programme: 'I think he's slowly drifting away from songwriting because he feels limited by the form. More and more of his work will probably come out in poetry and free verse, and I wouldn't be surprised if he stopped singing altogether.'

Yet here was Dylan, back at Freebody Park, now the star of the show, his fame almost overwhelming this most communal of musical gatherings. No longer a perennial presence on the scene, appearances were events, as they became when he turned up in Chicago and Detroit earlier that summer. Otherwise, Dylan seems to have spent the six weeks between Studio A and Newport where he felt most comfortable these days, a former artist's colony two hours upstate, still well off the beaten track. Even in Woodstock, though, he couldn't settle, writing Irwin Silber in June, 'I've been on the constant move an readjustment lately. havent been in any one place too long. am still lookin for someplace t go to figure out where i should go. I seem t have these many thousand of bedrooms across the country but no place t really sleep in yet.'

His latest bolthole was a room above the local Cafe Espresso, where he liked to play chess and chat with the owner Bernard Paturel, and his wife, Mary Lou, with whom he'd struck up a conversation after Tom Paxton played at the cafe and introduced him. As Mary Lou told Steve Turner, 'He later moved in with us and started writing. He dedicated one of his albums to us.' The album in question was *Another Side*,† though when he 'started writing' in earnest

---

* F'rinstance, he does nothing with one promising opening couplet: 'Well, the Devil said t meet him down on fifth an main / when I came to meet him, the street corner's in flames.'
† The dedication reads: 'Thank you Bernard, Marylou, Jean Pierre, Gerard Philip and Monique for the use of their house.'

at the Espresso it was done, and all that was needed was material for the rear sleeve.

With his papers from Europe by his side for reference, he now placed his favourite typewriter above the Espresso, rarely writing by hand save to correct or embellish. The poems poured out of him, inevitably providing a glossary on some of the songs therein. Thus, the chains 'on the others around him' in 'Plain D' becomes the reason why 'he had t go away … t a far off land', renouncing former ambition. Offering an explanation for the album's title, he insists he 'cannot go chargin over the battlefield / for i am no leader'.

And just as with the verses he gave Columbia the previous fall, he couldn't help but insert autobiographical references, the most startling of which was a poem that was supposed to start 'some other kinds of songs', but ended up being cut (for space, not censorial reasons):*
'i used to hate enzo'. Enzo Bartocciolo was someone Suze had met in Italy, and would end up marrying. In the poem, Dylan writes, 'my beloved one met him / in a far-off land / an' she stayed longer there / because of him', which was at least partly true.

Other references to Suze pepper the pages, including one about 'my last true love … who knows me better than anyone … [and] has seen the changes in me'. He excises some others, as he does a reference to Judy Rubin, who 'broke my little out of high school heart' because she was 'the pawn of her parents', a conscious echo of the situation with Suze. He also reimagines an internal conversation with his father that probably mirrored one from a misspent youth:

> 'yes, father, you've told me many times
> 'the lord has given. the lord shall take away.'
> an my only reply t you is
> 'who are these lords?
> what gives them the right?
> can i send them to hell if they do me wrong?
> or must i live blindly
> obeyin respectabilty.'

---

* Six of the eleven poems he intended for the album sleeve ended up being omitted, before appearing in 1973's *Writings & Drawings*, in an alternate sequence.

The one departure from such free-verse expeditions in these pre-Newport weeks was one of his most overtly Poetic (with a capital P) lyrics, 'Gates of Eden', found among the papers he left with the Paturels, handwritten in fair copy, almost perfectly intact and included in the 2005 *Bob Dylan Scrapbook*. Once again he had raised the bar on himself. What had been a clumsy clash of juxtapositions in 'My Back Pages' now truly adhered to a Beat (and by proxy, Blakean) sensibility. His muse had returned as 'the motorcycle black madonna two-wheeled gypsy queen', and Dylan couldn't wait to show the results to Allen Ginsberg, whose early collection of poems, *Gates of Wrath*, may even have lit the match.*

Namechecked in the *Another Side* notes, reaffirming Dylan's bond with the Beats, Ginsberg would spend time with Dylan on the West Coast in September, having previously been invited up to Woodstock in the company of Aronowitz, where he heard some new songs – presumably including 'Gates Of Eden', which left a deep impression on him – a moment in time captured in a series of photos by *Look* photographer, Douglas Gilbert.

Dylan seemed willing to taunt his fans with a glimpse of the upstate Bobby, inviting not one, but two photographers that summer to do portfolios there, even as it remained his secret Edenic garden. For Gilbert, the assignment was not always easy or enjoyable:

There was one incident where, early on ... I remember asking him to do something ... [and] I used the phrase, 'I want to make this look real' ... He stopped and looked me in the eye and said, 'Nothing's real, man.' ... At the end of a day I would be [left] feeling extremely frustrated ... [at] how difficult [the process] was ... [Just when] I would think I was beginning to get a little closer insight, he would turn it around ... It was like he wasn't letting me [get] that close.

---

* Though *Gates of Wrath* was not published until 1972, Ginsberg notes in a 'Hindsight' to that edition, '*Gates of Wrath* MS was carried to London by lady friend early fifties ... and I had no complete copy till 1968 when old typescript was returned thru poet Bob Dylan – it [had] passed into his hands years earlier.' As we know, Dylan was in London in May 1964.

And yet Dylan seemed content to let Gilbert photograph him with Ginsberg and his lover Peter Orlovsky, Al Aronowitz and fellow musician John Sebastian; perhaps because, as Dave Marsh notes in his insipid introduction to Gilbert's 2005 collection of Dylan snaps, 'If it didn't say Cafe Espresso in the window, the group of people, including … Mason Hoffenberg and Dylan's future wife, Sara Lowndes [sic], sitting at the red-checked table cloth, might be anywhere.'

Hoffenberg explained his own presence in 1973: an invitation from Dylan, proferred in Europe. But a disappointed Mason found these Woodstock women were not the kind of obliging 'chicks' the Dr Dunlap in him grooved on:

> He said if I ever got back to the States, to [come] stay with him in Woodstock. Which I did when my family broke up. I thought I was going to have a ball, because Dylan was real famous then, with girls climbing all over him. But … Grossman had this sign in the driveway that said, 'If you have not telephoned, you are trespassing.' And Dylan was very uptight. He's not really into balling groupies … Girls were going berserk to get to him and he was doing things like hiding in the closet whenever the door opened. Albert had this … concubine … named Sally. And Sally had a friend living there, a nice Jewish girl being helpful, doing things like picking up Dylan's notebooks and putting them away.

The 'nice Jewish girl' was Dylan's future wife, Sara, formerly married to photographer Hans Lownds. Born Shirley Marlin Noznisky in Wilmington, Delaware on October 28th, 1939, she lost her father, a scrap-metal merchant, in a 'grudge' shooting when she had just completed high school. When her mother died, five years later, she dropped out of college and came to New York, where she worked as a waitress, photographic model and film production assistant, as well as a Playboy bunny, all to make ends meet while she brought up her daughter, Marie, born in 1961, just as she and Hans were separating.

For Dylan, who had just lost a child, the mother/daughter combination offered him a glimpse of a more familial existence, the introduction having come from Grossman's beguiling girlfriend. Sally Buehler was another strikingly beautiful Jewish-American princess who had met Sara when she was working for documentary-maker D. A. Pennebaker at Time-Life and doing a stint at the Playboy club, shortly before Sally herself met Dylan's manager.

Pennebaker, for one, was not surprised when Sally 'started hanging out with Albert. All the young women were interested in being Playboy bunnies, because there was a lot of action there, [and] people were trying to get Sally to do it, but she seemed kind of vulnerable ... Albert was going to be her protector.' As for Dylan, it was Sara – who was known to Suze, who 'just knew, [as] a Scorpio [myself] ... she was in for it' – that centred him, even if it would take her a good two years to fix his moral compass.

It was also Sally's idea to bring Sara up to Bearsville, playing matchmaker for the maudlin singer who was moping around Grossman's estate mourning the loss of Suze. She even implied, to Hajdu, that she had been briefed by Bobby (and Albert) to find a certain type, 'He didn't like people prying into ... things that were really closest to him. If he was really serious about [someone], she had to be unknown ... He [had] just had a taste of a very public relationship.'

Though Sara was hardly another buxom blonde, she was another of Dylan's identifiable types; what he later characterised as 'witchy women'. As Woodstock neighbour Norma Cross observed, 'It was almost like she was surrounded by mist. She was very involved in mystical or spiritual things. We were all throwing the I Ching in those days, but Sara went beyond that.' She also had a mind of her own. As her son Jakob let slip in 2000, 'I don't think she's been affected by the things [that went on] around her. She was too strong for that stuff, that lifestyle you see ... other "wives-of" pursuing.'

That summer, Dylan and Sara started to become close, though not so close that Joan Baez was jettisoned or Sara stopped seeing other men.* Indeed, Sara had to make herself scarce when Baez came to visit after the unofficial coronation of the King & Queen of Folk at this year's Newport Folk Festival the last weekend in July, and then

---

* David Boyle told Barney Hoskyns he was carrying on with both Sally and Sara that summer: 'Those were the free-love days. The first night up there I got with Sara [while] Sally and I had a fling for about a month or two, [before] she told me she and Albert were getting married.'

resumed their liaison ten days later, unaware that Dylan had spent the time in Hawaii with another corporeal muse, Bonnie Beecher.

With Suze out of the picture, and seemingly unaware of the others on his 1964 scorecard, Baez had begun to believe she and the boy wonder had a future together. In a letter she wrote him after leaving Woodstock that August, she even expressed the hope that maybe someday she'd have his baby, something they must have talked about.

So when Dylan finally chose Sara – as he would – her rival never saw it coming. Neither did one of his closest confidants, Victor Maymudes, who asked him, 'Why Sara? Why not Joan Baez?', unaware that his boss was already looking for someone who 'could cook and sew / make flowers grow', even as he was telling himself, 'i will never chase a livin soul into the poisonous grasp of my own self love'.*

All of this lay some way off in the future. For now, Dylan needed to prepare for two important Newport rendezvouses – with the lovestruck Joanie, yes, but also with a former idol, Johnny Cash. It would also be the public unveiling – two weeks ahead of *Another Side*'s release – of the latest New Dylan to an audience filled to capacity with acolytes, Cash included.

Cash, like The Beatles, had been converted by *Freewheelin'*.† He immediately felt Dylan 'was one of the best country singers I had ever heard … before we had ever met. I knew he had heard and listened to country music. I heard a lot of inflections from country artists … I was in Las Vegas in '63/'64 and wrote him a letter telling him how much I liked his work. I got a letter back and we developed a correspondence.' Cash was already attempting the commercially hazardous trick of straddling the country/folk divide when he wrote to *Broadside* that March to rhapsodise about this protestin' prodigy:

> I got hung, but didn't choke … Bob Dylan slung his rope. I sat down and listened quick …

---

* The published version of this 1964 poem reads 'prison grasp' but the original manuscript reads 'poisonous grasp'.
† Robert Hilburn says John Hammond sent Cash Dylan's 'first' album in his authorized Cash biography. Not so.

> Gravy from that brain is thick ...
> Don't bad-mouth him, till you hear him
> Let him start by continuing, He's almost brand new,
> SHUT UP! ... AND LET HIM SING!

At the same time Cash wrote directly to Dylan, telling him it was June Carter, the love of his life, who 'first flipped me over you' by singing 'Girl From The North Country' 'eighty-three times a day'. Cash had an ulterior motive for corresponding – he needed songs to signal a conscious change in direction. An album of rerecorded Sun classics, a Christmas album, an album of hymns and the featured guest on a Carter Family album of standards – the sum total of his recent output – suggested someone treading water creatively.

Dylan must have been greatly flattered when his teen idol asked to 'hear the songs you have for me'. And when that didn't result in a set of Witmark acetates, Cash wrote again, flattering him, 'There ain't never been a writer got thru to me like you.' He even mentioned 'Walls Of Redwing', which suggests someone at Columbia or Witmark had obliged. 'Being half-assed attuned', he remained convinced Dylan had a song for him but might be thinking he'd be 'afraid to use it'. And so, he asked outright for a 'shut-your-damn-mouth-and-listen' song, unaware that Dylan had stopped writing those kind of songs.

They would finally meet in Joan Baez's Newport motel room in late July, and according to Cash, 'It was like we were two old friends. There was none of this standing back, trying to figure each other out.' Tony Glover, who was also there, later wrote, Cash 'was kinda nervous 'cause of this room full of freaks, some of whom had been smoking dope'.

It was certainly quite a gathering. Joan Baez, Sandy Bull and Jack Elliott were all as anxious as Cash, it seems, to hear some of Dylan's new songs. But as far as Dylan was concerned, there was only one person he needed to impress. And the feeling was mutual. Glover recalled 'Joan set[ting] up a little portable machine, and that's where Bob gave Johnny "It Ain't Me Babe" and "Mama You've Been On My Mind" ... Afterward, Johnny took Bob aside and gave him his guitar – an old country gesture of admiration.'

Cash, who was already performing 'Don't Think Twice' in his set, now had a trilogy of 'Suze' songs he could make his own. All three would feature on *Orange Blossom Special*, the February 1965 album that would signal a much-needed re-engagement with contemporary songwriting on Cash's part.

Dylan also played 'Tambourine Man' for this rapt audience, but refrained from demoing it for the Man in Black. It evidently made a deep impression on Cash because five months later he was still asking Dylan for a copy of the song. He also evidently struggled to discern the words to 'Mama You Been On My Mind' – 'The colour of the sun cut flat an' coverin'', for starters – until he ran into Baez again and she obliged with a full set of lyrics, despite previously earmarking the song for herself. The race to record Dylan's detritus was ramping up as the likes of Odetta and Judy Collins joined Baez and Cash in an almost unseemly rush for contemporary relevance.

The set Dylan played on the Sunday night (July 26th) at Newport – most of it released on a Sony DVD in 2007 – suggested he still had his hand on that plow, even if the old guard had now lost his train of thoughts. 'To Ramona', 'Chimes Of Freedom' and 'Tambourine Man', the primary fare in a five-song set, perplexed the many and infuriated a few.

For Paul Nelson, there on behalf of *Little Sandy Review* – and about to become managing editor at *Sing Out!* – it was a vindication of everything he had argued for a year earlier, as he commended Dylan for electing 'to show off his more personal, introspective songs rather shoot the obvious fish in the barrel', a clear nod to their previous discussion.

Fellow Minnesotan, Tony Glover, was equally delighted by the new material but noticed that the reaction out front was mixed: 'Instead of all the political material everybody expected, he did songs from *Another Side* ... You could tell the audience was puzzled, but they didn't want to be thought uncool by anybody, so they applauded just as vigorously.'

If Dylan had thought he might be lauded by his earliest media supporters for daring to change, he was soon disabused. Irwin Silber wrote a highly presumptuous open letter in *Sing Out!*, accusing him of losing 'contact with people' and writing 'maudlin' songs, the tone of which stung Dylan enough for him to write four decades later that Silber acted 'as if he alone ... had the keys to the real world'. Even Robert Shelton, while content to bask in Dylan's presence onsite, wrote of his disappointment at what he saw as a 'lack of control [in] his stage manner [and] his raucously grating singing'. If Dylan was not amused, for once Shelton had a point – he *was* bobbing and weaving like (and almost certainly because) he was either high or slightly drunk. His singing that Sunday night was an early manifestation of his later 'arena' voice; more declamatory, less nuanced.

Unfortunately, what these worthy critics had yet to realize was that he was no longer 'theirs'; that their words were increasingly mere background hum against the swelling tide of Dylanmania. As the festival organizer, George Wein, later remarked to Elijah Wald, 'We were learning first-hand that the so-called national "folk boom" had more to do with celebrity than with any deep grass-roots interest.'

In Dylan's case, there was really no other word for it. Attendant West Coast photographer Jim Marshall recalled, 'Crowds [now] followed him everywhere and a kind of wariness was just beginning to creep into his life and his relationship with the press.' The closer one was to the eye of the storm, the more surreal the experience, Glover noting in a 1972 memoir:

> It was starting to get weird around Dylan by then ... He was starting to be a kind of 'star' in people's eyes, and they would follow him in the parking lots and lobbies ... One afternoon, [we were] just sitting around the hotel, he was on guitar and vocal, Bobby Neuwirth was on maracas and vocal, and I was on harp [i.e. harmonica]. We were doing Rolling Stones songs like 'King Bee' and 'Tell Me', [and] when we finished, from outside the door came applause. We opened the door, and there were twelve or fourteen people huddled in the hall.

An inevitable collision of the folk revival with skiffle-infused English R&B reached critical mass that weekend at Newport when – according to Jack Elliott – he and Dylan 'were sitting in the front seat of Bob's blue Ford station wagon saying [our] goodbyes. The car's radio was playing ... The Animals' electrified version of "The House of the Rising Sun".'

Supposedly, both folksingers pointed at the radio and exclaimed, 'That's *my* version!' It was neither. Though the Geordie lads certainly knew Dylan's (as well as Josh White's and The Vipers') revamp of the traditional song, theirs had soul, brother. Although Dylan would tell

The Animals' John Steel, the following January, that he had 'first heard [their version] when he was driving and he stopped the car and jumped up and down, he liked it so much', he was confusing it with the occasion he had first heard The Beatles in Colorado. Elliott's account fits better, not least because the single had just been released stateside, though it was already top of the UK charts.

Also probably mistaken about the sequence of events that summer was Al Aronowitz, who suggested it was only after seeing The Beatles in September that Dylan 'asked my wife to drive him over to Rondo Music on Route 22 ... [where] he rented an electric guitar and took it back to my house'. Doug Gilbert had already snapped Dylan earlier that summer playing an electric guitar in tandem with John Sebastian on harmonica and acoustic, confirming that it was hearing The Animals and/or his friend John Hammond Jr's new album which sent him back to the future.

If an infuriating lack of session information for Hammond's *So Many Roads* makes it impossible to definitively state who was the donkey and who the cart, Hammond told Ben Edmonds that his first electric blues album, recorded some time that summer, came about because he had become 'friendly with a group called Levon & The Hawks':

> They'd play the wild blood'n'guts clubs on the Jersey shore and then come to New York and play places like Joey Dee's Starlite Lounge. They were an insanely good live band. So I got Robbie Robertson to play guitar, Levon Helm drums and Garth Hudson organ. I'd seen Mike Bloomfield, and thought he'd be great alongside Robertson. But ... he didn't want to play guitar! ... [He] decided he'd rather play piano ... Bob stopped by, which was not unusual, checking it out, and you could tell he was really digging it.

According to Danny Kalb, who had just played with the anagrammatic Bob Landy(!) on Elektra's *Blues Project* album, the experience made enough of an impression on Dylan for him to want to talk about it when the pair ran into each other at the Cafe Figaro that summer: 'Bob was really excited about what John Hammond was doing with electric blues ... He was telling me about ... his going to Chicago [to check out Bloomfield], and playing with a band.'

What tipped Dylan over the pop precipice, though, was an August 28th rendezvous now replete with the resonance of hindsight. At the time, it was just the forty-third most popular US album act being introduced to the number-one cultural phenomenon of the decade by that cultural facilitator par excellence, Al Aronowitz. It had still taken some arranging, with one particular Beatle playing coy. Lennon, the prickliest member of the combo, when asked by Aronowitz, 'Do you want to meet Dylan?' replied, 'Sure. *If* he wants to meet us.'

It was a telling qualification Aronowitz would have to address: 'Bob and The Beatles all needed room to swashbuckle, but nobody wanted to step on anybody else's ego ... As soon as I got to know John well ... I started telling him that he ought to meet Bob. [But] John kept saying he wanted to wait until he was Dylan's "ego equal".'

Dylan was also slightly wary of being sucked up by the whirlwind swirling around the Brits' every waking moment. Indeed, according to Maymudes, Dylan's minder for this meeting, 'At first Bob said very little. He cannot talk to a group of people except from the stage, and ... John Lennon was the same way ... [getting] tongue-tied speaking to small groups.'

For Dylan, just fighting his way through the lobby of the Delmonico Hotel had been an eye-opener. These boys' fame was at a level that made his Newport 'notoriety' seem risible by comparison and his natural response was to send it up: Lennon recalled the following April that when Bob first 'came up to the hotel room ... he kept answering our phone, saying, "This is Beatlemania here."'

Eventually, everyone began to relax, at which point either Dylan or Maymudes suggested they roll some joints and get high. The folksinger had, not unnaturally, assumed they were operating on the same heightened plane as all the musicians he hung out with – hence the bridge to 'I Wanna Hold Your Hand', 'I get high [x3]'. Except The Beatles actually sang 'I can't hide' [x3] in their thick Scouse accents. Time to turn 'em on.

But just as Maymudes began to roll everyone a joint, Dylan seemed inclined to keep his wits about him. According to Victor, 'He just [drank] alcohol and took a few hits here and there, but not a whole joint like the rest of us.' McCartney, on the other hand, took a long, deep toke and was soon, in his own words, 'wandering around looking for a pencil because I discovered the meaning of life that evening and I wanted to get it down on a bit of paper ... Mal [Evans, their road manager] handed me the little bit of paper the next morning ... and on it was written, in very scrawly handwriting: THERE ARE SEVEN LEVELS.'

Meanwhile, George Harrison began asking his drug buddy about the girl on the cover of the album that had made him a believer. Dylan explained it was his ex-girlfriend and that she still lived downtown, at which point Harrison asked for her number, promptly ringing it to invite her to the party. Suze was with her friend, Sue Zuckerman, an equally rabid fan of the Fab Four. It was her who answered the phone in Suze's apartment to someone with a pronounced Liverpudlian lilt:

> The maybe-George reassured us. 'We're here at the Delmonico Hotel with Bobby Dylan. He told us to invite you over.' In the background we heard a voice, [sounding] suspiciously like Ringo's, yelling: 'Bring girls!' [So] a few minutes later Suze and I were driving uptown to Park Avenue at 59th Street with the four bemused male friends who happened to be with us that evening ... There were still hundreds of young people surrounding the Delmonico when we arrived at about midnight ... When Bobby picked up the phone, Suze immediately got on the line. They argued for almost ten minutes [as he] insisted that only females were welcome.

Suze later wrote, 'Bob was annoyed that I had brought other people with me ... I hung up the phone and went home.' He still could not believe she would no longer accede to doing things on his terms, even if it meant not meeting The Beatles. The girl on the year-old album cover was long gone.

Despite – or perhaps because of – a lack of girls, Bobby and The Beatles bonded that night. Three weeks later, Bob, Al and Victor stood in the wings while The Beatles tried to make themselves heard at a benefit concert at the Paramount. To no avail. As Maymudes noted, 'The audience was so loud, you [simply] could not hear the band.' That would not change. When John mockingly enquired of Dylan in May 1966 – at the height of his electric apostasy – 'What about you, Bobby? The girls still screaming for you?' Dylan showed he had lost none of his desire to send up Beatlemania, 'Oh yeah, the girls and the boys are screaming at what we're doing, but not in the same way as for you.'

In August 1964, though, Dylan was still biding his time, telling Tami Dean in another amphetamine-fuelled letter, 'have still got my eyes on the future an am not letting go of my visions', as he plotted his next seven moves,* one of which still involved a possible return to writing a book, i.e. emulating Lennon.

Back in May, he had spoken to *Melody Maker*'s Max Jones about a book of Barry Feinstein's pictures where he would provide a series of captions 'that coincide with the photographer's ... mood. All the pictures were shot in Hollywood: shots of everything ... from the beautiful sign on the hill to Marlon Brando speaking while someone holds up a sign saying "Nigger-Lover".' Sure enough, an internal fact sheet circulating at Macmillan that summer announced the May 1965 publication of a book called, initially, *Hollywood Stark Naked* and then *The Rottenest Town In The USA*:

> A fierce, funny, wild tour of Hollywood, full of the raw impact of Bobby Dylan's folk songs. In this book, two spokesmen of the new wave proclaim their feelings in pictures and words of the sham and hypocrisy of Hollywood, the phoniness, the flatulent expression of all that is wrong with the world, as epitomized by Hollywood. It's all told in twenty-three scenes. For each group (in some cases there is just a single photograph), Bobby Dylan has written a verse. Some of these are merely six lines long, some are a number of pages [*sic*]. They are by turns descriptive, impressionistic, documentary, but all bear the unmistakeable imprint of Dylan and his special genius.

The project was already well advanced. Indeed, among the 'Paturel papers' is an early attempt to write a caption for the infamous Brando shot. By November, Macmillan had a contract and a redrafted press release, confirming the May 1965 publication of the rebranded book – scheduled to be called *Pictures And Words*. By now it had become 'the first book by Bob Dylan, whose literary gifts have long been evident in his folk song compositions. In sometimes bitter, sometimes

---

* As Maymudes noted of his regular chess partner, 'He [always] took his time to make [his] move'.

funny – always unabashed – prose, Dylan peels the lid off the sham, the hypocrisy, the fatuousness of Hollywood ... PICTURES AND WORDS is expected to generate a storm of interest and controversy', Feinstein having been relegated from collaborator to contributor.

It was surely this book – and not the one which would become *Tarantula* – that Dylan discussed the August day he brought Baez to Macmillan's downtown offices. Editor Bob Markel got 'the distinct impression ... Dylan wanted to show her off to me ... And he wanted to show me off to her, to impress her [with the idea] "I'm going to be an Author with a capital A." ... Beyond that, he was really uncertain what the hell he was doing ... They both seemed to have a very short attention span, and [soon] got bored and left.'

The person Dylan was really looking to impress and/or infuriate – by proxy – was back in Woodstock, eating from Grossman's well-stocked fridge, drinking his wine and enjoying the company of a wife for whom Dylan continued to have a yen.* Richard and Mimi Fariña had rolled into town a couple of days before Baez headlined the August Forest Hills Music Festival. Tensions between the foursome were never far from the surface, Baez acknowledging as much in a letter to her parents, 'Mimi and Dick aren't too cool, but it comes and goes.'

Partly it was a case of, in Mimi's words, 'Dick [being] terribly envious of Dylan, because of his tremendous success ... The one edge he had ... was as a serious writer.' The trip to Macmillan was partly intended to show that even in this field, Dylan could better Dick. However, the two alpha males' rivalry wasn't so fierce that Dylan had abandoned collaborating with Fariña on a movie script. According to Izzy Young, in his regular *Sing Out!* column, the subject matter had changed somewhat, now being 'concern[ed with] a lot of people you [subscribers] read about, including myself'.

Suffice to say, this idea went the way of all flesh and almost all Dylan movie projects. The Fariñas left the Grossmans' Bearsville retreat at the end of August with Richard still shy of a book deal, and Dylan anxious to get back to writing some songs, joking to Tami

---

* A John Byrne Cooke photo of Dylan propping himself against a coolly confident Mimi, arm casually draped around her, at the nearby motel, during the July 1964 Newport festival suggests the attraction was mutual.

Dean about how 'a hard rain rotted all my onions last week. gonna write a song about it when i get the time.'

However, another distraction loomed. Dylan had arranged for a second photographer to come to the cabin while the Grossmans were away, meaning any songwriting session would have to again be put on hold. In fact, when the photographer in question, Daniel Kramer, suggested he photograph him at work, he got very short shrift:

> I suggested photographing him doing the things that seemed most natural for him – working, writing music, or playing the guitar. Dylan told me that the pictures I wanted wouldn't work out, since he was always alone when he wrote and that it would be silly to make a picture of him posing at the typewriter* ... We ended up at an outdoor table at Bernard's Cafe Espresso ... [Dylan] play[ing] chess at a table shaded from the sun by an overhanging roof. I realized early on that the chess game was not a gimmick.

It had been barely a fortnight since Dylan and Baez had visited *Look* to see the layout for Gilbert's feature, but when the story was spiked, Dylan gave Kramer – another photographer-fan who saw his potential early – his chance, still looking for a photographer who worked on instinct, like him. Kramer knew he was on the right path when he saw the sign put there by the gruff Grossman, 'IF YOU HAVE NOT TELEPHONED, YOU ARE TRESPASSING'.

Despite Kramer's earlier faux pas, Dylan 'invited me to do what I needed to do to get some pictures and disappeared into the house. I ... found him sitting at a dining booth in the kitchen reading a newspaper. He ... never acknowledged my presence. This set the pace. Apparently he was not going to do anything, especially for my camera.'

The fact that Dylan introduced Kramer to Bernard Paturel before day's end suggested he had passed some kinda test. The young photographer would go on to shoot the iconic covers for *Bringing It All Back Home* and *Highway 61 Revisited*, before being dropped almost as abruptly as Gilbert, replaced by someone the 'nice Jewish girl' had once dated. Like both his predecessor and successor, Kramer would have to learn

---

* Douglas Gilbert had, in fact, already snapped this very image, one I used for the cover of *Revolution In The Air*.

the rules of engagement with the fledgling folk star by observation. He would not be allowed to meet either Baez or Sara for a while yet. For now, he had to content himself with shots of Dylan and one of the Paturels' children, Sally's bikini bottom or a skulking minder.

Dylan had let the Baez sisters fly the coop before inviting Kramer to audition for the role of quasi-official photographer. He was beginning to shape his public image, much to the annoyance of Village habitués like Izzy Young, who thought it all a sham: 'In concert at [the] Philharmonic [Hall], he came out with blue jeans. And [yet] at the party afterwards, he had on a regular suit. In other words, the blue jeans were a costume for him.' If so, the whole counterculture would soon follow suit.

Meanwhile, Dylan ensured the man behind the lens never saw his Mr Hyde, dispenser of 'truth', who used his tongue to dissect artifice and lash out at the Unhip. Maymudes, though, knew that man well, even on occasion goading him to show his face, a process described in Maymudes' memoir: 'If we did actually get into a conversation with someone [uncool], we would dismantle him or her ... making them explain themselves and tell us why they were the way they were. This ... became a thing for us.'

Maymudes and Neuwirth would both come to believe this alter-Dylan was partly their creation. Unbeknownst to either, this Bobby had always been there. As school chum John Bucklen noted, even the boy he knew back in Hibbing 'was a master of the put-on ... There was [already] a current of hostility.'

In a seemingly conscious act, Dylan now allowed his social circle to contract considerably. Some who had known the Village Bob very well longed to get back to the garden. Others, like Barry Feinstein, realized 'He [now] had an image to maintain, and he protected it.'

Suze preferred to take the more charitable view, believing 'he was trying to find a balance within himself when everything was off-kilter'. She certainly knew he had a temper, and though she 'was never on the receiving end of one of his tirades', she witnessed a few. But for those who had encountered only the friendly, funny folk obsessive, it came as something of a shock when he did flip the switch:

Michael Bloomfield: I'd never been around anyone famous, and I didn't even know how famous he really was. Dylan and Albert Grossman and this guy Bobby Neuwirth, they were beginning to get isolated. Dylan couldn't deal with people anymore ... And all those people who used to be his buddies, he was getting way [more] famous than I think he ever thought he'd get – fast. [He]'d play these little mind-fuck games with everyone [he] came into contact with, and talked very put-downy to everyone. It was character armour, done in self-defense.

Being a friend or confidant was not necessarily a defence, either. If anything, Dylan felt compelled to discover how far said friendship could be stretched. Even someone as Hip to what was Happening as Aronowitz, friend to the stars, was considered fair game:

Hipper-Than-Thou was the favourite head game of the Dylan crowd and Bobby [Neuwirth] was maybe the game's mosty vicious hardballer ... When he got finished putting you down, you could crawl out the door through the keyhole ... Bob and Bobby ... would forever put me on, [while] I was dazzled by their quick-draw tongues. Some of the scenes they put on were hilarious. Sometimes, they were like kids pulling the wings off insects.

And woe betide anyone who did what Dylan did – that is, write songs for a living. Bloomfield well remembered one time he was 'in a room with Dylan and Phil Ochs and David Blue ... and they would play their songs [before] he'd say, "Well, have you heard this?" ... They knew their stuff just wasn't as good.' Len Chandler, who saw him take Ochs apart on another evening, was less taken aback, 'Dylan was always brutal. [He] had a real hatchet mouth, and it was always very competitive between him and Phil.'

Not even sleeping with the man granted immunity. Mimi and Richard Fariña were present at the Cafe Espresso one evening in late August, the night before the Baez sisters were due to depart, when suddenly Dylan began laying into Joan about her appearance, and he would not let up.* No one quite knew where that person came from, unless he crawled out of a second bottle of Beaujolais, but the result

---

* He would do something similar at a party in London the following May, this time singling out Baez's singing for his disapprobation in the presence of a bemused Marianne Faithfull.

was predictable: Joan in tears and an unimpressed Mimi berating a Bobby she did not recognize. As with Suze's once-smitten sister, seeing the way Dylan treated her sibling would alienate a former ally.

With no apology forthcoming, Joan left the following morning, writing to Dylan from the road a couple of days later. In the letter, which Dylan kept, she is clearly fighting – and failing – to keep her feelings in check, lest she come across as uncool. At one point she quotes 'I Still Miss Someone' as a way of expressing the way she feels; at another, she self-deprecatingly calls herself a 'flat-chested ... phantom queen', her reflection of the way Dylan saw her.

Rather than overuse the L-word, she insists she digs him, but in the end she can't help herself, gushing about those moments when they had lain face to face, smoking and talking. Then suddenly she is all business, telling him all the things he has to do, like read his contracts – something she is fully aware he had failed to do in the past – before pushing him to 'start writing the movie and ... a book', just because she wants to read it.*

She signs off by acting like a surrogate mother, telling him to eat some yoghurt and brush his teeth, before surrendering to her true feelings, unleashing the L-word four times. Even knowing that they have a rendezvous the following week in Monterey, the girl can't help it.

One somehow doubts Dylan spilled his own guts by return post. His most revealing prose piece about their relationship was not the poem he donated to her second *In Concert* LP (1963), a dissertation on beauty that sees the only true beauty as 'ugly, man'; but rather a satirical letter he wrote 'on her behalf' to her parents from Woodstock that August. In it he depicts himself as 'you-know-who' and has Joanie ostensibly claiming she did everything she could to avoid him, but 'pulled back the blankets' at the Foremans' and 'who do you think was hiding under the quilt?' Here was the worst nightmare for any mother – Dylan – 'his hair ... down past his waist ... wearing this monster sweater that stank like he hadn't taken a bath for a year'.

The letter – belatedly published in Baez's own memoir, *And A Voice To Sing With* – provided a refracted version of their relationship as

---

* She had already read parts of an abandoned autobiography, which he had left at her place the previous fall.

seen through Dylan-as-parent eyes. It was both endearingly witty and mildly disturbing, though it would be hard to imagine Dylan writing such a letter to Suze's mother, even in mock seriousness. He preferred correspondents to be in on the joke, hence the four letters he wrote across a nine-month period in 1964 to Tami Dean, a precocious painter-fan from Denton, Texas – whom he calls his 'methedrene pen pal lover' in letter two* – passages of which are a presentiment of the surrealist screeds splattered across side one of his next LP:

> i mix up crazy phantoms.
> exchange their eyes bust into plate glass predictions.
> get in two timed position.
> try t make it with the manacans ...
> i get chopped off head no hair under armpit.
> go dancing back t where i'm better known.
> arrive in a flurry ...
> my head back on backwards i stumble out door.
> wave bye bye get hit by loose lion.
> knock down cop comes ...
> says what's wrong with your head.
> i call him kimosabee in broken french.
> arrests me as a trespasser.
> i say i'm folksinger in real life.
> he dont wanna hear it.
> i say i'm poet storyteller.
> he grabs my throat.
> says theres a noose waiting.
> i say i got influence round here ...

In fact, this quartet of letters – written between March and November – are the best indication we have of a marked transition in writing style, Dylan edging towards the expectant *Tarantula*. By the fourth letter to Dean, he is shuttling between prose and free verse, using couplets that tarantella to a different tune, like 'cleopatra's sister

---

* 'Methedrene' is a deliberate misspelling of 'Methedrine', the trade name of amphetamine, something Dylan was certainly taking by this point, even if Tami was not. He also calls her his 'dope fiend angel'.

opens her mouth at the manhole / tries t grab mayor wagner's son.'
A November 1964 letter to Glover also sees him talk about 'bob dylan' for the first time in the third person, a sign that the separation of Self which would become irretrievably pronounced by the time he entered middle-age was making its first baby steps. It also contains the central image to a notable song he will write later that month, 'Farewell Angelina':

> I write by candlelight. hardly never during the day/
> bob dylan he plays makes bread facing kind fond people menace in their bathtubs/
> they call him names an pay outrageously just t see what he looks like . . . bob dylan he laughs/
> it is all a joke see me in the sky. the sky is on fire.

By now, he is edging away from the 'jotting down notes' approach used for the Feinstein project, which he would unconvincingly claim in 2008 'was something that sort of happened spontaneously'. Unbeknownst to Feinstein, Dylan had arranged a further meeting with editor Bob Markel that fall, to discuss an entirely different project. This time Dylan asked Markel if they could meet 'after dark as he felt he couldn't travel in broad daylight . . . There was no book at the time . . . [Indeed,] he was uncertain what the book would be.' Markel later mistakenly recalled, 'We gave him an advance for an untitled book of writings'. This was not the case – not now or any time soon. It seems Dylan had taken at least one piece of advice from Baez to heart.

What Markel probably saw were parts of something Dylan was calling *Walk Down Crooked Highway*, an excerpt of which appeared in the January 1965 edition of *Sing Out!*.* What is apparent, even in this brief passage, is that Dylan has started creating character studies of the weird and wonderful. In this instance it is Laura, who 'ponders on historical documents. memorizes who gets biggest laugh. invites friends over t discuss matters. tells them not t answer the phone no

---

* This edition would have been on the stands by early December 1964, so must have been sent by November. So when Dylan writes at the end he is getting 'ready to travel west', he may mean this literally.

matter what, then goes out t phone booth an calls herself.' If Markel was looking for a clue as to its thesis, a brief dedicatory poem at the outset offered none:

> justice. humility. freedom. the tortures of laugh[ter]
> are inside here somewhere
> he who reads this in the rain, tho, is bound t get the pages wet.

By year's end Dylan would quietly drop another 1964 persona from his prose poems: he who dispensed advice in a series of aphorisms such as 'watch for cave ins an dont be too good to nobody / they might get wrong idea / sneer at graveyard', advice he gave to Tami Dean in a letter; or, 'do not say or do anything that / he who [is] standing in front of you / watching cannot understand ... do not sign on any dotted line ... do Not create anything / it will be misinterpreted', advice he gave to Geraldine 'on Her Miscellaneous Birthday', published as programme notes for his Halloween Philharmonic Hall concert.* Only fleetingly does the same didactic tone appear among the extant *Tarantula* typescripts in Tulsa, though one passage from an April 1965 draft contains vestiges:

> stay all nite out & be born with something – cast off everything youve been taught ... discover your language & use it – be violent for that is the shape of things – do this & they will search your room – learn first hand that the inventions of others fade at accomplishments – learn this & you will be driven onward – this will bring new inventions & mystify the masses – some will sneak into your body ... do only what you know how to do but transform this useless knowledge to devour all subjects for all subjects are & will remain the same subjects – when others criticize, this is the time for sleep – you'll need all the sleep you can get – you will escape passion & know that your silence is the key – the key to the world's matrimony – there shall be no divorce in your soul & others will hate you for law & unity breed divorce.

---

* Incongruously, Dylan included this poem amongst the *Times They Are A Changin'* material in *Writings & Drawings*, though it belongs with *Bringing It All Back Home*.
† The live album would go through at least two incarnations, the first of which would later become the bootleg LP, *His Gotham Ingress*.

Instead, he fed such a world view into the *Bringing It All Back Home* songs, three of which were part of his Halloween Philharmonic Hall showcase – 'Mr Tambourine Man' (familiar enough to the audience to be greeted by applause), his latest social manifesto, 'It's Alright Ma', and 'Gates of Eden'. All he needed now was another seven or eight and he might have a worthier successor to the patchy fourth album.

Time to return to the starting point. The book, a movie, even a provisional *In Concert* album – all would now be put on hold.[†] Whatever stones had been in his passway he now brushed aside to let months of fermenting song-ideas through, starting at Joan's Carmelian hideaway in late November and continuing back at the Paturels', where the journey 'back home' had begun six months earlier. He had made up his mind. He was going to put that new electic guitar to good use, and the carpers and critics could all go hang themselves.

2.3

November 1964 to April 1965: Walking Down A Crooked Highway

> He doesn't put himself out. And he never tries to change anyone. He accepts or rejects them as he expects them to treat him ... He always wants to know what you think and what you are thinking about ... He is scared of being alone, [yet can] cut himself off and write even with a lot of noise around him.
>
> Nico, 'The Real Bob Dylan', *Disc*, September 18th, 1965

> He's a mysterious cat ... When you're talking to him you just know that he's seeing everything. His little eyes are seeing every bit of truth and every bit of bull and he's categorizing it, working with it, understanding it.
>
> Mike Bloomfield, June 1968

> The thoughts he shared were usually unfinished ... [and came] in quick startling images ... He would stand [there] thinking, his mouth working, his knees flexing ... right, left, right, left. He seemed to function from the center of his own thoughts ... and like a madman he was swallowed up by them.
>
> Joan Baez

> As his life got more surreal, his writing got more surreal.
>
> David Blue

*

On June 23rd, 2011, Christie's in New York were due to conclude a 325-lot auction of 'Fine Printed Books and Manuscripts' with seven lots of Dylan typescripts and manuscripts from the watershed year, 1965. With estimates set between $15,000–20,000 (for a handwritten rewrite of 'Visions Of Johanna's final verse) and $90,000 (for three hand-corrected typescripts – 'Maggie's Farm', 'I'll Keep It With Mine' and '115th Dream'), it was mouth-watering fare. The provenance was unimpeachable, too: 'Albert Grossman, gift of Bob Dylan'.

Except it wasn't a gift, it was an oversight. On the morning of the auction, all seven items – almost all reproduced in the usual handsome catalogue – were removed from sale, to be returned to their rightful owner, Mr Dylan. A marker had been put down. Leaving valuable manuscripts at someone else's house did not amount to a transfer of ownership. Dylan evidently felt widow Sally – the intended beneficiary – had benefited enough from his largesse.

More importantly, the Dylan office's swift action ensured the papers became part of the official archive, not hanging on the wall of some local Hard Rock Cafe or dot.com billionaire. Before 2011, Dylan's dilatory disregard for his personal history, and reluctance to pay for his own handiwork, ensured all auctioned manuscripts had passed into private hands. When the Margolis & Moss papers, from fall 1963, were first put up for sale, Dylan insisted that he had no memory of writing this material and then, when offered the opportunity to buy it, lost interest when he realized copies of the material had been widely circulated. And in the nineties, the Paturels were allowed to sell their collection of 1964 manuscripts privately, a belatedly lucrative form of rent collection.

As a result of Dylan's failure to keep tabs on his own work, for the uniquely fecund fifteen-month period in which Dylan essentially wrote and recorded *Bringing It All Back Home*, *Highway 61 Revisited* and *Blonde On Blonde*, we are reliant on scraps modern Percys rescued from the fire of Dylan's imagination. So focused was he on moving forward, he simply would not allow himself time to collect the detritus that could connect the dots on surely the greatest creative burst in the history of popular song. And on those rare occasions when he did, he duly lost what he had gathered.*

---

* On page 125 of Taschen's 2018 edition of Daniel Kramer's photos is Dylan at the January 1965 sessions, with multiple hand-corrected typescripts on the music stand in front of him. All seemingly lost now.

He also misplaced all but one of the notebooks from this era, though he used them frequently. Kramer photographed him writing 'in his small black notebook ... for a while during the car trip to Philadelphia' in October. The ever-observant Daniel also 'photographed him when for just a few minutes he played with some melodies on a backstage piano', spending enough time with him to see he 'spent a great deal of time writing new material'.

And yet, at that night's show, the only post-*Another Side* song performed would be 'It's Alright, Ma'. The days of previewing new songs in concert had almost passed. Instead, he continued 'to function from the center of his own thoughts', which he kept to himself until ready to spring them on an increasingly chaotic, existential world.

Though Dylan would use what the Paturels called the white room through the fall of 1964, he seemingly scooped up whatever he worked on before turning them into the fair drafts he took to the sessions. A solitary rough draft of 'Subterranean Homesick Blues', which survived long enough to be reproduced in 1973's *Writings & Drawings*, confirms Mary Lou's recollection of him bringing 'just his guitar and a typewriter', as he continued composing to the clatter of keys.

Not that he entirely hid himself away in the room with black curtains, or stopped using sounding boards. Mary Lou specifically recalls 'If You Gotta Go, Go Now' as one instance where 'he'd ... come downstairs and try the songs out on us'. That was one which stuck. How could it not? It was a perfect send-up of the British Pop 45s now dominating the Hot Hundred, albeit with the kinda lyrics not allowed on air in a country that still thought Doris Day was as pure as the driven snow. (This was two years before The Stones rewrote the chorus to 'Let's Spend The Night Together' to keep Ed Sullivan's censor happy, and Dylan's tag line was equally unambiguous, 'Or else you gotta stay all night'.)

Bernard Paturel occasionally hung around long enough to see how Dylan worked. To his amazement, the bardic Bob would usually start by playing the melodic framework – often a simple blues – over and over again until it was lodged in his head, and then he would start to sing and/or type 'disconnected phrases with a poetic feeling'.

However, little of what widow Sally hoped to sell for six figures in 2011 comprised a series of 'disconnected phrases'. The likes of

'Maggie's Farm', 'I'll Keep It With Mine', 'Subterranean Homesick Blues', '115th Dream', 'Outlaw Blues' and 'Farewell Angelina' – the bulk of her hoard – were fair copies, left behind in the Grossmans' colour-coded 'blue bedroom'. If 'Maggie's Farm', 'Subterranean Homesick Blues' (aka 'Look Out Kid') and 'Farewell Angelina' all received handwritten final verses, the others remained largely pristine.

The one important exception was the 'Love Minus Zero' typescript, which was more akin to the published typescript of 'Subterranean Homesick Blues'. Still called 'My Love She Comes In Silence', the single-page lyric paid witness to the war typewriter and pen waged for the soul of this important song. The fact that everything in the finished artefact is contained herein suggests it came with relative ease. Which isn't to say Dylan didn't discard some promising images in the culling. In the draft, 'pride' – presumably his own – 'hangs down on chains', yet 'she offers no solutions' and 'never steps into the center of [the] light'. She is a force of nature, 'ture [sic] as ice or fire', so much so that neither moneylenders nor 'the merchants [who] sell perfection from the shadows of the cave-in' can lay a glove on her.

This is not just a love song; it is in a sense his first wedding song, directed at Sara, another guest the Grossmans' invited to attend the private ceremony which tied Sally and Albert 'till death do part' on November 12th, 1964 in Woodstock. Both Bob and Sara were part of the select list, though according to at least one eye-witness, Dylan seemed to pay more attention to Sally than Sara on the day. Likewise Sara certainly knew that when Dylan left for the West Coast the following week, he had a bed in Carmel waiting for him.

Dylan was sure that the tab for this particular Californian sojourn could be paid in song. Indeed, he seems to have been untypically generous with his largesse, letting Baez record and release two quite superb songs penned on this visit, 'Farewell Angelina' and 'Love Is Just A Four-Letter Word', either one of which she could have taken personally, but insists she didn't: 'There was no way to be sure if he was really writing about me – I wouldn't ask him and he wouldn't tell me. The songs he was doing weren't really about anybody or anything in particular.'

'Farewell Angelina', in particular, seems with hindsight like a test run for the final parting of a star-crossed couple, only one of whom can see 'the sky is on fire'. As previously, Dylan seems to have been inspired by a record in Baez's collection, the tune being taken wholesale from the quasi-traditional 'Farewell To Tarwathie', composed in the 1850s by Aberdeenshire poet George Scroggie, but collected orally by Ewan MacColl.*

Baez shared his passion for such songs; unlike Sara, who seemed indifferent to his chosen vocation. At the three January 1965 sessions, while Sally eagerly accompanied her new husband, her friend remained singularly absent.

For now, Dylan earmarked 'Farewell Angelina' for this next album, unsure how many more spontaneous screeds he had in him. Even after the faucet continued flowing freely through January, he would tell Daniel Kramer, just before the sessions, he had written eighteen songs for the album, but was only admitting to twelve, and was 'holding the others back for next time'. His reasoning? 'How do I know I can do it again?'

He said something similar to Max Jones in a contemporary phone interview. Yet if he was holding songs in reserve, he soon forgot them. 'Love Is Just A Four-Letter Word' is the only documented song from this period which – perhaps because of its problematic final verse – went unrecorded. Even Baez held off recording it till after it appeared in 1967's *dont look back*, even though Dylan admitted on camera, 'That was a good song.'

Sally's typescripts also offered other stray thoughts, including the confessional 'life is just a mess up / i like t get messed up too', and the cryptic 'I've taken [the] peace pill / I drink war juice / drugs bug the doctors / now I'm ready for you', but no complete songs. The only other 'lost' song, 'You Don't Have To Do That', Dylan does attempt at the first *Bringing It . . .* session, but abandons after the first verse, never reaching the verse which accuses her of 'go[ing] out with other people / now [do] you wanna make me jealous?'

---

* Presumably, the LP was *Whaling Ballads* by Ewan MacColl and A. L. Lloyd (Riverside, 1957). Dylan has written at the top of the Grossman typescript in pencil: 'Ewan MacColl Tune'.

This January 13th, 1965 Columbia session, would prove a real pick'n'mix of styles as Dylan seems at times to be demoing his entire new album – save for the three songs debuted live – in a session which starts at seven in the evening – like the one six months earlier, resulting in *Another Side*. The eleven songs he completed in the time allocated – supposedly, a mere three hours – would actually have made for a better album.*

Whereas Dylan used everything, good, bad and indifferent, from the previous session, this time he uses less than zero, instead returning to eight of the eleven songs over the following two days, in every instance with other musicians to hand. Two songs to which he does not return – an inspired 'I'll Keep It With Mine' and the six-verse 'Farewell Angelina' – he leaves imperfect, living proof he has given up any attempt at perfection.

Though neither are 'pulled to master', two cuts from the 13th – solo versions of 'Subterranean Homesick Blues' and 'It's All Over Now, Baby Blue' – are lodged with Witmark nine days later, forming the basis for the songbook versions. In that registration, Dylan makes it plain one of them was his first mathematical song, calling it:

Love Minus Zero
No Limit

'Love Minus Zero' would be the song with which he would bookend the first session and open the second. It was clearly important to him, as evidenced by the fact he returned to it twice, despite telling Wilson after take one breaks down, that he can't 'do any song as good as I can do it the first time', laying bare an aesthetic applicable for all subsequent albums. The breakdown comes about largely because Dylan has co-opted John Sebastian into playing bass, under the mistaken impression he could:

---

* 'I'll Keep It With Mine' / 'It's All Over Now, Baby Blue' / 'Bob Dylan's 115th Dream' / 'Subterranean Homesick Blues' / 'Outlaw Blues' / 'On The Road Again' / 'Farewell Angelina' / 'If You Gotta Go, Go Now' / 'California' / 'Love Minus Zero' / 'She Belongs To Me'.

John Sebastian: I told [Dylan] I wasn't a bass player. But he just said, 'Don't worry, it'll be fine.' I ... was handed a Fender bass, and did the best I could. I don't want to use the word 'tentative', because if Dylan wasn't committed he didn't perform, but I got the distinct impression that this session was for Bob to hear himself and consider his options ... I don't know that we came away with any keepers that day.

Other first-day takes, though, were very nearly 'keepers', after Dylan returned to both 'Love Minus Zero' and 'She Belongs To Me' (attempted solo initially) at session's end. And this time Bruce Langhorne weaves a six-string spell around Dylan, while Sebastian on the former, Bill Lee (playing stand-up) on the latter, burble away at the bottom end. Both takes were pulled, appearing on an out-takes reel alongside 'It's All Over Now, Baby Blue'.* After these successes, Dylan wraps up the largely acoustic session by hinting at what the next two days will hold with a raucous remake of 'Outlaw Blues' – one of three whimsical blues he had attempted that evening solo.† On this take he co-opts Al Gorgoni on electric guitar, John Sebastian on harmonica and 'Joe Mack' on bass, to wallop out an ur-blues sound he could co-opt for this album and the next.

Both 'Outlaw Blues' and 'On The Road Again' will get the full band treatment in the days to come. 'California' – save for a verse donated to 'Outlaw Blues' – will have to await that state's bootleggers for release. All three songs interchange imagery, proof that, as Nico would remark nine months later, 'He used to write all the time, even with the studio full of people.'

Whatever his initial intentions, he had cut usable (semi-)acoustic takes for all but one of the songs that would feature on side one, just in case he should stumble when he plugged in. The one moment of

---

* All three feature on the classic 1969 Dylan bootleg LP, *Stealin'*, evidently taken from said out-takes reel.
† The other two, 'On The Road Again' and 'California' – like 'I'll Keep It With Mine' – were done at the piano.

friction came when Wilson got a little too smart for his own good, provoking an incident which stuck in Kramer's memory:

> Wilson noticed that Bob had a habit of wandering away from his microphone position that adversely affected the quality of the sound. On this day, the mikes and booms were surreptitiously arranged to keep Bob on his spot, and at some point during the session, Bob realized this and called out in mock anger to be released from his confinement.

The 'mock anger' may not have been quite so staged. In a later account, Kramer suggests Dylan cut the song short, then bellowed, 'Can't we get rid of some of these things?' before taking to moving some obstacles himself (not captured on tape). He calms down soon enough, but maybe it is this which prompts Dylan to switch from piano to guitar throughout the session, keeping Wilson and engineer Roy Halee constantly on edge, and driving Halee quietly up the wall. Certainly something prompts Dylan to say, at one point, 'No, no, I'm not gonna do it,' before trying and quickly abandoning 'You Don't Have To Do That', and then announcing, 'I'm gonna play ... piano.'

For now, he needs Wilson and he knows it. Wilson has been pushing him – in person and via Grossman – to plug in for some months, even going into Columbia's 20th Street studio the previous month, where he 'tried ... overdubbing ... a Fats Domino early rock'n'roll thing on top of what Dylan had done [with "House of the Rising Sun", which is] where I first consciously ... started to try to put [folk and rock] together'.*

Though the results were unconvincing, Wilson continued to pitch such a fusion, telling Grossman at one point, 'If you put some background to this [guy], you might have a white Ray Charles with a message.' By January 1965, Dylan didn't need convincing, while Wilson knew full well he had something vital to bring to the party, as he highlighted in a 1967 interview, when he was pushing rock music to its very sonic limit with The Velvet Underground: 'My [main] contribution to the Dylan group things was to find good musicians who had the skill of session musicians and the outlook of young

---

* This 'electric' overdubbed version was featured on the *Highway 61 Interactive* CD-ROM (1995).

rock'n'rollers – men who sympathised with what he was doing.' It took until 2017 for Dylan to concur, acknowledging it was Wilson who 'brought in musicians like Bobby Gregg and Paul Griffin to play with me. Those guys were first class, they had insight into what I was about. Most studio musicians had no idea.'

Thankfully for the future of music, on January 14th and 15th, 1965 these alpha males agreed to work from the same page for now, and probably the same reference tapes. Kramer's photos suggest it was all good-humoured, and that Dylan was revelling in the experience – as was Bruce Langhorne, the most experienced at gauging Dylan's intentions and very much *Dylan's* choice:

> Bob would just step to the microphone and launch into a song. No warning, no explanation, no nothing. We'd just leap in and try to keep up. Somehow everybody found a way to tune in to what Bob was going for. He didn't really know what he wanted, but his absolute certainty about the song he was singing pulled us all behind in its wake. He didn't try to *arrange* people's performances. It was spontaneous, almost telepathic. We had to catch the moment, because there was no going back and fixing things with overdubs.

Not that it was entirely ad hoc. It couldn't be. Yet, according to electric guitarist Ken Rankin, 'There was minimal soundcheck; they got basic balances and checked the mike. It was all completely loose. There was no rehearsal to speak of, no charts, and no instructions I can recall. Dylan would just start playing, and you'd better be ready. We did our best to fall into a groove behind him. There might be two takes ... It was almost a blur.' To which Langhorne concurs, 'We didn't do any rehearsal, we just did first takes.'

Yet *somehow* everyone sounds like they are all working from the same prompt book. 'Love Minus Zero' takes up where it left off the previous evening, but with the metronomic Bobby Gregg added to the mix, while 'Subterranean Homesick Blues' – the second song that first afternoon – is all there from take one, which would have been a keeper if Dylan had not tripped himself up vocally.

Presumably, the musicians had been played the previous day's version and were expected to take their cue from it. This seems to have been the pattern throughout. The results speak for themselves, as does Langhorne: 'It was [all] amazingly intuitive and successful ... [and] Dylan was the thread that held everything together. His intent and his inertia – in Physics terms – was very easy to hook onto.' And it wasn't just the musicians who were caught up in the moment:

> **Daniel Kramer**: Watching the band come together and watching Bob orchestrate what was happening, I was ... impressed ... Musicians not used to playing with Bob had to adjust to his particular style and method of delivery ... They had to be sensitive and flexible, and open to changing or abandoning an idea quickly ... It was crucial to use musicians who could really meet the challenge and accommodate Dylan's needs. As a matter of fact, some musicians were replaced after the first day.

But even these A-list musicians weren't miracle-workers. So when Wilson suggested they record an insert on the fade-out to 'Love Minus Zero' to allow Dylan to add a harmonica coda, one of them expresses disbelief, asking Wilson, 'Insert what? From the top or the fade?' When he is told, 'The fade,' he fires back a sarcastic, 'Thanks for telling us.' When Dylan is co-opted into the conversation, he washes his hands of the plan – 'I have no idea. I'm just gonna play harmonica' – quietly sure it will never sync up. And nor does it. The previous take is just faded down to slot on a seven-track side A.

Which still leaves the thorny question of the *Marie Celeste* of Dylan session tapes: an evening session on the 14th for which the tapes have been mislaid – or erased. Some have suggested it never happened, though AFM records have a three-hour session on file, with John Hammond Jr, Bruce Langhorne, John Sebastian and John Boone all present and correct. And it was seemingly documented by Kramer, who snapped photos of Sebastian, Hammond and Boone at Studio A – with Sebastian visibly playing the electric piano, perhaps on 'I'll Keep It With Mine'.

So there was such a session.* Six songs were logged, including 'I'll Keep It With Mine' and 'It's All Over Now, Baby Blue', neither of

---

* Kramer, in his 1967 photobook, states that 'Mr Tambourine Man' was attempted on the 14th. This evening session is the only possibility. John 'Stephen' Boone, destined to become bassist in Sebastian's Lovin' Spoonful, writes in his memoir that he played on these sessions.

which had been attempted that afternoon. Perhaps they never ran tape because nothing came together.

Certainly Sebastian, Hammond and Boone were all deemed surplus to requirement when Dylan resumed work the following afternoon, wrapping up proceedings in a historic three-hour session where he went electric, then acoustic, then electric again. All through the afternoon, he never let up. Kramer was again in awe: 'His method of working, the certainty of what he wanted, kept things moving. He would listen to the playbacks in the control booth, discuss what was happening with Tom Wilson, and move on to the next number. If he tried something that didn't go well, he would put it off ... In this way, he never got bogged down – he just kept on going.'

Actually, he does get temporarily 'bogged down' on the all-important 'Mr Tambourine Man', having had the byrd-brained idea of trying it with drums, perhaps convinced Bobby Gregg could play on anything. Well, *almost* anything. After two breakdowns, Dylan exclaims, 'Ah, the drums are driving me mad. I'm going out of my brain,' and decides 'me and Bruce'll just play it'.

The problem seems to be that the drums were, as Dylan says, 'very loud in one ear', perhaps because he had refused to reposition himself at the other end of the studio and/or wear headphones. In-house engineer Roy Halee looked on, outwardly calm but quietly smug:

> Dylan was not easy to work with in the studio. He liked to do things very quick and [was] very disorganized. He'd say, 'I want to do a vocal over here by the drums,' and stand next to the drummer. And you'd say, 'Hey, look, it's kinda hard to isolate you by the drums when ... he's beating his brains out.' But he didn't care ... [] ... I know enough about recording at this point [to know] that the singer can't go over and stand next to the drums ... [But] he wants to. So you do what he wants! ... [Because you're already] skating on thin ice with this guy.

If Halee senses he is 'on thin ice', Wilson's own flotilla has also started to crack. Before the first take of 'Tambourine Man', Dylan berates Wilson for starting recording when he isn't ready, 'If you'd look at me, Tom, you'd see when I wave my hands.' Where things nearly – or off-tape, really? – get heated is on the second song that day, 'On The Road Again', when Wilson calls a halt during take eleven (in reality take four, plus several nanosecond false starts), saying, 'That tempo's too fast to squeeze in those words, Bobby.' Dylan is fuming, 'Hey man, *c'mon*! [It's] the way we're gonna do it!' Just to prove he is right, he starts again at the exact same tempo and after the briefest of false starts, nails it at the very same, word-perfect clip.

Wilson, though, continues to chance his arm. Dylan has barely started 'It's Alright, Ma' when he cuts in, 'Bob, can you back up just a little?' Dylan almost downs tools, 'I really don't feel like doing this song.' Wilson refuses to rise to the bait, 'Suit yourself. I'm with *you*,' at which point Dylan smashes into an exhilirating, spiky, near-perfect take two, barely pausing to catch his breath before executing 'Gates Of Eden' with similar elan. It is the third single take master at a session which began auspiciously, the band spilling straight into 'Maggie's Farm' first time, something that will prove beyond the musicians at Newport in July despite a whole night of rehearsals.

Once Dylan stops Gregg from alternating between drums and tambourine, he also dispatches 'Mr Tambourine Man', which has hung around for ten long months. 'It's All Over Now, Baby Blue' comes next, another first take, before every able-bodied musician, including the otherwise unemployed backing singer Angeline Butler, lends a hand on 'If You Gotta Go, Go Now'. Four takes later, Dylan has an authentic pop song.

And yet this potential hit would not be earmarked as the lead single. That would be 'Subterranean Homesick Blues', once he'd done his own market test by calling Nico up in Paris, playing it to her over the phone and asking her what she thought: 'I had to say ten times how good it was before he was sure [I meant it].'

Still unconvinced, Dylan proceeded to invite The Animals – then on their first American tour – to his manager's Gramercy apartment to hear some acetates of what he'd just recorded accompanied by 'a few flagons of wine'. Eric Burdon later told an English journalist, 'He couldn't make up his mind whether to release ["Subterranean Homesick Blues"] as a single. [We] assured him it was right.'

The 45 would be in the shops by March 8th, signalling a shift as seismic as the one Dylan acolyte Marc Bolan would make five years later by electrifying 'Ride A White Swan'. If Bolan's blockbuster lit the blue touchpaper on Glam, Dylan's debut chart single stalled at thirty-nine stateside. It would be The Byrds' debut 45, a jingle-jangle pop expurgation of 'Mr Tambourine Man' – released five weeks later – which would set the seal on Dylan's passage into pop consciousness and trigger a naming contest for what he had spawned. Meanwhile, Dylan had another listening session – this time of the complete album – to attend:

> **Eric Andersen**: I was there when Dylan [played] the first acetate of *Bringing It All Back Home*. It was at Albert Grossman's town house in Gramercy Park – me, Bob, Joan Baez, my first wife Debbie Green, Bobby Neuwirth. It was the first time anybody had heard the album. Bob put it on this rickety old record player and turned it up. He was obviously happy ... He [had] got people tapping their feet and listening to the lyrics at the same time ... Bob felt he'd succeeded in pushing himself to someplace new, a place he'd never been before.

Andersen couldn't help but think back to when he'd 'played us "Chimes Of Freedom" ... [which] seemed like a lifetime ago, but it was only a few months'. One person singularly absent from this convivial gathering – after being along for the whole 'road trip' a year earlier – was Paul Clayton, no longer an Inner Circle member. Despite Dylan's gesture the previous February, Clayton and/or his music publisher had gone after him for a share of 'Don't Think Twice', requiring a legal report on Dylan's behalf to decide whether to settle. The report, by a Harold Barlow, was delivered on January 20th, just five days after Dylan recorded 'It's All Over Now, Baby Blue'. It was unequivocal: 'Bottom Line. Plaintiff's claim has no basis in fact and must be rejected.'*

The report said nothing about ostracizing the instigator. Yet this seems to have been another consequence. Ironically, it is Clayton to whom the memorable phrase 'If you can't write, rewrite; and if you can't rewrite, copyright' was widely attributed in folk circles. And here he was trying it on with an old friend, even if there remained those, like Barry Kornfeld, who felt 'he could have given Paul some money ... [that is, if] Bobby was[n't] one of the stingiest sons of bitches'.†

Others never imagined Dylan was going to leave it at that. When Clayton heard 'It's All Over Now, Baby Blue', he told Steve Wilson he

---

* Barlow was nothing if not thorough. He even interviewed Clayton's old tutor, the eminent folklorist, Arthur Kyle Davis.
* Not as stingy as Paul Simon, though, whom Kornfeld successfully sued for monies owed.

thought it 'might be about him'.* If the lyric *was* directed at a man, he was clearly gay ('Your lover who just walked out your door / Has taken all his blankets from the floor').† 'Baby Blue's inclusion on the album put paid to the equally barbed, equally valedictory 'Farewell Angelina', which Baez scooped up, the irony of her singing it not yet apparent to her.

Meanwhile, Dylan (and Neuwirth) continued holding court at the Kettle of Fish where, as Suze sometimes saw, they 'pronounced sentence and declared truth to whoever approached them'. One regular attendee later claimed Dylan, Neuwirth and David Blue would often head up to Times Square to catch a late movie, choosing 'to go to see comedies in order to discipline themselves not to laugh'. No one was safe. When Eric Burdon agreed to meet Dylan there, 'No sooner had he said, "Hi, man," than he tried to chat up my girl.'

Suze, who saw less and less of him as the months passed, realized 'he had succumbed to [his] demons'. But there was one occasion at the Kettle when he just talked to her 'about drugs, fame, faith, mysticism, women'. And on that occasion he told her there were very few women 'he respected' – just her and Sara really. At that moment, she knew his relationship with this other 'Scorpio sphinx' was serious.

All of which makes Sara's appearance, peeking round the cabin door, in a March photo shoot for the front cover of his new book so incongruous. She was meant to be Dylan's 'back street girl' (two years before Jagger codified such a type). Thankfully, he had yet to sign a contract for said book, and could always change his mind. (He did.) Meanwhile, he irredeemably muddied the waters by casting Sally Grossman – according to Aronowitz, one of three wives, his own included, 'in love with Bob ... a little too much' – as the woman in red on the album cover. Stretched out on the sofa Dylan would later foolishly exchange for an original Warhol, the sultry Sally was duly mistaken by some for Dylan in drag – suggesting it was them, not the photographer, who'd been at the lysergic Smarties.

As for the trick effect which made Dylan seem out of focus – taken by some to intentionally evoke the drug haze these songs supposedly

---

* Dylan told Tony Glover in 1971 that the song was about David Blue. I'm not convinced. After all, he went on to claim 'Tangled Up In Blue' was inspired by Joni Mitchell's *Blue*.
* Clayton would take his own life in April 1967, still unreconciled to his sexuality.

embodied – it was, in Kramer's own words, 'something I had to create by hand. I built a rig that enabled me to rotate the camera ... I wanted it to feel like the universe moving around him. The Columbia art director [John Berg] didn't like it ... He resented being presented with a guy who'd never done an album cover. But Albert Grossman said in no uncertain terms that I was doing it.'

In fact, Grossman, who was enjoying his growing power, was having lunch with Kramer at Columbia when the photographer 'explained ... I would not be able to shoot the cover and why ... [Albert] took [me] by the arm and off we went to the art director's office, where Mr Grossman proceeded to make a series of predictions [regarding] what ... would happen if I did not get this assignment.'

By now, both Dylan and Grossman had very clear ideas about how they wanted the visuals to look and brooked no interference. Fellow pop star Eric Burdon had the rare privilege of sitting in on a picture-selection session at Albert's at this time. He noted, '[Dylan]'s got a big colour projector there, and he and his manager take a lot of care choosing the right type of picture of him to be released. Not necessarily the ones that make him look best – but the type of picture [they like]; most of them ... very way-out.'

Now all Dylan needed to do was give the label his sleeve notes – hopefully tailored to a single 12x12 sleeve this time – and the Columbia pressing-plant could start rolling out what is still Dylan's most innovative album. He may have gone on to make better artefacts – two in the next fifteen months – but he would never again break the mould the way he did on *Bringing It All Back Home*, fusing sensibilities kept apart for centuries. He had attached poetry with a balladic sensibility to the big beat, taken it onto the AM airwaves and declared open season on a song's subject matter.

And yet no sooner had he written the bulk of his most radical album, than he promptly returned to the almost formless be-bop prose of *Tarantula*, which he now presaged publicly with his third set of sleeve notes, which again needed to be pruned by the powers that be. Lost to the scissors is maggie's scheme 'to rob this dimestore' which is interrupted by the grafitti-artist/narrator's entrance:

> I come rambling
> my head fixed on

> sleepy john estes. jayne mansfield,
> so forth / maggie's friend
> stops an wants t know didnt he see
> me at this hootenanny in puarta villarta ...

Dylan was now talking about his new book, caught up in the fleeting belief he had cracked another code. When *Melody Maker*'s Max Jones called him in early March for an update on activities, he told him the book with Feinstein would be out in the fall (he was out by forty-three years) and that he was 'in the country now, working on another book ... It's not really a novel, just bits of information. It's called *Bob Dylan Off The Record*.' It still had that title when he spoke to Paul Jay Robbins in LA at month's end, when his enthusiasm for the book remained audibly intact:

Paul Robbins: You have a book coming out. What['s] the title?
BD: Tentatively, *Bob Dylan Off The Record*. But they tell me there's already books out with that ... title. The book can't really be titled, that's the kind of book it is. I'm also going to write the reviews for it.
PR: Why write a book, instead of [just] lyrics?
BD: I've written some songs which are kind of far out, a long continuation of verses, stuff like that – but I haven't really gotten into writing a completely free song ... I wrote the book because there's a lot of stuff in there I can't possibly sing ... all the collages. I can't sing it because it gets too long or it goes too far out ... Something that had no rhyme, all cut up, no nothing, except something happening, which is words.
PR: You wrote the book to say something?
BD: ... Certainly not any kind of profound statement.

For now, he was taking all comers into his confidence, even telling Robert Shelton before a Paul Butterfield Blues Band gig at the Village Gate that he was 'contracted to write two books for Macmillan, is writing a play and considering acting in a movie or two'. And when Martin Carthy calls, he informs him 'he is writing a John Lennon-type book', the first public indication that the huge success of Lennon's *In His Own Write*, published the previous March, had shaped his thinking as to the type of book he could get away with, seemingly taking McCartney's introductory comment that 'none of it has to make sense' to heart.

At a 2001 press conference he referred to the fact that 'John Lennon had just published his book [sic] at that time', only to squarely place the blame for his own deal at Grossman's door: 'I never had any intention of writing a book. [But] I had a manager who was asked: He writes all those songs ... maybe he writes books. And he ... replied: Sure he writes books ... He made the deal and then I had to write the book. He often did things like that.'

'Tis a gross distortion of the facts. Grossman played a part, but only to ensure Dylan didn't give his book to the hip but hopeless City Lights on a handshake. He then stepped in to play hardball with Macmillan, some of whose staff seemed to think it was a done deal until a memo came down from on high in June, directed at those who 'had already completed a review list for SIDE ONE. Please understand that this book is no longer on the list for fall. As a matter of fact, we do not yet have a contract.'

With Grossman on the case, the final contract was still being negotiated. Dylan, meanwhile, stocked up on typewriter ribbons as he hammered out a draft which changed its name three times in three months. Rather than staying off the record, Dylan had decided to write a two-sided tome, the first half of which would be called *Side One's Prayer Book Number Zero*; the second, *Side Two. Number Green. & Black Nite Falling*. The former is the title on page one of the earliest complete draft, now housed in Tulsa.

In one of the crueller jokes posterity has recently played, Dylan kept but a single typescript lyric from the wild mercury years, but folder after folder of drafts to *Tarantula*, the combined weight of which serve to confirm what the published book itself suggested: Dylan may be a fine editor of lyrics, but when it comes to prose, he needed more objective sounding boards than paid minders or a salaried backing band. When he read passages of the finished book to Australian actress Rosemary Gerrette the following April, she found it 'unintelligible, avant-garde, like the backs of his record covers. [But] the boys [in the band] all thought it was really groovy.' By then, the title had changed to *Tarantula*.

Indeed, by April 28th, 1965 it had assumed this single-word title, as Dylan informed Maureen Cleave during a Savoy hotel-room mini conference:

Cleave: As in spiders?
BD: As in spiders.
Male journo: What's it about?
BD: It's just a book of some kind of writing ... a stream-of-consciousness thing.

The following year, when asked at another London press conference, this one at the Mayfair, how long it had taken to write, he reverted to mythmaking: 'Oh, about a week, off and on.' When asked if it was finished, he misunderstood: 'It wasn't finished last year ...' – which was true – '[but] I only worked on it for a few days' – which was not. He worked on it nigh-on continuously through early May. For a while, he even retained some kinda handle on its obtuse literary code.

Like Lennon, he indulged his love of wordplay, though with less punning.* Where the Scouser called Enid Blyton 'Enig Blyter', Dylan preferred someone speaking 'in a peter lorry voice' or being 'head over heals' in love. But just like Lennon, his parodies failed to suggest an intimate knowledge of the classics. His language was all his own. When he wrote 'to be or not to be, that is digestion', and credited it to 'Little Billy Come', he was merely testing the coordinates for 'Desolation Row'.

Elsewhere in this first full draft, from spring 1965, he tapped into a vein of anti-intellectualism he would mine throughout 1965–6, describing 'the old folks' home, the college [and] the orphan factory' as 'all the same residense'. Meanwhile, an equally entrenched atheism leads him to depict Jude as 'a stoned freak from the other side of the tracks, [who] goes totally beserk when he sees this fish climb out of the water an fetch a piece of bread.'

---

* Dylan even anticipates Lennon by creating someone who 'moves about like a walrus & has to sleep with a wife that feels like a walrus & he's forced to be a walrus for a buncha nagging kids'.

References to traditional songs also abound. 'yonder stands lil maggie. with a shotglass in her hand / casting away her beatniks like some lowdown gambling man' could almost be a lost couplet from 'Tombstone Blues'. While a passage like 'the lonesome home rambler, fetching camp like gypsy davy, the undercover hobo with the pretty things watching – from the hips on down, onward then, to the lipreading of aretha's moment' could almost serve as a glossary on the comment he had made to Robbins: 'There's a lot of stuff in there I can't possibly sing ... because it gets too long or it goes too far out.'

Another draft from 1965 – which calls the second section *Falcon's Mouth Book Number Zero* – goes to town on the Child Ballad references: '*lord randall* on time's square. fanny blair on the fire hydrant. willy moore, the shoemaker, counting his thumbs / the crippled fiddler, hauling his nail an nine tails to the bookcases – *sir james* rising over morningside an hey lawdy mama, the dunce, driving the bus of open tuning / *matty groves*, with his mattress, hitch-hiking with *edward*, who cuts hedges for his wages / *barbara allen*, growing out of the cinders.'

The *Side One* draft also confirms 'aretha' was there almost from day one, while a partial typescript, probably from 1964, has an opening which suggests he is already intent on writing a book the folks back home won't understand, but Allen Ginsberg – he of the 'hydrogen jukebox' – might:

> 1. aretha / holy jukebox. darla, queen of dance. tombs of brilliance bore me. an other's that never laugh / blast the polls. the conceited competition – from the clowns of petty politics t the kings of preaching tou[n]ghs of liberation ... an all their backers / Daisy writes from lisbon / ace of spades comes up sneaky back room smoke / counting numbers that've come in today / Suzie Q the angel. absurdness and the rest of God / ... sing, aretha / sing their sins on mainstreet into its sewer / sing misty if you can. sing without t s eliot's touch / sing in the sewer. the madness of sunshine / sing for the barber ...

Another important link at this stage is Maria, perhaps a nod to his stepdaughter. No fewer than nine chapter titles reference her: 'Beginning With Maria', 'Say Hello to Maria', 'Maria Nowhere', 'Making Love on Maria's Friend', 'Proposition to Falling Maria', 'Maria an the Mirror of Constant', 'Maria an the Mexican Jealousy', 'Everybody Down on Maria' and 'A False Eyelash in Maria's Transmission', all of which will later be tweaked or discarded.

The one place where he overtly takes a leaf from Lennon and riotously runs with it are the letters. In Lennon's six-line 'A Letter', the art-school wag asks for 'a stabbed undressed envelope' and signs off 'hop[ing] this fires you as you keeler. An admirrer.' This approach could have inspired Dylan to pen the series of satirical epistles which will be the most accessible part of *Tarantula*. The funniest and most important of them – the 'butter-sculptor' letter – is already in this early draft, Dylan seemingly anticipating the controversies to come. Elsewhere, he takes particular delight in imagining the kind of love letter someone else must have received:

> so he won't let you look at anyone else huh? well that's called love, baby, that's called true love. you say he buys things for you all the time ... yeah, well, that's called comedy / in any case, i would-not worry about it none, you've probably got him head over heals. i know him very well. he likes his mashed tomatoes with peanut butter an not too much salt. see you when the moon is down. your faithful hump, Hank.

Perhaps surprisingly, there is even a letter addressed to his mother – 'mother say go / in That direction / an write the greatest book of all'.* And by the final chapter, numbered 69, aretha has returned, still singing of tree-cutters:

> but what's the worth? foreign country, the rejective re-
> ceptive, sits crosslegged on a table in the woods / burning
> a questionaire an the legs of the table / as the song shall
> die, the singer with it – you know, because you shall sing
> the song / meantime, some shell of me is on this totem pole.
>   aretha, lady godiva of the migrants,
>   she's singing /
>   she's singing
>   a
>   lumberjack song.

---

* Dylan will later change 'book' to 'deed', a revealing switch.

Already, though, Dylan is expressing doubts that what he is doing is as worthwhile as, say, 'discover[ing] a rubber dolly in the defence factory. i would like to do something of value like grow some daisys on the desert ... but i am just a guitar player.'

Despite such protestations, he would allow the book to torment him for the next eighteen months, before abandoning it. For most of that time he would have to fend off questions about publication, having mentioned it rather too often in the first flush of a transitory enthusiasm. Here was a medium he would have to wait four decades to conquer, and then only by returning to the liar's autobiography he'd started out to write.

For now, he thought he had the answer to every question. He even handwrites in pencil, on one of the spring 1965 drafts, the imaginary question 'When were you first disillusioned with Folk Music?', as well as his answer, 'When I saw everybody laughing at Jesse Fuller's jokes.'

Here was a more suitable outlet for his wit – sending up the press, present or not. That winter, he concocted a whole press conference in cahoots with J. R. Goddard, which the latter ran in the *Village Voice* as if it was a genuine happening, and not a by-product of Mr Send-Up.

Cavalier, a short-lived rival to *Playboy*, also happily ran a page-long interview entirely about one of Dylan's ties, the visual evidence provided by a complicit Kramer, who also convinced Dylan to write *Tarantula*-esque captions to a photo portfolio he gave another short-lived US periodical, *Pageant*. And if he needed a straight man, there was always his old friend, Robert Shelton, who was writing a feature on Dylan for *Cavalier*, for which Dylan forewarned him, 'I'm in the show business now. I'm not in the folk-music business. That's where it's at. So is Roscoe Holcomb, Jean Ritchie, Little Orphan Annie, Dick Tracy, all the way up to President Johnson.' The penny still failed to drop.

As Dylan probably knew – and if he didn't, the irascible Izzy did – Shelton had become 'terrifically bitter ... [because Dylan] doesn't talk to him anymore. He says, I made him ... I got him jobs, I boosted him', all of which was true. But to the new Bobby, Shelton was someone who had played the Dylan card too often. And others like Irwin Silber viewed him similarly, stating in 2001: '[When] the folk boom unfolded ... he was already in place at the *New York Times*. And so he became an authority [on something] for which he wasn't really qualified. But he wallowed in it ... There was an arrogance to the way in which he appointed himself ... as sort of the definitive judge when it came to what was good, what was bad.' Shelton's reviews of Dylan at Newport and the Philharmonic Hall had certainly annoyed the singer. He was about to be put on and cast out, in that order.

Not that Dylan displaying a cruel streak in the company of friends was anything new. As Shelton himself told Max Jones in 1966, 'Dylan always liked play[ing] games on people'. But even Ramblin' Jack Elliott was shocked when he tagged along to an uptown nightclub after Dylan's first national TV appearance in a year, on Les Crane's February 17th chat show, where Dylan previewed 'Baby Blue' and 'It's Alright, Ma', and demolished Les (or 'Less', as he calls him throughout their conversation) with some razor-sharp wit.

At the club, though, Elliott saw Dylan being unconscionably mean when 'some girl fan ... wanted to get his autograph and talk to him ... He was making fun of her, trying to make her feel miserable. [He] kept saying, "Through the hoop! Through the hoop!" and holding up this imaginary circus hoop.' The Swiftian satirist was now lashing out in all directions, searching for 'a balance within himself when everything was off-kilter'.

After agreeing to do a short joint tour of the north-east with Baez in early March – now he had proven beyond all reasonable doubt that he was fully her equal as a concert draw – he proceeded to upset those who once booed him for interrupting their Queen. Joan well recalls 'the kids ... calling out for him to do the songs that meant something to them, like "Masters Of War" and "With God On Our Side" ... reaching out to him, and he [just] didn't care'. Dylan later told Shelton, 'It was like playing in a funeral parlor.'

Perhaps the audience was mourning the end of an era. Joan certainly began to sense the sky was folding, as evidenced by the first three songs on her next album – all Dylan valedictions from the past year ('Baby Blue', 'Farewell Angelina' and 'Daddy, You Been On My Mind') – and her wanton use of Langhorne's distinctive guitar sound, last heard when she was invited to an exclusive unveiling of Bobby's latest quantum leap.*

---

* Track #4 would be the Celtic folksong 'Wild Mountain Thyme', a song they sang in tandem at these shows.

As for her former beau, he couldn't wait to head west for a Columbia promotion party arranged by Billy James in LA to celebrate the release of his album, the charting of his single and the imminent release of 'Mr Tambourine Man' by another of James's clients, The Byrds.

LA scenester Kim Fowley recalls just how incongruous the new Dylan looked at what, to his mind, was 'one of those in-crowd meet and greets where they have tiny sandwiches and everyone stands around acting gay-effete'. And yet, 'here comes Bob Dylan, ... a scruffy guy who might have slept on somebody's sofa that day'.

He was probably just savouring the moment, using the opportunity to make it up with James (over the Svedberg farrago) and posing on the steps outside with The Byrds, caught in preflyte. The following day, Dylan returned to the Santa Monica Civic Auditorium, the site of the first shoots of Dylanmania fourteen months earlier, itching to perform the likes of 'Love Minus Zero', 'She Belongs To Me' and 'Baby Blue'. Yet even as West Coast adulation was a-growin', John Lennon was telling *Melody Maker*, 'I think Bob Dylan's music will grow steadily in this country, but I can't see him becoming the kids' new craze. I'm not saying the kids in this country won't grow to like his stuff, but there can't really be Dylanmania.'

Three weeks after the Santa Monica show, the UK charts showed Lennon to have been mistaken. Dylan had his first number one album: the first artist of any kind in twenty-five months to top said chart who was not The Beatles or The Stones. The album in question was not even the folk-pop album he had just recorded, but rather the one which had blown The Beatles away in their Parisian suite fifteen months earlier, *Freewheelin'*.

If English Dylanmania wasn't likely to result in quite so many damp knickers as Beatlemania, one reporter at the opening show of his imminent English tour rightly noted 'The times [really] are a-changin' ... when a poet and not a pop singer fills a [concert] hall.'

Not just a poet. A novelist and film-maker. For Dylan was finally making a movie. When he flew into the eye of this cultural storm on April 26th, he had a film crew with him to document his arrival, and a script on his lap.

Actually, the script was for *Christmas On Earth Continued*, the second film by underground film-maker and friend Barbara Rubin, who was on the flight at Dylan's behest (as was her friend Kate Heliczer) hoping to make connections in London, having been promised by 'Bobby [he] will give John Lennon the script and make much talk', as she optimistically reported in a letter the following day to Jonas Mekas. For Dylan's own film, a documentary, no script would be required – just the odd prop.

2.4

April to June 1965: Call Me Vérité

He hides his true feelings completely and never really lets you know what he feels.

Dana Gillespie, July 1965

He doesn't split people into blacks and whites. To him, people are people. He accepts them as they come ... He can be a great tease, he'll [happily] make fun of people – but ... there is nothing malicious about him ... Bob [also] has an eye for ... the Scandinavian type ... [and] he likes reading – especially poetry ... He'll talk on any subject under the sun. Often, during a conversation, he will appear preoccupied. You think he isn't listening to a thing you are saying, then he will surprise you by coming up with a pointed comment.

Martin Carthy, April 1965

When it was just us he was perfectly comfortable, perfectly relaxed and perfectly easy. But once the place was full of people there was a little gear change and he became the Public Person.

Anthea Joseph, to author

Bob puts on a show of scorn for the teenybopper adoration of The Beatles, but ... Bob is very competitive. He laughs at John, Paul, George and Ringo for performing while being drowned out by the screeches that always prevent the audience from ever actually hearing a Beatles concert. He sneers at the idea of living a life while being mobbed by fans. 'Who wants to be imprisoned in a hotel room?'

Al Aronowitz

Q: Would you be annoyed if the girls screamed at you like they do at The Beatles?
Bob Dylan: I would not play.

Varsity questionnaire, May 1965

*

The period between Dylan arriving at London airport on April 26th, 1965 and playing the second of two sold-out shows at the Royal Albert Hall on May 10th is surely the most well-documented fortnight of his career, thanks in no small part to D. A. Pennebaker's all-seeing 'Eye'. What we see in *dont look back*, the 1967 film of that tour, and the reels and reels of out-take footage that now reside at Tulsa, is 'somebody who has come to the end of one road, knows there's another road there, but doesn't exactly know where it is'.

What we don't see is a man finding that next springboard. Hence, perhaps, Dylan's rather dismissive 1978 description of said film, 'It seems like I wasn't doing anything but living in hotel rooms, playing the typewriter and holding press conferences for journalists.' He also reluctantly recalled some 'throwing [of] bottles' in there, an incident he tried his best to persuade Pennebaker to remove, telling him, 'All that stuff in the room with the glass, you don't need to have that. That's so noisy.' Pennebaker replied, 'It matters to the story,' and he had right to final cut.

It stayed in – as did much of the footage with Joan Baez, who was there because Dylan had also invited her along. Again, when Pennebaker screened a rough cut of the movie for Dylan in April 1966, an attendant reporter recalled Dylan saying, 'We'll have to take all that stuff of Joan out ... She was only there a few days.' And yet, she remained. In fact, Pennebaker's main concern was that there might be no story to tell. He knew he had 'to take it on faith the film would not be a series of press conferences, and getting in and out of concert halls ... [Thankfully,] Dylan was going through some kind of change, and I knew that if I could stick with him I'd see something of it.'

What he saw was not only 'somebody who has come to the end of one road', but someone who, by the end, wants *out*. Yet a number of hints as to where he is going shall end up on the cutting-room floor, such as a telling conversation with his producer Tom Wilson and Albert Grossman in his Savoy hotel room, while watching Britain's leading R&B band, John Mayall's Bluesbreakers – with their new guitarist, Eric Clapton – on a children's TV show.

Dylan is audibly enthused, 'That's his new guitar-player – cat looks like Wyatt Earp. Wow. He's one of the grooviest guys we've seen so far. Hey, we'll do "Maggie's Farm". [Mayall] said they could reproduce "Subterranean Homesick Blues" better than the record.' Grossman, who has already 'dissed' those 'people [who] listen to [The] Dave Clark [Five] and think it's rock'n'roll', doesn't think the Bluesbreakers doing his client's new single is such a good idea, but his client is adamant: 'I think they could [do it].'*

Though the final film famously opens with Dylan's innovative promo video for that single – widely recognized as the first of its kind – no explanation is offered for its inclusion. Yet the idea had been raised by Dylan the first time he, Neuwirth and Pennebaker met at the Cedar Tavern in New York, in March, as proof that he wasn't about to play the media game:

D. A. Pennebaker: [The video] was Dylan's idea, actually, and a neat idea. He said ... 'We'll draw up these cards and we'll play back th[is] song I've just written and I'll throw the cards up, or something.' ... []
... It would be a take-off of what The Beatles had to do when they had to play [along to] the playback ... Dylan wanted to put a little needle into that, by doing it as a gag.

In person, though, he put the needle away. At no point in *dont look back* does Dylan play on his relationship with The Beatles, even though that relationship was now the key dynamic in Pop. But he couldn't wait to play them his new single, which had been reviewed that week in *Disc* by Penny Valentine, who called Dylan out in no uncertain terms, describing it as 'a very strange record that's a cross between Chuck Berry and Rick Nelson's "Waiting At School [*sic*]" – with an

---

* Pennebaker produced a companion one-hour documentary for the 2006 DVD release, calling it simply *Dylan '65 Revisited*. It offers a more benign portrait of the pop idol, as if in direct response to Dylan's 1978 comments. This exchange still ends up on the cutting-room floor, the comment about Clapton only finally appearing in the 2018 documentary, *Life In 12 Bars*.

ORCHESTRA no less ... I have a strange feeling that Mr Dylan is having a good laugh at us all', a view echoed by one of the Liverpool gals Dylan invites up to his Adelphi hotel room in *dont look back*.

Valentine, the regular *Disc* singles reviewer, was spot on – Dylan's new 45 really was a cross between Chuck Berry's 'Too Much Monkey Business' and Ricky Nelson's 'Waitin' In School' ('Headin' down to the drugstore to get a soda pop / Throw a nickel in the jukebox, then we start to rock ...'), Valentine being one of a number of savvy sisters-in-spirit who saw pop journalism as a way to the very heart of pop culture. Ditto, Maureen Cleave, whom Dylan initially fails (or pretends to fail) to recognize as someone who interviewed him the year before, when he'd been playing the straight man:

Maureen Cleave: Where do you live?
Bob Dylan: Some [of the] time in New Orleans. Some time in New York City.
MC: What sort of house do you have in New Orleans? One with a balcony?
BD: [Actually] I live out in the country. Outside New York. I stay with friends.
MC: People say you have houses.
BD: No, I don't. I'd tell you if I did.
MC: What happened to your motorcycle?
BD: I still have it. The battery's dead [by now], I guess. I'll have to get another one.

The penny now seems to drop. So when Cleave asks if a song like 'Subteranean Homesick Blues' 'come[s] quickly', the songwriter answers with a degree of candour. 'They come very fast. I write down the idea [in] say an hour, and then I just fill them in as time goes by with all these things,' before he turns personal, 'I saw what you wrote last year.' A delighted Cleave asks him, 'Did you like it? I put a lot of trouble into that.' Rather than answering, Dylan asks her if he's changed. When she assures him, 'You're exactly the same,' Dylan disarmingly informs her, 'I'm gonna marry you.'*

---

* Could it be Dylan already knows about her and Lennon's clandestine affair, which will later inspire 'Norwegian Wood' – and, therefore, by proxy, '4th Time Around'?

The whole exchange would form part of Dylan's first Savoy hotel press conference, during which he is also asked 'What do you think about the [English] pop scene?' His response is a knowing one: 'This is the one place where [singers] weren't regarded as some kind of freaks. That never happened in America. You never found rock'n'roll groups in the *news*. On the front pages.'

By now, he knew he was more than just a person of interest to the pop papers. If he didn't quite know what to make of the interest, the media really didn't know what to make of him. They were used to getting access, and they were used to cooperative subjects. *Dont look back* conveys just how quickly Dylan went from enjoying games with the media to wanting to be left alone.

Initially, he willingly plays along. When one reporter asks him, the morning after landing, 'What do you do with your money?' he fails to feel the tug of someone having his leg pulled as Dylan replies, 'A lot of cigarettes. I don't drink hard liquor. I make a lot of beaver skins. I make about 500 rabbit furs a year.'

Sometimes, Dylan would even let reporters in on the gag. When another Mr Jones asks him why he wears dark glasses, he adopts a soon-familiar mantra, 'I have very bad eyes.' He then hands the glasses to the journalist, 'Wanna get a kick? Here, see the world as Bob Dylan sees it.' When the journalist admits it is making him cross-eyed, Dylan snaps, 'Imagine what it does to my eyes.' It is all said in jest and though he can't resist sending up the process (and the press), it is all very gentle. Even when asked by a particularly impudent male reporter if he and Joan Baez were 'romantically involved', he pulls the rug away from Joan – who was thankfully not present – by replying, 'Just good friends. I have no one special girl.'

It would be just the beginning of a chastening fortnight for the unfortunate lady. At a reception laid on for Dylan at the Dorchester on the very first evening, Dylan had run into the dyed-blonde bombshell Dana Gillespie, who remembered they 'started talking almost as soon as I walked in ... He was fairly blatant about [his interest], and made some remark about my 44-inch bust.' Dana was soon, as she put it recently, 'seeing Dylan romantically, though horizontally might be a more accurate description.'

Dana, too, would have to pass a test as to whether she was cool enough to be part of the 'in' crowd, and Pennebaker was there to document it as Dylan and Neuwirth do a number on her in his suite, Dylan telling her, 'You have a fantastic set of hair. It's the size of the hair.' But the person who once proclaimed he was 'a freak for tits' isn't looking at the lady's hair. Dana challenges Dylan, 'Are you laughing at me?' Neuwirth defuses the situation, 'Just 'cause we laugh all the time, doesn't mean we're laughing at people. Nobody puts someone in a room just to laugh at them. [You] just ask 'em to leave.' An unconvinced Dana warns them both, 'I have a starting pistol in there.'

Having crossed some invisible Rubicon, Dana gained enough confidence to end up 'keeping [his] bed warm … [though] I think he just wanted someone warm to keep him company.' Just fifteen, she would 'slip out of his bed in the early hours and sneak back to my parent's house' in South Kensington.

The person she described to *NME*'s Keith Altham the following month was 'a kind of tramp, who would rather do his travelling in comfort, and enjoys kicking conformity and convention in the teeth. Most of the time he walks around in jeans, a shirt and a pair of hideous, thonged sandals … For a long while he wore my black corduroy jacket over here and I wore his grey jacket. Later I discovered he had left his passport in the pocket.'

If Dylan's blatant interest in Gillespie's assets cannot have sat easily with the wounded Queen of Folk, nor can the fact that he was soon coming on to English pop's latest chanteuse, Marianne Faithfull, in Joan's presence. When Baez responded by singing 'high vibrato' versions of 'Here Comes The Night' and 'Go Now', Faithfull witnessed Dylan's cruel side as he held 'up a bottle as she sang a high note, and drawled, "Break that!" She just laughed' – presumably between gritted teeth.

The meeting with Marianne the motorcycle madonna had been arranged by John Mayall, someone hip enough to be ushered into the inner sanctum even as Dylan's hotel room at the Savoy became the temporary headquarters of Anglo-American pop culture. How Dylan became aware of the Bluesbreakers is not clear, though possibly he had heard of them from Paul Rothchild, the Butterfield Blues Band producer, who had been told about 'the charismatic role a young guitar player for John Mayall's Bluesbreakers named Eric Clapton had in the mythology of English blues bands' by his Boston buddy, Joe Boyd, who had been spending time in Britain tour-managing blues acts.* Whatever the connection, Mayall was apparently summoned to the Savoy:

> He didn't know too much about who was over here, but apparently the one person he wanted to meet was [me] ... I went over to the Savoy hotel, which was just a total circus ... Dylan would go off at tangents – he'd be talking, then he'd go off into a corner and write something down. But he was so surrounded with his entourage that it was hard to get more than five minutes [alone] with him.

If Dylan's ego needed stoking – and I'm not sure that it did – The Beatles turning up to pay homage and hang out the first day he hit town only served to fan the flames. According to Dana, 'The Beatles came [to the Savoy] with their respective girls and everyone got very high on wine ... the only thing Dylan ever drinks. He seemed to get on very well with John Lennon – they both share the same sense of humour ... [But] at one point all the boys got up and went into the bedroom for a chat. We were told it was a staff party in there and girls were not admitted.' One suspects the 'staff party' was a spliffing affair.

Below the surface banter, though, some present felt more than a little uptight. Patti Boyd remembers there were 'so many people there, it was kinda chaotic. People with cameras, his whole gang ... I seem to remember Bob later on wanting to meet John, just the two of them', a bond which was further solidified when he visited the Lennons that evening at their Weybridge home. Lennon evidently wanted to talk privately. The hotel suite was not the place for that.

On another occasion, Lennon recalled, there were 'all these freaks around us ... Ginsberg and all those people. I was anxious as shit.' This was presumably the time Dylan introduced Rubin and Heliczer to this potential investor, with Heliczer remembering that Dylan and Lennon were 'talking gobbledegook' and appeared to be 'high as kites'. Baez, writing to her sister the week after arriving, also noted, 'The

---

* Dana thinks it might have been her who tipped Dylan off, 'I definitely would've talked about Eric, as I raved about him wherever I went ... I'm sure I would've said something, especially as I had also met John Mayall [by] then.' She is also of the opinion that Marianne 'had the hots for Dylan and was quite keen to pull him.'

Beatles [were] a little confused by Bobby, he got so drunk and they all had to [try to] be ha ha funny.'

Throughout all the networking and glad-handing, the Midwest refugee and the guys from Liverpool's ginnels reaffirmed a mutual respect and admiration. But for Dylan, this was just the beginning. He met with Phil May of The Pretty Things, the Bluesbreakers, assorted Stones and an ex-Animal, in Alan Price, who according to Dana, 'turned up at the [first] concert, in Sheffield. Bob always has a piano in his dressing room, so Alan began to play and sing blues numbers on it ... [But when] Bob asked him why he left The Animals ... he slammed the piano lid down and refused to talk about it.' Dylan might actually have appreciated the irony of Price becoming *persona non grata* for taking the arrangement credit (and therefore the publishing) for 'House Of The Rising Sun' from the other Animals.

The meeting that the media seemed most interested in, though, involved Dylan and Britain's very own New Dylan, Donovan, about whom Dylan was asked the minute he stepped off the plane. He professed ignorance, telling a kid at the Savoy reception, 'I've never seen him ... never heard of him ... For all I know, Donovan might be a new kind of food.' Yet two weeks before Dylan's arrival, Martin Carthy had said that his friend didn't 'give a damn about the singers who have copied his style', suggesting Carthy may have already given him the heads-up on this arch imitator.

Donovan's 'Catch The Wind' was already climbing the charts when the Prince of Folk landed, only for *Melody Maker* to slip it into a pile of supposedly hot-off-the-press singles they asked Dylan to review for their weekly 'Blind Date' column. He said he thought Donovan sounded 'a bit like he's holding onto a tree trunk, wearing a patch over one eye', but didn't reveal whether this was a good thing.

He was soon as curious to meet Donovan as vice versa, and on the evening of May 4th, Mr Leitch joined Dylan, Baez, Mayall and Faithfull in the Dylan hotel suite for a song-swapping session. It was no contest, and eventually Dylan stopped playing his new songs to the awed acolyte and put on his new record, which confirmed that the various supplicants coming to his hotel door were trailing in his dust creatively.

If the media, predictably, remained stuck in 1963, Dylan was more interested in what people thought about his new record than the shows he was playing, requiring Faithfull to be a private *Jukebox Jury*: 'After every track he would ask, "Did you understand what I was getting at?" or "What was that all about?" I got quite flattered. He has this huge pile of "cue cards" with the meaning of his songs written on them, so that if anyone asks what "Subterranean Homesick Blues" is about, he just holds up the appropriate card. He ... takes himself very seriously.'

Dylan was simply looking to wrestle free of the stereotypical straitjacket that lazy tabloid journalists thought they could wrap him in. When a reporter at the Savoy reception tried to put him in the folk box, Dylan explained he was rooted in so much more: 'I started playing country and western music ... Then I started playing rock'n'roll music ... then I started playing folk music ... and I sorta combined all three somewhere,' which was remarkably close to the truth. Not for the first time, he wouldn't be believed. When another reporter at the same reception asked if he would describe 'The Times They Are A-Changin'' as a folk song, he was adamant, 'That's not a folk song.' Nor was it.

Playing with Mayall was intended to be part of a planned breakout. When Dylan watches the Bluesbreakers on TV, he clearly states, 'They're gonna be on my show with me,' meaning the national TV show we see Grossman negotiating for in *dont look back*. Likewise, his interest in Marianne Faithfull was not entirely carnal. As she informed Keith Altham, 'Dylan invited me to dinner ... saying that he wanted me to appear on his TV show.'

In the end, these plans would be sabotaged by an impromptu studio session and Dylan being taken ill, thus losing valuable time to 'prep' anything more ambitious than a solo concert, which is what the BBC thought they had bought. Solo concerts were, after all, the ostensible reason he was 'over here' and why Pennebaker had agreed to tag along:

> I didn't know that he was going to leave acoustic. I did know that he was getting a little dragged by it. It was definitely a bore for him to have to go on stage every night while the rest of us were sitting around getting high in the green room ... [] ... [But] *dont look back* wasn't really about music ... Dylan maybe thought it was gonna be about music ... The film was originally two hours and had more music in it, but I knew the real film [would be] focused ... on the thing that was Dylan.

That 'thing' was spinning out of control. Faithfull, while admitting she was smitten by the man, found it a daunting experience just being around him and his inner circle: '[They] were all so hip, so devastatingly hip. [And] they were all so fucking high. Every five minutes or so someone would go into the bathroom, and come out speaking in tongues.'

Increasingly, the ever-widening chasm which separated Dylan from normality was artificially induced, and it was making it impossible to be around him for anyone tired of others taking drugs and staying up late. Which meant Baez, for whom 'the tour in England was … just hideous; partly because everybody was doing drugs'.

She was not the only one who once knew him biblically that was concerned. Nico, who would herself be a junkie for the last twenty years of her life, had now made her way to England to become Rolling Stones manager Andrew Loog Oldham's new diva. She thought, 'He looked terrible. Bob was completely drugged up and moody and arrogant as ever. I had not seen him so thin and white, like a matchstick.' While Donovan still remembers, 'Bob and his team were [all] on amphetamine, and so it was really intense – [he had that] jawline with the muscles sticking out.'

Even his fans were concerned. The Liverpool gal who, in *dont look back*, swoons 'Pinch me' when he waves to her from his Adelphi hotel room, asks him flat out if he takes drugs, only for Dylan to disingenously deflect, 'I don't take anything. I don't even eat,'* a statement Baez confirms was largely true: 'Bob was being spoiled to death … ordering heaps of food and letting it pile up around him … [while] the room was filled with sycophants who praised each new line that he peeled off the typewriter.'

The typewriter certainly earned its keep on this trip, Dylan seemingly able to listen to Baez suck the life out of several of his songs while typing a set of notes for that year's Newport Folk Festival programme ('Alternatives To College'). He also used it to give the readers of the teen-girl magazine *Jackie* a glimpse of the real me.

---

* The raw footage Pennebaker shot makes it clear that Dylan was far kinder to the two Liverpool girls than the 1967 film suggested, even letting the more attractive one try on his sunglasses, after observing, 'All you people talk like The Beatles.'

Asked to contribute a list of love and hates, he reeled off a number of genuine pet preferences for its hormonal readership:

loves:
Wandering. I often drift away from my base without telling anyone.
Beaujolais. The only thing I drink.
Writing. No – I don't mean letters. Just writing about anything around me.
Photography. I kind of dabble in that.
Originality in anybody. Makes such a big difference when they've got their own ideas to give out.
Freedom. It is the greatest if you don't have to account to anybody.
Good poetry. Don't really know what that is, but it's got to mean something.
Playing rock'n'roll piano.
My friends. My real friends, I mean.
Negro Blues. They make shivers run up my spine. These guys know what it's all about.
hates:
Writing letters. I just never do that.
Rules. Why should we have them?
Racial hatred. What's got into folk that they've got to feel superior to others?
Not having anybody to sing to.
The importance that money has in our society.
Intolerance of any sort – Well, it's everybody's world, isn't it?
Going into a smart restaurant. Always terrifies me.
Ties. Well, maybe that's not true. I just can't be bothered with them.
<u>That strange feeling when you come into a room that something's gone wrong.</u>
The American way of glorifying death. Sick, sick, sick!

The penultimate entry, underlined, certainly suggests the opening for 'Ballad Of A Thin Man' ('You walk into the room ... see somebody naked') was already forming at the back of his mind. It took him twenty-one years to suggest in concert that the song was aimed at 'people who ask questions all the time', and that it was his 'response to something that happened over in England'. Meanwhile, another piece he was tapping out was quietly dismissive of a former confidante:*

> i stayed awake for three hours & ten minutes last nite with Pearl – she claims to have walked by a rooming house i once lived in – had nothing in common me & Pearl / i shared her bor[e]dom & had nothing to give her – i was drunk & entertained myself.

This was the precursor to a rare moment when Dylan and Baez did actually connect, the cameras capturing them breaking into the kind of Americana they both grew up loving; not folk, but country. Dylan even sings 'Remember Me (When The Candlelights Are Gleaming)', a song he played the Gleasons on his first New York home tape, a lifetime ago. But when they duet on 'Wild Mountain Thyme', Baez repeatedly threatens to drown Dylan out, rather confirming why he no longer wishes to share a stage with her.

Baez would chastise herself in the 2009 American Masters documentary, *How Sweet The Sound*, for 'letting myself be demoralized by him not asking me onstage with him', after Dylan informed Shelton, 'I told her [up] front that she couldn't sing with me ... before we left ... the States ... There is no place for her in my music ... and it would have been misleading to the audience.' He goes further in *No Direction Home*: 'I hope[d] she'd see the light sooner or later.'

And it seems she did, because the day after their hotel jam session and the 'breaking glass' incident reminded her of something similar at the Cafe Espresso, it all came out in a letter to Mimi, informing her she was leaving Dylan's entourage because:

> He has become so unbelievably unmanageable that I can't stand to be around him. Everyone traveling with him is going mad – He walks around in new clothes with a cane – Has tantrums, orders fish, gets drunk, plays his record, phones up America, asks if his concert tonight is sold out – stops [the car] every morning to buy all the newspapers that might have his name in them. He won't

---

* I date this prose-poem – typed on the reverse page to a section of <u>Tarantula</u>, pp. 94–98 – to his English visit based on the use of A4, a strictly English paper-size.

invite me to sing with him even when the kids yell out my name ...
It's shocked me completely out of my senses and I'm fed up. Pride
enters, too ...

Baez was hardly the sole witness to Dylan's demon child during this fortnight in the limelight. The evening before the first Albert Hall show, someone at one of the nightly parties in his suite started throwing glass bathroom shelves out of the window. He promptly lost it. For those attending, even Anthea Joseph, it was quite a shock: 'I'd never seen him lose his temper before. It was really quite frightening. He went up like a little torch. And rightfully so.'

Of course, those who had spent *real* time with Dylan – like Neuwirth – had long known about his short fuse. As Maymudes notes, 'He could lose control more than other people and go off.' This time he quickly calmed down, leaving Grossman to deal with the inevitable complaint from the other guests, the poor floor manager being subjected to this pompous blowhard calling him 'a tiny, infinitesimal fool'. Tom Paxton, there that night, was disgusted that 'some of the people in Bob's coterie were ... awful to the hotel employees, who [were just] try[ing] to do their job.'

Actually the relationship with the Savoy seems to have quickly turned fractious, a hotel spokesman rather sniffily telling *Disc* on Dylan's departure, 'He had all his meals in his room and he certainly wouldn't have been allowed in [the restaurant], dressed as he was, although he was often seen wandering around the main hall in jeans and sandals.' He returned to the Mayfair the following year.

Baez, on the other hand, was the perfect guest as she largely kept to her own room except when, despite her protestations to her sister, she travelled to Birmingham with Dylan and John Mayall, the evening after she wrote Mimi, to attend the fourth of her mystery tramp's eight English concerts. She still loved to see him play.

Though hardly the most arduous of schedules, for Dylan the tour was a new and not entirely welcome experience. Until now, touring had been largely anathema. He preferred an occasional festival set or headlining showcases in the US cities where his reputation was strongest, but not show after show. It wasn't good for his morale – or his art. Hence, perhaps, his jaundiced response to a question by a reporter at the Savoy who asked whether 'people listen intelligently' to him: 'If you tell people a certain thing that they agree with, you [are] just flatter[ing] their intelligence and they clap.'

Was this something he first encountered playing to Baez's audiences? If so, the wholly positive reaction in England did nothing to ameliorate a nagging inner doubt, one he would not articulate until *Highway 61 Revisted* was released, and he was asked by the late, great Nora Ephron – then a journalist – what made him turn to electronic music: 'It was a sure thing. I was getting very bored ... I couldn't go out and play like that. I was thinking of quitting ... I knew what the audience was gonna do, how they would react. It was very automatic.'

How ironic, then, that when he next played Manchester's Free Trade Hall, a year and ten days later, disgruntled fan after disgruntled fan compared that evening's apocalyptic fare pejoratively with the autopilot performance he gave on May 7th, 1965 – and, indeed, all six provincial dates on his 1965 tour. Even in London, where he slightly upped his game – lest The Beatles, who attended both shows, should leave unimpressed – the set was by the numbers, as were the gags. And it was affecting his mood generally, so that by the time he sat down with a reporter from *Time* magazine, Horace Freeland Judson, the afternoon before the first Albert Hall show, he was spoiling for a fight.

Judson, who would become a leading historian of molecular biology,* blundered his way into the room, determined – in the words of Anthea Joseph, clearly visible in the background – to 'treat Bob as some sort of curiosity, not as a serious artist'. Anthea knew what was coming – 'By this time I'd learnt that he could pull strips of skin off people, verbally' – Judson did not.

Judson later told a former student Dylan 'just went nuts and started yelling', having become convinced that 'Grossman and Pennebaker instructed Bob to conduct himself in that way to spice up the film'. Actually, Pennebaker had no shortage of footage of Dylan 'pull[ing] strips of skin off people'. When it came to condescension, though, Judson was in a league of his own. The unedited footage reveals the

---

* Whereas the equally chastened 'Science Student', Terry Ellis, who tangles with Dylan backstage at Newcastle City Hall three days earlier, would take the altogether more lucrative route of co-founding his own record label – Chrysalis Records – and managing Jethro Tull.

lead-up to the scene where Dylan compares himself (favourably) with Caruso and proves that Judson got what he deserved, having not even done him the courtesy of listening to his music in advance:

Horace Judson: Are you playing to the same people as The Beatles?
Bob Dylan [looking annoyed]: I don't know. It's [my] first time playing around the country. [cuts]
HJ: I'd say you're saying something about age.
BD: What would you base that on?
HJ: 'The Times They Are A-Changin''.
BD: That's just one song. If you don't know what I do, it's just impossible.
HJ: I've listened to three or four songs ...
BD: I've made five albums. On each of those albums, there's forty-four minutes. And each of those minutes ...
HJ: I'm trying to find out what you think you're doing.
BD: I just do it. Do you know anything about the scenes in the United States? Unless you know those *scenes*, you're gonna have a hard time putting me in a place. You can [try and] say everything based on that one song, but other people are gonna be disturbed about it because they're going to know better. And they'll know *Time* magazine. I had a bigger record than that. It's called 'Subterranean Homesick Blues'. What about the words [on that]? What about the idea? If you took the first record I made and put drums and lead guitar on it – which you can do – you'll find it's the same songs I'm doing now. Same songs. Have you been down to the Marquee and the Flamingo?
HJ: What would I see?
BD: Just pop music ... You know anything about the San Francisco scene of writers? You're just taking the half of me – taking the music part of it. There's a whole other idea which hasn't anything to do with pop music. Just because I play the guitar, I'm a pop singer [to you]. Why do you necessarily have to stay in step? People like blue and they don't like any other colours. Maybe they haven't seen that [other] colour before. Maybe they just haven't seen me before.

Grossman took this as his own cue to lay into Judson, asking him to justify why Dylan should give him the time of day. By now Dylan is done, having argued his corner devastatingly, while keeping his own doubts about the worth of what he is giving the sell-out audiences strictly to himself, leaving Pennebaker (as always) to decide whether to roll film: '[Dylan] never asked [me] to do anything ... I hung out with everybody all the time but I didn't shoot all the time. Often I just sat and listened.' This time, thankfully, he did roll tape, and kept rolling till even Judson realized he was not cut out to be a reporter.

Gillespie, another witness who saw him mete out verbal lashings, insisted to Altham, 'I've never seen him [being] deliberately insulting to a reporter. Although I have seen him annoyed when some journalists insist on asking questions like "Where were you born?" and "How old are you?"'

Daniel Kramer, back in the USA, had already noticed that Dylan 'would often answer reporters in a way that would make it obvious he felt the questions were silly or naive. He was asked by one reporter, what do you really want to do? "Go to college, learn to make money, and be a success," he told her.' Likewise, when *NME* gave him a whole questionnaire of such questions, for their 'Lifeline' column, he just sent the whole idea up, describing his taste in music as 'sort of peanut butter'.

Yet Dylan came clean at the time to a couple of students who came to interview him for the Sheffield University paper, 'Newspaper reporters, they're just hung-up writers, frustrated novelists [who've] got all these preconceived ideas about me, so I just play up to them.' If Dylan certainly placed Judson in this camp, Kramer had already noticed 'The youngest interviewers ... had the best chance. Dylan seemed to have the most patience with these people ... After a concert at Princeton, Dylan granted interviews first to a high-school girl and then to a young man who was reporting for the first time for his college newspaper.'

Which is why the most straightforward interview Dylan gave during his May visit was one he wrote out for a Cambridge University student, who wanted something for 'the students here [who] want to know something about your songs, rather than just about your private life – that's all we've got out of the national papers'. Dylan took the time to respond at length, then forgot to mail his replies. Found among his papers when the Savoy cleared out his suite in June, it shows a Dylan trying to live outside the law and still be honest:

> **Q**: Does it usually take you a long time to write your songs? Are you suddenly seized with inspiration or do you have to sit down for hours and work at them?
> **BD**: Songs come in ideas / people good bad indifferent, situations anything / takes me short time to write it out / usually changes somewhat constantly.
> **Q**: You're quoted as saying, I can't listen to my old songs anymore. Why not?
> **BD**: Old songs tend to be motivated by private desires.
> **Q**: Which is your favourite of all the songs you've written?
> **BD**: NONE – All of them / I have no favourites, just some of them I like less.
> **Q**: You're also quoted as saying, Nobody influences me anymore. What about Woody Guthrie?
> **BD**: Woody's language doesn't appeal to me anymore – his words are group words / his ideas are fake / I have no faith in better world coming / I live now in this world.
> **Q**: What do you mean when you say you don't write *about* anything?
> **BD**: I write inside out + sometimes the dimensions cross. I can't write *about* the tree, I must write *of* the tree.
> **Q**: What do you think as the function of your songs? Simply to entertain, or to make people think about what you've got to say.
> **BD**: Myself to satisfy.
> **Q**: Why don't you like being identified with Civil Rights movement, or with anything in particular?
> **BD**: Life is too big for any ONE thing ...
> **Q**: Do you sometimes write words for their sound, rather than for what they say?
> **BD**: Sometimes Yes / but not just that simple.
> **Q**: Now that your records are reaching the hit parade, do you think you might ... write more songs that will definitely have commercial appeal, rather than songs motivated by your conscience?
> **BD**: No.
> **Q**: Do you like the idea of people coming to your concerts and buying your records because you're fashionable, rather than because they appreciate your poetry?

With Joan Baez, on top for once (Getty Images).

The Queen of Folk & The Prince of Protest try for that high lonesome sound, 1964 (Getty Images).

At the motel pool, Newport Folk Festival, July 1964, with his girlfriend's sister, Mimi (John Byrne Cooke).

Dylan sings to Sally Grossman and the back of Allen Ginsberg's head in his Woodstock cabin, summer 1964 (Douglas R. Gilbert).

Dylan dances circles round the LA press while Columbia publicist Billy James enjoys the spectacle, December 16, 1965 (Getty Images).

Dylan at the Whisky A-Go-Go, April 1966 (Getty Images).

Dylan arrives at Copenhagen airport, with Rick Danko lagging behind and D.A. Pennebaker shooting the piano player (The John Bauldie Estate).

Dylan studiously ignores Tom Waits' Danish cousin at the Copenhagen press conference, April 30, 1966 (The John Bauldie Estate).

'I have glass in the back of my head ... and I can't see too well on Tuesdays.'
The man behind the shades, Mayfair Hotel, London, May 3, 1966 (Getty Images).

BD: It doesn't matter why ...
Q: Did you have any say in having 'Times They Are A-Changin'' and 'Subterranean Homesick Blues' released as singles aimed at the hit parade?
BD: No say in 'Times They Are A-Changin'' – that was recorded three years ago for an album / SHB was taken off new album.

After another short sabbatical, songs had now started forming in his head again. But the line between song and prose poem remained blurred. He continued writing – or typing – pieces in the style of 'Alternatives To College' and the *Highway 61* sleeve notes, one of which reads like an incantatory prototype for 'Sad Eyed Lady Of The Lowlands':

what about those silver bells you promised me oh St Claude &
where are they now these hunchbacks & heroes – their women – their
sons & daughters – oh where are they now these possessions &
winnings of slaughter – oh where is great boneparte, the cornwalls
& iron walls – these battles & gods, the lions & teeth of arena –
where is colonel mckinley & the killers of john wilkes booth oh
where is he now? where is john wilkes booth[?]
oh where are these tall gentlemen of the weapon? where are their
weapons – their swollen tongues & their syph[i]lis – where are their
reporters – the little men who snapped so absurdly to attention &
obscurity / the parades & confetti & mussolini – oh St Claude so
young with apostrophes you walk & plan to bomb these museums &
cease the songs – the singers of the meathouse – oh where is great
stonewall jackson now?

But perhaps his most unexpected use of the typewriter occured the day of the final London concert, when Dylan sat in his hotel room and tapped out a reworked version of the 'jack o'diamonds' section

---

* This scene would be included as an extra on the 2015 Blu-Ray edition of *dont look back*.
† Though the Carruthers single died a death, a promo copy given to Max Jones at *Melody Maker* was borrowed by his son Nic, to work up with his school band, Emil and the Detectives, whose guitar-vocalist was none other than Richard Thompson, who co-opted the song when he co-founded Fairport Convention. Fairport recorded it on their eponymous debut, thus creating a need for the song's publishing to be accounted for.

from his *Another Side* sleeve notes, while his friend-turned-actor Ben Carruthers explained how he wanted to make it a single.* Dylan told him he didn't mind what he did with it. Indeed, when the single became a matter of copyright dispute in 1973, Witmark were able to produce a contract signed by Carruthers that very May day, 'assigning an unpublished musical composition, written by Bob Dylan and Ben Carruthers, entitled Jack O'Diamonds to M. Witmark'.†

For the first time, the line between one of Dylan's poems and a lyric had become invisible. If Pennebaker caught the moment, he was also there – rolling film – when Tom Wilson, Grossman, Dylan, Neuwirth and Alan Price discussed how the music business worked, and Grossman opined, 'The [British pop] scene's gotta be dumb. I know all the agents, and *they're* dumb.' Wilson had just flown in. Clinging by his fingernails to his job as Dylan's producer, he got to hear his meal-ticket play him an early 'It Takes A Lot To Laugh' (aka 'Phantom Engineer') at the piano.

It was perhaps a song that Dylan was looking to record, confirmation of something a local CBS spokesman had told the *NME*, that '*if* ... [he felt] sufficiently inspired to write some new material, he planned to record' some of it in London during the fortnight separating the end of the tour from a one-hour BBC TV 'in concert'. Hence, Wilson's presence. Dylan also hinted at work in progress in his last interview of the tour: 'I have ... things ready ... [but] nothing's finished, ... [so] what shape it'll take has yet to be decided.'

When the time came to record with the Bluesbreakers at Levy's in New Bond Street – originally Oriole Records, recently acquired by CBS – on May 12th, the shape of the new material had still 'yet to be decided', and he ended up spending most of the session trying to get a usable version of a song he'd rejected from *Bringing It All Back Home*.

The engineer, Mike Ross-Trevor, had 'got the impression CBS wanted a new single from him and [tried] to pin him down in London during some time off. The evening started with Dylan doing promotional chats for the CBS annual conference: "Hi, I'm Bob Dylan. I want to thank all you salesmen for selling my records ... " [before the] session started with John Mayall's Bluesbreakers. Eric Clapton was in the line-up and there were about twenty people crammed into the room, including Joan Baez and Paul Jones. That must have been the first time [Jones] heard "If You Gotta Go, Go Now" ... Dylan wasn't that happy at being forced to record so he stalled a lot of the time, hoping it would drift by ... He was singing and playing the piano, and after every take he made me move it to another part of the room, [which] had to be a wind-up, because it made absolutely no difference to the sound ... It was a ramshackle affair and there wasn't a great deal of dialogue between him and Mayall's band, [who] were ... just jamming behind him.'

Among the 'twenty people' in attendance were other notable singers: Baez and possibly Nico, Nadia Catouse, Sydney Carter, Manfred Mann's Paul Jones (who later asked for a copy of the song, which then became a Top Ten hit). Yet Dylan seemed to grow dispirited quite quickly, not helped by comments from Neuwirth to the eager pup on guitar, 'You're playing too much blues, man. He needs to be more country!'

According to Bluesbreakers drummer, Hughie Flint, the entire session 'was just messing around. I don't think we played a complete number ... I'd never seen so much wine, and everybody got very pissed, very quickly, no one more so than Dylan'. Yet Clapton suggested there was other content, 'We did a lot [sic] of blues songs, which ... he was making up ... sitting at the piano and we just joined in.'* Eventually, Dylan staggered out into the night with Wilson and Ms Catouse, having been at the Beaujolais – 'the only thing I drink' – too long.

The only tape ever to emerge from Levy's has Dylan's Miami Sales Convention message and a brief snatch of a ramshackle 'If You Gotta Go, Go Now'. Yet Ross-Trevor claimed he kept 'a seven-and-a-half-inch mix-down' of the song (which he later lost), suggesting there *was* a complete version. One would hardly bother to mix what circulates.

The multitracks, the engineer insists, were then sent to New York. Which begs the question, why wouldn't Wilson simply take them with him? We know Wilson soon returned to the States because nine days later, he was back at Columbia creating a composite version of the same song from four electric takes cut at the January sessions. This rather suggests Dylan intended it as the follow-up to

---

* Clapton and Dylan wouldn't meet again till the Delaney & Bonnie tour in 1970. If 'Phantom Engineer' was attempted that evening in 1965 – as I think it probably was – it would certainly explain why Dylan and Clapton reprised the song at rehearsals for 1992's so-called 'Bobfest'.

'Subterranean Homesick Blues', perhaps feeling that he needed a stop-gap single but had as yet no new songs he was itching to record.

All that would change the very day Wilson went into Columbia's New York studio, May 21st, when Dylan held another of his infamous Savoy hotel parties, this one announcing his return from a week-long Portugeuse holiday with Sara Lownds, who had again snuck in the back door after the public Dylan had done his bit.

He had spent the week doing a great deal of soul-searching. As he admitted, months later, 'I was going to quit singing. I was very drained ... I was playing a lot of songs I didn't want to play. I was singing words I didn't really want to sing.' The idea had been at the back of his mind for most of his time in England, and hinted at in conversation with Sheffield University student, Peter Roche:

> **BD**: I see myself sleeping in the future. I plan to take a big long sleep for sixty years and then wake up and go to town. I don't plan the future. I do what I'm doing now. A year from now I could be doing something else completely. I'm more interested in writing than I am in performing on the stage.
> **PR**: Lennon seems more interested in writing.
> **BD**: I just do this 'cause I can't do anything else.

Even as he asked himself the self-same rhetorical question he raised back in January, 'How do I know I can do it again?,' he spent some quality time with Sara, who 'always responded' when he needed her help. Unbeknownst to them both, Sara was now with child, Dylan's child, a clear sign the relationship had entered a new phase. Sara had seen off her only serious rival.

When Baez – due to headline a London concert on the 23rd – called to see how her ex-lover was, Sara opened the door. It was the first time they met face to face; indeed, the first time Baez knew of her existence. For Joan, it was the end, at least until she and Dylan got to rake over the coals on camera in 1975 for the ill-fated *Renaldo & Clara*, with her dressed in a wedding gown, engaging in an exchange which sounded like something from the Savoy:

> **BD**: It really displeases me [that] you went off and got married.
> **JB**: You went off and got married first – and didn't tell me.

BD: Yeah, but I married the woman I loved.
JB: And I married the man I thought I loved.
BD: That's what thought has to do with it. Thought will fuck you up. See, it's heart, not head.

Baez had previously slipped a note under Dylan's door, saying that she didn't like to keep phoning but that 'a whole lot of that four-letter word ... L-O-V-E is riding the airwaves up all the stairways and lifts day and night. Get well.' She had heard that 'her Bobby' was laid up in bed, having been taken ill with 'food poisoning', and was unable to attend her concert or record his own BBC broadcast. By the following month, though, the love-light was out, as she told an English tabloid, 'I left Bob when I came to London ... I got tired of his antics. I thought he cared, but I was wrong.'

Nico was another concerned party who had also heard the news and come calling. Her note told him she would be performing 'Mr Tambourine Man' on *Ready Steady Go*, and to 'get well' so he could write some more songs for her (having foolishly held off recording 'I'll Keep It With Mine', allowing an attuned Judy Collins to cover it first):

> I am very sad today because you are supposedly in bad shape & I did not know that ... I want you to be strong. Please, please, you promised to write me songs & I want to sing your songs, they are the only ones that make sense to me & my life depends on them – Will you please let me know if you are staying at your Hotel or not? It seems to be a big secret! You were not there today, when I went to get my coat – so it seemed anyway ... Ciao, Nico.

The next time their paths would cross, Nico would be in New York singing with a band of Lower East Side degenerates, the only New Yorkers capable of keeping pace with the pre-accident Dylan.

After the Savoy party, Dylan wasn't just avoiding former paramours. He was keeping a very low profile. He had even hired a private nurse to attend to him at the hotel, rather than checking into St Mary's Hospital, Paddington. The story given to the press to explain the postponement of his BBC concert, food poisoning, never made much sense.

Meanwhile, across the pond, the rumour mill was working overtime (a dry run for a certain motorcycle accident), Izzy Young informing a *Sing Out!* intern that news had reached him, 'via Peter Orlovsky, from Ginsberg, that [Dylan] had gotten the clap from this girl'. Though this was hardly likely to lead to a week in bed, something had laid Dylan low the day after that homecoming party. And it seems to have been something they were putting in the wine, because another guest at the soirée had started acting awfully weird.

Vince Taylor, the English rock'n'roller who had recorded perhaps the first great British rock'n'roll 45, 'Brand New Cadillac', had not taken his cue from Dylan, who had gone to hospital the next day. Instead, Taylor turned up at a concert in Paris, where he stunned his French fans by informing them, 'You all think I'm Vince Taylor. Well, I'm not. My name is Mateus, I'm the new Jesus, the son of God.' He had lost his mind – thanks to a double dose of LSD – inadvertently providing the spark for David Bowie's 1972 alter-ego, Ziggy Stardust.

Still legal in the UK, dosing people with LSD – usually surreptitiously – had become the new fun social activity. Both Harrison and Lennon, as well as their wives, had been 'dosed' by their dentist at a dinner party just eighteen days before Dylan came to town. And, like Taylor, they were never the same again. As Harrison later said of that evening, 'There was no way back after that. It showed you backwards and forwards and time stood still ... [It] suddenly wipes away all you were taught or brought up to believe.' That experience inspired Lennon to write 'Help', a departure of sorts for a Fab Four 45.

Dylan's own experience of a bad acid trip – crucially not his first trip – seems to have prompted his own Rimbaudian 'ecstatic flight through things unheard of, unnameable'. He came out the other side not with something as trite as, 'Help me if you can, I'm feeling down', but rather the raw, existential howl, 'How does it *feeeel* to be on your own?'

The way Dylan described this epiphany on a number of occasions over the next year, he found himself 'writing this song, this story, this long piece of vomit about twenty pages long, and out of it I took "Like A Rolling Stone"'. At some point, he found himself 'at the piano

---

* He also suggested to Ralph J. Gleason, 'I always sing when I write, even prose, and I heard it like that.'

and on the paper it was singing, "How does it feel?"* Initially, though, 'It was ten [sic] pages long, it wasn't called anything, just a rhythm thing on paper, all about my steady hatred, directed at some point that was honest.'

Of those multiple pages, perhaps one survived – a stray A4 sheet preserved in the Tulsa archive. It has no lines from 'Like A Rolling Stone' but it does seem to contain an early portrait of Miss Lonely:

the world passes you by ...
& cannot accept you as its power
you stand among the vulchers / you know that tho
i know ... youre too beautiful for words
you cannot be imprisoned.

He proceeds to embellish the above portrait in pencil, noting that 'the feeling of having no place to go, the unwanted feeling / can be felt by every person ... it is a / paralyzing feeling'. Thus spake the voice of experience. As he continued directing his 'steady hatred ... at some point that was honest', it seemed like a continuation of something expressed on another typed sheet at this time:

you hang pictures on the wall of people who all adore you ...
you can fool your companions but you cant fool me. i'm too smart for ya
you give everybody orders / to get what you want done ...
youve been raised in castles yet your minds in the gutter. you borrow
peoples' brains an promise that they'll all get them back tomorrow.

This US letter-size sheet also contains a couplet destined for 'Phantom Engineer' – 'dont my [gal] look good when shes coming after me / if i dont finish you know my baby will', whereas, on the 'Miss Lonely' A4 sheet, equally non-linear thoughts flower into other songs, using a similar equation. 'From A Buick Six' is there, specifically, 'i got these women / but my soulful mama, you know she's like the ladies that renoir paints'; as are two verses that became 'Tombstone Blues':

in the tunnel waits Hubert & his wife made of stone
lead[ing] stray children / they have of their own
but instead raise vegetables & after theyre grown

>   eat them or let them go rotten
>   i wish i could write you the melody so plain
>   that could save you dear lady & from going insane / the pain
>   your useless knowle[d]ge & wisdom
>   cigarette ashes. they cover the beach.

But no actual, identifiable prototype for 'Rolling Stone' appears. Perhaps the real working draft was not typed, but handwritten, like the four-page manuscript sold at Sotheby's in New York on June 23rd, 2014 for $2.1 million. The manuscript in question is certainly the song Dylan described in a 1966 conversation, 'It [was] twenty pages [long], but it's [now] concise, and it changes from the first two verses to the third verse to the last verse. But it's not what you think it's about. It's not about any specific incident.'*

The most worrying incongruity was its appearance on notepaper from the Roger Smith Hotel, in Washington DC. It is inconceivable that he would have had this with him in London, and none of the 'other' *Highway 61* MSS from Woodstock are on headed paper. Some of the lyrical anachronisms also ring alarm bells. 'You used to clown around with Jackhoman [sic] John in Lonesome Town' appears to reference 'Brother John', a 1976 Neville Brothers song; while the couplet 'You never listened to the man who could jump, jive and wail / Never believed 'm when he told you he had love for sale' namechecks a 1930 Cole Porter composition, a trope Dylan adopted when he was forty-four, not twenty-four.

However, it was only when an indisputably genuine typescript of 'Like A Rolling Stone' was partially reproduced by *Rolling Stone* in their report on the Tulsa acquisitions in 2016 that it became apparent 'Rolling Stone' had followed the normal pattern for the era, i.e. was typed first, probably typed again (and again), and only then hand-corrected. The Tulsa typescript is the perfect paradigm of the approach Dylan described to Cleave three weeks earlier: 'I write down the idea [in] say an hour, and then I just fill them in as time goes by with all these things.'

---

* Sotheby's catalogue for the auction quotes rather selectively, from my own report on the manuscript which the vendor himself commissioned, concerned it might not be genuine. It certainly doesn't resemble any previously authenticated 1965 ms.

At this formative stage, it remains a series of images, unrefined, in kernel form: 'just another juggler / did tricks for you / youve studied all these great theories on life / & now you find out they dont mean a thing'; 'you never understood / all your friends that used to brag / turned out to be just method actors all [dressed] in drag,' and this evocative if unhoned image, 'when you ain't got nothing – you got nothing to lose / youre strength must lie now in your lonesome blues'. He has yet to connect it all up with that unforgettable final line, 'You're invisible now, you got no secrets to conceal.'

Here is very much a work in progress, not a way of joining up dots after the fact. Though the paper used is standard American letter-size, it feels like something he could have typed out in London, just before he finally recorded his hour-long BBC broadcast and flew home with his pregnant girlfriend.

He now had his follow-up to 'Subterranean Homesick Blues'. He just needed to follow the sound. And in the time it took to return across the pond, he figured out who could corral the song he now heard in his head. Not Eric Clapton, but rather his American equivalent, Chicago's own axiomatic axeman, Michael Bloomfield, whom he now invited up to Woodstock, keen to play him the song and hear his thoughts:

> I didn't even have a guitar case. I just had my Telecaster. And Bob picked me up at the bus station and took me to this house where he lived ... Sara was there ... and she made very strange food, tuna fish salad with peanuts in it, toasted ... He had this tiny old wooden house in Woodstock, New York way out in the country. It was a little two-room hut, like a log cabin ... in the woods ... The first thing I heard was 'Like A Rolling Stone'. He wanted me to get the concept of it, how to play it. I figured he wanted blues, string bending, because that's what I do. He said, 'I don't want you to play any of that B.B. King shit, none of that fucking blues, I want you to play something else.' ... It was very weird, he was playing in weird keys which he always does, all on the black keys of the piano ... [] ... [I thought] What the heck does he want? We messed around with the song. I played the way that he dug and he said it was groovy ... I was in Dylan's house for about three days learning the songs. [But] I had no identification with the material at all. I mean, I had never heard music like this before.

Bloomfield was nonplussed because Dylan had stumbled on 'things unheard of, unnameable'. Could he really help translate such 'things' from page to vinyl? That was the challenge for Dylan – something he was already talking about when he first arrived at the Savoy: 'to see if I could write a lot of the stuff I was writing on paper and sing it; combine the [two forms] instead of keeping them separate – writing and singing'. This was virgin territory, a journey into darkest Abyssinia for the great explorer. So, how did it feel?

2.5

June to September 1965: The Rites Of Summer

Bob could string words together with God-like power and he also could charm the rattles off a snake's ass. Often seeming to speak in parables, a lot like the liner notes he wrote for his early albums ... he was always incredibly stimulating. But at the same time he could be moody and mysterious and unpredictable and cranky and nasty.

Al Aronowitz

I think the conflict that came into Dylan's life was that he wanted to be Elvis, a rock'n'roll star. He [also] wanted to be Lightnin' Hopkins [and] to be Woody Guthrie ... He had the voice – a voice of race – [to] be like these singers *and* a pop star. [But] it was a dilemma, trying to be all those things.

Liam Clancy

The thing about Bobby is that he always wanted to be a rock'n'roll singer ... When he achieved fame as a folksinger, he thought he might be able to change and become accepted as a rock singer, too.

Dana Gillespie, May 1966

I used to go after a song, seek it out. But now, instead of going to it, I stay where I am and let everything disappear and the song rushes to me ... What I'm doing now you can't learn by studying; you can't copy it.

Bob Dylan, November 1965

By the spring of 1965, nascent rock bands were beginning to flex their undeniable commercial muscle in the studio, demanding the hours, and sometimes the days, to realize their latest pitch to posterity, no matter how many rolls of the dice it took. In April, The Kinks went into the studio to cut not one but two singles – 'Set Me Free' and 'See My Friends' – trying to replicate a streak of three consecutive number ones between August 1964 and February 1965. When 'See My Friends' came out a little too experimental, they returned three weeks later, and cut a klassic.

A week after that remake, The Rolling Stones tried cutting their latest, '(I Can't Get No) Satisfaction', at Chess in Chicago, and when that didn't work, took it to LA to break the mould. The Who would record 'My Generation' no fewer than four times between August 16th and October 13th, trying to ensure they didn't f-f-fade away. Even the ever-efficient Beatles recut breakthrough song 'Norwegian Wood' nine days after spending four and a half hours working on it, the day before The Who definitively defined their generation.

Such is the musical context surrounding the two afternoons it took to capture 'Like A Rolling Stone' (June 15th/16th) after Dylan temporarily abandoned the song at the end of day one without capturing a complete take, the blame for which has been placed squarely at Tom Wilson's door by one vital component, about whom early on the 15th Dylan tells us, mid-song, the woman killing him alive 'ain't as good as this guitar player I got right now':

> **Michael Bloomfield**: The producer was a non-producer ... a black guy named Tom Wilson. He didn't know what was happening, man! ... We did twenty alternate takes of every song, and it got ridiculous because they were long songs ... It was never like: 'Here's one of the tunes, we're gonna learn it, work out the arrangement,' that just wasn't done ... It was just like a jam session, it really was ... [] ... I was there man, I'm telling you it was a result of chucklefucking, of people stepping on each other's dicks until it came out right.

It was certainly déjà vu for Wilson *and* Dylan, who were presiding over their second session in five weeks to result in no product worth a Columbia label. But to suggest Dylan was wholly the injured party would be to deny his complicity in the chaos. Before the first session, he had already made a critical misjudgement, instructing Bloomfield, 'You talk to the musicians, man. I don't want to tell them anything.'

Bloomfield, for all his undoubted talent, was a mere studio novice. With the exception of this diffident bluesmaker, the musicians were all veterans of January's sessions: Bobby Gregg, Joseph Macho, Al Gorgoni, Frank Owen and Paul Griffin.

> **Michael Bloomfield**: All these studio cats are standing around. I come in like a dumb punk with my guitar over my back, no case, and I'm telling people about this and that, and this is the arrangement and do this on the bridge. These are like the heaviest studio musicians in New York. They looked at me like I was crazy ... But Bob remained completely isolated from that. He just sang his tunes and they fitted the music around him ... I never saw any communication between Dylan and the band ... [] ... I could probably have put a more formal rock'n'roll sound to it, or at least my idea of one, but I was too intimidated by that company.

Nor does Dylan seem to have fully processed the chastening experience at Levy's, having again arrived at a session with only one finished song and, in Bloomfield's words, 'No game plan. The day before, he was still writing the songs.' When Dylan successfully completes the second semi-improvised blues jam of the day, he actually boasts, 'We recorded that song and I don't even have any words for it, man!' The song in question '(Sitting On A) Barbed Wire Fence', was a semi-improvised piano boogie searching for a home.

Yet the session had started promisingly with a complete first take of 'Phantom Engineer' that steams into town fuelled up by Dylan's pounding piano. The musicians were used to Dylan's rapid-fire methodology, shuttling from song to song, refusing to get bogged down. But this time it took ten takes, four of them complete, to get 'Phantom Engineer', and six takes, three of them complete, to get 'Barbed Wire Fence'.

Only at this juncture does Dylan bring in the main course, 'Like A Rolling Stone', still in waltz time (3/4) and in need of an arrangement. Five takes are logged on that first day, but it is mostly a case of Levy's Revisited, the musicians 'just messing around' until Wilson calls time on the day's work, rightly sensing that they would need a full three-hour session the following afternoon to get this one right.*

---

* Columbia records confirm both sessions were scheduled in advance, hence presumably why Dylan took his time getting to 'Like A Rolling Stone'.

At least he had already introduced one innovation – an important one – possibly at Dylan's behest: continually running tape. So when, after a couple of rehearsals, a musician calls out, 'Are we rolling?' Wilson can say, 'Yeah, we're continually rolling,' thus allowing us fifty years later to hear the transition from chucklefucking to pure serendipity.

It confirms what Bloomfield later admitted, 'It happened almost by mistake'; day two, remake take four. Enter Al Kooper, who has pointed out, 'You can hear Tom Wilson [say], "OK, this is take seven [sic]. Hey! What are you doing in there?" ... That was the moment he could have just thrown me out and rightfully so. And you know what? He didn't.' At the time that Kooper commandeered the organ stool, they still haven't managed a full take of 'Rolling Stone'.

In fact, day two starts with Dylan in reflective mood, muttering into the mike (and maybe to himself), 'I'm just me, you know. I can't, really, man. I'm just playing the song. I don't want to scream it, that's all I know.'* Frank Owen has gone, as has Al Gorgoni – evidently both Dylan's decision. In their place, he has brought in 'Tambourine Man' himself, Langhorne, on stand-by. But when Dylan switches to guitar – possibly at the suggestion of Grossman, who asks to hear just his guitar in the mix – and Griffin to piano, there is suddenly a great gaping hole where the organ once was. Kooper, who had snuck into the session hoping to supplant Gorgoni, seizes the moment and ends up replacing Owen.

Immediately, the organ makes its presence felt. It also frees Griffin to play all around the song, masking the moments where bass and/ or drums lose their way. One more rehearsal, in which Gregg finally finds a use for that snare drum – the one which 'sounded like somebody'd kicked open the door to your mind', to quote Bruce Springsteen – then, ker-pow.

Even hearing 'Remake Take Four' now, surrounded by false starts, breakdowns and car crashes, it comes out of nowhere. And goes straight back there. Another eleven takes will be logged, only one of them complete. But having exhausted everything in his locker, Dylan

---

* For some reason this rehearsal take, 1.55, has been omitted from the 'complete' 18-CD set of 1965–66 sessions, *The Cutting Edge*. Not enough room?

pushes the envelope to see how far it can go. *This* far. Time to hear the playback, and get some feedback.

The studio has begun to fill with friends and other strangers. Even John Hammond Jr has popped in with a Canadian guitarist – in case they were in short supply – who, in his 2016 memoir, suggests this was the first time he met Dylan:

> **Robbie Robertson**: [They] were listening to the playback of a song they had just cut. Sitting in the corner silently was Dion ... John went over and [greeted Dylan] ... You could barely see his eyes through the dark glasses he wore, but there was high voltage in the room coming from his persona. Bob [turned] to John, 'You wanna hear something ... You never heard anything like this before.'

The excitement in the room – captured by legendary photojournalist Eugene Smith – did not abate even when everyone decamped to Grossman's Gramercy Park apartment with a hot-off-the-press acetate of the song. As Dylan recalled in 1987, 'Different people kept coming and going and we played it on the record player all night. My music publisher [presumably Artie Mogull] just kept listening to it, shaking his head saying, "Wow, man, I just don't believe this."'

Even after he drove back to Woodstock to be with his pregnant girlfriend, he still wanted people he knew to share the high. According to another displaced Village folkie, John Herald, 'Anybody he knew who passed by the Cafe Espresso, Dylan would run out and say, "I've got this great new song. It's going to be really big, you've got to hear it." Then he would take them inside and play it for them.'

He also played it to his favourite ladies, though for Sally Grossman it was only when the song came 'on the radio for the first time ... riding around with ... Sara in the car when she was pregnant' that she realized just how profound a statement her girlfriend's husband had made. Dylan stated as much in 2000: 'I didn't feel like radio had ever played a song like that before. I know I'd never heard a song like that before. And everything I'd done up to that point had led up to writing a song like that.'

For once, even Columbia tapped into the zeitgeist, releasing the record just twelve days after it was recorded and mixed by Tom Wilson; not that he was about to receive any share of the plaudits. In fact, he was getting the boot. Dylan – in the role of Pontius Pilate – later insisted, 'Tom had always been there – I had no reason to think he wasn't going to be there – [but] I looked up one day and [he] was[n't] there.' Nothing could be further from the truth. The smoking gun is a letter to Grossman from Ken Glancy at Columbia, the day they started the revolution without Wilson, June 28th:

> Dear Al, Because of the somewhat ridiculous circus in which we find ourselves regarding Bob and yourself versus [sic] engineering, A&R men &c., &c., I am alarmed by what appears to be a steadily developing pattern of confusion over our mutual responsibilities. I feel we have extended ourselves considerably beyond contractual provisions to provide an agreeable working climate for Bob, but in the light of what has been going on for the last few months, I am asking that we ... come to certain decisions which I feel must be made. Until then the status is quo.

If the unreliable Kooper has suggested 'Tom and Albert didn't get along at all ... that was why he got the boot', only Wilson and Dylan really knew what the problem was. All Wilson himself ever said was that, 'after cutting "Like A Rolling Stone", [we] fell out ... He said, "Maybe we should try Phil Spector."'

Dylan was still considering working with Spector – who was one of the few who noticed 'Like A Rolling Stone' was actually based on a traditional Mexican folk song, 'La Bamba' – six months later. A less suitable producer for Dylan would be hard to imagine. Spector was a taskmaster, a control freak and a perfectionist; whereas, in the words of fired guitarist Al Gorgoni, 'Tom was more of an executive producer, [with] a concept and ideas approach. As I recall, he didn't come into the studio with the musicians, he [just] let it all happen.'

It would take Dylan twelve years to realize the error of his ways, telling Ron Rosenbaum, 'I haven't felt comfortable in a studio since I worked with Tom Wilson.' Meanwhile, Wilson was determined to show the world that the folk-rock sound was not a Dylan trademark. On July 22nd he took two vital components of its first incarnation – Al Gorgoni and Joseph Macho – added Vinnie Bell and drummer Buddy Saltzman, and dubbed them all onto Simon & Garfunkel's acoustic version of 'The Sound Of Silence', achieving what 'Like A Rolling Stone' could not – a number one single, Wilson's first and last.

The person Dylan seemed to have in mind as Wilson's replacement had been making hits of his own for years. Johnny Cash told English reporter Norman Jopling, the week before 'Like A Rolling Stone' was cut, 'There's a chance [Dylan] may come to Nashville and let me produce an album with him – if the A&R men agree. I've got my own ideas about the Nashville sound and I'd like to try it with Bob.'

In fact, the two singers had cooked up a plan to do sessions in Nashville some months earlier, Cash writing to Dylan in early February to say they could meet there on 'March 10th for four days, if you feel [like] it. I could show you what there is [that's] worth your while.' In the end, it clashed with the Dylan/Baez tour. Indeed, it would be eleven months before Dylan made it to Music City USA, by which time Wilson's replacement was claiming the credit, the habit of a lifetime.

While the politics of Columbia slowly resolved itself – Grossman doubtless making it crystal clear his client wouldn't be entering any Columbia studio till he got his way – and with 'Like A Rolling Stone' steadily climbing the charts, Dylan finally bought a place of his own on the outskirts of Woodstock, a large, rambling property called Hi Lo Ha, through Davasee Enterprises, a business front Grossman had set up (still in use today).

Despite claiming, in an early *Tarantula* draft, not to be talking 'about anything anymore – not even with francine, the fall girl, who … walks like modigliani paints', Dylan increasingly came to see Sara as his safe-house in a storm. Here, in the woods, with his wife-in-waiting, he began writing the songs that would make up his next album, having already depicted Highway 61 as 'the wrinkled delta. calculated majestic'.

With the song 'Highway 61 Revisited' itself, he merely had to decide which characters to include and who to kill off, dispensing ultimately with 'bony mcfony [who] had a thousand friends / & talks to himself'; 'josephine from the lonesome / [who] makes the top of your head explode'; and 'luke the jerk [who] couldn't go no where'.

With song ideas a-plenty, he typed up working drafts of 'Queen Jane Approximately', 'Ballad Of A Thin Man' and 'Highway 61 Revisited' while staying in the blue bedroom, prior to moving into Hi Lo Ha. Of these, the one that travelled furthest is 'Queen Jane', which begins life with a single line at the bottom of the 'Highway 61' typescript, 'Won't you come see me, Lord Jim?', before being transferred to a new sheet, which begins with the idea 'youre scared more of yourself then [sic] you are of your ... creations', going on to warn her about those who 'tell you that they understand your pain'.* By now, she is Queen Jane, another character from the Child cosmology, as he starts to hand-correct the verses, flipping the page to pen an ending by hand.

Even if we assume Dylan wasn't just yanking chains when he said, at a September 1965 press conference, 'Queen Jane is a man', the contemporary 'Ballad Of A Thin Man' draft serves to confirm he'd entered a demi-monde of Warholian debauchery: 'you fought so hard / your whole life to get blessed / by those who make you undress'. He had also written in his notebook, as a potential song title, 'She Ain't No Woman, She's A Man'.† The theme was one Dylan would flirt with long enough to give those absurd 'misogyny hunters' the merest scraps.

Meanwhile, Izzy Young, reporting the latest scuttlebutt to his favourite *Sing Out!* intern, stated that Dylan had been seen frequenting certain bars, 'making a lot of different sexual, homosexual scenes, pot scenes, [as if] he wants to have every experience open to man'. Perhaps it was background research for 'Ballad Of A Thin Man'. If so, it was because he planned to deconstruct those who 'ask obnoxious questions & ... expect all the answers in just one word'.

Song after song is teeming through his brain, the first of which might have been 'about Tom Thumb'. This song, which lit the way to *Highway 61*, was at this point called 'Just Like Juarez', preserved in a typescript much like the one for 'Like A Rolling Stone'. Again, it seems, he wrote 'down the idea [in] an hour, and then fill[ed it] in as time goes by with all these things', its starting point being abstract to the ninth power:

just like juarez / Easter
wearing a charity belt on Rue Morgue Avenue
zero

---

* His concern with others' pain has already featured in the earliest version of 'Tombstone Blues', where the 'melody so plain ... would cancel your pain'.
† Presumably, this is the song that became 'Jet Pilot', recorded in October 1965.

negativity & the gravity / pulls you right thru
they got some hungry women there / they really make a mess out of you
Mexico City & the smoky kerosine.

At this stage, sweet Melinda 'keeps a cape hidden in her room'. Otherwise, the lines can be readily filled in. It is just the final image that gets jettisoned; the enticing thought, 'next time stay with the devil / he don't play so rough' (to rhyme with 'enough').

Nine months later, he told Mr Jones's Antipodean cousins how this breakthrough came about:

> 'Just Like Tom Thumb's Blues' is a line I crossed about a year and a half ago, and once I crossed that I didn't have to worry any more. Everything became one. The words and the song itself became one whole thing, while before that it was just plain basic simplicity, you know, songs of the dimension – I wrote ... in New York City for specific personal reasons.

Unlike in 1964, none of the above songs (finished or not) would be debuted at 1965's Newport Folk Festival the last week in July. Instead, Dylan stuck to the songs he brought back from London – his new A-side, 'Phantom Engineer', a 'Tombstone Blues' missing a chorus, which was debuted to 9,000 at Saturday's Contemporary Songs workshop, and the new single.

The reaction to Dylan's appearance at the Saturday workshop was another indication he was fast transcending the scene, taking its collegiate audience with him. As Tony Glover wrote in 1972, '[1965] was the year you could tell it was almost over – the audience wasn't there to have a good time as much as to be satiated. They came hungry and demanded to be fed, and by God they were going to write the menu!'

Scheduling other workshops at the same time didn't help. As Joe Boyd recalls: 'People were complaining, "Turn up the Dylan one, we're getting bleed from the banjo one on the other side."' Before Dylan even mounted the stage, he found himself pursued by 'a herd of people' until, in the words of one companion, Patrick Sky, 'we started running across the field. When we got to this fence, Donovan and I made it over, but Dylan couldn't. We reached over and grabbed him by the seat of the pants and dropped him over just as the crowd got there. It was frightening.' Such was the aura he was now projecting. Welcome to full-on Dylanmania!:

> **Joe Boyd**: Instead of this blue-jeaned, work-shirted guy who'd arrived in 1964 to be the Pied Piper, he arrived rather secretively; he was staying in a luxurious hotel just on the outside of town, and he arrived with Bob Neuwirth and Al Kooper. That was the entourage, Neuwirth, Kooper and Dylan. And they were all wearing puff-sleeved duelling shirts – one of them was polka dot ... They wore sunglasses. The whole image was very, very different.

Film director Murray Lerner – onsite to make a documentary of the festival – certainly noticed 'the way Dylan was dressed, in the leather'. To him, it signified 'motorcycle[s], a tinge of Hell's Angel'. Others, including a *Broadside* reviewer, seemed to take umbrage: 'His black leather sports jacket, red shirt, tapered black slacks and electric guitar startled some ... and dismayed many.'

It wasn't just Dylan and his new music that was drowning tradition in the tide that weekend. When the Paul Butterfield Blues Band – with Michael Bloomfield riffing away – plugged in to play an afternoon blues workshop, Maybelle Carter and Mike Seeger were forced to abandon an autoharp workshop. Alan Lomax – self-proclaimed arbiter of all things Americana – hardened any divisions with his snotty introduction to Butterfield's combo:

> Us white cats always moved in [on the blues], a little bit late, but tried to catch up. I understand that this present combination has not only caught up but passed the test ... I'm anxious to find out whether it's true or not ... Anyway, this is the new blues from Chicago.

As he descended the stage an incandescent Grossman, now managing the Butterfield band, told Lomax he had 'done the worst MC job ever'. Never one to back down when in the wrong, Lomax threatened to 'bust [him] in the mouth', to which Grossman replied, 'I don't want a bust in the mouth from no faggot,' at which point these giant egos began throwing mile-wide haymakers. According to

Izzy Young, discussing the weekend's events the following Monday, 'There was a movie-camera guy standing right there, who decided not to [film] the moment 'cause he probably would've been killed ... They were tussling in the dust ... Shelton wrote about the ... fight ... but the *Times* censored it.'

For the good of the festival, the organizers tried throwing a blanket of silence over the incident, even as Lomax convened an emergency board meeting to ban Grossman from the grounds. Festival organizer George Wein was obliged to explain the facts of life while Boyd sat and took notes: 'If they banned Grossman, Dylan, Peter, Paul & Mary, Kweskin, Odetta and Butterfield would leave with him ... There was, moreover, a documentary film crew onsite recording everything for posterity.'

Said film crew also documented Dylan's soundcheck Sunday afternoon, ahead of the live debut of his brand of 'folk-rock', which Shelton erroneously described in the festival programme as a 'fusing [of] his own lyrics with the cadences and drive of Chuck Berry tunes'. The rock version of 'This Land Is Your Land' Dylan vamped during the soundcheck demonstrated 'not much was really sacred'.

Far from seeing the Butterfield Blues Band as a threat, Dylan had co-opted Bloomfield, bassist Jerome Arnold and drummer Sam Lay into the ad hoc band he had hastily assembled that Saturday evening. Again he let Bloomfield do the heavy lifting:

> **Nick Gravenites**: They were ... bringing various people that could play electric into the house [at Nethercliffe] ... Dylan was over in the corner, and Michael knew all the chords and would audition these people. If they didn't know what to do, bam! he got somebody else ... Dylan would [occasionally] come over and clarify some chord.

Given the hit and miss nature of his 'electric' sessions to date, Dylan was taking a *huge* risk, to a potentially unforgiving audience. The audition became an all-night rehearsal – with the Butterfield trio joined by Al Kooper, tagging along at Dylan's insistence, and Barry Goldberg on electric piano. Bloomfield soon began to doubt the wisdom of Dylan's decision: 'This schwartze Jerome ... is fucking up everything. We're practicing there in a room, and Odetta's staring at us, and Mary Travers is there, and ... it's sounding horrible.'

Dylan, though, was having a ball, as a providentially placed journalist got to witness; '[Odetta] bounced up and down, striking a tambourine while ... Bobby Dylan, standing in high-heeled boots to match his long hair, blasted away on an electric guitar ... No one knew what to make of the situation. Bobby Dylan pounding away as if he were a rock'n'roll idol. Facial expressions. His gyrations. Roaring amplifiers. "This is folk music?" someone asked.'

For Dylan, Sunday evening couldn't come soon enough. He alone knew what to expect. Yet he had no experience of how the music would sound out front. This was hardly Hibbing High School. The one thing all parties agree – Joe Boyd included – is that it was loud: 'I mean, by today's standards it wasn't very loud, but by those standards of the day it was the loudest thing anybody had ever heard. The volume. That was the thing, the volume.'

And the loudest instrument of the lot was the guitar: not Dylan's guitar – the one sold at Christie's, New York in December 2013 for a million bucks – which was barely audible, but Bloomfield's guitar. As Eric Von Schmidt recalled, 'It was obvious that Bloomfield was out to kill. He had his guitar turned up as loud as he could possibly turn it up, and he was playing as many notes as he could possibly play.'

Ramblin' Jack Elliott thought 'it sounded like horseshit', while Tony Glover took the view 'the sound was really fucked [because] the guitar was too loud, [so] there was a lot of shouting but most of it was, Turn up the vocals, or, Fix the mix'. Ed Ward, in his Bloomfield biography, explained that the live set-up was simply not up to it:

> What made Dylan's electric set sonically problematic wasn't the ineptitude of the technicians. The Newport stage was raked – that is, it sloped toward the audience. There were no stage monitors in those days, and the PA speakers were set at the sides of the stage. Dylan's vocals came through the PA speakers, but there was no way to feed the electric instruments into the PA. Anyone sitting directly in front of the stage heard the amplified sound coming right at them, while Dylan's voice came only through the PA speakers. For many in the audience, it made for a bizarre listening experience.

At this point, Pete Seeger and/or Alan Lomax bellowed to Boyd, 'You've got to turn it down! It's far too loud! We can't have it like this. It's just unbearably loud.' Boyd patiently explained that only the desk could turn the sound down, and in order to get to the desk, one would have to 'climb on top of a box and get over the fence from backstage'. He was so instructed.

It took Boyd, who was at least as tall as Seeger, until the start of 'Like A Rolling Stone' to make it across, only to find 'Grossman, Neuwirth, Yarrow and Rothchild all sitting at the sound desk, grinning ... I relayed Lomax's message and Peter Yarrow said, "Tell Alan Lomax," and extended his middle finger ... By this time all I could see was the back of Pete Seeger disappearing down the road past the car park.'

According to legend, the do-gooder was heading off to find an axe to cut the electric cable. In reality, he was heading for his car, which provided some form of sound insulation. Once there, according to festival organizer George Wein, he 'rolled up all the windows, and sat there tears rolling down his cheeks'. His equally high-strung wife Toshi burst into tears in Wein's arms.

In the end, as Boyd can confirm, 'There was no ax wielded.' Instead, while 'Mr Lomax spat with fury', Dylan's three-song set came to an end. Bloomfield was just relieved to get through it: 'I thought we were boffo, smasheroo ... I said, "Bob, how do you think we did?" And he said, "They were booing. Didn't you hear it?" I said, "No, man, I thought it was cheers." He didn't seem pissed [off]. He [just] seemed perplexed.'

Dylan confirmed at a December 1965 West Coast press conference, 'They certainly booed, I'll tell you that. You could hear it all over the place.' Yet to this day, no one present can agree on *why* he was booed, Dylan himself saying, thirty-five years later, 'Whatever it was about, it wasn't about anything that they were hearing.' Later that evening he asked Tony Glover what he'd thought. Glover remembered in 1972, 'He was a little surprised people were so uptight, [but] he was more annoyed that the sound was not that good.' At least Dylan could put *that* right readily enough. The sound would never again be a reason to boo.

The ever-contrary Al Kooper prefers to believe a lot of 'college kids ... migrated there to see Dylan, and ... watched a lotta stuff that they didn't particularly wanna see. And then when he played, [it was just] fifteen minutes ... They weren't happy.' And Noel Stookey agrees,

'Nobody booed until he walked off stage ... I was standing there, and the audience was excited about Dylan going electric.'

At the time, though, most witnesses thought that the reaction got progressively worse, not helped by the order of the set, which concluded with the unrecognizable 'Phantom Engineer', made doubly disorienting because bassist Arnold missed the change and turned the beat around, leaving the others to either compensate or carry on. Dylan did one, Bloomfield the other.

According to Caryl Mirken, writing in *Broadside*: 'By his third – and most "radically" rock'n'roll – song there was loud jeering and cat-calls from some parts of the audience. Then a regular battle between boos and cheers. Bob was obviously quite perturbed.' Paul Nelson, who was up close, camera in hand, agreed with Mirken that he 'looked ... like he was quite moved and upset by it, and I was only about ten feet away'. Nelson's shot of Dylan with what appears to be a tear rolling down his cheek – actually a bead of sweat – would later be used as 'proof' that the audience reaction got to him. Even the predetermined brevity of the set was attributed to a hostile reaction by the *Boston Broadside*'s Ed Freedman:

> Peter Yarrow tries to convince the audience that he had only allotted time for three songs; somebody else said it was because he was sick or because he couldn't get together with Butterfield's band, but the real reason was rather obvious: he left the stage because he was being booed by a large segment of the audience ... who don't like electrified, amplified, reverberated, echo-chambered, rock'n'rolled Bob Dylan.

Freedman was one of those who convinced himself it was a chastened Dylan who returned to sing two songs acoustically. Dylan later told Glover, 'I went back on solo and sang Mr Tambourine Man and Baby Blue because that's what the crowd wanted to hear ... That's all they wanted to hear – so I went and sang it for them. It was the easy thing to do.' Little did they realise he had returned unbowed. In reality, he was still making a point, ending with 'Mr Tambourine Man', the song he was castigated by Silber and co. for singing the previous year at Newport.

Nelson returned to the *Sing Out!* office the next day to tell everyone there about 'the Dylan fiasco', Richard Reuss's summer diary recording that Sunday's set had 'made a very great impression on [Nelson] ... He kept saying how dramatic it was and how it overshadowed everything else ... "Dylan was absolutely the greatest," Paul said, ... But he got a stone-cold reaction. People yelled, You stink, and, Throw away the electric guitar as his old fans turned on him. He left after three numbers with tears running down his face ... You could tell he was hurt.'

Dylan later refuted this version of events, telling Scaduto, 'I did *not* have tears in my eyes. I was just stunned and probably a little drunk.' At least the straight press, the few that were there, rushed to his defence, with Arthur Kretchmer the most far-seeing of the reviewers, writing in the *Village Voice* the following week:

> Bob Dylan was booed for linking rhythm and blues to the paranoid nightmares of his vision ... The irony of the folklorists and their parochial ire at Dylan's musical transgressions is that he is ... this generation's most awesome talent. And in eighty years you will read scholarly papers about his themes (terror, release).

The *Providence Journal*'s Charlie Bakst also highlighted an undeniable fact: 'Dylan now sings rock'n'roll, the words mattering less than the beat. What he used to stand for, whether one agreed with it or not, was much clearer than what he stands for now. [Which is] maybe himself.' In Greenwich and Cambridge circles, there remained a phalanx of folkies who still thought they could bring a chastened Dylan to heel, including those who had once slept with him.

Joan Baez explained to *Broadside*, 'Tonight Bob was in a mess. [But] he's really very good. People just don't understand his [new] writing.' Meanwhile, Barbara Dane told Nelson and Tony Glover (who called at the *Sing Out!* offices, post-festival, to talk about a harmonica book): 'Dylan ha[s] to realize that his audience expected a certain thing from him which in many cases filled a need in his audience. If he wished to switch his style so drastically, he had to realize that much of his audience ... would seek to find their fulfillment in someone else ... Actually it was a very good experience for a young artist like Dylan to go through.'

Afterwards, Dylan seemed slightly stunned, sitting backstage on the lap of Cambridge mother-hen, Betsy Siggins, who remembers, 'He did not say one word ... He seemed to be exhausted, kind of overwhelmed.' And at the traditional post-festival party, when Maria Muldaur asked, 'Do ya wanna dance?' he looked up and said, 'I would, but my hands are on fire.' Even Bloomfield, who 'saw him afterwards, [thought] he looked real shook up and I didn't know the nature of what made him all shook up'.

By the next night, when their paths crossed again, 'at this party', the old Bobby was back: 'He's sitting next to this girl and her husband, and he's got his hand right up her pussy, right next to her husband, and she's letting him do this.' By then, Dylan had probably penned an unnostalgic return to 4th Street: 'You say I let you down / You know it's not like that.'

Grossman may have bitten the dust, but his client had won him the war of words. Days later Alan Lomax, writing to a friend, complained, '[Dylan] more or less killed the festival ... As soon as he [finished his set], 4,000 people rose as one man and left the grounds ... the rest of the evening was a shambles ... That boy [sure] is destructive.' One new buzz word was folk-rock, another was bandwagon:

> **Donovan**: [Dylan] was doing this great thing with electric guitars. It lasted a while and was fantastic, man. Electric guitars and folk, do they mix? Sure, if you want them to. Why not? Dylan uses electric guitars because he likes it that way. He doesn't care what people think.
>
> **Phil Ochs**: Dylan as usual was doing ... what any real artist should, that is performing the music he personally felt closest to and putting his own judgement before that of his audience ... The people that thought they were booing Dylan were in reality booing themselves in a most vulgar display of unthinking mob censorship.
>
> **Paul Nelson** [in a letter to Jon Pankake]: By God, [Dylan] was so great in those three numbers! ... I'll bet my critical judgement I'm right (and particularly so because Irwin [Silber] hated it), and I'll stand by Dylan and his new songs.

The above reactions – all of them from people who were *there* – came in the immediate aftermath of the Rhode Island storm. Jac Holzman, founder of Elektra Records (originally a folk label), who stood alongside Nelson at Newport, decided his label needed a reboot: 'This was electricity married to content. We were hearing music with lyrics that had meaning, with a rock beat ... All the parallel strains of music over the years coalesced for me in that moment.' For Joe Boyd, who would go on to produce even more folk-rock masterpieces than Tom Wilson, 'This was the birth of Rock. So many taste crimes have been committed in rock's name since then that it might be questionable to count this moment as a triumph, but it certainly felt like one [that night] in July 1965.'

Dylan, meanwhile, needed to find a new producer for himself. Or at least, someone whom the label thought of as a producer, who would keep tape rolling and leave him largely to his own devices. He probably asked Cash for suggestions. Patti Page producer Bob Johnston – working out of Nashville – was doubtless on the shortlist, Cash later depicting Johnston as someone who 'likes to sit back and watch an artist produce himself ... [He] is smart enough to know when he gets an artist who believes in himself to let him run with it.'

That certainly describes Dylan in the summer of 1965. According to Johnston – and a fair few snake-oil salesmen could have learnt something from sharing a baloney sandwich with him – Columbia's head of production told him Wilson was on the way out: 'I went to Wilson and I said, Bill Gallagher just called me in and said they're going to get rid of you, and that Grossman hates you ... He said, "Hell, I knew that ... Be my guest. I'm out of here anyway."'

Wilson was already plotting his move to Verve, tired of Columbia's by-the-book approach. Johnston's audition would be the first *Highway 61 Revisited* session: July 29th, 1965. He brought with him a single innovation, which at least solved the perennial problem of Dylan moving about when recording:

> Everybody else at the time was using one [vocal] microphone. Which means you have to sacrifice something. If you're gonna have a band, you can't have the band playin' full tilt. If you've got him in the middle you can't understand everything with different [engineers] in there raising the guitar up, raising the drum up, and shit like that. What I did was [use] three microphones because he was always jerking his head around. I put the microphone on the left, center and right [so] it didn't matter where in the fuckin' room he went.

It was an ingenious solution. Other than this, Johnston kept his thoughts to himself. Tony Glover, who was invited to a Dylan session for the first time, soon realized, 'Johnston was from the John Hammond school of production; call out take numbers, keep the logs, make phone calls, and stay out of the way. The only people I heard making comments about the takes were Albert and Neuwirth.'

Al Kooper, to whom Wilson had been a good friend, considered the new incumbent to be more akin to a cheerleader, 'The kinda guy that just pats you on the back and says you're fantastic, and just keeps you going.' Much the same thought occured to the new boy Kooper had brought in on bass:

Harvey Brooks: As I was [about] to learn, this was a case of just go for it – you were only going to get one or two shots, maybe, at each song... [When] Bob comes into the studio... [everyone] starts listening to ... what he wants to do. He ran the whole session. Bob Johnston was there just to keep it going. He was supposed to say if somebody was in tune or out of tune, but that was a useless concept, to try and get *anything* in tune ... Johnston may have been ... keeping the tape rolling, but it was all Bob Dylan deciding what felt right and what didn't.

Beneath the bluff exterior, Johnston had few illusions about why he was chosen and approved (to remain in that chair for the next half decade). As he informed *Disc*, at the end of his tenure, 'I don't consider myself a record producer... I don't believe in microphones, or booths, or calling out "Take 43". I just let the machines go ... The sequencing lies with him. He's the boss, ... Dylan is a perfectionist. He won't settle for second best. The sound has to be there; the vocal has to be there.'*

For that first session, Johnston didn't even have Roy Halee to hold his hand and make the whole thing blend.† Unsurprisingly, it was not a roaring success. After six hours – a morning and an afternoon session – they had got just three songs, one of which, 'Phantom Engineer', gave up the ghost only after three Newportesque remakes. The first

---

* Less of a perfectionist in the studio than Dylan would be hard to imagine.
† Thankfully, Halee would be back for the next two *Highway 61* sessions.

of these is an absolute hoot as Dylan loses it at something another musician is doing, exclaiming, 'What the fuck are we doing with this song, man!' After the merriment subsides, he wonders aloud, 'It's not such a terrible song.'

It remained the song which got him booed off at Newport until after the lunch break, when he stayed behind to work on a slower, more soulful arrangement. It immediately worked. They did it three times, to prove it was no fluke, but as Brooks says, 'If the feel was there and the performance was successful, that's all he cared about.'

Mike Bloomfield, on the other hand, still knew that his boss wasn't much of a team player, and this sense of separation was holding the process back: 'From my experience with Dylan's rock-band sessions, he never really gets with the band. We just learnt the tunes right there, he sang and we played around him. He never got with the band so that we could groove together. There was no real empathy with the beat, or between Dylan's singing and the groove of the band.'

Ample evidence to support Bloomfield's assertion is to be found on the very next song, 'Tombstone Blues', which should hardly have required half of the morning and a chunk of the afternoon to capture. Just as they are starting to 'groove together' on take eleven (really take ten), with Bloomfield riding the riffs after every chorus, Dylan fails to wait for Bloomfield's solo to end, thus blowing the whole take. He then has the temerity to blame Bloomfield, 'Hey, dig, man, you're doing too much.' Bloomfield reins himself in for the final take, which has none of that 'B.B. King shit', and is all the worse for it.

The rest of the afternoon is devoted to a song with the bile not yet dry. 'Positively 4th Street', Dylan's riposte to the recidivists at Newport, was very much a case of 'Dylan deciding what felt right and what didn't', because they actually nailed the song on the first full take, but at a more sedate pace, with Kooper still fumbling for the light switch, and a vocal where the only thing one gets from it is sorrow.

It will take eight more takes for Dylan to find that cutting-edge vocal, and for Kooper to become a fairground attraction, with one 'long breakdown' (take six) down to the new bassist, Russ Savakus – a replacement for Joe Macho Jr – who holds his hands up at the end of the take, 'I fucked up.' In fact, he was finding the whole thing hard going and at the end of the day, he quit. Harvey Brooks, who knew him well (and was his replacement), thinks he was 'hav[ing] some difficulty with the style of music'. Given that Dylan brought Russ back to play stand-up on the final track, it was clearly not personal.

By then, Brooks had already had his crack at the same track, an eleven-minute opus called 'Desolation Row', Dylan asking him and Kooper to stay behind on the Friday afternoon, hoping to capture it cold. Without any credible manuscript version, placing Desolation Row's composition chronologically is a challenge, but by July 30th it is one line shy of finished ('get him to feel more assured' for 'the boiled guts of birds').

The historical figures that flit across its stage read like refugees from his soon-to-be-discarded novel; perhaps they were. As he said in 1966, 'After writing ["Like A Rolling Stone"], I wasn't interested in writing a novel or a play.' Hamlet's suicidal girlfriend, though, came from an abandoned song idea: 'Ophelia lift your head up / I cannot stay with you / I cannot insult you / By saying I need you.'

Unfortunately, first time around, having tuned his bottom string to D to get the same modal effect as 'It's Alright, Ma', Dylan forgot to retune the other strings. Glover noticed straight away, 'By the [end of the] first verse ... it was obvious that Bob's guitar was rather painfully out of tune. Both Neuwirth and I pointed it out, but Albert didn't want to stop the take ... I realized he did that to let him get it out of his system.'

I think not. The fact that Dylan went on to record a full band version at the third session and then pulled the Kooper/Brooks take to a production master, suggests he intended to include it on the album.* It certainly has the superior vocal (Dylan's usual criteria for inclusion), and if he was squeamish about out-of-tune guitars, he'd have fixed up the intro and released take two of 'Queen Jane Approximately', not take seven.

The fact that Dylan tried this epic with Kooper and Brooks, guitar and bass; then electric piano (Kooper), guitar (Bloomfield), Brooks and Gregg; and even with piano and stand-up bass, before finally

---

* This production reel, widely bootlegged as *Highway 61 Revisited Again*, has recently been described as a 'rough mix publisher's tape', whatever the hell that is. It is clearly not so, since the songs on it were copyrighted in three stages, with two different sets of rights, and the songs play to the end, unfaded, a sure sign of a production reel.

cutting it with acoustic and stand-up, illustrates how Dylan's vision shaped the sound picture at every turn.

Though Dylan cleared the studio before he recorded that first 'Desolation Row', he allowed Suze (and Glover, it would seem) to remain. Sally had invited Suze to the session – at Dylan's behest – planning to drive up to Woodstock for the weekend. Suze had arrived to find the session already in progress and her former boyfriend 'quiet, intense and twitchy behind his dark glasses'. Also there was photographer Jerry Schatzberg, an ex-boyfriend of Dylan's current girlfriend. Sara had phoned him when she heard he wanted to photograph her Bobby. As Schatzberg said, 'He's very suspicious of people, but because Sara said I was cool, I had an entree,' and Daniel was consigned to the lion's den.

When Dylan returned to the studio the following Monday (August 2nd), it was key personnel only. Time to get down to business. He wanted a minimum of distractions as he wrapped up the album in a double session; starting at eight in the evening, it would go on until the tolling ended. Another marathon, with its fair share of train wrecks, by 3 a.m. he had five more songs: 'Highway 61 Revisited', 'Just Like Tom Thumb's Blues', 'Queen Jane Aproximately', 'Ballad Of A Thin Man' and a soon-discarded electric 'Desolation Row'. Phew!

Dylan was still not satisfied. In his head, he heard background vocals on 'Tombstone Blues', so he brought the Chamber Brothers in, fresh from Newport. But after he dubbed them on, he changed his mind. He also recalled Savakus on stand-up, his preferred instrument, to jazz up an acoustic 'Desolation Row', leaving it to Johnston to dub on some flamenco flourishes, courtesy of Charlie McCoy, after which he was ready to play the finished artefact to his main rivals for the hearts and minds of a generation.

Nine days after completing his second album in eight months – and a week after The Beatles released a second album spent treading water, *Help!* – Dylan arrived at the Warwick Hotel with Al Aronowitz, brought along to arbitrate. If McCartney would later admit Dylan's latest single 'showed all of us that it was possible to go a little further', this evening Aronowitz saw the Mersey Beat collective close ranks:

[Bob] has already recorded his next electric album ... 'I brought along a dub so you could hear it,' Bob says, telling The Beatles about the album. Still, too many beats pass before John finally says, 'Well, let's 'ear it.' Dylan hands me the acetate and says, 'Here, Al! You play disc jockey.' ... As I carry the dub over to the turntable, Dylan tells about playing the Newport Folk Festival with an electric backup band. 'Yeah,' I comment, 'They booed him—' 'Naw, naw,' Dylan interrupts me sharply, 'That's not what happened!' ... When *Highway 61* finishes, The Beatles don't stampede to congratulate Bob. Certainly not in the same way that fawning fans like myself ha[d] told him that the album knock[ed] us on our asses. The collective consciousness of the single, larger Beatles organism seems to be saying, 'Yeah, it's okay.'

If Dylan was fazed by the united foursome, he wasn't about to show it. He was already thinking how best to present the material live. For that, he would need a standing band. One of his reference points was Ricky Nelson. Both guitar legend James Burton and bassist Joe Osborn had cut their teeth in the Nelson school of frat-rock. And behind this pair Dylan envisaged the pummelling beat of Mickey Jones. Jones was currently playing with Johnny Rivers, whom Dylan had caught at the Whisky on his first LA trip in February 1964. But as Dylan ruefully recalled in 1969, 'Mickey couldn't make it immediately and ... Jim Burton was playing with a television group at that time.'*

With Bloomfield committed to the Butterfield Blues Band, and prestigious shows at the Forest Hills Stadium and the Hollywood Bowl booked in four to five weeks' time, he was certainly cutting it fine. But for now serendipity was his gimp, and Mary Martin – a secretary at Grossman's office – its maître d'.

She recommended a band she knew from her home town of Toronto. A Canadian native, she had been pushing The Hawks, formerly Ronnie Hawkins' backing band, to anyone who would listen, including Grossman, who duly introduced them to Richard Alderson, 'ask[ing] me if I wanted to produce them ... [But] they weren't really great [and] they didn't have any original songs.' If they had any potential, it was raw potential.

---

* Burton has confirmed that Grossman called but it 'was like a three-month tour, and there was no way I could get off and do a three-month tour, so I had to bow out'.

Dylan was not walking wholly blind. Even if he didn't witness the *So Many Roads* session/s – and the jury is still out – he certainly knew the album and the man who made it, John Hammond Jr. Hammond's ringing endorsement would have counted for far more than Martin's soft-shoe sales pitch. According to Robbie, in 1969, it was just a case of the stars aligning: 'We just fell in with the man. There were never any hassles or strict schedules, simply a series of get-togethers ... I don't even remember that phone call ... from Dylan in the beginning.' By 2015, though, he had regained an almost perfect recall:

> I got a message from Albert Grossman's office, asking me to come up to the city on our next day off to meet with Bob Dylan ... Bob filled me in on his recent experiment playing electric ... at the Newport Folk Festival ... Bob claimed to have considerable experience with rock'n'roll, mentioning ... that he'd played with Bobby Vee for a while ... [He] left the room and came back a minute later, carrying an acoustic guitar case. 'Hey man, you wanna go somewhere ... There's something I wanna play you.'

Their destination was Grossman's downtown apartment, where Dylan proceeded to play Robertson an acetate of the album. Robbie sensed that same separation of singer and musicians as Bloomfield, but blamed it on the band for not 'keep[ing] up with his epic poetic energy'. Never short of self-confidence, Robertson told Dylan he thought he could do better. On his return to New Jersey and a residency at Tony Mart's, he told Hawks drummer Levon Helm he had ended up 'playing a little rough. Dylan seemed to want it that way.'

No sooner had Robertson secured the gig than he began pitching to the folk-rocker to use the whole ensemble, but Dylan knew he wanted Brooks and Kooper representing key elements of the album sound. He just needed a guitarist and, soon, a drummer. When his first choice – probably Mike Nelson, a local favourite – quit, Levon was allowed to fill the breach: 'I got behind the drums ... and we began, ragged at first. Real ragged. We worked out parts for eight or nine songs ... I couldn't believe how many words this guy had in his music.' According to Robertson, 'As soon as Levon got behind the drums for our first ... rehearsal, Bob could tell he was the real deal.' Actually, it was Helm who would need convincing he wasn't wasting his time.

These two sell-out shows would showcase the new album and the new Dylan. They would also be an acid test for the relative Hipness of audiences on the two coasts, one the East spectacularly failed. The location – a windy open-air stadium in Queens, more used to tennis players learning to play than inventors of folk-rock – didn't do Dylan any favours. But at least this time he'd rehearsed and, learning from Newport, reversed the equation, beginning with forty-five minutes of acoustic music to lull the 'folknik crowd, who neither needed nor wanted an explanation for Dylan's conversion to rock'n'roll', to quote *Variety* reviewer, Herm Schoenfeld.

This proved necessary because the minute Murray 'the K' Kaufman, an incendiary choice for MC, introduced the band, 'Kaufman's close association with the "Top 40" school of pop earned some vigorous boos from a large section'. Paul Nelson, in the bleachers, saw a woman walking out, muttering 'Joan Baez wouldn't sell out like this.' At least he knew he was in the right place. Others who had shared the journey this far were equally blown away, including Suze, who 'remember[ed] talking to [Bob] afterward ... wonder[ing] if I was as complimentary as I felt'.

Ever the optimist, Dylan had even rehearsed two possible encores: 'Baby Let Me Follow You Down' and 'Highway 61 Revisited'. But by opening with 'Tombstone Blues' and doing 'From A Buick Six' and 'Just Like Tom Thumb's Blues' third and fourth – all unreleased and, on first listen, quite impenetrable – he was hardly meeting his (former) fans halfway. If not quite Stuttgart 1991 – where an eight-minute 'New Morning' contained not a single intelligible line – it was a test New York seemed bound to fail.

After the show Jerry Schatzberg, duking it out with Kramer to officially document the day visually, was sat in the limo with an animated Dylan, and remembers, 'He just kept cursing them out, "Fuck 'em, I don't care. That's the way I'm going."' But he did care. When a girl at Grossman's post-gig soirée admitted she had not particularly liked the new music, Dylan wanted to know why she hadn't booed.

At least the Forest Hills audience could hear every word, unlike those at The Beatles' own show the following night, at the venue Dylan was heading for next. Somewhat pointlessly, The Beatles tried to record both Hollywood Bowl shows. Dylan did not. Thankfully, someone who knew it had an in-house PA ran tape, and it confirms *LA Times* journo Charles Champlin's contrasting assessment of the two shows, 'The monumental difference [being] that his vast audience paid Bob Dylan the compliment of pin-drop silence while he was performing.'

Perhaps they were as nonplussed by the five new songs – an acoustic 'Desolation Row' and four all-electric previews – as the New Yorkers, but the LAers had the good grace to listen, even if Robertson thought the audience may have been simply 'distracted by its own agenda'. Dylan seemed delighted by the way the band had gelled over the two gigs. When *Free Press* journalist Paul Jay Robbins asked him why he didn't play lead guitar himself, he retorted, 'Robbie does things I can't do, which the songs need done.' If, in the fullness of time, he'd be proven right, right now Robbie stayed firmly in the shadows, offering little of Bloomfield's bluesy bluster onstage.

Dylan just needed to explain what had happened at the Bowl to a West Coast media even more uninformed than its East Coast counterpart, conducting his first American press conference on September 4th at the Beverly Hills Hilton, when one brave soul asked him if he thought 'anything of consequence happens at these things'. Dylan's reply would become the sustaining motif for nine months of relentless press coverage: 'Interviewers will write my scene and words from their own bags ... no matter what I say.'

At least Billy James, who set the whole thing up, took the opportunity to introduce Dylan to Phil Spector, an historic meeting of the mutually curious. In fact, the whole trip to LA was one rendezvous after another for pop culture's 'public writer number one'. One was with old friend Bonnie Beecher, who was co-running the Fred C. Dobbs cafe, to which Dylan brought The Byrds.

P. F. Sloan – who had just written 'Eve of Destruction' for Barry McGuire, another old friend now riding his shirt tails to the top of the charts – did not fare so well. According to Harvey Brooks, Sloan had agreed to the meeting but 'lasted about ten minutes before Dylan dismissed him with the tag "derivative" burned into his brain'. Sloan later told Sounes he was distracted by 'two women [who came] in from the bedroom half-naked – topless – [sat] down like bookends on the couch, and [didn't] say a word ... I can only imagine that Bob had set this up.' Perfectly possible.

Dylan was starting to up the ante with his mind games. As Aronowitz candidly confessed, 'To be the constant targets of digs from Bob was the price each of us paid for hanging out with him ... [and] Bob liked to feel big by making his hangers-on feel small.' Arthur Kretchmer, in his positive *Village Voice* review of Newport, was one of the first to express distaste at the way Dylan now 'surrounds himself with flunkies who feed him lines and laugh when he repeats them. At dinner he rotates the chicks at the place of honour next to himself.'

If being in Hollywood afforded Dylan the opportunity to work on the movie-star mind-fuck, he still had a lot to learn. When he finally met Marlon Brando – another long-standing hero – at a party somewhere in the Hills, after the Bowl, he was stunned when Brando told his gorgeous girlfriend, Pat Quinn, that he was 'going home with the black bitch' (a reference to Miles Davis's wife) – perhaps taking that protester's placard a tad literally. Quinn apparently drove over to the Chateau Marmont in retaliation, knocked on Dylan's door and said, 'Well, here I am.'

But if Dylan was not quite movie-star material, he was indisputably king of the folk-rock fad and, in Aronowitz's words, 'some kind of messiah to each of us', which is perhaps why he increasingly took the view 'he who is not for me is against me'. On returning to New York he bumped into the man who had spurned his offer to become his lead guitarist, preferring to play 'East/West'. In Dylan's company – sticking to him like sand and glue – was Robbie Robertson, whom Dylan seemed to have forgotten had once made an album with a perplexed Bloomfield:

> Prior to that Newport thing he was always introducing me to his friends as 'the best guitar player in the world'. It was sort of funny. Then one day I saw him with Robbie Robertson, his new guitar player, at the Cafe Au Go Go ... He introduces me to Robbie, who I [obviously] already knew, and Bob says 'Hey, Mike, I want you to meet the best guitar player in the world.' I think that's what Bob is all about. He wants loyalty. If you say you're going to do something with him and you don't do it, ... he figures he's being betrayed.

Betrayal was a theme Dylan would look to mine to the hilt for the foreseeable, starting the week after the Hollywood Bowl with the release of 'Positively 4th Street', the ultimate *j'accuse* in song. A week earlier, tickets had gone on sale for his next retort to the recidivists. He was on a mission for the soul of folk. On October 1st, he would return to Carnegie Hall, two years on from being the Prince of Protest.

On the day of the Bowl show, tickets had also gone on sale for two shows in Texas in three weeks' time. All he needed was a band. When Kooper quit, post-Bowl – perhaps sensing that he had better seize the opportunity to make a name for himself and not just the boss – it left Dylan a matter of days in which to find his fifth electric band in four months. It was hardly time enough to assemble one. It would have to be an outfit that had been left on the shelf, watching the pop world pass them by.

2.6

September 1965 to March 1966: Both Kinds Of Music

He changed ... I would see him consciously be that cruel, man. I didn't understand ... that constant insane sort of sadistic put-down game.

Michael Bloomfield

As soon as Robbie and the others got with Dylan, I fell out of touch ... They had been the coolest guys – wide-open, full-throttle – but all of a sudden, I was just a complete idiot to them.

John Hammond Jr

Bob soaked up everything and glommed onto whatever taught him something new.

Suze Rotolo

Dylan has his ears open all the time. He is always listening to, and looking at, what's going on.

John Steel (The Animals), February 1965

Dylan was always entirely open; he listened to everything – Ozark music, Gregorian chants, blues and rock'n'roll – and also Coltrane.

Tom Wilson, September 1967

People ask me how come I'm using a rock'n'roll band ... If I told people why, it would be all over!

Bob Dylan to Barry McGuire, December 1965

We're just playing the best music we know how – that other stuff is the [audiences'] problem.

Robbie Robertson, to Tony Glover, November 1965

*

Robbie Robertson, who in the fullness of time would break up The Band because *he* was tired of gigging, has always insisted it was his own fierce loyalty to his fellow Canadians that forced Dylan's hand, and made him agree to The Hawks becoming his touring band. In his 2015 memoir, he relates a night at the Kettle of Fish, post-Bowl, when Dylan asked him straight, could he do the upcoming tour? 'I told him again that The Hawks were a close unit and we were on our own mission.' Not so, according to the man at the Helm. It was him, not Robbie, who on hearing that Kooper had quit, apparently gave Grossman an ultimatum: 'Take us all, or don't take anybody'.

Whoever is telling it like it was – and my money's on Levon – the pair's ambitions had previously led them to quit their gig as Ronnie Hawkins' backing band in 1964, striking out on their own. A year later, they had hit a a dead end. With only one stillborn single to their name – of strictly historical interest – they were playing a New Jersey nightclub six nights a week just to make ends meet. In truth, tapes of the 1964–5 Hawks suggest they would have struggled to make commercial headway anyway, anyhow, anywhere.

And yet Dylan took a leap of faith – albeit an enforced one – after Harvey Brooks flew straight back to New York from LA to rehearse for a three-week gig in Detroit with Chico Holiday (booked before Dylan recruited him). When a blithe Brooks phoned Grossman's office from Detroit's Cadillac Square Hotel the following week, to ascertain when rehearsals were beginning again, he was informed that The Hawks had filled the void. His services were no longer required.

It was Newport all over again. Another all-night rehearsal (or two) would have to suffice before Dylan rolled the dice for a third time in two months in the high-stakes game of Going Electric. Flying 'by private plane' to Toronto on September 15th, just nine days before he was due to play Austin, Dylan arrived to 'rehearse with Levon and The Hawks, a local rock'n'roll group that will back him on his current tour. In the city for two days, Dylan checked into a midtown motor hotel ... to work on his book *Tarantula*[!], and spent much of his evenings and early mornings at the Friar's Tavern, where the group was playing', or so *Variety* breathlessly reported in the following week's issue.

Dylan had not travelled alone. He had brought Sara, to meet his mum, visiting from Minnesota. The first night at Friar's, Sara accompanied Dylan. She apparently told Robertson how much she liked the band, before taking a taxi to the hotel, leaving her partner to Levon and the gang. According to Robbie, that night's audition-cum-rehearsal was do or die:

> We played the songs with no concrete beginnings or endings. Bob would usually start strumming away to set the tempo, and we would stagger in when we got a feel for the rhythm. I suggested that when we neared the end of the song, Bob could give me a nod [to] signal ... we were coming in for a landing. We ran through about ten tunes before Bob ... called it a night ... 'Yeah, that sounds pretty good.'

Levon's expeditionary force would accompany the folk-rocker for the next nine months, though Helm himself would surrender after two, convinced they should go back to the drawing board/rehearsal room. He was particularly frustrated by Dylan's penchant for stop-start arrangements: 'He would suddenly stop and break the beat, and we'd get confused and not know where we were.* We'd look at one another and try to figure out if we were playing great music or total bullshit.'

Figuring that out would perforce occupy every musician still standing. Having been thrown in at the deep end, Robertson, Danko, Manuel and Hudson had to sink or swim. Initially, they suspected they were merely rearranging deckchairs on the *Titanic* while the captain sang 'Which Side Are You On?':

> **Robbie Robertson**: It was hard. There were times out there when you were just playing to the heavens ... Everything you had, you were laying out. And they'd ... boo. People acted like it was a sin. I have great admiration for Bob for not backing out of the thing ... [] ... His friends, his advisers, everyone said, 'Just get rid of these guys ... [] ... This is death. They're killing your career.' But Bob didn't do it. He either knew something that they didn't know, or he just didn't have the heart to tell us.

---

* This is surely a direct reference to the fall 1965 electric arrangement of 'It Ain't Me Babe'.

A lot of the time The Hawks were playing blind, lacking many of the same reference points as their new leader. As the most soulful Hawk, Richard Manuel, observed in 1971, 'I hadn't heard much Dylan stuff before then. I'd heard other [pop] albums, but prior to that we were very much into nightclub rock'n'roll,' which was Bandspeak for being completely out of the loop. Listening to a 1965 Levon and The Hawks set was like hearing a band in cryogenic storage since BBI (Before the British Invasion).

Perhaps that's what appealed to Dylan. He had, after all, left the rock'n'roll arena himself when 'the whole field got taken over into some milk', in order to do something antithetical, nay heretical. Now he was determined to bend the pop world – bound by Britbeat as it was – to his internal vision. And if that meant a period of transition, or 'total bullshit', so be it. Even in the period when the jury was out, Dylan was impervious to criticism. He just wanted to get out there and play:

> **Robbie Robertson:** We were ready to work [at songs]. But Bob didn't like to work. We'd run over a song and he'd say, 'I guess that's how it is. That's fine.' And we'd say, 'Well, it could be a lot better.' ... We rehearsed in front of audiences rather than before we went out. And that was very odd for the guys in the band. It was like going out in your underwear or something ... That might have been why they were booing. [1983]

In a gesture of unstinting generosity, Dylan agreed to a second night of post-Friar's rehearsals on the 17th, taking a break around 2 a.m. to remind the *Toronto Star*'s Robert Fulford and his readers, *plus ça change, plus c'est la même chose*:

> **Bob Dylan:** If you listen to the early records and the recent ones, you can see the band really makes no difference.
> **Robert Fulford:** Then why change?
> **BD:** To get rid of some of the boredom. I mean, I might write a symphony next year. I don't know what I'm going to do.
> **RF:** What about your followers' indignation?
> **BD:** ... If they come to do their thing, whatever it is – [whether] they come to boo, or clap, or cheer – well ... they couldn't have a reaction in the world that would scare me.

If Fulford was nonplussed, he did not let on. His reaction was certainly receptive compared to the sheer incomprehension that greeted Dylan a week later, at a press conference in Austin, local DJ Judith Adams providing an account of proceedings to Ralph J. Gleason, describing Dylan as 'quiet, gentle and immensely patient', even when 'someone ... inquired if he were trying to change the world with his songs. He finally asked her if she knew what he was saying in his songs and she admitted she didn't, really.'

In a scene that would be replayed many times over the next nine months, Dylan spent the afternoon in Austin explaining his music to a Sanhedrin of Mr Joneses before playing to an audience split between believers and non-believers, using a half-acoustic, half-electric format that was not just an exercise in contrasts but, post-intermission, a cathartic release for the frontman who, one *Texas Ranger* noted, 'jump[ed] across the stage, sometimes walking right up to the soloist in the middle of their solos and grinning in their faces'.

Thankfully, the audiences in both Austin and Dallas seemed largely receptive to Dylan's good news. Even the one agnostic in the band, its drummer and former bandleader, admitted in 1971 that the experience of playing with Dylan made him 'realize there was a lot more to music than just chords and a tight rhythm section'.

Seemingly determined to disprove that ol' chestnut – 'How does one get to Carnegie Hall?' 'Practise, practise' – Dylan and his band jetted into New York two days later, after just two onstage rehearsals, to play a sold-out show at Manhattan's most prestigious concert hall. Such was Dylan's level of excitement that he forgot to take his guitar case with him. No matter. His Sunburst Strat was hardly in the live mix.

The Hawks were determined to stick to the agreed set. They didn't need any neophyte rocker throwing them curve balls here, of all places.* If reviews were mostly upbeat, one jaundiced editor didn't think much of what he heard, using his regular column in *Sing Out!* to lambast the former folk messiah:

Half of the program [was] done 'straight', with unamplified guitar [*sic*], the second half to the accompaniment of a painfully neurotic

---

* An uncorroborated list for the Carnegie concert sourced by Krogsgaard lists an electric 'Can You Please Crawl ...' Five days later in Studio A, The Hawks clearly don't know the song well enough to have played it live.

electrified supporting cast. Apparently this was the statement that Dylan will be making at similar concerts throughout the country in the coming months ... [which] is basically a philosophy of alienation and paranoid fear ... a death-wish set to music.

Dylan had already crossed said sourpuss – Irwin Silber – off his list. But even the seditious Silber had to admit to 'total acceptance at Carnegie Hall. Perhaps those ... enamoured of the "old" Dylan didn't bother to ... get ... tickets.' The *Village Voice*'s Jack Newfield, a champion of the 'new' Dylan, suggested the show was more like a Damascene conversion: 'At the beginning there were a few boos, perhaps a conditioned response ... [but] on this third try, it became clear he had sold his new style to his fans.'

Now was surely the time to take his new band into the studio and cut a follow-up to 'Positively 4th Street' – at this juncture a nightly prelude to 'Like A Rolling Stone'. Dylan did just that, booking one afternoon (the 4th) and two evenings (the 5th and 6th) at Studio A. Time to see if his new band could pick things up as readily as the trio who helped Hammond make *So Many Roads*.

But there was a glitch. Dylan seemed to have mislaid the songs he'd been working on between Toronto and Texas. Wherever could they be? The answer was, in the guitar case he'd left behind on the Lodestar, which contained working drafts to new lyrics like 'Uranium Sunday' and 'Inside The Darkness Of Your Room'.

What he could remember of the former would constitute the basis of the one song he would complete to his satisfaction on October 5th, 'I Wanna Be Your Lover', even if some of the mislaid lines were never quite surpassed, 'i'm all fixed up / my eyes can see / but oh these headaches are killing me' and, 'there's guns in my ears but they never go off / my mouth tastes funny – all i do is cough' for starters.

'Inside The Darkness Of Your Room' – the hand-corrected typescript of which failed to make its $12,000 reserve when auctioned by Christie's in December 2013 – is of even greater historical import. It's the foundation stone for that bridge to *Blonde On Blonde*, with its embittered portrait of 'pretty mary / she's going to be killing the first boy that hurts for her / there he stands / with his mouth (teeth) in his hands, crying to put his love into words for her', while, 'maid marian's drunk / she's trying to smile / she used to be so warm / but she's lost her style'; all set against a backdrop of 'all the clocks ... exploding' and 'the four horsemen of the apocalipse [sic] ... dancing on the fingertips / trying to get home before he flips'. In the end, 'there's nothing left but me and you, lady ... inside the darkness of your room'. Truly mouth-watering stuff, save to chequebook collectors impressed only by the finished article, preferably handwritten.

Without the latter lyric, and only a vague idea of the former, Dylan entered the studio on the 5th – having cancelled the session the previous day, perhaps hoping to reconstruct two other songs he'd left behind, 'Pilot Eyes' and 'Medicine Sunday'. He may even have intended to make up the remaining lyrics in the studio, a practice he later told Ginsberg he adopted 'round '65': 'He used to go into a studio ... and babble into the microphone then rush into the control room and listen to what he said ... write it down ... maybe arrange it a little bit, and then rush back out in front and sing it [again].'

What is there on the October 5th tape suggests Dylan decided to 'demo' four single-verse songs (including 'Can You Please Crawl Out Your Window?), before picking out a possible A-side. Dylan informed Johnston before 'Medicine Sunday', 'We're just gonna do one verse'; ditto 'I Wanna Be Your Lover', 'Just one verse and play it back.' He even recorded a truncated 'Can You Please ...', of which there was already a finished version. After a second aborted take, he asks for 'a monitor that won't feedback'. Halee, the returning engineer, tells him no can do, before Johnston enquires, 'D'you want headphones?'

For The Hawks, the experience was positively disorienting. After one song Robertson claims he asked Dylan if they could take a few minutes, 'so that the boys and I could put together a more solid arrangement'. Bob replied, 'I think we got it ... I got another song I'd like to get to,' determined not to get stalled.

Though the session does get bogged down in magnetic mush, Dylan perseveres, electing to capture 'I Wanna Be Your Lover' – his postmodernist deconstruction of a Beatlesque love song – for which he had a full set of lyrics all along. After a single rough rehearsal, they cut four complete takes and pulled the third. It has taken six hours but Dylan has a single, and a potential hit, should he choose to put it out. He won't.

A photo taken that night at Ondine's – an after-hours club partly owned by Jerry Schatzberg – suggests a good time was being had by all, Dylan not feeling the pressure to produce one jot. But when, a couple of weeks later, he met Eric Burdon there, The Animals frontman noted 'He looked very ill. I would say he's working too hard and should ease up.' Photos from this period confirm an almost ghostly visage now surrounds Dylan, burning away the puppy fat for good. It wasn't work – he was only gigging at weekends – but the fact that even when at play, he would stay out well after dark.

When he flew to Minneapolis for a Friday show in early November, he spent the night before trawling Dinkytown looking for Glover. Having failed, he instead picked up two coeds, with whom he rode around. One of them later related how he 'refus[ed] to answer any "fan" questions ... [but] asked especially about ... the write-ups he received ... He wore shades most of the evening until my friend commented on how brilliant the sunlight was – causing ... a discarding of the glasses ... Everywhere, [my friend] had to go in first to see if the path was clear, then the group followed.' After dropping both girls off, unmolested, Dylan continued driving around town until early morning. 'Twas a normal day.

Then there were the all-night sessions, not in the studio but at the Chelsea Hotel, where he tended to stay when he was in Manhattan, or electing to join other friends who burned the candle at both ends around town. One such night owl was Brian Jones of The Stones, with whom Dylan and Robertson spent three consecutive evenings in early November, including the 9th, when the lights went out all over New York. Dylan would spend it jamming with Jones, Bill Wyman, Robertson and Neuwirth in the City Squire Hotel; in Jones's case till his lips bled, and in Dylan's case until he saw Martians, prompting him to suggest, 'Let's turn on. What better time? The little green men have landed.'

The night before, he was snapped by Don Paulsen having dinner with Jones, Schatzberg and a radiant Sara – a rare social sighting – and on the 7th, Dylan and Jones had gatecrashed a Wilson Pickett session, offering to write the soul brother a song. Jones even features in a semi-fictional account of 'A Night With Bob Dylan', published anonymously in the *Herald Tribune* that December.* It portrayed a helter-skelter existence where failure to entertain meant expulsion, in

---

* The essay was apparently Aronowitz's work, but with input from a Dylan who shared his wavelength.

this instance of Brian's friend, Milly, who 'one way or another, was thrown out' of the limo.

It wasn't the only time that fall Dylan's mercurial mindset lay behind a published piece. He famously rewrote a *Playboy* interview done with Nat Hentoff, after a copy editor mangled the original. He was still annoyed five years later, when he told Glover, 'We did the interview on tape, and then they just took it right off the tape, and any time they felt like changing it, or thought I should say something else, they'd just put it in.' That original – later booklegged – had shown a surprisingly unguarded Dylan talking about drugs ('To know any drug … it's not gonna fuck you up … I mean, LSD is a medicine'); and dismissing those who took his songs personally, 'I don't really worry too much about people who say they've been hurt by me, because ninety-nine times out of a hundred, it's not me that hurts them.' The comedy script Hentoff and Dylan concocted, run with no hint of a put-on, appeared alongside *Playboy*'s other scoop that March, *Octopussy*'s debut in print.

Days when they didn't load up the Lodestar to go and be booed were spent checking out R&R, not resting and recuperating. Dylan was living on the edge, my friend, catching music and chasing ghosts. Yet he somehow missed the two most exciting New York acts to emerge in many a moon.

Jimi Hendrix, who was still playing with Curtis Knight, recalled meeting Dylan at the Kettle of Fish at this time but 'we were both stoned [out] of our minds … we just hung around, laughing'. By the time Hendrix became Jimmy James, leader of The Blue Flames, Dylan had left the city. They never met again, despite the crucial role *Highway 61 Revisited* played in unlocking Hendrix's muse.

The fact that Dylan failed to see The Velvet Underground was just bad timing – he was on the West Coast when (with Al Aronowitz's help) they were booked to play a December residency at the Cafe Bizarre. Barbara Rubin, the lady massaging Dylan's head on the rear cover of *Bringing It …*, was also much taken with the Velvets, introducing them to Warhol, as she did Dylan. But Dylan's interest in that downtown demi-monde would wane as fatherhood beckoned.*

---

* Although Dylan never checked the Velvets out, Robertson did. He also caught Hendrix, taking Brian Jones with him. Jones told ex-Animal Chas Chandler about this amazing guitarist. The rest, as they say, is history.

It has recently been suggested (by Greil Marcus, among others), that the evening of the blackout (November 9th) served as inspiration for 'Visions Of Johanna', a song certainly composed in its immediate aftermath. If so, Robbie was there, but it was not an all-boys affair. Some kinda psychosexual drama was being played out, involving the mysterious 'Louise' and a 'little boy lost [who] takes himself so seriously [and] brags of his misery'. This certainly could be Brian Jones, whom Dylan described to Neuwirth the following May, on camera, as 'very paranoid ... He wouldn't dig [this film]. He'd [just] dig himself – the way he looked.'

Perhaps Dylan even started sketching out 'Visions' that evening, or the next, because as Robbie confirms, 'Bob wasn't someone who went off into a corner to seclude himself during his creative process. He sat down at the typewriter right in front of you. Lyrics came flying out of that machine ... The radio could be playing.' If it was, it was presumably tuned to 'a country music station'.

Possibly Dylan's greatest song, and the one that flicked the switch to reveal another portal inside the darkness of her room, 'Visions Of Johanna' was composed in two stages, most of it coming in a single amphetamine rush of inspiration, save for the final verse, a not uncommon situation. Indeed, he would bemoan, in the *Biograph* notes, those instances when 'sometimes you'll ... be very inspired, and you won't quite finish it for one reason or another ... and you ... leave a few little pieces to fill in, and you're trying always to finish it off. Then it's a struggle.'

The near-perfect 'Visions Of Johanna' may not sound a likely candidate, but it surely was. Shortly before a late November session Dylan returned to the final verse and wrestled it to the ground – probably while staying over at the Grossmans' Gramercy pad, which is how a handwritten manuscript ended up in Sally's possession. Initially, he 'mourns this death of infinity / used by (the) nightingale(s) of the road(s) / (he) who've taken (who takes) back everything which (that) was owed'. Enter The Peddler, who 'steps to the road / Everything's gone which was owed / But the nightingale – he's left his code'.

Close but no cigar. Resolution would only come with the rolling of tape. Hopefully those veterans of two months' boogieing and booing could now cut the mustard. This time, at least Dylan would cover his bases, hoping to help The Hawks unlock the code. He first played it to Robbie, not yet daring to risk it in concert. Instead, they worked up 'Phantom Engineer's natural successor, 'Long Distance Operator', debuting it at the late November shows with the departing Helm, and playing it all through December, with the incoming Bobby Gregg.

By the time they got to Washington on November 28th, Helm was ready to bail, never 100% convinced that Dylan and The Hawks were a natural fit. Part of the problem was that Dylan, far from worrying about any negative reception, was revelling in it. Helm had begun 'to think it was a ridiculous way to make a living ... The more Bob heard [booing], the more he wanted to drill these songs into the audience ... We didn't mean to play that loud, but Bob told the sound people to turn it up ... He'd bend and grind, stage front, miming Robbie's solos.'

None of this was Levon's imagination. A Minneapolis reporter described Dylan's November homecoming performance thus: 'When the lights went off for the second half ... the "New Dylan" appeared on stage. Now he was visibly ... a little happier, as he bounced around the stage ... giving last-minute instructions to his "big beat" electrified rock'n'roll band.' It was all starting to wear on Helm's nerves.

When The Hawks played their own home town ten days later, it was to an even more vitriolic reaction from both press and punters. Robertson recalls, 'A dark wave passed over The Hawks ... Levon was completely pissed off.' A week later, they played two shows at Boston's Bay Theater – previously diehard Dylan territory – and, to Helm's deep dismay, 'We were seriously booed [both nights] ... That's when it started to get to me. I'd been raised to believe that music was supposed to make people ... want to party. And here was all this hostility coming back at us.'

With a month on the West Coast looming, Helm knocked on Robertson's Washington hotel door to inform him, 'I'm leaving tonight. I can't do this no more ... I don't like this damn music, and I don't trust Albert Grossman.' Robertson did his best to keep Helm onside, assuring him, 'Lee, we're gonna find this music. We're gonna find a way to make it work so that we can get something out of it.' It was no good. The Levon-less Hawks would have to soldier on without him – as would Dylan.

When Robbie summoned up the nerve to tell his boss, Dylan just laughed, 'He's really going to Arkansas? What's Levon going to do *there?'* The bulletproof Bobby merely called up a namesake, asking to resume their recording association and if he was doing anything in December. What he didn't tell the metronomic Gregg – but did inform Allen Ginsberg, backstage in San Francisco – was that they would be sticking to the same set: 'We can't take a chance with the new drummer.'

And yet, when he did spring 'Visions Of Johanna', his most complex song to date, on Gregg at Studio A, two days after Helm headed south for the winter, he confidently rode through hedgerow and heather. His partner in rhythm, Rick Danko, did not fare so well, Dylan chewing him out after a second false start on 'Can You Please . . .', 'If you don't know it, man, don't stay in front. You're not playing the right chords.'

The decision to rerecord this 'old' song had been partly forced on Dylan by a 'pirate' version by The Vacels that Buddah rush-released at the end of September, advertised in that week's *Billboard* as 'the first single of the great new Bob Dylan song', which was not strictly true. Columbia had accidentally released Dylan's version, from the *Highway 61* sessions, thinking it was 'Positively 4th Street'. They hastily recalled it, but not swiftly enough to dissuade these doo-woppers from mutilating the Dylan original, minus that trademark sneer.

'Can You Please . . .' was neither complex nor new to Gregg – and after three complete takes Dylan's remake was in the can. But 'Visions of Johanna' (aka 'Freeze Out') was an entirely different truck of fish. Initially, Dylan seemed to think it might be another six-minute 45, telling the Bay Area press three days later, 'I thought of releasing it as a single but they would have [had to]cut it up.'*

If he ever thought he was going to cram 'Freeze Out' onto seven-inch vinyl, he would certainly have to speed it up. Initially, this is exactly what he tries to do, even as he instructs the band, 'It's not hard rock.' Eventually, he slows it right down, adding a harpsichord, possibly played by Al Kooper (in attendance as an insurance policy). After fourteen takes, five of them complete, he has a stately half-sister of the 'Johanna' he will ultimately choose. This elusive lady won't find a home till 1970, on one of the great Dylan vinyl bootlegs, *Seems Like A Freeze Out*.

---

* When Dylan released 'Like A Rolling Stone' stateside, *Melody Maker* famously ran as a front-page story, 'Thank Goodness We Won't Get This Six-Minute Bob Dylan Single In Britain'. CBS-UK did release it, and it went to number four.

It had been a struggle to garner just two tracks from a session that ran from 2.30 p.m. to the wee hours. Yet this was essentially the same band who sent jolts of electricty through Dylan nightly. Perhaps it was not really their fault, but rather a character flaw in Dylan, one Michael Bloomfield had previously noticed: 'When he wants [to], he can get into a good rock'n'roll groove, with electric instruments, and shout and be a really great rock'n'roll singer ... in the old Elvis Presley style ... [but] he won't let himself work with the band. He always seems to be fighting the band.'

Meanwhile, he held off copyrighting 'Visions of Johanna' until Grossman set up a new publishing concern, his Witmark deal having expired between 'Like A Rolling Stone' and *Highway 61*.* He also finally put his name to a Macmillan contract for the book he had spent much of the last year bashing out. How ironic that he should commit to its publication at the very moment he began doubting its worth. As he wrote in one of the trimmed sections:

> i keep starting to say some-
> thing but i realize everything's
> been said. i realize that any
> story of mine with meaning could
> at the most only amuse you as you
> eat your candy at bedside / yester-
> day i was so disturbed about this, that
> i figured to shock you – but i realized
> then that i'd have to keep the shock
> up at regular intervals for it to
> be effective an frankly, i just dont
> have that kind of time.

Having barely signed the contract, he confided in Nat Hentoff, 'I've a book coming out but it's very average to me. I can't really be excited about it. I've worked on it hard at certain times. But now it's all done, it means very little.' A couple of months later he informed Ralph J.

---

* In the interim, he licensed the *Highway 61* songs to Witmark, while reserving the right to stop them appearing in songbooks.

Gleason, another trusted journalist, it was all 'stuff which I had written ... which wasn't song ... just on a piece of toilet paper', which the well-read *San Francisco Chronicle* writer undoubtedly interpreted as a reference to Kerouac's notorious 'toilet roll' draft for *On The Road* – even if Dylan just meant it was crap.

When Dylan discussed the book with the *Saturday Evening Post*'s Jules Siegel the following April, Siegel perceived, 'He couldn't bring himself to publish it. He was afraid ... he'd be attacked by the critics. Ginsberg had told him the academic people were laying [in wait] for him.' Dylan also came to feel 'It had no story. I'd been reading all these trash books, works suffering from sex and excitement and foolish things.' Yet he continued carrying the proofs around with him until this *Tarantula* – whose 'triangle and symbol sits black on your back' – died from exhaustion.

One can't help wondering what his bride-to-be thought of a work suffering from 'sex and excitement', or if Dylan even showed it to her. Perhaps he still thought of Sara as someone who would 'be home when I want her to be home ... be there when I want her to be there ... will do it when I want her to do it'; which is what Victor Maymudes claims Dylan told him when he asked, 'Why Sara? Why not Joan Baez?' If that seems cold even for 1965 Dylan, when Sara introduced him to one of her few confidantes, the lady in question found him 'unbearable – offhand to the point of rudeness, bad-tempered, surly and moody as a spoilt child'.

And yet here they were, in a Long Island registry office on November 22nd, being married by New York State Supreme Court Justice Manuel Levine. Afterwards, there was a small party in a private banquet room at the Algonquin hotel, to which the likes of Neuwirth, Aronowitz and Robbie were invited – because Sara liked them – but Maymudes was not. He still gave this Scorpio sphinx the creeps.

Four days later, responding to a question from *Chicago Daily News* reporter Joseph Haas, Dylan blew smoke: 'Getting married, having a bunch of kids, I have no hopes for it.' Even when the wedding story broke, halfway through December, he continued to deny the 'marriage rumours'.* Meanwhile, Sara was due to give birth in a matter of

---

* Even at a May 1966 press conference he kept up the pretence, see chapter 2.7, and even as late as 1971 stated, 'I just didn't think anybody needed to know that.'

weeks. Dylan just had to hope he'd be back from the West Coast in time to play the dutiful dad.

The West Coast had become something of a commercial stronghold in the past two years. And thanks to Dylan's generosity – funding the purchase of a portable reel-to-reel for Allen Ginsberg – decent recordings of shows from San Francisco and San Jose allow listeners to now hear how The Hawks handled the challenge, post-Helm.* Despite reviewers complaining they couldn't hear the words in the second half, on San Jose Dylan is enunciating the lines with real 'tonal breath control'. Gregg has also made a difference, carrying the songs rather than playing around them, as Helm had.†

Supposedly, Dylan made his uncharacteristic gesture to Ginsberg partly because he had offered to record fans' comments after the show, something he singularly failed to do – forcing Dylan to do it himself later on in the world tour (with dramatic results). Actually, the Bay Area shows would have provided a wholly unrepresentative market sample. As one reviewer wrote of the Berkeley audience, 'There were no boos ... As a matter of fact, there was quite a bit of applause ... [which] extended to his five associates.' Gleason was even more effusive: 'Dylan's rock'n'roll band ... went over in Berkeley like the discovery of gold.'

Ginsberg did, however, take the opportunity to record their backstage conversation, during which Dylan became quite animated about his current music: 'I don't know what the fuck it is I do. I didn't set out to do this, I can tell you that. But ... the songs aren't bullshit songs.' This was probably what he wanted to say at two West Coast press conferences, one in LA, arranged by Billy James, the other in San Francisco, arranged by Gleason – both filmed, providing rare visual proof that the circus was in town:

> Reporters and journalists and TV cameras all had come to see a freak in a sideshow, all had come to be entertained. Instead, they

---

* Though they are listed as such in the Ginsberg archive at Stanford, one of the electric sets, given to Garth Hudson by Ginsberg, was previously marked Berkeley, and the poet told me personally he taped that show. Ginsberg certainly attended one or both Berkeley shows.
† For all of Helm's musical credentials, it cannot be coincidence that almost all of Dylan's best work with The Band would be done without him.

found a man – Dylan ... Some round-looking people tried to squeeze their questions into little square pegholes and hoped that Dylan would follow after. They tried to pin him down: How exactly do you write your songs and poems. 'I just sit down and write and the next thing I know, it's there.' ... People asking foolish and irrelevant questions found that they received their answers in direct accordance. Why did you come to California, Bob? 'I came to find some donkeys for a film I'm making!' Are you gonna play yourself in the film? 'No, I'm gonna play my mother ... We're gonna call it "Mother Revisited"!'

The LA press conference was the more ill-tempered, hence the ironic tone of *KRLA-Beat*'s pro-Dylan report (above). But even the largely good-humoured Bay Area affair – which began with future film director, George Lucas, admitting the cover to *Highway 61* bothered him – saw Dylan swim through a sea of confusion, with only the occasional life raft thrown him by the likes of Gleason and Ginsberg.

In fact, LA seemed to treat Dylan with greater disdain in general, Dylan checking out of the Chateau Marmont because, as he told Ginsberg, 'We had a lot of bullshit ... They didn't want me staying there.' The exclusive hotel probably didn't appreciate him playing a spinet piano Phil Spector had sent him over to use while living and dying in LA.

But if the hotel manager found Dylan's after-hours tinkling distracting, it was as nothing to the roar The Hawks made after the intermission of his Santa Monica concert, which prompted even an enthused Marlon Brando to inform the singer, 'When I was a young man ... I stood just a few feet away from a railroad track as a long freight train went roaring by. I made myself just stand there until it passed. That was the loudest thing I have ever witnessed. Until tonight.'

Dylan apparently responded, 'We usually play much harder than this,' a view endorsed by many a scribe in the next six months. Yet only Zelda Heller of the *Montreal Gazette* did enough research to ascertain it was quite deliberate: 'At first it seemed that the amplifiers ... had been accidentally turned up too loud. For it was impossible to hear anything he sang, or rather shouted, as if trying to be heard above them. But it seems that he had carefully prepared the balance and the volume at rehearsals during the afternoon.'

Dylan ended up talking with Brando for three hours, as well as discussing with Spector the idea of Phil producing the author of 'Howl'. If he was on the lookout for someone more technically minded than Johnston, Terry Melcher was in town and a certified Columbia producer. Perhaps the subject came up when Dylan popped in to see him record The Rising Sons, a band right up Dylan's alley, featuring Ry Cooder and Taj Mahal.

Afforded a four-day window between shows, he was enjoying hanging out with old friends like Barry McGuire (who thought he looked 'so fragile – so frail') and Billy James, while being feted by the likes of Brando. But when he returned to LA after a second set of three Bay Area shows, added due to popular demand, it was straight down to business: three shows in three days (17th–19th) preceded by an afternoon press conference.

This time he decided to rent the Castle, an old-style mansion in Hollywood, ensuring greater privacy and – on the evidence of the LA press conference, where he looks shattered, and not a little wasted – allowing him to party with the she-creatures of the Hollywood Hills.

The all-night parties evidently carried on for a few days after he concluded his public commitments, allowing the musicians and road manager Jonathan Taplin to relax. Possibly also there was Warhol 'superstar' Edie Sedgwick, whom Taplin remembered, 'because she was one of the few people who could stand up against [Dylan's] weird little numbers ... He was always in an adversar[ial] relationship with women. He tested people, perhaps to find out about himself.'

The reference to 'everybody that cares ... goin' up the Castle stairs' – in a song Dylan wrote immediately after his LA visit – has been taken as a direct reference to Edie – who was certainly in Dylan's company, this time in New York, on December 28th. She is a prime candidate for the woman in 'She's Your Lover Now', also on the receiving end of one of Dylan's 'weird little numbers'.

For a brief moment, Dylan seemed fascinated by this ill-fated starlet, whose ghostly presence also flits across 'Leopard-Skin Pill-Box Hat' and 'One Of Us Must Know', two other songs he wrote that January. He soon set out to record all three, starting with another marathon session on January 21st, intended to capture an epic counterpoint to 'Visions of Johanna', the full four-verse 'She's Your Lover Now'. It was not to be.

The 'She's Your Lover Now' session, now released – expletives deleted, but otherwise complete – on the eighteen-CD *Cutting Edge* set, is the car crash which convinces Dylan to jettison The Hawks and revert to The Cash Plan. The idea when he entered the studio, as he told WBAI DJ Bob Fass five days later, was 'to make an album' – though Lord knows how. He simply did not have the songs, nor a drummer he could rely on.

Yet it would be wrong to place the major portion of the blame for not realizing this masterful song at the drummer's door. It was Dylan who seemingly decided to make today's session an audition for Bobby Gregg's replacement.* Sandy Konikoff had been Robertson's suggestion, though in the latter's memoir he claims he 'could see the mismatch immediately. Sandy even tuned his small-combo drum set in a tight, jazzy sort of style.' Robertson went over during the session and warned him, 'Rule number one, don't swing. Never swing. Flighty fills and jazzy grooves don't work here.'

It is probably Konikoff who, after thirteen stillborn takes, summons up the nerve to say, 'It's not our fault it's not together, man. It's *different* every time.' Whereas it was Dylan who couldn't decide whether to do the song in 6/8 or 4/4 time. By then, he had blown up, not once, but twice; once at himself, bemoaning after take twelve, 'I'm losing the whole fucking song!' before laying into the band two takes later, 'I don't give a fuck if it's good or not, just play it together, make it all together. You don't have to play anything fancy ... Just one [take] that's together.'†

That 'one take together' would never come. When a close-but-no-cigar take fifteen breaks down on the final verse, he admits defeat, 'I can't do this.' He even apologises to the band, 'I'm sorry. It was my fault.' Rather than simply doing an insert for that final half-verse, he ushers everyone out the door and records the song solo, pouring out all his angst from a sad and lonesome day into a performance left unreleased (but not unbootlegged) for half a century.

---

* Gregg was essentially a session musician. The West Coast tour he had surely agreed to do as a favour to Dylan.
† The version of the 'complete session' on the eighteen-CD *Cutting Edge* boxed-set (2015) expurgates the part where Dylan loses his cool.

When sessions resumed the following Tuesday, he partly covered his bases. Temporarily returned to the fold are three key components from the *Highway 61* band – Bobby Gregg, Paul Griffin and Al Kooper – Dylan having effectively fired his touring band save for the one Hawk he wanted all along, Robertson, and bassist, Rick Danko. But if he hoped this might make things run smooth as a rhapsody, he was soon disabused.

It would take twenty-four takes, only five of them complete, to relate the next chapter in Her story, '(Sooner Or Later) One of Us Must Know'. That he was still stuck in the same adversarial relationship was clear from the song's final couplet, 'And I told you as you clawed out my eyes / that I really didn't mean to do you any harm.' Where he was dredging up such anger and pain from – just nineteen days after Sara gave birth to Jesse Byron Dylan – he thankfully never entrusted to analysis, à la Springsteen. All we can say is that even as he embraced fatherhood, he was determined to put *someone* straight, sooner rather than later.

A sequel of sorts to 'Can You Please ...', 'One Of Us Must Know' would be Dylan's fifth assault on the airwaves in a year. He promptly took an acetate of the completed song to WBAI to play to Bob Fass, who convinced him to stick around long enough to take a battery of calls from insomniacs across the five boroughs, including this fascinating exchange with Caller 35:

Caller 35: I guess you were probably being pretty sincere [back] then, and since then your music has changed ...
Bob Dylan: No, I haven't changed, you've changed. My music hasn't changed. I'm just using other people playing with me. Same music.
C35: Come on, don't goof on me.
BD: ... The songs are the same! [But] 'With God On Your Side' is contained in two lines of something like 'Desolation Row'. That whole song is in there in two lines. I mean, if you can't pick it out or single it out, that's not my problem.
C35: [So] it's a lot more subtle ...
BD: It's not more subtle! It's just more to the point. It doesn't spare you any time to string the thing together ...
C35: [So] when you were writing these more obvious protest [songs], like '[Only A] Pawn In Their Game' ...

BD: Well, I did it because that was the thing. That's what I was involved in. There's no big hoax or any kinda secret thing happening, or any kind of plan from the beginning. I [had] played rock'n'roll music when I was sixteen ... I quit doing it because I couldn't make it ... Old people that smoked cigars and hung around in certain bars uptown, around Tin Pan Alley; well, that used to be the music thing. But it's not that anymore. I don't know what I was thinking about two or three years ago. [Do] I have to explain it to you? It's not so complicated, man. You don't even have to ask why – it's very simple. But I just don't feel like sitting here talking about it right now.

If Dylan was prepared to jive callers, he was more honest with Fass, that long-standing late-night staple of the New York airwaves, admitting, 'We've just made ... a single ... [It's] the only thing we came out with in three days.' He had also decided his fourth single in seven months would be his last single-as-a-single – for now. He was tired of jumping on, and off, his own bandwagon. As he admitted in 2000, 'I didn't really like that sound ... folk-rock, whatever that was. I didn't feel that had anything to do with me. It got me thinking about the *Billboard* charts and the songs which become popular, which I hadn't thought [about] before.'*

The real problem was more prosaic. As he expressed it in 1969, 'Right after "Positively 4th Street", we cut some singles and they didn't really get off the ground ... They didn't even make it on the charts.' He meant 'Can You Please Crawl ...' and 'One Of Us Must Know', neither of which dented the Top Thirty, though Columbia – in their haste to hit the Christmas market – shipped the former in a scarcely believable eight days.

All of which makes Phil Ochs's comment to Dylan three weeks later at Jerry Schatzberg's photostudio – 'I don't think it'll sell' – a lot less clairvoyant. It already wasn't selling. Nonetheless, Schatzberg recalls, 'Dylan didn't take too kindly to it.' What probably really stung was being told, 'It's not as good as your old stuff', a barb that prompted Dylan to retort, 'You're crazy, man, it's a great song. You only know protest.' He sat there quietly seething until it was time to go clubbing,

---

* 'We tried making singles in New York. I'm not gonna make singles anymore' – London press conference, May 3rd, 1966.

at which point he offered Ochs a lift and then ordered him out of the limo, having come up with the perfect rebuttal: 'Phil, you're not a songwriter, you're just a journalist.' On his way to an Arthurian rendezvous with Andy Warhol and Edie Sedgwick, he'd decided Ochs was not hip enough to join such rarefied company.

Dylan hadn't expected his latest 45 to fare worse than 'Subterranean Homesick Blues'. What it presaged he didn't know, though one young fanzine editor took the view, 'The music business geniuses will probably look at the charts, notice how poorly Dylan's [new single] is doing, and announce: "Don't play it, the Dylan trend is over."' Such a notion, true or not, was worrying to Dylan and his label, who scheduled his next single – setting the world of women to rights – for Valentine's Day 1966, hoping to buck the downward trend. Ten days later, the prescient 'zine editor, eighteen-year-old Paul Williams – a sophomore at Swarthmore – dropped off the first two issues of his mimeographed 'zine, *Crawdaddy*, at the Philly theatre Dylan was playing that night.*

The first rockzine of its kind, *Crawdaddy* would tap into enough of a latent demand to convince Williams to quit formal education, and for a more businesslike 'rock fan' on the West Coast to form *Rolling Stone*, ultimately stealing his thunder. For now, it was Williams's 'Can You Please...' comment which struck a chord. When he returned to his dorm another student hollered the immortal line, 'Hey Williams!! Bob Dylan called you!':

> I returned the call ... Bob [had] read the magazines and liked them. I was invited to come to his hotel room that afternoon ... Dylan was friendly and open and talkative ... I didn't interview him – I didn't own a tape recorder – and I was so pleased by his friendliness and respect for what I was trying to do with my magazine, that I didn't want to spoil things by playing 'journalist'. He told me about obscure blues singers I should check out [and] mentioned his long-time interest in rock'n'roll as though affirming ... my thesis that rock music was as worthy of being talked about seriously as any other musical form.

---

* Also there that night was a nineteen-year-old Patti Smith, whose 1974 recollection was that 'he played with such urgency – as if he had a stilted lifeline'.

Far from always being a truculent traducer of doubting Thomases, Dylan continued reaching out to anyone who seemed sincere, even if they came in a suit and tie. When the thirty-year-old Martin Bronstein turned up to the Montreal show with Canadian Broadcasting Corporation credentials and a reel-to-reel, he might as well have been wrapped in swaddling:

> A new aural experience is the kind[est] way to describe the sound that met my ears backstage. Caterwauling is a little closer to my true feelings ... Center stage, bathed in a strong white spotlight, was this skinny Jewish kid with an Afro playing a guitar and producing a nasal ululation ... And then he would breathe into this thing strapped around his neck, creating a sort of musical asthma. I suddenly had the feeling that this was all a put-on, a huge practical joke. But then the song ended, and the audience reaction reached a decibel level that would have drowned out several Concordes. This was real ... and somehow it had passed me by.

Bronstein's curiosity had been piqued. Although he was previously as oblivious to Dylan as Jesse Byron currently was, he somehow avoided a verbal roasting as he ventured backstage to meet a Dylan patiently prepared to set him straight, even when the first question was: did you take your name from Dylan Thomas ('That's ... a rumor made up by people who like to simplify things'). It gets worse: Was 'Blowin' In The Wind' the 'breakthrough for you'? ('That wasn't it, really ... I would have to say ... "Like A Rolling Stone" because ... I'd never written anything like that before and it suddenly came to me that that was what I should do. I mean, nobody had ever done *that* before.'). Even his final question – 'When did you realize this success was happening to you?' – didn't ruffle the folk-rocker's feathers:

> **Bob Dylan**: Not too long ago really. I never really realized it before four, five, six months ago, that I couldn't go into a restaurant. I didn't really know it was that bad. It does tricks with your head where you can't go someplace, where everybody else can go and be left alone. I mean, you can't go down to the all-night drugstore and just sit there

all night, and my whole life I'[d been] used to staying out all night in public places. It's all gone now, you know.

Bronstein was one fortunate son. He encountered a Dylan neither manic from the methamphetamine, nor weighed down by the Nembutal his medicine man on 68th Street was now prescribing. But just to show what Dylan was up against, Bronstein's producer promptly rejected the resultant interview because 'the guy was practically inarticulate'. Actually, it was one of the more revealing interviews this Nobel writer ever gave.

Seemingly bereft of any national pride, the Canadian media were particularly unforgiving of the Helm-less Hawks, even if the *Ottawa Journal's* Sandy Gardiner sensed that he couldn't dent Dylan's unswerving self-belief: 'The Hawks played as though they were the featured attraction ... but you can be good without being loud. Dylan didn't seem to mind the racket. Despite all the commotion on stage, he remained nonchalant – a man wrapped up in his music, oblivious of what was around him.'

Still unwilling to meet naysayers halfway, Dylan had devised a way to make the experience doubly disorienting: opening with a brand-new song that had no fixed words but simply spat electricity at each and every madding crowd. At least Robertson was in on the joke, aware that making 'Tell Me, Momma' the opener 'meant not only were we going into hostile territory for our electric part of the show, but we were also starting the set with a funky, unfamiliar, aggressive and not particularly melodic tune'.

Konikoff, though, was struggling to hit Dylan's funny bone, and when during one particularly fraught soundcheck he tried to put a jazzy cymbal splash on 'One Too Many Mornings', he was told by the boss in no uncertain terms, 'Don't do that. Don't *ever* do that.' His days were numbered.

In fact, though Dylan continued to revel in the other Hawks' company, they were also deemed surplus to requirement when he started afresh on the album he had yet to get off the ground, having admitted to himself – and Robert Shelton's tape recorder – 'In ten recording sessions, man, we didn't get one song ... It was the band ... I didn't want to think that.'

If anyone else had been whispering in his ear to this effect, it was Bob Johnston. The drawling producer was determined to get him to come to Nashville and work with the A-team, even to the point where he was prepared to piss off New York's finest, one of whom recalled how Johnston's 'bias toward Nashville musicians ... became an underlying topic [throughout] the entire [*Highway 61*] session[s] ... He kept talking about how cool Nashville is ... [which] was a bit disparaging for us.' It could well be the real reason why Grossman came up to him and said, 'If you ever mention Nashville again, you're gone.'

It certainly wasn't because Dylan had an aversion to the idea. As early as December 1965, the *Herald Tribune*'s William Bender, clearly the recipient of inside info, announced the folk-rocker 'would like to take guitars, harmonicas and "electricity" to Nashville, Tennessee, to get what is known in the trade as the "Nashville Sound" – something that has to do with "presence" of a recording's sound, but that also depends on the superb country-Western and rhythm and blues instrumentalists who now gravitate to Nashville.' Dylan coming out of three days' recording in January with a single 'releasable' song was just the cue Johnston had been waiting for.*

On February 14th, Dylan flew into Nashville with Grossman and Al Kooper at his side. What he didn't perhaps realize was that this was a town built on tall stories and whopping lies – hence Johnston's affection for the place. By October, one Nashville musician was already describing Dylan's first day thus:

> Everybody was introduced and he asked us if we'd mind waiting a while. They had stopped at an airport in Richmond, and he didn't have a chance to finish his [new] material. He asked us if we'd mind waiting a minute while he worked on a song. So we all went out and let him have the studio to himself. He ended up staying in there working on that song for six hours ... He finally told us to come in and we cut it. It turned out to be fourteen minutes long ... The whole session followed a pattern like that. We'd go outside for a long time while he worked on a song, then we'd come back and record it.

---

* 'She's Your Lover Now' did make it to the so-called 'LA Band Tape', a widely bootlegged compilation of *Blonde On Blonde* out-takes, probably compiled in LA (see Paul Cable for contents). A copy ended up in Garth Hudson's archive, labelled accordingly.

The musician was Charlie McCoy. The song was 'Sad Eyed Lady Of The Lowlands'. One problem: Dylan didn't record said song on the 14th, but rather on the 16th, at about 4 a.m. (Al Kooper calls it 'the definitive version of what 4 a.m. sounds like.' No argument here.)

On day one, Dylan recorded '4th Time Around', 'Visions Of Johanna' and 'Leopard-Skin Pill-Box Hat' and was done by 9.30 p.m. 'Visions Of Johanna', a strong candidate for his finest recorded performance, was captured in one breathless seven-minute take, after just a couple of false starts. '4th Time Around' could have been the same, if only Dylan had put his trust in the musicians and recorded an insert to the second take, after blowing the last three lines of an otherwise near-perfect version.

Instead, it took him another eighteen takes to get back there, thus setting the pattern for the sessions to come. Songs were either captured quickly, with nary a pause – like 'Visions' and 'Sad Eyed Lady' – or required dental equipment, like '4th Time Around', 'Stuck Inside Of Mobile' and 'Leopard-Skin Pill-Box Hat', the last of which he would have to revisit for a third time in March, after spending a whole session trying to graft on a knock-knock joke and then having the gall to inform the musicians, 'Hey, we're spending too much time on it.' For Al the Amaneunsis, the real eye-opener was how the A-team took everything thrown at them in their stride:

Al Kooper: In New York where I was raised, all the sessions I played on … it was three songs in three hours. I had never seen what they did in Nashville. They just hired the musicians and they were booked until we were done that day, or night, or whenever it was. They didn't have any other distractions, there was no breaks, just whatever it was and I had never worked like that in the studio. [2010]

Which isn't to say the musicians weren't taken aback when Dylan, having exhausted all the songs he'd written in advance by the end of day one, spent three sessions – booked and paid for, from the 15th into the 16th – writing a set of lyrics he later claimed he wrote after 'staying up for days in the Chelsea Hotel'.

Keyboardist Bill Atkins can still 'remember him sitting at the piano in deep, deep meditative thought. He was creating, writing. So we were just on hold as musicians, on the payroll, on a master session

... just hanging out.' McCoy was similarly stunned: 'We sat there from 2 p.m. [actually, 6 p.m.] till 4 a.m. the next morning and we never played a note. This was unheard of. Everybody was on the clock.'

But this also told the musicians, here was someone extra-special. As Atkins notes, 'That's the kind of budget they had for him.' At least the result, when it came, was a song which would occupy an entire LP side, the seductive, ever so slightly soporific 'Sad Eyed Lady'. Now they just needed to get it on tape. And it was with this in mind that Johnston gave Nashville's most highly paid, ultra-competent musicians their first and last pep talk:

> I told everybody if they quit playing they were gone ... because I could overdub anybody but Dylan. But if you quit with him ... he'[ll] go to the count and play something else. So they came out ... And Dylan said, 'It goes like this. C, D, G' ... And he went out there and started counting off ... 1, 2, with that foot, and it was gone. When we got through, he said 'Let's hear it back.' ... [It was] fifteen, sixteen minutes.

If the pep talk was meant to put the fear of God in the musicians, it succeeded. As McCoy avers, 'Everybody's sitting there [think]ing, please don't let me make a mistake. He just started playing it and kind of left it up to us to decide what to do.' Drummer Ken Buttrey suggests there came a point, about three-quarters of the way through take one, when fear turned to sheer incredulity:

> He ran down a verse and a chorus ... and said, 'We'll do a verse and a chorus then I'll play my harmonica thing. Then we'll do another verse and chorus and I'll play some more harmonica, and we'll see how it goes from there.' That was his explanation of what was getting ready to happen ... Not knowing how long this thing was going to be, we were preparing ourselves dynamically for a basic two- to three-minute record. Because records just didn't go over three minutes ... After about ten minutes of this thing we're cracking up at each other, at what we were doing. I mean, we peaked five minutes ago. Where do we go from here?

Remarkably, the song was cut in three takes, all complete, all with that same druggy vibe. In fact, Johnston admitted he became a little worried: Dylan 'never left the studio ... and he kept ordering milkshakes and malts, candy bars ... I thought, "Well goddamn, he's a junkie." But he wasn't, he was just gettin' energy.' One somehow doubts any such combination, minus 'powerful medicine', could have kept Dylan going through not one, but two *all-night* sessions.

In the case of 'Stuck Inside Of Mobile', they also started recording at 4 a.m. But this time it took three hours and twenty takes to recreate the perfection of 'Visions'. It meant just four tracks from four days' work, though this amounted to thirty minutes of music. Add 'One Of Us Must Know' to the equation, and he had an album as long as *Pet Sounds* – an artefact the Beach Boys had been working on for the past seven months – and twice as futuristic.

When Dylan rejoined The Hawks, cooling their Cuban heels in New York, he was audibly enthused by his experience, telling a receptive Robbie, 'These guys didn't know me, they didn't know this music – I went in there, and they just all get in a huddle, and they figure it out so quickly and come up with an arrangement, a whole idea for the song.' So enthused was he that he began making plans to return in three weeks to 'complete' the album – a fateful decision with unforeseen consequences.

This time he co-opted Robertson. According to Kooper, it was 'for [Dylan's] comfort level, rather than just go[ing] in there cold'. He could have raised that comfort level even more by arriving with some completed songs. Instead, he brought mostly scraps of songs, half-formed verses and a list which read:

(i)   'if nothing comes outa this, you'll soon know' song ('Pledging My Time')
(ii) 'guilty for just being there' song ('Temporary Like Achilles')
(iii) 'i did it so you wouldn't have to (do it)' song ('You Go Your Way')
(iv) 'White Love' song
(v)   'Yellow Monday' song*

---

* A hoard of *Blonde On Blonde* manuscripts and typescripts, all from the March 1966 set of songs, were auctioned piecemeal in the late 1980s and early 1990s. Clearly genuine, they nonetheless lack any provenance. In 2020 a set of copyright sheets for the March songs, hand-corrected by Dylan, also emerged.

Somehow he spun all this into eight songs for eternity at his Nashville motel. To help things along, he had a piano put in his hotel room; not for him, but so that Kooper could 'go up to his room and he would teach me the song ... I would play the song over and over for him and he would write the lyrics.' The first result, 'Absolutely Sweet Marie', started proceedings in style, highlighting Kooper's contribution to the 'wild mercury sound'.

By now, Kooper was a trusted lieutenant: 'We had spent a lot of time together. Off-hours time together. Just sitting around bars and shit like that. Going to the movies.' It became his job to 'talk to the musicians', Bloomfield having long resigned that commission, as well as making suggestions in the studio, one of which was to add horns to the 'i did it so you wouldn't have to' song:

> **Al Kooper**: Dylan refused to overdub things. He just wanted to play it live right there, ... [But] I said to Bob, 'Horns would be really nice on this.' And he said, 'Well, there's no horns here.' [At which point,] Charlie McCoy says, 'I play trumpet.' So Bob said, 'I don't want to overdub anything,' [and] Charlie said, 'I can play the bass and the trumpet at the same time.' And Bob and I looked at each other, and Bob [started] laughing, [to which] Charlie said, 'No really, I can,' [and promptly] played the bass and the trumpet [parts] at the same time ... Our jaws hit the floor. [2010]

As the sessions proceeded, McCoy would become an increasingly important factor, even playing harmonica on 'Obviously 5 Believers' because Dylan 'couldn't sing and play [the riff] at the same time, [and] what he wanted – the riff on it – is not what he does'.

When Dylan played the real McCoy 'Rainy Day Women' on the piano, Charlie told him, 'Goddamn, that sounds like a Salvation Army band.' It prompted Dylan to enquire if he could find a slide trombone player who could emulate the 'Sally Army' on the intro in the middle of the night. He had someone there inside seventeen minutes, they rehearsed the song once, cutting it in a single take.

And a single, it soon was, Columbia pulling out all the stops to get the song out in a fortnight. This time they struck gold, with what was little more than a novelty song, outselling even 'Like A Rolling Stone' stateside. Twenty years later Dylan finally explained to Bob Fass what he meant by 'Everybody must get stoned':

> It's like, when you go against the tide. You might in different times find yourself in an unfortunate situation and do what you believe in. Sometimes people just take offence to that ... Throughout history ... people have taken offence to who[ever] come[s] out with a different viewpoint on things. And being stoned is a way of saying that.

But a far better indicator for the rest of the forthcoming album's contents was to be found on the B-side, recorded two days earlier, after a single breakdown and one full-blown rehearsal. It left one eyewitness, bluegrass picker Pete Rowan, unimpressed, turning to Johnston and saying, 'I don't know why he keeps using those same old chord changes and ... rock'n'roll things over and over again.' The slightly manic blues jam was at this juncture called 'What Can You Do For My Wigwam'. Within two takes, it became the slow and easy 'Pledging My Time'.

Most of the other songs also came quickly, whether by luck or judgement, or a combination of the two, with six songs cut in a marathon session that ran from 6 p.m. on the 9th through 7 a.m. It included that single-take 'Rainy Day Women' and a one-stop 'Leopard-Skin Pill-Box Hat', with Robertson unleashing a coruscating lead honed over weeks of live performance. The contagion to get things done affected even Johnston, who before 'Obviously 5 Believers' tells the musicians, 'All the way through. One take is all we need on this, man.' It took two takes, both complete, but they sure weren't hanging about.

The only song that really suffered from the previous month's All Night Blues was 'Just Like A Woman', mainly because it clearly wasn't finished, either lyrically or melodically, when Dylan started teaching it to the band at 2 p.m. on March 8th. Ten hours and eighteen takes later, after a brief interlude looking for a wigwam, he had that rat-a-tat opening, a well-crafted cryptic bridge, an opening couplet for the ages ('Nobody feels any pain / Tonight as I stand inside the rain ...') and a portrait of someone (beginning with E?) composed of 'fog, amphetamines and pearls'. Jettisoned along the way was the *ménage à trois* element there in the original typescript – 'how come you both lied to me?'

Before he left for St Louis, a delighted Dylan took McCoy aside and informed him 'he'd probably cut everything he did down here from now on'. McCoy took this as a momentary enthusiasm, but Dylan would not record albums anywhere else for another four years. As of now, he had a single to okay and a return to Dylanmania – in both its positive and negative guises – to negotiate.

2.7

March to May 1966: I've Been All Around This World

He will make attempts to like people even when it's obvious to him that they dislike him. His evaluation of silly questions and a questioner's evaluation of a silly question may be different, [but] I think it's ludicrous for one human being to ask another human being: 'Don't you have any feelings?'

Billy James, December 1965

Journalist: How much money do you make, Bob?
Bob Dylan: I don't know how much money I make and I don't ever want to find out. When I want some money, I just go and ask for it, and then I use it. When I want some more I go and ask for some more.

LA press conference, December 16th, 1965

Dylan twisted my head all around. He made me realize that you didn't have to write only 'my boyfriend's gone' songs; you could write things with meaning and emotion.

Jackie Deshannon, September 1965

I used to remember Albert as a nice-looking businessman, the kind of middle-aged man you would meet in a decent restaurant in the garment district. Then, a while after he signed Dylan, I met him again. I just couldn't believe what had happened. 'Albert!' I screamed, when I finally recognized him, 'What has Bobby done to you?'

Gloria Stavers, editor of *16* magazine

*

The pace was now unrelenting. Still playing triple clusters of shows, Dylan flew direct from Nashville to St Louis, for the first of three consecutive gigs across Missouri, Nebraska and Colorado, then back to New York, where he met with Jerry Schatzberg to pick an album cover. Meanwhile Grossman took a meeting with Columbia, who thought it was about a new contract. Actually, Albert was still fuming about the old one, asking when a previously agreed bump in Dylan's royalties, from 4% to 5%, would be honoured.

Columbia, who had been pushing for talks about Dylan's next contract since early February, were stymied. They thought they had got away with it, it having been three years since they verbally agreed to the royalty hike, which was supposed to be 'retroactive to the commencement of his contract' and was a condition of Grossman *not* challenging the October 1962 letter of reaffirmation Dylan misguidedly signed. Three years later, it was hardly an insignificant sum. Columbia, though, weren't about to start honouring verbal promises. As far as the label was concerned, they weren't worth the paper they were written on.

Ordinarily, Grossman would have been a fearsome adversary. But while Dylan and Grossman continued demonstrating the ball-juggling skills they'd acquired in the last year, they had taken their eyes off the main prize. Specifically, one or both of them made a huge error of judgement, agreeing to the first set of *Blonde On Blonde* sessions starting just fourteen days before the final year of Dylan's original Columbia contract began.

Because, if Dylan *had* held back those February and March tracks, they would have constituted the fulfilment of his Columbia contract, something he could have insisted upon *if* Grossman and/or his legal eagle, David Braun, had advised him to hold Columbia to ransom before they did the same to them. But Dylan wasn't thinking about the loot. It seems he'd been telling the truth the previous December, when he sat in one of Columbia's LA Studios and said, 'I don't know how much money I make and I don't ever want to find out.'

He relied on Grossman to handle the folding stuff. And handle it he did. Eighteen years later, in the inevitable legal deposition when Dylan countersued his ex-manager, the now-business-savvy artist would mount the famous I Was An Idiot defence: 'Grossman told me that I could rely on him, and I did rely on him, to read documents, to explain them to me, and to tell me if it was all right to sign them.'

Back in March 1966, Dylan was more concerned about what artwork to wrap his latest offering in. His most recent photo session had been a month earlier. He wanted to see what Jerry had snapped. When Schatzberg produced a sequence shot in Manhattan's meat-packing district when it was nine below zero, Dylan said, 'I like that slightly blurry one,' even though it was that way because it was taken while both of them froze right to the bone. Schatzberg admits, 'I would never have suggested to Columbia that out-of-focus image' (due to past experience with record companies). Once again, the decision-maker would be asked if the blurriness was meant to 'represent a drug trip?'

Dylan also insisted the cover shot was spread across the fold, front and back, and for the album's title to appear only on the spine (a trick he probably picked up from The Rolling Stones, who'd adopted this Andrew Oldham innovation on their first two UK albums). By now, he knew he wanted it to be a double album, even if he did so by stretching a point, making the thirteen-minute 'Sad Eyed Lady' occupy a whole side, when The Rolling Stones' latest, *Aftermath* – released mid-April, a month before *Pet Sounds* and two months before *Blonde On Blonde* – included the eleven-minutes-plus 'Goin' Home' alongside five more tracks on a single side.

Ordinarily, Columbia would now have gone into overdrive to get Dylan's album into the racks by the end of April. But it seems he wasn't happy with how the rough mixes sounded and wanted to remix some tracks in LA, when he got there the first week in April. Even then, it took two and a half months to get it out. Was the ensuing delay a case of 'by th[is] time Dylan had the power', or were Columbia hoping to get a third single into the shops before the release of what was a big commercial gamble?*

For now, the album was on hold, as Grossman – wheeling and dealing on other media fronts – allowed its release to drift into the summer. By then, he hoped Dylan might have not one but two films

---

* In 1966 double albums that were neither anthologies nor concerts were rare beasts. Columbia hedged their bets in some countries by also issuing the album in two individual volumes. The domestic sales through September 1973 of *Blonde On Blonde* (312,656) versus *Highway 61* (430,705) confirm the commercial challenge.

ready for release, having signed a deal with CBS's main TV rivals, ABC, to do a TV special called *The World Of Bob Dylan* for a $200,000 advance. He had even set up an independent production company, Hamlet & Trinien Productions, Inc., which agreed 'to produce and furnish for exclusive telecast ... an original one-hour color film special ... for telecast during the 1966-67 telecast season. Said special program shall star Bob Dylan and ... also feature guest performers ... Messrs Rasky and Dylan are approved as producer-director and writer respectively.'

Harry Rasky, who had just finished a film about Castro's Cuba, was apparently ABC's suggested director. According to Rasky in 1998, 'They chose me as a free-minded guy, but the minute Dylan found out I had been asked by ABC to do the film, he thought I was the voice of authority.'

Rasky would have to be replaced. But by whom? Fortunately, when Dylan arrived in LA at the end of March – after three north-east shows brought the curtain down on six months criss-crossing North America before hitting alien shores – he was met by a familiar face, who wanted to show him last year's film. After two screenings of a rough cut for *dont look back*, Dylan mustered the nerve to ask Pennebaker to join him in the bear's pit again:

> We had a meeting in Los Angeles and Bob said, 'You got your movie and now I want you to help me make mine ... [] ... but this time there's gonna be none of this artsy fartsy ... *cinéma-vérité* shit. This is gonna be a *real* movie.' He had some kind of vision of it, but no idea how to get it.

Despite some reservations, the documentary-maker agreed to make his film for him, and to meet him in Sweden at the end of April. One down, two to go. Now Dylan just needed a drummer and a wizard soundman, and they were ready for Oz. A leaf through his back pages got him the men he wanted, starting with Johnny Rivers' drummer, Mickey Jones, who'd been on his radar since Rivers opened the Whisky A Go-Go in February 1964. Rivers recalls Dylan 'would come upstairs to the dressing rooms ... and shoot the bull with the guys in the band', eyeing up his intended target.

Bob had phoned Mickey personally from New York with an offer he couldn't refuse – but almost did. Weeks later, Dylan recalled Jones's response: 'I been playing with Johnny for a while, and my hair's a bit long at the back, I hope you don't mind.' He'd just about stopped laughing when he touched down in LA. For Dylan, it was all about the drums. As he said in 1997, 'My guitar playing just plays with the drums. In my group, the drummer is the lead guitar player. I play on the structure of where the drum plays.'

On March 31st Jones met the others at Columbia's Studio D, to rehearse for a week before blasting off across the Pacific. But if Dylan was about to let Jones off the leash, he also needed a soundman who took no prisoners. The man whom he called had already worked for a number of Grossman acts and knew Dylan from his younger days, having recorded the Second Gaslight Tape. He immediately got what Dylan had in mind:

> **Richard Alderson**: [Dylan]'s whole idea on that tour was to hit everybody over the head with the loudest rock'n'roll band that he could do … People were not understanding what he was doing. So he figured he would pound them over the head. That's why he took … Mickey Jones – because he was a loud, powerful drummer. Regardless of what anyone says, that is why Mickey Jones was the drummer … It's the only time that happens with Dylan. Mickey was just too much of a redneck to give a shit – he just plays the way he plays. [And] because he was loud … and aggressive … it made for great music.

It helped that The Hawks had finally embraced Dylan's performance aesthetic en masse. As Robertson later said, 'By the time we did … Australia and Europe … we had discovered whatever this thing was. It was not light, it was not folky. It was very dynamic, very explosive and very violent.' It was just a case of integrating Jones into the brotherhood.

When not breaking in Mr Jones, approving the final mixes of *Blonde On Blonde* or okaying Pennebaker's vision of a tour from another lifetime, Dylan tapped into the West Coast scene at its most vibrant. On April 2nd, he turned up to see Tiny Tim perform with *The Phantom Cabaret Strikes Again*, in the company of Barry McGuire. As Tim recorded in his diary, Dylan 'autographed my copy of "Positively 4th Street" … as I sang it in front of him', minus the sneer. The following night he caught The Byrds at The Trip, riding eight miles high despite their latest 45 being banned for being a 'drurg song', their protestations notwithstanding.

He was still enjoying being the public Dylan, and when *Teen* columnist/photographer Earl Leaf invited himself to join the *Teen* star, 'sitting at a far dark booth with [his] cronies', he got into the kind of verbal sparring match he planned to transport to the boxing arenas of Australia. Leaf's contemporary account, for all its self-aggrandizement, has an authentic ring:

> He claims to be indifferent to what people write or say about him, but he listened all ears when I repeated some of the Dylan stories and opinions I'd written in these columns. He took it as praise when I said he had a distorted, deceptive and devious mind that races along a slippery track ... I reminded him he mocked or duped his interviewers [at the LA press conference in December] with wry fabrications ... 'Yeah, man, that's right! Some of their campy and very personal questions blew my mind,' he allowed. 'Say, if I laid nine put-ons and one truth on you, could you tell which is which?' 'Sure, man,' I boasted, 'I've been alerted to your wavelength.' ... We hollered into each other's ears about music, poetry, people, freedom, loneliness, faith, honor, ethics and philosophy.

Once again, Dylan had rented the Castle from owner Tom Law. But this time Tom's wife, Lisa, a respected LA photographer, got to snap Dylan in Hollywood. She even witnessed that mind working overtime, offering the one anecdotal piece of evidence that Dylan was still tapping out lyrics, his methodology unchanged: 'He was writing all the time. I photographed his desk with his typewriter. He didn't crumple papers up and throw them in the trash or I would've kept them! He would type a song and then write over it and add things.'

Any such papers would not survive the world tour. Nor were any of them offered to other interested parties, or heard outside hotel rooms and soundchecks. Instead, Dylan planned to play others the songs he'd just recorded in Nashville. On his final night in LA, he returned to the Whisky looking to burn his last LA candle for a while, in the company of Tom and Lisa Law, Robbie Robertson, Mickey

Jones and D. A. Pennebaker, each of whom has a different version of what happened 'The Night Dylan Met Otis Redding'.*

Although everyone agrees Dylan went backstage, according to Lisa Law, 'Bob asked Otis if he wanted one of his songs'; Mickey Jones has Bob telling Otis, 'Man, I've got a song that's perfect for you,' before picking up a guitar and playing Otis 'Just Like A Woman'; Robbie has 'Bob play[ing] the acetate of "Just Like A Woman" ... [Otis] absolutely loved it'; while D. A. Pennebaker suggests: 'Otis wanted to get Dylan ... Anything that connected with Dylan, [he] would have done at the drop of a hat.' Take your pick, *Rashomon*.

Suffice to say, though Otis really dug what he heard, he never recorded the song, even if Dylan left him one of a plentiful supply of acetates he was carrying. At least the folk-rocker had finally okayed an album he hoped would keep him ahead of the stiff competition, as 1966 threatened to become The Year of The Rock Album.

He was also steeling himself for two months away from Sara and son, and forty nights without sleep, all for the cause of the Big Boo. The carousel was due to begin again with a dry-run in Hawaii and two weeks in Australia, an English-speaking enclave still stuck in the fifties, with a thriving folk scene and a tabloid media which made England's look streetwise. Both tribes thought the Dylan who landed at Sydney airport on April 12th had a target on his forehead. The few eyewitnesses sympathetic to the artist could only watch and learn.

Australian actor Lex Marinos was one of those who loved every minute of the ensuing press conference as 'Dylan's defiant anti-publicity stance ... bewildered and outraged the local chapter of the fourth estate. At the time, the roles of interviewer and interviewee were well defined and ... suddenly this little smartarse decided to change the rules [as] he constructed and deconstructed and reconstructed his image himself.'

Equally delighted was an anonymous reporter who championed the singer's combative responses for the US-based *Datebook*: 'Bless Dylan, our ambassador of the put-on. When he arrived in Australia on his recent round-the-world tour, he was met with the usual mob of square reporters with the usual nowhere questions ... So these

---

* Although Otis was the headliner, Dylan would have been just as keen to see Taj Mahal, the opening act.

reporters make this great fuss over his arrival, then they come on like they've been living in caves for three years. What does Dylan do? He puts them on.'

Most of the local reporters, though, bristled at Dylan's verbal barbs and impenetrable wall of otherworldliness, glinting off shades which perennially shut out the light. Uli Schmetzer of the *Sydney Sun* recalls being 'furious [that] Dylan did not take me serious[ly] but made fun of all my questions. He was probably high on something.'

Schmetzer only found out that the American had plenty of people fighting his corner the next day, when 'a delegation of Dylan fans, all girls, turned up at the *Sun* office, when I [just about] talked them out of thrashing me'. Lines were being drawn, and could not be erased, save by Generation X. However, when a journalist showed he, or she, was on his wavelength, Dylan allowed a glimpse inside the darkness of his room. Thus the *Sydney Morning Herald*'s Craig McGregor, after writing a witty piece about Dylan's 'anti-interview' at the airport, got invited backstage during the first show's intermission, only to receive quite a shock:

> He is squatting down on his heels on the floor, electric guitar already around his neck. ... Dylan mumbles hello. Yeah, he dug what I wrote. People don't understand what he's into. He's got the band because the songs needed it; he wanted something to fill in the spaces between the words. He is jumpy, nervous, unable to keep still ... It occurs to me, for the first time, that he is stoned, and not on grass: he isn't anything like the calm, self-possessed guy I saw at the airport ... [Rather, he is] edgy, twitchy, hyperactive: 'Hey, come up to [the] hotel room after tomorrow's show [*sic*], huh?' He's got the acetates on his next album, he wants me to hear them.

McGregor was a rare outsider, allowed to see Dylan emerging from his acoustic chrysalis. But to those who saw the change nightly, it was always something to behold. They included the not-so-little drummer boy, who noticed right away how he would start 'to get pumped up. He ... could not wait to get out there and rock'n'roll ... Sometimes we all got off in a rather unusual way ... Our attitude was *fuck* the audience.'

As far as the soundman was concerned, the change simply highlighted a shuffling of the singer's multiple personae: 'It was like he changed personalities from one half of the concert to the next. He came out a different guy. He acted different. He carried himself different. It was amazing. Really animated – jumping around and carrying on, obviously trying to incite the crowd to [display] the very thing he's annoyed by.'

Despite setting both Sydney shows in a boxing arena, Alderson was delighted by the results: 'That was the biggest place of all, but [it] wasn't bad[-sounding], considering the stage rotated. Most of the places in Australia we didn't have problems with the volume. They were [okay] acoustically.'

The professional soundman's point of view was not entirely shared by those out front. Audience member George Westbrook remembers, 'The PA system was much larger and more potent than anything seen or heard in Australia before. There's no doubt that the volume took the audience by surprise. ... [Some]one said, "I'd like to kill that drummer."' Possibly that someone was the *Australian*'s Edgar Waters, whose opening-night review marked both Jones and Alderson down for murder city night:

> The drummer is odd man out in the rock group ... He bashed away at drum and cymbal with a solid left and a solid right, as though he hated his instruments. He makes Ringo Starr seem to have, by comparison, the subtlety of an Indian tabla player. The guitarists were with the drummer in spirit, and so was the sound control man, who stood a few feet away from where I sat, with the pleasure shining through his attempts to keep a deadpan face, as the solid waves of sound battered at my eardrums until they throbbed and ached (and went on throbbing for half an hour after it was all over).

Another punter, David Pepperell, recalled that even in cosmopolitan Sydney, 'the booing and catcalling was ... vicious during the second set ... It was a rump of a couple of hundred people [but] ... it was organised. They were all sitting in the same place ... As soon as he walked out with the band they started yelling and booing ... Others in the crowd were trying to drown them out.' Dylan didn't need any Prussian Guard to come to his aid. He knew he'd win the battle of Sydney, as was confirmed by the PA tape officially released in 2015. Even at this formative stage, the Mk 4 Hawks' sound is a primal roar, against which protestations become mere background static, signifying nought.

Afterwards, Dylan agreed to attend a party at local academic Don Henderson's house. Henderson's partner, Margaret Kitamura, remembers, 'Dylan just turned up with his band and ... acoustic guitar. He asked us straight away, "How was it? How was it?" We said, "It was great." ... "Too loud, though, huh? Too loud?"' Was he genuinely curious, or just goading the great and the good of academia, a demographic of whom he remained innately suspicious? Probably a bit of both.

The rest of the evening, thankfully, passed off without further incident. But Australia's folkies were just warming up. Two nights later, in Brisbane, Frank Neilsen witnessed a repeat performance from Dylan's side of the divide: 'There was a large contingent of ardent folk addicts, part of the [Brisbane] Folk Centre ... There was a lot of booing, catcalling and ridiculous behaviour. And people like us were yelling, "Shut up." ... It was almost fisticuffs ... The dissent all came from one direction behind us, one big group.'

Such orchestrated antipathy would become a feature of the whole world tour, mainland Europe excepted. But they knew not their enemy. Dylan was not about to turn it down, or change course midstream.

By the time he got to Melbourne on April 17th, he was enjoying himself – perhaps even a little too much. By now the whole druggy vibe permeating the artist and crew was attracting the unwelcome attention of reactionary authorities, and when road manager Bill Avis picked up the chief of police's (possibly underage) daughter at a party after the first show, Dylan came dangerously close to having someone 'put his ass in stir'. According to Robertson, it was Grossman who saved him by hiding 'the chunk of hash we had' in 'his British gentleman's hat'. Maymudes, on the other hand, gives Dylan the credit for using his head – and his hat:

> Bob was really the prize catch – if they could snag a huge celebrity on drug charges, they would be local heroes ... We all headed out to Bob's [room]. I had no chance to warn him ... I started pounding on the door ... I spoke quickly, 'Bob, look, [Bill] got busted with some hashish, and the police want to search your room.' ... Bob turned around and walked to the side table. He grabbed something and dropped it into

his hat, right as the cops pushed the door open and pressed in. Bob put the hat on his head just as the police began their search of the room. They didn't find anything.

According to local poet Adrian Rawlins – who had just left Dylan's hotel room, high as a kite but senses intact – 'Albert [simply] took the remaining hash and threw it down the incinerator.' Maymudes' roommate, Alderson, also had the presence of mind to flush his own supply down the toilet. But just a a few hours earlier, all of the superhuman crew had been in Dylan's hotel suite, party to tonight's descent into regions unknowable in the company of Rawlins, who later wrote:

> He taught us to smoke hashish pure, over silver foil over whisky; we drank whisky, then tea (brought in elaborate silver service), then Coca-Cola, then water. Dylan and I talked for over six hours. ... He talked and talked, telling me intimate details about his childhood, about his cultural affiliations, about his world view: he mentioned visiting Henry Miller at his home in Pacific Palisades; how he felt that the older writer mocked him; he [told me], 'I don't like Ernest Hemingway ... I don't like *Time* magazine.' ... About six-thirty in the morning he said he had a song he wanted me to hear. He took the borrowed guitar and played 'Sad Eyed Lady Of The Lowlands' ... [after being] most loquacious about 'Desolation Row', a still epochal song inspired by Jack Kerouac's *Desolation Angels*. Initially, the song began as sixteen pages of lyrics. Bob set himself the task of reducing this ... to four pages without any loss of meaning.*

In what became the Antipodean pattern, Rawlins had first shown his face at Melbourne's airport press conference, a relatively sedate affair, save for one of Dylan's amusing little riffs on pop art, which according to him 'lasted only three months. After three months people stopped painting soup-can labels. After three [more] months people stopped buying paintings of soup-can labels. After [another] three

---

* Rawlins may well mean 'Like A Rolling Stone', unless Dylan applied the technique to both songs.

months people stopped buying soup! In fact, they picketed the supermarkets. I know, 'cause I was there.'

Rawlins, Australia's answer to Allen Ginsberg, did as McGregor had, striking up a conversation with someone in Dylan's retinue – in this instance, Robbie – while the main man plucked metaphorical wings off poorly briefed pressmen. Once Robertson vetted him, and checked out a recent drug charge for possession, he was introduced to Dylan, after which he became tour guide, court jester and pot buddy – until the bust, for which his own recent brush with the law was somehow held responsible, not Avis's stupidity.

When Rawlins returned to the hotel mid-afternoon on the 20th, he found Dylan 'highly agitated' and the bonds he thought they'd formed the previous evening sundered. Even a glowing review of the Melbourne shows in *Farrago* could not mend the breach. Indeed, when Rawlins forwarded said piece to Dylan in Britain three weeks later, the reply he received read: 'I really resent the lame and pleading tone of that piece of shit you sent me.' So much for shared wavelengths.

Bust or no bust, on the evidence of that evening's (broadcast) acoustic set – a legendary 1974 TMQ bootleg – the all-important supply chain remained intact. Dylan was pilled to the gills and yet utterly mesmeric. In the second half, he again came to life, dedicating 'Thin Man' to Mrs Sphinx and eliciting teenybopper screams for 'Just Like Tom Thumb's Blues'. One student reviewer still insisted he heard 'the sound of footsteps heading towards the exit ... throughout the "folk-rock" part of the performance'.

Dylan was nearing the end of his Aussie jaunt – or so he thought. When their flight to Stockholm, the day after their April 23rd concert in Perth, was cancelled, he found himself with forty-eight unscheduled hours of downtime in which to rest and regenerate – or get more fried than your average plantain. He chose the latter, attended by another would-be acolyte looking to bask in the afterglow of his invisible halo.

Rosemary Gerrette, identified by Scaduto merely as 'an Australian actress', was at Perth's press conference because she aspired to be a writer and wished to see for herself these 'reporters who ask ad infinitum questions like what do God, people, life mean to him'. Actually, the now-ubiquitous press conference provided some of the more light-hearted exchanges between Dylan and a still-uncomprehending Antipodean media:

> **Q**: You don't dress very traditional. Why do you wear your hair long?
> **BD**: For the same reason that you wear yours short ...
> **Q**: What about Allen Ginsberg? Do you count him among your friends, and an influence?
> **BD**: Yes, he's a good friend of mine. I like what he does.
> **Q**: Is he still held in such high esteem as he was when he was first published?
> **BD**: Yes. He's a man held in high esteem, but he's not really accepted by the literary world. But he will be in time. He's the best poet, to me, anywhere in the world. He's certainly better than any of the Russian poets or the other European poets. He writes on paper. I'm not a poet, you see. I feel that to write poetry, it should sing off the paper. I don't have to worry about that because I sing it to myself. So I can't really be classified as a poet.
> **Q**: Songs like 'Ballad Of A Thin Man' and 'Just Like Tom Thumb's Blues' – do they mean anything to you at all?
> **BD**: 'Just Like Tom Thumb's Blues' means more to me than, say, 'Times They Are A-Changin''. Although I don't put down any of these other songs I wrote. I know I wrote them and I know nobody else did write them.

Gerrette was determined to pen a column or seven that would give Dylan the benefit of the doubt and declare his genius. But even the insightful piece she wrote for the *Canberra Times*, 'Dylan – Man In A Mask', was necessarily whitewashed, omitting her private conviction that 'Dylan was on some kind of drugs. He said it was pot. [When] I said to him I had never had marijuana, [he was shocked] ... I don't think he [had] ever met anyone who was so not into anything.' Little did she realize, the pot was a mere palliative. More 'powerful medicine' was needed.

An old friend of Rawlins, Gerrette was the last Australian allowed through that pot-infused portal. Summoned to Dylan's hotel after the concert, she 'sat for six hours while Dylan played me ... a pile of unreleased acetate[s], which he carries around with him ... He made me ask at once if I missed a word or its meaning ... He knew every word ... He loved those songs ... On stage he didn't seem to be trying. Yet he asked me eagerly what I thought of his concert.'

If this was one ritual she got to share with McGregor and Rawlins (and others in Europe), far rarer was the opportunity Dylan granted her 'to listen to a composing session. Countless cups of tea ... Things happened, and six new songs were born. The poetry seemed already to have been written.' All of this she wrote about, as well as Dylan's ongoing battle to cope with his new-found fame. He told her, 'People don't value their obscurity. They don't know what it's like to have it taken away,' before insisting 'he was interested in [the] Self ... You go down into the deeper self and go through it all and come out the other side, and then you're going to *know*.' Rimbaud went to Abyssinia, Dylan came to Australia. Both ended up 'dealing with slaves'.

She also omitted the part where Dylan justified his 'truth attacks', saying it was his way of 'being honest ... telling things and expressing things the way you really want to ... He was saying that small unkindnesses were not necessary, but when it came to things that involved your feelings, things you had to tell people, then it was okay to be cruel, if necessary ... He was saying he could be cruel – we should all be cruel – to show someone what was wrong with [his or] her life.'

Gerrette herself was soon on the receiving end of one such blow-up, as Dylan threw her out of his hotel room at seven in the morning, suddenly enraged by her presence. He'd had enough of Perth, pretty women and pressmen. Now he just hoped to sleep till Stockholm. The mood swings were becoming harder and harder to control, just as he was heading for a Scandinavian rendezvous with his favourite documentary-maker and his handheld camera/s.

This time there would have to be some ground rules for what DA could and could not film. At least Dylan had control of the final cut. Hence, perhaps, his response on the one occasion in Europe when Robertson inadvertently allowed himself to take a hit of hash from Maymudes on film, only to exclaim, 'I forgot all about The Eye and the hash.' Dylan insists, 'I don't give a shit, man. It's my film.' Though they were never going to use that *vérité* moment, the final cut still opens with Dylan snorting some unknown substance from a dining-room table and laughing hysterically. Maybe he really didn't 'give a shit'.

He also didn't 'give a shit' about all the money he was earning, though the subject still seemed to obsess reporters at each and every press conference – and he had three more to circumnavigate before his three-week British tour started on May 5th. The first of these, in Stockholm, was largely benign, but when a girl reporter said she'd heard 'you're on a lot of money and you say you don't care about it, [so] what do you do with it?' Dylan already knew his reply. He was saving up 'to buy Australia'.

If Dylan was hoping to increase his revenue streams he was going about it the wrong way – putting his trust in Grossman and tying himself to his manager with ever-stronger bonds. Barely had he arrived in Stockholm, dog-tired and jet-lagged, than his (*and* Grossman's) lawyer, David Braun, arrived from New York with papers, setting up a jointly owned music publisher, to be called Dwarf Music.

He had got out of jail, more by luck than judgement, with the Witmark deal back in 1962. Now he chanced his arm again, and was not so lucky. Just as Braun was explaining the new set-up, which would become Dylan's primary source of income for the foreseeable, Grossman 'came … racing into the room, while I was explaining [it] to Bob and terminated the discussion. He indicated there was no need for me to explain [the documents] fully … that Bob knew what they were about.'

Dylan may have remained in the dark a while longer, but back in the Village Izzy Young was telling anyone who would listen just 'how Grossman really makes his fortune – he owns part of Dylan's songs and then he sells it to Peter, Paul & Mary, and he owns [part of] that; then he's part of Music Publishing Holding Corporation … Every time it hits the wall, he gets another slice.'*

Nearer to thee someone else was waving a large red flag, endangering his very livelihood by informing Dylan, 'he was giving away the rights to his songs when he handed them over to Albert to publish'. Not only did Victor tell him he was 'splitting fifty-fifty the proceeds from the publishing of the songs … [but] in addition, Albert had complete control over who could use the songs, commercially'. At some point in Europe Maymudes chose to brave the wrath of Grossman to explain the facts of life. A disbelieving Dylan refused to

---

* This is a verbatim quote from a July 1965 interview Richard Reuss conducted.

accept Maymudes' word, and effectively froze him out. He took the hint and returned stateside. They would not speak again for several years.

But even as he continued to see no evil, hear no evil, Dylan was having to 'learn to live with, not [exactly] subterfuge ... but a way of comunication', that Pennebaker, for one, noticed Grossman had begun to develop. By the time DA arrived in Sweden, 'Albert was playing a very difficult game with Bobby, and I know it caused some problems ... Towards the end, both were telling me different stories about things, and they didn't agree.'

Dylan decided to ask the most successful song partnership in history about their own music company, Northern Songs. He got nowhere, prompting this verbal blast directed at Lennon on their notorious drive around London – famously filmed – that May: 'Do you remember what you said to me when I played you this song?* [I asked] What's your publishing company? I had to go and find out. You laughed and Paul McCartney looked the other way. You wouldn't tell me.'

Perhaps Lennon was simply too embarrassed to admit that he and McCartney had been shafted royally by that smiling assassin, Dick James, and that what he knew about song-publishing law could be written on a penny black stamp and still leave room for the collected insights of Philip Norman. Dylan would have received similarly short shrift from Jagger and/or Richards, who the previous summer had made a Faustian pact with part-time accountant and full-time crook, Allen Klein, which would ensure they ended the decade as broke as they started it.

These were the days when Dylan would happily sign off on putting together an expensive new sound system for the European shows, while leaving the Australian sound system in Oz so that Grossman could set up a PA rental company down under (which never happened).

As a result, Richard Alderson had to fly from Perth to New York, purchase the necessary, and fly on to Stockholm, where he 'was still putting the equipment together on the stage fifteen minutes before the concert ... That sound system never worked as well as the first one ... I was so crazed getting it together and it wasn't

---

* He may well mean '4th Time Around', based as it was on what was only a northern song.

quite right ... There wasn't enough time to get it right. I was also getting burnt out.'

Dylan, on the other hand, spent his first day and a half in Sweden orchestrating a series of scenes for the TV movie he was now committed to making for ABC, who had advanced Braun $30,000 on April 22nd to cover running costs. Never short of ambition, Dylan informed a sceptical DA, 'He was going to do things totally differently from the way they'd been done; he was gonna revamp network schedules; he was gonna revamp movies; he was gonna make everything in a new way.' What he failed to explain to Pennebaker was exactly how:

> He was [going to] get a big pot boiling, with everybody at odds and uncertain and confused and even a little annoyed and then film that ... in various ways. It's a way for people who aren't film-makers, but are consummate dramatists in one way or another, to create a kind of scene for a film. They're not writing scenes [which] is an art in itself. So Bob just simply said, 'I'll get a lot of people together and we'll see what happens.' ... [] ... He'd occasionally say, 'Shoot that, shoot some of this over here.' That kind of direction. [Or] he would ... get people to say things or set up situations. For instance, he would get rooms filled with strangers who appeared out of nowhere ... I don't know what he was smoking, but he was pretty far up in the air a lot of the time!

Dylan had been listening to another cineaste whose ideas, in Pennebaker's professional opinion, 'tend[ed] to be sort of intellectual ideas ... not visual ideas ... He was very influenced by Howard [Alk]'s film ideas.' Despite Alk (whom Dylan had known since 1963) and his wife Jones shooting a lot of *dont look back* – under Pennebaker's direction – Alk's directorial CV remained as blank as the canvas he and Dylan hoped to paint pictures on.* Pennebaker thought they were missing a trick: 'Making home movies ... simply doesn't interest me very much ... I'm not sure how to ... make other people's home movies for them ... And in a way, we were doing that.'

---

* I refer interested readers to the 'Profile of Howard Alk' I wrote for *Telegraph #18*, later impertinently re-edited by Michael Gray in the *All Across The Telegraph* anthology.

The first scene they shot confirmed this would not be *dont look back* Mk 2. Dylan arranged a scene involving a drop-dead-gorgeous Swedish blonde who echoed someone from his youth, an unbusinesslike boyfriend, and Dylan himself. In *Eat The Document* – the 1968 movie Dylan and Alk made out of Pennebaker's out-takes, hence the title – we see Dylan trying to buy the girl from her boyfriend while Rick Danko mutters, 'Swedish girls got no business sense.'

But the original 1967 cut of the unreleased *Something Is Happening* – the version of the film ABC saw in rough cut – has an altogether wittier *mise en scène* and opening sequence. Dylan starts to wall the blonde in with cement bricks, all the while telling her, 'You'll be like one of those Egyptian queens ... that have been sealed off for 200,000 years. Would you like to be like that? Cleopatra? Elizabeth Taylor? Same thing.' She seems unperturbed. He finally completes the wall, at which point he gives her a potted plant, saying, 'This is for you. [For] if you get hungry. I'm gonna leave you here now. I'll see you next time I'm here. *I'm sorry for everything I've done and I hope to remedy it soon.** I hope to make everything good again. I have to go now. My friend is leaving without me. See you again,' at which point Danko cycles into shot on a tandem, which Dylan mounts before pedalling off into the distance. Cut.

There was more, too, Dylan asking the blonde, 'Are you one of these people with time on their side? If so, we're gonna have to bring our relationship to a very abrupt end ... The first time I saw you, I thought you were one of those people who has to understand everything. But I [now] know I was wrong. You're not one of those people.'

When she takes all he throws at her in her stride, Dylan engages the boyfriend in conversation, 'I'm looking for Hamlet's grave.' The name of the original production company; Dylan's imminent visit to Elsinore, the setting for Shakespeare's play; and a report that the film's original title was *Hamlet Revisited*, all suggest a developing interest in the Jacobethan play on Dylan's part. The boyfriend's response, 'I thought he was a fictitious character', suggests he agreed with the Danish prince that life was but a joke.

Whether ABC's audience would have been amused, we will never know, because that original version was junked, while the end

---

* This italicised line appears in *Eat The Document*, out of context.

product Dylan and Alk compiled without Pennebaker's input – which at times did rather smack of 'other people's home movies' – made The Beatles' own 1967 'home movie', *Magical Mystery Tour*, look well conceived.

At least Dylan now felt he'd made a start on a film he intended to cram with the beautiful people. That evening, he invited another vivacious female reporter, Pi Ann Murray, up to his hotel room, having asked 'if I would like to be part of the film being made by a team which was following him during this whole tour ... [to be] filmed in colour. [I] assume[d] it was my pink stockings and sweater which made him ask me ... We drank ... tea, [and] listened to Bob's records':

> [And] when he had played the records, he started to talk. What a storyteller! He stretched each story into a wilder and more bizarre one than the one before, he smoked constantly (Marlboro), holding a cup of tea which was growing ever more tepid. After a few hours he wanted to start the filming. We went to the bathroom, Bob and I, and there he wanted me to wash my hands while talking in Swedish [as] he spoke in English and sauntered around.

This footage now resides in Tulsa. Again Dylan is playing his little games. In this scene a (presumably bursting) Robbie is trying to get into the bathroom to, er, change his shirt:

> **Robbie Robertson**: C'mon, man. I'm getting very hungry. I'm gonna have to come in here for a while. [Starts to take off shirt. Girl continues talking in Swedish, washing her hands]
> **Bob Dylan**: You don't have to be mean.
> **RR**: I've been waiting outside the door since this morning.
> **BD**: I'll see you later. Just don't bother her. [To the girl] This guy's from Rangoon.

One doubts ABC would have felt they were getting their $200,000 worth had Dylan delivered a full hour of such high jinks. But for now, he was having fun sending up aspects of this goldfish-bowl existence. Over the next six days he would get more apposite fare by shooting press conferences in Stockholm, Copenhagen and London, affording him a tried and tested forum for verbal jousting with a whole lot of unpaid extras, cast as sacrificial lambs, something his director well understood:

> **D. A. Pennebaker**: [The press] were sent to do a story on this guy who'd arrived [in town] ... They didn't know much about him. It was just a day's story. Dylan's sense, in a way, was [like] pearls before swine – if they didn't know who he was or why he was, it wasn't anything he was going to try to mend. He just went [along] with them as if it was some sort of comic show of misperceptions. [2016]

If Dylan really wanted to get 'everybody at odds and uncertain and confused and even a little annoyed', he would have few better opportunities. A paradigmatic reflection of the sixties' societal spasms, these conferences resulted in what Dylan later called 'a distorted, warped view of me – "The spokesman of the generation." "The conscience of a ... " [&c.] – I just couldn't relate to it. [But] as long as I could continue doing what ... I loved to do, I didn't care what kinds of labels were put on me.'

Asked in Stockholm if he considered himself 'the same type of singer as Pete Seeger', he bristled at the comparison: 'He sings railroad songs. I sing mathematical songs.' Asked about those who dislike his electric music, he dismissed them as 'people who don't have any sex appeal'. When some foolhardy soul asked him if he's 'the ultimate beatnik', he turned the question around:

> **BD**: What do you think? I won't tell anybody.
> **Journalist**: I haven't any opinion ... I haven't heard you sing.
> **BD**: You haven't heard me sing and here you are, asking me all these questions ...
> What sort of questions would you ask Mozart?
> **Journalist**: I'm interested in you, and in Swedish audiences.
> **BD**: I'm interested in Swedish audiences, too, but I'm sure they're not interested in these dumb things.
> **Journalist**: Well, they've seen a lot of dumb things in the papers. I thought you could straighten them out.
> **BD**: I can't straighten them out. I don't think they have to be straightened out ...

Journalist #2: Are you trying to put over some kind of message or just singing from within?
BD: That's right ...
Girl Journalist: Someone [once] said your new songs are only written for yourself. No one else could possibly understand [them].
BD: That's not true. Ask anybody here.

When one brave journalist tried to inject some levity into proceedings by suggesting 'this interview could have taken place on Desolation Row', Dylan refuses to play ball: 'It couldn't have taken place there. There are no interviews on Desolation Row.' Proceedings break up with everyone's mutual misunderstandings intact and plenty of footage for the film. If Dylan's goading has failed to hit all the marks, he knew he could try again in two days' time in Copenhagen.

This time, though, some of Hamlet's children cried wolf. Indeed, it would be the press conference, not the concert, that provided Dylan's Danish battleground. The show at the KB-Hallen – the first to be recorded by Richard Alderson, who begins taping all the shows on his trusty Nagra for the film – will meet with near-unanimous roars of approval in the land of Sven Grundtvig and the *Danmarks Folkeviser*. Its dramatic finale left *Politiken*'s Ole John, for one, breathless with admiration:

> A complete transformation takes place. Dylan becomes intense, the hall comes alive, and everything is important ... A chill runs down one's spine. He doesn't sell any alibis but keeps moving towards a constantly stronger calling. His music finally becomes more real and true as he reaches and surpasses his best recordings ... I think many people left the concert completely stunned.

Alderson's partial tape captures this intensity. Remarkably, he ends up capturing almost all of these 'nightly rituals' through May, even when Columbia screw up their more hi-tech efforts, whilst still doing the job he was paid for: the sound. He quickly figured out when to change reels: 'I had a good sensibility of how people were gonna react after the first couple of concerts.'

Copenhagen and Stockholm were noble exceptions. There were no breaks between songs while audience members vented their frustration,

Scandinavia proving to be the line of least resistance. The Danes in particular took Dylan's brand of folk-rock in their stride, being fully briefed and up to speed – as were their reporters, who caught Dylan wholly unprepared for their knowledge and keen intellectual curiosity. When he met questions with condescension, they returned it redoubled, as one report filed after the fractious conference confirms:

> Dylan drinks tea. Dylan refuses to answer. Mumbles through his fingers. The air is filled with the journalists' attempts to explain Dylan to the man himself: 'I understand you, it must be awful ... but why do you give press conferences when it's such a pain for you?' Other journalists stand behind his back, trying to say mean things and frequently using the word 'fuck'. All is doomed to fail. It's going to end soon, he says to one of the tour managers ... The press – a bunch of people arriving at a precise time, an opportunity for him to test his resistance, his ability to strike back ... The fear of the journalists turns into spite: if he can be mean, so can we. A mirrored image of reality.

The April 30th Copenhagen conference started with Dylan pulling out a notebook and announcing, 'I have some questions, some things I need to find out here ... Are there any reporters here?' Almost immediately the jig is up. After a girl reporter plaintively complains, 'You're supposed to answer the questions,' Tom Waits's Danish cousin calls out the name of the game: 'He wants to reverse the process.' This isn't going to be as easy as Dylan initially thought. The latter journalist wants answers and determinedly perseveres, even when Dylan gets noticeably tetchy:

> **Journo**: This is a sincere question and I don't want any projected images. Can I ask what period you developed your social conscience?
> **BD**: ... It was 1942.
> **Journo**: You were one year old in 1942. Are we going to proceed along these lines then?
> **BD**: We're gonna proceed along the lines *you* set up, not me ... Are you telling me what I'm supposed to be? I'm not going for that. I'm not any kid.
> **Journo**: Well, you're behaving like one at the moment.
> **BD**: Why don't you get mad [then].

Journo: I'm giving you a fair chance.

BD: You don't have to give me any fair chance. I don't need a fair chance ...

Journo: Do you assume this attitude of superficiality because you think it's impressive?

BD: I don't think it's impressive, but I don't have anything to gain or lose by being here talking to you.

Dylan soon finds a focal point for the footage Pennebaker is shooting, having taken a shine to a blonde girl reporter with her own set of shades and a short bob haircut. Her very first entry into these intemperate exchanges seeks an explanation: 'I don't understand, if it's so awful for you to do these press conferences ...' But before she can complete her question, Dylan asks for her favourite piece of music – something he asks every questioner. She tersely offers, 'The Fourth Symphony. You happy now?' When Dylan opens up the debate by asking, 'Is there anybody here who knows exactly what I do, the music I play and what it is I do?' the girl's reply reflects a collective rising annoyance, 'Really, we do, but you won't believe us.'

Dylan announces that the conference 'can start now. But [pointing to the girl behind the shades] she's gonna answer all the questions I can't answer.' She doesn't let the remark go, interjecting, 'You're not very nice to us.' When that draws a smile, she notes, 'You're smiling for a change.' Dylan now wants to know all about her, 'What paper are you from?' She names a magazine from West Zeeland. He claims, 'I've heard of that paper. They sell it on 42nd Street. You can buy it from a little man with a crutch.'

Just as he is clicking into gear, recognizing a worthy adversary, the conference winds down. When he turns around, she is gone. But he isn't gonna leave it at that. He goes in search of the girl who had stayed for so long, only to find her sitting outside a cafe, having coffee with a man. When Dylan calls out to her, she replies, in perfect English:

Girl: I'm having cake. You wanna join us?
BD: I dunno. I see you got your boyfriend.
Girl: He's not my boyfriend.
BD: You sure?
Girl: He's my photographer.

BD: You gonna ask me a bunch of questions or you gonna take off your shoes?
Girl: I'll take off my shoes, if you like.
BD: That sounds like a pretty good proposition ...
Girl: Can you jump? [There is a wall between them]
BD: I can't jump. I'm down here on the gravel.
[He climbs over the wall to join her, handing her a piece of paper.]
BD: I'll give it back to you 'cause I'm a bad guy ...
Girl: I'll keep it, as a memory of you.
BD: You Danish people. I come in, answer all your questions, I ask one question – just one question ...

It's fabulous footage, Dylan acting free and easy, showing that public persona at both its best and worst, a boor turned gentleman, but not one frame of their banter will end up in the film. The single shot of the girl in *Eat The Document* (from the conference) has her saying, 'Well, I don't know if I'll accept that'. We never find out what she has been asked to accept. A crutch?

Another opportunity to capture a conference in conflict is scheduled for four days' time in London. On this occasion, rested and ready to rumble, he has a better idea of what to expect, even offering to let anyone so inclined to 'suck my glasses' as photographers snap the archetypal Dylan image on the Mayfair balcony before proceedings commence.

The conference itself starts very sedately, with a tabloid journalist asking, 'Are you [more] interested in writing songs or another medium?' 'I'm interested in writing songs.' But when he is asked about 'Rainy Day Women', he is as unhelpful as can be, insisting, 'That's about the Venezuelan women.' When that doesn't work, he takes a different tack: 'It's very hard to explain [it] unless you've been to north Mexico for six months at a time.'* If, by now, the journalists are starting to sense this is not going to be '65 Revisited, what really sends the whole conference off the rails is an innocuous question about his wife:

---

* Back in Stockholm, he'd also been asked about 'Rainy Day Women', which he explained 'happens to be a protest song ... It borders on the mathematical. It deals with a minority of cripples and Orientals. And the world in which they live. Very protesty. One of the most protesty things in my protesty years ... It has to do with God.'

Q: You just got married, haven't you? Is this your wife?

BD: You can't call her that. It'd be very misleading if I answered yes and I'd be a fool if I answered no.

Q: But you are married, yes?

Q2: Do you mean a common law wife?

BD: Is that what they call it? How many [common law] wives can you have?

Q: As many as you like, that way.

Q2: So can we say you're married?

BD: You can say anything you want ... I can't marry. I have medical problems. I'd be a liar if I answered the way you want me to say. I have glass in the back of my head. My toenails don't really fit right and I can't see too well on Tuesdays.

Q: What do you do on Mondays, Bob?

BD: I'd be a liar if I answered that.

Girl: So you're not married. [Referring to his shades] You can see me, I can't see you. It's very disconcerting, Will you get married?

BD: Are you married?

Girl: No.

BD: Why?

Journo: She's living in sin. She's answered your question, answer hers. Surely if you're [just] married, you're the happiest man in the world ...

Q: Did you borrow the glasses from Roy Orbison?

BD: Would you like to look at the world through these eyes? Through these sunglasses? They're prescription. I'm not trying to come on like a beatnik or anything. I've got very mercuryesque eyes.

Journo: Another medical problem ...

BD [to girl]: You can look through my glasses and maybe you won't ask if I'm married anymore ...

Q: Which one's your wife?

BD: You'll meet my wife. I'll introduce you to him later ...

Q: Your publicist just stood up and said you're anxious to answer any question.

Q2: Are there any questions you'd like to answer?

BD: I answered it to the best of my ability ... I brought my wife last time, no one paid any attention to her ...

Max Jones: I read you no longer sing protest songs. Is that true?

BD: Who said that? All my songs are protest songs. Every single one of them. All I do is protest.
Q: What are you going to protest about on this trip?
BD: You name it and I'll protest about it.
Q: Marriage? ...

Having flat-out refused to answer a simple question, Dylan never fully regains his grip on proceedings. The journalists are not amused, one of them taking it out on Grossman at the end: 'Why doesn't he start talking, dribbling on like this [about] a question like, are you married?' Grossman stonewalls him, 'Who has to know?'

The afternoon's events have put the kibosh on any further on-the-record meetings with the press, even though Dylan knows he is making a rod for his own back. As he later tells a rich old lady backstage in Edinburgh, 'Oh man, they give me bad reviews. We don't meet the press, you [see].' Yet the reporters from Britain's music press were delighted by the Mayfair face-off. *Disc & Music Echo* pointed out that 'he is [only] rude to people whom he considers ask stupid questions ... Dylan is also a very sympathetic man with a vast sense of humour.' *Record Mirror*'s Richard Green wisely decided to just sit back and watch:

> Until [this afternoon], I'd always thought that *Juke Box Jury* was the funniest thing ever. But Dylan's handling of the press left that standing. Asked if he had any children, he said, 'Every man with medical problems has children.' Asked what his medical problems were, he said, 'Well, there's glass in the back of my head and my toenails don't fit properly.' Dylan's bunch of assorted film cameramen and sound recordists were happily enjoying the farce, which was obviously being staged for their benefit.

Dylan did not get off so lightly when he decided to go for a stroll to Speakers' Corner, camera crew in tow, perhaps looking for material for a song. Once there, he is quickly recognized by a particularly po-faced anarchist who challenges him, 'Why don't you talk about banning the bomb?' Dylan replies, 'I['ve] done all that.' This prompts the anarchist to show his true colours, 'How could you turn from one of the greatest protesters to one of the greatest elitists in history?' Dylan can only say, 'Gee, I'm sorry.'

The smug anarchist continues to upbraid him, 'What are you Americans doing in Vietnam?' Dylan deflects, 'I dunno. I'm not there.' The anarchist will not let him be – 'You're not protesting' – so Dylan sets him straight, 'If you think you can do anything about it, you're wrong.' He could just as easily have said, 'Of war and peace, the truth just twists,' before leaving the man to his black and white world.

He now makes his way back to the Mayfair, and a more welcome rendezvous with Dana Gillespie, whom he is trying to help use her ballsy pipes to get in the charts – offering to put her together with Manfred Mann to record one of his songs.* It never comes to pass. Instead, he has to listen to the latest offering of one of the few friends Dana acknowledged – on Dylan's behalf – to a passing reporter that month: 'He likes Paul McCartney, John Lennon, Keith Moon and Marianne Faithfull and her husband [John Dunbar]. But he has very few close friends [here].'

What Dylan wasn't about to inform John or Paul – but did tell an American journalist a week later – was that he considered The Beatles 'nice fellows. But they're not as good as [Percy Sledge]. They're not *that*,† are they? ... When you're all alone, [would] you listen to "All My Loving" or "Blue Suede Shoes"? Which is the greatest of the great? "Heartbreak Hotel" you can listen to ... alone.' Of the English singers, it was Steve Winwood who impressed him the most, so much so he told the young prodigy's bandleader, Spencer Davis, '[He] sounds like a twelve-year-old Ray Charles.'

He was less impressed by a new track McCartney had come all the way to the Mayfair to play him. It had been a month to the day since Roger McGuinn had played him 'Eight Miles High' and Dylan asked, 'How'd you come up with that?' McGuinn explained he'd 'been listening to a lot of Coltrane. Trying to interpret that in my own way on the twelve-string guitar.' Dylan wanted to know *why* – as in why bother? 'Probably because I like it. Don't you like John Coltrane?' 'Sure, but I don't try to copy his stuff.' Ouch.

Robertson's implausible account of the meeting with McCartney suggests he wasn't really there. But Marianne Faithfull was, and remembers, 'Paul got a very cool reception. I saw him come in ...

---

* Evidently, it was a new one because he tells her, 'You haven't heard the song'.
† He is playing Sledge's 'When A Man Loves A Woman' at the time.

with an acetate of a track he'd been working on which was very far out for its time, with all kinds of distorted, electronic things on it. Paul was obviously terribly proud of it, he put it on the record player and stood back in anticipation, but Dylan just walked out of the room.'

At this stage, the song McCartney played was called 'Mark One'. In due time it would appear as the closing track on *Revolver*, 'Tomorrow Never Knows'. Pennebaker's own take on the meeting was that 'McCartney showed up and brought [electronic] stuff to [play] him, but Dylan's very afraid of anybody that appears to have a kinda intellectual sense of things.' It wasn't fear, this time, it was a feeling that this wasn't 'the greatest of the great' – it wasn't Percy Sledge. And nor was it. It was a one-chord drone set to bits of the Tibetan Book of the Dead. To disguise the lack of a tune and copped words, McCartney (principally) and Lennon piled on special effects from the Abbey Road tape library.

Given that the foursome recorded the utterly magnificent 'And Your Bird Can Sing' and 'I'm Only Sleeping' the same day they mixed said acetate, Paul clearly didn't know what was likely to impress Dylan. And though he says he 'was happy to pay homage', he clearly resented the fact that 'it was a little bit An Audience With Dylan in those days: you went round to the Mayfair hotel and waited in the outer room while Bob was in the other room'. Dylan rightly remained convinced he was still leader of the pack, and had a band that could leave the best of British in its wake. What he probably didn't expect was dozens of fans turning up nightly for whom the worst epithet they could direct his way was, 'You sound like The Rolling Stones'!

2.8

May 1966:
Man, I'm Not Even Twenty-Five

French journalist: Does any kind of dope provide inspiration?
BD [to interpreter]: Ask him if he's ever taken dope. [He answers in the affirmative] Well, then he should know.

Paris press conference, on his twenty-fifth birthday

Dylan was visibly vibrating. I should imagine it was the exhaustion and a good deal of substances. He was totally away, there was a yawning chasm between him and any kind of human activity.

Johnny Byrne

Like other poets, from Rimbaud to Dylan Thomas ... Dylan has a kindred genius for afflicting his body and health. At twenty-four, he already has a prematurely tired, wizened look. [Yet] he'll brush aside the concern of his friends, indicating that everybody dies sometime.

Robert Shelton, July 1965

Filming ... the 1966 tour turned out to be hard. Dylan was supposed to be in charge, but he was as wild as I'd ever seen him: all-night sagas of traipsing around shooting this and that, and none of it made sense. He was in over his head and he was vamping, and I didn't know what to tell him.

D. A. Pennebaker

He was very surprised at the reaction of the English audiences. He thought England was far ahead of any other country in pop music and he just couldn't understand why he was booed and catcalled.

Dana Gillespie, July 1966

Judas, the most hated name in human history! If you think you've been called a bad name, try to work your way out from under that. Yeah, and for what? For playing an electric guitar?

Bob Dylan, 2012

*

A week after the fiftieth-anniversary celebrations for Ireland's Easter Rising subsided, another kind of 'terrible beauty' took place around the corner from Dublin's General Post Office at the Art Moderne 2,000-seat Adelphi Theatre. Dylan was playing his first concert in Ireland, and although the previous week music fans' weekly bible, *Melody Maker*, had run the unambiguous headline 'Dylan Brings Own Group,' no one seemed too sure what it meant or what reaction awaited the latest revolutionary to risk Eire's opprobrium.*

There were certainly some dissenters present, Dylan being subjected to a brief slow handclap and audible taunts either side of 'Thin Man', as well as at the end of 'I Don't Believe You' and 'Baby Let Me Follow You Down'. No question, he was perturbed, complaining the very next day to a Belfast journalist about 'the lousy reception he'd been given in Dublin'. (Weeks later, Robertson informed an English journalist, 'They were [actually] holding up Stop The War signs.')

A cursory scan of reviews in the *Irish Times*, *Sunday Independent* and *Dublin Evening Herald* would lead one to think he'd faced down an entire Irish Rebellion. The worst of the lot – factually and grammatically – would be the *Evening Herald*'s 'JK'. He concluded, 'The 2,000-odd who came to hear him will remember it as the Night of The Great Let-down.'

It would take fifty years, and the release of Alderson's tape, to prove JK made it all up. The local fans, though, knew from the outset, using the letters page to give JK both barrels, Dermot Meleady pointing out how he 'childishly exaggerated ... a small amount of unpleasantness ... In fact, the only remarks shouted during the amplified second half were when somebody called for the microphone to be turned down,

---

* The attendant article informed readers: 'The group ... will accompany the singer for half of each concert and he will do the other half alone.'

this being followed by the shouts of "stuffed golliwog" &c., which, it must be emphasised, were completely isolated. The only mob action was an outburst of slow-handclapping which could be traced to one or two rows.' 'Disgusted of Foxrock', while also affirming that 'there was some booing and even jeering ... doubt[ed] if there were forty people responsible [whereas] JK would lead us to believe the whole audience was participating.'

Still, the damage was done. Both *Melody Maker* and *Disc*, rather than sending correspondents, paraphrased reviews from the *Independent* and the *Evening Herald* and reported them as fact. Any dialectic would have to wait. For now, the British daily press preferred to exaggerate the nightly conflict – save for one night in Manchester when all hell really did break loose, and the only reporter on hand was Parisian. It was left to fans to write in, suggesting there were lies, damn lies and tabloid reports.

Photographer Barry Feinstein – there to document each nightly drama visually – notes that Dylan 'was interested in what the music press had to say about him, [but] it didn't really affect him ... Nonetheless ... [he] would get pissed off once in a while.' Dublin was one such an occasion, Dylan complaining the evening after that 'the southern press ... [had] slayed him because of his non-cooperation'. He also joked to Johnny Cash – who was on his own British tour that month – 'Wait till you get to Belfast and Dublin. You won't talk so smart then.'

If he hadn't already made up his mind to avoid any more on-the-record conversations, the Irish press's petulance led to a blanket ban on press interviews, for which the one written explanation – a scrawled note to a journalist turning down his request for an interview – was positively poetic:

>   time now is pushed &
>   I most definitely ...
>   would not want to see
>   someone whose making
>   love with my songs to hear [that]
>   my mind now is in Del Rio – New York –
>   & North Mexico – it gets this
>   way when I play on tour –
>   ... my heart and veins are
>   not here in England.

Yet far from shutting himself off from feedback, the *Eat The Document* out-takes – now deposited in Tulsa – reveal a Dylan feeding his need for verbal jousting almost nightly, just not on the record and not to any emissaries from tabloids or music papers. They also suggest how revealing a documentary it could have been had Dylan not been consumed by post-traumatic hindsight.

That night in Dublin he talked for a long time on camera to an Irishwoman who seemed determined to get to know the 'real' Dylan, physically and psychologically ('You're asking me to take off my clothes. You'd be frightened to death if I took off my clothes'). The result is one of the more gentlemanly versions of his patented truth attack:

Bob Dylan: It's weird, this saviour business, you realize that [don't you?] The evangelist stardom. I could be the saviour you want me to be if I lived my whole life on the stage, like that. [But] you don't understand what you heard tonight. You're just looking for things [that aren't there] ... Like [when] a tree falls, it happens to you, like hunger happens to you ... You heard me sing tonight for two hours. Ask me if you think I was right about something I said to you, something I told you ... You think I'm trying to hurt you ... You think I want to make fun of you. You think I got something against you. You're paranoid ... You want me to get down on my knees and cross my heart and ask forgiveness and feel sad ... You ask, did I believe in ... love? I'd ask if you believe in love. And you wouldn't know how to answer me. You'd say, yes you do, but you'd try to think in your mind the grooviest words to *prove* that you believe in it ... The greatest image of love you could think of ... I don't think you would ... mean the same word I mean ... You think I've never known love? You feel sorry for me ... I ain't gonna try and correct you. I bet I've known greater love. What's your greatest love? I'll tell you my greatest love. What's your greatest, warmest feeling you've ever received. A Home Sweet Home sign? You see it all the time. 'Tony Curtis has fallen in love with Ursula Andress. See Hercules and his greatest love affair.'
Irish Girl: I mean the love between a woman and a man.
BD: Is that the only kind of love that there is? ... What do you think about love? [When] you've fallen in love – the world is great. When it rains, it's really sunshine. It's heaven.

IG: So you've been in love.
BD: No, I just know what people say.
IG: So you've never known that?
BD: What you don't know is that love is cold.

Even in the semi-darkness of his hotel room, it's riveting stuff, as Dylan endeavours to hold up a metapahorical mirror to the misguided girl: 'As time goes on, you're getting weirder and weirder ... I'm gonna bring over a mirror pretty soon, with a glass of water in front of it.' Here was a visual motif he intended for the film, having previously asked reporters at the Mayfair to 'look in the mirror one time before [you] leave this room', and in a more heated exchange with a Parisian pseud, 'I'm just telling you there's a mirror in the back of you and it's gonna bounce back right through, unless you acknowledge it.' Yet the Dublin girl refuses to back down, throwing his own words at him:

IG: How does it feel to be on your own?
BD: ... You're putting [those words] where they don't belong ... Alone's got nothing to do with it. Do you take great pride in being alone? Do you take great romantic misery in it? Do you like to be alone?
IG: Sometimes.
BD: Did you know that every person living now, did you realize that they're *all* alone.

Already Dylan was feeling desperately homesick. When a sly Belfast reporter snuck backstage the following night, he agreed to chat – 'not an interview ... we're just gonna have a lil' talkie!' What he talked about was mainly 'guitars and homesickness. He claimed to have no feelings about the tour. All he wanted to do was go home.'

Back in London, Pennebaker captures another conversation with a translator who wants to put Dylan's work into Italian. Dylan admits his mind is on other things: 'I just wanna go home. I don't wanna go to Italy. I don't wanna go anywhere no more. I just wanna go home. I'll do short lil' tours from now on. But it's waste, decay, to play like this. You end up crashing in a private airplane. In the mountains of

Sicily. I'm sorry to look at you this way but I just wanna go home. The songs are the furthest thing from my mind.'

Dana Gillespie, a welcome presence in the inner sanctum, suggested at the time that his reluctance to talk to the press was because 'Bobby is only interested in the international, glossy magazines like *Time*, *Paris Match* [&c.]. He's really very concerned about publicity, but ... only reads the glossies.' Perhaps so. Of the two journalists who got to travel with him for two or three days, Jean-Marc Pascal – who travelled from Sheffield to Manchester, and then to Paris – was writing for French 'glossy', *Salut Les Copains*. Also admitted to the inner sanctum was Michael Braun, author of the 1964 bestseller *Love Me Do* on Beatlemania, who joined him in Bristol for his first mainland UK concert and was still there in Cardiff, two nights later, at which point Dylan lights into him, 'Tell me what you do. You've been with us for three days and absolutely nobody knows what you do.' Said verbal challenge comes at the end of another feisty hotel-room exchange, during which Dylan asks, 'Are you sure you understand me?' Braun confesses, 'There's a couple of blocked passages, but it's been a long day.' Actually, every attempt at something more formal, Dylan stonewalled:

Q: Are you here to do your act in Wales?
BD: Don't get salty. Are you gonna use it in your article?
Q: I just thought it was incumbent on me.
BD: What do you think I'm doing here in Wales? Do you think if I knew what I was doing in Wales, I'd be here? ... I got a weird feeling tonight. I never thought in a million years I'd get to Wales. I started thinking [about] Richard Burton, Tom Jones, that chick Shirley Bassey ...
Q: Dylan Thomas?
BD: ... All these people think I got my name from Dylan Thomas ... I know you know [different], but there's a lot of people think it happened.

Despite Braun's best efforts, the glossies evidently passed on anything the scribe delivered, perhaps feeling that the answers were still blowing across the Bristol Channel. Meanwhile, Pennebaker's Eye remained all-seeing and all-knowing, documenting everyone who came and went.

But not a foot of film from his exchanges with the Dublin girl, Michael Braun, the Italian translator or an altogether more pugnacious exchange with an Okie writer in Paris will end up in *Eat The Document*. Did the post-accident Dylan not like the person captured by the Eye's celluloid mirr'r?

The George V truth-attack, in particular, suggests Horace Judson got off lightly. Once again the trigger is a journalist admitting he doesn't really know Dylan's work well, prompting a patently lonely Dylan to use his verbal bayonet:

BD: You're one writer I've never seen anything you've written. You don't know how to write. You can't write ... you like to sit and drink red wine while you write ... on a cosmic rug underneath your chair with a lamp aimed down at your desk watching the dawn come up. With your girlfriend and your wife ... and people talking two rooms away from you. And when you get scared, you can go in there and talk about writing 'cause they're all doing the same thing you are ... I'm not here to discuss any of those things with you. I'm here to look at your shirt and buy your belt. That's about all. I made a record called *Highway 61 Revisited* – it's an album. Have you heard it?
Writer: Uh-huh.
BD: Have you listened to it a lot? Have you heard a song called 'Just Like Tom Thumb's Blues'?
Writer: No, I heard a song called 'Everybody Must Get Stoned' [*sic*].
BD: ... You've never listened to one of my records *alone* ... you've never let me talk to you ... you've never let me stand in front of you and untie one of your tennis shoes ... and try to buy your fingers, man, and try to con your teeth ... you'd walk out of here crippled if I had a mind to do it. I don't really care [how many people listen to my songs].
Writer: I think you do.
BD: I'm a rock'n'roll singer, man ... I find myself in this accidental position. I'm fortunate because I make a lot of money and it's all I really wanna do. No hobbies. No outside interests ... You have no language. Don't call me lonely. I will glady admit that I am lonely but you don't know what that even means. I'm not even gonna let you tell me what it is because it's gonna be some lame-ass word. I'm gonna have to kick you out ...

Writer: You're alone.
BD: Did I say I wasn't alone?
Writer: That's how you play [with] words, and fool people.
BD: You don't know anything about the words that I write ... I can do things that would astound you. I can do things that would make you stop what you are doing.
Writer: I can astound me. Never in your life have you astounded yourself.
BD: Well, I feel very privileged. I've always been very uptight about it, but after seeing you, I know it's not so bad, after all. The day that I astound myself, man, that's the day that I'll grow a beard, man, and take my shoes off and straighten my feet and take a slow, slow train to Fuji and starve to death amongst the scorpions.

By Paris, on May 24th, Dylan had reached the end of his tether. As he admitted to Jeff Rosen in *No Direction Home*, 'I'd had it with the whole scene ... Whether I knew it or didn't know it, I was looking to just quit for a while ... Just being ... expected to answer *questions*.'

One trigger that invariably set Dylan off in such exchanges was name-dropping, specifically literary name-dropping – like the pompous public schoolboy in *Eat The Document* who suggests he should 'read a few good poets' (and in the out-takes, suggests he should 'stay away from Kerouac and people like that'). Pennebaker felt part of it was down to a foreshortened education: 'He's fantastic in ... absorb[ing] everything he can get into, but he makes funny mistakes and intellectuals catch him at it and it makes him nervous ... like somebody that had skipped third grade ... and d[oes]n't know certain [obvious] things.'

As a result, he had – and to some extent still has – an anti-intellectual streak a mile wide,* evidenced by a revealing remark he'd made to Earl Leaf in early April: 'Philosophy's only a crock. It's just a belief or theory that some cats are hung up on. That intellectual garbage grabbed me when I was thirteen, but now it shuts me down.' He was now almost painfully aware of the mortality rate among writers,

---

* Witness some of his statements at the height of his evangelical phase in the late seventies, and indeed his portrayal of Freud and Marx as 'enemies of mankind' in the masterful 2020 song, 'My Version of You'.

commenting in an Edinburgh hotel room about how they usually develop 'until they just level off and pass away to obscurity or else die a violent death'.

In late spring 1966 (just as in 1960), he seemed to particularly have it in for T. S. Eliot. When Adrian Rawlins had asked him, in Melbourne, if he had read Pound and Eliot, Dylan snorted, 'Yeah, man, Allen gave me the books. I read three pages ... That's not where it's at!' Also, after the Dublin girl asks what some lyric means, he snaps, 'T. S. Eliot would use words [like] "mean". What do you care what I mean? I don't know how a song comes out on stage.'

After playing 'When A Man Loves A Woman' in his Cardiff hotel room, Dylan informs the Bristol-based expat, 'T. S. Eliot's not as good as [Percy Sledge],' before laying into Robert Graves (who was beholden to Eliot for the publication of his most important book, *The White Goddess*): 'There's somebody [who's] very well respected – [an] old miserly gentleman who's very kind, with a piano in his stomach. A lot of very serious people think Robert Graves is fantastic, but he's not as good as *that*.' He saves his most sustained attack on Eliot for the bemused Italian translator:

> People lay different books on you. You have this poet T. S. Eliot, a banker-poet who went to England. He's a shuck, a terrible, horrible poet. He wrote words you cannot believe. The literary people are sexless people ... The literary world is one dimension[al] – just people who sit around cocktail tables and discuss things. I have no respect for it. Understand? I'm not telling you to do these songs in any great magnetic way. [My stuff] is not a shuck. It's done for absolutely nobody. I know nobody's gonna understand these songs ... because they're looking to understand them ... Man, I don't know if I'm even getting through to you at all. Laws of opposites – admitting that everything is its own opposite – that's what we're dealing with here. They're not intellectual songs – if they happen to you, they happen.

All this revelatory footage – most of it nocturnal – simply serves to confirm a statement Dylan made on his next tour, eight years later: '[On] the last tour, we were going all the time, even when we weren't going. We were always doing something else, which is just as draining as performing. We were looking for Loch Ness monsters, staying up for four days running – and making all those eight o'clock curtains, besides.'

Even when the hotel room was free of journalists, part-time girlfriends or fellow music-makers, music remained at the fore. Rosemary Gerrette's description of an after-hours session in Perth – 'he and the lead guitarist work on a tune and Dylan's leg beats time with the rhythm, continuously, even when the rhythm is in his own mind' – was replayed in Britain several times, just not in hotels that were soundproofed or tolerant of noise. As a result, they usually ended up curtailed, though not before Robertson discovered 'that Bob probably knew more songs than anybody walking the earth'.

In Belfast, they have barely started playing when the desk calls up with a complaint. Dylan, wrapped in his own solipsistic bubble, responds, 'It's the middle of the night in Ireland, huh. Where I come from, it's only three-thirty in the afternoon. We're just looking for something to do. We're still up. So you can't blame us.' He then turns to Robertson and suggests 'we go to Richard's room. Is that the dawn coming up? It *is* the dawn. I wanna go home, man. I've never wanted to ... I *wanna* go home.'

In Edinburgh, in the wee small hours, Dylan asks Robertson, 'What's that song we were playing the other night? We should do that song,' and starts to sing, 'Beg, steal or borrow / Got a hold on you ...', at which point the hotel sends up the night supervisor to register another complaint. Much to Dylan's chagrin, there was a whole world of people not living his vampiric existence, 'This happens all over ... You know, I'm not gonna be able to finish those songs.'

At least he found time two days earlier on a rainy Glasgow afternoon to indulge in an off-the-cuff composing session with Robertson while cameras (and the Nagra) rolled, proof that Dylan was still receiving his muse's communiqués and the pain was still inspirational. At one point he even starts to vamp a blues that could describe a muse who's still killing me alive: 'She ain't good-looking ... She got one foot out the window / One foot on the floor, one foot in the kitchen ... She knows I love her.'

They capture four new songs, three of which will be cut up across *Eat The Document*, while the one with perhaps the most potential, 'If I Was A King' – a cross between 'Willie o' Winsbury' and '4th Time Around' – would not appear until 2016's *Cutting Edge*, and then only on audio.

None of these songs, though, were to be realized. Indeed, this seems to be something of a *modus operandi*. After trying the potentially exquisite 'I Can't Leave Her Behind' in two different keys, Dylan tells Robbie, 'That's good enough. We can slash away all the prehistoric trivia which came with that [later],' before enquiring, 'What else can we do?' When Robertson breaks into a blues, Dylan does not rise to the bait: 'Yeah, yeah, I heard it. It's done.' He simply isn't in the mood to finish anything. Eleven years later, he explained what he was reaching for, in his second *Playboy* interview:

> It was the sound of the streets ... I symbolically hear that sound wherever I am ... Usually it's [at] the crack of dawn. Music filters out to me in the crack of dawn ... You get a little spacey when you've been up all night, so you don't really have the power to form it, but that's the sound I'm trying to get across. I'm not just up there recreating old blues tunes or trying to invent some surrealistic rhapsody.

For speedball repartee, though, a pre-concert piano jam with Johnny Cash in Cardiff would be hard to top. Cash was having his own drug-intake issues at this time, culminating in an afternoon in London when he burst in on Richard Alderson, who 'had a vial of amphetamine pills sitting on my dresser ... John saw [the vial] and took the whole thing and locked himself in my bathroom for a whole day [while] June [Carter] was trying to find him.' According to Cash's road manager, Saul Holiff, in Hilburn's authorised Cash biography, Cash bailed on a show in Paris to go on a 'wild escapade' with Dylan. But when Cash got bombed he became monosyllabic, which was not what Dylan was hoping for. He wanted some quickfire repartee to fill that 'guest' slot in his film. The best he got was:

> **Bob Dylan**: 'Big River' – you wrote that song about a one-eyed man, didn't ya? I know you did. A man who couldn't catch any fish, I heard from an old lady down in Memphis.
> **Johnny Cash**: Ah, she told you. I didn't know I was going to be exposed. I shouldn't have walked up the bluff and raised a few eyebrows.
> **BD**: I'll sing one of those countless country-folk-protest songs with you. It's nice to be here with a real protester for a change ... I'm very proud of my protesting. It has earned me a brass ring in the nose, and

three pairs of clean socks, plus thousands and thousands of lampshades just lined up in front of me.

When Cash proves to have little else to offer, Dylan resorts to a series of country duets on songs Cash has already recorded, but doesn't seem to know. Alderson thinks the plan was to 'record some precious shit, but nothing ever happened because they were so ... *stoned*'.

Thankfully, in Dylan's case the drugs only made his performances more edgy, more confrontational. By now, Robertson had realized that Dylan was 'maintaining his performance level with the help of amphetamines ... but these particular pills Bob had were ... much smoother; you didn't get too wired ... Nonetheless, in time all of this shit catches up with you.' What didn't help was the inability of Dylan's chauffeur/drug mule, Tom Keylock, to follow the simplest instructions:

Richard Alderson: Dylan ... hated LSD [but] he drank a lot of red wine and he took these little amphetamine pills. But we had this guy in Britain called Tom Keylock and we would always send him out for drugs in Britain and he would never come back with what we sent him for. We'd send him for hash and he'd come back with kif, and we'd send him for kif, he'd come back with heroin. He always came back with something, but he never came back with the right thing.

It is Keylock, doing his day job of minder-driver, who is at the wheel as Dylan tells John Lennon, before the London shows, 'I could vomit into the camera ... It'd be a good ending. We could call it *Cooking With Bob Dylan*,' surely a reference to injecting substances, which not surpisingly got cut from the film. All Dylan would admit to, after the fact, was that 'the strain got pretty tough ... Everyone else was having a good time and some really unhealthy things cropped up.'

Pennebaker, invariably the straightest guy in the room, knew 'there were a lot of drugs going down that I didn't know about, [even though] I was carrying for everybody'. Soon enough he recognized the effect it was having on them all – especially Dylan: 'I don't know what kind of chemicals he and Robbie were putting down but I'm telling you it made him very irascible and very peculiar. He never slept – and I just couldn't take it after a while ... There was a lot of weird behaviour on that trip, [but] ... the pressures were enormous.'

If the days were starting to drag, there was one hour each day when it all came together, and Dylan felt whole. As his redneck, bedrock drummer recalled, 'As soon as he strapped on that black Telecaster, he was ready to rock. He would jump around in the dressing room. He could not wait to get on that stage ... Sometimes Bob would hardly face the audience in the electric set. He played to the band ... where his focus was.'

The ever-observant Eye also couldn't help but notice the change: 'You could see right away that the difference [between acoustic and electric sets] was night and day in terms of his performance.' He soon began to tailor the footage he was shooting to take account of this: 'I'd gotten tired of just shooting anything that took place and [so] I started making a film the only way I know ... I was caught up in it a little bit and made a film [my way] over three or four days and then I kinda let it go.' Inevitably, it brought him into conflict with Alk and, to an extent, Dylan:

> I wasn't opposed to the film he was making ... I just didn't exactly know how to do it. So I started making [my] kind of film ... You can see that sometimes ... He thinks I'm shooting this thing the way he wants it to be shot [and I'm not] ... [] ... I began to think we couldn't film that [drama] with long lenses. I had to get out on stage, put a wide angle lens on the camera and get into it, myself. That was a big decision. It meant the first time Dylan came out on stage and I was standing there with a camera, he almost flipped.

Dylan had no such problem with Don documenting conversations backstage as he changed from the creature he was, never quite knowing what the reaction might be. On one occasion Alderson asks if he read a review that alleged people walked out. He jokes, 'One paper said *everybody* walked out. I'm gonna walk out. That's what I should do – in the first half, when they're all so quiet ... I['ve] decided I'm gonna tell 'em, Dylan got sick.'* On another, someone asks, 'You gonna do any folk songs in the first half?' Dylan loves the idea, 'Yeah. I'm gonna

---

* He delivers on this threat, telling a Glaswegian audience, 'Bob Dylan got very sick backstage, and I'm here to take his place.'

do some folk songs. I'm gonna give it to them – "Boo! We want the real Bob Dylan."'

In fact, he was doing one folk song nightly, 'Baby Let Me Follow You Down', in a way which might have even shocked Bert Berns. At the concert after Cardiff, in Birmingham, he responded to shouts of 'Stop trying to be a pop star' and 'Play some folk music' by sneering, 'Aaah, folk music. If you want folk music, I'll play you some folk music ... I'll sing you a folk song that ma granddaddy sang to ma mother when she was a little girl. It goes like this!'* The *Redbrick* reviewer suggested, 'If his mother had heard what followed, the chances are that Bob would never have been born.'

If Mr *Redbrick* thought this was sacrilege, he should have heard a backstage session in which Dylan parodied, first, 'Blowin' In The Wind' – 'The answer, [my friend,] is slowing in the pin' – and then 'Masters Of War', a song he wrote a couple of miles away but never sounded like this: 'Come you bastards of CORE / You that have all the fun ... You tell me to run, you bastards of CORE / I've learnt all the things that you said you'd save / And now you've done it / Edgar Allan Poe would shit in his grave.'

Another feature of the backstage banter is Dylan's concern with what the crowd outside look like. On one occasion, someone says, 'They all have short hair,' apparently not a good sign. Dylan is constantly dispatching Keylock to go talk to them. In one instance, he asks, 'What's the audience like?' and Keylock replies, 'Pretty good. I asked a couple of kids, they said they liked big bands. When I asked them what they'd read in the papers, they said they didn't know.' Dylan clearly wants to know if they'd bought into any tabloid bullshit. In Paris, he asks Keylock if he was 'here with The Stones? Different to The Stones? Older?' On loan from the Dartford renegades, Keylock informs him he has nothing to fear out front – as long as he tunes up.

At another point Dylan turns to Neuwirth and asks, 'Have you seen these people?' Neuwirth unhelpfully suggests he should give them 'a little drug-rock music'. Neuwirth is enjoying the conflict almost as much as Dylan and wants it to continue. He even hits on the idea of

---

* For once, Richard Alderson was a little too slow making the reel change before 'Baby Let Me Follow You Down', and missed Dylan's brief rap from his otherwise exemplary tape of the show.

interviewing audience-members *on camera*, just as soon as Pennebaker is out of the way. Sure enough, after Birmingham the obliging filmmaker heads for France, claiming in 1999, 'I got so frustrated I quit and went to Cannes ... I was never quite sure what I was meant to be doing.' In fact, the trip was prearranged. He was looking for someone to distribute *his* Dylan film. And once Don was out of the way, Neuwirth and Alk had carte blanche to go forth and find the naysayers, which they did before both Liverpool and Leicester, locating one particularly self-satisfied couple in Leicester:

> **Girl**: He sounds almost like any other group with this band behind him.
> **Her Boyfriend**: It's just a noise, instead of the words and the meaning.
> [Off-camera: Do you have tickets for the concert?]
> **Girl**: Yes, [but] it's not the original Bob Dylan, that's for sure.
> [Off-camera: He was booed last night in Liverpool.]
> **Boy**: It was in the second half when he was booed. So, it would seem [that] what we think is believed by others.

The home of The Beatles had indeed turned into something of a battleground, even if Dylan couldn't make out some of the supposed barbs (including, bizarrely, 'Woody would be turning in his grave'), the Scouse accent defeating him. Indeed, he confessed to The Hawks, pre-show, 'I always have this strange idea that if I stand and listen [closely], I'll be able to hear. [Laughs] Time goes by, and I'm trying to listen to what people are yelling, and I [just] can't.' Expecting trouble, he proceeds to give them what was presumably a minor variant on a regular pep talk: 'Just get ready to play ... Start in fast tonight, be ready to play – at all times ... I'll be ready ... [so] don't worry about me.'

One student, later a world-famous playwright, Willy Russell, recalls the electric set that night being 'so much better [than the first half]. He had become more and more angry and he was funnelling ... that anger towards the audience.' He certainly was – as evidenced by the one track from the world tour released in real time, an apocalyptic 'Tom Thumb' from Liverpool.

Yet those on his side were still very much in the majority, and audibly rooting for him. As T. Hardern of Nantwich informed *Disc*,

'At his Liverpool concert the audience appreciated the quiet sense of humour he showed to hecklers. No trace of the arrogance they try to pin on him. Incidentally, all the kids round us were digging the new Dylan very much.' On the same page was a letter from Barbara Ellis, who travelled to Liverpool *and* Sheffield. Both nights, she witnessed 'this ... little man, looking quite defenceless in spite of his backing group, fac[ing] a barrage of insults from a large section of the audience with a tolerance and humour the press could well take an example from'.

As he headed closer and closer to the northern marches, it became blatantly obvious that the response, at least from those who had come not to listen but to heckle, was highly orchestrated:

Richard Alderson: Someone had primed the audience [in some of these places] into an anti-folk-hero thing. They were all ready for Bob when he arrived. There must have been something in the press. The audience couldn't have reacted that way unprompted.

By the time they got to Manchester on May 17th, Dylan had decided it was time to capture the conflict on multitrack. He had hoped to do some of this the night before in Sheffield, but recording the electric set in the requisite fidelity proved beyond the wit of his own record label. Once again, Alderson showed the professionals how to do it: '[Columbia] brought all this gear, and all these microphones, and a whole crew, and I'm just by myself, taping off the PA feed ... [but] I listened to [their] tapes and they [didn't] have the ambience of the tapes I got, the depth of everything. It's the sound mix of the hall – that's all it was.'

When Dylan returned to his hotel room after the show, he listened to Alderson's tape of the electric set, which an attendant Gallic reporter called 'a nightly ritual'. Robertson, talking in 1987, also remembered 'listen[ing] to these tapes, and say[ing], Jeez, you know, this is very passionate. And it's people doing this with all their hearts. I don't know what more you['d] want.'

The Columbia boffins would get a second shot at taping this historic tour at the Free Trade Hall (which they managed to call the Royal Albert Hall on the tape box), a historic venue built on the site of the 1819 Peterloo Massacre that had inspired Shelley's famous aphorism 'Ye are many – they are few', almost the perfect motif for this performance.

The decision to try recording again had obviously been made at the last minute because the first three rows of a sold-out show now had to be removed, one eyewitness recalling, 'The stage was completely covered with equipment which was even spread out in front of the stage, on the floor.'

Hall manager, 'AS', was incensed by this imposition, complaining to promoter Tito Burns, 'The patrons attending paid to hear and see a concert, not a recording session.' He was even more 'annoyed ... by the arrogant and overbearing manner adopted by the persons employed on the recording. We were practically held to ransom – if recording was not permitted, then no concert, practically sums up the situation.' Grossman spelt it out to AS by adding an extra 'S'.

The show would go on. Manchester had been the first to sell out, outside of London, which Dylan was evidently aware of, because he wonders aloud as he jumps into the car post-gig, 'Jeez, I don't understand how they [manage to] buy the tickets up so fast.' What he would not have been aware of was that this was the first 'pop' concert at this prestigious concert-hall in six years. The last one had ended in a full-scale riot when the entertainment on offer changed out of all recognition. A sick Billy Fury had been replaced by the family entertainer, Joe Brown (the equivalent of replacing Sun-era Elvis with Paul Anka), the predictable result of which was that the place was trashed.*

Although the new Dylan was playing the same venue as the previous May, then he had been a folk act. And some of those who had paid top-dollar seemed to think he still was. One of 'the few' storming out during 'Like A Rolling Stone' would tell Bobby Neuwirth, 'We paid to see a folksinger.' What they had got instead was the loudest band in Christendom, fronted by an apostate incarnate. Rick Sanders, working the hall, described the volume as 'something that I'd never heard before, especially being so close up to it. I was just blasted out of my skin. It was physical rather than just listening to music.'

The acoustics of the venue were just perfect for this kind of music, and the volume merely enhanced the dynamics captured on tape. This

---

* The equally challenging Ornette Coleman Trio actually played the Free Trade Hall three days before Dylan in May 1966, a performance broadcast on the Home Service.

time there would be no snafus, after Dylan made an appearance that afternoon for 'a short soundcheck with his band, [as] the two cameramen and two soundmen film[ed] around him.' This was going to be one well-documented show. Pennebaker himself was back from Cannes to resume filming; Alderson was still rolling tape; Feinstein even snapped the moment Dylan walked onstage for the electric set – after an acoustic half that didn't quite have the same otherworldly quality as Sheffield – ready to rock the rafters, surrounded on every side (including behind him, onstage) by paying punters. What happened next is best described by eyewitness, John Kappes:

> Bob appeared onstage and the band very quickly followed him. ... The drummer seemed to be the odd one out ... Bob appeared to be enjoying himself, smiling quite frequently and during guitar riffs etc. was dancing around in front of the drums, extraordinary for a folkie! The slow handclapping gradually spreads and at the start of 'Baby Let Me Follow You Down', the band seemed not to take Bob's lead. He looked to his right and then to his left to Robbie Robertson, I thought he was going to walk off! The song then took off. I can also remember ... the incoherent talking into the microphone [before 'One Too Many Mornings']. Everyone was shushing, [thinking] he's trying to say something. The noise grew louder and louder, people were walking out and one fellow walked by the stage with his hands over his ears, within a few feet of Bob who, I am sure, saw him. People around me were arguing amongst themselves ... People were shouting, 'Ignore them Bobby!', 'You're still great!' and similar things. At the end of each song Bob would make deep bows and blow kisses with both hands to the audience as if acknowledging tremendous acclaim. While this was all going on, the band continued as if nothing was happening. Robbie Robertson always seemed to have that half-smile. There was also a long pause before 'Ballad Of A Thin Man' – [because] someone was leaning onto the front of the stage waving a piece of paper at Bob.

The 'piece of paper' contained just six words, 'Tell the band to go home.' The woman who wrote it, a hard-hearted Barbara, seemed to think Dylan was oblivious to the effect his performance was having. But Rick Sanders quickly realized 'the long tune-ups were [an act of] defiance. Very calculated ... Whatever he was on had him operating on a very different velocity to anyone else – even the band.' The one journalist who'd elected to document the second most important concert in rock history, Jean-Marc Pascal, felt only admiration for the frontman as a war of words ensued:

> From the audience, a restless one, come several epithets that can be heard above the huge sound of the rock'n'roll group; words like 'Play some folk songs …' and 'Go get some work with The Rolling Stones …' and 'Traitor …' and 'We don't need you! We already have The Animals, and The Beatles', while the rest of the audience which doesn't participate in the rout, applauds, clasping hands and feet, shouting approvingly. Undaunted by the noise, … the object of both animosity and marks of allegiance, keeps singing … Bob Dylan has long ago accepted his fate.

But even Pascal failed to reference the defining moment of this concert – and all concerts since Forest Hills. Just before 'Like A Rolling Stone', as Dylan indulged in another act of defiant tuning-up, someone shouted for Child Ballad 26 – JUDAS!! The person responsible, a student from Keele called Keith Butler, couldn't believe what Dylan was doing to these 'lovely songs':* 'I was emotional, and I think my anger just welled up inside of me. It was "One Too Many Mornings" that really sent me over the top.' It was the cue for further taunts, resounding support for Dylan and the man himself telling The Hawks to 'play fucking loud'! It was the end for the disenchanted 'few' among this audience. It was time to leave. Dozens headed for the exit, only to be confronted in the foyer by a cameraman, a brave Jones Alk and a delighted Bobby Neuwirth, wanting to know what they thought. They let fly:

'It was a load of rubbish. He's taking everyone for a ride. He knows this. I know this. But the other turds in there didn't. Simple as that.'

'It was worse than The Beatles.'

'It was worth 12/6 for the first three-quarters of an hour. But if you pay to see a pop group, you [would] pay to see The Beatles. I came to see Bob Dylan play folk music.'

'Bob Dylan was a bastard in the second half.'

---

* Another candidate later claimed responsibility but he was in the balcony and couldn't remember Dylan's retort, convincing me to discount his version as scarcely credible.

'I can go to any dance hall in the Pott[erie]s and listen to that crap.'

'I hope he spews up all his guts on the way home.'

'Dylan was shit. I'd accept it from The Stones, but I don't accept it from Dylan.'

While Pennebaker positioned himself on the horseshoe of the Free Trade Hall circle to film the dramatic finale, capturing as much of 'Like A Rolling Stone' as he could, Alk and Neuwirth were asking a retinue of blunt northerners, 'What do you want from him?', 'What didn't you like about it?' and, most enticing of all, 'If you could tell him anything, what would you tell him?'

After someone suggests, 'It's like he's drugged,' a hilarious series of non sequiturs ensues – 'What's wrong with being drugged?' – 'Pass the pills round' – before the original critic complains, 'He's changed from what he was.' Neuwirth asks the angry Mancunian to 'sum it up in one word'. He gets three: 'Shit. Rubbish. Crap.'

By now, the final chords of 'Like A Rolling Stone' can be heard, and the people streaming for the exit are far more positive about what they have seen, forcing Neuwirth to ask the teeming fans, 'Anybody think he was rubbish?' With a cue like that, a steaming mad student from Keele leans over content concertgoers to shout, 'I've heard third-rate pop groups better than that.' Neuwirth calls Butler over, and out it pours: 'It was a bloody disgrace. He wants shooting. He's a traitor.' Meanwhile, a particularly perceptive girl whispers to her friend, 'I bet they only show [those] that say crap.'

Dylan had already jumped into a limo for the 200-yard journey to the Midland Hotel, admitting he couldn't 'hear anything. I d[id]n't even wanna get in tune,' while Robertson remarks, 'They yell in this weird nasal tone.'

The showdown of all showdowns has somehow passed the press by. Only the local letter-writers feel the urge to memorialize this momentous performance, a Mr McCann apologizing to Dylan in the *Evening News* on behalf of 'Manchester people' for 'a childish display of audience participation ... Certain members of the audience jeered and slow-clapped him ... even after he had apologised for playing too loud'.* Meanwhile, in the *Oldham Evening Chronicle*, a self-proclaimed 'Dylan Fan' concluded, 'Bob put his feelings over to the knockers just

---

* He has evidently misheard and/or misunderstood Dylan's command to 'play fucking loud'.

great. When someone shouted out to him "Judas!", he just calmly went to the microphone and quietly drawled, "Ya liar!"'

Dylan knew it was history in the making, and asked for an acetate to be cut of the electric set. In so doing, he inadvertently gave an enthralled IBC engineer the opportunity to dub it himself. Anyone and everyone who heard it over the next four years thought it should have a wider audience, and ultimately it did; first, on more bootlegs than a Kentucky whiskey still; finally, in 1998, as *The Bootleg Series Vol. 4*. How had something this dramatic taken thirty-two years to be released?

For Dylan and The Hawks, though, it was *not* the end. Not by a long chalk. As they headed further north, toward the very font of traditional ballad-singing, the response only grew more vituperative – and not just onstage. In a hotel room, probably in Glasgow or Edinburgh, Tom Keylock remembered room service came with extra vitriol: 'The waiter come[s] in, "Put it down there," I sign for it, and he [suddenly] says, "I want to talk to him! [To Dylan] You're a fucking traitor to folk music!" ... Albert looked at me, "Get him out of here!" I shoved open the door and shoved him out.'

In Glasgow, unlike in Manchester, the Scottish *Daily Mail* reported it all: 'There were shouts of "rubbish" from the purists and "shut up" from the beat fans', and the now nightly 'slow handclap when he launched into "Leopard-Skin Pill-Box Hat"'. What the reporter didn't catch was the moment when Dylan, in his own words, 'was walking off the stage ... [and] a chick rushed up. She came right up and punched the shit out of my face. Happened so fast I thought it was a guy.' Robertson saw it, but couldn't quite believe it: 'There was a ramp coming off the stage – [she] jumped right up.' The experience was shocking enough for Dylan to comment on it five years later for a planned interview in *Esquire*:

> At some place ... instead of a drop in front of the stage there was a [ramp]. Very strange – you could just walk right into the audience from the stage. And this big chick stormed the stage, she just came right up ... really meant to have it out – the electric music wasn't working for her [I guess].'

At least in Edinburgh, Dylan found a new fan, an octogenarian from the hotel whom he invited backstage beforehand. She wondered whether there would be a seat for her. Dylan assured her, 'There will be. A lot of people don't like electronic music, and some of them who really don't like it, they just walk out. So you'll get their seat.'

During the concert, another *Daily Mail* reporter noticed, 'Dylan repeatedly turned his back on the audience and posed for his personal cine-photographer.'* By Newcastle, the last provincial date, Dylan was inclined to chide his critics, prefacing a ramped-up 'Thin Man' with 'C'mon now, you know I'm a sick man. Leave me alone.' Yet that pleading figure was nowhere to be seen a couple of minutes later as he pumped the piano and punched the air, declaiming, 'Something is happening ... and it's happening to *you*, isn't *it*, Mr Jones!'

The next morning he boarded a flight to Paris – after standing in line with all the straight people on the tarmac, looking like *The Man Who Fell To Earth* – during which he interrogated Jean-Marc Pascal on his likely reception: 'What am I going to do in a country where no one understands what I'm saying? Do you think they'll boo me at the Olympia? What sort of questions will they ask me at the press conference?' Jean reassured him, 'Nothing original, you can be assured. What do you think about the Vietnam war? Why have you changed your style of music? What do you think about long hair?' He now knew what to do, 'Fine. Stupid questions deserve stupid answers.'

What he didn't expect was to be waylaid at Le Bourget airport by a group of fans looking to conduct their own mini press conference. One of them even gave him a list of questions once compiled by Marcel Proust, only for Dylan to make it plain what he thinks of the idea: 'Why'd he ask all these dumb questions? Who's your favourite painter? *That's* a question Proust would ask of somebody? What quality do you prefer in a woman?' The thick-skinned fan offers to send him the book. Meanwhile, another fan wants to know whether he thinks he'll be misunderstood: 'What do I care? We don't play English music or French music or Russian music. We play American music.'

L'experiénce turned out to be good practice for the 'real' Paris press conference, conducted in a ballroom of the George V, the following afternoon. Covering his bases, Dylan brought a visual prop, a ventriloquist's puppet he'd picked up that morning in the local flea market. Barry Feinstein, who witnessed the showdown close up, noted, 'If

---

* This seems to be the occasion Pennebaker surprised Dylan by filming onstage.

[journalists] asked him something sensible, he gave them a decent answer ... [but] every time one of the [French] journalists asked him a [dumb] question, he put his ear to the puppet's mouth and pretended to listen to the answer. Then he would tell the press. It drove them nuts.' The result was confusion, and mutiny from stern to bow:

Q: Why do you have a doll sitting next to you?
BD: He just sneaks up on me.
Q: Is it a symbol, mascot or fetish?
BD: It's a religion ...
Q: Do you think you could build a career in France?
BD: In what? Ridicule?
Q: Do you think you'll be understood when you sing tomorrow?
BD: No ...
Q: Don't you think your first records were much better than the ones you do now?
BD: Who said that? You? [To interpreter] Ask him if he's American.
Q: I'm French.
BD: That's probably why you think that ...
Q: Which American singers do you rate?
BD: Bessie Smith. Ma Rainey. Memphis Minnie. Billie Holiday. Nancy Sinatra. I like everybody ...
Q: Do you always live as a beatnik?
BD: What do you mean beatnik? [To interpreter] Ask him what he means.
Q: Someone who travels whenever he feels like it.
BD: Tell him, that's very kind of him ...
Woman Journo [in English]: Do you find yourself involved in the great questions America must face? I mean, the negro problem, Vietnam and so on.
BD: Why do people ask me these questions? ...
Q: Is there anything you're quite sure of?
BD: Ashtrays, doorknobs, windowpanes ...

Monsieur Jones hadn't done his homework. Finally, exasperated by Gallic ignorance and the gall of French editors for sending along almost entirely non-English-speaking reporters, Dylan turns to the poor interpreter and says, 'I don't mind them asking questions about anything, but I mind them asking questions about my music, because they don't know anything about my music. Tell 'em not to ask me anything about my music. They don't in other places,' lines he should perhaps have used in *Eat The Document*. When this doesn't work, he answers all the 'stupid' questions in one fell swoop: 'I don't belong to any movement. I've only got some ideas in my head and I tell them. I don't support anybody's causes. No revolution ever came about because of songs.'

None of the footage shot at the conference is deemed worthy enough for the film, which is again on Dylan's mind. A two-day break from performance allows him to shoot a couple more improvised scenes involving two heavily made-up girls, one dressed as Batgirl, and a mock fall from the balcony. Hardly cutting-edge stuff, almost all of it ending up on the cutting-room floor. What doesn't would stop the film making sense.

The real drama will once again happen onstage in a theatre of world renown – L'Olympia – or backstage, as Dylan held court to French pop royalty and a single expat writer. Mason Hoffenberg has shown up with a new wife, much to Dylan's delight, flanked by French folkie Hugues Aufray, rocker Johnny Hallyday and *chanteuse* Françoise Hardy.

He proceeds to yank his friend's Yankee chain, 'C'mon Mason, be the old Mason. You haven't changed too, have you?' before announcing, 'I'm twenty-five years old at this minute.' It's quite true. Robert Allen Zimmerman is celebrating a quarter-century on earth, and can't quite believe he's made it this far. To celebrate the occasion he asks a photographer to 'take a picture of me, and Johnny [Hallyday] and Mason ... He's one of the great Parisian writers. We're doing this for a talent-show contest – help all the young kids along.'

Yet it is the diffident Hardy – someone he'd referenced as far back as the *Another Side* sleeve notes – whom he is primarily fixated on, whispering to her after the backstage has been cleared in a surprisingly self-conscious way:

> I wish I could talk French, so I could talk to you ... Do you have good seats, Françoise? I wanna talk to you as much as I can, 'cause I don't know when I'll ever see you again. Things are like that. I don't have to go [yet]. Hey, please sit down, Françoise. I won't hurt you. I won't

start the concert till I'm sure you're where you need to be. Don't take this personal – I'm not coming on [to you] or anything. I just want you to know that I know who you are and I think you're very beautiful. I don't know what you're all about or anything like that, but if you ever don't wanna hurt, you can always come see me. Any time.

He was misreading the situation. Françoise wasn't worried for herself, she was concerned about him: 'I wasn't aware of all the drugs and everything but I had this bad feeling about him. He was so thin. He was very frail. He really seemed to be sick. He wasn't well in himself. I honestly thought he was at death's door.' Nor was she mistaken about the shape he was in – or how smitten he was: 'After the concert ... he invited me to come to his room alone ... He played me two songs that hadn't even been released at the time, "Just Like A Woman" and "I Want You". I was delighted! But he wasn't in love with me, he was in love with my image, which is different.' He should have known just how that felt.

By the time he finally took the stage, the hour was getting late. As Keylock told me, 'He was in a bit of a state with his pills ... He wouldn't come out of the dressing room. Albert and Tito [Burns] couldn't get him out. ... It took me about fifteen minutes to get him onstage.' This was just the beginning of his travails. His acoustic guitar refused to stay in tune, and he was growing increasingly frustrated. Even as he tried to compensate by applying pinprick precision to those convoluted lyrics, the breaks between the songs grew longer and longer, and the audience grew increasingly restless. Just before 'Just Like A Woman' someone shouts something negative and he snaps:

I'm doing this for you. I don't care. If you want to hear it that way, I'll play it that way ... [more shouting] You just can't wait, can ya? You have to go to work at ten [p.m.], huh? It's a drag for me, too. But that's folk music for ya! It does this all the time ... Anyone have another guitar? My guitar's broken. It got broke on the way here. It's happened many times before. Nothing to be alarmed about. Didn't you bring a magazine to read or something? ... In the meantime, you can go to the bowling alley [starts the song but abandons it, prompting further heckling] Oh come on, I wouldn't behave like this if I came to see you

... It's fun to just watch me tune it. Hey, I wanna get out of here as fast as you want to get out of here.

But if he thinks he had lost the audience in the acoustic set, the roar of applause after 'Mr Tambourine Man' tells him all is forgiven. Whether he is in such a forgiving mood himself is another matter entirely. He stamps backstage for a showdown with Alderson, who meets Mr 'Who Threw The Fucking Glass' for the first time. According to a demented Dylan, the main problem was not the guitar, but the monitors:

You could've stopped the fucking show. It's the worse thing I ever wanna go through, man. I'm gonna walk off the fucking stage next time. Fuck it ... I could not hear shit, man. I was beating the guitar, [thinking the] strings are gonna go any second. Can't even hear the fucking guitar to put it in tune. That can't ever happen again, man ... Even in the last song, all I could hear was the song. I'm not playing this half if I'm hearing it this way. You're gonna stay out there and fix this son of a bitch till it works. I don't care if those people go home, man. The show is not gonna go on ... I should've pulled it on the first song but you let me go all the way to the fucking end song ... Richard, I don't want you to think I'm pissed off at you. [But] I'm not gonna go back onstage. That vocal mike is out. I'm not gonna go back on for the second half. You tell Fred Perry to stick his fifteen-minute intermission up his ass. ... It was the worst thing since I was twelve years old, man.* I called four times, 'Get me off the stage.' It's the best [sound] system in the world, but it failed ... from the first song. I couldn't hear nothing.

Alderson, to his credit, refuses to take any of this personally and talks Dylan down. But he could see that 'he was [now] burning himself up'. Thankfully, the singer finally strapped on his Telecaster and poured his frustrations into the music, delivering an electric set that ranks with Manchester, without a gram of hostility from this French audience. As in Scandinavia, they seem delighted by the new sound, not even rising to the bait when Dylan has a fifty-foot American flag

---

* Is this a reference to the Golden Chords at Hibbing High School, by any chance?

draped across the back of the stage when the curtain opens. The message is clear: 'We don't play English music or French music ... We play American music.'*

Once again the local press was determined to spin their own web of perceived hostility. *Paris Jour*, remembering the Treaty of Versailles, printed their headline in English, 'Dylan Go Home!' It took a German journalist, from *Pop* magazine, to point out that 'the little orchestra played with remarkable precision and with swing. Bob on the other hand seemed to be a little out of control, the general presumption [being] that he performed on dope.'

General or not, it was a presumption no other paper voiced, even if those who had known the bright young thing of yesteryear were in little doubt. McCartney, for one, remembered calling at the Mayfair hotel in the days after Paris: 'People would come out and say ... Bob's taking a nap or make [other] terrible excuses, and I'd say, "It's okay, man, I understand, he's out of it."'

Likewise, when Dylan and Lennon took a spin around Hyde Park to film something for his TV movie, trying – in Pennebaker's words – 'to invent something that would be amusing in some way' – a concerned Don noticed 'Dylan was ... in such a terrible state that after a while I don't think he knew what he was saying.' After the drive, Dylan stayed slumped in his seat until (John and) Don 'picked him up and hauled him upstairs and got him into his room. We laid him down on his bed ... He looked dead. We went downstairs and back outside, and John said, "Well, I think we just said goodbye to ol' Bob."'

Thankfully, he just had one more show to get through, the second of two sell-outs at London's Royal Albert Hall.† Backstage before that final show, Robertson turned to ask, 'You got one more show left in you?' He replied, 'I'm just getting warmed up.' But Robbie noticed 'his eyes looked dark and hollow'. Pennebaker, too, concluded, 'He was like a fighter ... trying to survive ... in spite of all the things he put into himself.' *NME*'s Tony Tyler, allowed backstage beforehand,

---

* The booing that accompanies this moment in *Eat The Document* has been dubbed on from another concert.
† The first London show had passed off largely without incident, even if the *Telegraph* accused him of 'show[ing] signs of a man who does not care whether he communicates'.

recalls, 'He looked heavily out of it. His eyes were rolled up inside his head. He was in no fit state to perform ... Suddenly, he made a convulsive jerk and knocked the [tea] all over Dana Gillespie, who was sitting on the floor beside him ... He was really good, though – especially in the second half.'

Lennon, expecting the worst, was astounded by Dylan's performance, having heard 'all that stuff about [him] being booed ha[d] been exaggerated. I saw [both] London concerts and about five or six people booed ... and everyone else in the audience was shutting them up.'

Actually, on that final night, things *did* get a little heated. And Dylan, far from being 'a little out of control', was out of his mind and out to antagonise. Dana Gillespie, for one, realized, even before he explained it to her, that 'when the audience booed and jeered his rock numbers in London, he just rocked [it] up more to annoy them'.

Dylan knew this was his last chance to get a few things off his chest, and before 'Visions Of Johanna', he decided to give the press a piece of his mangled mind, 'This is a typical example of what your English newspapers would call a *drurg* song. I don't write *drurg* songs ... I wouldn't know how to ... It's just *Not* a *Drurg* song. It's just vulgar to think so.' He also set some paying punters straight before 'I Don't Believe You', delivering his longest rap to date:

> This is a song I wrote about three years ago. I like all my old songs. I never said they were 'rubbish' [said in a northern accent]. I don't use that word. It's not in my vocabulary. I wouldn't use it if it was there on the street to use for free ... This music, ... no matter what it is, if anybody out there could offer any advice on how it could be played better or the words improved, we['d] appreciate all suggestions. Other than that, we like these songs. I'm only saying this because this is the last night we're here and I luuuve England a lot, but we did this in the States from September on, and we've been playing this music since we were ten years old and folk music happens to be a thing which ... was very useful y'know ... I realize it's loud music but if you don't like it, well, that's fine ... But the thing is, it's not English music you're listening to. It might sound like English music, if you've never heard American music before ... What you're hearing now is the sound of the songs. You're not hearing anything else. You can take it or leave it.

It doesn't matter to me, it really doesn't ... If you disagree, I'm not gonna fight you ... Anyway, this happens to be an old song, called 'I Don't Believe You'. It used to go like that and now it goes like this – and rightfully so!

Then, just before 'Tom Thumb's Blues' he singles out some hecklers down front and tells them, 'You don't want me to do it, I don't care ... We'll just play the music and leave. And [pointing at] you and you and you can just go out and read some books.' Increasingly, though, he is slurring his words and losing the thread. Before one final 'Rolling Stone', he signs off by insisting his backing band are 'all poets' and that they've 'enjoyed every minute of being here'. He sounds dead on his feet, almost literally.

Twelve years later, he will find himself back in Australia, the starting point of all this insanity, on his second and last world tour. Sat in his Brisbane hotel – talking to a fellow survivor, Craig McGregor – he admits for the first time, 'I was straining pretty hard and couldn't have gone on living that way much longer. The fact that I made it through what I did is pretty miraculous.' Amen.

After that final London show, on May 27th, it was time to wrap up the gear, clean out the hotel room and process all the film.* And yet, for a man who had been desperately homesick three weeks earlier, he seemed in no great hurry to head home; to life and life only. Indeed, he took the time to shoot one more reel, one more scene – no playacting, just him alone, looking straight into the camera, getting a few things off his chest:

> I know I am being distorted. But ... I always know what I'm gonna say. I could say, 'This is the Bob Dylan Show', and they wouldn't know what it was, but they'd say, 'I see he sells a lot of records. We didn't know he did *this*! He really is very good. We should bring him to Hollywood.' Nobody who's looking at me now has got any idea what they're seeing ... And [yet] they have the gall to think it's *me*!

---

* Keylock would be paid extra to remove all evidence of pills and the like from Dylan's room after he left London.

Winterlude #2 (June/July 1966): Off The Road Again

> [This] was the time that he was most caressed and possessed by the various drugs that he was taking. The effects on him were that he was pretty displaced.
>
> Carly Simon

The last documented sighting we have of a pre-accident Dylan 'at work' comes courtesy of the diary of Beatles' driver, Alf Bicknell, who records two nights – May 28th–29th – spent 'in the company of the boys and Bob Dylan, watching some of his home movies that he is turning into a film' (though George, for one, just 'wanted to sit down and sing and play with Bob').

These screenings could well have had a greater import – assuaging some of ABC's concerns. As the executive producer of the *Stage 66* series, Hubbell Robinson, later said, 'We didn't know what we had because when we saw the film ... it wasn't yet edited.' What he saw was quite possibly the same as John, Paul, George and Ringo. Also privy to some of the same footage around this time was Mason Hoffenberg, who described a very different film to what was released in a 1973 *Playboy* feature:

> They had this terrific film team travelling with him, shooting miles of film ... And a good film editor named Howard Alk was going to put it together ... But every time they cut to Dylan, it was like a commercial ... It would have been a great film if they ... showed the scene around him, what it was like for him to tour. The guys in The Band were great, because the pressure wasn't on them ... but they kept arbitrarily returning to Dylan, and ... he's not a movie actor ... There was a great picture in those miles of film.

According to Harry Rasky, who was still ostensibly the film's producer, he – and Robinson – had flown into London to meet with the man at the Mayfair, where Dylan told him, 'We're going to do things my way.' In 1998, Rasky described 'one unusual experience – attending a private late-night screening of *dont look back* [sic] with Dylan and The Beatles. When it was over ... [I] discovered The Beatles [were] asleep.' Shortly afterwards, Grossman 'paid him ... to leave' London job-less.

It was going to be Dylan's film all the way. And his manager approved. According to Robbie, Grossman 'had no problem sticking this in ABC's face ... [After] Albert screened it for ABC, their response was, "Are you crazy? We can't show this on television. It's too weird. Nobody will get it, and we don't get it."'

Robbie's account certainly sounds like the response Rasky and Robinson would have given on seeing the 'roughs' in London, at a time when Dylan and Grossman were still preaching from the same pulpit, determined to make 'a splendid rebuke to everything that the dumbness of TV represented'.

Yet by the time Dylan finally crawled back to Woodstock, some time in June, probably after a short break in Spain with Sara, he had perhaps realized he had better produce something ABC *could* screen, even if he knew not how. Making a rare sortie to the city to review the footage shot, he turned expectantly to Pennebaker, who 'spent two or three days looking at stuff in the studio and then he said, "Well, I want you guys to go ahead and make some sort of a rough edit to get an idea of what you did because ABC is coming after it." ... So Neuwirth and I started to edit something together ... a twenty- or thirty-minute thing.'

If Dylan was temporarily washing his hands of one irksome project, he faced the prospect of another hitting the streets in October to widespread incomprehension and wholesale brickbats unless he did something about it. Probably on the same trip into the city, Dylan called in at Macmillan's to see Bob Markel, taking 'a break from some film-editing he was doing. We talked a little about the book, and about Rameau and Rimbaud, and Bob promised to finish "making a few changes" in [the next] two weeks. A few days after that, [he] stopped working.'

It was way too late to start 'making a few changes'. The galleys of *Tarantula* were already abroad, promotional badges had been made and covers printed, a state of affairs which would come back to haunt Dylan, who knew nothing of the exigencies of book production. He just knew he wanted out, but had yet to find a way.

He did, thankfully, have a greater grasp of the record industry, going out of his way to ensure that even before *Blonde On Blonde* hit the streets *finally* – on June 20th* – there would be vinyl evidence of the aural havoc he had just unleashed. On June 10th, Columbia released their third 'preview' on 45, 'I Want You'. However, at the last minute Dylan pulled the intended B-side, 'Tombstone Blues', replacing it with another song from *Highway 61*, 'Just Like Tom Thumb's Blues', which used to sound like that, but never sounded like this: a soundtrack to the end of the world, recorded in Liverpool one evening in May.

Although it was Alderson's tape, he was out of the picture: '[Columbia] never talked to me. They probably resented the fact they were putting my mono tape in preference to theirs ... I remember listening to a test pressing and thinking they did a really bad job mastering ... [But I also] remember thinking, "Maybe I fucked up."'

Actually, it sounded magnificent; not so much edge-of-the-seat as edge-of-the-precipice; prompting the English music press's six-minute man to rear his head again, this time for *Record Mirror*, calling it 'probably the worst thing by Bob on record'. And that was that – the last official representation of this audio Apocalypse for nineteen years, plenty of time for the legend to ferment.

There was also a plan to release the 1966 arrangement of 'Baby Let Me Follow You Down', just not with Dylan himself wailing the words. Grossman had a new potential protégé, a precocious young singer-songwriter called Carly Simon, and on June 25th, 1966, Dylan – evidently still in town – phoned an awestruck Simon to invite her down to Grossman's office to discuss making a record.† She arrived to find Dylan was still eight miles high:

---

* A comment Dylan makes at the London press conference on May 3rd – 'I have an album record in the States' – suggests he doesn't yet know about the delayed release.
† A day (or two) before, Dylan had popped in to see his old friend John Hammond Jr recording his new album, *I Can Tell*. He probably continued on to a party at the Chelsea Hotel, attended by at least two characters from *Blonde On Blonde*, Brian Jones and Edie Sedgwick. Simon did indeed record the song, with Robertson audibly on lead guitar, but it doesn't sound like The Hawks.

If talking to Bob Dylan on the phone paralyzed me, being in the same room made me ... even more awestruck ... Thank God he was stoned, which meant I didn't have to worry too much about making a good impression ... Bob went on and on about the glory, the sheer magic, that was Nashville, and told me that if and when I recorded an album, Nashville was the place to be ... Then he recommended a song that he said would be perfect for me, 'Baby Let Me Follow You Down' ... [] ... [It] seemed like he was very high on speed: very, very wasted and talking incoherently, saying a lot about God and Jesus.

He wasn't just talking 'about God and Jesus'. He was writing about them, too, on a new typewriter, tapping out seemingly random thoughts which read like aphorisms, one of which was: 'Evil is not done, it is imagined', a line from Jean-Paul Sartre's biography of Jean Genet, an artist who very nearly *was* hung as a thief. Sartre explained that he wrote the book 'to prove that genius is not a gift but the way out that one invents in desperate cases'. Another phrase Dylan typed, 'Occide Moriturus', is a term from Jung's *Psychology of the Unconscious*, in a section where the psychologist states that any 'step towards a new life means, at the same time, the death of the past life'. Seems somebody was busy being reborn.

If Dylan was looking for answers from these modern philosophers, he may also have been turning to one from more classical times. Another typed saying reads 'That which is not the City of God is itself the City of God', which could and should be from St Augustine of Hippo's *Civitas Dei*. But it isn't. Nevertheless, the fourth-century author of *Confessions* may already be haunting his dreams – as may Christ, about whom he writes, 'O son of heaven! Who knows thy age[?] ... We don't owe thanks to life! explain we do not deserve death!'

Further evidence of mortality preying on his mind in the weeks before a near-death experience is provided by a single, typed song title (not expanded upon) – 'Sweet Black Darkness'. But, just as with the fall 1963 Margolis & Moss typescripts, there are no song lyrics among the papers from the two months which separate the private screening of footage from 'the road' and a back brake locking on the road.

It seems unlikely this would have worried Dylan. There had been similar hiatuses between *Times* ... and *Another Side*, and *Bringing It* ... and *Highway 61*. Fortunately, just as the Margolis & Moss papers provide a serendipitous peek into the post-JFK Dylan in retreat, so the Tulsa papers start to make their presence felt just as he is disappearing from view in the early summer of 1966.

Tulsa, of all places, had been on Dylan's mind as recently as May 23rd, when he had launched another truth-attack on an Okie émigré at Paris's George V hotel, an exchange which included this admission from Dylan: 'I don't speak with a nothing Midwest accent, [but] I've been to Tulsa, Oklahoma and I found the highway. I know it as good as I know this room.' The conversation continues along similar lines:

> **Writer**: Maybe I'm where you were many years ago. The times have changed.
> **BD**: Yeah, but I was cute. You're not cute … How many years of college have you had?
> **Writer**: None. One semester. I went to South-Western College in Oklahoma.
> **BD**: And you were a freak, [weren't you?] And you had to split … I can't help that you [haven't] gotten over the barrel, man. But I made my records and I did what I had to do when I made those records that were heard [even] in Oklahoma.

But Dylan was no longer sure he wanted to be that person who 'took me out of where I was in and [led me somewhere] I could make money'. Already, an inner voice is whispering in his ear, warning him about ' Greed / Trust … reduced to essentials', two lines he wrote at the bottom of a business letter to Grossman dated July 20th.

It seems he was finally getting around to dealing with a backlog of correspondence that week. Drafts of two letters from this time, seemingly never sent, have survived: one to Allen Ginsberg, the other to Paul Williams. The note to Allen starts out as a straight 'thank you' for the signed copy of *Kaddish*, a spoken-word album Allen released in June, which Dylan says he has 'listened to … & read liner notes'. It ends with two lines that could have appeared in one of *Tarantula*'s absurdist epistles: 'i must Admit allen, youve made the strangest / lieutenant with the horse in flames.'

Yet it is positively prosaic compared to the passage Dylan inserts into a long, unfinished letter to Williams, thanking him for *Crawdaddy* #4, which had appeared mid-July with Dylan on the cover and a six-page article called 'Understanding Dylan', penned by Paul, that ends with him calling the freshly minted *Blonde On Blonde*, 'a cache of emotion, a well-handled package of excellent music and better poetry, blended and meshed and ready to become a part of your reality'. Spot on. And then Dylan unexpectedly veers off into the thorny wilds of his own imagination, returning to the Bible for inspiration – knowing he'd have been burnt at the stake for expressing such sentiments half a millennium earlier:

> it must seem silly to you as a critic (but youre Really not you no) all the bullshit of habits & people telling their dreams in dreams where everyone else is also telling their dreams & habits to large grey figures & common working men – & of course empty woman-superlady (the lady without a back or stomach; have you ever seen her?) who of course leads the dreamer up to Moses the Fucker who at the time is fucking someone else but pauses just long enough to say hi to the dreamer – call him God.

The primary purpose of writing to Williams seems to have been to convince him that he was no mere critic, Dylan cajoling the college dropout to 'write other things ... for you know (you must), that this magazine could only expand & ...' Which is where it ends. Though it would be pure speculation to suggest that fate, in the form of a locked wheel, intervened, the timeline fits. Perhaps there was still a price to be paid for blasphemy.

If Williams never saw the letter, he did unwittingly take Dylan's advice to 'write other things', after rock's first critical magazine expanded into something that was no longer his inside eighteen months. In 1968, he sold his interest in it and resigned. By then, Dylan had stopped writing to critics, even good critics. Indeed, he had barely been seen in public since July 29th, 1966, the day he went for a spin on his cherished Triumph, and nearly met his Maker, wearing a 'pinebox for all eternity'.*

---

* The line, from 1979's 'Saving Grace', I always took to refer to the motorcycle accident.

Acknowledgements

Well, here I am back at the coalface, dark as a dungeon, with a long list of people who have helped to light the way. And once again, head of the class among those who've shown the generosity of spirit to let my every little query eat into their working day is Glenn Korman of Studio Archives, Brooklyn, one of the most knowledgeable audio archivists on the planet.

Other pukka archivists who have responded to my endless queries with nary a pause, suggesting avenues and garnishing many an outlandish authorial theory with actual facts include Parker Fishel of the New York Dylan office, Thomas Tierney at Sony Music, Todd Harvey at the Library of Congress and, last but certainly not least, chief librarian at the Dylan archive in Tulsa, Mark Davidson.

Indeed, thanks to all at the George Kaiser Foundation, the Woody Guthrie Center and the Gilcrease Museum in Tulsa for hospitality and helpfulness in spades. Special thanks to Michael Chaiken, curator of the Dylan archive, who has been a tireless cheerleader for this whole project.

Jeff Rosen has tried to be as helpful as a man in his invidious position, managing the unmanageable, can realistically be. Thanks, as always, for untying some of those bonds, J. The next French press is on me!

Rock writers, past and present, have heard and noted some important echoes, illuminating occasional unexplored byways for my benefit. So here's a nod of unrecoupable indebtedness to the late Al Aronowitz, Ben Edmonds and Paul Williams, and a wink to the alive'n'kickin' (last time I checked) Pete Doggett, Robert Hilburn, Barney Hoskyns, Robert Gordon, Daryl Sanders and Elijah Wald. Rave on, guys.

We now come to the secret seven, a cabal of serious Dylan scholars, not one of whom is academically accredited. Yet each of 'em knows more about Dylan and his work than the entire academic world could muster in toto. Six of you, I have known for three decades and more – Mitch Blank, Glen Dundas, Rod McBeath, Bill Pagell, Arie De Reus and the ageless Ian Woodward; while spring chicken Zac Dadic of Brisbane, Australia, now carries the torch.

In this wholly new take on 'His Bobness', new interviews with friends and other strangers who've known the man Alias are less of a feature than in the original *Behind The Shades*. As memories have grown weak and anecdotes have taken on a life of their own, far from the facts, I have primarily turned to new-found archival material to plug the historical gaps.

But I have still enjoyed trawling the past with Dylan's childhood chum, Louie Kemp; friends from the Village days, Steve Wilson and Barry Kornfeld; the ever-delightful Patti Boyd; and that great soundman, Richard Alderson, who made seminal recordings of Dylan in 1962 and 1966. The collective memory may now play tricks, but the above have all come to my aid in reconstructing the Dylan they knew, so that I may know.

Thanks also to all the others I've interviewed down the years for projects galore; those I have continued cherry-picking here, and those who are now just part of the back story.

Meantime, a tip of the hat and a French Quarter slap on the back goes to Marcus Whitman, who back in the Eighties tracked down a lot of important people from Dylan's pre-New York past and interviewed them for a college film project. Despite losing touch long ago, when I tracked Marcus down, he was as generous with his invaluable (and still underappreciated) archive of interviews as he had been to Wanted Man, back in the day.

As manuscripts and audio-*vérité* have now begun to replace and/or reconfigure memories, I have been given access to some remarkable (and some more questionable) documents thanks to Richard Austin at Sotheby's, Ed Kozinski at Gottahaveit, Bernie Chase at the Halcyon Gallery, and the ever-incorrigible Peter McKenzie. Thanks also to Barry Ollman, George Hecksher, Justin Martell and the Morgan Library.

Other archives mined include the Kingston court records, the New York Public Library and the premier photographic collection for Dylan and all things rock-related, Getty Images in New York, curated for many years by the memory man himself, Mitch Blank.

Scott Curran's private archive of Rock Literature was, as ever, on tap. The internet even on occasion stepped up, in the form of Rock Back Pages and the old curiosity shop that is Expecting Rain. Fanx.

Which just leaves the following lengthy list of helpers, regulars *and* occasional interlopers, who have responded to e-mails, phone calls and the occasional metaphorical truncheon with patience and forbearance: Bill Allison, for friendship's sake; Graham Ashton of Birmingham; Derek Barker at *Isis*; Joel Bernstein of Rock Ridge; Victor Bockris, somewhere off the Gulf Coast Highway; Joe Boyd of Little Venice; Harvey Brooks of Zion; Ian and Isabel Daley, especially for our recent Dylan journeys together; Michelle Engert of D.C. for past favours; the late lamented Barry Feinstein and his unique Eye; Dana Gillespie for her Basques and Blues; Raymond Foye and Allen Ginsberg for dinners and diners; John Kappes for setting down memories of a night like no other; David Kinney, historian of Dylanology; John Lattanzio of Monash; Gene Lafond of windswept Minnesota; Raymond Landry of Louisiana law; Richard Lysons, a proud Mancunian, for giving the Free Trade Hall its due; Bev Martin of Madison and the Mid West; Andy and Pia Muir, for answering the call, whenever and whatever the cause; Lisa O'Neill, a rare academic who thinks outside the box; Adrian Rawlins for a riotous tour of an Oz winery and some hazy half-remembered anecdotes; Pete Rowan from the Bay Area and beyond; Bob Spitz, another Bob biographer, for letting me reach out; Rob Whitehouse of *Look Back* and house visits; and Sean Wilentz of Princeton, a bona fide historian.

Finally thanks to The Shed, for its ever-reliable wifi and wonderful lattes; to my agent Stateside, Matt Bialer; and to my editors on this (ongoing) odyssey, Jörg Hensgen and Philip Marino, for sharing the ride and even occasionally taking the wheel.

Roll on, one and all, till the end of the line ...

Clinton Heylin, October 2020

Notes on Sources

Below are the primary resources for *A Restless, Hungry Feeling*. Where a quote has the following code, ... [] ..., it indicates that it is a composite of two (or more) quotes from the same person. To save time, space and energy, the various biographical sources, below, have each been given a capital-letter code – e.g. [AA] – to indicate where it has been used in the relevant chapter/s. I have included both official and unofficial publications of Dylan's own words, as many of his more important poems and unpublished lyrics were booklegged in the 1970s and 1980s. The *Some Other Kinds of Songs* bookleg has now been incorporated into Olof Björner's *About Bob Dylan* website, seemingly with permission or at least the tacit consent of the copyright-holder.

The manuscripts listed below pertain to material which exists *outside* the official Dylan archive in Tulsa, the resources of which remain vast and, as yet, not fully catalogued. Of the Dylan fanzines, a vital resource for Dylan researchers for well nigh forty years, just the two asterisked – both based in the UK – remain current. Finally, a note of thanks to the various contributors to the 'Reference Resources' section for blazing a trail, in most cases unaware that the Internet would place most or all of their work into the public domain without attribution or recognition, for the Internet 'experts' (an oxymoron) to misuse. As they say, no good deeds go unpunished.

A disclaimer: The considerable collection of Dylan manuscripts housed at the Gilcrease Museum in Tulsa were, when I inspected them, divided into approximately 130 boxes, containing a variable number of individual folders. Because the material, when it was acquired by the George Kaiser Foundation back in 2016, had been given a somewhat scattershot arrangement – the exigencies of history having been sacrificed in favour of confidentiality – the numbering system given to it was often arbitrary and at odds with the internal evidence.

The Covid crisis has enabled the Bob Dylan Archive to recatalogue all this material, led by the indefatigable Mark Davidson. But it means that the Box and Folder numbering system I used during my on-site research no

NOTES ON SOURCES 463

longer applies, and therefore citing the Box and Folder numbers I used would be both confusing and pointless. Suffice to say, if an unpublished quote is not sourced in the following notes, it is from Tulsa. Once again, I gratefully acknowledge the archive's continued help and support in this project.

Biographical portraits and oral histories:
Aronowitz, Al – *Bob Dylan and The Beatles* (1st Books, 2003) [AA]
Baez, Joan – *And A Voice To Sing With: A Memoir* (Summit Books, 1987) [JB]
Bicker, Stewart P. – *Friends & Other Strangers: Bob Dylan In Other People's Words* (pp, 1985) [F&OS]
Davis, Clive with James Willwerth – *Clive: Inside The Record Business* (Ballantine Books, 1976) [CD]
Dylan, Bob – *Chronicles Volume One* (Simon & Schuster, 2004) [CHR]
Dylan, Bob – transcript of *No Direction Home* interviews, 13–16/12/00, in *Every Mind Polluting Word* [NDH]
Hajdu, David – *Positively 4th Street: The Lives and Times of Joan Baez, Bob Dylan, Mimi & Richard Fariña* (Farrar, Straus & Giroux, 2001) [DH]
Helm, Levon with Stephen Davis – *This Wheel's On Fire: Levon Helm and the Story of The Band* (William Morrow, 1993) [LH]
Heylin, Clinton – *Dylan Behind The Shades: Take Two* (Viking, 2000) [CH]
Hoskyns, Barney – *Small Town Talk* (Faber & Faber, 2016) [BH]
Kemp, Louie – *Dylan and Me: 50 Years of Adventures* (Westrose Press, 2019) [LK]
MacKay, Kathleen – *Bob Dylan: Intimate Insights* (Omnibus Press, 2007) [KM]
Maymudes, Victor with Jacob Maymudes – *Another Side of Bob Dylan* (St Martin's Press, 2014) [VM]
Robertson, Robbie – *Testimony* (Crown Archetype, 2016) [RR]
Rotolo, Suze – *A Freewheelin' Time* (Aurum, 2008) [SR]
Scaduto, Anthony – *Bob Dylan* (W. H. Allen, 1972) [AS]
Shelton, Robert – *No Direction Home* (New English Library, 1986) [RS]
Spitz, Bob – *Bob Dylan. A Biography* (McGraw-Hill, 1987) [BS]
Sounes, Howard – *Down The Highway: A Life of Bob Dylan* (Grove Press, 2001) [HS]
Van Ronk, Dave with E. Wald – *The Mayor of MacDougal Street. A Memoir* (Da Capo, 2005) [VR]

Dylan's own published works:
Dylan, Bob – *Bob Dylan Himself* (Hal Leonard, 1965)
Dylan, Bob – *Tarantula* (Macmillan, 1971)
Dylan, Bob – *Writings & Drawings* (Knopf, 1973)
Dylan, Bob – *Lyrics 1962–1985* (Knopf, 1985)
Dylan, Bob – *The Bob Dylan Scrapbook: An American Journey 1956–66* (Simon & Schuster, 2005)

Dylan, Bob & Barry Feinstein – *Hollywood Foto-Rhetoric: The Lost Manuscript* (Simon & Schuster, 2008)

Dylan, Bob – *The Lyrics* (annotated edition, edited by Christopher Ricks) (Simon & Schuster, 2014)

Dylan, Bob – *In His Own Write: Personal Sketches 1962–65* (bookleg, 1980)

Dylan, Bob (ed. John Tuttle) – *In His Own Write: Personal Sketches Vol. 2* (bookleg, 1990)

Dylan, Bob (ed. John Tuttle) – *In His Own Write: Personal Sketches Vol. 3* (bookleg, 1992)

Dylan, Bob – *Some Other Kinds of Songs* (bookleg, 1987)

Dylan, Bob – *Whaaat? The Original Playboy Interview* (bookleg, 1988)

Dylan, Bob – Handwritten manuscript versions of 'Blowin' In The Wind', 'The Times They Are A-Changin'', 'Mr Tambourine Man', 'It Ain't Me Babe', 'Subterranean Homesick Blues' and 'Like A Rolling Stone', sold privately or by auction 2012–14

Dylan, Bob – Misc. songs published in *Broadside* fanzine, issues 1–43, February 1962–4 (q.v. 'Bob Dylan's Publications In Broadside Magazine 1962–65', by David Pichaske, the *Telegraph* #20)

Dylan manuscripts:

The Paturel 'Another Side' MSS, circa May–July 1964, including 'some other kinds of songs' & 'Gates of Eden', Morgan Library, NYC

The 'fair copy' *Blood On The Tracks* notebook, July–August 1974, Morgan Library, NYC. Reproduced in facsimile in *More Blood, More Tracks* boxed set (2019) (author's own transcript from his copy of same)

'Poems Without Titles', circa 1960, sixteen-page folio of poems, partially reproduced and transcribed in auction catalog (Item #21, Christie's, New York, 21/11/05)

The 'Sally Grossman' MSS, circa 1965, reproduced in facsimile in the Christie's, NYC, catalog of 'Fine Printed Books and Manuscripts' 23/6/11 (withdrawn from sale, the items now reside in the Dylan archive, Tulsa)

The 'Jet Pilot' MSS, circa October 1965, Auctioned at Christie's, NYC, 6/12/13, reproduced in facsimile at www.pbs.org/opb/historydetectives/investigation/bob-dylan-guitar

'It's A Hard Rain's Gonna Fall', handcorrected typescript, reproduced in facsimile in Sotheby's catalogue, London Rock'n'Pop auction, 29/9/15

Book of Dreams, Dylan's 1974 tour diary, Morgan Library, New York (private transcript)

'Most Likely You Go Your Way', hand-corrected typescript, March 1966, reproduced in Sotheby's catalogue, London auction, 10/12/13

'Just Like A Woman', typescript and handwritten bridge, March 1966, reproduced in Christie's catalogue, London auction, 30/9/99

Handwritten draft of 'Absolutely Sweet Marie', auctioned at Sotheby's, 1990s

Typescript from March 1966, 'You Cant Get Your Way Alla Time' and handwritten verse for 'Absolutely Sweet Marie'

Handwritten manuscript for 'Obviously 5 Believers', March 1966

'Restless Farewell', draft typescript, October 1963, private collection

Handwritten drafts of 'Queen Jane Approximately', 'One of Us Must Know', 'Ballad of a Thin Man', and 'I Want You'; typewritten drafts of 'Subterranean Homesick Blues' and '115th Dream', in *Mixing Up The Medicine* 1965–6 (included with *Cutting Edge* set)

'I'm Not There' typescript, reproduced in the *Telegraph* #24

Typed letter to Lawrence Ferlinghetti, 28/4/64, Bancroft Library, Berkeley. Reproduced in *Words Fill My Head*

Four-page poem, beginning 'Oh yes I could've gotten the money ...', *circa* winter 1963, Suze Rotolo collection, reproduced in facsimile in auction catalog

The Margolis & Moss MSS: misc. autobiographical poems, draft originals of eleven Outlined Epitaphs, an incomplete play and 'Liverpool Gal', all *circa* 1963

Dylan inscribed gift-book to Suze Rotolo on her twentieth birthday, 20/11/63, reproduced in Christie's auction catalog, *circa* 2005

'Tony Glover's Bob Dylan Archive', RR Auction Catalog, 19/11/20

Reference resources:

Anon. ('Artur') – *Every Mind Polluting Word: Assorted Dylan Utterances* (online)

Cable, Paul – *Bob Dylan: His Unreleased Recordings* (Dark Star, 1978)

Dundas, Glen – *Tangled Up In Tapes* (pp, various editions 1987–99)

Dunn, Tim – *The Bob Dylan Copyright Files 1962–2007* (AuthorHouse, 2008)

Heylin, Clinton – *Bob Dylan: The Recording Sessions 1960–94* (St Martin's Press, 1995)

Heylin, Clinton – *Bob Dylan Day By Day 1941–1995* (Schirmer Books, 1996)

Krogsgaard, Michael – 'Bob Dylan: The Recording Sessions', published initially in the *Telegraph* and the *Bridge*; now available (uncorrected) online

Maus, Christoph with Alan Fraser – *Bob Dylan Worldwide: An Anthology of Original Album, Singles & EP Releases 1961–81* (Maus of Music, 2016)

'Rolling Stone' (eds.) – *Rolling Stone: Cover To Cover 1967–2007* (Bondi, DVD-ROMx4)

Roques, Dominique – *The Great White Answers: The Bob Dylan Bootleg Records* (pp, 1980)

Van Estrick, Robert – *Concerted Efforts* (pp, 1982)

Websites:
About Bob Dylan
Expecting Rain
Rocksbackpages.com

Dylan fanzines:
The Bridge (67 issues to date)*
Isis (205 issues to date)*

Endless Road (7 issues)
Homer The Slut (11 issues)
Judas! (19 issues)
Look Back (27 issues)
Occasionally (5 issues)
On The Tracks (17 issues)
The Telegraph (56 issues)
Who Threw The Glass (8 issues)
Zimmerman Blues (10 issues)

Useful anthologies of Dylan-related material:
Cott, Jonathan – *Dylan: The Essential Interviews* (Simon & Schuster, 2006)
Heylin, Clinton (attributed to Carl Benson) – *The Bob Dylan Companion: Four Decades of Commentary* (Schirmer Books, 1998)
Fong-Torres, Ben – *Rolling Stone Rock'n'Roll Reader* (Bantam, 1974)
McGregor, Craig (ed.) – *Bob Dylan: A Retrospective* (Morrow, 1972)
Percival, Dave (ed.) – *The Dust of Rumour* (pp, 1985)
Percival, Dave (ed.) – *This Wasn't Written In Tin Pan Alley* (pp, 1989)

Other books used as resources:
Avery, Kevin (ed.) – *Everything Is An Afterthought: The Life & Writings of Paul Nelson* (Fantagraphics Books, 2011)
Balfour, Victoria – *Rock Wives* (William Morrow, 1987)
Banauch, Eugen (ed.) – *Refractions of Bob Dylan* (Manchester University Press, 2015)
Barker, Derek – *Bob Dylan Under The Influence* (Chrome Dreams, 2008)
Barker, Derek – *Too Much of Nothing* (Red Planet, 2018)
Barker, Derek (ed.) – *Isis: A Bob Dylan Anthology* (Helter Skelter, 2004)
Bell, Ian – *Once Upon A Time: The Lives of Bob Dylan* (Mainstream, 2012)
Flanagan, Bill – *Written In My Soul: Rock's Great Songwriters Talk About Creating Their Music* (Contemporary Press, 1986)
Gillespie, Dana – *Weren't Born A Man* (Hawksmoor, 2021)
Gray, Michael & Bauldie, John (ed.) – *All Across The Telegraph: A Bob Dylan Handbook* (Sidgwick & Jackson, 1987)
Gray, Michael – *Song & Dance Man III: The Art of Bob Dylan* (Cassell, 2000)
Guthrie, Nora & Woody – *My Name Is New York: Ramblin' Around Woody Guthrie's Town* (PowerHouse Books, 2015)
Heylin, Clinton – *Rain Unravelled Tales: A Rumourography* (omnibus edition) (pp, 1985)
Heylin, Clinton – *Revolution In The Air: The Songs of Bob Dylan 1957–73* (Constable, 2009)
Heylin, Clinton – *Judas: From Forest Hills To The Free Trade Hall* (Route, 2016)
Miles – *Bob Dylan In His Own Words* (Omnibus Press, 1978)

Pickering, Stephen – Dylan: A Commemoration (pp, 1971)
Reineke, Hank – Ramblin' Jack Elliott: The Never Ending Highway (Scarecrow Press, 2009)
Ribacove, Sy & Barbara – Folk-Rock: The Bob Dylan Story (Dell, 1966)
Schumacher, Michael – There But For Fortune: The Life of Phil Ochs (Hyperion, 1996)
Sheehy, Colleen J. & Swiss, Thomas (eds.) – Highway 61 Revisited: Bob Dylan's Road From Minnesota To The World (University of Minnesota Press, 2009)
Warner, Simon – Text, Drugs and Rock'N'Roll: The Beats and Rock Culture (Bloomsbury, 2013)
Woliver, Robbie – Bringing It All Back Home: Twenty-Five Years of American Music at Folk City (Pantheon, 1986)
Zollo, Paul – Songwriters On Songwriting (Da Capo Press, 1997)

Unpublished Resources:
Misc. internal Macmillan memos pertaining to Hollywood Foto-Rhetoric and Tarantula, 1964-6 (courtesy of Bob Bettendorf)
Tape Identification Data for Dylan's Columbia studio reels 1961-74 (with the exception of Pat Garrett & Billy The Kid sessions) (also misc. master & mix reels 1967-74)
Richard Reuss – Diary from summer 1965 and interviews with Izzy Young & Paul Nelson, July 1965
American Federation of Musicians Sheets for Self-Portrait, Planet Waves* & Blood On The Tracks sessions (* – from Dylan archive, Tulsa)
Letter to author from Jahanara Romney (Bonnie Beecher), 30/3/91
Bob Dylan Recording Contracts with Columbia Records: 26/10/61 (courtesy of Naomi Saltzman)
Grossman, Albert – Estate Papers, filed at county court offices, Kingston, NY, specifically as pertaining to 'The Management Agreement', 'The Witmark Agreement' and '1970 Settlement Agreement'
Chaiken, Michael – private notes on John Bucklen tapes

That all-important intro ... 2-3-4.
Biographical sources: AA; CHR

Dylan quotes:
Mikal Gilmore, Rolling Stone 22/11/01
'Tony Glover's Bob Dylan Archive', RR Auction Catalog, 19/11/20

Audio-video sources:
Studs Terkel, WFMT 26/4/63
Rolling Thunder Revue, Netflix, 2019

Secondary resources:
'Masked & Anonymous', Andrew Motion, review on Sony.com

Prelude – July 29th, 1961: Down By The Riverside
Biographical sources: BTS; CHR; SR

Dylan quotes:
Studs Terkel, WFMT 26/4/63

Contemporary published sources:
Preview of Riverside concert, *New Jersey Record* 22/7/61
Karman, Pete – Riverside concert review, *New York Mirror* 6/8/61
Shelton, Robert – 'Folk Music Heard On 12-Hour Show', *New York Times* 31/7/61

Audio-video sources:
Dylan's five-song set at the Riverside Church, NYC 29/7/61
Forty-two non-Dylan tracks from *Saturday of Folk Music*, WRVR-FM 29/7/61, recorded by Mel Bailey, Dylan archive, Tulsa

Secondary resources:
Delaney, Samuel R. – *The Motion of Light In Water* (Arbor House, 1988)
Green (née Zuckerman), Sue – *Critics At Large* (online), 3/3/11

1.1 – January to May 1961: Big City Blues
Biographical sources: AS; BTS; CHR; DH; HS; KM; NDH; RS; VM; VR

Dylan quotes:
'Song To Woody', 'Gleason MS', courtesy of Barry Ollman, and introduction, *Sing Out!* 10–11/62, © Bob Dylan
'Talkin' New York', handwritten draft, in *The Bob Dylan Scrapbook*, © Bob Dylan
'Talkin' Folklore Center', Folklore Center broadside, 1962, © Bob Dylan
'In The Wind', Peter, Paul & Mary sleeve notes, fall 1963, © Bob Dylan
'Message to ECLC', December 1963, © Bob Dylan
Izzy Young's notebooks, 20/10/61 and 23/10/61 (*Other Scenes* 12/68)
Gil Turner, *Sing Out!* 10–11/62
Studs Terkel, WFMT 26/4/63
The Whitakers', Glover Tape 17/7/63
Anon., *Gargoyle* 2/64
Ron Rosenbaum, *Playboy* 3/78
Randy Anderson, *Minnesota Daily* 17/2/78
Bob Fass, WBAI 21/5/86

Interviews with others:
Berger, Dave –*Telegraph* #43
Elliott, Ramblin' Jack – Reineke, *Ramblin' Jack Elliott: The Never Ending Highway* (Scarecrow Press, 2009)
Hammond, John Jr – *On The Tracks* #9
Houston, Cisco – Leslie Claypool 8/4/61 (transcribed on ciscohouston.com)
Kornfeld, Barry – interview with author
McKenzie, Eve –*Telegraph* #56
McKenzie, Peter – interview with author
Rotolo, Suze – Green (née Zuckerman), Sue, *Critics At Large* (online), 3/3/11
Rotolo, Suze – Balfour, *Rock Wives*
Stookey, Noel – MacKay, *Bob Dylan: Intimate Insights*
Young, Izzy – Richard Reuss, July 1965
Young, Izzy – *Mojo*, 2010 (op. cit. Rock Back Pages website)
Zimmerman, Beattie – November 1990 interview (online)

Contemporary published sources:
Cassidy, Joseph & Jack Smee – 'Park Songfest In Village Boils Into Slugfest', *New York Daily News* 10/4/61
Goddard, J. R. – *Village Voice* 26/4/62
Seeger, Pete (introduction to) Guthrie, Woody – *California To The New York Island* (Oak Publications, 1960)

Audio-video sources:
The Gleason Tape, East Orange, NJ 6/2/61
John Lee Hooker at Gerde's Folk City 29/3/61 (Cynthia Gooding archive)
Columbia session tape 24/4/62
Studs Terkel, WFMT 26/4/63
The Whitakers', Glover Tape 17/7/63
Bob Fass, WBAI 21/5/86

Unpublished material utilized:
Dylan's inscribed copy of *California To The New York Island*

Secondary resources:
Brand, Oscar – *The Ballad Mongers: Rise of the Modern Folk Song* (Funk & Wagnalls, 1962)
Murray, Charles Shaar – *Boogie Man: The Adventures of John Lee Hooker* (Viking, 1999)

1.2 – Summer 1953 to January 1961: On The Road To Damascus
Biographical sources: AS; CHR; HS; LK; NDH; RS; VR

Dylan quotes:
Poems Without Titles, circa 1960, sixteen-page folio of poems, partially reproduced and transcribed in auction catalog (Item #21 Christie's, NYC 21/11/05), © Bob Dylan
'Song To Bonny', copy of handwritten MS, enclosed with letter from Bonnie Beecher to author, 30/3/91, © Bob Dylan
'East Colorado Blues', *In His Own Write: Personal Sketches Vol. 2*, © Bob Dylan
The Margolis & Moss MSS, misc. autobiographical poems, circa 1963, © Bob Dylan
The Whitakers', Glover Tape 17/7/63
'I Am My Words', Andrea Svedberg, *Newsweek* 4/11/63
Perth press conference 23/4/66 (transcript from *Music Maker* 6/66)
Barbara Kerr, *Toronto Sun* 26–29/3/78
Ron Rosenbaum, *Playboy* 3/78
On-stage rap, Warfield Theater, San Francisco 18/11/80
Jeff Rosen, *No Direction Home* DVD, 13–16/12/00
Austin Scaggs, *Rolling Stone* (online edn) 17/11/04
'Tony Glover's Bob Dylan Archive', RR Auction Catalog, 19/11/20

Interviews with others:
Abrams, Harvey – *Isis* #94–6
Beecher, Bonnie –*Telegraph* #36
Brown, Hugh – *Isis* #97
Bucklen, John – *On The Tracks* #8
Cohen, Rich – *Duluth Tribune* 29/6/86
Friedman, Steve – *Duluth Tribune* 29/6/86
Glover, Tony – video interview with Marcus Whitman, mid-1980s
Gotlieb, Stan – online posting (op. cit. Bell, *Once Upon A Time*)
Joelson, Ron – *Highway 94 Revisited* sleeve notes
Kalb, Danny –*Telegraph* #47
Kemp, Louie – interview with author
Koerner, 'Spider' John – *Isis* #86
LaFond, Gene – interview with author
Michaels, Mike – University of Chicago magazine 7–8/12
Morton, Dave *Isis* #102–3
Morton, Dave – video interview with Marcus Whitman, mid-1980s
Nelson, Paul – *Isis* #90–2
Nelson, Paul – interview with author
Pankake, Jon – *Isis* #88
Propotnick, Jim – *Highway 94 Revisited* sleeve notes

Ray, Dave – video interview with Marcus Whitman, mid-1980s
Scroggins, Bob – *St Paul Almanac* 28/10/14
Waldman, Jerry – *Duluth Tribune* 29/6/86
Wallace, Karen – transcribed interview, courtesy of David Kinney,
Wallace, Terri – interview by sister, Karen, regarding St Paul Tape, *circa* mid-1980
Weber, Harry – Shelton, *No Direction Home*
Whitaker, Dave – *Isis* #87–8
Whitaker, Dave – *Telegraph* #26
Zimmerman, Abraham – *Duluth News Tribune* 20/10/63
Zimmerman, Beattie – Barker, *Isis: A Bob Dylan Anthology*

Contemporary published sources:
Nelson, Paul & Jon Pankake, *Little Sandy Review* #2, Summer 1960
Nelson, Paul & Jon Pankake, *Little Sandy Review* #11, May 1962

Audio-video sources:
'The St Paul Tape', Karen Moynihan's Apartment, May 1960
'The Madison Tape', with Danny Kalb, January 1961
'Bonnie, Why'd You Cut My Hair?', from 'The Minneapolis Party Tape' 5/61
The Whitakers', Glover Tape 17/7/63
Eat The Document raw footage, 171 cans, Dylan archive, Tulsa
Rolling Thunder Revue (Criterion DVD, 2021)

Unpublished material utilized:
Unproduced screenplay for *When Billy Broke His Head* (excerpted online)

Secondary resources:
Axelrod, Mark – 'The Fraternity Days & Nights of Bob Dylan', *Isis* #166
Bell, Ian – *Once Upon A Time: The Lives of Bob Dylan* (Mainstream, 2012)
Cleeper, P. M. – 'Dylan's Fortune', *This Week* Magazine 27/3/66
Engel, Dave – *Just Like Bob Zimmerman's Blues: Dylan In Minnesota* (River City Memoirs, 1997)
Ginsberg, Allen (introduction to Kerouac, Jack) *Pomes All Sizes* (City Lights, 1992)
Kerouac, Jack – *On The Road* (Penguin Modern Classics, 2000)
Levitan, Stuart D. – *Madison In The Sixties* (Wisconsin Historical Society Press, 2018)
Thompson, Toby – *Positively Main Street: An Unorthodox View of Bob Dylan* (Coward-McCann, 1971)

1.3 – May to October 1961: The Kindness Of (Friends & Other) Strangers
Biographical sources: AS; BS; CHR; DH; KM; SR; VR

Dylan quotes:
'California Blue Eyed Baby', The McKenzie song MSS, George Hecksher Collection, Morgan Library, NYC, © Bob Dylan
'VD Seaman's Letter', The McKenzie song MSS, George Hecksher Collection, Morgan Library, NYC, © Bob Dylan
Izzy Young notebooks 20/10/61 and 23/10/61 (*Other Scenes* 12/68)
Billy James, CBS December 1961 (transcript from *Every Mind Polluting Word*)
???, *Gargoyle* 2/64
Horace Judson, *dont look back* DVD (interview conducted 9/5/65)
'Thirty Questions To Bob Dylan', Rod MacBeath, *Bridge* #24. (see *Salut Les Copains*, September 1966)
Jeff Rosen, *No Direction Home* DVD, 13–16/12/00

Interviews with others:
Crabb, Earl – online posting
Glover, Tony – video interview with Marcus Whitman, mid-1980s
Hammond, John Jr – *On The Tracks* #9
Hammond, John Sr – *Melody Maker* 15/5/65
Kretchmer, Arthur – *Montreal Gazette* 12/1/74
Langhorne, Bruce – interview with author
McKenzie, Eve – *Telegraph* #56
McKenzie, Peter – interview with author
Nissenson, Jack – *Montreal Gazette* 12/1/74
Rotolo, Suze – Balfour, *Rock Wives*
Shelton, Robert – *Isis* #156
Shelton, Robert – Max Jones, *Melody Maker* 19/2/66
Young, Izzy – Richard Reuss, July 1965
Zimmerman, Abraham – *Duluth News Tribune* 20/10/63

Contemporary published sources:
Nelson, Paul & Jon Pankake, *Little Sandy Review*, May 1962.
Shelton, Robert – 'A Distinctive Folk Stylist', *New York Times* 29/9/61

Audio-video sources:
'The Indian Neck Folk Festival', Branford, CT 6/5/61
'The Minneapolis Party Tape' 5/61
'1st Bailey Home Tape', Bailey's Apartment, NYC 24/6/61
'The First Gaslight Tape', Gaslight Cafe, NYC 6/9/61
Gerde's Folk City, New York 1/10/61, Cynthia Gooding archive, Tulsa
dont look back, BluRay edition
Tony Glover – video interview with Marcus Whitman, mid-1980s

Unpublished material utilized:
The McKenzie song MSS, April to September 1961, George Hecksher Collection, Morgan Library, NYC, including three typescripts with handwritten chords: 'Dead For A Dollar', 'The Preacher's Folly' and 'Red Travelin' Shoes' (see Heylin, *Revolution In The Air*, pp 39–55, for a full description of content), © Bob Dylan
Cynthia Gooding's handwritten set list for Dylan and the Greenbriar Boys at Gerde's 1/10/61.
Bob Dylan Recording Contracts with Columbia Records 26/10/61, 1/7/67, 1/8/74 (courtesy of Naomi Saltzman)

Secondary resources:
Cable, Paul – *Bob Dylan: His Unreleased Recordings* (Dark Star, 1978)
Hammond, John Sr – *On Record: An Autobiography* (Summit Books, 1977)
Levitan, Stuart D. – *Madison In The Sixties* (Wisconsin Historical Society Press, 2018)
Paxton, Tom – *The Honor Of Your Company* (Cherry Tree Music, 2000)
Prial, Dunstan – *The Producer: John Hammond & the Soul of American Music* (Farrar, Straus & Giroux, 2006)
Shelton, Robert – 'The Charisma Kid', *Cavalier* 7/65
Von Schmidt, Eric & Jim Rooney – *Baby Let Me Follow You Down: The Illustrated Story of The Cambridge Folk Years* (Anchor Press, 1979)
Woodward, Ian – 'Did Dylan Seek Work with Hill & Range?', *Isis* #165
Young, Izzy with Scott Barretta – *The Conscience of the Folk Revival: The Writings of Israel Young* (Scarecrow Press, 2012)

1.4 – November 1961 to March 1962: The Balladeer Fires Broadsides
Biographical sources: BS; CHR; DH; HS; SR; VR

Dylan quotes:
'Let Me Die In My Footsteps', *Writings & Drawings*, © Bob Dylan
'Man of Constant Sorrow', arrangement of trad. song, *Bob Dylan Himself* (Hal Leonard, 1965), © Bob Dylan
'Ballad For A Friend', *Bob Dylan Himself* (Hal Leonard, 1965), © Bob Dylan
Izzy Young's notebooks, 20/10/61 and 23/10/61 (*Other Scenes* 12/68)
Billy James, CBS December 1961 (transcript from *Every Mind Polluting Word*)
Edwin Miller, *Seventeen* 9/62
Freewheelin' Mk 1 sleeve notes, reproduced in *Telegraph* #8
Anon., *Gargoyle* 2/64
Frances Taylor, *Long Island Press* 17/10/65
Glover Tape 11/8/62
Glover Tape 17/7/63
Dedication, *Writings & Drawings* (Knopf, 1973)

Jeff Rosen, *No Direction Home* DVD, 13–16/12/00
Robert Hilburn Interview, Amsterdam, 10/11/03 (transcript, *Every Mind Polluting Word*)

Interviews with others:
Cohen, John – *The Times* 28/8/63.
Glover, Tony – video interview with Marcus Whitman, mid-1980s
Hammond, John Sr – *Fusion* 31/10/69
Kornfeld, Barry – interview with author
McKenzie, Eve –*Telegraph* #56
McKenzie, Pete – interview with author
Ray, Dave – video interview with Marcus Whitman, mid-1980s
Rotolo, Suze – Balfour, *Rock Wives*
Rotolo, Suze – Green (née Zuckerman), Sue, *Critics At Large* (online), 3/3/11
Young, Izzy – Richard Reuss, July 1965

Contemporary published sources:
Young, Izzy – 'Frets & Frails', *Sing Out!* 4/62

Audio-video sources:
Carnegie Recital Hall 4/11/61 (complete twenty-two-song concert), Dylan archive, Tulsa
Columbia session tapes 20/11/61 and 22/11/61
'First McKenzie Tape', the McKenzies' apartment, NYC 23/11/61
Minneapolis 'Hotel' Tape 22/12/61, recorded by Tony Glover
Leeds Music Demos, Duchess Music, NYC 5/1/62 and 18/1/62
Columbia session tape with Harry Belafonte, Webster Hall, NYC 2/2/62
Folksinger's Choice, WBAI, NYC, February 1962
The Whitakers', Glover Tape 11/8/62
The Whitakers', Glover Tape 17/7/63

Unpublished material utilized:
A single-page MS, provisional LP listing, with illustration, *circa* November 1961

Secondary resources:
(Christie's) catalogue copy for sale of McKenzie Tape 23/11/61, NYC
Arem, Jocelyn (ed.) – *Caffe Lena: Inside America's Legendary Folk Music Coffee house* (pH Books, 2013)
Bell, Ian – *Once Upon A Time: The Lives of Bob Dylan* (Mainstream, 2012)
Cable, Paul – *Bob Dylan: His Unreleased Recordings* (Dark Star, 1978)
Heylin, Clinton – *It's One For The Money: The Songsnatchers Who Carved Up A Century of Pop* (Constable, 2015)

Paxton, Tom – *The Honor Of Your Company* (Cherry Tree Music, 2000)
Prial, Dunstan – *The Producer: John Hammond & the Soul of American Music* (Farrar, Straus & Giroux, 2006)
Redpath, Jean with Mark Brownrigg – *Giving Voice To Traditional Songs: Jean Redpath's Autobiography* (University of South Carolina Press, 2018)
Russell, Ted – *Bob Dylan NYC 1961–64* (Rizzoli, 2015)
Young, Izzy with Scott Barretta – *The Conscience of the Folk Revival: The Writings of Israel Young* (Scarecrow Press, 2012)

1.5 – April to October 1962: How Many Roads, So Many Roads
Biographical sources: BH; BS; DH; KM; SR; VM; VR

Dylan quotes:
'It's A Hard Rain's Gonna Fall', handcorrected typescript, reproduced in facsimile in Sotheby's catalogue, London Rock'n'Pop auction, 29/9/15, © Bob Dylan
Four-page poem, beginning 'Oh yes I could've gotten the money …', *circa* winter 1963, Suze Rotolo collection, reproduced in facsimile in auction catalog, © Bob Dylan
'Bob Dylan's Blues', unedited version, Columbia Studio A, NYC, 9/7/62
Letter to Suze Rotolo 26/7/62, quoted in *A Freewheelin' Time*
Glover Tape 11/8/62
Studs Terkel, WFMT 26/4/63
Glover Tape 17/7/63
John Cohen & Happy Traum, *Sing Out!* 10/68
Jeff Rosen, *No Direction Home* DVD, 13–16/12/00
'Tony Glover's Bob Dylan Archive', RR Auction Catalog, 19/11/20

Interviews with others:
Alderson, Richard – New York 24/3/14
Colby, Paul – *The Bitter End: Hanging Out At America's Nightclub* (2002)
Glover, Tony – video interview with Marcus Whitman, mid-1980s
Hammond, John Sr – *Melody Maker* 7/8/68
Kornfeld, Barry – interview with the author
Mandell, Steve – *Madison In The Sixties*
McKenzie, Eve – *Telegraph* #56.
Mogull, Artie – *No Direction Home* DVD
Morton, Dave – video interview with Marcus Whitman, mid-1980s
Rotolo, Suze – Balfour, *Rock Wives*
Sebastian, John – *Mojo* 2/05
Shelton, Robert – Max Jones, *Melody Maker* 19/2/66
Wilson, Stephen – interview with the author
Young, Izzy – Richard Reuss, July 1965

Contemporary published sources:
Nelson, Paul & Jon Pankake, *Little Sandy Review*, May 1962
Hentoff, Nat, review of Bob Dylan, quoted in *Sing Out!* 10–11/62
Hentoff, Nat – *Playboy* 6/63

Audio-video sources:
Gerde's Folk City, NYC 16/4/62
Columbia session tapes 24/4/62 and 25/4/62
'Blowin' In The Wind', Witmark demo, NYC, June 1962
Columbia session tape 9/7/62
Glover Tape 11/8/62
'The 2nd Gaslight Tape', Gaslight Cafe, NYC early October 1962
Glover Tape 17/7/63
Tony Glover – video interview with Marcus Whitman, mid-1980s

Unpublished material utilized:
Grossman, Albert – Estate Papers, filed at county court offices, Kingston, NY
Hammond, John Sr – Columbia internal memo to David Kapralik 9/10/62
Rotolo, Suze – letter to her mother, Mary 10/7/62

Secondary resources:
'Ad for Folk & Jazz Concert', *Columbia Daily Spectator* 10/4/62
Eliot, Marc – *Death of A Rebel: Phil Ochs* (Anchor Books, 1979)
Eliot, Marc – *Rockonomics* (Omnibus Press, 1989)
Hentoff, Nat – *Wall Street Journal* 29/12/04
Paxton, Tom – *The Honor Of Your Company* (Cherry Tree Music, 2000)
Woodward, Ian – 'Dylan In Montreal in 1962', *Isis* #190

1.6 – May 1941 to June 1959: Have You Heard The News?
Biographical sources: CHR; DH; HS; LK; SR; VM; VR

Dylan quotes:
'Good poem, bad poem', from 2007 Morgan Library exhibition, reproduced in *Isis* #191, © Bob Dylan
'All American Boy', 1967, © Bob Dylan
Izzy Young's notebooks, 20/10/61 and 23/10/61 (*Other Scenes* 12/68)
Billy James, CBS December 1961 (transcript from *Every Mind Polluting Word*)
Nat Hentoff, *New Yorker* 24/10/64
Perth press conference 23/4/66 (transcript from *Music Maker* 6/66)
Klas Burling, Swedish Radio 28/4/66 (transcript from *Ghost of Electricity*)
???, 'Thirty Questions', *Salut Les Copains* 9/66 (translation in *The Bridge* #24)

Dylan, Bob – *Tarantula* (Macmillan, 1971)
Barbara Kerr, *Toronto Sun* 26–29/3/78
Philippe Adler, *L'Express* 9/7/78 (English translation in *4th Time Around* #3)
Kurt Loder, *Rolling Stone* 21/6/84
Scott Cohen, *Spin* magazine 11/85
Jon Bream, *Minneapolis Star & Tribune* June 1986
Nick Krewen, *Long Island Voice* 11/9/97
Alan Jackson, *The Times* 15/11/97
Best Album of 1997 Award acceptance speech, Radio City Music Hall, NYC, 25/2/98
Jeff Rosen, *No Direction Home* DVD, 13–16/12/00
Robert Hilburn Interview, Amsterdam, 10/11/03 (transcript, *Every Mind Polluting Word*)
Theme Time Radio Hour, xFM, 2007
Douglas Brinkley, *Rolling Stone* 14/5/09
Bill Flanagan 22/3/17
'Tony Glover's Bob Dylan Archive', RR Auction Catalog, 19/11/20

Interviews with others:
Becker, Bob – *Highway 94 Revisited* sleeve notes
Berg, Bill – interview with the author
Bucklen, John – *On The Tracks* #8
Ron Joelson – *Highway 94 Revisited* sleeve notes
Louie Kemp – interview with author
Mestek, Pat – *Duluth Tribune* 29/6/86
Odegard, Kevin – interview with the author
Propotnick, Jim – *Highway 94 Revisited* sleeve notes
Vee, Bobby – radio interview 4/6/76 (transcribed in Bicker, *Friends & Other Strangers*)
Vee, Bobby – Random Notes, *Rolling Stone* 17/8/72
Zimmerman, Abraham – *Duluth News Tribune* 20/10/63
Zimmerman, Abraham – Barker, *Isis: A Bob Dylan Anthology*
Zimmerman, Beattie – *Duluth News Tribune* 20/10/63
Zimmerman, Beattie – interview 11/90, online transcript.
Zimmerman, Beattie – interview with Minnesota Historical Society, quoted in *Highway 61 Revisited: Bob Dylan's Road From Minnesota To The World*

Contemporary published sources:
Hematite 1957, Hibbing High School

Audio-video sources:
R'n'R medley by The Jokers, Terlinde Music Shop, St Paul, MN 24/12/56
Zimmerman–Bucklen home tapes, *circa* 1957–58
Transcript of Cynthia Gooding's *Folksinger's Choice* 2/62 – *Isis* #43

Unpublished material utilized:
Rotolo, Suze – letter to her mother, Mary, 10/7/62
Various 1959 Hibbing High School Yearbooks, inscribed by Bob Zimmerman, courtesy of Bill Pagell and Barry Ollman
Chaiken, Michael – private notes on Bucklen tapes

Secondary resources:
'The Drunkard's Son', handwritten lyric in Bob Zimmerman's hand – *Isis* #44
Engel, Dave – *Just Like Bob Zimmerman's Blues: Dylan In Minnesota* (River City Memoirs, 1997)
Gordon, Robert – *It Came From Memphis* (Faber & Faber, 1995)
Scaduto, Anthony – *New York Times* magazine 26/11/71

1.7 – October 1962 to April 1963: A New World Singer In Ye Olde Worlde
Biographical sources: AS; BS; CHR; DH; HS; SR

Dylan quotes:
Four-page poem, beginning 'Oh yes I could've gotten the money ...', *circa* winter 1963, Suze Rotolo collection, reproduced in facsimile in auction catalog, © Bob Dylan
'Liverpool Gal', Margolis & Moss MSS, 1963, © Bob Dylan
Postcard to Suze Rotolo from Italy, January 1963, reproduced in auction catalog
Letter to Suze Rotolo, October 1962, quoted in *A Freewheelin' Time*
Studs Terkel, WFMT 26/4/63
Tony Glover Tape 17/7/63
???, *Boston Broadside* 30/10/63
Perth press conference 23/4/66 (transcript in *Music Maker* 6/66)
Mikal Gilmore, *Rolling Stone* 22/11/01
Bill Flanagan 22/3/17

Interviews with others:
Alderson, Richard – 'The Gaslight's Soundman', *New York* 24/3/14–6/4/2014
Augenblink, Ivan – telephone interview with author
Bloomfield, Michael – *Hit Parader* 6/68
Carthy, Martin – *Disc* 10/4/65
Carthy, Martin – *Telegraph* #42
Donaldson, Willie – interview with Pete Silverton, 1996 (Rock Back Pages)
Hammond, John Sr – to Anthony Scaduto
Hammond, John Sr – *Melody Maker* 15/5/65
Hammond, John Sr – *Melody Maker* 17/8/68
Jones, Elvin – *Dylan In The Madhouse*, BBC4 documentary, broadcast 26/9/05

Joseph, Anthea – interview with the author
Kooper, Al – interview by Harvey Kubernik, 2010 (Rock Back Pages)
Langhorne, Bruce – interview with the author
Nelson, Paul – interview with the author
Nelson, Paul – Richard Reuss, July 1965
Saville, Philip –*Telegraph* #45
Saville, Philip – Caspar Llewellyn-Smith, *Observer* 18/9/05
Whitaker, Dave –*Telegraph* #26
Wilson, Tom – Chris Charlesworth, *Melody Maker* 31/1/76
Young, Izzy – Richard Reuss, July 1965

Contemporary published sources:
Radio Times, 12–18/1/63
Broadside #14 (October 1962)
???, *Scene* magazine, January 1963
Denver, Nigel – 'An Open Letter To Bob Dylan', *Folk Music* #4 (2/64)
Shelton, Robert – review of Town Hall concert, *New York Times* 13/4/63
Solomon, Linda – review of *Freewheelin'*, *Village Voice* 25/7/63

Audio-video sources:
Columbia session tapes 26/10/62, 1/11/62, 14/11/62, 6/12/62, 23/4/63
Broadside demos, the Friesens, NYC November 1962
Witmark demos, NYC, November 1962
'Ballad Of The Gliding Swan', in *Dylan In The Madhouse*, BBC4 documentary, broadcast 26/9/05
'Masters Of War', demo version for Alan Lomax, with spoken intro, 2/63
Town Hall, New York (complete show) 12/4/63
Glover Tape 17/7/63
Eat The Document raw footage, 171 cans, Dylan archive, Tulsa

Unpublished material utilized:
Hammond, John Sr – Columbia internal memo to David Kapralik 9/10/62
Letter from David Braun to Walter Dean, 13/3/63 (Columbia archives)

Secondary resources:
Details of an eleven-track Witmark acetate in Suze Rotolo's collection, *circa* 1963, in Christie's auction catalog, New York, 4/12/06
Barker, Derek – 'One Time In London', *Isis* #83
Devlin, Polly – unattributed article in *Sunday* magazine, February 2006
Eliot, Marc – *Death of A Rebel: Phil Ochs* (Anchor Books, 1979)
'Tony Glover's Bob Dylan Archive', RR Auction Catalog, 19/11/20

Harvey, Todd – *The Formative Dylan: Transmission & Stylistic Influences 1961–3* (Scarecrow Press, 2001)
Lawlan, Val & Brian, 'Doing The London Waltz', in *Steppin' Out* (pp, 1987)
Ledeen, Jenny – *Prophecy In The Christian Era* (pp, 1995)
Paxton, Tom – *The Honor Of Your Company* (Cherry Tree Music, 2000)
Prial, Dunstan – *The Producer: John Hammond & the Soul of American Music* (Farrar, Straus & Giroux, 2006)
Woodward, Ian – 'Dylan's Part in Madhouse On Castle Street', *Isis* #127
Woodward, Ian – 'Entering The Madhouse', *Isis* #175
Woodward, Ian – 'Dylan's London Album', *Isis* #196–7

1.8 – April to Nov. 1963: He's Not The Messiah, He's A Very Naughty Boy
Biographical sources: BH; DH; HS; SR

Dylan quotes:
Four-page poem, beginning 'Oh yes I could've gotten the money …', *circa* winter 1963, Suze Rotolo collection, reproduced in facsimile in Christie's auction catalog, New York, 4/12/06, © Bob Dylan
'For Dave Glover', Newport Folk Festival programme 7/63, © Bob Dylan
Nat Hentoff, 'Dylan Skips CBS Over Birch Talk', *Village Voice* 16/5/63
Max Jones, *Melody Maker* 23/5/64
Tony Glover Tape 17/7/63
Jack Smith, *National Guardian* 22/8/63
???, *Boston Broadside* 30/10/63
Ray Coleman, *Melody Maker* 22/5/65
Robert Hilburn, *LA Times* 4/4/04

Interviews with others:
Bloomfield, Michael – *On The Road With Bob Dylan*
Diaz, Cesar – interview with the author
Fass, Bob – *On The Tracks* #13
Feinstein, Barry – *Early Dylan* (Bullfinch Press, 1999)
Glover, Tony – video interview with Marcus Whitman, mid-1980s
James, Billy – interview with the author
Kornfeld, Barry – interview with the author
Nelson, Paul – interview with the author
Rotolo, Suze – Green (née Zuckerman), Sue, *Critics At Large* (online), 3/3/11
Simon, Paul – *NME* 30/7/65
Wilson, Tom – *Fusion* 31/10/69
Young, Izzy – Richard Reuss, July 1965

Zimmerman, Abraham + Beattie – *Duluth News Tribune* 20/10/63
Zimmerman, Beattie – Barker, *Isis: A Bob Dylan Anthology*

Contemporary published sources:
'Rich Brute Slays Negro Mother', Roy H. Wood, reproduced in *Broadside* #23
'Talkin' John Birch Blues', mimeographed broadsheet by Izzy Young, May 1963
'Farmer Sentenced In Barmaid's Death', *New York Times* 29/8/63 (q.v. *Isis* #143)
Report on Medgar Evers' funeral, *New York Times* 16/6/63
Nelson, Paul & Jon Pankake, 'Flat Tire … The Freewheelin' Bob Dylan', *Little Sandy Review* #27
Denver, Nigel – 'An Open Letter To Bob Dylan', *Folk Music* April 1964
Hentoff, Nat – *Village Voice* 14/3/63
Hentoff, Nat – *Playboy* 6/63
Seeger, Pete – Account of Greenwood voter rally, *Broadside* #30
Svedberg, Andrea – 'I Am My Words', *Newsweek* 4/11/63
Welles, Chris – 'Bob Dylan: Angry Young Folk Singer', *Life* 10/4/64

Audio-video sources:
The Bear, Chicago 25/4/63
'Only A Pawn In Their Game', Greenwood, Miss., 6/7/63
Tony Glover Tape 17/7/63
Newport Folk Festival, Freebody Park, RI 26–28/7/63
Columbia session tapes 6/8/63, 7/8/63, 12/8/63, 23/10/63, 24/10/63
Forest Hills Stadium, Forest Hills, NYC 17/8/63
Carnegie Hall, New York 26/10/63
Steve Allen Show, Los Angeles 25/2/64
Rolling Thunder Revue, Netflix, 2019

Unpublished material utilized:
Copyright file on 'Blowin' In The Wind' and Lorre Wyatt, Dylan archive, Tulsa

Secondary resources:
'A Regular Old Southern Maryland Boy', Peter Carlson, *Washington Post Magazine*, 4/8/81
'The Case of Hattie Carroll', David Simon, *Baltimore Sun*, 7/2/88
'A Lonesome Death Revisited', Michael Yockel, *Baltimore*, March 2004
Dunaway, David King – *Pete Seeger: How Can I Keep From Singing* (McGraw-Hill, 1981)
Feinstein, Barry; Kramer, Daniel; Marshall, Jim – *Early Dylan* (Bullfinch Press, 1999)
Updike, John – *Concerts At Castle Hill* (Lord John Press, 1993) (pp. 39–40)

Wald, Elijah – *Dylan Goes Electric!* (Dey St, 2015)
Ward, Ed – *Michael Bloomfield: The Rise & Fall of An American Guitar Hero* (Chicago Review Press, 2016)
Woodward, Ian – 'Dylan's non-appearance on Ed Sullivan', *Isis* #149
Woodward, Ian – 'Dylan at the March at Washington', *Isis* #172

Winterlude #1 (November/December 1963): Off The Road
Biographical sources: AA; AS; SR

Dylan quotes:
'Restless Farewell', draft typescript, October 1963, © Bob Dylan
'Message To ECLC', December 1963, © Bob Dylan
'to sis and gordon ...', *Broadside* #38 (20/1/64), © Bob Dylan
Margolis & Moss MSS: misc. autobiographical poems, draft originals of eleven Outlined Epitaphs, an incomplete play and 'Liverpool Gal', all *circa* 1963, © Bob Dylan
'loves/hates', *Jackie* #80, 17/7/65, © Bob Dylan
Inscribed gift-book to Suze Rotolo on her twentieth birthday, 20/11/63, reproduced in Christie's auction catalog, New York, 4/12/06.
Nat Hentoff, *New Yorker* 24/10/64
Scaduto, Anthony – *Bob Dylan* (W. H. Allen, 1972)
'Tony Glover's Bob Dylan Archive', RR Auction Catalog, 19/11/20

Interviews with others:
Ginsberg, Allen – Anne Waldman, in *Highway 61 Revisited: Bob Dylan's Road From Minnesota To The World*
Kornfeld, Barry – interview with the author
Pennebaker, D. A. –*Telegraph* #16

Audio-video sources:
Columbia session, NYC 31/10/63

Unpublished material utilized:
Memo from Tom Wilson to 'Linda', re acetate version of *Times They Are A-Changin'*

Secondary resources:
Dylan book inscription to Suze Rotolo, on her twentieth birthday, 20/11/63 reproduced in Christie's auction catalog, New York, 4/12/06.
Weberman, A. J. – 'Notes On *Eleven Outlined Epitaphs*', from bookleg edition, *circa* 1970

2.1 – January to June 1964: Becoming Withdrawn

Biographical sources: AA; AS; BH; CHR; DH; HS; KM; SR; VM; VR

Dylan quotes:
'to sis and gordon ...', *Broadside* #38 (20/1/64), © Bob Dylan
'Chimes of Freedom', handwritten draft on hotel stationery, in *The Bob Dylan Scrapbook*, © Bob Dylan
Typed letter to Lawrence Ferlinghetti, 28/4/64, Bancroft Library, Berkeley, reproduced in *Words Fill My Head*, © Bob Dylan
The Paturel 'Another Side' MSS, *circa* May–July 1964, including 'some other kinds of songs' & 'Gates of Eden', Morgan Library, NYC, © Bob Dylan
???, *Gargoyle* 2/64
Nat Hentoff, *New Yorker* 24/10/64
Martin Bronstein, CBC 20/2/66
Bill Flanagan, *Written In My Soul* (interview conducted in March 1985)
Bill Flanagan 22/3/17

Interviews with others:
Andersen, Eric – *Mojo* 2/05
Blue, David – *Mojo* 2/05
Hoffenberg, Mason – *Playboy* 11/73
Kornfeld, Barry – interview with the author
Langhorne, Bruce – interview with the author
Lennon, John – *Melody Maker* 9/1/65
Lennon, John – *NME* 23/4/65
Morton, Dave – video interview with Marcus Whitman, mid-1980s
Nico – *Disc* 18/9/65
Rotolo, Suze – Balfour, *Rock Wives*
Wilson, Steve – interview with the author

Audio-video sources:
Steve Allen Show, Los Angeles 25/2/64
'Von Schmidt Home Tape', Sarasota, FL, April 1964 (unedited version from personal collection)
Royal Festival Hall 17/5/64, unedited Pye recording
Columbia session tape 9/6/64
Witmark demos, NYC June 1964
Eat The Document raw footage, 171 cans, Dylan archive, Tulsa

Unpublished material utilized:
'Mr Tambourine Man', draft in Dylan's handwriting on Royal Orleans notepaper
Letter from Albert Grossman to Walter Dean, August 1963, Sony archives

Secondary resources:
Aronowitz, Al – *Melody Maker* 1/12/73
Cable, Paul – *Bob Dylan: His Unreleased Recordings* (Dark Star, 1978)
Coltman, Bob – *Paul Clayton and The Folksong Revival* (Scarecrow Press, 2008)
'Tony Glover's Bob Dylan Archive', RR Auction Catalog, 19/11/20
Schumacher, Michael – *There But For Fortune: The Life of Phil Ochs* (Hyperion, 1996)

2.2 – June to November 1964: Meet The Beat
Biographical sources: AA; BH; CHR; DH; JB; RR; SR; VM

Dylan quotes:
'Mama You Been On My Mind', May 1964, © Bob Dylan
'some other kinds of songs', *Another Side* sleeve notes, August 1964 (unedited version published in *Writings & Drawings*, 1973), © Bob Dylan
Letters to Tami Dean, March to November 1964, *Telegraph* #16, © Bob Dylan
'Advice To Geraldine On Her Miscellanous Birthday', Philharmonic Hall program 31/10/64, © Bob Dylan
Max Jones, *Melody Maker* 23/5/64
Letter to Irwin Silber, June 1964, Paturel papers
'Tony Glover's Bob Dylan Archive', RR Auction Catalog, 19/11/20

Interviews with others:
Bloomfield, Michael – Ward, *Michael Bloomfield: The Rise & Fall of An American Guitar Hero*
Bucklen, John – *On The Tracks* #8
Cash, Johnny – to Harvey Kubernik, *Rock Back Pages* 1975 and 5/09
Dylan, Jakob – *Once Upon A Time*
Fariña, Mimi – *Positively 4th Street*
Hammond, John Jr – *On The Tracks* #9
Hammond John Jr – to Ben Edmonds, *Mojo* 2/05
Hoffenberg, Mason – *Playboy* 11/73
Kalb, Danny – *Telegraph* #47
Lennon, John – *NME* 23/4/65
Markel, Bob – *Positively 4th Street*
Markel, Bob – *Telegraph* #52
Marshall, Jim – *Early Dylan* (Bullfinch Press, 1999)

McCartney, Paul – *Mojo #1*
Nelson, Paul – interview with the author
Paturel, Mary Lou – to Steve Turner, 1990 (Rock Back Pages)
Steel, John – *Melody Maker* 6/2/65
Taplin, Jonathan – *Small Town Talk*
Yarrow, Peter – *Small Town Talk*
Young, Izzy – Richard Reuss, July 1965

Contemporary published sources:
Cash, Johnny – letter, *Broadside* #41
Ochs, Phil – Newport Folk Festival programme, July 1964
Shelton, Robert – review of Dylan at Newport, *New York Times* 7/64.

Audio-video sources:
Newport Folk Festival, Freebody Park, RI 24/7/64 and 26/7/64

Unpublished material utilized:
Letters from Cash to Dylan, 1964, Dylan archive, Tulsa
Press release for *Hollywood Stark Naked*, Macmillan, summer 1964
Press release for *Pictures and Words*, Macmillan, November 1964

Secondary resources:
Feinstein, Barry; Kramer, Daniel; Marshall, Jim – *Early Dylan* (Bullfinch Press, 1999)
Gilbert, Douglas with Dave Marsh – *Forever Young: Photographs of Bob Dylan* (Da Capo, 2005)
Glover, Tony – excerpt from unpublished memoir, Mariposa Folk Festival program, August 1972
Kramer, Daniel – *Bob Dylan: A Year and A Day* (Taschen, 2018)
Reineke, Hank – *Ramblin' Jack Elliott: The Never Ending Highway* (Scarecrow Press, 2009)
Silber, Irwin – 'An Open Letter To Bob Dylan', *Sing Out!* 11/64
Wald, Elijah – *Dylan Goes Electric!* (Dey St, 2015)
Zuckerman, Sue – *Critics At Large* 3/3/11

2.3 – November 1964 to April 1965: Walking Down A Crooked Highway
Biographical sources: AA; DH; JB; SR

Dylan quotes:
'My Love She Comes In Silence', Christie's auction catalog, New York 23/6/11, © Bob Dylan

Max Jones, *Melody Maker* 20/3/65
To Maureen Cleave, Savoy hotel press conference 28/4/65, *dont look back* raw footage
Paul Jay Robbins, *LA Free Press* 17–24/9/65
London press conference 3/5/66 (transcript from ETD footage by author)
Rome press conference 23/7/01 (transcript from *Isis* #99)
Bill Flanagan 22/3/17

Interviews with others:
Andersen, Eric – *Mojo* 2/05
Bloomfield, Michael – *Hit Parader*, 6/68
Blue, David – *Mojo* 2/05
Burdon, Eric – *Disc* 6/11/65
Fowley, Kim – interview with the author
Halee, Roy – *Songtalk* 4/90
Halee, Roy – *Sound On Sound* 2005
Kornfeld, Barry – interview with the author
Kramer, Daniel – *Early Dylan* (Bullfinch Press, 1999)
Kramer, Daniel – *Mojo* 2/05
Langhorne, Bruce – *Mojo* 2/05
Langhorne, Bruce – interview with the author
Lennon, John – *Melody Maker* 9/1/65
Nico – *Disc* 18/9/65
Paturel, Mary Lou – to Steve Turner, 1990 (Rock Back Pages)
Rankin, Ken – *Mojo* 2/05
Sebastian, John – *Mojo* 2/05
Shelton, Robert – *Melody Maker* 19/2/66
Wilson, Steve – interview with the author
Wilson, Tom – *Melody Maker* 2/9/67
Wilson, Tom – *Melody Maker* 31/1/76
Young, Izzy – Richard Reuss, July 1965

Contemporary published sources:
Dylan, Bob – 'Walk Down Crooked Highway', *Sing Out!* January 1965 (misdated on cover, January 1964)
Dylan, Bob – captions to a photo-essay by Daniel Kramer, *Pageant* 3/65
Gerrette, Rosemary – *Canberra Times* 7/5/66
Shelton, Robert – 'The Charisma Kid', *Cavalier* 7/65

Audio-video sources:
Columbia session tapes 13–15/1/65
dont look back, raw video footage 4–5/65, Dylan archive, Tulsa

Unpublished material utilized:
Internal Macmillan memo, June 1965

Secondary resources:
Sally Grossman MSS, Christie's auction catalog, New York 23/6/11
Eliot, Marc – *Death of A Rebel: Phil Ochs* (Anchor Books, 1979)
Ford, Roger – 'The Bringing It All Back Home sessions', *Isis* #184
Goodman, Fred – *The Mansion On The Hill: The Head-On Collision of Rock and Commerce* (Times Books, 1997)
Kramer, Daniel – *Bob Dylan* (Castle Books, 1967)
Kramer, Daniel – *Bob Dylan: A Year and A Day* (Taschen, 2018)
Mekas, Jonas (ed.) – *Film Culture #80: The Legend of Barbara Rubin* (2018)
Reineke, Hank – *Ramblin' Jack Elliott: The Never Ending Highway* (Scarecrow Press, 2009)
Woodward, Ian – 'Dylan, The Byrds & Like A Rolling Stone', *Isis* #119

2.4 – April to June 1965: Call Me Vérité
Biographical sources: AA; DH; HS; RS; VM; RS

Dylan quotes:
'Lifeline' questionnaire, *NME* 22/5/65, © Bob Dylan
'Loves and Hates of Bob Dylan', *Jackie* 17/7/65, © Bob Dylan
'Like A Rolling Stone', four-page handwritten draft on Washington hotel notepaper, © Bob Dylan
Studs Terkel, WFMT 26/4/63
Jenny De Yong & Peter Roche, *Darts* 5/65
'Blind Date', *Melody Maker* 8/5/65
Varsity questionnaire, May 1965. *Isis* #102
Ray Coleman, *Melody Maker* 22/5/65
Nora Ephron, McGregor (ed.), *Bob Dylan: A Retrospective* (interview conducted in September 1965)
Nat Hentoff, *Playboy* March 1966
Jules Siegel, *Saturday Evening Post* 30/7/66
Ron Rosenbaum, *Playboy* 3/78
spoken intro to 'Thin Man', Nagoya 8/3/86
Jeff Rosen, *No Direction Home* DVD, 13–16/12/00

Interviews with others:
Baez, Joan – *How Sweet The Sound* DVD
Bloomfield, Michael – *Hit Parader* 6/68
Bloomfield, Michael – *On The Road With Bob Dylan*

Boyd, Patti – interview with the author
Carthy, Martin – *Disc* 10/4/65
Donovan – 'The Green Man', *Q* 7/2020
Faithfull, Marianne – *NME* 14/5/65
Flint, Hughie – *Telegraph* #36
Gillespie, Dana – *NME* 9/7/65
Gillespie, Dana – *News of the World* 31/8/81
Gillespie, Dana – *British Blues Review* 2/90
Gillespie, Dana – interview with the author
Gillespie, Dana – *Weren't Born A Man*
Joseph, Anthea – interview with the author
Judson, Horace – online posting on EDLIS 17/10/98
Mayall, John – *Telegraph* #36
Pennebaker, D. A. – *Melody Maker* 17/6/72
Pennebaker, D. A. – *Telegraph* #26
Pennebaker, D. A. – *Who Threw The Glass* #4 (Summer 1993)
Pennebaker, D. A. – *Gadfly* 4/99
Pennebaker, D. A. – *Time* 26/2/07
Ross-Trevor, Mike – *Word* 5/04
Siegel, Jules – interview with the author
Young, Izzy – Richard Reuss, July 1965

Contemporary published sources:
Valentine, Penny – review of 'Subterranean Homesick Blues', *Disc* 24/4/65
NME 8/5/65
Disc Weekly 4/9/65

Audio-video sources:
dont look back, raw video footage 4–5/65, Dylan archive, Tulsa, including Dylan/Baez hotel jam session 4/5/65
'1965 English Tour', soundboard recordings, 30/4/65–10/5/65, 1965 Copyright Collection (official download)
dont look back: The Out-takes (Tambourine Man Video), 2xDVD
Levy's Recording Studio, London, with John Mayall's Bluesbreakers 12/5/65
Eat The Document raw footage, 171 cans, Dylan archive, Tulsa
How Sweet The Sound DVD
Rolling Thunder Revue, Netflix, 2019

Unpublished material utilized:
Invoice for John Mayall's Bluesbreakers, for session work 12/5/65

Secondary resources:
Baez, Joan – letter to her sister, Mimi, in *Positively 4th Street*
Barker, Derek – 'Auction Block', in *Isis* #102 (includes transcripts of letters from Baez and Nico to Dylan at the Savoy in May, and facsimile of the *Varsity* questionnaire)
Bauldie, John (ed.) – 'Dylan's London Album', in *Positively Tie Dream* (Ashes & Sand, 1979)
Cooper, Chris & Keith Marsh – *The Circus Is In Town: England 1965* (pp, 1987)
Dalton, David with Marianne Faithfull – *Faithfull by Faithfull* (Little, Brown, 1994)
Heylin, Clinton – *All The Madmen: A Journey To The Dark Side of British Rock* (Constable & Robinson, 2012).
Kramer, Daniel – *Bob Dylan: A Year and A Day* (Taschen, 2018)
Mekas, Jonas (ed.) – *Film Culture #80: The Legend of Barbara Rubin* (2018)
Sheff, David – *The Playboy Interviews with John Lennon & Yoko Ono* (Playboy Press, 1981)
Woodward, Ian – 'Dylan's 1965 London Recording Session', *Isis* #120

2.5 – June to September 1965: The Rites Of Summer
Biographical sources: AA; AS; BH; HS; KM; LH; RR; SR

Dylan quotes:
'Highway 61 Revisited', typed draft, Dylan archive, Tulsa, © Bob Dylan
'Queen Jane Approximately', handwritten/typed drafts, Dylan archive, Tulsa, © Bob Dylan
'Ballad Of A Thin Man', typed draft, Dylan archive, Tulsa, © Bob Dylan
'Just Like Tom Thumb's Blues', typed draft, Dylan archive, Tulsa, © Bob Dylan
Hollywood press conference 4/9/65 (transcript from *Rain Unravelled Tales*)
Paul Jay Robbins, *LA Free Press* 17–24/9/65
Margaret Steen, *Toronto Star Weekly* 29/1/66
San Francisco press conference 3/12/65 (transcript from *Rolling Stone Rock'n'Roll Reader*)
Martin Bronstein, CBC 20/2/66
Perth press conference 23/4/66 (transcript from *Music Maker* 6/66)
Jann Wenner, *Rolling Stone* 29/11/69
Ron Rosenbaum, *Playboy* 3/78
'Like A Rolling Stone', 100 Greatest Singles #2, *Rolling Stone* 8/9/88
Jeff Rosen, *No Direction Home* DVD, 13–16/12/00
'Tony Glover's Bob Dylan Archive', RR Auction Catalog, 19/11/20

Interviews with others:
Alderson, Richard – interview with the author
Baez, Joan – *Broadside* #61

Bloomfield, Michael – *Hit Parader* 6/68
Bloomfield, Michael – *On The Road With Bob Dylan*
Bloomfield, Michael – Ward, *Michael Bloomfield: The Rise & Fall of An American Guitar Hero*
Boyd, Joe – *Telegraph* #31
Brooks, Harvey – *Telegraph* #47
Cash, Johnny – *The Other Side of Nashville* DVD
Donovan – *NME* 10/9/65
Gillespie, Dana – *NME* 6/66
Glover, Tony – video interview with Marcus Whitman, mid-1980s
Gorgoni, Al – interview with the author
Gravenites, Nick – Ward, *Michael Bloomfield: The Rise & Fall of An American Guitar Hero*
Grossman, Sally – to Steve Turner, 1990 (Rock Back Pages)
Herald, John – *Small Town Talk*
Johnston, Bob – Marcus, *Like A Rolling Stone*
Johnston, Bob – *Disc* 7/11/70
Kooper, Al – Harvey Kubernik, *Rock Back Pages* 2010
Kooper, Al – *Minneapolis City Pages* 2010
Kooper, Al – interview with the author
Lerner, Murray – interview with the author
Muldaur, Maria – Von Schmidt & Rooney, *Baby Let Me Follow You Down: The Illustrated Story of The Cambridge Folk Years* (1979)
Nelson, Paul – interview with the author
Ochs, Phil – *Village Voice* 12/8/65
Robertson, Robbie – *Record Mirror* 13/9/69
Sky, Patrick – Schumacher, *There But For Fortune: The Life of Phil Ochs*
Springsteen, Bruce – speech at Rock'n'Roll Hall of Fame induction 20/1/88
Wilson, Tom – *Melody Maker* 31/1/76
Young, Izzy – Richard Reuss, July 1965

Contemporary published sources:
Bakst, M. Charles – *Providence Journal* 26/7/65
Champlin, Charles – review of Hollywood Bowl, *LA Times* 6/9/65
Freedman, Ed – *Boston Broadside* 18/8/65
Kretchmer, Arthur – review of Newport, *Village Voice* 5/8/65
Mirken, Caryl – *Broadside* #61 (15/8/65)
Nelson, Paul – 'What's Happening' in *Sing Out!* November 1965
Schoenfeld, Herm – *Variety* 1/9/65
Shelton, Robert – Newport Folk Festival program, July 1965
Shelton, Robert – review of Dylan at Newport, *Cavalier* 11/66

Audio-video sources:
The Other Side of Nashville documentary, DVD
Columbia session tapes 15/6/65 and 16/6/65
Newport Folk Festival, Freebody Park, RI 24–5/7/65
Columbia session tapes 29/7/65, 30/7/65, 2/8/65, 4/8/65
Forest Hills Stadium, Forest Hills, NYC 28/8/65
Hollywood Bowl, LA 3/9/65

Unpublished material utilized:
Letter from Ken Glancy to Albert Grossman 28/6/65
Reuss, Richard – Folk Scene Diary, summer 1965

Secondary resources:
Boyd, Joe – *White Bicycles: Making Music In The 1960s* (Serpent's Tail, 2005)
Boyd, Joe – letter to the *New York Observer* 5/11/98
Dunaway, David King – *Pete Seeger: How Can I Keep From Singing* (McGraw-Hill, 1981)
Ford, Roger – 'The Highway 61 Revisited Sessions', *Isis* #185
Glover, Tony – excerpt from unpublished memoir, Mariposa Folk Festival program, August 1972
Glover, Tony – sleeve notes for *No Direction Home: The Bootleg Series Vol. 7*
Heylin, Clinton – *Judas: From Forest Hills To The Free Trade Hall* (Route, 2016)
Holzman, Jac – *Follow The Music: The Life & High Times of Elektra Records* (FirstMedia, 1998)
Jopling, Norman – *Shake It Up Baby! Notes From a Pop Music Reporter 1961–72* (RockHistory, 2015)
Kramer, Daniel – *Bob Dylan: A Year and A Day* (Taschen, 2018)
Marcus, Greil – *Like A Rolling Stone: Bob Dylan At The Crossroads* (Faber & Faber, 2005)
Schatzberg, Jerry – *Dylan By Schatzberg* (AccArt Books, 2018)
Sloman, Larry – *On The Road With Bob Dylan* (Bantam, 1978)
Wald, Elijah – *Dylan Goes Electric!* (Dey St, 2015)
Ward, Ed – *Michael Bloomfield: The Rise & Fall of An American Guitar Hero* (Chicago Review Press, 2016)
Wein, George – *Myself Among Others: A Life In Music* (Da Capo, 2009)

2.6 – September 1965 to March 1966: Both Kinds Of Music
Biographical sources: BH; HS; LH; RR; RS; SR; VM

Dylan quotes:
'Sally Grossman' MSS, *circa* 1965, reproduced in facsimile in the Christie's, NYC, catalog of 'Fine Printed Books and Manuscripts' 23/6/11 (withdrawn from sale, the items now reside in the Dylan archive in Tulsa), © Bob Dylan

'Jet Pilot' MSS, *circa* October 1965, auctioned at Christie's, NYC, 6/12/13, reproduced in facsimile at www.pbs.org/opb/historydetectives/investigation/bob-dylan-guitar, © Bob Dylan

Typescript from March 1966, 'You Cant Get Your Way Alla Time' and handwritten verse for 'Absolutely Sweet Marie', © Bob Dylan

'Just Like A Woman', typescript and handwritten bridge, March 1966, reproduced in Christie's catalogue, London auction 30/9/99, © Bob Dylan

Robert Fulford, *Toronto Star* 18/9/65

Nat Hentoff, the original *Playboy* interview, published as *Whaaat!* (interview conducted in October 1965)

Joseph Haas, *Chicago Daily News* 27/11/65

San Francisco Press Conference 3/12/65 (transcript from *Rolling Stone Rock'n'Roll Reader*)

Los Angeles Press Conference 16/12/65

Ralph J. Gleason, *Ramparts* 3/66

Bob Fass, WBAI 26/1/66

Martin Bronstein, CBC 20/2/66

Robert Shelton, March 1966, *No Direction Home*

John Cohen & Happy Traum, *Sing Out!* 10/68

Jann Wenner, *Rolling Stone* 29/11/69

Cameron Crowe, *Biograph* sleeve notes (interview conducted in September 1985)

Bob Fass, WBAI 21/5/86

'Tony Glover's Bob Dylan Archive', RR Auction Catalog, 19/11/20

Jeff Rosen, *No Direction Home* DVD, 13–16/12/00

Interviews with others:
Bloomfield, Michael – *Sloman: On The Road With Bob Dylan*
Bloomfield, Michael – *Hit Parader* 6/68
Burdon, Eric – *Disc* 6/11/65
Ginsberg, Allen – *Melody Maker* 18/3/72
Helm, Levon – *NME* 1971.
Helm, Levon – *Modern Drummer* 8/84
Johnston, Bob – *Nashville Scene* 7/3/96
Johnston, Bob – *Rock Back Pages* 5/09
Kooper, Al – 'Dylan In Nashville', *Mojo* 7/16
Kooper, Al – Harvey Kubernik, *Rock Back Pages* 2010
Kooper, Al – interview with the author
Manuel, Richard – *Disc* 29/5/71
McCoy, Charlie – *Hit Parader* 10/66
McCoy, Charlie – Harvey Kubernik, *Rock Back Pages* 2010
McCoy, Charlie – Adam Sherwin, *Independent* 24/6/15

Robertson, Robbie – 'Music From Big Pink', Tony Glover, in *Eye* 10/68
Robertson, Robbie – *Rolling Stone* 27/4/87
Rowan, Pete – *Journal of Country Music* Vol. 7 #3 (12/78, interview from 1966)
Siegel, Jules – interview with the author
Steel, John – *Melody Maker* 6/2/65
Taplin, Jonathan – Plimpton & Stein, *Edie: An American Biography* (1988)
Wilson, Tom – *Melody Maker* 2/9/67

Contemporary published sources:
Variety 22/9/65
Berkeley Barb 10/12/65
KRLA Beat 22/1/66 (report of LA press conference 16/12/65)
'Dylan's Return', *Twin City A Go Go* 11/65 (reprint: *Occasionally* #5)
'The Big Beat of Folk-Rock-Protest', *Cavalier* 3/66
Gardiner, Sandy – *Ottawa Journal* 21/2/66
Gleason, Ralph J., 'The Children's Crusade', *Ramparts* 3/66
Gleason, Ralph J. – Judith Adams' account of Austin press conference, *San Francisco Chronicle* 9/65
Gleason, Ralph J. – review of Berkeley concert, *San Francisco Chronicle* 6/12/65
Heller, Zelda – *Montreal Gazette* 21/2/66
Mann – 'A Personal Observation' (reprint: *Occasionally* #5)
Newfield, Jack – review of Carnegie Hall concert, *Village Voice* 10/65
Paxton, Tom & Henrietta Yurchenco – 'Bob Dylan: News or Noise', *Sounds & Fury* 4/66
Shelton, Gilbert – *Texas Ranger* 11/65
Silber, Irwin – 'Fan The Flames' in *Sing Out!* 1/66
Williams, Paul – *Crawdaddy* #2

Audio-video sources:
Columbia session tape 5/10/65
Columbia session tape 30/11/65
San Francisco press conference 3/12/65
Allen Ginsberg's backstage conversation with Dylan, San Francisco, 12/65
Allen Ginsberg Californian audience tapes x2, 4–12/11/65
Los Angeles press conference 16/12/65
Columbia session tapes 21/1/66, 25/1/66, 27/1/66
Columbia session tapes 14–17/2/66
Columbia session tapes 7–10/3/66
Eat The Document raw footage, 171 cans, Dylan archive, Tulsa
Bob Fass WBAI radio show 26/1/66

Secondary resources:
Bronstein, Martin – *Observatory* 15/6/98
Fong-Torres, Ben – *Rolling Stone Rock'n'Roll Reader* (Bantam, 1974)
Ford, Roger: 'Cutting Edge Sessions October 1965 to March 1966', *Isis* #186–9
Glover, Tony – 'Big Pink', *Eye* 10/68
Heylin, Clinton – *Judas: From Forest Hills To The Free Trade Hall* (Route, 2016)
Lange, Kees De & Ben Valkhoff – *Plug Your Ears: A Comprehensive Guide To Recordings of Jimi Hendrix* (pp, 1993)
Sanders, Daryl – *That Thin, Wild Mercury Sound: The Making of Blonde On Blonde* (Chicago Review Press, 2019)
Schatzberg, Jerry – *Dylan By Schatzberg* (AccArt Books, 2018)
Smith, Patti – 'Depletion Behind A Positive Mask', *Creem* 4/74
Stein, Jean & George Plimpton – *Edie: An American Biography* (Random House, 1988)
Williams, Paul – *Performing Artist: The Music of Bob Dylan Vol. 1* (Underwood-Miller, 1990)
Williams, Paul (ed.) – *The Crawdaddy Book* (Hal Leonard, 2002)
Williams, Paul – *Watching The River Flow* (Omnibus Press, 1996)
Wyman, Bill – *Stone Alone* (Viking, 1990)

2.7 – March to May 1966: I've Been All Around This World
Biographical sources: HS; KM; RR; VM

Dylan quotes:
LA press conference 16/12/65 (transcript from video footage by author)
Melbourne press conference 18/4/66
Perth press conference 23/4/66 (transcript from *Music Maker* 6/66)
Stockholm press conference 28/4/66 (transcript from raw ETD footage by author)
Copenhagen press conference 30/4/66 (transcript from raw ETD footage by author)
London press conference 3/5/66 (transcript from raw ETD footage by author)
London press conference 4/10/97 (*Mojo* 2/98)

Interviews with others:
Alderson, Richard – interview with the author
Deshannon, Jackie – *Cavalier* 3/66
Faithfull, Marianne – Dalton, *Faithfull*
Gillespie, Dana – *NME* 6/66
James, Billy – *KRLA Beat* 22/1/66
Jones, Mickey – *Isis* #79
Jones, Mickey – *Telegraph* #55
Law, Lisa – Michael Simmons, *Mojo* 6/16
McCartney, Paul – *Mojo* #1

Pennebaker, D. A. – *Gadfly* 4/99
Pennebaker, D. A. – *Melody Maker* 17/6/72
Pennebaker, D. A. – *Telegraph* #16
Pennebaker, D. A. – *Denver Post* 17/10/98
Pennebaker, D. A. – *New York Times* 19/5/16
Rasky, Harry – *Denver Post* 17/10/98
Robertson, Robbie – *Crawdaddy* 3/76
Robertson, Robbie – *NME* 17/6/78
Young, Izzy – Richard Reuss, July 1965

Contemporary published sources:
Datebook 7/66.
Gerrette, Rosemary – *Canberra Times* 7/5/66
Green, Richard – *Record Mirror* 14/5/66
John, Ole – *Politiken* 2/5/66
Kullenberg, Annette – 'A Picture of Our Time With Many Senses', *Idun Veckojournalen* 13/5/66 (English translation *Occasionally* #4)
Leaf, Earl – 'My Fair and Frantic Hollywood', *Teen* 7/66
Tillman-Murray, Pi Ann, *Idolnytt* 7/66
Waters, Edgar, *Australian* 16/4/66

Audio-video sources:
Eat The Document raw footage, 171 cans, Dylan archive, Tulsa, including Stockholm, Copenhagen and London press conferences
Soundboard and audience recordings 13/4/66–1/5/66, *The 1966 Live Recordings*

Unpublished material utilized:
Log for LA recording sessions, 30/3/66
Printout of contents for *Eat The Document* raw footage, 171 cans, Dylan archive, Tulsa
Tiny Tim's diary for 1966, courtesy of Justin Martell

Secondary resources:
Bauldic, John   *The Ghost of Electricity* (pp, 1989)
Dadic, Zac – 'Australia 1966 Approximately' Pts 1–3, *Isis* #185–7
Heylin, Clinton – *Judas: From Forest Hills To The Free Trade Hall* (Route, 2016)
Heylin, Clinton – 'A Profile of Howard Alk', *Telegraph* #18
Hols, Lars – *Dylan In Sweden* (pp, 1991)
McGregor, Craig (ed.) – *Bob Dylan: A Retrospective* (Morrow, 1972)
Rawlins, Adrian – *Through The Looking Glass: A Collection of Writings on Bob Dylan* (The All Night Cafe, 1994)
Schatzberg, Jerry – *Dylan By Schatzberg* (AccArt Books, 2018)

2.8 – May 1966: Man, I'm Not Even Twenty-Five
Biographical sources: DH; RR

Dylan quotes:
'A Note From Bob', Rod MacBeath, *Bridge* #49
Paris press conference 23/5/66 (transcript from raw ETD footage by author)
'Thirty Questions To Bob Dylan', Rod MacBeath, *Bridge* #24 (see *Salut Les Copains*, 9/66)
Ian Brady, *Top Pops* 30/8/69
John Rockwell, *New York Times* 8/1/74
Ron Rosenbaum, *Playboy* 3/78
Craig McGregor, *Sydney Morning Herald* 18/3/78
Jeff Rosen, *No Direction Home* DVD, 13–16/12/00
Mikal Gilmore, *Rolling Stone* 27/9/12
'Tony Glover's Bob Dylan Archive', RR Auction Catalog, 19/11/20

Interviews with others:
Alderson, Richard – interview with the author
Byrne, Johnny – Green, *Days In The Life: Voices From the English Underground.*
Feinstein, Barry – *Early Dylan* (Bullfinch Press, 1999)
Gillespie, Dana – *NME* 6/66
Hardy, Françoise – *Word* #25 (3/05)
Jones, Mickey – 'Manchester Revisited', *Isis* #79
Jones, Mickey – *Telegraph* #55
Keylock, Tom – interview with the author
McCartney, Paul – *Mojo* #1
Pennebaker, D. A. – *Denver Post* 17/10/98
Pennebaker, D. A. – *Melody Maker* 17/6/72
Pennebaker, D. A. – *Who Threw The Glass* #4 (Summer 1993)
Pennebaker, D. A. – *Gadfly* 4/99
Pennebaker, D. A. – *Small Town Talk*
Robertson, Robbie – *Rolling Stone* 27/4/87
Russell, Willy – radio interview with Spencer Leigh, courtesy of Spencer Leigh

Contemporary published sources:
Young, Andrew – review of Glasgow concert, *Scottish Daily Mail* 20/5/66
Anon.– 'Dylan Faces Another Night of Cat-Calls', review of Edinburgh concert, *Scottish Daily Mail* 21/5/66
Ellis, Barbara – *Melody Maker* 11/6/66
Gerrette, Rosemary – *Canberra Times* 7/5/66
Hardern, T. – Letter to *Disc* 28/5/66

McCann, Mr – letter to *Manchester Evening News* 21/5/66
'Dylan Fan' – *Oldham Evening Chronicle* 25/5/66
'Talking To A Modern Myth', *Ulsterweek* 12/5/66
'JK' – 'The Night of the Great Let-Down', *Dublin Evening Herald* 6/5/66
Dublin Evening Herald letters page, 19/5/66 and 21/5/66
Pascal, Jean-Marc – *Salut Les Copains* 7/66
(Pascal, Jean-Marc) – 'A Plea For A Better Dylan', *Hullabaloo* 12/66
Shelton, Robert – 'The Charisma Kid', *Cavalier* 7/65
Pop magazine 1/7/66
Letter from AS to Tito Burns, Free Trade Hall archive, Manchester Central Ref. Library (Lee, *Like The Night*)

Audio-video sources:
Eat The Document raw footage, 171 cans, Dylan archive, Tulsa, including Paris press conference 24/5/66
Mono soundboard recordings of all concerts, Dublin 5/5/66 to London 27/5/66, *The 1966 Live Recordings*
Three-track soundboard recordings of Royal Albert Hall, London 26/5/66 and 27/5/66, *The 1966 Live Recordings*
'Judas' shout at Manchester Free Trade Hall, isolated three-track Columbia tape

Unpublished material utilized:
Printout of contents for *Eat The Document* raw footage, 171 cans, Dylan archive, Tulsa
Correspondence with Graham Ashton re Birmingham 12/5/66
Correspondence with John Kappes re Manchester 17/5/66

Useful resources:
Bauldie, John – *The Ghost of Electricity* (pp, 1989)
Feinstein, Barry – *Real Moments* (Omnibus Press, 2008)
Green, Jonathon – *Days In The Life: Voices From the English Underground 1961–71* (William Heinemann, 1988)
Heylin, Clinton – *Judas: From Forest Hills To The Free Trade Hall* (Route, 2016)
Lee, C. P. – *Like The Night: Bob Dylan and the road to the Free Trade Hall* (Helter Skelter, 1998)
MacDonald, Ian – *The People's Music* (Pimlico, 2003).

Winterlude #2 (June/July 1966): Off The Road Again
Biographical sources: BH; RR

Interviews with others:
Hoffenberg, Mason – *Playboy* 11/73

Markel, Bob – *Telegraph* #52
Rasky, Harry – *Denver Post* 17/10/98

Contemporary published sources:
Review of 'I Want You' 45, *Record Mirror* 7/66
Paul Williams, 'Understanding Dylan', *Crawdaddy* #4

Audio-video sources:
Eat The Document raw footage, 171 cans, Dylan archive, Tulsa

Useful resources:
Barker, Derek – *Too Much of Nothing* (Red Planet, 2018)
Bicknell, Alf with Garry Mars – *Baby, You Can Drive My Car* (#9, 1990)
Hilburn, Robert – *Johnny Cash: The Life* (Little, Brown, 2013)
Markel, Bob – introduction to *Tarantula* (Macmillan, 1971)
Simon, Carly – *Boys In The Trees: A Memoir* (Constable, 2015)
Williams, Paul (ed.) – *The Crawdaddy Book* (Hal Leonard, 2002)

Index

ABC (American Broadcasting Company), 205, 399, 412, 413, 453
About Bob Dylan, 6
Abrams, Harvey, 60
'Absolute Sweet Marie' (Dylan), 393
Acuff, Roy, 122, 159
Adams, Camilla, 35n
Adams, Judith, 370
Adelphi Hotel, Liverpool, 315, 321
Adelphi Theatre, Dublin, 425
Aftermath (The Rolling Stones), 398
'Ain't Gonna Grieve' (Dylan), 183
Alderson, Richard, 12n, 142, 146, 360, 400, 404, 411, 416, 425, 434, 439, 441, 448, 455
Algonquin Hotel, New York, 379
Alk, Howard, 204, 222, 412, 414, 435, 442, 453
'All American Boy' (Bare), 168
'All Over You' (Dylan), 198
Allen, Steve, 224, 249–50
Almanac Singers, 41
Alper, Joe, 118
'Alternatives To College' (Dylan), 321, 329
Altham, Keith, 317, 320, 327
Amazon, 6
American Ballads & Folk Songs, 97
American Songbag, 245
Amram, David, 209
'Anathea' (Collins), 184, 185
'Ancient Memories' (Dylan), 263; *see also* 'My Back Pages'
And A Voice To Sing With (Baez), 283–4
'And Your Bird Can Sing' (Lennon/McCartney), 423
Andersen, Eric, 254, 300
Anderson, Randy, 26
Animals, The, 199, 274, 299, 319, 366, 373
Anka, Paul, 440

'Anna Fehrer' (trad.), 184
'Annie Had A Baby' (Glover), 50
'Another Man Done Gone' (Odetta), 62
Another Side Of Bob Dylan (Dylan), 231, 257, 259, 260–64, 266, 271, 273, 293, 330, 447
Another Side Of Bob Dylan (Maymudes), 8
Anthology of American Folk Music, 85
'Are You Walking And A-Talking For The Lord?' (Hank Williams), 155
Arnold, Jerome, 349, 352
Arnold, Kokomo, 129
Aronowitz, Al, 9, 166, 253, 255, 257, 276, 277, 282, 301, 312, 339, 364
  on alcohol consumption, 261
  on The Beatles, 246, 276, 359
  and break up with Suze (1964), 253, 255
  on cruel streak, 282, 363
  at Dylan's wedding (1965), 379
  on electric conversion, 275
  Gilbert's photographs (1964), 269
  Ginsberg, relationship with, 236, 268
Asch, Moses, 35n, 38, 89–90
Astral Weeks (Morrison), 108n, 206n
Atkins, Bill, 390–91
Auden, W. H., 186n
Autray, Hugues, 258, 447
Augenblink, Ivan, 183–4
Augusta, Georgia, 244
Augustine of Hippo, 456
Austin, Texas, 367, 370
Australia, 400, 401, 402–9, 452
Australian, The, 404
Avakian, George, 96
Avalon, Frankie, 173
Avis, Bill, 405, 407
Avril (dancer), 42–3, 78
Aznavour, Charles, 197

'Babe, I'm In The Mood For You' (Dylan), 133, 134
Baby Let Me Follow Me Down (Von Schmidt), 91, 185
'Baby Let Me Follow You Down', 107, 108, 109, 112n, 126, 196, 362, 425, 437, 441, 455
'Baby Please Don't Go' (Williams), 113, 115, 116n
'Baby, Let Me Lay It On You' (trad.), 90
Bacall, Lauren, 249
'Backwater Blues' (Smith), 74, 104
Baez, Joan, 7, 42, 105, 184, 189, 202, 203, 223, 248, 265, 271, 282–4, 288
   Cash, meeting with (1964), 272
   cave incident (c.1965), 48
   'Daddy You Been On My Mind', 257, 309
   England tour (1965), 27, 313, 316, 317, 318–19, 321, 323, 324, 332–3
   'Farewell Angelina', 291–2, 301, 309
   Forest Hills show (1963), 217–18
   Hammond and, 92
   Hootenanny boycott (1963), 205
   'It's All Over Now, Baby Blue', 309
   letters to, 231, 283
   'Love Is Just A Four-Letter Word', 291, 292
   Maymudes on, 271, 379
   at Newport Festival, 217, 270, 353
   record deal, 92
   Rotolo and, 219–20, 251
   tour (1963), 219
   tour (1965), 309
   Town Hall show (1961), 105
   'Troubled & I Don't Know Why', 218
   Washington Civil Rights March (1963), 220
Bailey, Lillian, 84, 104
Bailey, Mell, 17–18, 84, 104
Baker, Ellen, 20, 56, 70–71
Baker, Etta, 131, 132
Bakst, Charlie, 353
Balfour, Victoria, 101
'Ballad For A Friend' (Dylan), 48, 83, 115
'Ballad In Plain D' (Dylan), 258, 259–60, 262, 267
'Ballad Of A Gliding Swan' (Jones), 190
'Ballad Of A Thin Man' (Dylan), 15, 322, 345, 346, 359, 407, 408, 425, 441, 445
'Ballad Of Donald White, The' (Dylan), 83, 209
'Ballad Of Emmett Till, The' (Dylan), 119–20, 128, 216
'Ballad Of Hollis Brown' (Dylan), 147, 179, 192, 206, 225, 226

'Ballad Of Tim Evans' (MacColl), 61
de Balzac, Honoré, 37
'Bamba, La' (trad. arr. Valens), 344
Band, The, 8, 367
Banjo Barons, The, 227
Banjo Tape (1963), 181n
Bare, Bobby, 168
Barlow, Harold, 300
Barnes, George, 177
Bartocciolo, Enzo, 267
'Battleship Of Maine, The' (trad.), 103
Beach Boys, The, 392, 398
Bear Mountain, New York, 80
Bear, The, Chicago, 204–5
Bearsville, New York, 265, 270, 279
Beat Generation, The, 197
Beatles, The, 246–8, 275, 310, 312, 313, 314, 325, 411, 422, 442, 453–4
   Delmonico meeting (1964), 276–8
   Freewheelin', views on, 247, 310
   Hard Day's Night, A, 249
   Help!, 334, 359
   Highway 61, views on, 359–60
   Hollywood Bowl shows (1965), 362
   Magical Mystery Tour, 414
   Revolver, 423
   Savoy meeting (1965), 318–19
'Beautiful People, The' (Dylan/Wynn), 20–21
Becker, Bob, 171
Beecher, Bonnie, 60–61, 64, 70–71, 76, 84, 112–13, 194, 249, 251, 363
Behan, Dominic, 194
Behind The Shades (Heylin), 3, 15, 122
Belafonte, Harry, 35n, 61, 69, 105, 116, 214
Belfast, Northern Ireland, 425, 426, 428, 433
Bell, Ian, 6, 10, 110
Bell, Vinnie, 344
Bender, William, 389
Bennington, Massachusetts, 87–8, 220
Berg, Bill, 165
Berg, John, 302
Berger, Dave, 26
Berger, Glenn, 11
Berkeley, California, 244, 248, 249
Berliner, Jay, 206
Berns, Bert, 199, 437
Bernstein, Ellen, 11
Berry, Chuck, 51, 314, 315, 349
Best American Poetry, 27
Bicknell, Alf, 453

INDEX

Big Bopper, 168, 169
Big Pink, New York, 255
Bikel, Theodore, 210–11
Billboard, 92, 124, 151, 199, 200, 216, 377, 385
Biograph (Dylan), 246, 375
Bird, Annie, 18, 20, 209
Birmingham, England, 324, 437
Bitter End, The, New York, 37, 142
Björner, Olof, 6
'Black Cross' (Lord Buckley), 104, 113
'Black Crow Blues' (Dylan), 258, 262
'Blackjack Blues' (Charles), 64
Blonde On Blonde (Dylan), 2, 12, 289, 371–2, 377–8, 382–4, 388–95, 397–8, 455
Blood On The Tracks (Dylan), 11, 12, 14
Bloomfield, Michael, 174, 222, 275, 288, 363, 364, 378
    Bear show (1963), 204
    on cruel streak, 281–2, 366
    Forest Hills show (1965), 360
    Highway 61 album (1965), 340–41, 342, 357, 358, 361
    Hollywood Bowl show (1965), 360, 363
    on 'Like A Rolling Stone', 337
    Newport Festival (1965), 348, 349, 350, 352, 354
'Blowin' In The Wind' (Dylan), 129–30, 134–6, 137, 192, 199, 206, 216, 228–9, 387, 437
'Blue Eyed Baby' (Dylan), 140
'Blue Moon of Kentucky' (Monroe), 160
Blue, David, 241, 254, 282, 288, 301
Blues Project, 275
Bluesbreakers, The, 314, 317, 320, 330–31
Blyton, Enid, 305
Bob Dylan (Dylan), 80–81, 103, 105–10, 123, 124–7
Bob Dylan Himself (Dylan), 81–2, 114, 185
Bob Dylan Off The Record (Dylan), 303
Bob Dylan Scrapbook, The (Dylan), 14, 268
'Bob Dylan's Blues' (Dylan), 133, 134, 183n
'Bob Dylan's Dream' (Dylan), 205, 215
'Bob Dylan's 115th Dream' (Dylan), 289, 291, 293n
'Bob Dylan's Secret Archive' (*New York Times*), 13–14
Bogart, Humphrey, 249
Bolan, Marc, 126, 299
Bonaparte, Napoleon, 23
'Bonnie Lass Of Fyvie, The' (trad.), 103
'Bonnie, Why'd You Cut My Hair?' (Dylan), 71, 77

Bono, 59
Boone, John, 297, 298
Bootleg Series, The (Dylan), 11, 15, 113, 183n, 444
'Boots Of Spanish Leather' (Dylan), 132, 194, 198, 215, 225
'Boppin' The Blues' (Perkins), 161, 162
Boston Broadside, 216, 352
Boston, Massachusetts, 80, 90, 91–2, 202–3, 376
Bouchillon, Chris, 31
Bound For Glory (Guthrie), 27, 33, 40, 70
'Bound To Lose' (Dylan), 183n
Bowie, David, 334
Boyd, Joe, 317, 347, 348, 349, 350–51, 354
Boyd, Patti, 318
Brand, Oscar, 39–40, 42, 110
Brandeis University, 205
Brando, Marlon, 248, 278, 364, 381–2
Branford, Connecticut, 77, 80, 90, 205
Braun, David, 177, 178, 185, 197, 397, 410, 412
Braun, Michael, 429–30
Brecht, Bertolt, 218, 234
'Brennan On The Moor' (trad.), 117
Brickman, Marshall, 73
Bringing It All Back Home (Dylan), 280, 286, 287, 289–302, 310, 330, 374
Brinkley, Douglas, 13, 188n
Brisbane, Queensland, 405, 452
Bristol, England, 429
British Broadcasting Corporation (BBC), 186, 189, 190, 191, 192, 195, 320, 330, 333, 337
Broadside, 120–21, 130, 181–2, 211, 219, 231, 236, 241, 271, 348, 352, 353
Broadside Ballads Vol. 1, 121
Broadside Reunion, 121
Bronstein, Martin, 387–8
Brooks, Harvey, 356, 357, 361, 363, 367
Broonzy, Big Bill, 39, 87, 177
'Brother John' (Neville), 336
Brown, Hugh, 32n, 69, 70
Brown, Joe, 440
Brown, Maxine, 173
Bucklen, John, 57, 94, 161, 162, 165, 168, 281
Buckley, Jeff, 85
Bull, Sandy, 77, 272
Burdon, Eric, 299, 301, 302, 373
Burns, Tito, 440
Burton, James, 360
Butler, Keith, 442, 443
Buttrey, Kenneth, 391
Byrds, The, 257, 299, 310, 363, 400–401

502　INDEX

Byrne, Johnny, 424
Byron, Lord, 180

Cable, Paul, 77, 113, 259, 264
Cafe Bizarre, New York, 374
Cafe Espresso, Woodstock, 266–7, 269, 280, 282, 323, 343
Cafe Wha?, New York, 30, 31, 36, 44, 45
Cafe Yana, Boston, 91, 203
Cahn, Rolf, 80
'California' (Dylan), 293n, 294
'California Brown Eyed Baby' (Dylan), 78–9, 81, 82
California to the New York Island (Guthrie), 38, 82
Cambridge University, 327–9
Cambridge, Massachusetts, 78, 90–91
Camp Herzl, Webster, 49–54, 157, 163, 167
Camp, Hamilton, 142, 144
'Can You Please Crawl Out Your Window?' (Dylan), 371, 372, 377, 384, 385–6
Canadian Broadcasting Corporation (CBC), 243, 387
Canberra Times, 408
Candy (Southern/Hoffenberg), 258
'Car Song' (Guthrie), 80n
Cardiff, Wales, 429, 434, 437
Carmel, California, 223, 287
Carnegie Hall, New York, 34, 74, 147, 184, 227–8, 365, 370–71
　Chapter Hall, 34, 35, 79, 89, 110, 199
Carroll, Hattie, 223–4
Carruthers, Ben, 330
Carter, Maybelle, 348
Carter, Sydney, 331
Carthy, Martin, 192, 194, 257, 265, 303, 312, 319
Caruso, Enrico, 87, 326
Cash Plan, The, 383
Cash, Johnny, 82, 161, 231, 271–3, 345, 355, 426, 434
Cash, June Carter, 272, 434
Cashbox, 125
Cassady, Neal, 52, 70, 157
Castle, Hollywood, 382
Castner, Lynn, 60
Cat Iron, 60
'Catch The Wind' (Donovan), 319
Catouse, Nadia, 331
Cavalier, 308
CBS, 92, 205–7, 248, 330, 399
Cedar Tavern, New York, 314

Central City, Colorado, 66–7, 70, 222, 244
Cesaroni, Giancarlo, 193
Chamber Brothers, 359
Chandler, Chas, 374n
Chandler, Len, 79, 211, 282
Chaplin, Charles, 35, 88, 147
Chapman, Graham, 3
Chapter Hall, New York, 34, 35, 79, 89, 110, 199
Charles, Ray, 64, 94, 295, 422
Charley River Valley Boys, 39
Charlottesville, Virginia, 244
Charters, Ann, 144n
Chelsea Hotel, New York, 373, 390, 455
chess, 142, 252, 266, 278n, 280
Chess Records, 161, 340
Chicago Daily News, 379
Chicago, Illinois, 1, 26, 72–3, 203–4, 222, 266
Child Ballads, 84, 102, 306, 346, 442
'Chimes Of Freedom' (Dylan), 14, 243, 246, 249, 254, 257, 261, 262, 273, 300
'Chimes Of Trinity, The' (trad.), 243
Chris Barber Jazz Band, 151
Christie's, 14, 59, 288–9, 350, 371
Christmas On Earth Continued, 310
Chronicles Vol. 1 (Dylan), 3, 6, 8, 9, 10, 15, 57, 60, 87
　on Baez, 105
　on Beat Generation, 59
　on Chicago, 26
　on childhood, 152, 155, 156, 157
　on Columbia, 13n, 93, 95, 98
　on Cotten, 38n
　on Dalton, 30n
　on Dixon, 130
　on Golden Chords, 164
　on Guthrie, 32
　on Holzman, 90
　on Houston, 35n
　on Johnson, 4, 5, 115
　on Koerner, 63
　on Leeds Music, 136
　on Lomax, 102
　on Minneapolis, 55
　on New York, 31
　on Niles, 61
　on Rotolos, 20, 251
　on Van Ronk, 111
　on Vee, 173
　on Young, 39
Chronicles Vol. 2 (Dylan), 8, 188
Chrysalis Records, 325n

INDEX

City Lights Books, 58, 59, 119, 242, 304
Civil Rights Movement (1954–68), 119–20, 209–10, 216, 219–20, 235, 446
Clancy Brothers, The, 87, 117, 194
Clancy, Liam, 76, 83, 139, 339
Clancy, Patrick, 41
Clapton, Eric, 314, 317, 330, 331
Clayton, Paul, 37, 61, 84, 131, 132, 234, 244–5, 249, 251–2, 300–301
Cleary, Ann and Marty, 122
Cleave, Maureen, 258, 305, 315, 336
Cleeper, P. M., 56, 58
Club 47, Cambridge, 91, 92, 203
'Cocaine Blues' (trad.), 19, 74
Coen Brothers, 85
Cohen, Dick, 55
Cohen, Herb, 141
Cohen, John, 119, 131, 144
Colby, Paul, 37, 142, 144–5
Cold War, 157
Coleman, Ray, 220
Collins, Judy, 66, 107, 184–5, 257, 273, 333
Coltrane, John, 129, 200, 366, 422
Columbia, 4–5, 13, 32, 81, 147, 148
  Another Side album (1964), 259, 261–4
  Bob Dylan album (1961–2), 105–9, 111–12, 113, 123, 125, 124–7
  Blonde On Blonde album (1965–6), 372, 377–8, 382, 388–95, 397–8
  Bringing It album (1965), 293–302, 310
  contracts, 4–5, 90, 92–8, 99, 109, 127, 145, 148, 177–9, 197–8, 397–8
  Freewheelin' album (1962–3), 127–9, 134, 177, 182, 198–201
  Highway 61 album (1965), 340–45, 355–9, 377
  'I Want You' single (1966), 455
  'Mixed Up Confusion' single (1962), 148, 174–7, 179
  Times album (1963–4), 225–7, 231, 232–3
  World Tour recordings (1966), 416, 439
'Columbus Stockade' (Guthrie), 78
'Come Back, Baby' (trad.), 94
Compulsion, 157
Condon, Richard, 209
'Confidential' (Morgan), 162
Conley, Walt, 66, 67
Conoby, Tom, 54
Conway Twitty, 172
Cooder, Ry, 382
Cook, Peter, 9, 188

Cooke, John Byrne, 279n
Copenhagen, Denmark, 414, 416, 417–19
copyright collections, 11
CORE (Campaign of Racial Equality), 119, 437
'Corrina Corrina', 128, 139, 140, 141, 175, 179
Corso, Gregory, 58, 59, 69
Cotten, Elizabeth, 38, 131–2
Count Basie, 93
Country Gentlemen, The, 39
Court, John, 107, 176
'Courting Is A Pleasure' (trad.), 19
Cox, Courtney, 214
Crabb, Earl, 87
Crane, Les, 309
Crawdaddy, 386, 457–8
Cross, Norma, 270
'Crossroad Blues' (Johnson), 114
Crudup, Arthur, 148, 149, 151
Cuban Missile Crisis (1962), 145, 180, 189, 209
'Cuban Missile Crisis' (Dylan), 182
'Cuckoo Is A Pretty Bird, The' (trad.), 103
'Cuckoo, The' (trad.), 190
Cunningham, Arline, 135
'Cut Me Down, My Love' (Jones), 190
Cutting Edge (Dylan), 383, 433

Daffy, 248
Daily Mail, 444, 445
Dallas, Texas, 370
Dallas, Karl, 127
Dalton, Karen, 30, 43
Dane, Barbara, 43, 353
Danielson, Bill, 64
Danko, Rick, 368, 377, 384, 413
Danmarks Folkeviser, 416
Danny and the Juniors, 173
'Danville Girl' (Guthrie), 74
Datebook, 402
Davasee Enterprises, 345
Dave Clark Five, The, 314
Davidson, Mark, 14
Davis, Arthur Kyle, 37, 300n
Davis, Clive, 198
Davis, Gary, 18, 40, 76, 77, 87–8, 103
Davis, Miles, 364
Davis, Spencer, 148n, 422
Dawbarn, Bob, 191
Day, Doris, 290
De La Beckwith, Byron, 210
Dean, James, 155, 166, 169

Dean, Tami, 231, 255, 278, 279–80, 284, 286
Dean, Walter, 197, 248
'Death Of Emmett Till, The' (Dylan), 119–20, 128
'Death Of Robert Johnson, The' (Dylan), 5
Dee, Joey, 275
'Deep Water' (trad.), 19
Delaney, Samuel R. 18
Delmonico Hotel, New York, 276–8
demo tape (1961), 114
'Denise, Denise' (Dylan), 258
Denmark, 414, 416–19
Denver, Colorado, 26, 27, 28, 30, 66, 221, 222, 244, 246
Denver, Nigel, 196, 208
Deshannon, Jackie, 199, 254, 396
Desolation Angels (Kerouac), 406
'Desolation Row' (Dylan), 358, 359, 363, 384, 406, 416
Detroit, Michigan, 266, 367
Devlin, Polly, 191
Dharma Bums (Kerouac), 59
Diaz, Cesar, 202
Dickens, Charles, 35
Dickinson, Jim, 163
'Dignity' (Dylan), 15
DiMucci, Dion, 173
'Dink's Song' (trad.), 85, 97, 113
'Direct To You From Carnegie Hall' (Dylan), 226
Disc, 314, 356, 426, 438
Dixon, Delores, 35n, 43, 130
Domino, Fats, 160, 295
'Don't Let My Deal Go Down' (Dylan), 79
'Don't Think Twice, It's All Right' (Dylan), 147, 179–80, 199, 218, 222, 244, 272, 300
Donaldson, William, 188
Donovan, 319, 321, 347, 354
dont look back, 15, 87, 292, 313–16, 320, 325, 327, 330, 399, 400, 412–13, 454
'Dope Fiend Robber' (Dylan), 81, 83
'Down At Washington Square' (Dylan), 41–2
'Down On Penny's Farm' (trad.), 113
'Down The Highway' (Dylan), 133, 183n, 208
Down The Highway (Sounes), 3, 7
'Driftin' Too Far From Shore' (trad.), 159
'Drunkard's Child, A' (Rodgers), 160
'Drunkard's Son, The' (Snow), 159–60
Dublin Evening Herald, 425, 426
Dublin, Ireland, 425–8
Duchess Music Corp., 185

Duluth, Minnesota, 48, 49, 52, 54, 110, 152, 153, 167, 168
Duluth News Tribune, 228
Dunbar, John, 422
Dwarf Music, 410
Dyer, Geoff, 13
Dylan, Bob
    alcohol consumption, 45, 140, 181, 196, 261, 318, 435
    book writing, 302–8, 378–9
    chess hobby, 142, 252, 266, 278n, 280
    cruel streak, 251, 281–2, 301, 309, 363, 366
    drug consumption, 276, 321, 374, 405, 408, 424, 435, 448, 450, 452, 453
    electric conversion, 175, 275, 277, 294, 298, 331, 347–55, 359, 367, 425–44, 449–50
    girls, pursuit of, 167–8, 186, 194, 251, 301, 418–19
    harmonica playing, 64–5, 87–8, 116
    humour, 88, 120, 318
    letter writing, 230–31, 261
    name change, 137–8, 150, 208
    playwriting, 234–5, 242
    poems, 59, 131, 138, 144, 155, 158, 165, 184, 224, 230, 266, 286
    press, relations with, 316, 320, 327, 380, 403, 415–22, 425, 430, 445–7
    singing voice, 63, 87, 125, 274, 326
    songwriting, 48, 79, 143, 145, 155, 163, 207, 255, 266–7, 290, 372, 390–91
    temper, 324
    wedding (1965), 379
    see also album titles and songs
Dylan, Jesse Byron, 384
Dylan, Maria, 306–7
Dylan, Sara, 251, 269–71, 291, 332, 343, 359, 368, 373, 384, 454
Dylan '65 Revisited, 314n
Dylan Goes Electric (Wald), 12
Dylan in Minnesota (Engel), 153

Early 60s Revisited (Dylan), 18, 117n
'Earth Angel' (The Penguins), 162
'East Colorado Blues' (Dylan), 66, 67
East of Eden, 155
'East Virginia Blues' (trad.), 74, 213
'Easy Rider' (trad.), 74, 84
Eat The Document, 15, 413, 419, 427, 430, 431, 433, 447
Ed Sullivan Show, 86, 126, 205–7, 247, 290

Edinburgh, Scotland, 421, 432–3, 444
Edmonds, Ben, 275
Edwardson, Monte, 163–4
'Eight Miles High' (The Byrds), 422
Elektra Records, 89, 107, 202, 275, 354
'Eleven Outlined Epitaphs' (Dylan), 232, 238
Eliot, Marc, 181
Eliot, T. S. 59, 432
Elliott, Jack, 20, 25, 26, 68–9, 86, 104, 141, 191, 203, 253, 272
  on Animals, 274–5
  Another Side sessions (1964), 262
  Cash, meeting with (1964), 272
  Chapter Hall show (1961), 34, 35–6
  Gleasons', gatherings at, 33, 36
  Hootenanny boycott (1963), 205
  Issacson's, gatherings at, 100
  Les Crane Show (1965), 309
  Newport Festival (1965), 350
  Riverside broadcast (1961), 18, 19
  Talking Woody Guthrie, 70
Ellis, Barbara, 439, 441
Ellis, Terry, 325n
Elston Gunn & The Rock Boppers, 54, 168
Emerson, Ralph Waldo, 239
Emil and the Detectives, 329n
Emory University, 251
Engel, Dave, 153, 170
English, Logan, 18, 35n
Ephron, Nora, 325
Escott, Colin, 183n
Esquire, 444
Establishment, London, 188
Estes, Sleepy John, 60, 204
'Eternal Circle' (Dylan), 225, 226, 256, 257
'Eve Of Destruction' (Sloan), 363
Evers, Medgar, 209–10
'Every Time I Hear The Spirit' (trad.), 63
Exodus, Denver, 66, 184, 222
Expecting Rain, 6

F For Fake, 4
Fairport Convention, 329n
Faithfull, Marianne, 282n, 317, 319, 320–1, 422
'Farewell' (Dylan), 185, 194, 226
'Fare Thee Well' (Dylan), 198n
'Farewell Angelina' (Dylan), 285, 291–2, 293, 301, 309
'Farewell To Tarwathie' (trad.), 292
Fargo, North Dakota, 54, 170–72

Fariña, Mimi, 7, 42, 105, 195, 223, 279, 282–3, 323, 324
Fariña, Richard, 7, 84, 91, 93, 94, 95, 149, 189, 195, 196, 223, 248, 279, 282
Farrago, 407
Fass, Bob, 216, 234, 383, 384, 385
Faulk, John Henry, 134, 206
Feinstein, Barry, 221–2, 278, 281, 285, 303, 426, 441, 445
Ferlinghetti, Lawrence, 58, 231, 242, 255
'Fever' (Davenport/Cooley), 167
Fincher, Cynthia, 71
'Fixin' To Die' (White), 106, 109
Flanagan, Bill, 26
Flint, Hughie, 331
Flint, McGuinness, 120
Floyd, Pretty Boy, 32
Folk Music, 196, 208
folk process, 84
Folk Songs and More Folk Songs, 206
Folk Songs of North America (Lomax), 85
Folklore Center, New York, 29, 31, 34, 39, 40, 83, 117
Folksinger's Choice, 115, 120, 150
Folkways, 35n, 85, 89, 90, 111, 121
'Folsom Prison Blues' (Cash), 82
'For Dave Glover' (Dylan), 215, 230
Ford, Ernest Jennings, 178
Foreman, Clark, 42
Foreman, Geno, 235
Forest Hills Stadium, New York, 217, 279, 360, 362
'4th Time Around' (Dylan), 315n, 390, 433
Fowley, Kim, 310
France, 132, 247, 258, 262, 334, 424, 429, 430, 431, 437, 445–50, 457
Free Press, 363
Free Trade Hall, Manchester, 439–44
Freedman, Ed, 352
Freewheelin' Bob Dylan, The (Dylan)
  cover art, 277
  recording of, 127–9, 133–4, 177, 182, 198–201, 205
  reception, 69, 208, 211, 226, 247, 271, 310
Freewheelin' Time, A (Rotolo), 8
'Freight Train Blues' (trad. arr. Dylan), 108
Friedman, Steve, 51, 52
Friesen, Sis, 120–21, 130, 181–2, 231, 237, 242
Friesen, Gordon, 120–21, 130, 181–2, 231, 237, 242
Frizzell, Lefty, 158

'From A Buick Six' (Dylan), 335, 362
Fulford, Robert, 369–70
Fuller, Jesse, 66, 308
Fury, Billy, 440

Gallagher, Bill, 355
Gardiner, Sandy, 388
Gaslight Cafe, New York, 30, 31, 45, 76, 80, 90, 95, 96, 130, 141–7, 180, 181
Gaslight Tapes
    First (1961), 80
    Second (1962), 146–7, 400
Gasoline (Corso), 59
'Gates Of Eden' (Dylan), 268, 287, 299
'Gates Of Hate' (Dylan), 134
Gates of Wrath (Ginsberg), 268
Genet, Jean, 456
George V Hotel, Paris, 247, 430, 445–6, 457
Gerde's Folk City, New York, 30, 34–5, 42, 43, 45, 82, 85, 93, 95–7, 100, 101, 125, 218
Germany, 260
Gerrette, Rosemary, 195n, 407–9, 433
'Get Where I'm Going' (Dylan), 81
Gilbert, Douglas, 268–9, 275, 280
Gilded Garter, Central City, 66–7, 222
Gillespie, Dana, 312, 316–17, 318, 327, 339, 422, 424, 429, 451
Gilmore, Mikal, 3, 4
Ginsberg, Allen, 37, 58–9, 306, 318, 334, 372, 377, 379, 380–81, 408, 457
    Christmas meeting (1963), 235, 236
    and 'Gates Of Eden', 268
    Gilbert photographs (1964), 269
    Howl, 58, 59, 144, 236, 382
    Kaddish, 457
'Girl From The North Country' (Dylan), 185, 194, 198, 201, 208, 212, 215, 272
'Girl I Left Behind, The' (trad.), 97
Glancy, Ken, 344
Glasgow, Scotland, 433, 444
Gleason, Bob, 31, 33, 34, 36, 39
Gleason, Ralph, 248, 334n, 370, 378–9, 380–81
Gleason, Sidsel, 31, 33, 34, 36, 39
Gleason Tape (1961), 27, 323
Glover, Tony, 15, 57, 65, 68–9, 72, 76, 94, 119, 122, 130
    Bob Dylan release (1962), 127
    on Cash, 272
    Gerde's recording (1961), 85
    and 'Girl From The North Country', 208

Guthrie, meeting with (1962), 130–31
    on Helstrom, 138–9
    Highway 61 sessions (1965), 356, 358, 359
    home tapes (1962–3), 135, 139–40, 212–16
    letters to, 231, 285
    Minneapolis Hotel Tape (1961), 5, 112–14
    Newport Festival (1964), 273
    Newport Festival (1965), 347, 350, 351, 352, 353
    poem to (1963), 215, 230
    Santa Monica show (1964), 249
    on 'The Times They Are A-Changin'', 202
'Go 'Way From My Window' (Niles), 61
'Go From My Window' (trad.), 256n
Goddard, J. R., 40, 124, 125, 308
'Going Back To Rome' (Dylan), 193
Goldberg, Barry, 349
Golden Chords, The, 163–4
'Golden Vanity, The' (trad.), 84
Gooding, Cynthia, 41, 85, 96, 97, 115, 120, 124, 150
Gorgoni, Al, 294, 341, 342, 344
Gorodetsky, Eddie, 51
'Gospel Plow' (trad. arr. Dylan), 108, 114
Gotlieb, Stan, 62
'Gotta Travel On' (Clayton), 37, 61
Gramercy Park, New York, 299–300, 343, 375
Grand Ole Opry, Nashville, 155–6, 160
Gravenites, Nick, 349
Graves, Robert, 191, 245, 432
'Great Chicagonian, The' (Dylan), 81, 82
Great Divide, The (Dylan), 103
'Great Ship, The' (trad., also called 'The Titanic'), 84
Great White Wonder, 85
Greece, 260
Green, Debbie, 300
Green, Richard, 421
Greenbriar Boys, 18, 77, 96
Greenhill, Manny, 185
Greenhill, Mitch, 203
Gregg, Bobby, 296, 298, 341, 358, 377, 383, 384
Greystone Asylum, New Jersey, 27–8, 33
Griffin, Paul, 296, 341, 384
Grimm's Fairy Tales, 155
Grossman, Albert, 7, 13, 107, 136–7, 141, 181, 211, 217, 396, 397, 410–11
    book deal affair (1965), 304
    Blonde On Blonde album (1965–6), 389, 398
    Bringing It album (1965), 295, 300, 302
    Daffy film proposal (1963), 248

Davasee Enterprises, 345
Ed Sullivan Show protest (1963), 207
England trip (1962–3), 191
England tour (1965), 314, 320, 324, 325, 326, 330
Freewheelin' album (1962–3), 200
Gaslight Tape (1962), 146–7
Hawks, relations with, 367, 376
Highway 61 album (1965), 343, 344, 361
manuscripts acquisition, 289, 291
'Mixed Up Confusion' single (1962), 148, 149, 176–9
Newport Festival (1963), 217
Newport Festival (1965), 348
Times album (1963–4), 226
Travelin' Hootenanny (1962), 145–6
World Tour (1966), 405, 410–11, 421, 454
Grossman, Sally, 253, 255, 269–70, 289, 290–91, 292, 301, 359
Grundtvig, Sven, 416
Gunnn, Elston, 54, 168, 170, 171
Gurwitch, Arnold, 185
Guthrie, Arlo, 34
Guthrie, Marjorie, 34–5
Guthrie, Nora, 32–3
Guthrie, Woody, 17n, 25, 32–3, 57, 87, 104, 115, 128, 142, 203, 214, 339
Almanac Singers, 41
Bound For Glory, 27, 33, 40, 70
at Brooklyn State Hospital, 44, 131
California to the New York Island, 38, 82
covers of *see* Guthrie covers
at Greystone Asylum, 27–8, 31, 32–3, 46
VD songs, 79
Guthrie covers, 65, 70, 86, 112
Bailey Tape (1961), 84
Bob Dylan sessions (1961), 108
Chapter Hall show (1961), 104
Columbia signing (1961), 95
Gleason Tape (1961), 27
Indian Neck festival (1961), 77
Madison Party Tape (1961), 74
Minneapolis University show (1961), 76
Minneapolis Party Tape (1961), 76–7, 80
St Paul Tape (1960), 61
WUCB show (1961), 73
'Gypsy Davey' (trad.), 27

Haas, Joseph, 379
Hajdu, David, 7, 80n, 91n, 93–4, 117, 127, 196, 270
Halee, Roy, 263, 295, 298, 356, 372

Hallelujah I Love Her So (Charles), 94
Hallyday, Johnny, 447
Hamlet & Trinien Productions, 399
Hamlet Revisited, 413
Hammerman, Tova, 60
Hammond Jr, John, 44, 93, 105, 143, 265, 275, 297, 298, 343, 361, 366, 371, 455n
Hammond Sr, John, 4–5, 32, 89n, 99, 103, 116, 127, 146, 148
Bob Dylan album (1961–2), 105–9, 111–12, 113, 125, 127
contracts, 90, 92–8, 177–9, 197–8
Freewheelin' album (1962–3), 128, 129, 134, 198, 200
'Mixed Up Confusion' single (1962), 148, 175–6, 177, 179
'Hammond's Folly', 127
'Handsome Molly' (trad.), 19
Handy, William Christopher, 18
'Hang Me Oh Hang Me' (trad.), 190
'Hang Your Head Tom Dooley' (trad.), 169
Hank Snow Salutes Jimmie Rodgers, 160
Hard Day's Night, A, 249
'Hard Rain's A-Gonna Fall, A' (Dylan), 119n, 142, 144–5, 147, 182, 199, 236, 254
'Hard Times In New York Town' (Dylan), 113, 123
'Hard Travelin'' (Guthrie), 19, 70
Hardy, Françoise, 447
Harker, Dave, 170
Harrison, George, 277, 334
Hawaii, 402
Hawkins, Ronnie, 367
Hawks, The, 275, 360, 361, 367–9, 372, 375–6, 380, 381, 383, 384, 388, 392, 400, 442
'He Was A Friend of Mine' (trad. arr. Dylan), 48, 80–81, 90, 97, 98, 103, 109, 114
Heliczer, Kate, 311, 318
Hell, Richard, 13
Heller, Zelda, 381
Helm, Levon, 361, 367, 368, 376, 380
Help! (The Beatles), 359
'Help!' (Lennon/McCartney), 334
Helstrom, Echo, 138–9, 164, 168, 194
Hemingway, Ernest, 406
Henderson, Don, 405
Hendrix, Jimi, 374
Hentoff, Nathan, 121, 125–6, 200, 205, 206, 232, 261, 374, 378
Herald, John, 20n, 25, 343

'Hero Blues' (Dylan), 226, 233
Herrmann, Bernard, 4
Hester, Carolyn, 91–4, 95, 96, 127
Heylyn, Peter, 6
Hi Lo Ha, Woodstock, 345
Hibbing, Minnesota, 49, 51, 56–7, 71, 88, 137–8, 150, 151–70
Hifi Stereo Review, 125
'Highway 51 Blues' (Jones), 103, 108, 109
Highway 61 Interactive (Dylan), 295n
Highway 61 Revisited (Dylan), 13, 280, 289, 325, 329, 340–47, 355–60, 374, 377, 381, 430
'Highway 61 Revisited' (Dylan), 345, 359, 362
Hilburn, Bob, 13, 122, 225, 271n, 434
His Gotham Ingress (bootleg), 286n
Hoffenberg, Mason, 258, 260, 262, 269, 447, 453
Hoffman, Gretel *see* Whitaker, Gretel
Hoikkala, Leroy, 163–4
Holiday, Billie, 93, 96, 446
Holiday, Chico, 367
Holiff, Saul, 434
Holinshed, Raphael, 11
Holly, Buddy, 149, 160, 168–9, 173
Hollywood Bowl, Los Angeles, 223, 360, 362–5, 367
Holscomb, Roscoe, 87
Holy Modal Rounders, The, 20
Holzman, Jac, 89, 90, 354
'Honey, Just Allow Me One More Chance' (Thomas/Dylan), 134, 183n
Hood, Clarence, 146
Hood, Sam, 141, 146
Hooker, John Lee, 44, 76
Hootenanny (magazine), 231
Hootenanny (TV show), 205
Hopkins, Lightnin', 102, 339
Hoskyns, Barney, 7
'House Carpenter, The' (trad.), 102, 107, 109
'House Of The Rising Sun' (trad.), 81, 86, 109, 111, 139, 274, 295, 319
Houston, Cisco, 33–5, 37, 142
How Sweet The Sound, 323
Howl (Ginsberg), 58, 59, 144, 236, 382
Howlin' Wolf, 115
Hudson, Garth, 275, 368, 380n, 389n
Hunstein, Donald, 105, 197, 199

I Can Tell (Hammond), 455n
'I Can't Leave Her Behind' (Dylan/Robertson), 434
'I Don't Believe You' (Dylan), 261, 425, 451
'I Hear A Train A-Rolling' (Dylan), 81, 82
'I Heard That Lonesome Whistle' (Williams), 74, 128
'I Shall Be Free' (Dylan), 182, 263
'I Still Miss Someone' (Cash), 283
'I Walk The Line' (Cash), 161
'I Wanna Be Your Lover' (Dylan), 371, 372
'I Wanna Hold Your Hand' (Lennon/McCartney), 276
'I Want My Milk' (Guthrie), 77
'I Want You To Be My Girl' (Goldner/Barrett), 161
'I Want You' (Dylan), 448, 455
'I Was Young When I Left Home' (Dylan), 83, 113–14
'I'll Keep It With Mine' (Dylan), 259, 289, 291, 293, 297, 333
'I'm A Rounder Till I Die' (trad.), 85
'I'm Only Sleeping' (Lennon/McCartney), 423
I'm The Man That Built The Bridges (Paxton), 80
'I've Got a Secret' (Neil/Cotten), 148–9
'If I Had To Do It All Over Again, Babe' (Dylan), 180
'If I Was A King' (Dylan), 433
'If You Gotta Go, Go Now' (Dylan), 290, 293n, 299, 330–31
Imperial Records, 161
In Concert (Baez), 283
In His Own Write (Lennon), 303–4, 305, 307
'In My Time Of Dyin'' (Blind Willie Johnson), 104, 107–8, 109
'In The Pines' (trad.), 104
'In The Still Of The Night' (Pruitt), 162
In The Wind (Peter Paul & Mary), 29
Indian Neck Folk Festival (1961), 77, 80, 90, 205
Inside Llewyn Davis, 85
'Inside The Darkness Of Your Room' (Dylan), 371
Ireland, 425–8
Irish Times, 425
'Is Your Love In Vain?' (Dylan), 89
Issacson, Miki, 99–100, 101
'It Ain't Me Babe' (Dylan), 255, 257, 259, 272, 368n
'It Rained Five Days' (Smith), 74
'It Takes A Lot To Laugh' (Dylan), 330, 331, 335, 341, 352, 356, 376
'It's All Over Now, Baby Blue' (Dylan), 293, 294, 297, 299, 300–301, 309, 310

'It's Alright Ma' (Dylan), 287, 290, 299, 309, 358
Italy, 132–3, 192–3, 260, 428–9

'Jack O'Diamonds' (trad.), 84
'Jack O'Diamonds' (Carruthers/Dylan), 330
Jackie, 231, 321
Jackson, Aunt Molly, 39, 105
Jackson, Mississippi, 209, 211, 214
Jagger, Mick, 301, 411
James, Billy, 29n, 87, 109–10, 113, 172, 207, 228, 310, 380, 382, 396
James, Dick, 411
James, Skip, 37
Jarry, Alfred, 119
'Jealous Lover, The' (trad.), 82
Jefferson, Blind Lemon, 84
Jefferson, Thomas, 133, 134
'Jenny Jenny' (Little Richard), 163n
Jerrusic, Charlotte, 72
'Jerry' (White), 62
Jet Set, 257
Joelson, Ron, 54, 63, 72, 151, 170–71
John B. Pimp script, 235, 242
John Birch Society, 32, 38, 120, 188, 198, 257
'John Brown' (Dylan), 147
'John Doe' (Almanac Singers), 41
John Mayall & the Bluesbreakers, 314, 317, 320, 330–31
John Wesley Harding (Dylan), 82
John, Ole, 416
John, Little Willie, 167
'Johnny's Gone To High Lea' (trad.), 84
Johnson, Lonnie, 116, 151
Johnson, Robert, 4–5, 108, 114, 115, 128, 129, 141, 147, 261
Johnston, Bob, 12, 355–7, 372, 388–9, 391
Jokers, The, 161–2, 250
Jones, Brian, 373, 374n, 375, 455n
Jones, Elvin, 190
Jones, LeRoi, 58
Jones, Max, 85, 127, 191, 242, 258, 278, 303, 329n
Jones, Mickey, 360, 399–401, 436, 442
Jones, Paul, 330, 331
Jones, Robert L., 77, 90
Joplin, Janis, 5
Jopling, Norman, 345
Joseph, Anthea, 192, 312, 324, 325
'Joshua Gone Barbados' (von Schmidt), 254–5
Journeymen, The, 114n

Judson, Horace Freeland, 325–6, 430
Jukebox Jury, 319
Jung, Carl Gustav, 456
'Just As Long As I'm In This World' (Dylan), 79
'Just Like A Woman' (Dylan), 394, 402, 448
'Just Like Tom Thumb's Blues' (Dylan), 346–7, 359, 362, 407, 408, 430, 452, 455

Kaddish (Ginsberg), 457
Kalb, Danny, 19, 20, 73, 74, 275
Kappes, John, 441
Kapralik, David, 127, 178
Karakash, Dave, 165
Karman, Peter, 17, 20, 244, 245, 251
Kaufman, Murray, 362
KB-Hallen, Copenhagen, 416
Kegan, Larry, 49, 50, 51, 52, 53, 54, 57, 157–8, 161, 162, 166
Kelley, Paula, 91
Kemp, Louie, 47, 49, 51, 52, 54, 55, 71, 72, 152, 154, 157, 167, 169
Kennedy, John Fitzgerald, 189, 219, 221, 233, 234–5, 457
Kent, Nick, 13
Kerouac, Jack, 28–9, 52, 58–9, 66, 67, 197, 222, 243, 379, 406, 431
Kerr, Barbara, 60, 66
Kettle of Fish, New York, 81, 110, 111, 142, 180, 301, 367, 374
Keylock, Tom, 435, 437, 444, 448, 452n
'Keys To The Highway' (Segar/Broonzy), 226
King & Queen, London, 188, 192, 196
King Of The Delta Blues Singers (Johnson), 4–5
King Records, 161
King, Ben E., 173
King, Martin Luther, 220
Kingston Quartet, The, 61
Kingston Trio, The, 41, 61, 105, 178, 217
Kinks, The, 340
Kitamura, Margaret, 405
Kittleson, Barry, 199
'Klan, The' (Conley), 67
Klein, Allen, 411
Knight, Curtis, 374
Koerner, Spider John, 61, 63, 202, 211
Konikoff, Sandy, 383, 388
Kooper, Al, 200, 342, 348, 349, 351, 356, 358, 361, 365, 367, 377, 384, 389, 390, 392, 393

Kornfeld, Barry, 44, 102, 143, 150, 179n, 202, 206, 233, 251, 252, 300
Kramer, Daniel, 280–81, 289n, 290, 292, 295, 296, 297, 298, 302, 308, 327
Krasilovsky, M. William, 137
Kretchmer, Arthur, 88, 353, 364
KRLA-Beat, 381
Krogsgaard, Michael, 106n, 201n, 370n
Krown, Kevin, 26–8, 66, 72, 113
Ku Klux Klan, 210
Kweskin, Jim, 77, 80, 249

LA Band Tape (Dylan), 389
'Lady Franklin's Lament' (trad.), 205
'Lady Of Carlisle, The' (trad.), 103
LaFarge, Peter, 86
LaFond, Gene, 51, 53
Landon, Grelun, 82n
Landy, Bob, 275
'Lang A-Growin'' (trad.), 84
Langhorne, Bruce, 18, 86, 175, 179–80, 253, 294, 296, 297, 342
Lauterbach, Ann, 27, 73, 78
Law, Lisa and Tom, 401
'Lawdy Miss Clawdy' (Price), 161, 162
'Lay Down Your Weary Tune' (Dylan), 223, 225, 227, 253
Lay, Sam, 349
Lead Belly, 34, 37, 56, 59, 116, 129, 142, 151, 169, 170
Leaf, Earl, 401, 431
'Leaving Of Liverpool, The' (trad.), 194
Lee, Bill, 129, 294
Lee, Brenda, 206
Leeds demos (1962), 117
Leeds Music, 80, 114, 116n, 120, 136, 185
Leftists, 86, 119
Leicester, England, 438
Leigh, Spencer, 6
Lennon, John, 157, 247, 276, 277, 303–5, 307, 315n, 318, 334, 411, 422, 435, 450
Lenya, Lotte, 218
'Leopard-Skin Pill-Box Hat' (Dylan), 382, 390, 395, 444
Lerner, Murray, 348
Les Crane Show, 155, 206, 309
'Let Me Die In My Footsteps' (Dylan), 122, 123, 128, 130
'Let The Good Times Roll' (Goodman/Lee), 161

'Let's Spend The Night Together' (Jagger/Richards), 290
Lethem, Jonathan, 13
Leventhal, Harold, 35n, 89, 135
Levine, Manuel, 379
Levitan, Stuart, 73, 78
Levon & The Hawks, 275, 360, 361, 367–9, 372, 375–6
Levy, Lou, 114, 115, 116, 117, 120, 185
Levy's, London, 330–31, 341
Lewis, Jerry Lee, 51, 54, 160, 170
Lewis, John, 19
Liar's Autobiography, A (Chapman), 3
Liberty, 199
Library of Congress, 76, 91
Lieberson, Goddard, 248
Life In 12 Bars, 314n
Life In Stolen Moments, A (Dylan), 158
Life, 58, 211
'Like A Rolling Stone' (Dylan), 137, 334–8, 340, 341–5, 346, 377n, 387, 393, 440, 442, 443, 452
Linz, Austria, 2, 3
Lipscomb, Mance, 102
'Little Maggie' (trad.), 215
Little Richard, 51, 54, 56, 160, 161, 165, 170
Little Sandy Review, 68, 69, 76, 125, 150, 208, 211, 212, 273
Liverpool, England, 315, 321, 438–9, 455
'Liverpool Gal' (Dylan), 194–5
Lloyd, Albert Lancaster, 85, 192, 292n
Logan, Josh, 86
Lomax, Alan, 20, 34, 85, 97, 102, 189, 348, 350, 351, 354
Lomax, John, 85, 97, 116
London, England, 126
  1962–3 visit, 185–92, 196
  1964 visit, 248n, 256, 257, 258
  1965 tour, 282n, 305, 313–37, 347
  1966 tour, 385, 414, 419–23, 428, 435, 440, 450–52, 453–4
London, Jack, 35n
'Lonesome Death Of Hattie Carroll, The' (Dylan), 184n, 223–5, 226, 246, 250, 257
'Long Ago Far Away' (Dylan), 140
'Long Distance Operator' (Dylan), 376
'Long Gone Lonesome Blues' (Williams), 159
'Long Time Gone' (Dylan), 140, 183
Look, 268, 280
Lord Buckley, 104, 113, 147

Los Angeles, California, 251, 310, 362–5,
        380–81, 382, 396, 399–402
'Lost Highway' (Payne), 85
Louisiana Hayride, 160
Love And Theft (Dylan), 2, 5, 114
'Love Is Just A Four-Letter Word' (Dylan),
        291, 292
Love Me Do (Braun), 429
'Love Minus Zero' (Dylan), 291, 293, 294, 296,
        297, 310
Lovin' Spoonful, The, 297n
Lownds, Hans, 269
Lownds, Sara *see* Dylan, Sara
LSD (lysergic acid diethylamide), 255, 301, 334,
        374, 435
Lucas, George, 381

MacColl, Ewan, 61, 85, 185, 192, 196, 292
Macho, Joseph, 341, 344, 357
Mack, Joe, 294
Macmillan, 278–9, 303–4, 378
Macmillan, Maurice Harold, 189
Madhouse on Castle Street, 187, 190, 191, 192, 195
Madison, Wisconsin, 18, 26, 27, 28, 30, 73, 78
'Maggie's Farm' (Dylan), 113, 289, 291, 299, 314
Magical Mystery Tour, 414
Maier, Reuben, 151
Mailer, Norman, 239
Malcolm X, 220
'Mama You Been On My Mind' (Dylan), 256,
        259, 263, 272, 309
'Man Of Constant Sorrow' (trad.), 77, 103,
        107, 108, 109, 114, 126n
'Man On The Street' (Dylan), 41, 80, 81, 82,
        84, 106, 108
Manchester, England, 325, 426, 439–44
Manchurian Candidate, The, 209
Mandell, Steve, 149
Manfred Mann, 331, 422
Manuel, Richard, 368, 369
'Many Thousands Gone', 129; *see also* 'No
        More Auction Block'
Marcus, Greil, 201, 375
Margolis & Moss papers, 242, 456
Marinos, Alexander, 402
Markel, Bob, 279, 285–6, 454
Marsh, Dave, 269
Marshall, James Charles, 274
Martin, Mary, 360
Martinson, Paul, 12

'Mary From The Wild Moor'(trad.), 85
Masked and Anonymous, 9
'Masters Of War' (Dylan), 147, 185, 189, 192,
        194, 197, 201, 208, 217, 222, 309, 437
May, Phil, 319
Mayall, John, 314, 317–18, 319, 320, 324
Mayfair Hotel, London, 186, 191, 258, 305, 324,
        419, 422, 423, 428, 450
Maymudes, Jacob, 8
Maymudes, Victor, 8, 37, 124, 141–3, 156, 166,
        239, 244, 250
    Australian tour (1966), 405
    Beatles, meeting with (1964), 276, 277
    chess games, 278n
    on cruel streak, 281
    European tour (1964), 258, 260
    Grossman, relationship with, 410–11
    on 'Mr Tambourine Man', 254, 255
    Rotolo, relationship with, 250–51
    on Sandburg, 245
    and Sara, 271, 379
    on temper, 324
Mazur, Barry, 135n
MCA, 126
McCartney, Paul, 247–8, 276–7, 304, 411, 422–3,
        450
McCoy, Charles, 359, 390, 391, 393, 395
McDarrah, Fred, 30
McEwen, Rory, 191
McGarrigle, Anna, 126, 196
McGear, Mike, 247
McGregor, Craig, 403, 452
McGuinn, Roger, 422
McGuire, Barry, 363, 366, 382, 400
McGuire, Mickey, 54
McKenzie, Eve, 25, 35, 78–9, 81, 94, 112–13,
        119, 132
McKenzie, Mac, 35, 78–9, 81, 112–13, 132
McKenzie, Peter, 27, 78, 81, 113
McLean, Donald, 169
McLean, James Yuille, 195
'Mean Ol' Mississippi Blues' (Dylan), 79
'Medicine Sunday' (Dylan), 372
Mekas, Jonas, 311
Melbourne, Victoria, 405–7, 432
Melcher, Terry, 382
Meleady, Dermot, 425
Melody Maker, 85, 93, 191, 220, 242, 247, 278,
        303, 319, 329n, 377n, 425, 426
Memphis Minnie, 446

Meredith, James, 181–2
Merenstein, Lewis, 108n
Meridian, Mississippi, 247
Mestek, Pat, 161
Mexico City Blues (Kerouac), 58–9
Michaels, Mike, 73
'Midnight Special' (trad.), 116
'Milk Cow Blues' (Arnold), 129
Millay, Edna St Vincent, 180
Miller, Henry, 406
Miller, Mitch, 96, 127
Million Dollar Quartet, The, 129
Mingus, Charles, 129
Minneapolis, Minnesota, 26, 46, 51–66, 67–72, 75–6, 373
   Blood On The Tracks sessions (1974), 12
   homecoming show (1965), 373, 376
   Hotel Tape (1961), 5, 112–14
   Party Tape (1961), 32n, 70–71, 76–7, 80, 84, 108
   St Paul Tape (1960), 37, 61, 63, 77
   University, 54–65, 67–8, 75–6
Mirken, Caryl, 352
'Mississippi River Blues' (Rodgers), 79
Mississippi Sheiks, 116
'Mixed Up Confusion' (Dylan), 175–7
Mogull, Artie, 135–7, 183, 343
MoMA, New York, 197
Monck, Edward 'Chip', 142
Montenegro, Hugo, 116
Montreal Gazette, 381
Montreal, Quebec, 126, 133, 196, 387
Monty Python, 3
Moon, Keith, 422
Moondog, 129
'Moonshine Blues' (trad. arr. Dylan), 225, 226
Moore, David, 203, 257
More Blood, More Tracks (Dylan), 11
Morrison, Van, 108n, 206n
Morton, Dave, 60, 62, 70, 139, 211, 213, 249
Morton, Jelly Roll, 149
Most, Mickie, 199
Mother Revisited (Dylan), 242, 248
'Motherless Children' (trad.), 140
Motion, Andrew, 9
'Motorpsycho Nitemare' (Dylan), 261
'Move It On Over' (Williams), 155–6
'Mr Tambourine Man' (Dylan), 246, 252–7, 259, 262, 273, 287, 297n, 298, 299, 310, 333, 352, 449

Muddy Waters, 149
Muldaur, Geoff, 203, 249
Muldaur, Maria, 86, 203, 209, 249, 354
'Muleskinner Blues' (trad.), 40, 66
murder ballads, 39, 41, 169
'Murder Most Foul' (Dylan), 234n
Murray, Pi Ann, 414
'My Back Pages' (Dylan), 256n, 263n, 268
'My Generation' (Townshend), 340
'My Life In A Stolen Moment' (Dylan), 29
'My Love She Comes In Silence' (Dylan), 291
'My Name Is John Johannah' (Harrell), 217
'My Son Calls Another Man Daddy' (House), 159

name change (1962), 137–8
Nashville, Tennessee, 345, 355, 389–95, 456
   Grand Ole Opry, 155–6, 160
National Enquirer, 3
National Guardian, 209
Neil, Fred, 30, 31, 36, 142, 148
Neilsen, Frank, 405
Nelson, Mike, 361
Nelson, Paul, 61–2, 68–9, 99, 145, 210, 224
   Bob Dylan review (1962), 125
   Forest Hills show (1965), 362
   Freewheelin' review (1963), 208, 211–15, 219
   Minneapolis University hootenanny (1961), 75–6
   Newport Festival (1964), 273
   Newport Festival (1965), 174, 352–3, 354
   on 'Only A Pawn', 210
   on topical songs, 174, 182, 203
Nelson, Ricky, 31, 314, 315, 360
Neuwirth, Bob, 77, 90, 91, 250, 251, 300, 301
   on cruel streak, 281, 282
   at Dylan's wedding (1965), 379
   England tour (1965), 317, 330, 331
   Highway 61 sessions (1965), 356, 358
   Newport Festival (1965), 348, 351
   New York blackout (1965), 373
   Santa Monica show (1964), 249
   'SHB' video (1965), 314
   on temper, 324
   World Tour (1966), 437, 440, 443, 454
Never Ending Tour, 2, 202
Neville Brothers, 336
New Directions Publishing, 119
New Left, 119
New Mexico, 17, 25, 35, 73, 110

'New Morning' (Dylan), 362
'New Orleans Rag' (Dylan), 226, 227
New Orleans, Louisiana, 244, 245–6, 315
New World Singers, The, 29, 130
New York City, New York
    Another Side sessions (1964), 259, 261–4
    blackout (1965), 373, 375
    Bob Dylan sessions (1961), 105–10
    Blonde On Blonde sessions (1965–6), 372, 377–8, 382–4
    Bringing It sessions (1965), 293–302
    Cafe Wha? shows, 30, 36
    Carnegie Hall shows, 79, 89, 104, 110, 184, 199, 227–8, 365, 370–71
    Columbia signing (1961), 90, 92–8
    Forest Hills shows, 217, 279, 360, 362
    Freewheelin' sessions (1962–3), 127–9, 133–4, 177, 201
    Gaslight shows, 80, 96, 103n, 130, 141, 146, 180
    Gerde's shows, 36, 43, 44–5, 82, 85, 93, 96, 97, 125, 129, 218
    Highway 61 sessions (1965), 340–45, 355–9
    McKenzie Tape (1961), 112–13
    'Mixed Up Confusion' sessions (1962), 148, 174–7, 179
    Philharmonic Hall show (1964), 281, 286, 287, 309
    Riverside broadcast (1961), 17–21
    Times album (1963–4), 225–7, 231, 232–3
    Town Hall show (1963), 198–9
New York Herald Tribune, 80, 373, 389
New York Mirror, 17, 20
New York Times, 11, 13–14, 17, 21, 85, 96–7, 124, 199, 207, 209, 211, 308
'New York Town' (Guthrie), 74
New Yorker, 261
Newcastle, England, 445
Newfield, Jack, 371
Newport Folk Festival, 12
    1963: 215, 216–18
    1964: 266, 270, 271, 272–5
    1965: 87, 321, 347–55, 357, 360, 361, 362, 364
Newsweek, 57, 208, 228, 232
Nico, 258–9, 288, 299, 321, 333
'Night With Bob Dylan, A' (Aronowitz/Dylan), 374
'Nightingale, The' (trad.) 194
Niles, John Jacob, 40, 61, 102, 169
'900 Miles' (trad.), 114

'1913 Massacre' (Guthrie), 39, 70
Nissenson, Jack, 75, 88
NME, 317, 327, 330, 450
No Direction Home, 28, 53, 68, 116, 129, 135n, 156, 157, 323, 431
'No Grave Can Hold My Body' (trad.), 84
'No More Auction Block' (trad.), 129
Norman, Philip, 411
'North Country Blues' (Dylan), 211, 225
North Platte, Nebraska, 221
Northern Songs, 411
'Norwegian Wood' (Lennon/McCartney), 315n
'Nottamun Town' (trad.), 189

O'Gorman, Ned, 93
Ochs, Philip David, 120, 141, 181, 182, 254, 266, 282, 354, 385–6
Odegard, Kevin, 12, 153, 166
Odetta, 56, 59, 61, 69, 193, 273, 349, 350
Oh Mercy (Dylan), 74
'Old Man' (Dylan), 41, 80, 81, 82, 84, 106, 108; see also 'Man On The Street'
Oldham Evening Chronicle, 443
Oldham, Andrew Loog, 191, 321, 398
L'Olympia, Paris, 445, 447–50
'Omie Wise' (trad.), 19, 85, 113, 120
'On My Journey Home' (trad.), 103
On The Road (Kerouac), 28–9, 58, 66, 379
'On The Road Again' (Dylan), 134, 186, 293n, 294, 298
Once Upon A Time (Bell), 6
Ondine, New York, 372
'One Morning In May' (Jackson), 39
'One Of Us Must Know' (Dylan), 382, 384, 385, 386, 392
One Sheridan Square, New York, 90, 99
'One Too Many Mornings' (Dylan), 223, 233, 388, 441, 442
'Only A Hobo' (Dylan), 226
'Only A Pawn In Their Game' (Dylan), 207, 209, 210–11, 216, 225, 384
Orange Blossom Special (Cash), 273
Orbison, Roy, 149, 420
'Original Talking Blues' (Bouchillon), 32
Orlovsky, Peter, 269, 334
Ornette Coleman Trio, 440n
Osborn, Joe, 360
Ottawa Journal, 388
Outlaw Blues (Leigh), 6

'Outlaw Blues' (Dylan), 291, 293n, 294
'Over The Road I'm Bound To Go' (Dylan), 81, 82
Owen, Frank, 341, 342
'Oxford Town' (Dylan), 181–2

Page, Patti, 355
Pageant, 308
Pankake, Jon, 61–2, 68–9, 70, 76, 125, 203, 208, 211, 354
Pareles, Jon, 13
Paris Jour, 450
Paris Match, 429
Paris, France, 132, 247, 258, 262, 334, 424, 429, 430, 431, 437, 445–50, 457
'Parting Glass, The' (trad.), 232
Pascal, Jean-Marc, 429, 442, 445
'Pastures Of Plenty' (Guthrie), 76
'Paths Of Victory' (Dylan), 182–3, 226
'Patriot Game, The' (Behan), 194, 217
Paturel, Bernard, 8, 266, 268, 278, 280, 287, 290
Paturel, Mary Lou, 266, 268, 287, 290
Paul Butterfield Blues Band, 303, 317, 348, 349, 352, 360
Paulsen, Don, 373
Paxton, Tom, 18, 19, 36, 79–80, 141, 143, 146, 266, 324
Peer, Ralph, 135
Penguin Book of the Beats, The, 144n
Pennebaker, D. A., 230, 270
  England Tour (1965), 313, 314, 316, 320, 325, 327, 330, 400
  World Tour (1966), 399, 402, 412, 415, 418, 423, 424, 428, 431, 435, 441, 443, 454
Pepperell, David, 404
'Percy's Song' (Dylan), 184n, 225, 227
Perkins, Carl, 160, 161, 162
Perry, Kathy, 139
Perth, Western Australia, 62, 174, 195, 407–9, 433
Pet Sounds (The Beach Boys), 392, 398
Peter, Paul & Mary, 29, 36, 207, 410
Phantom Cabaret Strikes Again, The, 400
'Phantom Engineer' (Dylan), 330, 331, 335, 341, 347, 352, 356, 376
'Philadelphia Lawyer' (Guthrie), 82
Philadelphia, Pennsylvania, 85, 290, 386
Philharmonic Hall, New York, 281, 286, 287, 309

Phillips, Cora, 132
Phillips, Sam, 161
Pickett, Wilson, 373
Pictures And Words (Dylan), 278–9
'Pilot Eyes' (Dylan), 372
Pine, Lester, 248
'Pirate Jenny' (Weill), 218–19
Pitt, Kenneth, 241, 257
Playboy, 206, 269, 270, 374, 434, 453
'Playboys & Playgirls, Ye' (Dylan), 182, 198n
Please Please Me (The Beatles), 248
'Pledging My Time' (Dylan), 394
Plymell, Charlie, 236
'Po' Lazarus' (trad.), 19
Poe, Edgar Allan, 155, 437
'Poem' (Dylan), 262
Poems Without Titles (Dylan), 59
Politiken, 416
Poniatowska, Elena, 23
Poole, Charlie, 39
'Poor Boy Blues', 114, 115
Poor Boys, The, 171
Pop, 450
Pope, Alexander, 7
Porco, Mike, 34, 45, 96, 101
Porter, Cole, 336
'Positively 4th Street' (Dylan), 357, 365, 377, 385, 400
Positively 4th Street (Hajdu), 7
Pound, Ezra, 432
Presley, Elvis, 129, 148, 149, 151, 160, 162, 173, 204, 339, 378, 440
Prestige, 81, 111
'Pretty Boy Floyd' (Guthrie), 70
'Pretty Peggy-O' (trad.), 102, 107, 109, 114, 126, 199
'Pretty Polly' (trad.), 80n, 103
Pretty Things, The, 319
Prial, Dunstan, 96, 179
Price, Alan, 319, 330
Princeton, New Jersey, 327
Propotnick, Jim, 63, 164, 165
Proust, Marcel, 445
Providence Journal, 353
Psychology of the Unconscious (Jung), 456
Puerto Rico, 216
Pull My Daisy, 197

'Queen Jane Approximately' (Dylan), 345, 346, 359
Quest, 243

Quinn, Pat, 364
'Quit Your Lowdown Ways' (Dylan), 134

Radosh, Ron, 73
'Railroad Bill' (trad.), 131, 189
'Railroad Boy' (trad.), 103
Rainey, Ma, 446
'Rainy Day Women' (Dylan), 393–4, 419, 430
'Ramblin' Gamblin' Willie' (Dylan), 81, 83, 109, 117, 128
'Ramblin' Round' (Guthrie), 108
Rameau, Jean-Philippe, 454
Ramone, Phil, 12
Rankin, Ken, 296
Rasky, Harry, 399, 454
Rawlins, Adrian, 406–7, 408, 409, 432
Ray, Dave, 64, 65, 68, 70, 111
Ready Steady Go, 333
'Ready Teddy' (Marascalco/Blackwell), 161
Rebel Without A Cause, 166
Record Mirror, 421, 455
Record, The, 17
Redbrick, 437
Redding, Otis, 402
Redpath, Jean, 43, 100–101, 102, 217
Reed, Jimmy, 70
Regents, The, 163
Rembrandt, 123
'Remember Me' (Wiseman), 27, 323
'Reminiscence Blues' (Dylan), 115; *see also* 'Ballad For A Friend'
Renaldo & Clara, 10, 332
Reporter, 125
'Restless Farewell' (Dylan), 232–3
Reuss, Richard, 99, 352
Revolver (The Beatles), 423
Rhodes, Jack, 130
Richards, Keith, 411
'Ride A White Swan' (Bolan), 299
Rimbaud, Arthur, 10, 118–19, 238, 239, 246, 253, 334, 409, 424, 454
Rising Sons, The, 382
Ritchie, Jean, 102, 104, 189, 194, 217
Rivers, Johnny, 360, 399
Riverside broadcast (1961), 17–21
Robbins, Paul Jay, 303, 363
Robertson, Robbie, 275, 343, 361, 363, 364, 366, 367, 368, 373, 384, 392
  at Dylan's wedding (1965), 379
  Redding, meeting with (1966), 401–2

Testimony (2016), 8
  on 'Visions Of Johanna', 375–6
  World Tour (1966), 405, 407, 414, 422, 433, 434, 435, 441, 443, 444, 454
Robertson, Jeannie, 102, 105
Robinson, Hubbell, 453
Roche, Peter, 332
'Rock Island Line' (Lead Belly), 151
Rockets, The, 164, 165, 171
'Rocking Chair' (Dylan), 81
'Rocks And Gravel' (trad. arr. Dylan), 127, 175, 177
Rodgers, Jimmie, 40, 79, 130, 160, 169
Roger Smith Hotel, Washington DC, 336
Rolling Stone, 14, 336, 386
Rolling Stones, The, 274, 290, 319, 340, 373, 398, 411, 423, 437, 443
Rolling Thunder Revue, 10, 12, 50
Rolls-Royce, 221–2
Romney, Hugh, 143, 144
Rosen, Jeff, 11, 135n, 157, 431
Rosenbaum, Ronald, 344
Rosenberg, Sam, 243
Ross-Trevor, Mike, 330, 331
Rothchild, Paul, 255, 317, 351
Rothschild, Charlie, 92, 96, 136
Rotolo, Carla, 20, 85, 102, 103, 132–3, 216, 219, 234, 244, 251, 260
Rotolo, Mary, 94, 99, 101, 102, 132–3, 260
Rotolo, Suze, 9, 20, 21, 43, 89, 97, 101–2, 117–18, 124, 130, 197, 281, 301, 366
  art, interest in, 60n, 197
  Baez, relationship with, 219–20, 251
  on Baileys, 84
  Bartocciolo, relationship with, 267
  Beatles and, 246, 277
  Bob Dylan album (1961–2), 105, 107, 109, 111
  Boston trip and, 203
  break up (1964), 250–56, 260
  Carnegie Hall show (1963), 228
  civil rights campaigning, 119, 219–20
  Ed Sullivan Show (1963), 207
  Forest Hills show (1965), 362
  Freewheelin' cover (1963), 277
  Freewheelin' Time, A (2008), 8
  Highway 61 sessions (1965), 359
  Italy trip (1962), 132–3, 139, 141, 142, 180, 193
  literature, interest in, 180, 191
  on live shows, 88
  Maymudes, relationship with, 250–51

Rotolo, Suze (*continued*)
   on name change, 150
   on One Sheridan Square, 99–100
   pregnancy (1963), 237
   Puerto Rico trip (1963), 216
   at Sheridan Square Playhouse, 218
   songs about, 132, 139–40, 180, 194, 199
   Virginia trip (1962), 131–2
   Woodstock trip (1963), 207
Rough and Rowdy Ways, 10
Rowan, Pete, 394
Rowe, Nicholas, 6n, 23
Roxreth, Kenneth, 58, 119
Royal Albert Hall, London, 313, 324, 325, 439, 450–52
Royal Festival Hall, London, 257
Rubin, Barbara, 310–11, 374
Rubin, Judy, 51, 60, 168, 237, 267, 318
Ruby, Jack, 234
Rush, Tom, 77
Russell, Ted, 118
Russell, William, 438
Rutman, Howard, 161, 162, 250

'Sad Eyed Lady Of The Lowlands' (Dylan), 329, 390, 391, 406
Sainte-Marie, Buffy, 77
'Sally Gal' (Dylan), 80n, 82, 97, 103, 113, 128
Saltzman, Buddy, 344
Salut Les Copains, 429
Salvation Army, 393
San Francisco, California, 48, 380
'San Francisco Bay Blues' (Elliott), 19
San Francisco Chronicle, 379
San Jose, California, 380
Sandburg, Carl, 245
Sanders, Daryl, 12
Sanders, Rick, 440, 441
Santa Monica, California, 249, 310, 381
Sarasota, Florida, 254
Sartre, Jean-Paul, 456
Satin Tones, The, 54, 165
'Satisfaction' (Jagger/Richards), 340
'Satisfied Mind' (Rhodes), 85, 130
Saturday Evening Post, 379
Savakus, Russ, 357–8, 359
Saville, Philip, 186–7, 190, 191
Savoy Hotel, London, 27, 105, 305, 314, 316–20, 324, 332–3, 338
Scaduto, Anthony, 3, 20n, 33, 66, 95, 136, 176, 353, 407

'Scarborough Fair' (trad.), 185, 194
Scene, 191
Schatzberg, Jerry, 359, 362, 372, 373, 385, 397, 398
Schmetzer, Uli, 403
von Schmidt, Eric, 80–81, 90, 112n, 195, 196, 218, 254–5, 350
Schoenfeld, Herm, 362
Scorsese, Martin, 12
Scroggie, George, 292
Scroggins, Bob, 64
Sebastian, John, 147, 149, 269, 275, 293, 294, 297, 298
Sedgwick, Edie, 382, 386, 455n
'See My Friends' (Davies), 340
'See That My Grave Is Kept Clean' (Jefferson), 84, 97, 103, 106–7, 109
Seeger, Charles, 38
Seeger, Peggy, 192
Seeger, Mike, 35n, 37–8, 348
Seeger, Pete, 35n, 37–8, 41, 92, 119, 120, 144, 145, 185, 205, 211, 350, 351, 415
Seems Like A Freeze Out (Dylan), 377
Sellers, Brother John, 18
September 11 attacks (2001), 5
'Set Me Free' (Davies), 340
'Seven Curses' (Dylan), 183n, 184–5, 199, 225, 226, 227, 233
Seventeen, 125
Shadow Blasters, The, 163n, 172
Shadows, The, 171, 172
Shakespeare, William, 6, 11, 23, 413
'She Belongs To Me' (Dylan), 293n, 294, 310
'She's Your Lover Now' (Dylan), 382, 383, 389n
Sheffield, England, 319, 327, 332, 439, 441
Shelley, Percy Bysshe, 439–40
Shelton, Robert, 7, 17n, 26, 75, 80, 85–6, 88, 90, 124, 172, 237, 303, 424
   on Baez, 323
   on *Blonde On Blonde*, 388
   Cavalier feature (1965), 308
   on 'Come Back, Baby', 94
   on 'Hammond's Folly', 127
   Hootenanny magazine, 231
   on 'House Of The Rising Sun', 81n
   on 'Many Thousands Gone', 130
   NYT review (1961), 21, 96–7
   Newport Festival (1964), 273–4, 309
   Newport Festival (1965), 349
   Philharmonic Hall show (1964), 309
   Redpath, relationship with, 100–101

Shepp, Archie, 129
Sheridan Square Playhouse, New York, 218
Shirelles, The, 173
Shoot The Piano Player, 197
Shot Of Love (Dylan), 50
Siegel, Jules, 379
Siggins, Betsy, 353
Silber, Irwin, 35n, 89, 231, 248, 266, 273, 308, 352, 371
Silo, 220
Silver, Jerry, 41
Silver, Judy, 196
Silver, Roy, 135, 136
Silvertone, 50, 159
Simon & Garfunkel, 344
Simon & Schuster, 3, 4
Simon, Carly, 453, 455
Simon, Paul, 217, 300n
Simple Twist of Fate (Odegard), 12
'Simple Twist Of Fate' (Dylan), 139
Sinatra, Frank, 233n
Sinatra, Nancy, 446
Sing Out!, 39, 82n, 117, 124, 126, 149, 192, 229, 231, 273, 279, 285, 334, 346, 352, 353, 370
Singer, Ethan, 195
Singers, London, 192, 196
'Sinner Man', 63
Sisario, Ben, 14
'Sitting On A Barbed Wire Fence' (Dylan), 341
'Sitting On The Railroad Track' (Dylan), 115
'Sitting On Top Of The World' (Mississippi Sheiks), 116
Sky, Patrick, 347
Sledge, Percy, 422, 423, 432
Sloan, P. F., 363
Small Town Talk (Hoskyns), 7
Smith, Bessie, 74, 104, 446
Smith, Eugene, 343
Smith, George Edward, 77
'Smokestack Lightning' (Howlin' Wolf), 115
Snow, Hank, 159–60
'So Long, It's Been Good To Know You' (Guthrie), 74
So Many Roads (Hammond), 275, 361, 371
Something Is Happening, 413
'Something's Burning Baby' (Dylan), 58
'Song To Woody' (Dylan), 19, 37, 39, 44, 77, 80, 81, 82, 106, 109, 116n
Sony, 5, 11, 15
Sotherby's, 109n, 144n, 336
'Sound Of Silence, The' (Simon), 344

Sounes, Howard, 3, 4, 7, 32, 42, 66n, 102, 210
'Spanish Harlem Incident' (Dylan), 256n, 261, 262
Speciality Records, 161
Spector, Phil, 344, 381, 382
Spitz, Bob, 3, 7, 80n
Spivey, Victoria, 18, 116
Spoelstra, Mark, 43, 77
Springsteen, Bruce, 96, 384
'St Louis Blues' (Handy), 18
St Louis, Missouri, 397
St Martin's Press, 8
St Paul Tape, 37, 61, 63, 77
St Paul, Minnesota, 51–2, 55, 67, 167
Stampfel, Peter, 20
'Standing On The Highway' (Dylan), 5, 114, 115
Stanley Brothers, 87
Stanley, Peter, 196
Starr, Herman, 137
Starr, Ringo, 277, 404
Stavers, Gloria, 396
Stealin' (Dylan), 294n
Steel, John, 275, 366
Stein, Etheldoris, 66
Steinbeck, John, 155
Steve Allen Show, The, 224, 249–50
Stewart, Rod, 126
Stockholm, Sweden, 407, 409–16
Stookey, Noel Paul, 36–7, 143, 351
Story, Gloria, 168
Stout, William, 18
Stuart, Joe B., 245
'Stuck Inside Of Mobile' (Dylan), 390, 392
Studio A, New York, 105, 128
Stuttgart, Germany, 362
'Subterranean Homesick Blues' (Dylan), 14, 290, 291, 293, 296, 299, 314, 315, 320, 326, 329, 332
Sullivan, Lorna, 71
Sun Records, 148, 149, 160, 161
Sunday Independent, 425, 426
Superior, Wisconsin, 152, 167
Supper Club, New York, 15
Sushi, Adele, 126
'Suzie Baby' (Vee), 171
Svedberg, Andrea, 228–9, 230, 232, 310
Sweden, 407, 409–16
Sydney Morning Herald, 403
Sydney Sun, 403
Sydney, New South Wales, 403–5

Taddei, Rod, 164, 165
Taft Hotel, New York, 130
Taj Mahal, 382, 402n
'Take Good Care Of My Baby' (King/ Goffin), 173
'Talkin' Bear Mountain' (Dylan), 80, 81, 82, 86, 91, 103, 128, 205
'Talkin' Central Park Mugger Blues' (Dylan/ Paxton), 80
'Talkin' Columbia' (Guthrie), 70
'Talkin' Folklore Center' (Dylan), 29
'Talkin' Hava Nagilah' (Dylan), 128
'Talkin' Hypocrite' (Dylan), 140
'Talkin' John Birch' (Dylan), 120, 128, 183n, 198, 199, 200, 201, 205–7, 227, 257
'Talkin' New York' (Dylan), 29, 31, 32, 46, 82, 109, 199
'Talkin' World War III' (Dylan), 201
Talking Woody Guthrie (Elliot) 70
'Tangled Up In Blue' (Dylan), 2
Taplin, Jonathan, 148, 265, 382
Tarantula (Dylan), 15, 154, 259n, 279, 284, 302–8, 345, 367, 454–5, 457
Taschen, 289n
Taylor, Cecil, 129
Taylor, Frances, 121
Taylor, Vince, 334
Teen, 401
'Tell Me, Momma' (Dylan), 388
Ten O'Clock Scholar, Minneapolis, 60–61, 62, 63, 64n, 162, 211
Terkel, Studs, 1, 144, 231
Terry, Sonny, 87
Testimony (Robertson), 8
Thal, Terri, 45, 80, 89, 91, 96, 135, 228
Thameside Four, The, 192
That Thin Wild Mercury Sound (Sanders), 12
'That's All Right Mama' (Crudup), 148, 151, 160, 175–6, 177, 179
Theme Time Radio Hour, 51, 161
'This Land Is Your Land' (Guthrie), 104, 349
'This Train Is Bound For Glory' (trad.), 82, 84
Thomas, Dylan, 36, 57, 58, 387, 424, 429
Thomas, Henry, 134
Thompson, Richard, 329n
Thornton, Terry, 216
Threepenny Opera (Brecht/Weill), 218–19
Till, Emmett, 119–20, 121, 216
Time Out Of Mind (Bell), 6
Time Out Of Mind (Dylan), 2

Time, 87, 208, 325–7, 406, 429
Times Square, New York, 29, 131, 301
'Times They Are A-Changin', The' (Dylan), 202, 220–21, 226, 227, 233, 320, 329
Times They Are A-Changin', The (Dylan), 225–7, 231, 232–3, 261
'To Ramona' (Dylan), 258, 259, 273
Together Thru Life, 135n
Tom Paine Award, 235
'Tombstone Blues' (Dylan), 306, 335, 347, 357, 359, 362, 455
'Tomorrow Is A Long Time' (Dylan), 131n, 139–40, 183, 199
'Tomorrow Never Knows' (Lennon/ McCartney), 423
'Too Much Monkey Business' (Berry), 315
Topic, 68
Toronto, Ontario, 197, 243, 360, 367
Toronto Star, 369–70
Town Hall, New York, 86, 105, 147, 181, 184, 198–9
'Trail Of The Buffalo' (trad.), 27
'Train A-Travelin'' (Dylan), 182
'Train For Auschwitz, The' (Paxton), 19
Traum, Artie, 41
Traum, Happy, 41
Travelin' Hootenanny, 145–6
'Travelin' Man' (Nelson), 31
Travers, Mary, 349
'Trees Do Grow So High, The' (trad.), 76, 84n; *see also* 'Young But Daily Growin''
Troubadour, London, 188, 192, 195–6
'Troubled & I Don't Know Why' (Dylan), 218
Truffaut, François, 197
'Trying To Get Home' (trad.), 103
Tulsa archive, 4n, 5, 14, 18, 95, 183n, 242, 256n, 258n, 286, 313, 335, 336, 414, 427, 457
Turner, Gil, 121, 122, 149
Turner, Steve, 266
Tyler, Tony, 450
Tyson, Ian, 84
Tyson, Sylvia, 81

Uhler, Max, 70
Underhill, Fred, 27, 73, 74
United Kingdom, 126
  1962–3 visit, 185–92, 196
  1964 visit, 248n, 256, 257, 258
  1965 tour, 282n, 305, 313–37, 347
  1966 tour, 385, 414, 419–23, 428–45, 450–52, 453–4

University of Chicago, 73
University of Minnesota, 54–65, 67–8, 75–6
University of Wisconsin, 38
Updike, John, 217–18
'Uranium Sunday' (Dylan), 371

Vacels, The, 377
Valens, Ritchie, 168
Valentine, Penny, 314
Van Ronk, Dave, 18, 19, 25, 31, 36, 40, 75, 83, 85, 86, 115, 119, 136, 139, 145
    'Car Car' duet (1961), 80n
    Carnegie Hall show (1963), 228
    on 'The Chimes of Trinity', 243
    on colouring books, 60n
    on Elliott, 150
    Gaslight residency, 143
    'He Was A Friend Of Mine', 80–81
    'House Of The Rising Sun', 81, 111
    'If I Had To Do It All Over Again, Babe', 180
Vanguard Records, 92
Variety, 205, 362, 367
Varsity, 313
'VD Seaman's Last Letter' (Dylan), 79
Vee, Bobby, 56, 65, 171–2, 361
Velvet Underground, The, 295, 374
Verlaine, Paul-Marie, 119
Verne, Jules, 155
Verve, 355
Vietnam, 422, 445, 446
Village Voice, 40, 124, 125, 199, 205, 207, 308, 353, 364, 371
Villon, François, 118, 119
Vipers, The, 274
Virginia, 131–2
'Visions Of Johanna' (Dylan), 289, 375, 377, 378, 382, 390, 392, 451
Vogue, 191–2

'Waitin' In School' (Burnette/Burnette), 314, 315
Wald, Elijah, 12, 274
Waldman, Anne, 220
Waldman, Jerry, 55
Walk Down Crooked Highway (Dylan), 285
'Walkin' Down The Line' (Dylan), 182–3, 199n
Wallace, Terri, 63
'Walls Of Redwing' (Dylan), 201, 203, 256, 257, 272

Ward, Edmund, 350
Warfield Theater, San Francisco, 48
Warhol, Andy, 301, 346, 374, 382, 386
Warner, David, 190
Warners Music, 137
Washington Civil Rights March (1963), 219–20
Washington Post, 14
Washington Square, New York, 41–2, 46n
'Wasn't That A Mighty Storm' (trad.), 90
Waters, Edgar, 404
Waynesboro, Virginia, 132
WBAI, 115, 216, 383, 384
'We Shall Overcome' (trad.), 42, 217
Weber, Harry, 63
Weill, Kurt, 218
Wein, George, 274, 349
Weinberger, Sybil, 90
'Weird Consumption' (Dylan), 262
Weissberg, Eric, 73
'Well, Well, Well' (Gibson/Camp), 252
Welles, Orson, 4, 157
Wells, Herbert George, 155
Wellstood, Dick, 175
West, Hedy, 43, 114n
Westinghouse syndicate, 206
Whaling Ballads (MacColl/Lloyd), 292n
'What Can You Do For My Wigwam' (Dylan), 394
'What Did The Deep Sea Say?' (Guthrie), 218
'Whatcha Gonna Do?' (Dylan), 182
Wheen, Francis, 13
'When A Man Loves A Woman' (Lewis/Wright), 432
When Billy Broke His Head, 47
'When God Comes And Gathers His Jewels' (Hank Williams), 155
'When The Ship Comes In' (Dylan), 218–19, 226, 227, 234, 246
'Which Side Are You On?' (Reece), 368
Whisky A Go-Go, Hollywood, 399, 401–2
Whitaker, Dave, 58, 59, 60, 70, 74, 138–40, 196, 211
Whitaker, Gretel, 60, 63, 74, 138–40, 211
White Goddess, The (Graves), 191, 432
White, Donald, 83, 121, 209
White, Josh, 30, 56, 62, 69, 274
Whitman, Marcus, 62
'Who Killed Davey Moore?' (Dylan), 203, 212
Who, The, 340
'Who's Going To Buy You Ribbons' (trad.), 244

'Whole Lotta Shakin' Goin' On' (Williams), 172
'Wild Mountain Thyme', 77, 323
Wild One, The, 23, 53, 166
Wilde, Oscar, 10
Wilentz, Sean, 13
Wilentz, Ted, 236
Wilkins, Roy, 209–10
'Will The Circle Be Unbroken?' (trad.), 103
Williams, Hank, 49, 50, 74, 77–8, 82, 85, 128, 149, 155, 158–60, 161, 169
Williams, Big Joe, 115, 116, 131
Williams, Paul, 386, 458
'Willie o' Winsbury' (trad.), 433
Wilson, Jackie, 173
Wilson, Steve, 124, 132, 143, 244
Wilson, Tom, 13, 216, 366
   Another Side sessions (1964), 261–4
   Bringing It sessions (1965), 293, 295–301
   firing of (1965), 343–5, 355
   Freewheelin' sessions (1963), 200, 201
   Highway 61 sessions (1965), 340–45
   Times sessions (1963), 225, 227, 233
   UK tour (1965), 314, 330, 331, 332
Winwood, Steve, 422
Wise, Omie, 19
Wiseman, Scott, 27
'With God On Our Side' (Dylan), 194, 203–4, 212, 213, 217, 225, 226, 309, 384
Witmark Music, 135–7, 140, 145, 181n, 182–3, 185, 259, 293, 378, 410
WNYC, 110
Wolcott, James, 13
Wood, Hally, 134
Wood, Roy, 224, 228
Woodstock, New York, 7, 8, 207, 209, 255, 258, 261, 265–71, 279, 288–92, 336, 337, 345
World Of Bob Dylan, The, 399
'Worried Blues' (Wood), 134
Writings & Drawings (Dylan), 14, 115, 231n, 267n, 286n, 290
WRVR, 17–18
WUCB, 73

Wyatt, Lorre, 228
Wyman, Bill, 373
Wynn, John, 20

Yarrow, Peter, 100, 207, 209, 241, 265, 351, 352
Yevtushenko, Yevgeny, 101
'You Don't Have To Do That' (Dylan), 292, 295
'You're No Good' (Fuller), 106, 107, 109
'Young But Daily Growin'' (trad.), 76, 84n, 104
'Young Craigston' (trad.), 84n; *see also* 'Young But Daily Growin''
Young, Izzy, 5, 35, 42, 69, 82n, 83, 96, 100, 117, 124, 346
   Carnegie Chapter Hall show (1961), 89, 104, 110
   Ed Sullivan Show protest (1963), 207
   Elektra Records story, 89
   Folklore Center, 31, 34, 39, 40, 83, 117
   Gerde's show (1961), 96
   on Grossman, 410
   on Kramer, 281
   and 'Let Me Die In My Footsteps', 121, 122, 123
   Newport Festival (1965), 349
   and 'Talkin' John Birch', 198
   Travelin' Hootenanny, 146
   Washington Square protest (1961), 41
'Your Cheatin' Heart' (Williams), 50
Yurchenco, Henrietta, 46n

Zantzinger, William, 223–5
Zimmerman, Abraham, 49, 55, 56, 71–2, 98, 138, 150, 154, 167
Zimmerman, Anna, 152, 153
Zimmerman, Beatrice, 45, 47, 49, 153, 167, 228, 368
Zimmerman, David, 156, 166
Zimmerman, Paul, 153
Zionism, 49
Zuckerman, Sue, 20, 43, 105, 109, 117–18, 203, 220, 277